RELAIS &
CHATEAUX®

Relais Gourmands

2000

427 HOTELS & RESTAURANTS

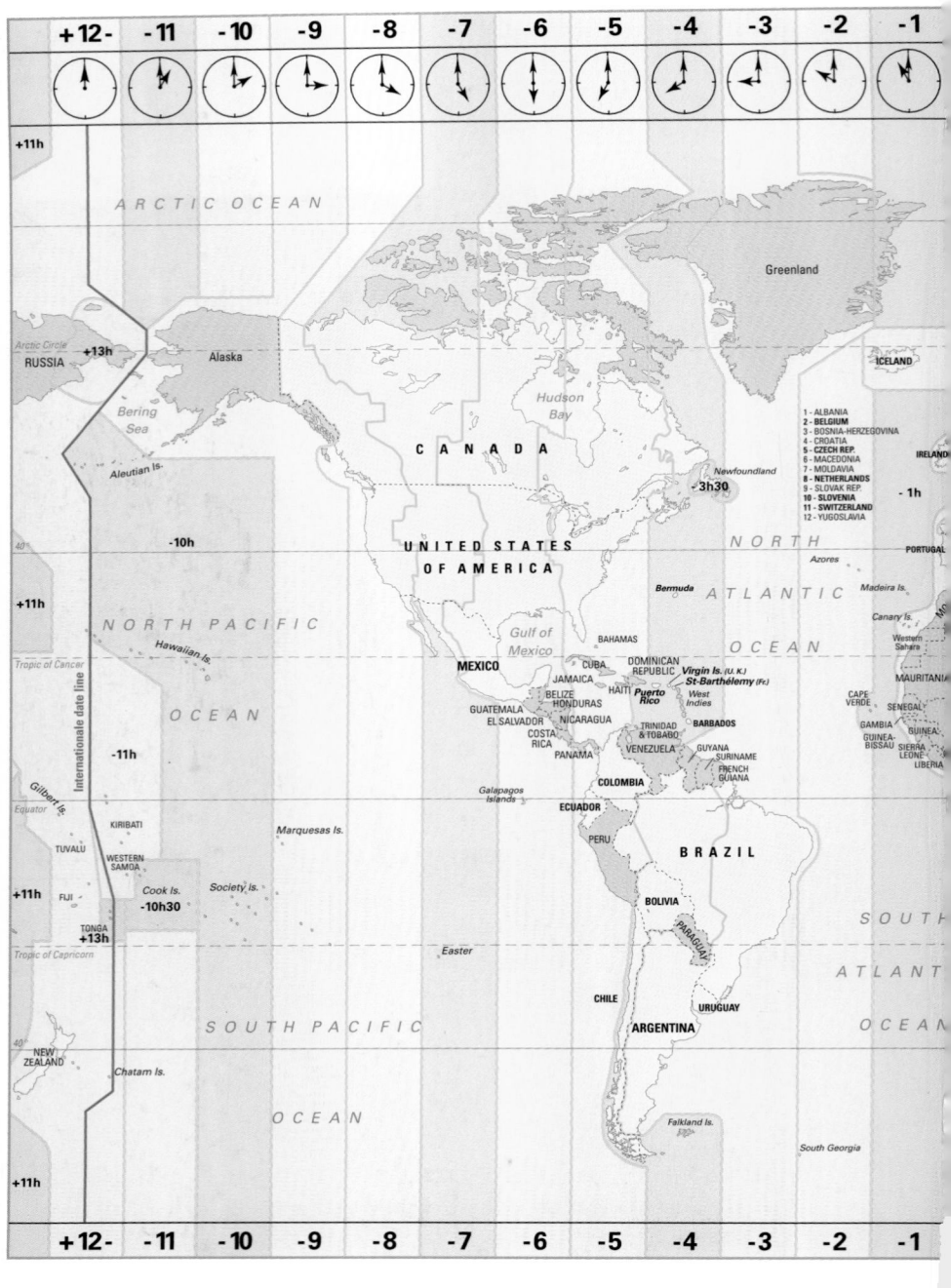

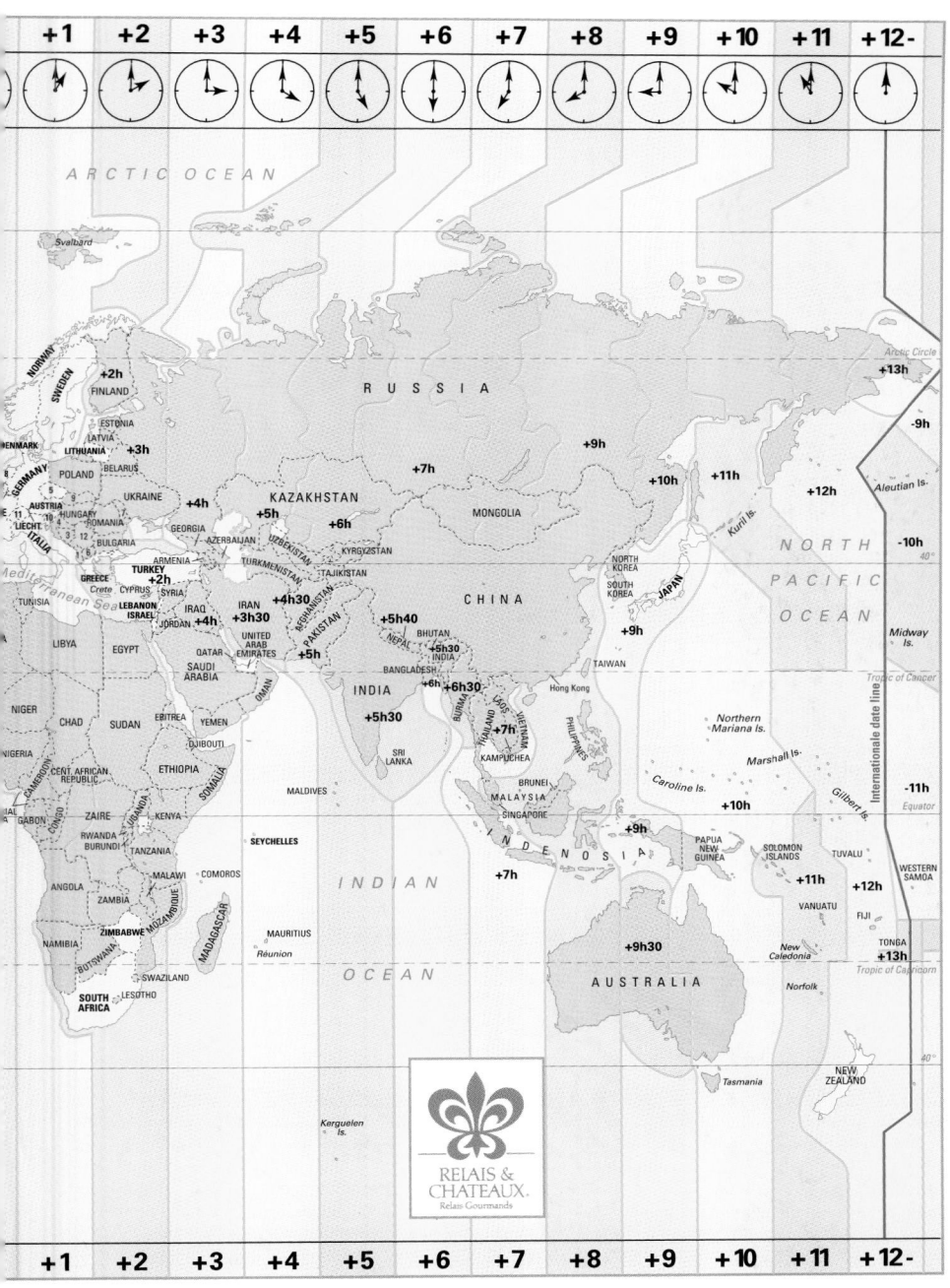

ICE CUBE

Chopard

Our clients know, as do tourism and hotel trade professionals, that the Relais & Châteaux have not waited for the coming of the third millennium to equip themselves with the tools of the future. Making ambitious plans for the future requires adaptation to technological progress which now means the Internet and this has helped us to optimise our Central Reservations Department.

But of greater importance than this efficiency, which our chain has strived for and defended inch by inch, encouraged in our boldness by our international identity, is the fact that our job has remained the same: serving you, our past and future clients whom we wish to always welcome as favoured guests in our residences.

Our difference has become an exclusive reference and the development phases which have sometimes revolutionised our habits have proved necessary for maintaining the values that we all share. It is not possible to endure without accepting change. The French-style art of living, incarnated by the Relais de Campagne 45 years ago, has been transformed into an art of providing a recognised and appreciated global welcome, with high standards and the concern for detail in services, consideration, charm and elegance in both welcome and atmosphere.

This is our story. Supported by their know-how, our establishments have acquired a style that has become the style of the Relais & Châteaux. Yet each one is different, none sacrifices its personality to comply with the rest. However, unity is preserved through the way in which we exercise our profession. Our association wishes to remain loyal to this spirit. Hence, our rigorous selection process and our great attachment to human-sized residences. The average capacity of our hotels is twenty-eight rooms.

Our aim is not to be perfect. Our professionalism is only aimed at satisfying you, our clients, by offering you a different experience. A moment of well-being not spoilt by anything, a moment during which we all hope that we give you a little more than you had hoped for. This is an appropriate year to remind you of our difference, as the year 2000 is also unique.

RÉGIS BULOT
Président International

www.cartier.com

Welcome

Character Charm Calm
Cuisine Courtesy

427 establishments in 43 countries
today share the five points of our promise.

We have designed this publication to guide you in your choice
and help you select the hotel
or restaurant that best matches your requirements.

Turn your back on time

Reverso

With its pure Art Deco features, unchanged since 1931, the Reverso has a unique identity. Especially when we add the final touch. By engraving your initials on its pivoting case, we invite you to turn your back on time as elegantly as you face it. Enjoy the gesture.

JAEGER-LECOULTRE

SUMMARY

AU–DELA DU STYLE,
L'EMOTION

PIAGET

GENEVE 1874

MISS PROTOCOLE

OR BLANC 18 CT, BRACELET

INTERCHANGEABLE

THE RELAIS & CHÂTEAUX BLAZONS

The Relais & Chateaux categories define three styles of hotel services and are identified by a fleur de lys of a different colour.

The Relais & Gourmands, with or without rooms, are restaurants that are known for the culinary mastery and inventiveness of their chefs.

 A beautiful establishment with a high level of comfort of the «relais de campagne» type.

The refined comfort of a magnificent residence.

 An exceptional establishment featuring the highest level service, amenities and furnishings.

Restaurants known for their excellent cuisine.

 The twofold pleasure of a comfortable establishment with an excellent restaurant.

•

A SOUGHT-AFTER DISTINCTION: THE WELCOME TROPHY

For 12 years now, Relais & Châteaux and Moët & Chandon have awarded the Welcome Trophy to a French establishment and to a foreign establishment which are distinguished by the excellence of their welcome and service.

This prize is given on the basis of the evaluation forms filled in by our Relais & Châteaux customers throughout the world.

In the guide, they are indicated by this symbol:

WELCOME TROPHY

WELCOME TROPHY 2000

Château de Bagnols (p. 175)   Albergo Giardino (p. 293)

Places to go? Sights to see? MasterCard® is accepted
at over 15 million places from New York to Paris
and lots of places in between.

www.mastercard.com

Please inquire about exclusive MasterCard® values by calling
Relais & Chateaux reservations, or visit our web site.

At your service

Directions
To rapidly locate the hotel or restaurant of your choice,
to find the Relais & Châteaux
in a favourite region, refer to:
- the index by country and by region (page 7)
- the alphabetical index (page 27)

Maps and plans
For each country (and in France in each region), a special map to help you locate
the establishments of your choice (index page 7)
For each hotel and restaurant, an access map gives you the main indications
to get there.

Information
Indicated on the cover of the guide, the pictograms are small symbols
that will help you to understand all the services offered
by each establishment.

Selecting activities
2 topical indexes will help you to choose your next destination.
- Leisure: selection of sports and outdoor activities proposed in the establishments (page 627).
- Fitness and beauty: hotels offering beauty treatments,
keep fit facilities or appropriate equipment (spa, balneotherapy...).
The sommeliers of the Relais & Châteaux and Relais Gourmands
also offer you their selection of World Vintages to drink in the year 2000 (page 607).

Meetings
The Relais & Châteaux will be pleased to help you organise your seminars,
conferences and receptions (information on pages 609 to 625).

Prices
The prices indicated are for information only and vary between low and high season.
They are given in local currency (indicated at the bottom of each page)
and in Euros for the countries of the corresponding zone.

A currency conversion table is available (page 48) to help you.

MOËT & CHANDON

Fondé en 1743

How to make a reservation?

The reservations may be made:

- directly at each establishment, at the numbers given on its page
  - through our central reservation department
  (details on page 15 and on the cover of the guide)
    - or on Internet : **www.relaischateaux.fr**
      - at your travel agency

The reservation conditions
(payment of a deposit, indication of your credit card number...)
will be given to you directly by the establishments or by our central department.

The conditions of cancellation or for shortening your stay are specific
to each establishment and will be specified to you when you make your reservation.

Offer a dream with Relais & Châteaux

- The Invitation Cheque
As a personal treat or a company reward,
Relais & Châteaux has the right formula (pages 21 and 471).
- Open a wedding list: your friends will be delighted to contribute
to your dream trip from Relais to Châteaux throughout the world.

For information and literature, ring (33) 01 45 72 90 01

Surf on
www.relaischateaux.fr
Since February 1995, the Relais & Châteaux site
tells you more about the establishments throughout the world

Arceau" watch
with crocodile strap.

TIME LASTS FOREVER.

HERMÈS
PARIS

RESERVATION

By internet   www.relaischateaux.fr
e-mail: resarc@relaischateaux.fr

By telephone and fax

EUROPE	Telephone	Fax
France	0 825 32 32 32	
Germany - Spain Italy - United Kingdom	00 800 2000 00 02●	(33) (0) 1 45 72 96 69
Sweden	009 800 2000 00 02●	
Other European countries	(33) (0) 1 45 72 96 50	

AMERICA	Telephone	Fax
USA - Canada	(1) 800 735 2478 ●	(1) 401 854 1612
Argentina	(54) 114 393 5350	(54) 114 393 2698
Brazil	0 800 11 8900 ●	0 800 11 8079 ●

ASIA-OCEANIA	Telephone	Fax
Japan	(81) 3 3475 6876	(81) 3 3475 3400
Australia	(61) 2 9247 8395	(61) 2 9247 8406

OTHER COUNTRIES	Telephone	Fax
	(33) (0) 1 45 72 96 50	(33) (0) 1 45 72 96 69

● *Toll-free numbers - Free calls*

By GDS

Relais & Châteaux establishments are accessible with code «WB» in the following GDS:
Amadeus, Apollo/Galileo, Worldspan and Sabre.

A brochure describing the codes of our establishments can be obtained from:
(33) (0) 1 45 72 96 69 (Fax)

Oh, the places you'll go.

We know you have places to go. And there are many ways you can get there with United Airlines Mileage Plus.

When you become a member, you can earn miles for free travel worldwide in a variety of ways — like while you enjoy luxury accommodations at any Relais & Châteaux hotel, estate or castle. You can earn 500 miles per qualifying stay, exclusively with Mileage Plus.

Or, earn miles with United Airlines or any of our 70 Mileage Plus partners. Your miles will add up quickly and you may choose from more than 700 destinations around the globe for your award travel.

You can also earn miles for car rentals, long-distance phone calls, cruises, hotel stays and more. In fact no other program offers more ways to earn free travel.

To join Mileage Plus, call your local United Reservations or join online by visiting United Airlines at www.ual.com.

/// UNITED AIRLINES

A STAR ALLIANCE MEMBER

How to obtain the Relais & Châteaux Guide

The Relais & Châteaux International Guide is updated annually.
It exists in 5 languages: English, French, German, Spanish and Japanese.

Our guide is at your disposal

- In the Relais & Châteaux establishments in the world (list p 7)

- In the Relais & Châteaux offices and sales representations in France, Germany, Great Britain and the USA and whose telephone numbers appear on the inside flap of the Guide's cover.

- On our internet site, you can also order the guide or send it to the person of your choice.

www.relaischateaux.fr

A participation for the packing and shipping cost is requested for all guides sent by mail.

Relais & Châteaux Guide is also available

- at the Paris Tourist Office: 127, avenue des Champs Elysées

- also at the different offices of «Maison de la France» in the world. List available on internet (www.franceguide.com)

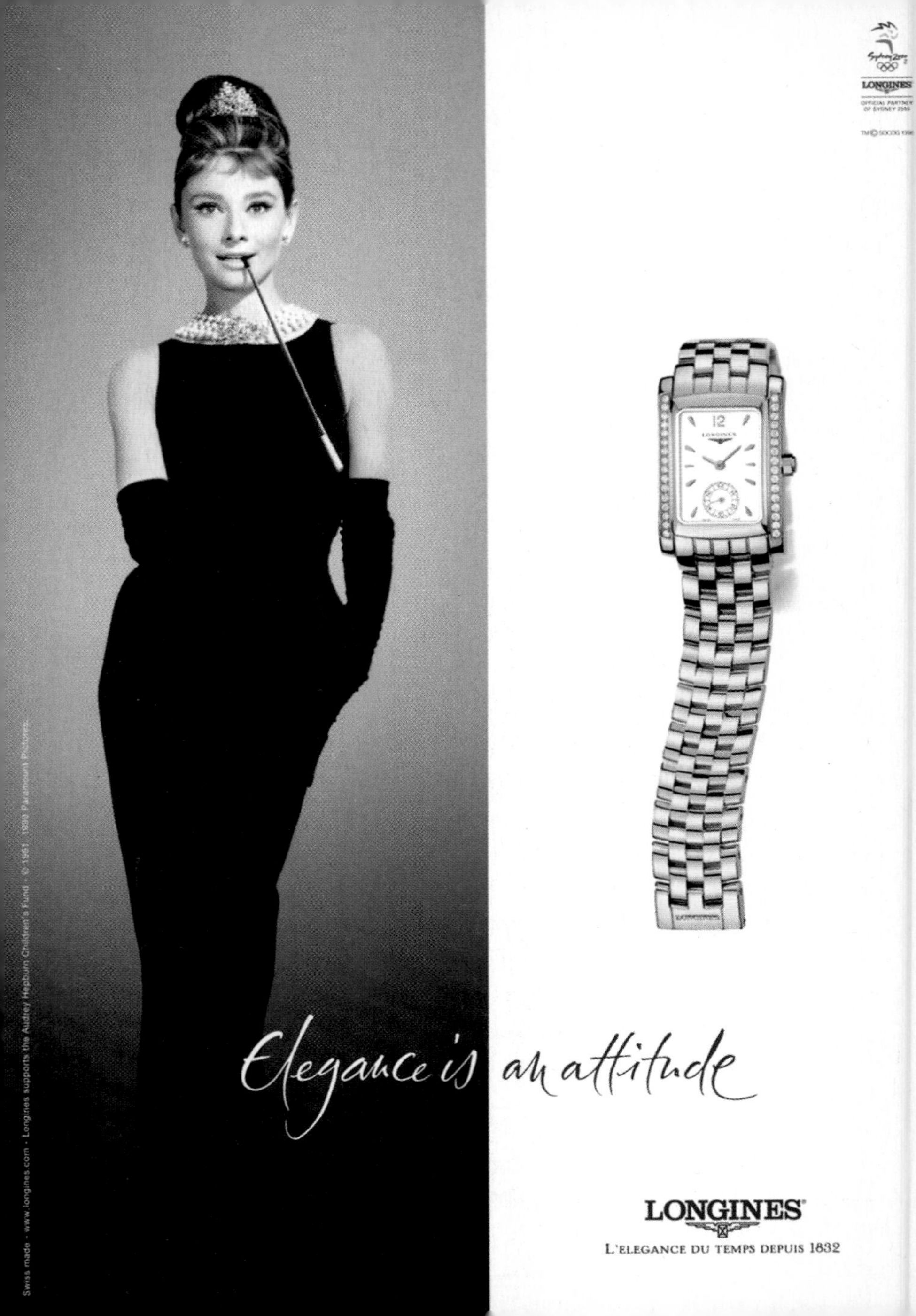

Elegance is an attitude

L'ELEGANCE DU TEMPS DEPUIS 1832

Choosing your Relais, information, reservations: www.relaischateaux.fr

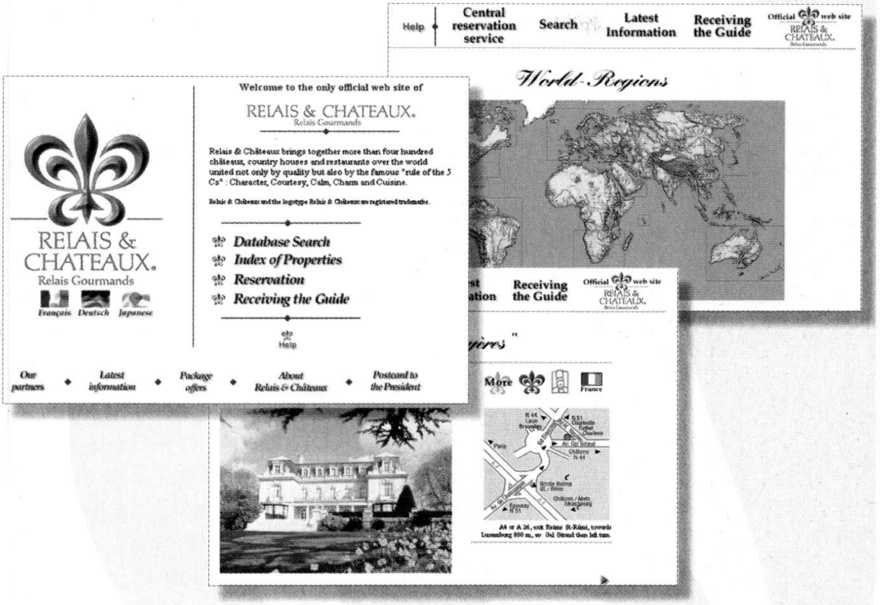

Welcome to the only official web site of

RELAIS & CHATEAUX
Relais Gourmands

Relais & Château brings together more than four hundred châteaux, country houses and restaurants over the world united not only by quality but also by the famous "rule of the 5 Cs" : Character, Courtesy, Calm, Charm and Cuisine.

Relais & Château and the logotype Relais & Château are registered trademarks.

- ❧ **Database Search**
- ❧ **Index of Properties**
- ❧ **Reservation**
- ❧ **Receiving the Guide**

Help

Our partners ◆ Latest information ◆ Package offers ◆ About Relais & Château ◆ Postcard to the President

Français   Deutsch   Japanese

| Help | Central reservation service | Search | Latest Information | Receiving the Guide | Official web site RELAIS & CHATEAUX |

World Regions

- ● Discover our establishments throughout the world
- ● Select your destination according to your criteria
- ● Visit… and reserve
- ● Order the guide, send it as a gift
- ● Consult our products and see what's new
- ● Stay in contact with us…

RELAIS & CHATEAUX.
Relais Gourmands

Orfèvre en chocolat

En vente chez les pâtissiers et confiseurs les plus renommés.
Available through well-known confectioners and patisseries.

MICHEL CLUIZEL • CHOCOLATIER • 201, RUE SAINT-HONORÉ 75001 PARIS

![Relais & Châteaux establishments photographs]

Relais & Châteaux Invitation Cheque:

re-inventing the art of giving

 An original and sophisticated formula allowing you to offer the person of your choice the freedom to select his or her own destination from among over 400 establishments throughout the world. An ideal gift for an important business or family event. For further information, ring (33) 01 45 72 90 01.

RELAIS &
CHATEAUX.
Relais Gourmands

15, rue Galvani 75017 Paris - Tel. (33) 01 45 72 90 01 - Fax (33) 01 44 09 72 30 - e-mail : rcr@relaischateaux.fr
International guide on request from (33) 01 45 72 90 00 or on Internet : www.relaischateaux.fr

THE YEAR 2000 RECRUITS

Welcome to the 31 establishments
joining the Relais & Châteaux this year.

These are indicated throughout the guide by the «since 2000» symbol.

SINCE
2000

This same symbol «since...» specifies the year of entry
of each establishment into the Chain.

L'ARNSBOURG
18, Untermuhlthal
57230 Baerenthal
page 149

France

France

LE HAMEAU ALBERT IER
119, impasse du Montenvers, BP 55
74402 Chamonix
page 195

OMBREMONT
RN 504
73370 Le Bourget-du-Lac
page 201

France

France

LE MOULIN DE LOURMARIN
(Opposite the château)
84160 Lourmarin
page 227

Le Club de Cavalière
83980 Le Lavandou
page 237

France

France

La Bastide Saint-Antoine
48, avenue Henri Dunant
06130 Grasse
page 241

Hof Van Cleve
Riemegemstraat, 1
B-9770 Kruishoutem
page 255

Belgium

Switzerland

Ermitage Am See
Seestrasse 80
CH-8700 Küsnacht
page 275

Villa Principe Leopoldo & Residence
Via Montalbano, 5
CH-6900 Lugano
page 295

Switzerland

Germany

Schloss Hubertushöhe
Robert-Koch-Str. 1
D-15859 Storkow
page 313

Germany

Burghotel Hardenberg
Im Hinterhaus 11a
D-37176 Nörten-Hardenberg
page 317

Germany

Germany

Hotel Burg Wernberg
Schlossberg 10
D-92533 Wernberg-Köblitz
page 325

Villino
Hoyerberg 34
D-88131 Lindau-Bodensee
page 339

Germany

Denmark

MOLSKROEN
Hovedgaden 16
DK-84000 Ebeltoft
page 365

RESTAURANT BAGATELLE
Bygdoy Alle 3
N-0257 Oslo
page 371

Norway

Lithunia

STIKLIAI HOTEL
Gaono Str. 7
2024 Vilnius
page 373

HOTEL BELLEVUE
Rue Grand Paradis 22
I-11012 Cogne
page 415

Italy

Italy

ROSA ALPINA
Str. Micura de Rü
I-39030 S. Cassiano
page 425

RISTORANTE AMBASCIATA
Via Martiri di Belfiore, 33
I-46026 Quistello-Mantova
page 429

Italy

VILLA LA MASSA
Via della Massa, 24
I-50012 Bagno a Ripoli
page 433

Italy

FORTALEZA DO GUINCHO
Estrada do Guincho
P-2750-642 Cascais
page 451

Portugal

Spain

POSADA DE LA CASA DEL ABAD
Plaza Francisco Martin Grohaz, 12
E-34160 Ampudia-Palencia
page 453

La Torre del Visco
Fuentespalda
E-44587 Tervel
page 463

Spain

Spain

Gran Hotel Son Net
E-07194 Puigpunyent-Mallorca
page 469

Bushmans Kloof
PO Box 53405
Kenilworth 7945
page 491

South Africa

South Africa

Le Quartier Français
CNR Berg-Wilhelmina Str.
Franschhoek 7690
page 495

The Marine Hermanus
Marine Drive
Hermanus 7200
page 497

South Africa

USA

The Wauwinet
120 Wauwinet Road - PO Box 2580
Nantucket, MA 02584
page 559

Jean Georges
One Central Park West
New York
New York 10023
page 567

USA

USA

The Fearrington House
2000 Fearrington Village
Pittsboro
North Carolina 27312
page 571

Les Nomades
222 East Ontario Street
Chicago
Illinois 60611
page 574

USA

Cindy
Crawford's Choice

Constellation
Stainless steel with
diamond-set bezel.
OMEGA — Swiss made since 1848.

Omega -- my choice *Cindy Crawford*

Ω
OMEGA
The sign of excellence

www.omega.ch

ALPHABETICAL INDEX OF ESTABLISHMENTS

27

29

Establishments	⚜	🍴	Page
Verniaz (La)	⚜		193
Vieux Castillon (Le)	⚜		215
Vieux Logis (Le)	⚜		124
Villa (La)	⚜		249
Villa Belrose (La)	⚜		236
Villa Florentine	⚜		183
Villa Gallici	⚜		230
BENELUX COUNTRIES			250
BELGIUM			253
Auberge du Moulin Hideux	⚜		262
Clos St. Denis		🍴	258
Hof Van Cleve		🍴	255
Hôtel de Snippe	⚜		253
Hostellerie Lafarque	⚜	🍴	261
Hostellerie Saint-Roch	⚜		259
Hostellerie Shamrock	⚜		254
Moulin des Ramiers	⚜		260
Restaurant Barbizon		🍴	256
Scholteshof	⚜	🍴	257
LUXEMBOURG			263
Gaichel (La)	⚜		264
Table des Guilloux (La)		🍴	263
NETHERLANDS			265
Kasteel Wittem	⚜		265
Manoir «Inter Scaldes»	⚜	🍴	267

Establishments	⚜	🍴	Page
Prinses Juliana	⚜	🍴	266
SWITZERLAND - LIECHTENSTEIN			268
SWITZERLAND			272
Albergo Giardino	⚜		293
Auberge du Raisin	⚜	🍴	282
Castello del Sole	⚜		292
Ermitage Am See	⚜		275
Georges Wenger Hôtel de la Gare	⚜	🍴	277
Grand Hôtel Park	⚜		286
Grandhôtel Schönegg	⚜		291
Hostellerie Alpenrose	⚜		285
Hostellerie du Débarcadère	⚜		280
Hostellerie du Pas de l'Ours	⚜		287
Hôtel de la Cigogne	⚜		279
Hotel Haus Paradies	⚜	🍴	298
Hôtel Rosalp	⚜	🍴	289
Hotel Splügenschloss	⚜		274
Hôtel Victoria	⚜		284
Hotel Walserhof	⚜	🍴	301
Hotel Walther	⚜		297
Les Sources des Alpes	⚜		290
Pont de Brent (Le)		🍴	283
Restaurant Bruderholz		🍴	272
Rest. de l'Hôtel de Ville - Ph. Rochat		🍴	281
Restaurant Jöhri's Talvo		🍴	296

GALERIES
Lafayette

DUTY FREE SHOPPING

WELCOME SERVICE

INTERPRETERS

PRIVATE WEEKLY
FASHION SHOWS

CURRENCY EXCHANGE
OFFICE

LAFAYETTE GOURMET:
DE LUXE GROCERY

RESTAURANTS

GALERIES LAFAYETTE - 40, BD HAUSSMANN 75009 PARIS. MÉTRO CHAUSSÉE D'ANTIN-LA FAYETTE
OPEN MONDAY THROUGH SATURDAY FROM 9:30 AM TO 6:45 PM
LATE NIGHT OPENING EVERY THURSDAY UNTIL 9 PM. TEL.: 01 42 82 36 40
http://www.galerieslafayette.com

35

Elite range

Enhance your wine collection

With passion, EuroCave has been combining art and functionality for over 20 years.

By recreating the natural and optimal conditions for wine storage, EuroCave offers the largest number of wine cabinets for preserving and serving wine.

By keeping your best wines in a EuroCave, each day you will combine visual delight with the confidence of knowing that your wines are safe.

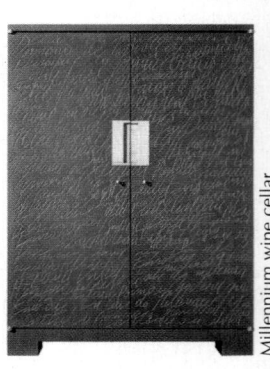

Millennium wine cellar

EuroCave®
World leader in wine cabinets

THE KEY TO TIME

CORUM

TABOGAN

On your wrist or bureau. A contemporary watch forever with you.
Steel or 18 carat gold. Automatic mechanical or quartz movement.
Registered model. Manufactured in Switzerland.

REGIONS OF FRANCE

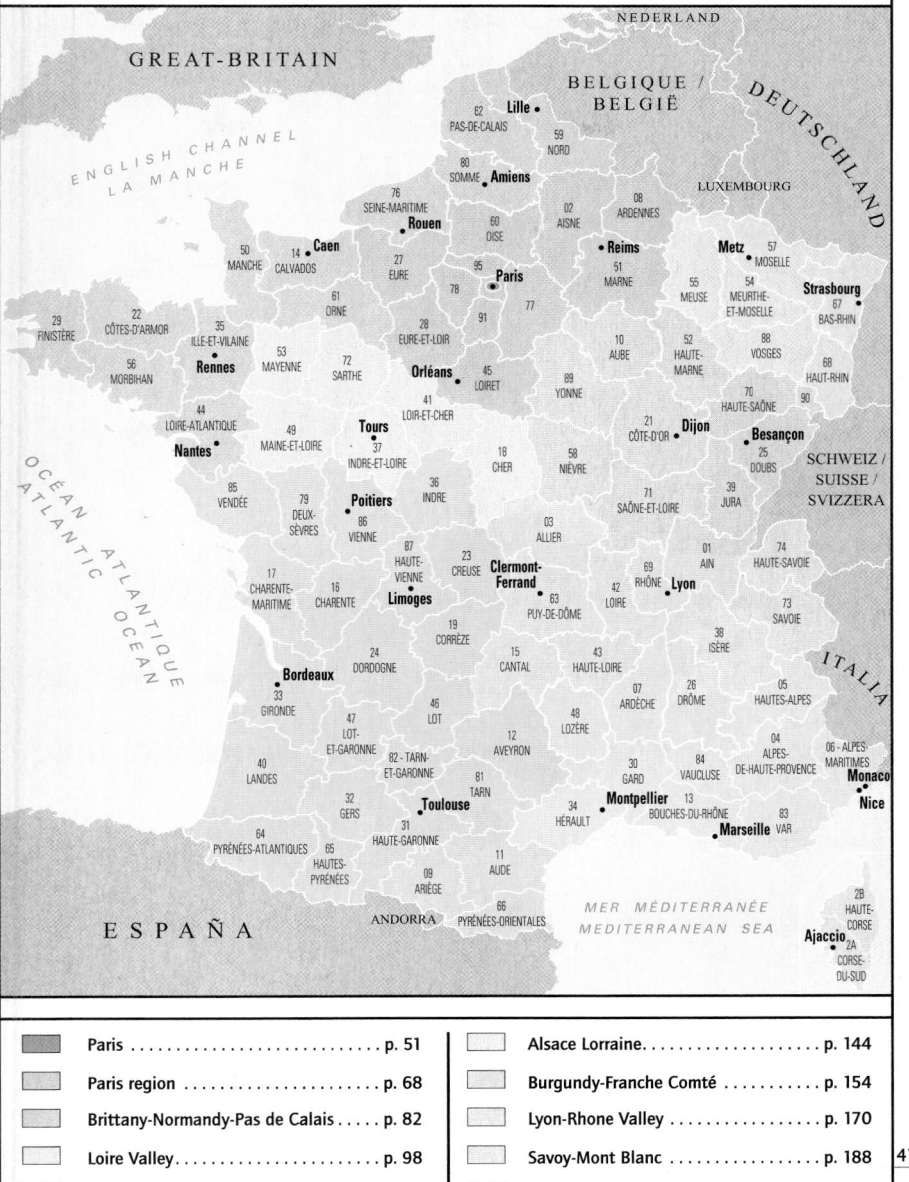

NEDERLAND

GREAT-BRITAIN

BELGIQUE / BELGIË

DEUTSCHLAND

ENGLISH CHANNEL
LA MANCHE

LUXEMBOURG

62 Lille
PAS-DE-CALAIS
59 NORD

80 SOMME • Amiens
02 AISNE
08 ARDENNES

76 SEINE-MARITIME
• Rouen
60 OISE

50 MANCHE
14 • Caen CALVADOS
27 EURE
95
78 • Paris
51 MARNE
• Reims
Metz 57 MOSELLE

61 ORNE
91
77
55 MEUSE
54 MEURTHE-ET-MOSELLE
Strasbourg
67 BAS-RHIN

29 FINISTÈRE
22 CÔTES-D'ARMOR
35 ILLE-ET-VILAINE
53 MAYENNE
72 SARTHE
28 EURE-ET-LOIR
Orléans
45 LOIRET
89 YONNE
10 AUBE
52 HAUTE-MARNE
88 VOSGES
68 HAUT-RHIN
90

• Rennes
44 LOIRE-ATLANTIQUE
49 MAINE-ET-LOIRE
Tours
37 INDRE-ET-LOIRE
41 LOIR-ET-CHER
21 CÔTE-D'OR
• Dijon
70 HAUTE-SAÔNE
• Besançon
25 DOUBS

56 MORBIHAN
• Nantes
85 VENDÉE
79 DEUX-SÈVRES
Poitiers
36 INDRE
18 CHER
58 NIÈVRE
71 SAÔNE-ET-LOIRE
39 JURA
SCHWEIZ / SUISSE / SVIZZERA

OCÉAN ATLANTIQUE
ATLANTIC OCEAN
86 VIENNE
87 HAUTE-VIENNE
23 CREUSE
Clermont-Ferrand
03 ALLIER
01 AIN
74 HAUTE-SAVOIE

17 CHARENTE-MARITIME
16 CHARENTE
Limoges
19 CORRÈZE
63 PUY-DE-DÔME
69 RHÔNE
42 LOIRE
Lyon
73 SAVOIE

• Bordeaux
33 GIRONDE
24 DORDOGNE
15 CANTAL
43 HAUTE-LOIRE
07 ARDÈCHE
26 DRÔME
38 ISÈRE
05 HAUTES-ALPES
ITALIA

47 LOT-ET-GARONNE
46 LOT
12 AVEYRON
48 LOZÈRE
30 GARD
84 VAUCLUSE
04 ALPES-DE-HAUTE-PROVENCE
06 - ALPES-MARITIMES
Monaco

40 LANDES
32 GERS
82 - TARN-ET-GARONNE
81 TARN
Montpellier
13 BOUCHES-DU-RHÔNE
• Nice

64 PYRÉNÉES-ATLANTIQUES
31 HAUTE-GARONNE
Toulouse
34 HÉRAULT
• Marseille 83 VAR

65 HAUTES-PYRÉNÉES
09 ARIÈGE
11 AUDE
MER MÉDITERRANÉE
MEDITERRANEAN SEA
2B HAUTE-CORSE

ESPAÑA
ANDORRA
66 PYRÉNÉES-ORIENTALES
Ajaccio •
2A CORSE-DU-SUD

▓	Paris .... p. 51	▓	Alsace Lorraine.................... p. 144
▓	Paris region .... p. 68	▓	Burgundy-Franche Comté .... p. 154
▓	Brittany-Normandy-Pas de Calais ..... p. 82	▓	Lyon-Rhone Valley .... p. 170
▓	Loire Valley....................... p. 98	▓	Savoy-Mont Blanc .... p. 188
▓	The Greater South West .... p. 110	▓	Provence-French Riviera-Corsica ...... p. 206

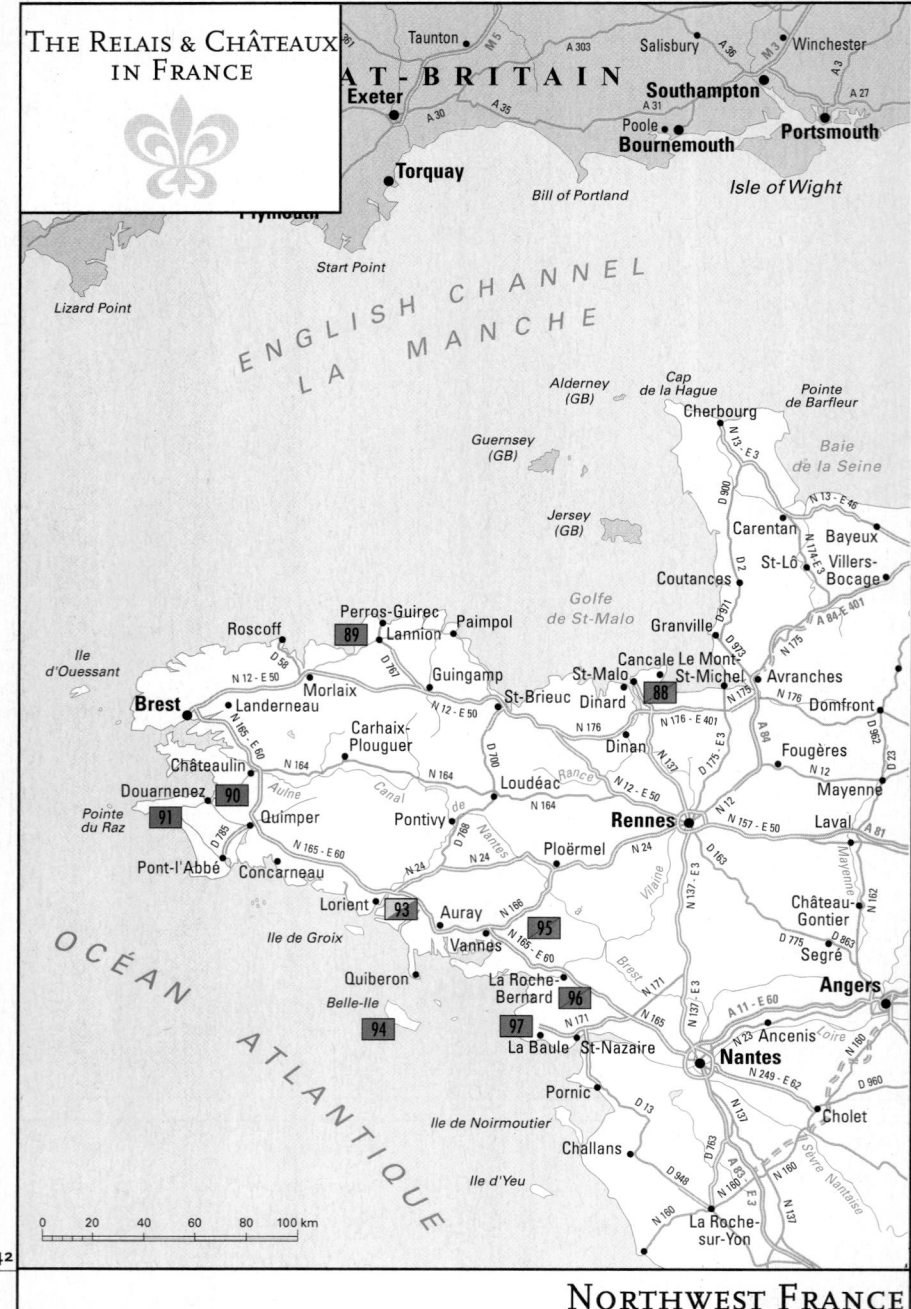

Taunton

GREAT - BRITAIN

Salisbury

Winchester

Exeter

Southampton

Poole

Portsmouth

Bournemouth

Torquay

Bill of Portland

Isle of Wight

Plymouth

Start Point

ENGLISH CHANNEL

Lizard Point

LA MANCHE

Alderney (GB)

Cap de la Hague

Pointe de Barfleur

Cherbourg

Baie de la Seine

Guernsey (GB)

Carentan

Bayeux

Jersey (GB)

St-Lô

Villers-Bocage

Coutances

Golfe de St-Malo

Granville

Roscoff

Perros-Guirec

Paimpol

Cancale

Le Mont-St-Michel

89

Lannion

St-Malo

88

Avranches

Guingamp

Dinard

Morlaix

St-Brieuc

Domfront

Brest

Landerneau

Carhaix-Plouguer

Dinan

Fougères

Châteaulin

Loudéac

Mayenne

Douarnenez

90

Aulne

Canal

Rennes

Laval

Pointe du Raz

91

Quimper

Pontivy

Ploërmel

Château-Gontier

Pont-l'Abbé

Concarneau

N 24

Segré

Lorient

93

Auray

95

Angers

Ile de Groix

Vannes

Quiberon

La Roche-Bernard

96

Belle-Ile

94

97

Ancenis

La Baule

St-Nazaire

Nantes

Cholet

OCÉAN

Pornic

Ile de Noirmoutier

Challans

ATLANTIQUE

Ile d'Yeu

La Roche-sur-Yon

0   20   40   60   80   100 km

42

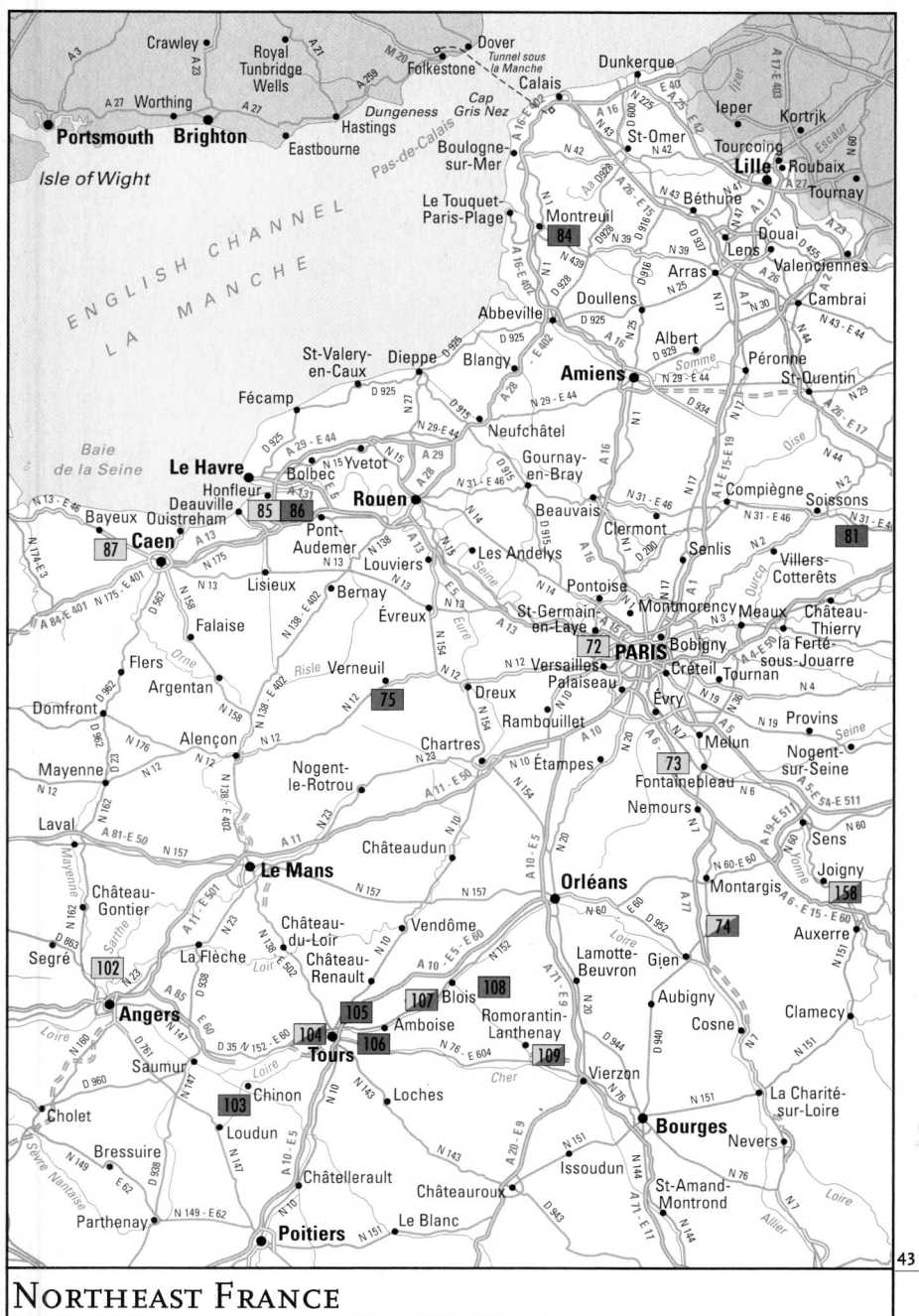

NORTHEAST FRANCE

43

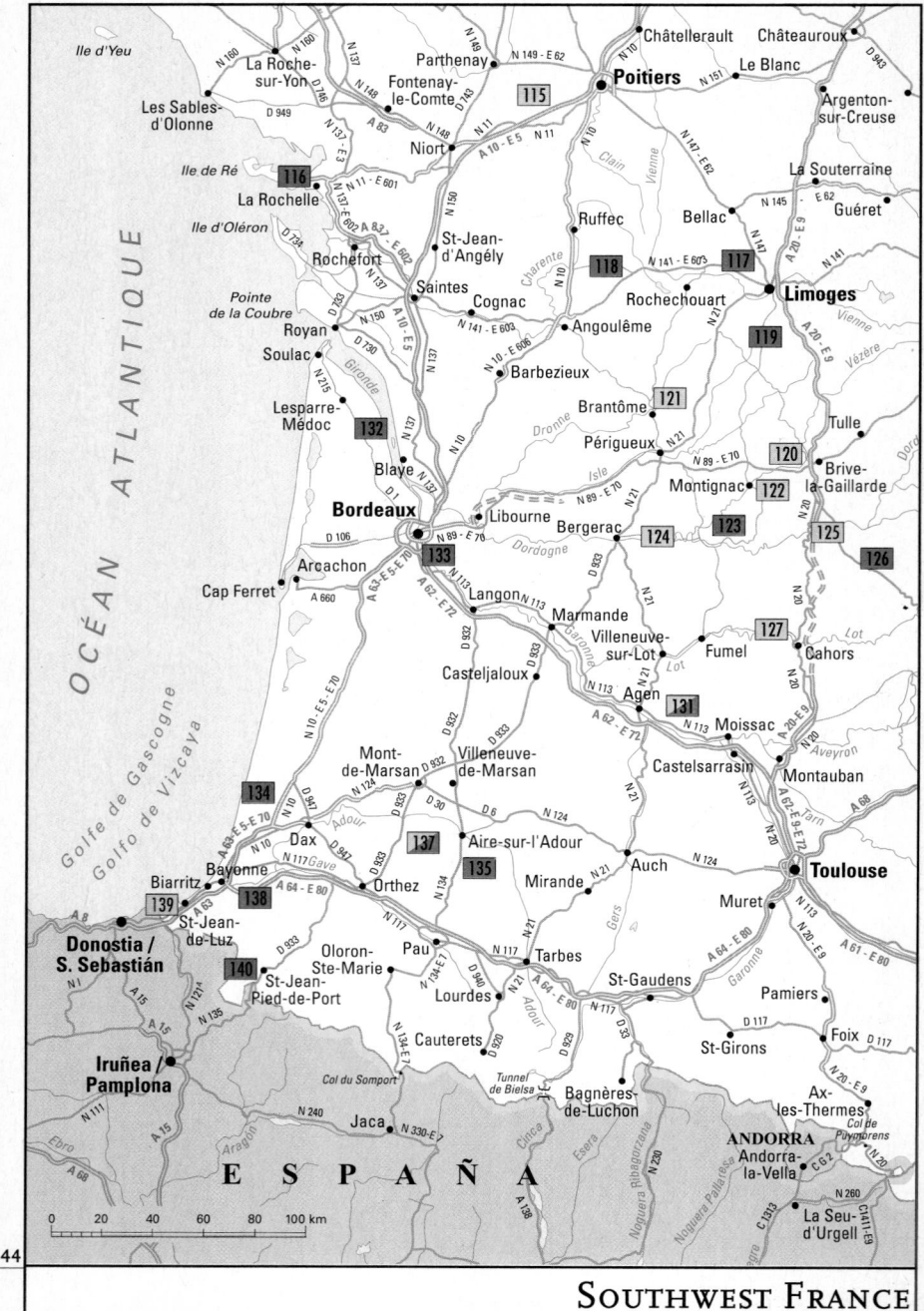

Île d'Yeu

Les Sables-
d'Olonne

La Roche-
sur-Yon

Parthenay

Fontenay-
le-Comte

Niort

Châtellerault

Châteauroux

Poitiers

Le Blanc

Argenton-
sur-Creuse

115

Île de Ré

116

La Rochelle

Île d'Oléron

Rochefort

St-Jean-
d'Angély

Saintes

Cognac

Ruffec

Bellac

La Souterraine

Guéret

145

118

117

Limoges

119

Pointe
de la Coubre

Royan

Soulac

Lesparre-
Médoc

132

Blaye

Barbezieux

Angoulême

Rochechouart

Brantôme

121

Périgueux

120

Tulle

Brive-
la-Gaillarde

Bordeaux

Libourne

Bergerac

124

Montignac

122

123

125

126

Cap Ferret

Arcachon

133

OCÉAN ATLANTIQUE

Langon

Marmande

Casteljaloux

Villeneuve-
sur-Lot

Fumel

Cahors

127

Golfe de Gascogne
Golfo de Vizcaya

Mont-
de-Marsan

Villeneuve-
de-Marsan

Agen

131

Moissac

Castelsarrasin

Montauban

134

Dax

137

Aire-sur-l'Adour

135

Mirande

Auch

Toulouse

Biarritz

Bayonne

139

138

St-Jean-
de-Luz

Orthez

Pau

Tarbes

Muret

Donostia /
S. Sebastián

140

Oloron-
Ste-Marie

Lourdes

St-Gaudens

Pamiers

St-Jean-
Pied-de-Port

Cauterets

St-Girons

Foix

Iruñea /
Pamplona

Col du Somport

Tunnel
de Bielsa

Bagnères-
de-Luchon

Ax-
les-Thermes

Col de
Puymorens

ANDORRA

Andorra-
la-Vella

Jaca

ESPAÑA

La Seu-
d'Urgell

0 20 40 60 80 100 km

44

SOUTHWEST FRANCE

EAST FRANCE

45

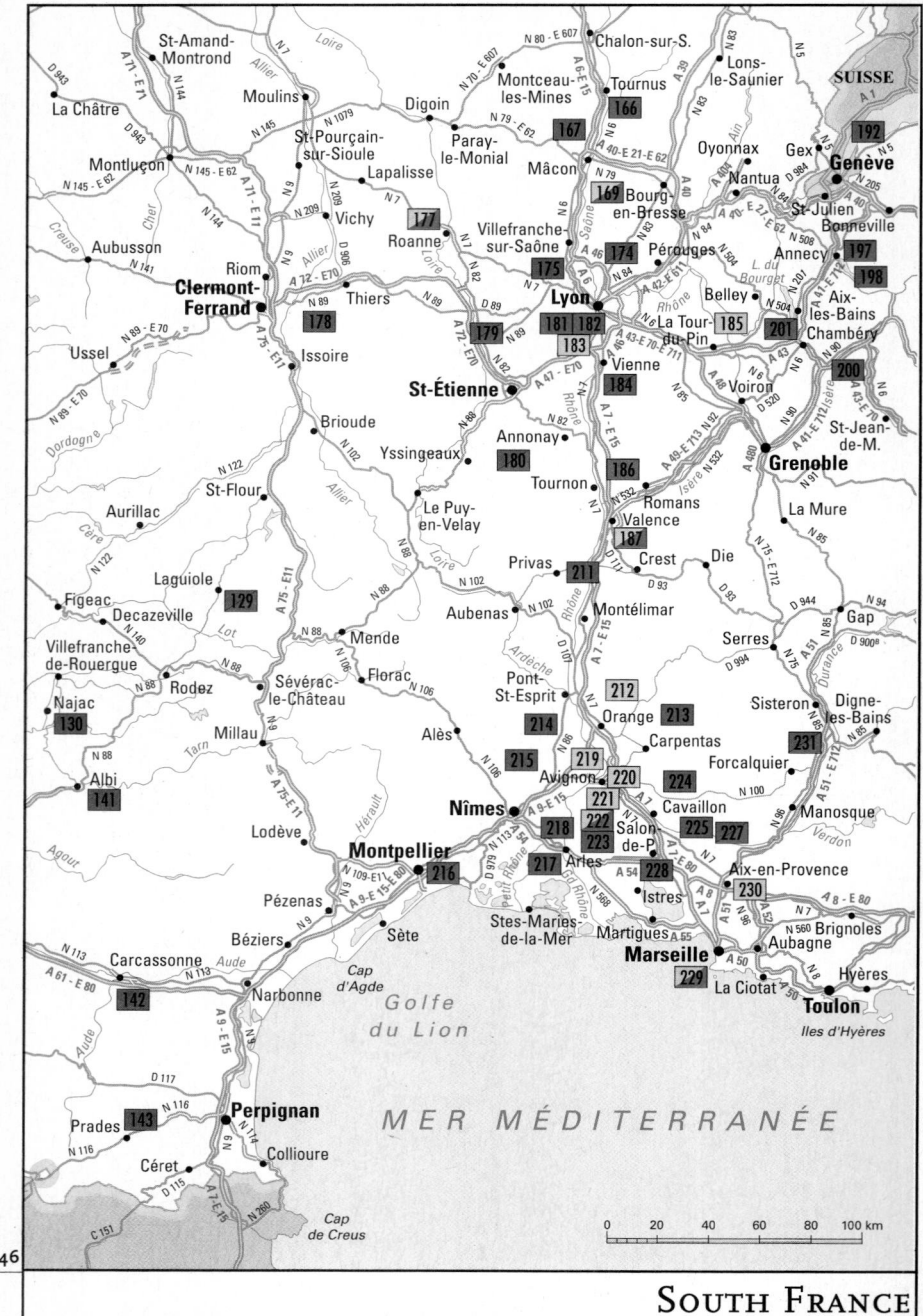

SOUTH FRANCE

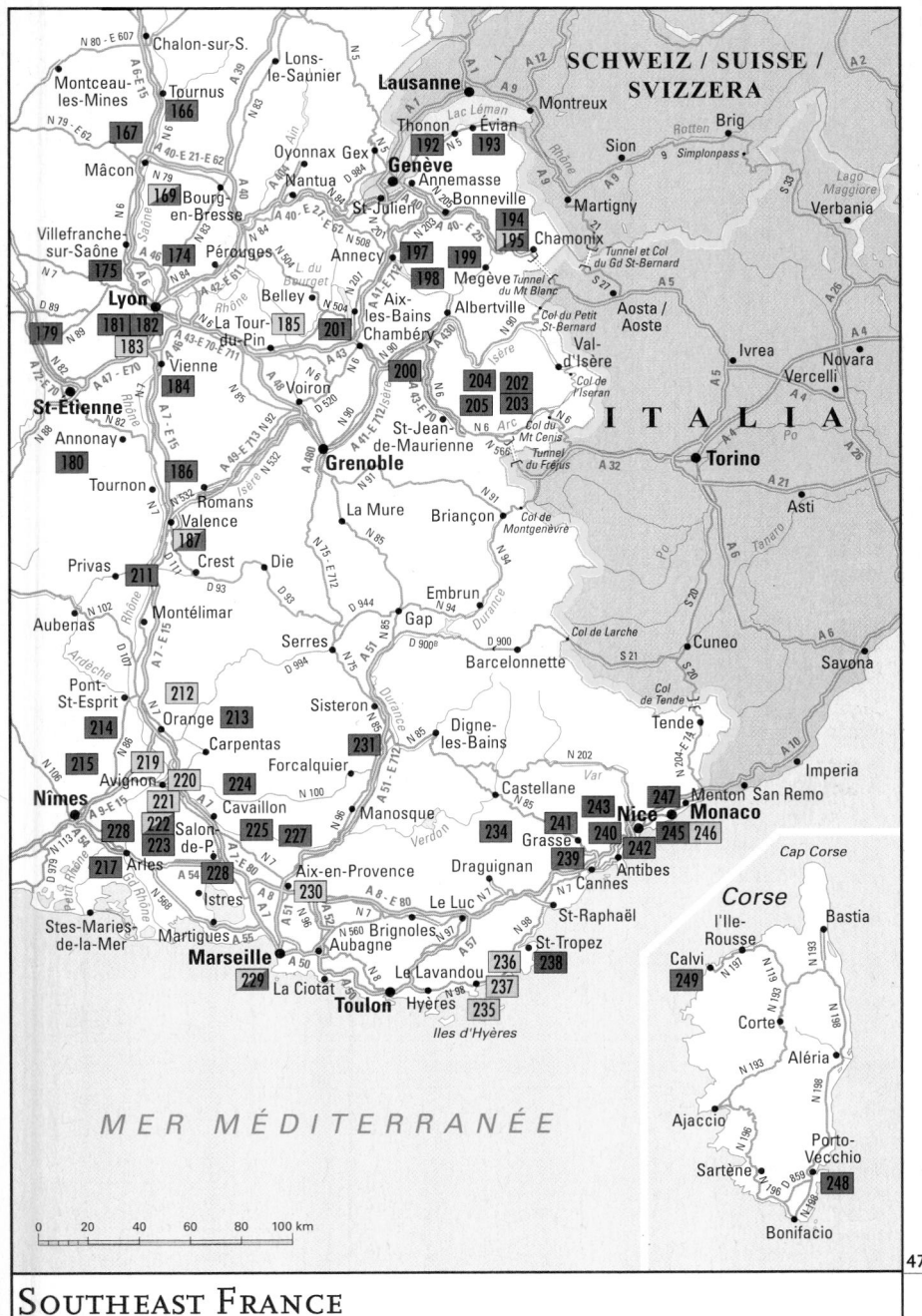

SCHWEIZ / SUISSE / SVIZZERA

ITALIA

Chalon-sur-S.
Montceau-les-Mines
Tournus **166**
167
Lons-le-Saunier
Lausanne
Montreux
Brig
Mâcon
Oyonnax Gex
Nantua
Thonon
Évian **193**
192
Genève
Annemasse
Sion
Simplonpass
Verbania
169 Bourg-en-Bresse
St-Julien
Bonneville
Martigny
Lago Maggiore
Villefranche-sur-Saône
174
Pérouges
197
Annecy
Chamonix
194
195
Tunnel et Col du Gd St-Bernard
175
Belley
198
Megève
Tunnel du Mt Blanc
Col du Petit St-Bernard
Aosta / Aoste
Lyon
181 182
183
La Tour-du-Pin
185
201
Aix-les-Bains
Chambéry
Albertville
Val-d'Isère
Ivrea
Novara
179
Vienne
184
200
204 202
205 203
Col de l'Iseran
Vercelli
St-Étienne
Voiron
St-Jean-de-Maurienne
Col du Mt Cenis
Tunnel du Fréjus
Torino
Annonay
Grenoble
Asti
180
Tournon
186
Romans
Valence **187**
La Mure
Briançon
Col de Montgenèvre
Privas
211
Crest
Die
Montélimar
Serres
Gap
Embrun
Col de Larche
Cuneo
Savona
Aubenas
Pont-St-Esprit
212
Orange **213**
Carpentras
231
Barcelonnette
Col de Tende
Tende
214
215
219
Avignon **220**
224
Sisteron
Digne-les-Bains
Imperia
Nîmes
221
222 223
Salon-de-P.
225 227
Cavaillon
Forcalquier
Castellane
Menton San Remo
247
Monaco
228
217
Arles
228
Aix-en-Provence
230
Manosque
Draguignan
234
Grasse
243
241
240
245 246
242
Nice
Antibes
Stes-Maries-de-la-Mer
Martigues
229
Istres
Aubagne
La Ciotat
Le Luc
Brignoles
St-Raphaël
Cannes
239
Marseille
Toulon
Hyères
Le Lavandou
236
237
St-Tropez
238
235
Iles d'Hyères

Cap Corse
Corse
l'Ile-Rousse
Bastia
Calvi **249**
Corte
Aléria
Ajaccio
Porto-Vecchio
248
Sartène
Bonifacio

MER MÉDITERRANÉE

0 20 40 60 80 100 km

SOUTHEAST FRANCE

TABLE OF EXCHANGE RATES

This table was established as of 31/07/99 by the services of the BFCE
It gives the indicative value of the currencies mentioned
(This rate must be adjusted to the value of the day when the transaction takes place)

WORLD

	Euro	GBP	USD	JPY (x100)
South Africa (ZAR)	0,151	0,100	0,162	0,186
Canada (CAD)	0,621	0,410	0,664	0,766
Denmark (DKK)	0,134	0,088	0,143	0,165
Dubai (AED)	0,255	0,168	0,272	0,314
Euro (€)	1,000	1,516	0,935	0,811
United Kingdom (GBP)	1,516	1,000	1,6202	1,869
Greece (GRD) (x100)	0,3	0,198	0,33	0,370
Iceland (ISK)	0,013	0,009	0,014	0,016
Japan (JPY) (x100)	0,811	0,535	0,86	1,000
Lebanon (LBP) (x100)	0,061	0,040	0,06	0,075
Lithuania (LTL)	0,235	0,155	0,250	0,290
Mexico (MXP)	0,0993	0,066	0,1062	0,122
Norway (NOK)	0,120	0,079	0,128	0,148
New Zealand (NZD)	0,496	0,327	0,528	0,612
Czech Republic (CZK)	0,027	0,018	0,029	0,033
Seychelles (SCR)	0,176	0,116	0,189	0,217
Sweden (SEK)	0,114	0,075	0,122	0,141
Switzerland (CHF)	0,626	0,413	0,667	0,772
USA (USD)	0,935	0,617	1,000	1,153

TABLE OF EXCHANGE RATES

This table was established as of 01/01/99 by the services of the Bank of France

VALUE OF THE EURO

		Values
	Germany (DEM)	1,95583
	Austria (ATS)	13,7603
	Belgium (BEF)	40,3399
	Spain (ESP)	166,386
	France (FRF)	6,55957
	Ireland (IEP)	0,787564
	Italy (ITL)	1936,27
	Luxembourg (LUX)	40,3399
	Netherlands (NLG)	2,20371
	Portugal (PTE)	200,482

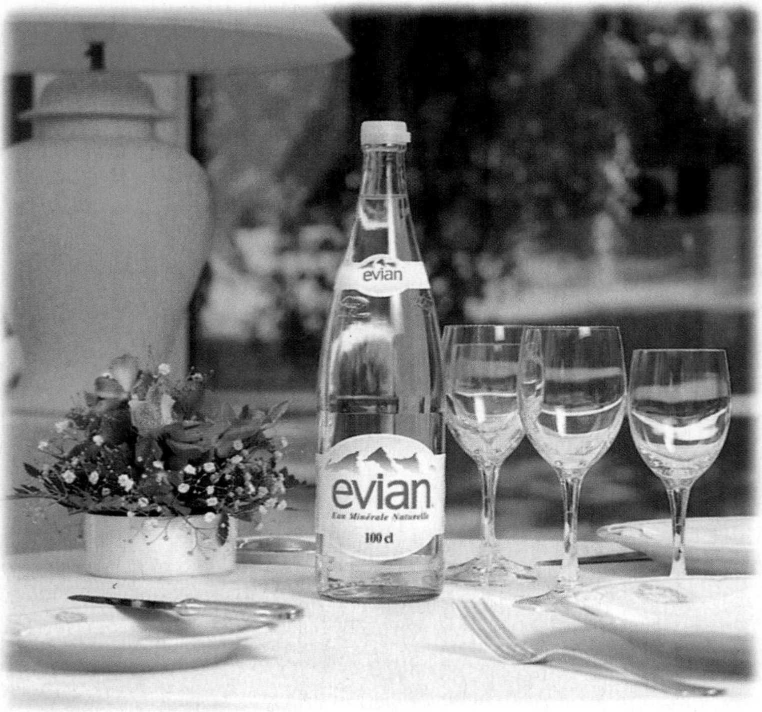

Evian. The mineral water on the world's finest tables.

RESTAURANT MICHEL ROSTANG

France

20, rue Rennequin
(angle rue Gustave Flaubert)
75017 Paris

Tel. : (33) 01 47 63 40 77
Fax : (33) 01 47 63 82 75
E-mail : rostang@relaischateaux.fr

*From Etoile, take av. de Wagram
and the 2nd left (rue Rennequin)
after place des Ternes.*

Owner : Michel Rostang
Weekly closing :
Saturday (lunch), Sunday
and Monday (lunch)
Annual closing :
1st fortnight in August

Orly (**Intl**) 20 km
Ch. de Gaulle (**Intl**) 25 km

Menus **690-890 FRF** s.i.
105-136 €
385 FRF (week lunch)
59 €
Carte **680-780 FRF** s.i.
104-119 €

yes

B rochettes de langoustines au romarin», «risotto de homard et petit épeautre», «canette de Bresse "Miéral" au sang» and the dazzling finale : «tarte chaude au chocolat amer». Virtuoso chef Michel Rostang, a Dauphinois who has become an honorary Parisian, creates a veritable symphony of flavours, elevating gourmet cuisine to its highest level. This elegant restaurant's wine list is truly exceptional.

55

Visa

HÔTEL DE VIGNY

SINCE 1993

Tel. : (33) 01 42 99 80 80
Fax : (33) 01 42 99 80 40
E-mail : vigny@relaischateaux.fr

9-11, rue Balzac
75008 Paris

France

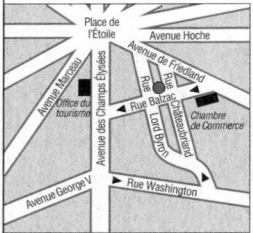

At the top of the Champs-Elysées, via rue Washington and rue Chateaubriand.

Owner : SA de Vigny
Director : Christian Falcucci
Open all year

✈	Orly (**Intl**) 15 km Ch. de Gaulle (**Intl**) 25 km
🍴	Carte **250-300 FRF** s.i. **38-46 €**
⚷	26 rooms **2 200-2 500 FRF** s.i. **335-381 €**
⚷	11 suites **3 000-4 500 FRF** s.i. **457-686 €**
☕	**100 FRF** s.i. **15 €**
🛎	yes
🎿	15 km

S tep behind the chic modern façade of the Hôtel de Vigny and discover a haven of calm and refinement far removed from the hustle and bustle outside. Enjoy a light meal or drink in the Art Deco ambience of the Baretto, sip a cup of tea in the mahogany-panelled lounge or savour a delicious breakfast in one of the artistically designed guest-rooms. Comfort, charm and impeccable service await you in the heart of Paris.

Visa

FRF : French franc

www.relaischateaux.fr/vigny

APICIUS

France

122, avenue de Villiers
75017 Paris

Tel. : (33) 01 43 80 19 66
Fax : (33) 01 44 40 09 57
E-mail : apicius@relaischateaux.fr

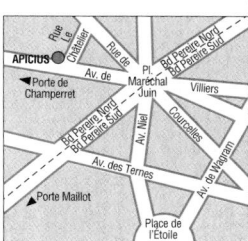

From Etoile, av. Mac Mahon,
av. Niel, to the left of place
du Maréchal Juin, av. de Villiers.

Owner : Jean-Pierre Vigato
Weekly closing :
Saturday and Sunday
Annual closing :
From August 1st to 30th

 Orly (**Intl**) 15 km
Ch. de Gaulle (**Intl**) 25 km

 Menu tasting **600 FRF** s.i.
91 €
Carte
starting at **500 FRF** s.i.
76 €
750-800 FRF s.i.
(wine included)
114-122 €

 yes

Gourmets flock to this elegant restaurant, named after the famous gourmet of Roman times, to savour Jean-Pierre Vigato's inspired cuisine. The menu is a celebration of pure flavours, offering «foie gras de canard poêlé en aigre-doux aux radis noirs confits» and «pigeon de ferme désossé et farci de vieux jambon et champignons». Savour the sublime «soufflé au chocolat noir», a veritable delight.

FRF : French franc

Le Divellec «La Cuisine de la Mer»

France

Tel. : (33) 01 45 51 91 96
Fax : (33) 01 45 51 31 75
E-mail : ledivellec@relaischateaux.fr

107, rue de l'Université
75007 Paris

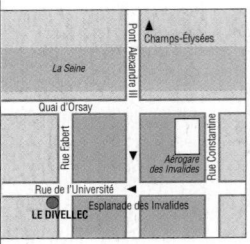

At the corner of rue de l'Université and the esplanade des Invalides.

Owner : Jacques Le Divellec
Weekly closing : Sunday
Annual closing :
From December 24th to January 3rd

✈ Orly (**Intl**) 15 km
Ch. de Gaulle (**Intl**) 25 km

🍴 Menus **290-390 FRF** s.i.
44-59 € (lunch only)
Carte **550-700 FRF** s.i.
84-107 €

🐾 no

This elegant restaurant, decorated in the style of a luxury yacht, is «moored» on the Invalides esplanade. Virtuoso chef Jacques Le Divellec stands at the helm, creating superb seafood cuisine with subtle Mediterranean accents. Gourmet guests will be enchanted by his «homard à la presse avec son corail» and «huîtres spéciales frémies à la laitue de mer». These culinary marvels are accompanied by the finest vintages.

  Visa

FRF : French franc

www.relaischateaux.fr/ledivellec

LE GRAND VÉFOUR

France

17, rue de Beaujolais
75001 Paris

Tel. : (33) 01 42 96 56 27
Fax : (33) 01 42 86 80 71
E-mail : vefour@relaischateaux.fr

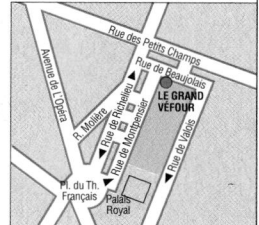

In the Palais-Royal gardens.

Owner : S.H. Concorde
Director : Guy Martin
Weekly closing :
Saturday and Sunday
Annual closing : August

 Orly (**Intl**) 15 km
Ch. de Gaulle (**Intl**) 25 km

 Menu **360 FRF** s.i. (lunch)
55 €
Carte **600-650 FRF** s.i.
91-99 €

 no

The 18th-century decor of this elegant restaurant, resplendent with gilt-edged mirrors and chandeliers, was once admired by Bonaparte, Victor Hugo, Colette, Malraux and Cocteau. Guy Martin carries on the gourmet tradition of Le Grand Véfour, with his sublime «ravioles de foie gras à l'émulsion de crème truffée», «tourte d'artichauts et légumes confits» and «sorbet aux amandes amères», served with the finest French wines.

67

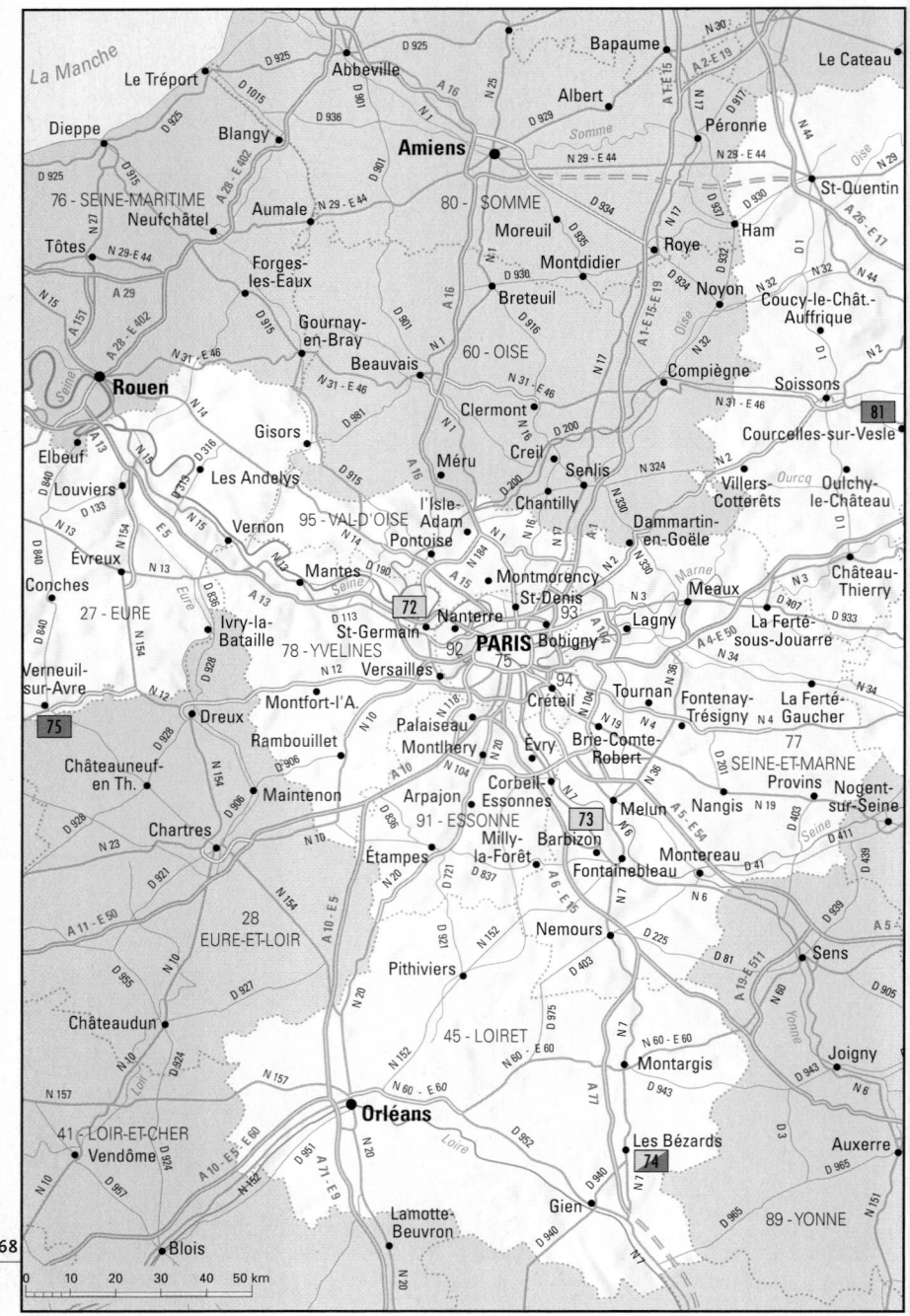

La Manche

Le Tréport
Dieppe
D 925
Blangy
D 915
D 1015
Abbeville
D 925
Bapaume
Albert
Le Cateau

76 - SEINE-MARITIME
Neufchâtel
Aumale
N 29 - E 44
Amiens
80 - SOMME
Somme
N 29 - E 44
Péronne
N 29 - E 44
St-Quentin

Tôtes
N 29-E 44
N 27
N 15
A 29
Forges-
les-Eaux
Gournay-
en-Bray
D 915
Moreuil
Montdidier
Breteuil
Roye
Noyon
Ham
Coucy-le-Chât.-
Auffrique

Rouen
N 31 - E 46
Beauvais
N 31 - E 46
60 - OISE
N 31 - E 46
Compiègne
N 31 - E 46
Soissons
81
Courcelles-sur-Vesle

Elbeuf
Louviers
Gisors
Clermont
Creil
Senlis
N 324
Villers-
Cotterêts
Oulchy-
le-Château
Ourcq

Les Andelys
Méru
Chantilly
N 330
Dammartin-
en-Goële
D 1
Château-
Thierry
D 933

Évreux
Conches
27 - EURE
Vernon
95 - VAL-D'OISE
l'Isle-
Adam
Pontoise
Mantes
Montmorency
St-Denis
Meaux
Marne
N 3
La Ferté-
sous-Jouarre

Ivry-la-
Bataille
78 - YVELINES
72
St-Germain
Nanterre
93
PARIS
75
Lagny
Bobigny
La Ferté-
Gaucher

Verneuil-
sur-Avre
75
Dreux
Montfort-l'A.
Versailles
92
94
Créteil
Tournan
Fontenay-
Trésigny
N 4

Châteauneuf-
en Th.
Rambouillet
Palaiseau
Montlhéry
Évry
Brie-Comte-
Robert
SEINE-ET-MARNE
77
Provins
Nogent-
sur-Seine

Maintenon
Arpajon
Corbeil-
Essonnes
73
Melun
Nangis
N 19

Chartres
N 23
91 - ESSONNE
Milly-
la-Forêt
Barbizon
Montereau

28
EURE-ET-LOIR
Étampes
Fontainebleau
N 6

Châteaudun
Pithiviers
Nemours
D 225
Sens

41 - LOIR-ET-CHER
Vendôme
45 - LOIRET
Montargis
Joigny
Auxerre
89 - YONNE

Orléans
Les Bézards
74

Lamotte-
Beuvron
Gien

Blois

68

0 10 20 30 40 50 km

PARIS REGION

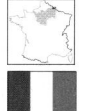

Establishments	Nearest major city	Relais & Châteaux	Relais Gourmands	Page
Auberge des Templiers	**Montargis**	⚜	👨‍🍳	**74**
Boyer «Les Crayères»	**Reims**	⚜	👨‍🍳	**79**
Cazaudehore et «La Forestière»	**St Germain en L.**	⚜		**72**
Château de Courcelles	**Soissons**	⚜		**81**
Hostellerie Le Clos	**Verneuil s/Avre**	⚜		**75**
Hotellerie du Bas-Bréau	**Fontainebleau**	⚜		**73**
Royal Champagne	**Epernay**	⚜		**77**

The Lange 1, in 18 k gold with outsize
date. Manually-wound 3-day power
reserve, 53 jewels, solid silver dial.

A. LANGE & SÖHNE

A combination of tradition and modern style. Fine works of art. Presented by a jeweller with the same philosophy.

VINTAGES TO DRINK IN YEAR 2000

CHAMPAGNE

**Wines recommended by the wine waiters
of the Relais & Châteaux and Relais Gourmands.**

* Index of world vintages to drink in year 2000 : page 607

	Name of wine	Wine to enjoy	Noble wine	Outstanding wine
	CHAMPAGNE			
White		1991	1990 - 1989	1988 - 1985
Rosé wines		1992	1990	1988 - 1986

CAZAUDEHORE ET «LA FORESTIÈRE»

SINCE 1973

Tel. : (33) 01 30 61 64 64
Fax : (33) 01 39 73 73 88
E-mail : cazaudehore@relaischateaux.fr

1, av. Kennedy
78100 St-Germain-en-Laye
(Yvelines)

France

From Paris, A13, 2nd exit, then RN 186 towards Saint-Germain, N 184 towards Pontoise.

Owner : Philippe Cazaudehore
Director : Philippe Cazaudehore
Weekly closing :
Rest. : Monday (except holidays)
Open all year

✈ Orly **(Intl)** 35 km
Ch. de Gaulle **(Intl)** 45 km

🍴 Menus
week lunch **300 FRF** s.i.
(wine included) - **46 €**
week-end **380 FRF** s.i.
(wine included) - **58 €**
Carte 450-500 FRF s.i.
69-76 €

⚷ 25 rooms
1 100 FRF s.i.
168 €

⚷ 5 suites
1 500 FRF s.i.
229 €

☕ 85 FRF s.i.
13 €

🐾 yes (extra cost **100 FRF** s.i.)
15 €

♪ 2 km

F rom this charming residence, nestling amidst rose gardens and forest groves, visitors can stroll along tranquil bridle paths to the Château de Saint-Germain-en-Laye where Louis XIV was born. «La Forestière», an idyllic rustic haven, offers exquisitely comfortable guestrooms, innovative cuisine, and an exceptional wine cellar. Enjoy lunch beneath the scented arbours in spring or dine beside a log fire in autumn.

FRF : French franc

HÔTELLERIE DU BAS-BRÉAU

France

22, rue Grande
77630 Barbizon
(Seine-et-Marne)

Tel. : (33) 01 60 66 40 05
Fax : (33) 01 60 69 22 89
E-mail : basbreau@relaischateaux.fr

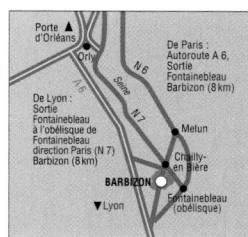

From Paris or Lyons, take highway A6, exit Fontainebleau, towards Barbizon (8 km).

Owners :
Jean-Pierre and Dominique Fava
Director : Tino Malchiodi
Open all year

✈ Orly (**Intl**) 40 km
Ch. de Gaulle (**Intl**) 80 km

🍴 Menus **400 FRF** s.i.
61 €
week lunch **365 FRF** s.i.
(drinks included)
56 €
Carte **600 FRF** s.i.
91 €

T his secluded hunting lodge, surrounded by a sea of greenery on the outskirts of Fontainebleau forest, is an oasis of comfort and tranquillity. Once a favourite retreat for the artists of the Barbizon school, the lodge's tastefully decorated rooms were more recently enjoyed by Emperor Hiro-Hito. A truly idyllic spot in which to savour gourmet cuisine and fine wines served in elegant crystal and silverware.

⊙ 12 rooms
1 000-1 700 FRF s.i.
152-259 €

⊙ 8 suites
starting at **1 900 FRF** s.i.
290 €

🍷 **100 FRF** s.i.
15 €

🍴 yes (extra cost)

🏃 Cély 3 km

 73

AUBERGE DES TEMPLIERS

Tel. : (33) 02 38 31 80 01
Fax : (33) 02 38 31 84 51
E-mail : templiers@relaischateaux.fr

Les Bezards
45290 Boismorand
(Loiret)

France

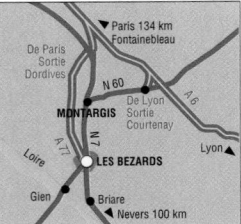

From Paris, A6 - exit Dordives,
then take A77 towards Nevers, exit
N° 19 Boismorand (2 km Auberge).

Owners : Dépée Family
Open all year

✈ Orly **(Intl)** 100 km
Vimory 20 km

🧭 GPS N 47° 48'
E 02° 44' 43"

🍴 Menus **320 FRF** (lunch)
49 €
420-750 FRF s.i.
64-114 €
Carte **480-680 FRF** s.i.
73-104 €

⚷ 22 rooms
650-1 380 FRF s.i.
99-210 €

⚷ 8 suites
starting at **1 500 FRF** s.i.
229 €

☕ 95 FRF s.i.
14 €

🍴 yes

♫ 2 to 25 km

T his former post house, beautifully
restored by the Dépée Family 50 years
ago, was one of the first Relais & Châteaux.
Savour a superb «marbré d'asperges vertes
au foie gras à la vinaigrette d'huile de
truffes» and enjoy prestigious wines in the
restaurant overlooking a magnificent park
full of hundred-year-old oaks. Explore the
Loire châteaux, the beautiful Sologne
forests and the vineyards of Sancerre and
Pouilly.

FRF : French franc

HOSTELLERIE LE CLOS

France

98, rue de la Ferté Vidame - BP 323
27133 Verneuil-sur-Avre Cedex
(Eure)

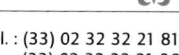
Tel. : (33) 02 32 32 21 81
Fax : (33) 02 32 32 21 36
E-mail : leclos@relaischateaux.fr

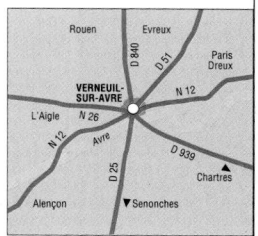

From Paris, A12/A13 towards Dreux and N12 until Verneuil; stay on N12 and turn right at the 1st light.

Owners :
Colette and Patrick Simon
Weekly closing :
Restaurant : Monday
Annual closing :
From Dec. 16th to Jan. 18th

This authentic Norman manor, with its impressive slate-roofed turrets and magnificent red brick façade, lies in a fortified village built by King Henry I in the early 12th century. The old-fashioned living room and the guestrooms filled with tasteful antique furniture are imbued with historic charm, while the dining room is decorated in stunning trompe l'œil. Superb cuisine is enhanced by an excellent wine list.

✈ Ch. de Gaulle (**Intl**) 110 km
Orly (**Intl**) 110 km

Menus **190-380 FRF** s.i.
29-58 €
Menu-Carte **300 FRF** s.i.
46 €
half-board
(week-end and holidays)

4 rooms
850-950 FRF s.i.
130-145 €

6 suites
starting at **1 200 FRF** s.i.
183 €

90 FRF s.i.
14 €

yes (extra cost)

7 km

Hunting, fishing,
mountain biking, fitness centre.

P

FRF : French franc

ROYAL CHAMPAGNE

France

51160 Champillon-Epernay
(Marne)

Tel. : (33) 03 26 52 87 11
Fax : (33) 03 26 52 89 69
E-mail : royalchampagne@relaischateaux.fr

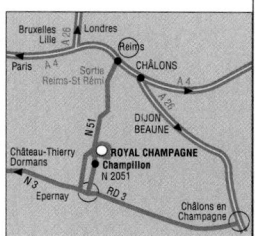

*From Paris : exit the A4 or A26
at Reims, exit St. Rémi, N51
towards Epernay, then towards
Champillon, N2051.
From Troyes : leave the A26 at
Châlons, exit St-Gibrien.*

Owner : Provital S.A.
Director : Alain Guichaoua
Open all year

 Orly (**Intl**) 130 km
Ch. de Gaulle (**Intl**) 130 km

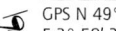 GPS N 49° 05' 34"
E 3° 58' 35"

Menus **195 FRF** s.i.
(lunch - except sunday)
30 €
280-380 FRF s.i. (dinner)
43-58 €
Carte **320-450 FRF** s.i.
49-69 €

This former coach inn is the ideal retreat for champagne enthusiasts who may select one of the Royal Champagne's two hundred and twenty varieties of bruts, rosés and exceptional vintages to accompany the excellent seasonal dishes. The tastefully decorated guestrooms and suites offer breathtaking views of the vineyards stretching away to the horizon and the river Marne shimmering in the distance.

26 rooms
880-1 350 FRF s.i.
134-206 €

3 suites
Season **1 500-1 800 FRF** s.i.
229-274 €

90 FRF s.i.
14 €

yes (extra cost)

practice

 Visa

77

Champagne POMMERY.
Ordinary days can have extraordinary moments !

BOYER «LES CRAYÈRES»

France

64, bd Henry-Vasnier
51100 Reims
(Marne)

Tel. : (33) 03 26 82 80 80
Fax : (33) 03 26 82 65 52
E-mail : crayeres@relaischateaux.fr

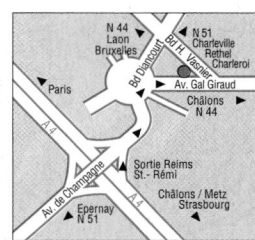

A4 or A26, exit Reims St-Rémi,
towards Luxemburg 800 m,
av. Gal Giraud then left turn.

Owner : Gérard Boyer
Weekly closing :
Rest. : Monday and Tuesday noon
Annual closing :
From Dec. 20th to January 10th

✈ Ch. de Gaulle (**Intl**) 130 km
Orly (**Intl**) 140 km

GPS N 49° 14' 52"
E 04° 02' 90"

🍴 Carte **600-750 FRF** s.i.
91-107 €

○ 16 rooms
1 390-1 990 FRF s.i.
212-303 €

○ 3 suites
1 990-2 550 FRF s.i.
303-389 €

☕ 128 FRF s.i.
20 €

🦃 yes (extra cost)

🏌 Gueux 5 km

Gérard and Elyane Boyer welcome you to an elegant turn-of-the-century residence set in English-style parkland. Blending tradition, comfort and refinement, the Boyers have created a luxurious gourmet retreat, where guests can relax in sumptuous rooms and savour superb cuisine. The «filets de rouget de roche grillés, sauce au thym, petite galette de pommes de terre dorées et ail doux caramélisé» is simply sublime.

www.relaischateaux.fr/crayeres

FRF : French franc

Visa

79

PIERRE FREY

Paris

CREATEUR · EDITEUR · FABRICANT
étoffes d'ameublement

Collection *Comoglio*

BRITTANY - NORMANDY PAS-DE-CALAIS

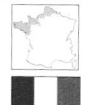

Establishments	Nearest major city	Relais & Châteaux	Relais Gourmands	Page
Auberge Bretonne (L')	La Roche Bernard	⚜	🧑‍🍳	96
Bretagne et sa Résidence (Le)	Vannes	⚜	🧑‍🍳	95
Castel Clara	Belle-Ile-en-Mer	⚜		94
Castel Marie-Louise	Nantes	⚜		97
Château d'Audrieu	Caen	⚜		87
Château de Locguénolé	Lorient	⚜	🧑‍🍳	93
Château de Montreuil	Montreuil/mer	⚜		84
Chaumière (La)	Honfleur	⚜		86
Ferme St-Siméon (La)	Honfleur	⚜		85
Goyen (Le)	Audierne	⚜		91
Hôtel de la Plage	Douarnenez	⚜		90
Maisons de Bricourt	Cancale	⚜	🧑‍🍳	88
Manoir de Lan-Kerellec	Lannion	⚜		89

CHÂTEAU DE MONTREUIL

Tel. : (33) 03 21 81 53 04
Fax : (33) 03 21 81 36 43
E-mail : montreuil@relaischateaux.fr

4, chaussée des Capucins
62170 Montreuil-sur-Mer
(Pas-de-Calais)

France

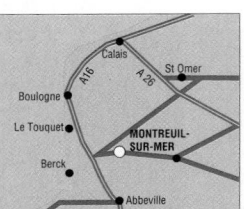

Opposite the Roman citadel of Montreuil-sur-Mer; from north first right, from south 3rd left.

Owners :
Christian and Lindsay Germain
Weekly closing :
Hotel/Rest. : Monday from October to April (except holidays)
Rest. only : Thursday at lunch all year long
Annual closing :
From mid-Dec. to end of January

✈ Ch. de Gaulle (**Intl**) 180 km
Lille 120 km

🍴 Menus **200-400 FRF** s.i.
30-61 €
Carte **350 FRF** s.i.
53 €

⊶ 13 rooms
950-1 100 FRF s.i.
145-168 €
1 800 FRF s.i.
(half board 2 p.)
274 €

⊶ 1 suite
1 850 FRF s.i.
(half board 2 p.)
282 €

☕ 80 FRF s.i.
12 €

🐕 yes (extra cost)

🏃 3 nearby

T his beautiful manor house, secluded behind elegant ramparts, offers comfortable rooms opening out onto exquisite landscape gardens. In this atmosphere of bucolic charm you will be enchanted by Christian Germain's cuisine, a delicious concoction of light sauces made with fresh local ingredients and garden vegetables and herbs. After sampling one of the fine wines you will find it hard to leave this earthly paradise.

Visa

FRF : French franc

www.relaischateaux.fr/montreuil

SINCE 1964

LA FERME SAINT-SIMÉON

France

Rue Adolphe-Marais
14600 Honfleur
(Calvados)

Tel. : **(33) 02 31 81 78 00**
Fax : **(33) 02 31 89 48 48**
E-mail : simeon@relaischateaux.fr

*From Paris A14, A13, A29, exit 3.
Cross Honfleur then take D513
by the coast.*

Owners : Boelen Family
Open all year

Deauville (**Intl**) 10 km
Ch. de Gaulle (**Intl**) 190 km

GPS N 49° 25' 32"
E 000° 13' 09"

The beautifully restored farm was the favourite retreat of 19th-century painters such as Monet, Sisley, Courbet, Boudin and Jongkind, who were enchanted by the ethereal light reflected in its estuary. The charm of bygone days still lingers on in the farm's tastefully decorated rooms. Savour delicious seafood and regional cuisine, relax in the elegant Italian palace decor of the spa or visit the picturesque port of Honfleur.

Menus **240 FRF** s.i.
(week lunch) - **37 €**
590 FRF s.i. - **90 €**
Carte **450-520 FRF** s.i.
69-79 €

25 rooms
790-2 690 FRF s.i.
120-410 €

4 suites
4 400-5 100 FRF s.i.
671-777 €

95 FRF s.i.
14 €

in some rooms

7 km

Beauty centre, bio-sauna face and body treatments, solarium, jacuzzis and special terrace service.

85

www.relaischateaux.fr/simeon

. FRF : French franc

Visa

LA CHAUMIÈRE

SINCE 1993

Tel. : (33) 02 31 81 63 20
Fax : (33) 02 31 89 59 23
E-mail : chaumiere@relaischateaux.fr

Route du Littoral
14600 Honfleur-Vasouy
(Calvados)

France

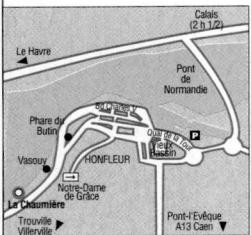

*From Paris A14, A13, A29, exit 3.
Cross Honfleur then take D513
by the coast.*

Owners : Boelen Family
Weekly closing :
Rest.: Tuesday and Wed. at lunch
Open all year

✈ Deauville (**Intl**) 10 km
Ch. de Gaulle (**Intl**) 190 km

🍴 Menus **190-380 FRF** s.i.
29-58 €
Carte **250-350 FRF** s.i.
38-53 €

☛ 8 rooms
990-1 350 FRF s.i.
151-206 €

☛ 1 suite
2 400 FRF s.i.
366 €

☕ **85 FRF** s.i.
13 €

🐕 in some rooms

🏊 6 km

Private access to the beach,
terrace service, forest walks,
sailing, fishing, polo.

T he Seine meets the sea at the foot of this magnificent half-timbered «chaumière» so typical of the Normandy region. Lie beneath the ancient oak-beamed ceilings and enjoy the bucolic charm of its eight cosy guestrooms, each individually decorated. The garden terrace is an idyllic setting in which to savour simple, traditional cuisine prepared with fresh ingredients from the sea and the surrounding countryside.

FRF : French franc

www.relaischateaux.fr/chaumiere

CHÂTEAU D'AUDRIEU

France

14250 Audrieu
(Calvados)

Tel. : (33) 02 31 80 21 52
Fax : (33) 02 31 80 24 73
E-mail : audrieu@relaischateaux.fr

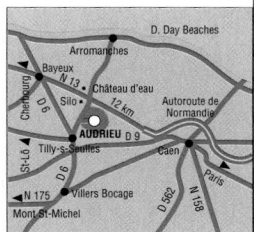

Caen-Bayeux expressway, exit 2nd interchange after Caen; D158 b.

Owners : Livry-Level Family
Directors : Jean-Marc Schnell, Angela Vallée
Weekly closing :
Restaurant Monday and Tuesday for lunch (except seminars)
Limited menu for guests on Monday evening in the high season
Annual closing :
From Dec. 23rd to Jan. 31st

S et amidst exquisite French gardens and acres of beautiful parkland, this magnificent 18th-century château is a protected historical monument. Gérard and Irène Livry-Level have lovingly preserved the original architecture of their ancestral home while embellishing its rooms with tasteful modern decor. Enjoy innovative cuisine and fine wines from the Loire and Central France in one of the three sumptuous dining rooms.

 Ch. de Gaulle (**Intl**) 250 km
Caen 12 km

 Menus 185-480 FRF s.i.
28-73 €
Carte 350-470 FRF s.i.
53-72 €

 25 rooms
790-2 050 FRF s.i.
120-313 €

 5 suites
2 300 FRF s.i.
351 €

 Continental 90 FRF s.i.
14 €
Buffet 135 FRF s.i.
21 €

yes (extra cost) except rest.

15 km

FRF : French franc

MAISONS DE BRICOURT

SINCE 1989

Tel. : (33) 02 99 89 64 76
Fax : (33) 02 99 89 88 47
E-mail : bricourt@relaischateaux.fr

1, rue Duguesclin
35260 Cancale
(Ille-et-Villaine)

France

*From Rennes, N137 via
Saint-Malo. Taxi service
between the 3 residences.*

Owner : Olivier Rœllinger
Weekly closing :
Rest. : Tuesday and Wednesday
and from December 15th
to March 15th
Open all year

✈ Dinard 20 km
Rennes 70 km

🍴 Le Relais Gourmand
Menu **260 FRF** s.i. (lunch)
40 €
Carte **480 FRF** s.i.
73 €
Le Coquillage
115-168-220 FRF s.i.
18-26-34 €

⚲ 16 rooms
750-1 500 FRF s.i.
114-229 €

⚲ 3 suites
1 000-1 600 FRF s.i
152-244 €

☕ **90 FRF** s.i.
14 €

🐴 yes (extra cost)

⚞ 12 km

Horseback riding (200 m).

Three idyllic retreats await you in the picturesque Saint-Malo region. Enjoy rustic elegance at «Les Rimains», a cottage facing the Cancale oyster beds and dine at «Le Château Richeux», the sea-front bistrot «Le Coquillage» overlooking Mont-Saint-Michel bay. Savour Olivier Rœllinger's gourmet specialities : «saint-pierre retour des Indes» and «homard aux saveurs de l'île aux épices» in his childhood home, an 18th-century «malouinière».

FRF : French franc

www.relaischateaux.fr/bricourt

MANOIR DE LAN-KERELLEC

France

Allée centrale de Lan-Kerellec
22560 Trébeurden
(Côtes d'Armor)

Tel. : **(33) 02 96 15 47 47**
Fax : **(33) 02 96 23 66 88**
E-mail : lankerellec@relaischateaux.fr

*Lannion, D 65 Trébeurden,
towards «Les Plages» /
Perros-Guirec, before village exit.*

Owners :
Luce and Gilles Daubé
Annual closing :
From mid-March to mid-November

 Brest (**Intl**) 80 km
Lannion 7 km

This 19th-century Breton manor, lovingly restored and decorated by Luce Daubé, lies on the Côte de Granit rose within walking distance of fine sand beaches. The guestrooms all overlook the sea while the cruiseliner-style dining room offers superb panoramic views of the coast and the local islands. Savour Loire wines and imaginative cuisine prepared with fresh ingredients from the sea and surrounding countryside.

 Menus **140-380 FRF** s.i.
21-58 €
Carte **230-450 FRF** s.i.
35-69 €

 16 rooms
550-1 700 FRF s.i.
84-259 €

 3 suites
starting at **2 000 FRF** s.i.
305 €

 80-120 FRF s.i.
12-18 €

 yes (extra cost)

St-Samson 5 km
several golf courses 50 km

Water-skiing, fishing, sailing,
mountain biking, jacuzzi,
strolling on the islands.

 **89**

FRF : French franc   Visa

Hôtel de la Plage

Since 1971

Tel. : (33) 02 98 92 50 12
Fax : (33) 02 98 92 56 54
E-mail : laplage@relaischateaux.fr

Sainte-Anne-la-Palud
29550 Plonevez-Porzay
(Finistère Sud)

France

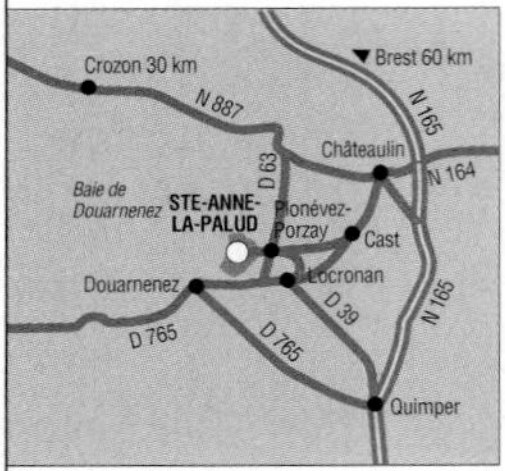

From Rennes, N165, exit Quimper Nord, D39 until Plonevez-Porzay, D61 towards Ste-Anne-la-Palud.

Owners : Le Coz Family
Directors :
Anne and Jean Milliau Le Coz
Weekly closing :
Rest. : Tuesday for lunch
(low season, except group)
Annual closing :
From mid-November
to the end of March

Brest (**Intl**) 80 km
Quimper 25 km

Menus **220-450 FRF** s.i.
34-69 €
Carte **300-550 FRF** s.i.
46-84 €

26 rooms
840-1 400 FRF s.i.
128-213 €

4 suites
1 100-1 400 FRF s.i.
168-213 €

80 FRF s.i.
12 €

yes (extra cost) except rest.

35 km

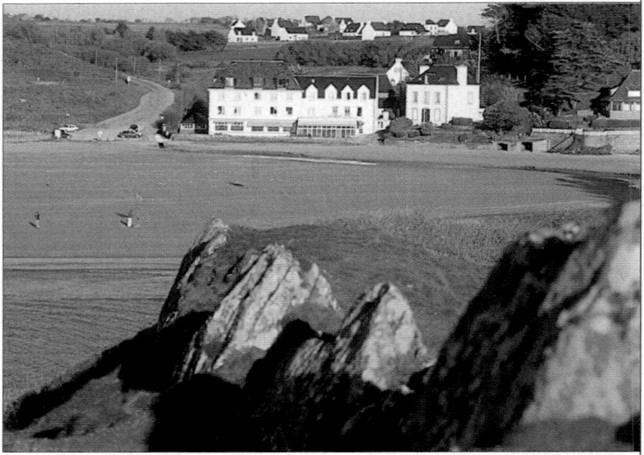

Contemplate the fiery splendour of a Breton sunset from the windows of this charming hotel, which has been welcoming guests with family-style hospitality since the 1920's. Savour excellent regional cuisine, prepared with the local fishermen's catch of the day, and enjoy fine Loire wines. After an invigorating stroll along the sandy shore, the soothing sound of the waves will lull you to sleep in your cosy guestroom.

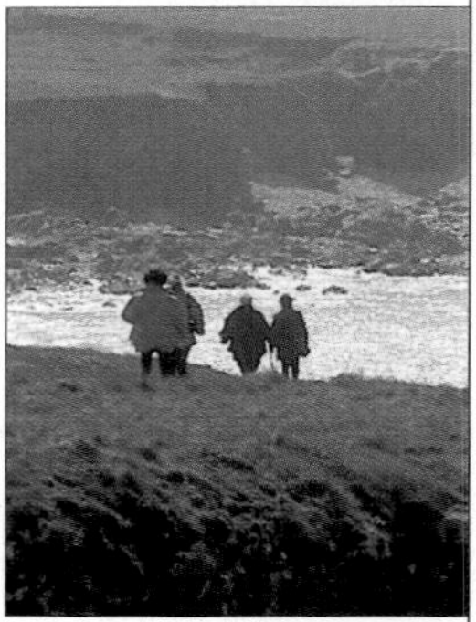

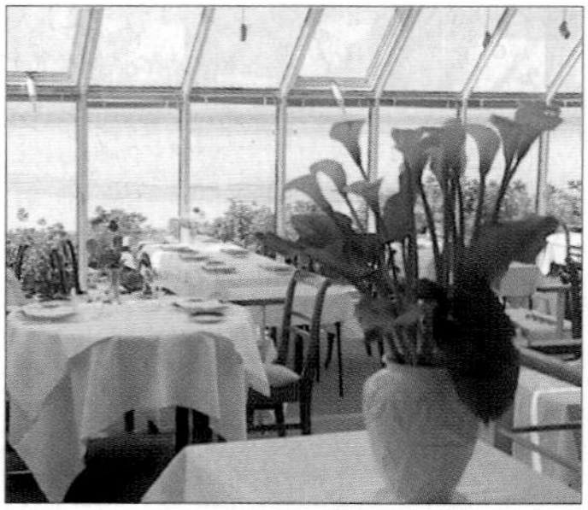

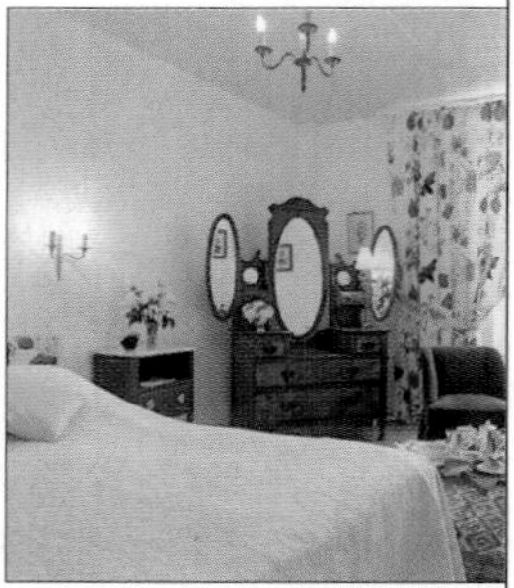

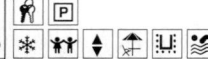

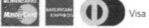

Visa

FRF : French franc

www.relaischateaux.fr/laplage

LE GOYEN

France

Place Jean Simon
29770 Audierne
(Finistère)

Tel. : (33) 02 98 70 08 88
Fax : (33) 02 98 70 18 77
E-mail : goyen@relaischateaux.fr

Océan Atlantique

From Paris : towards Chartres : A11.
From Mans : towards Rennes : A81.
From Rennes : towards Lorient : N165.
From Lorient : towards Quimper : N165.
From Quimper : towards Audierne : D784.

Owner : Adolphe Bosser
Weekly closing :
Restaurant : Mondays
(low season except holidays)
Annual closing :
End November to December 26th
and from the beginning of January
to the beginning of April
(except for seminars)

Le Goyen, which lies on the banks of a Finistère river, is an ideal starting point from which to explore the Breton hinterlands such as the Pointe du Raz and the Ile de Sein. This charming hotel, whose long white façades and flower-bedecked terraces overlook the picturesque port of Audierne, is renowned for its convivial atmosphere. Enjoy delicious fresh fish and shellfish accompanied by a remarkable selection of white Burgundies.

✈ Brest (**Intl**) 100 km
Quimper 20 km

🍴 Menus **160-420 FRF** s.i.
24-64 €
Carte **350-480 FRF** s.i.
53-73 €

🔑 21 rooms
430-800 FRF s.i.
66-122 €

🔑 3 suites
800-1 300 FRF s.i.
122-198 €

☕ **70 FRF** s.i.
11 €

🛎 yes

🏃 38 km

     91

FRF : French franc

Visa

SIEMENS

Live graciously, with Siemens, in your kitchen.

At the dawn of the twenty-first century, luxury and the fine art of living are more than ever privileged values to nurture in our daily lives. With this in mind, Siemens invites you to benefit from its series of household appliances, to make your kitchen a privileged and creative place, where work and pleasure go hand in hand. Ovens, hoods, gas or electric glass-ceramic cooking units, dish washers, refrigerators, are waiting for your talents, to cultivate for you enchanting experiences in gracious living.

www.siemens.de/hausgeraete

basile 04 76 51 35 35

CHÂTEAU DE LOCGUÉNOLÉ

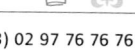

France

Route de Port-Louis
56700 Hennebont
(Morbihan)

Tel. : (33) 02 97 76 76 76
Fax : (33) 02 97 76 82 35
E-mail : locguenole@relaischateaux.fr

From Nantes or Rennes,
exit Port-Louis on the high-speed
route; then 2.5 km.

Owner : Alyette de la Sablière
Director : Bruno de la Sablière
Weekly closing :
Rest. closed on Monday
in winter (except for groups)
Annual closing :
From Jan. 2nd to Feb. 10th

This beautiful 19th-century castle and 18th-century manor stand in luxuriant parkland stretching 2km along a scenic bay. Historic furniture, wood panelling and tapestries recall the splendour of bygone days. The cuisine, pays tribute to Breton produce and local seafood. Savour the «poêlée de St- Jacques et bouquets, pomme de terre écrasée aux herbes, parfumée au rao-ram» enhanced by a superb wine list.

✈ Nantes (**Intl**) 160 km
Lorient 15 km

GPS N 47° 46' 14"
W 03° 17' 04

🍴 Menus **190-520 FRF** s.i.
29-79 €
Carte **350-450 FRF** s.i.
53-69 €

☞ 24 rooms
680-1 560 FRF s.i.
104-238 €

☞ 4 suites
1 370-2 300 FRF s.i.
209-351 €

🍷 90 FRF s.i.
14 €

🐾 yes (extra-cost)

🎣 16 km

Boarding pontoon, sailing,
fishing, water-skiing.

FRF : French franc

Visa

CASTEL CLARA

SINCE
1982

France

Tel. : (33) 02 97 31 84 21
Fax : (33) 02 97 31 51 69
E-mail : castelclara@relaischateaux.fr

Goulphar, Belle-Ile-en-Mer
56360 Bangor
(Morbihan)

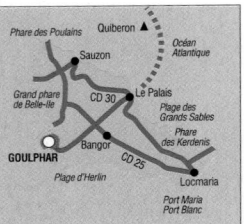

From Port Maria Quiberon,
45 min. crossing. At the Palais,
towards Goulphar (8 km).

Owner : SNHPET
Director : Claire Goumy-Meunier
Annual closing :
From Nov. 15th to Feb. 15th

✈ Nantes (**Intl**) 150 km
  Lorient 45 km

🍴 Menus **185-400 FRF** s.i.
  28-61 €
  Carte **280-460 FRF** s.i.
  43-70 €

⚷ 32 rooms
  940-1 650 FRF s.i.
  143-252 €

⚷ 11 suites
  1 390-3 490 FRF s.i.
  212-532 €

☕ **150 FRF** s.i.
  23 €

🐾 yes extra cost (except rest.)

♘ 8 km

Horse riding.

T his hotel, perched above the spectacular coast of Belle-Ile-en-Mer, offers breathtaking views of the ocean and the cliffs of Goulphar. It combines the charm of unspoiled natural surroundings with the height of luxury and refinement. The tastefully decorated rooms are spacious and peaceful, the seafood cuisine as invigorating as the climate. Stroll on the heather-covered hills or relax in the thalassotherapy institute.

P 🚻 ⬍ ✈ 🏨 🌊 ✒

MasterCard AMERICAN EXPRESS 🅓 Visa

FRF : French franc

www.relaischateaux.fr/castelclara

LE BRETAGNE ET SA RÉSIDENCE

France

13, rue Saint Michel
56230 Questembert
(Morbihan)

Tel. : (33) 02 97 26 11 12
Fax : (33) 02 97 26 12 37
E-mail : bretagne@relaischateaux.fr

From Nantes, take the N165, cross the «La Vilaine» river, D 139, follow signs.

Owner : Georges Paineau
Weekly closing : Monday all day and Tuesday noon (except July-August and holidays)
Annual closing :
3 weeks in January

I n this charming ivy-clad manor in the picturesque town of Questembert, Georges Paineau and his son-in-law Claude Corlouer create culinary master-pieces of extraordinary colour and flavour. Savour superb «turbot rôti aux étrilles écrasées, salpicon de légumes», exquisite «dos de cabillaud en croûte d'herbes au poivre de Setchuan» or try the «poitrine de pigeon laquée à la sauge». After your meal, retire to a pretty guestroom.

✈ Nantes **(Intl)** 80 km
 Lorient 60 km

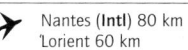 GPS N 47° 39' 37"
W 002° 26' 46"

🍴 Menus
210-295-395-490 FRF s.i.
32-45-60-75 €
Carte 380-530 FRF s.i.
58-81 €

⚷ 6 rooms
580-980 FRF s.i.
88-149 €

⚷ 3 suites
1 200-1 400 FRF s.i.
183-213 €

☕ 90 FRF s.i.
14 €

🐕 yes (extra cost)

🚶 12 km

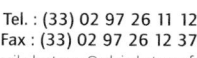

95

L'AUBERGE BRETONNE

SINCE 1994

Tel. : (33) 02 99 90 60 28
Fax : (33) 02 99 90 85 00
E-mail : aubbretonne@relaischateaux.fr

2, place Duguesclin
56130 La Roche-Bernard
(Morbihan)

France

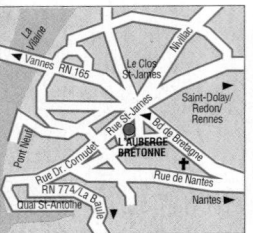

From Paris, A11 via Chartres, Angers, Nantes N165 towards Vannes.

Owner : Jacques Thorel
Weekly closing :
Rest. : Monday noon (from Sept. to June) and from Thursday morning to Friday 4pm
Annual closing : From January 4th to 26th and from November 13th to December 2nd

✈ Nantes (**Intl**) 60 km
Rennes 90 km

🍴 Menus **150-650 FRF** s.i.
23-99 €
Carte **320-450 FRF** s.i.
49-69 €

⚷ 8 rooms
500-1 500 FRF s.i.
76-229 €

☕ 90 FRF s.i.
14 €

🐴 yes (extra cost)

🏌 10 km

Polo, fishing, flying club...

This beautiful inn, lovingly restored by Solange and Jacques Thorel, is no longer a secret gourmet refuge. Today reservations must be made months in advance if you wish to savour the extraordinary «homard rôti au citron et au poivre, un blinis de blé noir» and exquisite «baba trempé à la chartreuse jaune, une crème glacée à la vanille». After enjoying one of the superb vintages, retire to a bright, comfortable guestroom.

FRF : French franc

www.relaischateaux.fr/aubbretonne

France

CASTEL MARIE-LOUISE

1, avenue Andrieu
44500 La Baule
(Loire-Atlantique)

Tel : (33) 02 40 11 48 38
Fax : (33) 02 40 11 48 35
E-mail : marielouise@relaischateaux.fr

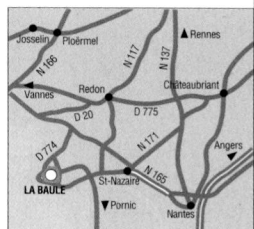

Nantes, N 165 towards La Baule, via St-Nazaire; Castel on the coast, near the Casino.

Owner :
Diane Desseigne-Barrière
Director : Louis Boutté
Annual closing :
From mid-January to
mid-February

 Nantes (**Intl**) 60 km
La Baule 4 km

 Menus
Lunch **220 FRF** s.i.
(except holidays, sundays,
July and August)
34 €
260-600 FRF s.i.
40-91 €
Carte **300-650 FRF** s.i.
46-99 €

S et amidst exquisite landscaped gardens overlooking a picturesque bay, this elegant Belle-Époque manor is just a short drive from the local casino. Its tastefully decorated guestrooms ensure a most comfortable stay. Savour refined cuisine, prepared with the very best regional products, in the convivial atmosphere of the restaurant or dine al fresco on the manicured English lawn. Fine Loire wines and vintage Bordeaux.

29 rooms
900-2 300 FRF s.i.
137-351 €

2 suites
starting at **1 900 FRF** s.i.
290 €

 105 FRF s.i.
16 €

yes (extra cost)

Saint-Denac 6 km

Bicycles, sports activities.

97

www.relaischateaux.fr/marielouise

FRF : French franc

Visa

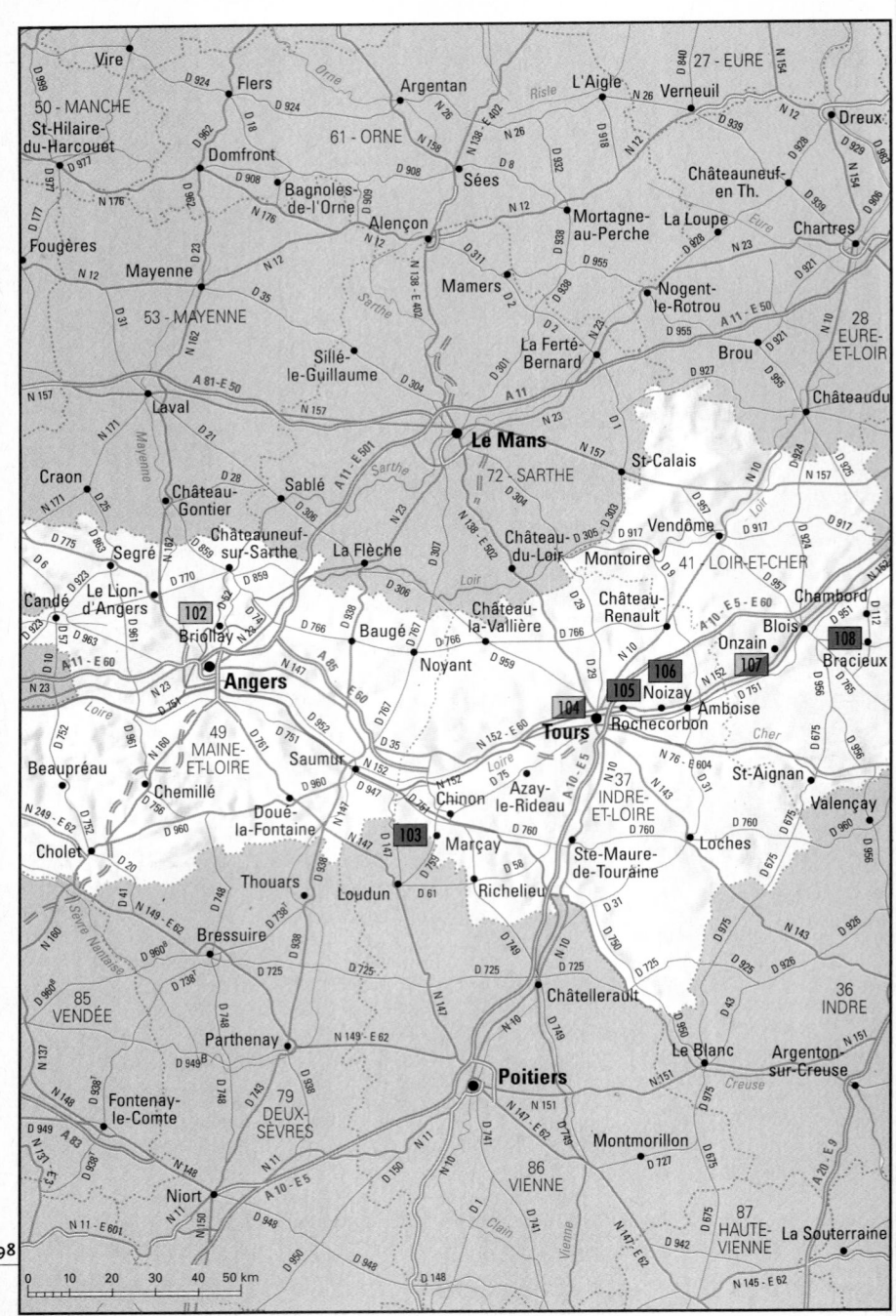

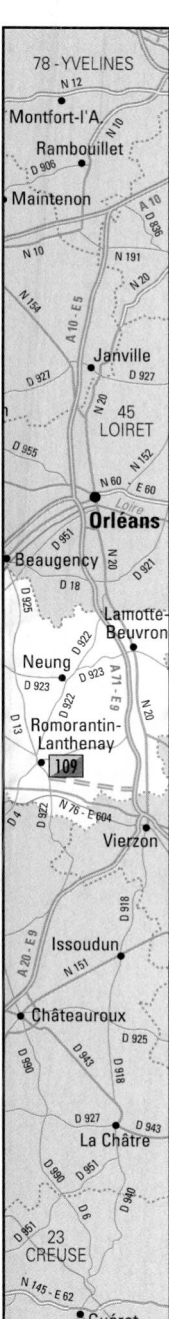

LOIRE VALLEY

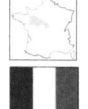

Establishments	Nearest major city	Relais & Châteaux	Relais Gourmands	Page
Bardet (Jean)	Tours	⚜	👨‍🍳	104
Bernard Robin - Le Relais	Chambord		👨‍🍳	108
Château de Marçay	Chinon	⚜		103
Château de Noirieux	Angers	⚜		102
Château de Noizay	Amboise	⚜		106
Domaine des Hauts de Loire	Blois	⚜	👨‍🍳	107
Grand Hôtel du Lion d'Or	Romorantin	⚜	👨‍🍳	109
Hautes Roches (Les)	Tours	⚜		105

MONT
BLANC

*Seeing the
world de-accelerate can
even change it.*

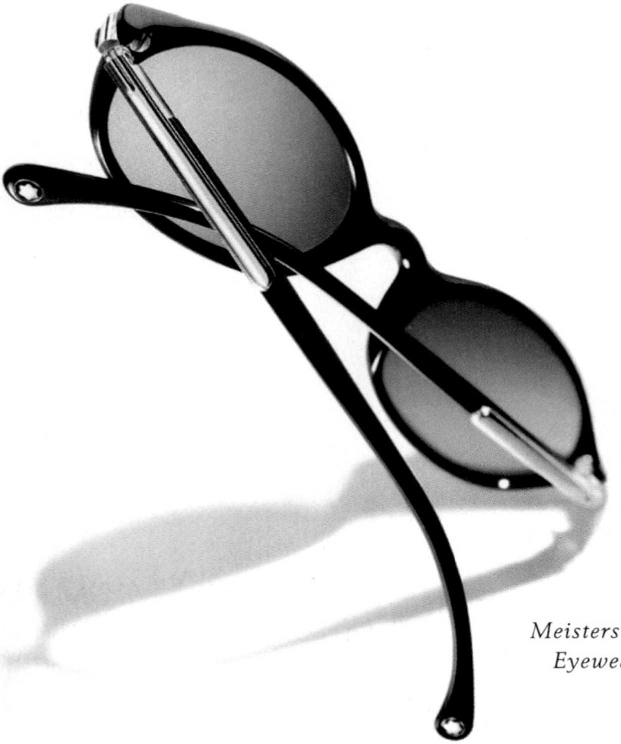

*Meisterstück
Eyewear*

THE ART OF WRITING YOUR LIFE

Writing Instruments · Watches · Leather · Jewellery · Eyewear

VINTAGES TO DRINK IN YEAR 2000

LOIRE

Wines recommended by the wine waiters
of the Relais & Châteaux and Relais Gourmands.

* Index of world vintages to drink in year 2000 : page 607

	Name of wine	Wine to enjoy	Noble wine	Outstanding wine
	LOIRE			
White	Anjou, Saumur	1998 - 1997	1996	1990
	Centre Loire, Berry nivernais : Sancerre, Pouilly-fumé	1998 - 1997	1995	1996 - 1990
	Pays Nantais : Muscadet	1998 - 1997	1996	1995
Red	Anjou, Saumur	1996	1995	
	Centre Loire, Berry nivernais : Sancerre, Reuilly	1996	1990 - 1989	
	Touraine : Chinon, Bourgueuil	1996	1990 - 1989	1976 - 1959
Medium sweet white wines	Anjou - Saumur : Coteaux du Layon	1996	1995 - 1990	1989 - 1959
	Touraine : Vouvray, Montlouis	1995	1985	1959 - 1947

CHÂTEAU DE NOIRIEUX

SINCE 1995

Tel. : (33) 02 41 42 50 05
Fax : (33) 02 41 37 91 00
E-mail : noirieux@relaischateaux.fr

26, route du Moulin
49125 Briollay
(Maine-et-Loire)

France

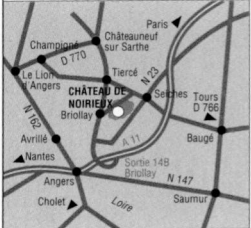

From Paris, A11, exit 14 Briollay, by D52 towards Soucelles by D109. From Nantes or Angers, A11, towards 14 B. Briollay via D52 then towards Soucelles via D109.

Owner : Michael Shen
Directors : Anja and Gérard Côme
Weekly closing :
Rest. : Sunday evening and Monday from mid-October to the end of April (except holidays)
Annual closing :
From February 15th to March 15th and from November 1st to 30th

✈ Nantes (**Intl**) 89 km
Orly (**Intl**) 280 km

GPS N 47° 34' 32"
W 000° 28' 04"

🍴 Menus 210 FRF (week lunch)
32 €
275-350-495 FRF s.i.
42-53-75 €
Carte 400-450 FRF s.i. - 61-69 €

⚷ 18 rooms
high sais. : 880-1 750 FRF s.i.
134-267 €
low sais. : 750-1 600 FRF s.i.
114-244 €

⚷ 1 suite
high sais. : 1 750 FRF s.i. - 267 €
low sais. : 1 600 FRF s.i. - 244 €

☕ 100 FRF s.i. - 15 €

🍽 yes (extra cost)

🧍 15 km

This elegant château, framed by luxuriant foliage and rhododendron bushes, offers picturesque views across the river Loire. After strolling through the winter garden or reclining in front of an elegant fireplace in the lounge, retire to a sumptuous Louis XIII or Regency guestroom hung with superb works of art. Savour refined seasonal dishes accompanied by fine wines and exceptional vintages from the Loire region.

Visa

FRF : French franc

www.relaischateaux.fr/noirieux

CHÂTEAU DE MARÇAY

France

37500 Marçay-Chinon
(Indre-et-Loire)

Tel. : (33) 02 47 93 03 47
Fax : (33) 02 47 93 45 33
E-mail : marcay@relaischateaux.fr

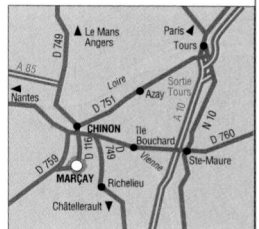

*A10, exit Sainte-Maure
towards Chinon Sud, then D 116,
village of Marçay.*

Owner : Philippe Mollard
Director : Bernard Beteille
Weekly closing :
Rest. : Sunday and Monday at
lunch from November 12th to
March 15th (except holidays)
Annual closing :
From mid-January to mid-March

The twin towers of this magnificent 15th-century castle, which lies near Chinon where Joan of Arc met King Charles VII, soar above a landscape that once enchanted François Rabelais. The château's tastefully decorated rooms, which blend wood panelling, sumptuous materials and period furniture, also offer every modern comfort. The refined cuisine is enhanced by an excellent selection of fine wines and Loire vintages.

 Tours 60 km

 GPS N 47° 06' 17"
E 000° 13' 16"

 Menus **300-450 FRF** s.i.
46-69 €
Carte **380-465 FRF** s.i.
58-71 €

 28 rooms
660-1 380 FRF s.i.
101-210 €

 6 suites
1 680 FRF s.i.
256 €

 100 FRF s.i.
15 €

yes

Roiffé St-Hilaire 15 km

103

www.relaischateaux.fr/marcay   FRF : French franc    Visa

JEAN BARDET - CHÂTEAU BELMONT

Tel. : (33) 02 47 41 41 11
Fax : (33) 02 47 51 68 72
E-mail : bardet@relaischateaux.fr

57, rue Groison
37100 Tours
(Indre-et-Loire)

France

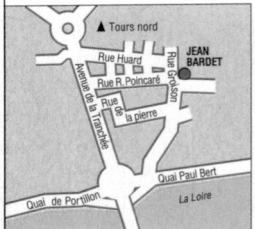

*A10 Tours-Nord, towards
the centre, av. Maginot,
av. de la Tranchée, 2nd left.*

Owners : Sophie and Jean Bardet
Weekly closing :
Restaurant : Sunday evening
and Monday from Nov. to
March / Monday at lunch
from April to Oct.
Open all year

✈ Orly **(Intl)** 250 km
  Tours 2 km

🍴 Menus **250-850 FRF** s.i.
  38-130 €
  Carte **550-700 FRF** s.i.
  84-107 €

⊶ 16 rooms
  750-1 400 FRF s.i.
  114-213 €

⊶ 5 suites
  1 800-2 300 FRF s.i.
  274-351 €

☕ **120 FRF** s.i.
  18 €

🍴 yes

🏃 7 km

Jogging, sports and
cultural activities.

This white Touraine stone residence, set amidst landscaped gardens, provides an idyllic refuge for gourmets and nature lovers all year round. Sophie Bardet welcomes guests with charming hospitality, showing them to their spacious, bright guestroom, while her husband Jean prepares exquisite seasonal cuisine. Savour divine desserts, excellent wines and the extraordinary «aumônière de légumes du potager de Jean Bardet».

 Visa

FRF : French franc

www.relaischateaux.fr/bardet

SINCE
1991

LES HAUTES ROCHES

France

86, quai de la Loire
37210 Rochecorbon
(Indre-et-Loire)

Tel. : (33) 02 47 52 88 88
Fax : (33) 02 47 52 81 30
E-mail : hautesroches@relaischateaux.fr

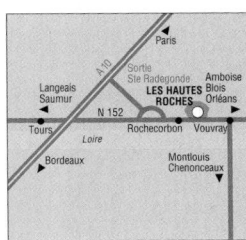

*From Paris, A10 exit Tours Nord,
Sainte Radegonde; then left
towards Vouvray.*

Owner : Philippe Mollard
Director : Didier Edon
Annual closing :
From the end of Jan. to mid-March

 Orly **(Intl)** 220 km
Tours 8 km

 Menus
165 FRF s.i. (week lunch)
25 €
220-290-375 FRF s.i.
34-44-57 €
Carte **300-400 FRF** s.i.
46-61 €

 15 rooms
695-1 350 FRF s.i.
106-206 €

 95 FRF s.i.
14 €

 yes

10 km

Mountain biking, hiking...

S ince the 11th century, the
Tourangeaux have carved into the
white chalk cliffs overlooking the Loire and
built their homes into the rock. Les Hautes
Roches has transformed these enchanting
cave residences into sumptuous rooms
with canopy beds and grand fireplaces. Its
lounges and dining room are housed in an
elegant 17th-century villa facing onto the
river. Enjoy romantic candelit dinners and
excellent Loire wines.

105

www.relaischateaux.fr/hautesroches

FRF : French franc

Visa

CHÂTEAU DE NOIZAY

SINCE 1992

Tel. : (33) 02 47 52 11 01
Fax : (33) 02 47 52 04 64
E-mail : noizay@relaischateaux.fr

Route de Chançay
37210 Noizay
(Indre-et-Loire)

France

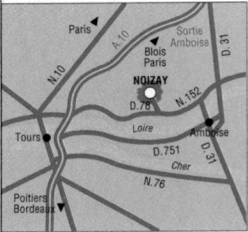

A10 exit Amboise / Château-Renault, D31 towards Amboise, N152 towards Vouvray-Tours, D78 Noizay.

Owner :
SCI Château de Noizay
Director : François Mollard
Annual closing :
From mid-January to mid-March

✈ Ch. de Gaulle (**Intl**) 230 km
Tours 18 km

🧭 GPS N 47° 25' 19"
E 000° 53' 30"

🍴 Menus
165-240-290-370 FRF s.i.
25-37-44-56 €
Carte **280-390 FRF** s.i.
43-59 €

🔑 14 rooms
Season : **685-1 450 FRF** s.i.
104-221 €
Off season :
550-1 160 FRF s.i.
84-177 €

☕ **95 FRF** s.i.
14 €

🐕 yes (except restaurant)

⛳ Ardrée 18 km

Hot-air ballon, helicopter,
VTT, quad.

This elegant 16th-century château, which lies in the heart of Touraine, was used as a refuge by the famous «Amboise conspirators» in 1560. The splendour of bygone days has been authentically recreated in the luxurious guestrooms, decorated with canopy beds and period furniture, accompanied by exquisite marble bathrooms. Savour superb cuisine accompanied by an excellent selection of Loire and Vouvray wines.

106

Visa

FRF : French franc

www.relaischateaux.fr/noizay

DOMAINE DES HAUTS DE LOIRE

France

Route de Herbault
41150 Onzain
(Loir-et-Cher)

Tel. : (33) 02 54 20 72 57
Reservation : (33) 02 54 20 70 43
Fax : (33) 02 54 20 77 32
E-mail : hauts-loire@relaischateaux.fr

From Paris A10 exit Blois then N152 towards Tours.
At the bridge of Chaumont towards Onzain.

Owners : Bonnigal Family
Director : Pierre-Alain Bonnigal
Weekly closing :
Rest. : Monday and Tuesday
at lunch (in March and Nov.)
Annual closing :
From Dec. 1st to March 1st

This magnificent hunting lodge, built in 1860 by the famous publisher Panckoucke, is secluded in tranquil parkland. Relish the calm of a cosy guestroom with painted beams, then savour exquisite gourmet delicacies such as «salade d'anguille croustillante à la vinaigrette d'échalote» or «pigeonneau du vendômois au jus de presse», accompanied by superb local wines. Visit the Loire valley by hot-air balloon or helicopter.

 Orly (**Intl**) 200 km
Tours 40 km

 GPS N 47° 30' 26"
E 1° 08' 47"

 Menus 320-420 FRF s.i.
49-64 €
Carte 350-550 FRF s.i.
53-84 €

 25 rooms
700-1 500 FRF s.i.
107-229 €

 10 suites
1 700-2 500 FRF s.i.
259-381 €

 100 FRF s.i.
15 €

 no ,

15 km

www.relaischateaux.fr/hauts-loire

FRF : French franc

Visa

BERNARD ROBIN – LE RELAIS

SINCE 1990

Tel. : (33) 02 54 46 41 22
Fax : (33) 02 54 46 03 69
E-mail : robin@relaischateaux.fr

1, av. de Chambord
41250 Bracieux
(Loir-et-Cher)

France

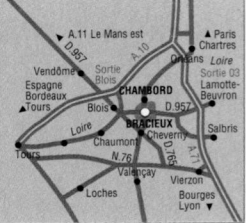

*From Paris, A10,
exit Chambord-Mer, Bracieux
on the road to Cheverny.*

Owner : Bernard Robin
Weekly Closing :
Tuesday evening and Wednesday
(except in July-August)
Annual Closing :
From Dec. 20th to January 20th

✈ Ch. de Gaulle (**Intl**) 180 km
Tours 80 km

⏴ GPS N 47° 33' 30"
E 1° 32' 22"

🍴 Menus **320-520 FRF** s.i.
49-79 €
Carte **250-400 FRF** s.i.
38-61 €

🛏 yes

🚶 Cheverny 9 km
Bich 15 km

Fishing, hunting in Sologne...

B ernard Robin has chosen to show-case his culinary creations in this picturesque residence near the Loire châteaux. Robin's «salade de pigeon et homard à la vinaigrette de légumes confits» and «queue de bœuf en hachis parmentier aux truffes» are veritable masterpieces, while the «lièvre à la royale» is simply sublime. The cellar is a treasure trove of local vintages, the service is impeccable and the hospitality unparalleled.

   Visa

FRF : French franc

www.relaischateaux.fr/robin

GRAND HÔTEL DU LION D'OR

France

69, rue Georges Clémenceau
41200 Romorantin-Lanthenay
(Loir-et-Cher)

Tel. : (33) 02 54 94 15 15
Fax : (33) 02 54 88 24 87
E-mail : liondor@relaischateaux.fr

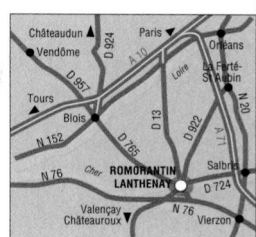

From Paris, A 10, A 71 to the north of Orleans, towards Bourges, exit Salbris and D 724.

Owners :
Colette and Alain Barrat,
Marie-Christine and Didier Clément
Annual closing :
From February 15th to March 24th

✈ Orly (**Intl**) 170 km
Ch. de Gaulle (**Intl**) 200 km

🍴 Menus 450-650 FRF s.i.
69-99 €
Carte 550-650 FRF s.i.
84-99 €

🔑 13 rooms
800-1 900 FRF s.i.
122-290 €

🔑 3 suites
1 500-2 200 FRF s.i.
229-335 €

☕ 110 FRF s.i.
17 €

🛗 yes

🍴 3 courses less than
30 minutes away

Loire castles, hunting, bicycle touring.

The owners of this beautiful Renaissance manor perpetuate the tradition of French hospitality and the art of good living. Didier Clément creates gourmet dishes of rare gastronomical delight such as «cuisses de grenouille à la rocambole», «langoustines bretonnes rôties à la graine de paradis» and «brioche caramélisée au sorbet d'angélique». Superb Loire wines and exquisitely comfortable rooms complete this picture of bliss.

109

FRF : French franc

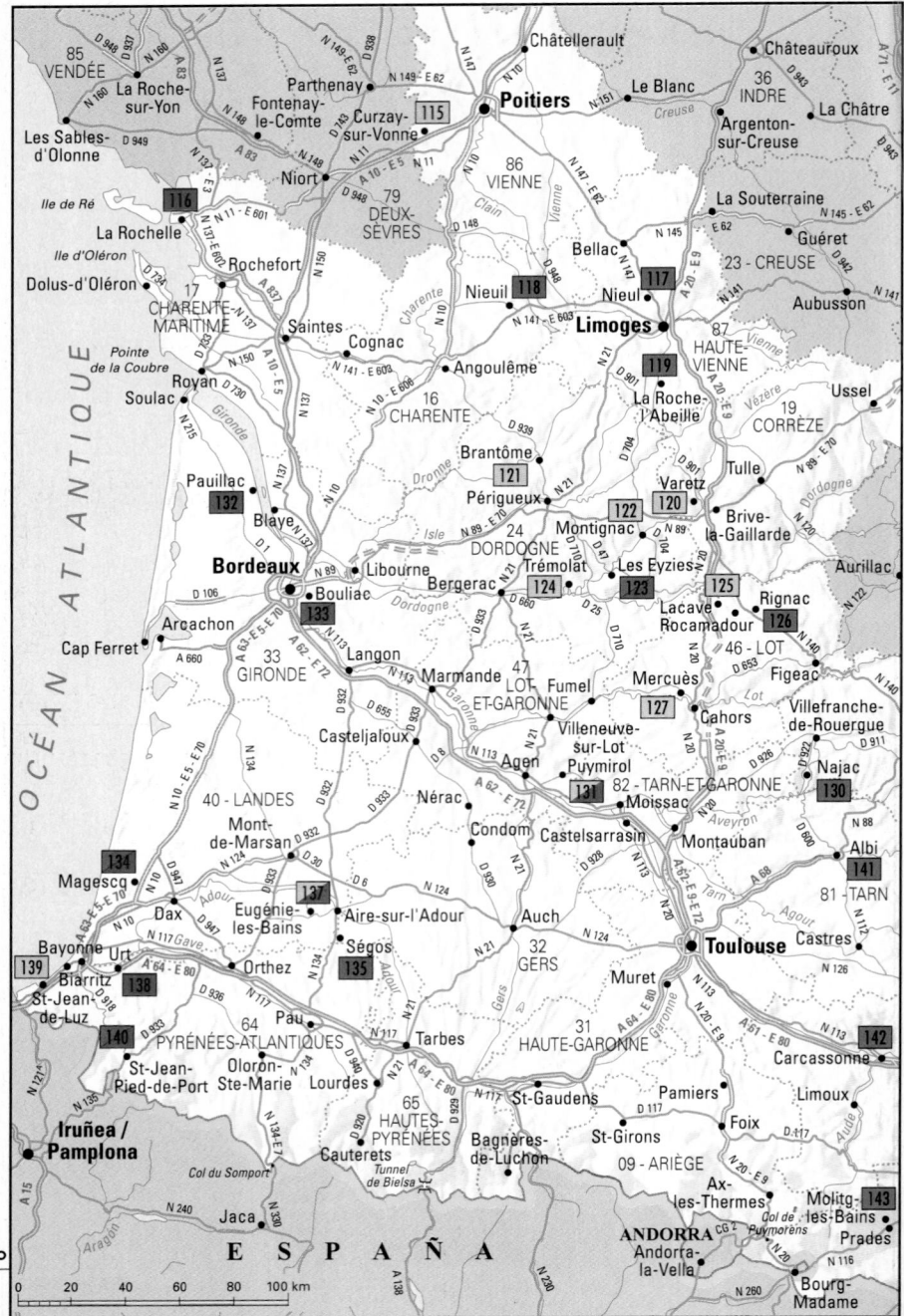

OCÉAN ATLANTIQUE

ESPAÑA

85 VENDÉE
La Roche-sur-Yon
Les Sables-d'Olonne
Île de Ré
La Rochelle
Île d'Oléron
Dolus-d'Oléron
Pointe de la Coubre
Soulac
Cap Ferret
Arcachon

Châtellerault
Parthenay
Fontenay-le-Comte
Curzay-sur-Vonne
Poitiers
Le Blanc
Châteauroux
36 INDRE
La Châtre
Argenton-sur-Creuse

Niort
79 DEUX-SÈVRES
86 VIENNE
Clain
La Souterraine
Guéret
23 - CREUSE
Aubusson

Rochefort
17 CHARENTE-MARITIME
Saintes
Cognac
Nieuil
Bellac
Nieul
Limoges
87 HAUTE-VIENNE
Angoulême
Ussel

Royan
16 CHARENTE
La Roche-l'Abeille
19 CORRÈZE

Pauillac
Brantôme
Périgueux
Varetz
Tulle
Brive-la-Gaillarde

Blaye
24 DORDOGNE
Montignac
Trémolat
Les Eyzies
Aurillac

Bordeaux
Bouliac
Libourne
Bergerac
Lacave
Rocamadour
Rignac

33 GIRONDE
Langon
Marmande
47 LOT-ET-GARONNE
Fumel
Mercuès
46 - LOT
Figeac
Villefranche-de-Rouergue

Casteljaloux
Villeneuve-sur-Lot
Puymirol
Cahors

Agen
Najac
130

Nérac
Condom
Castelsarrasin
82 - TARN-ET-GARONNE
Moissac
Montauban

40 - LANDES
Mont-de-Marsan
Albi
81 - TARN

Magescq
Dax
Eugénie-les-Bains
Aire-sur-l'Adour
Auch
32 GERS
Toulouse
Castres

Bayonne
Biarritz
St-Jean-de-Luz
Urt
Orthez
Ségos
Pau
Tarbes
31 HAUTE-GARONNE
Muret
Carcassonne

St-Jean-Pied-de-Port
64 PYRÉNÉES-ATLANTIQUES
Oloron-Ste-Marie
Lourdes
65 HAUTES-PYRÉNÉES
St-Gaudens
Pamiers
Limoux

Iruñea / Pamplona
Cauterets
Tunnel de Bielsa
Bagnères-de-Luchon
St-Girons
Foix
09 - ARIÈGE

Col du Somport
Ax-les-Thermes
Molitg-les-Bains
Prades

Jaca
ANDORRA
Andorra-la-Vella
Col de Puymorens
Bourg-Madame

0 20 40 60 80 100 km

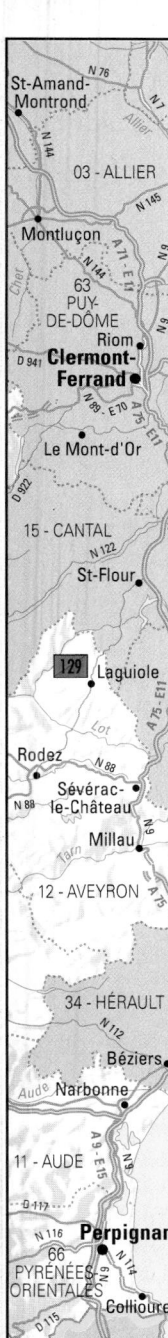

St-Amand-Montrond

N 76

N 7

N 144

Allier

03 - ALLIER

N 145

Montluçon

N 144 - E 11

N 9

Cher

63
PUY-DE-DÔME
Riom
D 941 **Clermont-Ferrand**

N 89 - E 70

A 75 - E 11

Le Mont-d'Or

D 922

15 - CANTAL

N 122

St-Flour

129 Laguiole

Lot

Rodez
N 88
Sévérac-le-Château
N 88

Millau

A 75

Tarn

12 - AVEYRON

N 9

34 - HÉRAULT

N 112

Béziers

Aude Narbonne

A 9 - E 15

N 9

11 - AUDE

D 117

N 116 **Perpignan**

66
PYRÉNÉES-ORIENTALES

N 114

D 115

Collioure

THE GREATER SOUTH WEST

Establishments	Nearest major city	Relais & Châteaux	Relais Gourmands	Page
Auberge de la Galupe	**Bayonne**		⌂	138
Bras (Michel)	**Rodez**	⚜	⌂	129
Chapelle St-Martin (La)	**Limoges**	⚜		117
Château Cordeillan-Bages	**Bordeaux**	⚜		132
Château de Castel Novel	**Brive**	⚜		120
Château de Curzay	**Poitiers**	⚜		115
Château de Mercuès	**Cahors**	⚜		127
Château de Nieuil	**Angoulême**	⚜		118
Château de Puy Robert	**Brive**	⚜		122
Château de Riell	**Perpignan**	⚜		143
Château de Roumégouse	**Rocamadour**	⚜		126
Château de la Treyne	**Rocamadour**	⚜		125
Domaine d'Auriac	**Carcassonne**	⚜		142
Domaine de Bassibé	**Pau**	⚜		135
Guérard (Michel)	**Pau**	⚜	⌂	137
Hôtel du Centenaire	**Sarlat**	⚜	⌂	123
Loges de l'Aubergade (Les)	**Agen**	⚜	⌂	131
Longcol	**Rodez**	⚜		130
Moulin de l'Abbaye (Le)	**Périgueux**	⚜		121
Moulin de la Gorce (Au)	**Limoges**	⚜		119
Parc Victoria (Le)	**Saint-Jean-de-Luz**	⚜		139
Pyrénées (Les)	**Biarritz**	⚜	⌂	140
Relais de la Poste	**Dax**	⚜	⌂	134
Réserve (La)	**Albi**	⚜		141
Richard Coutanceau	**La Rochelle**		⌂	116
Saint-James	**Bordeaux**	⚜	⌂	133
Vieux Logis (Le)	**Périgueux**	⚜		124

HOME SWEET HOME CINEMA !

DIGITAL WITH A DIFFERENCE

Get 5 speaker surround sound ...

From everything you listen to ...

Even mono programming ...

With the **NEW** BOSE® LIFESTYLE® 25 Digital ...

Audio home entertainment system ...

Visit your authorized BOSE dealer ...

Better sound through research®

Hear the difference. Ask for a demonstration.

VINTAGES TO DRINK IN YEAR 2000

BORDEAUX - SOUTH WEST LANGUEDOC-ROUSSILLON

Wines recommended by the wine waiters of the Relais & Châteaux and Relais Gourmands.

*Index of world vintages to drink in year 2000 : page 607

♟	Name of wine	Wine to enjoy	Noble wine	Outstanding wine
	BORDEAUX			
Dry white wines	Graves, Pessac Leognan	1996 - 1995	1993 - 1988	1990 - 1989
Sweet white wines	Sauternes (Barsac, Loupiac)	1983	1990 - 1989 - 1988	1975 - 1967
Red	Graves, Pessac Léognan	1994	1988 - 1986	1989 - 1982
	Libournais : Saint-Emilion, Pomerol...	1995 - 1993	1985 - 1983	1982 - 1978
	Médoc, Haut Médoc : Pauillac, Margaux Saint-Julien, Saint-Estephe	1993	1989 - 1988 - 1983	1986 - 1982 - 1970
	SOUTH WEST			
Dry white wines	Bergerac, Irouleguy, Gaillac	1998 - 1997	1995	
Medium sweet white wines	Jurançon, Gaillac, Côtes de Montravel, Saussignac, Bergerac	1997	1996 - 1995	1990
Sweet white wines	Jurançon, Pacherenc du vic-bilh, Monbazillac	1996 - 1995	1993	1990 - 1989
Red	Cahors, Madiran, Pécharmant...	1996	1995	1990 - 1989
	LANGUEDOC-ROUSSILLON			
White	Languedoc-Roussillon	1998 - 1997 - 1996	1994	1995
Red	Languedoc-Roussillon	1996	1994	1988 - 1986
Natural sweet wines	Muscats : Rivesaltes, Frontignan, Lunel Roussillon : Banyuls, Maury, Rivesaltes	1997 - 1996 1996 - 1995	1998 1991 - 1990	1978

113

Service from the heart
Le service avant tout

JCB Card's service from the heart.
Your passport to elegance wherever you may go.

Les cartes JCB vous offrent le service avant tout.
Votre passeport pour l'élégance, où que vous alliez.

JCB CARD

CHÂTEAU DE CURZAY

France

86600 Curzay-sur-Vonne
(Vienne)

Tel. : (33) 05 49 36 17 00
Fax : (33) 05 49 53 57 69
E-mail : curzay@relaischateaux.fr

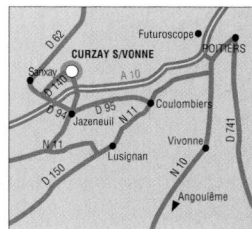

A10, exit 30. From Poitiers, towards Lusignan; at Coulombiers, towards Jazeneuil. From Niort, A10 exit 31 towards Lusignon, in Rouillé towards Sanxay.

Owners :
Brigitte de Gastines-Cachart and Eric Cachart
Director : Yves Van Wanghe
Open all year

 Poitiers 25 km

 GPS N 46° 29' 04"
E 000° 02' 55"

 Menus 190-380 FRF s.i.
29-58 €
Carte 260-410 FRF s.i.
40-62 €

 20 rooms
750-1 550 FRF s.i.
114-236 €

 2 suites
1 700 FRF s.i.
259 €

 80 FRF s.i.
12 €

yes (extra cost)

6 km

B uilt in 1710 by the banks of the Vonne river amidst 300 acres of superb parkland, the Château de Curzay is dedicated to seeing that guests have an unforgettable stay. The 22 individually-decorated rooms, the tree-lined paths, and the pool-side terrace in the shade of the 12th century towers all create a haven of calm. Located near Futuroscope, at Curzay enjoy a journey through time from the 18th to the 21st century.

   115

Restaurant Richard Coutanceau

SINCE 1988

Tel. : (33) 05 46 41 48 19
Fax : (33) 05 46 41 99 45
E-mail : coutanceau@relaischateaux.fr

Plage de la Concurrence
17000 La Rochelle
(Charente-Maritime)

France

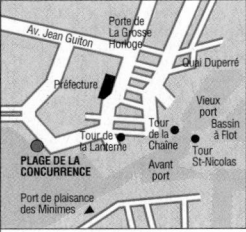

From Paris, A 10 exit 33 ;
N11, La Rochelle city centre,
follow the sign «La Plage».

Owner : Richard Coutanceau
Weekly closing : Sunday
Open all year

✈ Bordeaux **(Intl)** 200 km
La Rochelle 5 km

 Menus 230-430 FRF s.i.
35-66 €
Carte 290-375 FRF s.i.
44-57 €

 yes

 10 km

Fishing, sailing, hunting.

P 🚿 ❄ ♿

Virtuoso chef Richard Coutanceau is capable of drawing the most subtle flavours from seafood. His «tartare de langoustines aux huîtres spéciales», «homard breton à la coque ou en millefeuille» are extraordinary, while the «bar de ligne rôti sur sa peau croustillée au parfum de basilic et à la tomate confite» is a culinary masterpiece. The exceptional cellar includes a 19-year-old Pineau blanc which is served with dessert.

FRF : French franc

www.relaischateaux.fr/coutanceau

LA CHAPELLE SAINT-MARTIN

France

Nieul-près-Limoges
87510 Nieul
(Haute-Vienne)

Tel. : (33) 05 55 75 80 17
Fax : (33) 05 55 75 89 50
E-mail : chapelle@relaischateaux.fr

*From Limoges, towards
Angoulême N 141, airport, 4 km
after, on D 20.
From Paris exit 28.*

Owners : Dudognon Family
Director : Gilles Dudognon
Weekly Closing :
Restaurant : Monday
Annual Closing : January

Hospitality and impeccable taste are the twin emblems of this elegant bourgeois home set amidst acres of luxuriant parkland. The bright, sunny guestrooms, spacious lounges and convivial dining rooms are beautifully decorated with antique objects and period furniture. Inventive cuisine draws the very best from local produce and guests may choose from an excellent selection of Bordeaux and an extensive list of spirits.

Limoges (**Intl**) 4 km

GPS N 45° 53' 589"
E 001° 10' 724"

Menu **180 FRF** s.i.
27 €
Carte **300-400 FRF** s.i.
46-61 €

9 rooms
500-980 FRF s.i.
76-149 €

4 suites
1 300-1 500 FRF s.i.
198-229 €

75 FRF s.i.
11 €

yes welcome (except rest.)

10 km

117

www.relaischateaux.fr/chapelle

FRF : French franc

Visa

CHÂTEAU DE NIEUIL

France

Tel. : **(33) 05 45 71 36 38**
Fax : **(33) 05 45 71 46 45**
E-mail : nieuil@relaischateaux.fr

16270 Nieuil
(Charente)

From Angoulême: N141 towards Limoges; Suaux, exit on the left.

Owners :
Luce and Jean-Michel Bodinaud
Weekly closing :
Restaurant : Sunday evenings and Mondays (except for guests) and except in July/August
Annual closing :
From November 2nd to April 20th

 Bordeaux (**Intl**) 150 km
Angoulême 30 km

 GPS N 45° 53'
E 0° 31' 30"

 Menus
200 FRF s.i. (lunch) - **30 €**
260-350 FRF s.i. - **40-53 €**
Carte **280-380 FRF** s.i.
43-58 €

 11 rooms
750-1 600 FRF s.i.
114-244 €
half board - 2 pers. :
1 600-2 250 FRF s.i.
244-343 €

3 suites
1 600-2 400 FRF s.i.
244-366 €

80 FRF s.i. - **12 €**

yes (welcome)

La Preze 25 km

Fishing, mountain biking, beach buggy rental.

This former royal hunting palace, set in a magnificent 100-acre park, was once the property of François I. Today a warm welcome awaits you in the sumptuous suites and guestrooms, each individually decorated by the château's owners Luce and Jean-Michel Bodinaud. Savour delicious cuisine inspired by the Charentes countryside and choose from an excellent selection of Bordeaux and Cognacs. Art gallery and antique shop.

 Visa

FRF : French franc

www.relaischateaux.fr/nieuil

AU MOULIN DE LA GORCE

France

87800 la Roche-l'Abeille
(Haute-Vienne)

Tel. : (33) 05 55 00 70 66
Fax : (33) 05 55 00 76 57
E-mail : moulingorce@relaischateaux.fr

From Paris, towards
Brive-Toulouse, exit St-Yrieix,
D 704 La Roche l'Abeille.

Owner : Catherine Bertranet
Weekly closing :
Sunday evening and Monday
(from Oct. 1st to Easter)
Annual closing : January

✈ Limoges **(Intl)** 40 km

🍽 Menus 275-390 FRF s.i.
42-59 €
250 FRF s.i.
(at lunch only)
38 €
Carte 350-580 FRF s.i.
53-88 €

🗝 9 rooms
350-950 FRF s.i.
53-145 €

🗝 1 suite
1 300 FRF s.i.
198 €

☕ 75 FRF s.i.
11 €

🛏 yes

🎣 30 km

Fishing on the premises.

P astoral calm, bucolic charm, fishing... no wonder the writer Jean Giradoux cherished this part of the countryside. Enjoy an idyllic stay in one of the charming rooms, each named after a flower. The cuisine is like the establishment: warm, full or character and rich in bourgeois tradition: «œufs brouillés aux truffes», «lièvre "à la royale"» and «poêlée de langoustines au beurre de gingembre». Excellent wine list.

www.relaischateaux.fr/moulingorce   **FRF : French franc**   Visa

CHÂTEAU DE CASTEL-NOVEL

Tel. : (33) 05 55 85 00 01
Fax : (33) 05 55 85 09 03
E-mail : novel@relaischateaux.fr

19240 Varetz
(Corrèze)

France

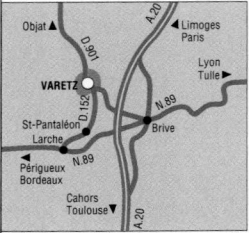

From Paris, A 10, then A 71 and A20 exit Vierzon until Brive, exit Brive nord, Varetz by D 901.

Owner : Albert Parveaux
Weekly closing :
Restaurant : 2 lunchs a week
Annual closing :
End of October to beg. May

✈ Bordeaux (**Intl**) 160 km
    Brive 5 km

🧭 GPS N 45° 11'
    E 001° 27'

🍴 Menus 240-450 FRF s.i.
    37-69 €
    Carte 350-450 FRF s.i.
    53-69 €

🗝 32 rooms
    690-1 365 FRF s.i.
    105-208 €

🗝 5 suites
    1 600-1 800 FRF s.i.
    244-274 €

☕ 90 FRF s.i.
    14 €

🏓 yes

⛳ 3 holes on the premises
    18 holes at 10 km

How could you fail to be enchanted by this elegant 15th-century «castel» ? French writer Colette once fell under its spell and moved in as lady of the manor. And when you experience the comfort and tranquil charm of the guestrooms and the idyllic park, you'll understand why. Traditional cuisine, prepared with fresh ingredients from the Limousin countryside, is complemeted by Cahors, Bergerac and vintage Bordeaux.

 Visa

FRF : French franc

LE MOULIN DE L'ABBAYE

France

1, route de Bourdeilles
24310 Brantôme-en-Périgord
(Dordogne)

Tel. : **(33) 05 53 05 80 22**
Fax : **(33) 05 53 05 75 27**
E-mail : moulin@relaischateaux.fr

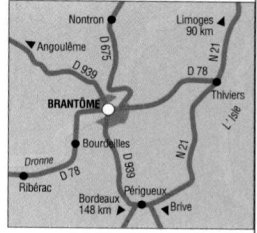

D 939 between Angoulême and Périgueux. In Brantôme, direction «l'Abbaye».

Owner :
SA Moulin de l'Abbaye
Directors :
Bernard and Yvette Dessum
Weekly closing :
Restaurant : lunch
(except weekend and holidays)
July and August :
Monday noon only
Annual closing :
From November 2nd to April 25th

«Le Moulin de l'Abbaye», «La Maison du Meunier» and «L'Abbé» are three romantic dwellings, steeped in history, on the banks of the Dronne river. This was the home of Abbé de Brantôme, author of «La vie des dames galantes». The charm of this region, known as the «Venice of the Perigord», is an inspiration for the palate in the elegant «Le Moulin» restaurant, on its riverside terrace or at the «Fil de l'Eau», its delightful fisherman's bar.

Bordeaux (**Intl**) 120 km
Périgueux 25 km

Menus
240-340-500 FRF s.i.
37-52-76 €
Menu-carte
340 FRF s.i.
52 €
Au Fil de l'Eau
120-150 FRF s.i.
18-23 €

16 rooms
900-1 050 FRF s.i.
137-160 €

3 suites
1 300-1 500 FRF s.i.
198-229 €

90 FRF s.i.
14 €

yes

25 km

121

FRF : French franc

CHÂTEAU DE PUY ROBERT

SINCE
1988

Tel. : (33) 05 53 51 92 13
Fax : (33) 05 53 51 80 11
E-mail : puyrobert@relaischateaux.fr

Route de Valojoulx
24290 Montignac-Lascaux
(Dordogne)

France

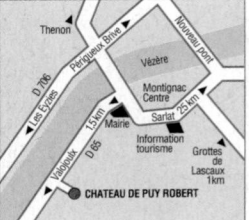

From Paris, A10 then A71 exit Vierzon, N20 Limoges, Brive, N89 Le Lardin St-Lazare, Montignac.

Owner : Albert Parveaux
Director : Vincent Nourrisson
Weekly closing :
Restaurant : Mondays noon and Wednesdays noon
Annual closing :
From October 17th to May 1st

✈ Bordeaux (**Intl**) 175 km
Brive 37 km

🧭 GPS N 45° 3' 8"
E 1° 9' 50"

🍴 Menus 215-445 FRF s.i.
33-68 €
Carte 330-450 FRF s.i.
50-69 €

⚷ 33 rooms
710-1 440 FRF s.i.
108-220 €

⚷ 5 suites
1 440-1 860 FRF s.i.
220-284 €

☕ 95 FRF s.i.
14 €

🛏 yes

🏃 45 km

Mountain-biking, canoeing.

This elegant neo-Renaissance château, which lies en route to Lascaux, makes an idyllic stopping place. The tiny boudoir, hidden in a turret overlooking the park, is simply one of the most romantic guestrooms imaginable. Savour inventive seasonal cuisine, prepared with the very best regional ingredients, and sample one of the excellent local vintages. Ideally located for visiting the region's famous prehistoric sites.

 Visa

FRF : French franc

www.relaischateaux.fr/puyrobert

France

24620 Les-Eyzies-de-Tayac
(Dordogne)

Tel. : (33) 05 53 06 68 68
Fax : (33) 05 53 06 92 41
E-mail : centenaire@relaischateaux.fr

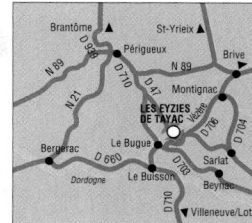

At the intersection of D 47
(Périgueux-Sarlat) and D 706.

Owners :
Mazère-Scholly Family
Weekly closing :
Restaurant : Tuesday noon and
Wednesday noon
Annual closing :
From Nov. to beginning of April

This elegant residence, set on the picturesque banks of the Vézère, where the painters of the Lascaux caverns once fished, is a haven of calm offering bright, comfortable rooms. The beautiful Dordogne countryside is the perfect place to savour Roland Mazère's inventive cuisine, based on regional and seasonal produce. Gourmets will be enchanted by his exquisite «terrine chaude de cèpes, risotto aux truffes».

✈ Bordeaux (**Intl**) 170 km
Périgueux 40 km

 Menus
325-470-615 FRF s.i.
50-72-94 €
180 FRF
(lunch except holidays)
27 €
Carte 370-550 FRF s.i.
56-84 €

⊶ 20 rooms
500-1 050 FRF s.i.
76-160 €

⊶ 4 suites
1 200-1 600 FRF s.i.
183-244 €

🍵 95 FRF s.i.
14 €

yes

25 km

Eyzies Prehistoric museum,
Lascaux caves, and Sarlat.

123

FRF : French franc

LE VIEUX LOGIS

France

SINCE 1955

Tel. : (33) 05 53 22 80 06
Fax : (33) 05 53 22 84 89
E-mail : vieuxlogis@relaischateaux.fr

24510 Trémolat
(Dordogne)

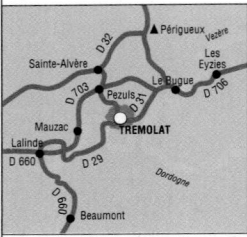

From Bordeaux, follow Sarlat D660; from Paris, Périgueux (N89) Le Bugue.

Owner : Bernard Giraudel
Director : Didier Bru
Weekly closing : Lunch
(except weekend and holidays)
July and August : Wednesday
noon only
Annual closing : From January 3rd
to February 12th

✈ Bordeaux **(Intl)** 120 km
Bergerac 32 km

⌖ GPS N 44° 52' 566"
E 000° 49' 732"

🍴 Menus **210-280-420 FRF** s.i.
32-43-64 €
Carte **350-400 FRF** s.i.
53-61 €
Bistrot **120-140 FRF** s.i.
18-21 €

⊶ 18 rooms
840-1 420 FRF s.i.
128-216 €

⊶ 6 suites
1 750 FRF s.i.
267 €

☕ **95 FRF** s.i.
14 €

⛨ yes

🏃 25 km

H enri Miller was so enchanted by this 17th-century Carthusian monastery of Perigord that he came to spend a week and ended up staying a month. You'll understand why when you discover this idyllic haven filled with birdsong and the babbling of the garden brook. Seasonal cuisine in the former tobacco drying room or under the linden trees. Regional restaurant at the «Bistrot du Logis».

FRF : French franc

CHÂTEAU DE LA TREYNE

France

46200 Lacave
(Lot)

Tel. : (33) 05 65 27 60 60
Fax : (33) 05 65 27 60 70
E-mail : treyne@relaischateaux.fr

A20 south of Souillac, D43, towards Lacave (6 km); Pinsac, after the bridge over the Dordogne.

Owner : Michèle Gombert
Director : Philippe Bappel
Weekly closing :
Rest.: Tuesday, Wednesday and Thursday noon
(except July-August)
Annual closing :
From Nov. 15th to Dec. 20th and from Jan. 5th to March 15th

This magnificent château (built in the 14th and 17th centuries) overlooks the Dordogne and blends the authenticity of the past with the comfort and quality of a landmarked site. Its French gardens extend into a 300-acre forest. Michèle Gombert has mastered the art of fine living, offering luxurious rooms, breakfast beneath the hundred-year-old cedars and dinner in the Louis XIII salon or on the riverside terrace.

✈ Toulouse (**Intl**) 180 km
Brive 40 km

GPS N 44° 51' 01"
E 01° 31' 38"

🍴 Menus 220-450 FRF s.i.
34-69 €
Carte 280-480 FRF s.i.
43-73 €

⚷ 14 rooms
750-1 950 FRF s.i.
114-297 €

⚷ 2 suites
starting at **1 950 FRF s.i.**
297 €

☕ 90 FRF s.i.
14 €

🐕 yes

🚶 10 km

www.relaischateaux.fr/treyne

FRF : French franc

CHÂTEAU DE ROUMÉGOUSE

Tel. : (33) 05 65 33 63 81
Fax : (33) 05 65 33 71 18
E-mail : roumegouse@relaischateaux.fr

Route de Rocamadour, Rignac
46500 Gramat
(Lot)

France

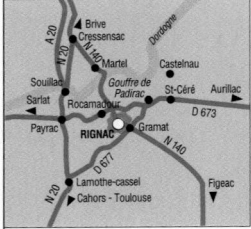

From Gramat, follow signs on N140. A20 exit Gramat.

Owners :
Luce and Jean-Louis Lainé
Director :
Laurent Garnier du Plessix
Weekly closing :
Rest. : Tuesdays (except July-August)
Annual closing :
From December 1st to April 20th (except Dec. 24th and 31st)

 Toulouse (**Intl**) 170 km
Brive 60 km

 GPS N 44° 48' 01"
E 001° 41' 21"

 Menus **185-330 FRF** s.i.
28-50 €
Carte **280-450 FRF** s.i.
43-69 €

 13 rooms
680-1 000 FRF s.i.
104-152 €

 2 suites
starting at **1 200 FRF** s.i.
183 €

 80 FRF s.i.
12 €

yes (welcome)

30 km

This elegant residence, which lies on the Compostelle pilgrimage route, is set amidst unspoiled natural surroundings. Luce and Jean-Louis Lainé have decorated their guest-rooms in styles ranging from Louis XIV to Napoleon III and their impeccable taste is reflected in the dining rooms which serve excellent local cuisine. Enjoy a candlelit dinner on the exquisite flowered terrace overlooking the Rocamadour plateau.

Visa

FRF : French franc

www.relaischateaux.fr/roumegouse

CHÂTEAU DE MERCUÈS

France

46090 Mercuès
(Lot)

Tel. : (33) 05 65 20 00 01
Fax : (33) 05 65 20 05 72
E-mail : mercues@relaischateaux.fr

A62 Bordeaux-Toulouse,
exit Montauban, A20 Cahors,
D911, Mercuès.

Owner : Georges Vigouroux
Director : Bernard Denegre
Weekly closing :
Rest. : Monday (all day)
and Tuesday noon
(except in July-August)
Annual closing :
From November 1st to Easter

F or twelve centuries the castle at Mercuès was the summer residence of the bishops of Cahors. Today the guestrooms, opening onto a breathtaking vista of vineyards, valleys and French gardens, have lost none of their feudal grandeur. In this kingdom of «foie gras», truffles and wine, the cuisine is rich and generous. Meanwhile, Georges Vigouroux's vintage Cahors age to perfection in the cathedral-like vaults of the cellar.

Toulouse (**Intl**) 102 km

GPS N 44° 29′ 75″
E 01° 24′ 04″

Menus
280-360-450 FRF s.i.
43-55-69 €
Carte **350-470 FRF** s.i.
53-72 €

22 rooms
850-1 500 FRF s.i.
130-229 €

8 suites
1 500-2 250 FRF s.i.
229-343 €

90 FRF s.i.
14 €

yes (hotel only)

30 km (9 holes)

127

FRF : French franc

Visa

DE L'EXCEPTION LA RÈGLE.

THE EXCEPTION IS THE RULE... SUSTAINING EACH EFFORT UNTIL THAT MOMENT OF PERFECT HARMONY WHICH MARKS THE CULMINATION OF ALL ENDEAVOUR... SEEKING OUT THE EXCEPTIONAL BECAUSE NOTHING LESS WILL DO... ALWAYS SEARCHING, NO STRANGER TO DOUBT... EMBRACING EACH DAY WITH PATIENCE ANEW... FOR TWO HUNDRED YEARS NOW, SUCH HAS BEEN THE DESTINY OF THE HOUSE OF LOUIS ROEDERER.

LOUIS ROEDERER

CHAMPAGNE

France

MICHEL BRAS

Route de l'Aubrac
12210 Laguiole
(Aveyron)

Tel. : (33) 05 65 51 18 20
Fax : (33) 05 65 48 47 02
E-mail : bras@relaischateaux.fr

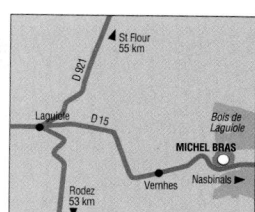

From Laguiole, towards Aubrac.
5.5 km turn left,
follow «Michel Bras» signs.

Owners :
Ginette and Michel Bras
Weekly closing :
Hotel : Monday
(except in July-August)
Rest. : Monday (all day), Tuesday,
Wednesday, Thursday for the lunch
July and August : Monday at lunch
Annual closing :
From November 1st to April 4th

This spectacular residence, a perfect blend of traditional and avant-garde architecture, is perched on a plateau overlooking the magnificent Aubrac countryside. It is here that the talented chef Michel Bras seeks out the herbs and plants which flavour his original gourmet specialities. Savour «gargouillou de jeunes légumes», «pièce de bœuf de l'Aubrac poêlée» and «biscuit tiède de chocolat coulant», accompanied by superb wines.

 Clermont-Ferrand (**Intl**) 170 km
Rodez 60 km

 GPS N 44° 44'
E 2° 55' 5''

 Menus
250-470-700 FRF s.i.
38-72-107 €
Carte **350-600 FRF** s.i.
53-91 €

15 rooms
980-1 750 FRF s.i.
149-267 €

100 FRF s.i.
15 €

yes (extra cost)

9 holes at 15 km

Hiking.

www.relaischateaux.fr/bras

FRF : French franc

129

LONGCOL

Tel. : (33) 05 65 29 63 36
Fax : (33) 05 65 29 64 28
E-mail : longcol@relaischateaux.fr

Route de Monteils
12270 La Fouillade/Najac
(Aveyron)

France

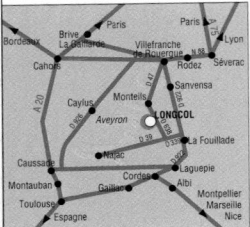

Villefranche-de-Rouergue,
D922 towards Albi, then
D39 towards Najac; 300 m later,
towards Monteils (D638).

Owners : Luyckx Family
Director : Bernard André
Weekly closing :
Restaurant: Monday and Tuesday
at lunch (except residents and
from June 15th to Sept.15th)
Annual closing :
From November 29th to
February 12th

✈ Toulouse (**Intl**) 120 km
Rodez 60 km

GPS N 44° 15' 28"
E 02° 00' 06"

🍴 Menus 210-295 FRF s.i.
32-45 €

🔑 18 rooms
650-900 FRF s.i.
99-137 €

🔑 1 suite
1 000-1 090 FRF s.i.
152-166 €

☕ 75 FRF s.i.
11 €

🐕 yes (extra cost) except rest.

🎿 60 km

This charming residence, once a fortified farm, lies at the entrance to the Aveyron gorges. The Luyckx Family have lovingly restored this unique site and today its elegant guestrooms, overlooking the pool or the picturesque valley, are the very height of refinement. Inventive and generous cuisine is set off by wines from Cahors and Gaillac. The medieval villages of Najac, Cordes and Albi la Rouge lie close by.

 Visa

FRF : French franc

www.relaischateaux.fr/longcol

LES LOGES DE L'AUBERGADE

France

52, rue Royale
47270 Puymirol
(Lot-et-Garonne)

Tel. : (33) 05 53 95 31 46
Fax : (33) 05 53 95 33 80
E-mail : aubergade@relaischateaux.fr

From Toulouse, A62 exit Valence d'Agen, towards Golfech Lamagistère via the N113 then D20, D248.
From Bordeaux, A62 exit Agen, towards Toulouse via the N 113 to Lafox then D 16.

Owners : Mr and Mrs Trama
Weekly closing : Monday
(low season) except holidays
Annual closing : February holidays

The rooms in this magnificent residence, decorated with impeccable taste by Maryse Trama, are a feast for the eyes, while her husband's cuisine is a feast for gourmet palates. Blending culinary tradition with modern innovation, Michel Trama invents marvels such as «papillote de pomme de terre au fumet de truffes», and «pied de cochon aux cèpes». Savour vintage Buzet and enjoy Havana cigars and old Armagnacs after dinner.

✈ Toulouse **(Intl)** 90 km
Bordeaux **(Intl)** 165 km

🍴 Menus
200-295-680 FRF s.i.
30-45-104 €
Carte **350-550 FRF** s.i.
53-84 €

🔑 10 rooms
750-1 410 FRF s.i.
114-215 €

100 FRF s.i.
15 €

yes (extra cost)

14 km

ULM, water-skiing, hiking, smokers' lounge.

131

FRF : French franc

Visa

CHÂTEAU CORDEILLAN-BAGES

France

Tel. : (33) 05 56 59 24 24
Fax : (33) 05 56 59 01 89
E-mail : cordeillan@relaischateaux.fr

Route des Châteaux
33250 Pauillac
(Gironde)

SINCE 1991

A10 towards Mérignac, beltway exit 7, N215 St-Laurent, Pauillac, D206.

Owner : Jean-Michel Cazes
Directors :
Alain Rabier, Thierry Marx
Weekly closing :
Rest.: Saturday noon and Monday
Annual closing : From Dec. 17th to January 31st

✈ Bordeaux (**Intl**) 45 km

📡 GPS N 45° 11' 29" E 000° 45' 12"

🍴 Menus **195-260-390 FRF** s.i.
(at noon except on Sunday)
30-40-60 €
evenings **195-295-390** FRF s.i
30-45-60 €
Carte **310-440 FRF** s.i.
48-68 €
Special menu for guests on Monday evenings :
260 FRF s.i. - **40 €**

⚷ 24 rooms
950-1 195 FRF s.i.
146-184 €
low season **760-955 FRF** s.i.
117-147 €

⚷ 1 suite
1 350 FRF s.i. - **208 €**
low season **1 080 FRF** s.i.
166 €

🍽 80-100 FRF s.i. - 12-16 €

🚫 yes

⛳ 4 courses 20-35 km

Y ou will be enchanted by the elegant exterior of this 17th-century château. Its bright, tastefully decorated rooms and its lounges, adorned with bouquets and old paintings, are also a feast for the eyes. Dine in the garden and savour the exquisite «Agneau de Pauillac» accompanied by one of the thousand Bordeaux awaiting you in the cellar. The château, which houses the Ecole de Bordeaux, also offers wine-tasting courses.

Visa

FRF : French franc

www.relaischateaux.fr/cordeillan

SAINT-JAMES

France

3, place Camille Hostein
33270 Bouliac
(Gironde)

Tel. : (33) 05 57 97 06 00
Fax : (33) 05 56 20 92 58
E-mail : stjames@relaischateaux.fr

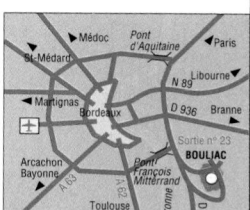

A 10, exit Artigues, leave beltway exit 23, towards Bouliac centre.

Owner : Hauterive - St James - S.A.
Director : Jean-Marie Amat
Annual closing : January

This superb contemporary architecture, designed by Jean Nouvel, overlooks the Garonne river and the Bordeaux countryside. After a stroll in the park, enjoy Jean-Marie Amat's gourmet delicacies accompanied by vintage Bordeaux. Savour the lamprey, «raviolis de cèpes» and «blanquette d'agneau» and the «petit homard sauté aux pommes de terre et aux gousses d'ail». Don't miss the «Bistroy» and the «Café de l'Espérance».

 Bordeaux (**Intl**) 20 km

 Menu **400 FRF** s.i.
61 €
Carte **390 FRF** s.i.
59 €
Café de l'Espérance
160 FRF s.i. - **24 €**
Le Bistroy
200 FRF s.i. - **30 €**

 15 rooms
season
1 000-1 100 FRF s.i.
152-168 €
off-season
800-900 FRF s.i.
122-137 €

 3 suites
season
1 500-1 700 FRF s.i.
229-259 €
off-season
1 300-1 500 FRF s.i.
198-229 €

 100-120 FRF s.i.
15-18 €

 no

 20 km

Sauna.

133

www.relaischateaux.fr/stjames   FRF : French franc   Visa

RELAIS DE LA POSTE

Tel. : (33) 05 58 47 70 25
Fax : (33) 05 58 47 76 17
E-mail : poste@relaischateaux.fr

24, avenue de Maremne
40140 Magescq
(Landes)

France

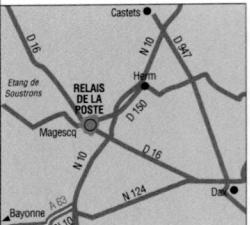

From Bordeaux, towards Bayonne, San Sebastian via A10, exit 10 Magescq.

Owners :
Jean and Jacques Coussau
Directors : Coussau Family
Weekly closing :
Monday evening and Tuesday
(except July and August)
Annual closing :
From Nov. 12th to Dec. 20th

✈ Biarritz (**Intl**) 45 km
Bordeaux (**Intl**) 130 km

🍴 Menus **300-400 FRF** s.i.
46-61 €
Carte **350-450 FRF** s.i.
53-69 €

☞ 10 rooms
600-950 FRF s.i.
91-145 €

☞ 2 suites
1 200-1 400 FRF s.i.
183-213 €

🍷 **70-90 FRF** s.i.
11-14 €

🍴 yes

🎣 15 km (18 holes)

Fishing, hunting, mountain-biking, horse-riding, thermal baths.

A stone's throw from the vast beaches of the Landes, this former posthouse perpetuates a certain idea of family tradition. The rooms with their contemporary decor and furniture, overlook a vast, calm and peaceful estate. Jean Cousseau proposes a whole range of regional products, in imaginative varieties, such as his «caviar d'Aquitaine et les blinis de maïs à la crème fleurette», his «foie gras de canard chaud aux raisins» or his superb collection of armagnacs.

 Visa

FRF : French franc

www.relaischateaux.fr/poste

DOMAINE DE BASSIBÉ

France

32400 Segos
(Gers)

Tel. : (33) 05 62 09 46 71
Fax : (33) 05 62 08 40 15
E-mail : bassibe@relaischateaux.fr

Bordeaux-Pau-Spain: 35 km
north of Pau, 8 km south
of Aire/Adour; D260 Segos.

Owners : Olivier and Sylvie Lacroix
Weekly closing :
Tuesday and Wednesday
for lunch (low season)
Annual closing :
From beginning of January
to the end of March

E arthen red tiles and elegant white façades gleaming in the afternoon sun, sylvan green ivy creepers framing the shutters: the colours of this spacious, picturesque residence appear to have been lifted from an artist's palette. Dinner, served in the old wine press or beneath the plane trees, features the rich traditional cuisine of the Gers region enhanced by excellent local wines : Madiran, Jurançon and Tursan.

✈ Bordeaux (**Intl**) 150 km
Pau 32 km

🛬 GPS N 43° 37' 65"
E 0° 15' 88"

 Menu **170 FRF** s.i.
26 €
Carte **245 FRF** s.i.
37 €

🔑 11 rooms
690-800 FRF s.i.
105-122 €

🔑 7 suites
980-1 100 FRF s.i.
149-168 €

☕ 75 FRF s.i.
11 €

🍴 yes

🎿 8 km

🏃 P 👫 ✈ 🔆 〰 **135**

www.relaischateaux.fr/bassibe

FRF : French franc

Visa

R i c h a r d
H e n n e s s y

Hennessy
COGNAC

EN 1765, RICHARD HENNESSY CRÉE LA MAISON QUI PORTE SON NOM. HUIT GÉNÉRATIONS DE SA FAMILLE
SE SONT SUCCÉDÉ POUR LUI RENDRE LE PLUS BEL HOMMAGE : "RICHARD HENNESSY",
CE COGNAC UNIQUE ISSU DES PLUS GRANDES RÉSERVES DE VIEILLES EAUX-DE-VIE AU MONDE.

MICHEL GUÉRARD «LES PRÉS D'EUGÉNIE»

France

40320 Eugénie-Les-Bains
(Landes)

Tel. : (33) 05 58 05 06 07
Fax : (33) 05 58 51 10 10
E-mail : guerard@relaischateaux.fr

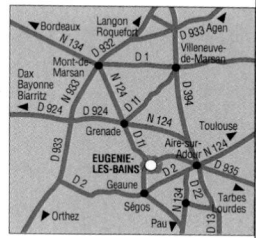

From Bordeaux A63,
RN134-Mont-de-Marsan;
N124 towards Grenade-sur-Adour.

Owners : C. & M. Guérard
Weekly closing :
Rest. Gastronomique: Wed. evening
(save bank holidays and high season)
Annual closing : From Dec. 4th to
21st and from Jan. 3rd to Feb. 23rd

I n the past century, Empress Eugénie was extremely fond of this elegant colonial hamlet where the white palace, «Les Prés», the «Couvent des Herbes» and the «Ferme aux Grives» gracefully court each other in balmy gardens of magnolias and verbena. Today, Christine and Michel Guérard delight guests with a rare symphony of herb gardens, climbing roses, magic springs, exotic fragrances, exquisite guestrooms and delicious flavours which distil a refined «Art de vivre».

✈ Bordeaux (**Intl**) 150 km
Pau 45 km

🍴 Cuisine de Jardin®
390 FRF s.i. (lunch) - **59 €**
Grande Cuisine Gourmande
600-820 FRF s.i. (evening)
91-125 €
Carte **500-700** FRF s.i.
76-107 €
Auberge Ferme aux Grives
195 FRF s.i. - **30 €**

🔑 30 rooms
1 100-2 000 FRF s.i.
168-305 €

🔑 10 suites
1 700-2 300 FRF s.i.
259-351 €

☕ **150** FRF s.i. - **23 €**

🐕 yes (extra cost) only
in «Couvent des Herbes»

⛳ 9 hole golf course 1,5 km

Ferme Thermale®, Fitness and Mineral water Spa, Beauty Centre, slimming cuisine, vegetable and herb gardens, vineyard, Maison Marine®.

FRF : French franc

AUBERGE DE LA GALUPE

SINCE 1998

Tel. : (33) 05 59 56 21 84
Fax : (33) 05 59 56 28 66
E-mail : galupe@relaischateaux.fr

Place du Port
64240 Urt
(Pyrénées Atlantiques)

France

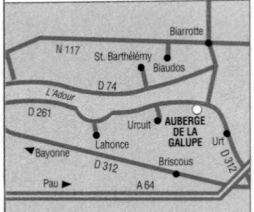

*From Bayonne, follow
the left bank of the Adour
towards the east. 15 km away
from centre of Bayonne (D261).*

Owner : Anne-Marie Parra
Weekly closing :
Sunday evening and Monday
Annual closing :
From January 10th
to February 14th

Biarritz (**Intl**) 20 km

Menus
245-360-550 FRF s.i.
37-55-84 €
Carte **290-450 FRF** s.i.
44-69 €

yes

15 km

Riding, fishing, canoeing...

This 16th-century barge inn, set on the picturesque banks of the Adour in the heart of the Basque country, welcomes gourmets from all over the world. Christian Parra, a poet and guitarist as well as a highly talented chef, concocts culinary masterpieces with regional market produce. His «anchois frais marinés aux herbes» and «boudin grillé et travers de cochon aux citrons blanchis» are exquisite and the wine list simply outstanding.

Visa

FRF : French franc

www.relaischateaux.fr/galupe

LE PARC VICTORIA

France

5, rue Cepé
64500 Saint-Jean-de-Luz
(Pyrénées-Atlantiques)

Tel. : (33) 05 59 26 78 78
Fax : (33) 05 59 26 78 08
E-mail : parcvictoria@relaischateaux.fr

*A 63, exit Saint-Jean-de-Luz nord;
towards the city centre,
in the lake district.*

Owner : Roger Larralde
Director : Richard Perodeau
Weekly closing :
Restaurant : Tuesday
Annual closing :
Hotel : Nov. 15th to March 15th
Rest. : Nov. 1st to April 1st

The recipe for a perfect vacation? An elegant 19th-century private manor house just a few steps from the beach. 12 tastefully decorated guestrooms and suites featuring magnificent Art Deco furniture and contemporary bathrooms. Spacious parkland with manicured lawns and ancestral trees. Exquisite culinary pleasures served in the summer dining room by the pool. The recipe for a perfect vacation? «Le Parc Victoria».

Biarritz (**Intl**) 15 km

Menus **230-380 FRF** s.i.
35-58 €
Carte **260-400 FRF** s.i.
40-61 €

8 rooms
900-1 400 FRF s.i.
137-213 €

4 suites
1 450-1 900 FRF s.i.
221-290 €

85 FRF s.i.
13 €

yes (extra cost)

2 km

Thalassotherapy (500 m),
horseback riding.

www.relaischateaux.fr/parcvictoria

FRF : French franc

LES PYRÉNÉES

SINCE 1988

Tel. : (33) 05 59 37 01 01
Fax : (33) 05 59 37 18 97
E-mail : pyrenees@relaischateaux.fr

19, place du Général de Gaulle
64220 St-Jean-Pied-de-Port
(Pyrénées-Atlantiques)

France

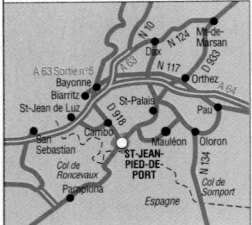

From Bordeaux A 63,
exit n° 5 at Bayonne,
D 932 Cambo-les-Bains, D 918.

Owners :
Mr and Mrs Firmin Arrambide
Weekly closing :
Tuesday (except from July 1st
to September 20th)
Annual closing :
From January 5th to 28th and
from November 20th to Dec. 22nd

✈ Biarritz (**Intl**) 50 km
Bordeaux (**Intl**) 240 km

🍴 Menus **250-530 FRF** s.i.
38-81 €
Carte **350-550 FRF** s.i.
53-84 €

🔑 18 rooms
560-920 FRF s.i.
85-140 €

🔑 2 suites
1 200 FRF s.i.
183 €

☕ **90 FRF** s.i.
14 €

🥢 yes

🏃 50 km

A nne-Marie and Firmin Arrambide welcome guests to the elegant rooms of this former coach inn set in one of the most beautiful villages in the Basque country. Les Pyrénées is renowned for its refined cuisine and gourmets will not fail to appreciate this talented chef's innovative creations. Savour «petits poivrons farcis à la morue», a remarkable «saumon frais de l'Adour grillé à la béarnaise» and superb wines.

Visa

FRF : French franc

www.relaischateaux.fr/pyrenees

LA RÉSERVE

France

Route de Cordes
81000 Albi
(Tarn)

Tel. : (33) 05 63 60 80 80
Fax : (33) 05 63 47 63 60
E-mail : reservealbi@relaischateaux.fr

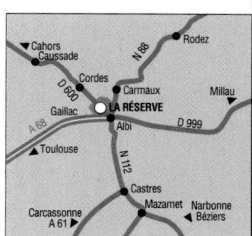

From Toulouse A68 until Albi.
At the Albi exit, D600 towards
Cordes.

Owner : SARL J. Rieux and Cie
Director : Hélène Hijosa-Rieux
Annual closing :
From November 1st to April 30th

This lovely residence near Albi, on the banks of the Tarn, is a haven of greenery. Air-conditioned and tastefully-decorated guestrooms overlook a park, pond, river and swimming pool. The dining room and terrace dominating the Tarn offer an idyllic setting for savouring a dutifully regional cuisine, or a «pool» luncheon. You will have the time to leisurely explore the magnificent city of Albi.

Toulouse (**Intl**) 78 km
Albi 8 km

GPS N 43° 56' 36"
E 2° 07' 07"

Menus
125 (lunch)-**160 FRF** s.i.
19-24 €
Carte **280-350 FRF** s.i.
43-53 €

20 rooms
550-1 450 FRF s.i.
84-221 €

4 suites
1 450-1 750 FRF s.i.
221-267 €

85 FRF s.i.
13 €

yes (extra cost)

2 courses 6 and 12 km

Toulouse Lautrec Museum,
Ste Cécile Cathedral.

www.relaischateaux.fr/reservealbi

FRF : French franc

Visa

DOMAINE D'AURIAC

SINCE 1970

Tel. : (33) 04 68 25 72 22
Fax : (33) 04 68 47 35 54
E-mail : auriac@relaischateaux.fr

Route de Saint-Hilaire, B.P. 554
11009 Carcassonne
(Aude)

France

*A61, exit Carcassonne ouest,
towards «centre-ville»
and Centre Hospitalier.*

Owner : Bernard Rigaudis
Director : Anne-Marie Rigaudis
Weekly closing :
Hotel/Rest.: Sunday evening and
Monday all day from February 13th
to May 31st and from October 1st
to Dec. 31st (except holidays)
Rest. only: Wednesday noon and
Monday noon, Friday noon from
June 1st to September 30th
Annual closing :
From January 2nd to February 10th

Toulouse (**Intl**) 100 km
Perpignan (**Intl**) 100 km
Carcassonne-Salvaza 7 km

GPS N 43° 11' 507"
E 002° 20' 175"

Menus **250-400 FRF** s.i.
38-61 €
Carte **335-395 FRF** s.i.
51-60 €

26 rooms
Season : **650-1 800 FRF** s.i.
99-274 €
Off-season : **500-1 300 FRF** s.i.
76-198 €

100 FRF s.i.
15 €

yes (extra cost)

18 holes

C arcassonne : 2000 years of history. With its fragrant park and only minutes away from the medieval city, the Domaine d'Auriac combines comfort with splendid regional cuisine and fine wines from the legendary vineyards. Swimming pool, tennis and 18-hole golf are ideal for relaxing; abbeys and Cathar sites will immerse you in history from the beautiful gourmet Aude region to the foot of the Cévennes and Pyrenees.

Visa

FRF : French franc

www.relaischateaux.fr/auriac

CHÂTEAU DE RIELL

France

Molitg-les-Bains
66500 Prades
(Pyrénées-Orientales)

Tel. : (33) 04 68 05 04 40
Fax : (33) 04 68 05 04 37
E-mail : riell@relaischateaux.fr

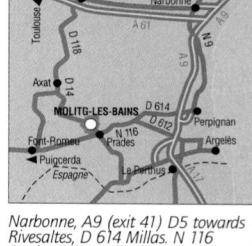

Narbonne, A9 (exit 41) D5 towards Rivesaltes, D 614 Millas. N 116 Prades, D14 Molitg-les-Bains.

Owner : Biche Barthélémy
Annual closing :
From Nov. 1st to April 1st

✈ Perpignan (**Intl**) 45 km

🍴 Menu **200 FRF** s.i.
30 €
Menu-Carte
350-450 FRF s.i.
53-69 €

🔑 19 rooms
995-1 400 FRF s.i.
152-213 €

🔑 3 suites
1 850 FRF s.i.
282 €

☕ **95 FRF** s.i.
14 €

 yes, except restaurant
(extra cost **95 FRF - 14 €**)

🏌 12 km (9 holes) - 45 km

P erched like a grandiose and elegant eyrie opposite the snow-capped peak of Mont Canigou, the Château de Riell guards the portals to the wild Catalan region. This intimate, comfortable haven, echoing with the sound of Pablo Casals's cello and Flamenco guitars, is an idyllic setting in which to savour noble vintages and delicious, sun-drenched cuisine. Its thermal baths endow you with an exquisite sense of well-being.

Thermal baths, sauna, horseback riding, hunting, fishing, climbing, canoeing...

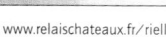
FRF : French franc

143

BELGIQUE /
BELGIË

LUXEMBOURG

DEUTSCHLAND

Givet

Bastogne

Bad Kreuznach

Charleville-
Mézières

Arlon **Luxembourg**

Trier

Sedan

Longwy

Neunkirchen

Kaiserslautern

08
ARDENNES

Stenay

Longuyon

Thionville

Saarlouis

Saarbrücken

Pirmasens

Vouziers

Hayange

Briey

Boulay-
Moselle

Forbach

Verdun

Metz

St-Avold

Sarreguemines

Wissembourg

Ste-Menehould

57
MOSELLE

149

51
MARNE

55
MEUSE

Pont-à-
Mousson

Château-
Salins

67 - BAS-RHIN

Haguenau

St-Mihiel

Sarrebourg

Saverne

Strasbourg

Bar-le-Duc

Commercy

Toul

Nancy 148

Lunéville

Molsheim

Obernai

150
151

St-Dizier

Vaucouleurs

54
MEURTHE-
ET-MOSELLE

Baccarat

Colroy-
la-Roche

152

153

Joinville

Neufchâteau

Charmes

Rambervillers

St-Dié

Sélestat

Ribeauvillé

Bar-
sur-Aube

52
HAUTE-
MARNE

Vittel

88
VOSGES

Col du
Bonhomme

Colmar

Chaumont

Contrexéville

Épinal

Gérardmer

Col de la Schlucht

68
HAUT-RHIN

Remiremont

Plombières

Le Thillot

Guebwiller

Langres

Luxeuil

Thann

Mulhouse

Recey

70
HAUTE-SAÔNE

90
TERRITOIRE-
DE-BELFORT

21
CÔTE-D'OR

Vesoul

Lure

Belfort

Altkirch

Basel

Montbéliard

Gray

SCHWEIZ /

Dijon

25
DOUBS

Maîche

Solothurn

SVIZZ

Besançon

Biel

Dole

Morteau

Neuchâtel

Aare

0 10 20 30 40 50 km

144

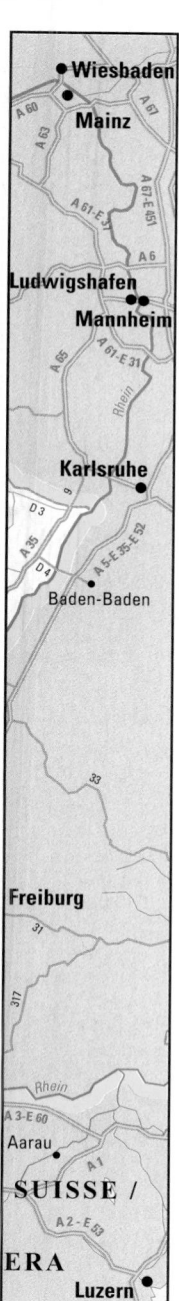

ALSACE LORRAINE

Establishments	Nearest major city	Relais & Châteaux	Relais Gourmands	Page
Abbaye La Pommeraie	Sélestat	⚜		153
Arnsbourg (L')	Bitche		👨‍🍳	149
Château d'Adoménil	Lunéville	⚜		148
Crocodile (Au)	Strasbourg		👨‍🍳	150
Hostellerie La Cheneaudière	Sélestat	⚜	👨‍🍳	152
Restaurant Buerehiesel	Strasbourg		👨‍🍳	151

We have been hosting the finest *sites* in the world for four years

Integra is a leading European provider of integrated e-commerce and Internet systems for enterprises requiring comprehensive e-commerce solutions. The Company's Integra-Commerce Technical Center provides an e-commerce infrastructure comprising all the components required to deliver, operate and maintain a fully functional e-commerce-enabled Web site. The Integra-Commerce Technical Center is a flexible and scalable e-commerce solution which may be linked to the merchant's back-office systems, such as enterprise resource planning systems, customer and marketing databases, as well as to third-party systems, such as call centers, credit card networks or delivery systems.

Integra operates more than 450 sites, its client range from pioneering Internet-based businesses to leading enterprises and include companies such as Cable & Wireless, Cetelem, Continent, Havas Voyages-American Express, Ikea, Lloyd's Register, Packard-Bell, Quelle and Relais & Châteaux. Integra provides its solutions through its partner network, Integra-Commerce Partners.

More information can be obtained from: www.integra-europe.com

integra - 29, rue du Colonel Avia
75015 Paris - France
Phone : +331.41.33.36.00
Fax : +331.41.33.36.33
Web : http://www.integra-europe.com

integra
Get ready for e-commerce !

VINTAGES TO DRINK IN YEAR 2000

ALSACE

**Wines recommended by the wine waiters
of the Relais & Châteaux and Relais Gourmands.**

* Index of world vintages to drink in year 2000 : page 607

♟	Name of wine	Wine to enjoy	Noble wine	Outstanding wine
	ALSACE			
Dry white wines	Gewurztraminer, Riesling, Tokay-Pinot Gris, Muscat	1997 - 1996	1990 - 1989	1985 - 1983
Red	Pinot Noir	1996	1995	1985
Medium sweet white wines	Vendanges tardives et sélection de grains nobles	1994	1990	1989 - 1976

CHÂTEAU D'ADOMÉNIL

SINCE 1990

Tel. : (33) 03 83 74 04 81
Fax : (33) 03 83 74 21 78
E-mail : adomenil@relaischateaux.fr

Rehainviller
54300 Lunéville
(Meurthe-et-Moselle)

France

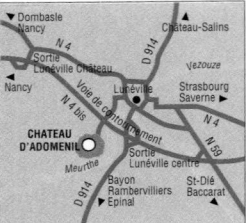

Nancy, exit Lunéville Château,
N4, take a right
at the Lunéville sign (3 km).

Owner : Michel Million
Weekly closing :
Sunday evening, Monday noon
and Tuesday noon : ·
from April 15th to October 31st
Sunday evening, Monday
and Tuesday for lunch :
from November 1st to April 14th
Annual closing :
From January 3rd to February 10th

✈ Louvigny 55 km

🍴 Menus **255-470 FRF** s.i.
39-72 €
Carte **430-480 FRF** s.i.
66-73 €

🔑 10 rooms
750-1 150 FRF s.i.
114-175 €

🔑 1 suite
1 300 FRF s.i.
198 €

☕ **80 FRF** s.i.
12 €

🛏 yes

🏇 practice on the premises

When the Duke of Lorraine created his own «petit Versailles» he built it in Lunéville. Standing close by in a spacious park, the Château d'Adoménil possesses the same architectural elegance. As the Lorraine light glints on the wood panelling and antique furniture of the château's interior, swans and mallards glide around the moat outside. Refined cuisine is enhanced by a rare Côtes de Toul or a fruity Gewurtztraminer.

P ❄ ⛵ ⊞ 〰

MasterCard ● Visa

FRF : French franc

www.relaischateaux.fr/adomenil

L'ARNSBOURG

France

18, Untermuhlthal
57230 Baerenthal
(Moselle)

Tel. : **(33) 03 87 06 50 85**
Fax : **(33) 03 87 06 57 67**
E-mail : arnsbourg@relaischateaux.fr

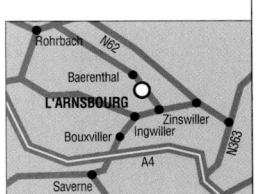

From Paris, Strasbourg or Germany, take the A4, exit at Haguenau. Follow signs to Sarreguemines N 62. At Philippsbourg, follow signs to Baerenthal. In Baerenthal, take the D 87 to Zinsviller (4 km).

Owners : Klein Family
Directors :
Cathy and Jean-Georges Klein
Weekly closing :
Tuesday and Wednesday
Annual closing :
From January 1st to 31st

✈ Strasbourg (**Intl**) 70 km

🍴 Menus **215-475 FRF** s.i.
33-73 €
Carte **395-500 FRF** s.i.
60-76 €

🐎 yes

🎿 20 km

Hunting, fishing.

For three generations the Klein family have contributed to making this charming Northern Vosge restaurant so renowned. Jean-Georges continues the tradition and invites you to savour dishes made with freshly gathered herbs and wild flowers. On the splendid veranda on piles overlooking a forest, savour «poitrine de pigeon, jus réduit à la livèche», one of his many culinary creations, enhanced by Grands Crus of Alsace.

P ♿

149

FRF : French franc
Visa

AU CROCODILE

SINCE 1984

Tel. : (33) 03 88 32 13 02
Fax : (33) 03 88 75 72 01
E-mail : crocodile@relaischateaux.fr

10, rue de l'Outre
67000 Strasbourg
(Bas-Rhin)

France

*From Paris, Colmar and Germany,
A4, exit place des Halles,
city centre, parking Kléber.*

Owners :
Monique and Emile Jung
Weekly closing : Sunday
and Monday except holidays
Annual closing :
From July 16th to August 7th
and from December 24th
to January 8th

✈ Strasbourg (**Intl**) 13 km

🍴 Menus **295-660 FRF** s.i.
45-101 €
Carte **450-600 FRF** s.i.
69-91 €

🐎 yes

Museums, cathedral, Christmas
market, astronomical clock.

E njoy the warm welcome and spirit
of this establishment. Discover the
refinement, the rich flavour and poetry of
the superb gourmet treats such as «cuisses
de grenouille et écrevisses au mille-chou»
enhanced by great French and international
wines. An unforgettable culinary experience.

   Visa

FRF : French franc

www.relaischateaux.fr/crocodile

RESTAURANT BUEREHIESEL

France

4, parc de l'Orangerie
67000 Strasbourg
(Bas-Rhin)

Tel. : (33) 03 88 45 56 65
Fax : (33) 03 88 61 32 00
E-mail : buerehiesel@relaischateaux.fr

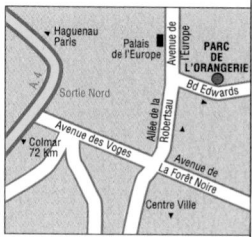

From the A4 - exit 51, towards the Palais de l'Europe, via av. des Vosges and allée de la Robertsau.

Owner : Antoine Westermann
Weekly closing :
Tuesday and Wednesday
Annual closing :
From January 1st to 19th and from August 1st to 23rd

✈ Strasbourg (**Intl**) 13km

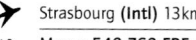 Menus **540-760 FRF** s.i.
82-116 €
Business menu **300 FRF** s.i.
(week lunch) **46 €**
Carte **480-620 FRF** s.i.
73-95 €

 yes

European Parliament, museums, cathedral, astronomical clock, Palais de l'Europe, Alsatian vineyards.

This elegant country house in the Orangerie park is an idyllic setting in which to enjoy superb gourmet cuisine. Antoine and Viviane Westermann's culinary talent and their intelligent use of local produce have placed their restaurant at the peak of gastromomic excellence. Savour «poulet de Bresse cuit comme un Baeckeoffe», «brioche caramélisée à la bière, glace à la bière et poire rôtie» and enjoy fine Alsatian wines.

P ⛾ ❄

Hostellerie La Cheneaudière

SINCE 1975

Tel. : (33) 03 88 97 61 64
Fax : (33) 03 88 47 21 73
E-mail : cheneaudiere@relaischateaux.fr

67420 Colroy-La-Roche
(Bas-Rhin)

France

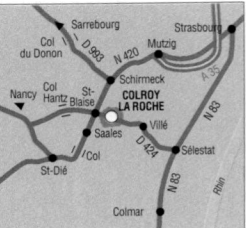

From Strasbourg, towards St-Dié via the Col, St Blaise La Roche, church on the left.

Owners : Mr and Mrs François
Director :
Fabienne François-Bossée
Open all year

✈ Strasbourg (**Intl**) 45 km
Colmar 45 km

🍴 Menus
Rest. «Les Princes de Salm»
590 FRF s.i. - **90 €**
Rest. «Les Pastoureaux»
290 FRF s.i. - **44 €**

🔑 22 rooms
season
800-1 650 FRF s.i.
122-252 €
off-season
700-1 200 FRF s.i.
107-183 €

🔑 7 suites
season
1 700-2 600 FRF s.i.
259-396 €
off-saison
1 300-1 900 FRF s.i.
198-290 €

☕ **90 FRF** s.i. - **14 €**
buffet **120 FRF** s.i. - **18 €**

🐕 yes (extra cost)

🏌 Rhinau 45 km

N estling between Alsace and the Vosges mountains, this picturesque residence features calm, comfortable rooms with breathtaking views of the mountains and forests. After relaxing in the sauna, jacuzzi or indoor pool, guests can choose between two restaurants, one offering gourmet cuisine, the other regional specialities. Enjoy «tartare de saumon frais d'Ecosse», «filet de chevreuil en habit de choux verts» and prestigious wines. Discovery weeks.

Visa

FRF : French franc

www.relaischateaux.fr/cheneaudiere

ABBAYE LA POMMERAIE

France

8, avenue du Maréchal Foch
67600 Sélestat
(Bas-Rhin)

Tel. : (33) 03 88 92 07 84
Fax : (33) 03 88 92 08 71
E-mail : pommeraie@relaischateaux.fr

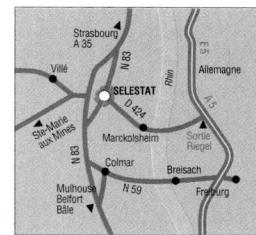

From Strasbourg, towards Colmar
via the A35 and N83,
exit Sélestat, then follow signs.

Owners :
Marcel and Arlette François
Director : Mireille François
Weekly closing :
Rest. : Sunday evenings
Open all year

T his noble residence, once part of the Baumgarten Cistercian abbey, blends modern luxury with the elegant charm of bygone days. Its spacious rooms offer magnificent views across the old town and the private park. Whether you savour cuisine in the Gastronomic restaurant or regional cuisine at the Winstub, both are lovingly prepared with the best regional produce. Excellent Alsatian wines, Rieslings and Pinots Noirs.

Strasbourg (**Intl**) 40 km
Colmar 15 km

Menu **290 FRF** s.i.
(wine included) - **44 €**
Carte **320-420 FRF** s.i.
49-64 €
Winstub **170 FRF** s.i.
26 €

10 rooms
800-1 200 FRF s.i.
122-183 €

4 suites
1 500-1 800 FRF s.i.
229-274 €

95 FRF s.i.
14 €

yes (extra cost)

30 km

153

FRF : French franc

Visa

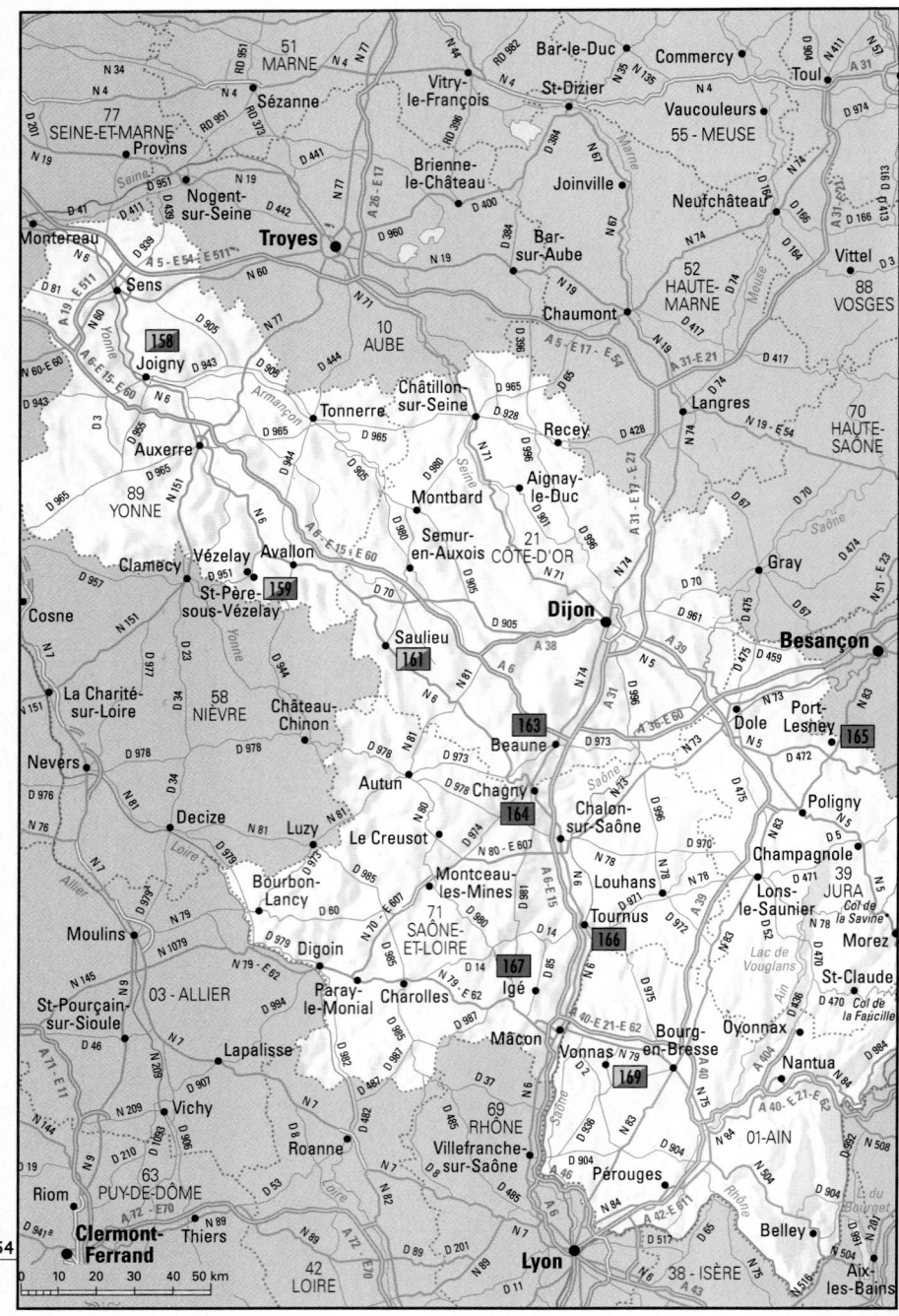

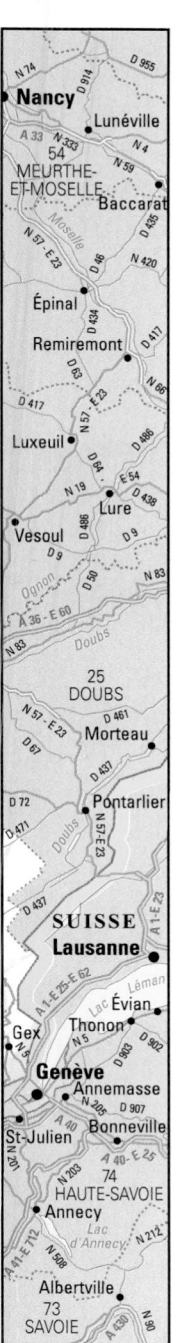

BURGUNDY
FRANCHE COMTÉ

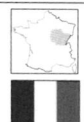

Establishments	Nearest major city	Relais & Châteaux	Relais Gourmands	Page
Blanc (Georges)	Mâcon		🍳	169
Château d'Igé	Mâcon	❀		167
Château de Germigney	Besançon	❀		165
Côte Saint-Jacques (La)	Joigny	❀	🍳	158
Espérance (L')	Vézelay	❀	🍳	159
Hostellerie de Levernois	Beaune	❀	🍳	163
Lameloise	Chagny	❀	🍳	164
Loiseau (Bernard)	Saulieu	❀	🍳	161
Restaurant Greuze	Tournus		🍳	166

Bon voyage.

www.mastercard.com

Please inquire about exclusive MasterCard® values by calling
Relais & Chateaux reservations, or visit our web site.

VINTAGES TO DRINK IN YEAR 2000
BURGUNDY - JURA

Wines recommended by the wine waiters
of the Relais & Châteaux and Relais Gourmands.

* Index of world vintages to drink in year 2000 : page 607

👤	Name of wine	Wine to enjoy	Noble wine	Outstanding wine
	BURGUNDY			
White	Chablis	1997 - 1994	1995 - 1992	1990 - 1989
	Côte Chalonnaise et vins du Maconnais	1998 - 1997	1996	1992
	Côte de Beaune : Meursault, Puligny-Montrachet	1994	1996 - 1992	1989 - 1983
	Côte de Nuits : Nuits-Saint-Georges, Marsannay	1996	1992	1990
Red	Côte Chalonnaise : Givry et Mercurey...	1996	1995	1990
	Côte de Beaune : Volnay, Pommard	1994 - 1993	1990 - 1989	1985
	Côte de Nuits : Gevrey-Chambertin, Vougeot, Vosne-Romanée	1996 - 1993	1990	1985 - 1978
	JURA			
White	Côtes du Jura, l'Etoile, Arbois	1998 - 1997	1995	1990
Red, Rosé wines	Côtes du Jura, Arbois	1998 - 1997		
Jaune	Château-Chalon		1989 - 1988 - 1985	1983 - 1982

La Côte Saint-Jacques

Tel. : (33) 03 86 62 09 70
Fax : (33) 03 86 91 49 70
E-mail : lorain@relaischateaux.fr

14, faubourg de Paris
89300 Joigny
(Yonne)

France

*From Paris, exit Joigny (A6)
or Sens (A5); from Lyons,
exit Auxerre Nord (A6).*

Owners :
Michel and Jean-Michel Lorain
Annual closing :
From January 3rd to 27th

✈ Orly (**Intl**) 120 km
Branches 30 km

⌖ GPS N 47° 59' 32"
E 3° 22' 27"

🍴 Menu **380 FRF** s.i.
(2 glasses of wine included)
week lunch - 58 **€**
Menu **580 FRF** s.i.
lunch - 88 **€**
Menu **780 FRF** s.i.
lunch-dinner - 119 **€**
Carte **690 FRF** s.i. - 105 **€**

🔑 16 rooms
Season **790-1 550 FRF** s.i.
120-236 **€**
Off seas. **660-1 290 FRF** s.i.
101-197 **€**

🔑 9 suites
Season starting at
1 890 FRF s.i. - 288 **€**
Off season starting at
1 690 FRF s.i. - 258 **€**

☕ 125 FRF s.i. - 19 **€**

🦮 yes

🎵 Roncemay 18 km

T hanks to the inspired creative
cuisine of Michel and Jean-Michel
Lorain, the Côte St. Jacques is now one of
the most renowned restaurants in France.
The entire family welcomes guests with
exquisite hospitality, showing them to
charming rooms nestling amidst garden
greenery on the banks of the Yonne or cosy
guestrooms in the main house. Enjoy
private cooking lessons and romantic boat
rides along the river.

Visa

FRF : French franc

www.relaischateaux.fr/lorain

L'ESPÉRANCE

France

89450 St-Père-sous-Vézelay
(Yonne)

Tel. : (33) 03 86 33 39 10
Fax : (33) 03 86 33 26 15
E-mail : esperance@relaischateaux.fr

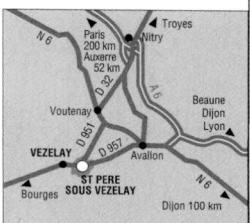

*From Paris, take the A6 to
exit Nitry, D 944 - D 32 towards
Vézelay; at Voutenay, take the N6.*

Owner : Marc Meneau
Weekly closing :
Restaurant : Tuesday and
Wednesday noon off-season
Annual closing : February

 Orly (**Intl**) 180 km
Auxerre 50 km

 GPS N 47° 27' 784"
E 003° 46' 285"

 Menus **400-700 FRF** s.i.
61-107 €
530 FRF s.i. (wine included)
81 €
Carte **600-800 FRF** s.i.
91-122 €

 30 rooms
700-1 400 FRF s.i.
107-213 €

 6 suites
starting at **1 700 FRF** s.i.
259 €

 140 FRF s.i.
21 €

 yes

Fishing, climbing, biking.

M arc Meneau has invented his own style of gourmet cuisine, based on the essential flavours of his native region. In the heart of the beautiful Burgundy countryside, savour «soupière de coquillages au caviar» and «tartine de Saint-Jacques à la moelle de caviar». The exquisite all «coco» dessert will delight hedonists, as will the vintage Burgundies and luxurious guestrooms.

159

www.relaischateaux.fr/esperance

FRF : French franc

L'authentique Chablis

Calcaire, marne, huîtres fossiles de 150 millions d'années, composent à Chablis un sol unique au monde : le kimméridgien. Né de cette puissance minérale, depuis onze siècles, un Chardonnay d'exception s'y épanouit tout en force et en finesse. Aujourd'hui, Michel Laroche, héritier passionné de cinq générations de vignerons produit la plus pure expression de ce terroir mythique,

l'authentique Chablis.

Wine
Spectator
Vin blanc de l'année
1998

Domaine Laroche
CHABLIS
depuis 1850

22 rue Louis Bro - 89800 CHABLIS - Tel : 33 03 86 42 89 00 - Fax : 33 03 86 42 89 29 - Internet : www.domainelaroche.com - E-mail : info@domainelaroche.fr

BERNARD LOISEAU - LA CÔTE D'OR

France

21210 Saulieu
(Côte-d'Or)

Tel. : (33) 03 80 90 53 53
Fax : (33) 03 80 64 08 92
E-mail : loiseau@relaischateaux.fr

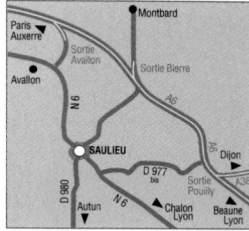

*From Paris, A6, exit Avallon
or Bierre. From Dijon or Lyons,
exit Pouilly- en- Auxois.*

Owner : Bernard Loiseau
Director : Dominique Loiseau
Open all year

 Orly (**Intl**) 200 km
Dijon 70 km

 Menus 490 FRF s.i.
(week lunch) - 75 €
680 FRF s.i. (except weekend
and holidays) - 104 €
450-980 FRF s.i.
69-150 €
Carte 650-900 FRF s.i.
99-137 €

 20 rooms
week 700-1 200 FRF s.i.
107-183 €
weekend 1100-1 900 FRF s.i.
168-290 €

 12 suites
week 1 200-2 000 FRF s.i.
183-305 €
weekend 1 800-2 700 FRF s.i.
274-412 €

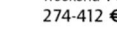 150 FRF s.i.
23 €

 yes

Chailly 27 km

Lakes, Morvan park,
vineyard visits, mountain biking,
fly fishing.

G ourmets flock to this idyllic country haven to savour the culinary marvels created by Bernard Loiseau. Drawing subtle flavours from the best local produce, Loiseau has a fine eye for detail and each dish is an artistic masterpiece. Savour the superb «Blanc de volaille fermière lardé de truffes et le foie gras chaud de canard au jus de truffe», accompanied by an excellent local wine, then retire to an elegant guestroom in this typical Burgundian residence.

161

www.relaischateaux.fr/loiseau   FRF : French franc

Grand Marnier®

Maison fondée en 1827

Cuvées GRAND MARNIER®.   Une histoire de Cognac et de temps.

GRAND MARNIER®
CORDON ROUGE

Cuvée du
CENTENAIRE

Cuvée du
CENT CINQUANTENAIRE

Finesse et subtilité

Harmonie et élégance

Complexité et puissance

HOSTELLERIE DE LEVERNOIS

France

Route de Combertault, Levernois,
21200 Beaune
(Côte-d'Or)

Tel. : (33) 03 80 24 73 58
Fax : (33) 03 80 22 78 00
E-mail : levernois@relaischateaux.fr

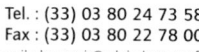

*From Lyons-Paris, exit 24-1
Beaune-Chagny; D970 towards
Lons-le-Saunier; Levernois,
signs «Jean Crotet».*

Owner : Jean Crotet
Weekly closing :
Restaurant : Tuesday, Wednesday
at lunch, Sunday evenings
(from Nov. 1st to March 31st)
Hotel : Tuesday evenings and
Sunday evenings
.(from Oct. 31st to April 1st)
Annual closing :
First half of March and
December 21st to 27th

This picturesque residence, set in a park of oaks, cedars and weeping willows, offers a variety of bright, comfortable rooms. Lulled by the sound of the river splashing against the ancient water-wheel, guests will enjoy undisturbed peace in this idyllic country haven. Savour gourmet cuisine, featuring delicacies such as «petits escargots de Bourgogne en cocotte lutée», and choose from more than 800 excellent vintages.

Dijon 50 km

GPS N 46° 59' 47"
E 004° 53' 01"

Menus **150-200 FRF** s.i.
(week lunch) - **23-30 €**
680 FRF s.i. - **104 €**
Carte **450-650 FRF** s.i.
69-99 €

15 rooms
1 100-1 600 FRF s.i.
168-244 €

1 suite
1 700-1 950 FRF s.i.
259-297 €

100 FRF s.i.
15 €

yes

100 m

163

www.relaischateaux.fr/levernois

FRF : French franc

Visa

LAMELOISE

SINCE 1990

France

Tel. : (33) 03 85 87 65 65
Fax : (33) 03 85 87 03 57
E-mail : lameloise@relaischateaux.fr

36, place d'Armes
71150 Chagny
(Saône-et-Loire)

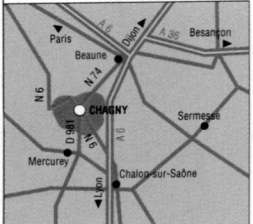

From Lyons, A6 exit Chalon-Nord,
RN 6, Chagny,
near the Post office;
from Paris, A6 exit Beaune.

Owner : Jacques Lameloise
Weekly closing :
Restaurant : Wednesday
and Thursday at lunch
Hotel : Wednesday
Annual closing :
From December 23rd
to January 28th

✈ Lyons (**Intl**) 150 km
    Dijon 50 km

🍴 Menus **420-630 FRF** s.i.
    64-96 €
    Carte **400-600 FRF** s.i.
    61-91 €

⚷ 16 rooms
    750-1 600 FRF s.i.
    114-244 €

☕ **100 FRF** s.i.
    15 €

🛏 yes

🚶 15 km

The Lameloise family has been established on the picturesque square of Chagny for over a hundred years now in a beautiful 15th-century house with gleaming wooden floors. Their renowned cuisine is inspired by Burgundy tradition, and the «raviolis d'escargots de Bourgogne dans leur bouillon d'ail doux» and «pigeonneau rôti à l'émiettée de truffes» are culinary masterpieces. The cellar is a treasure trove of fine vintages.

164

Visa

FRF : French franc

www.relaischateaux.fr/lameloise

France

Rue Edgar Faure
39600 Port-Lesney
(Franche-Comté)

Tel. : (33) 03 84 73 85 85
Fax : (33) 03 84 73 88 88
E-mail : germigney@relaischateaux.fr

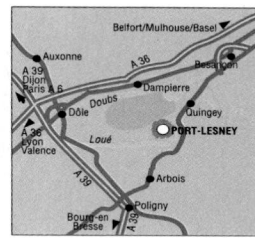

From Paris, A6 exit Dole, D405,
N5 towards Villiers-Farlay,
Mouchard. From Lyons, towards
Bourg-en-Bresse, A39, exit
Poligny, N83, towards Besançon.

Owners :
Roland and Verena Schön
Weekly closing :
Restaurant : Tuesday
Annual closing :
From January 4th to February 10th

 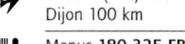

Geneva (**Intl**) 120 km
Dijon 100 km

This XVIIIth century manor was built amidst a landscape of forests and lakes. The comfortably restored rooms, have been redesigned by the interior designer, Roland Schön. An eclectic decoration, combining contemporary and Napoleon III styles. In the restaurant, you will succumb to the Franche-Comté products prepared in yellow Jura wine, alongside the light savours of the Mediterranean.

Menus 180-325 FRF s.i.
27-50 €
Carte 255-375 FRF s.i.
39-57 €

12 rooms
900-1 200 FRF s.i.
137-183 €

2 suites
1 300-1 500 FRF s.i.
198-229 €

80 FRF s.i.
12 €

yes

30 km (18 holes)

Hunting, fishing, climbing,
kayaking, mountain-biking,
walking, hot-air balloon.

Restaurant Greuze

SINCE 1978

Tel. : (33) 03 85 51 13 52
Fax : (33) 03 85 51 75 42
E-mail : greuze@relaischateaux.fr

Rue Albert Thibaudet
71700 Tournus
(Saône-et-Loire)

France

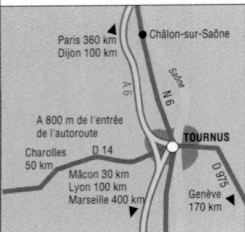

Highway A6, exit Tournus;
near the Saint-Philibert Abbey.

Owner : Jean Ducloux
Annual closing :
From November 20th
to December 8th

✈ Lyons (**Intl**) 100 km
Dijon 80 km

🍴 Menus **285-550 FRF** s.i.
43-84 €
Carte **300-550 FRF** s.i.
46-84 €

🐎 yes

♞ 15 km

Saint-Philibert Abbey, Greuze
and Bourguignon Museums,
Solutré museum, walks on the
banks of the Saône river.

Restaurant Greuze, named after the renowned 18th-century painter, has become a fashionable rendez-vous for gourmets and celebrities. For a quarter of a century, Jean Ducloux, one of the highest stars in the firmament of French gastronomy, has perpetuated culinary tradition with his «pâté en croûte Alexandre Dumaine», «quenelles de brochets Racouchot» and «poulet de Bresse sauté Jean Ducloux». Savour superb vintage Burgundies.

  Visa

FRF : French franc

www.relaischateaux.fr/greuze

CHÂTEAU D'IGÉ

France

71960 Igé
(Saône-et-Loire)

Tel. : (33) 03 85 33 33 99
Fax : (33) 03 85 33 41 41
E-mail : ige@relaischateaux.fr

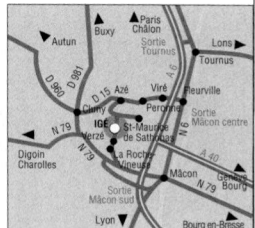

From Lyons, A6 exit Mâcon sud,
N 79 towards Moulins,
Montceau, exit La Roche Vineuse,
towards La Roche Vineuse, Verzé,
Igé.

Owner : Henri Jadot
Director :
Françoise Germond-Lieury
Weekly closing :
Rest.: Tuesday at lunch (except holidays)
Annual closing :
From Dec. 1st to March 1st

S et in a magnificent region full of Romanesque architecture, the feudal turrets of the Château d'Igé, fortified in 1235, offer superb vistas of the castle's floral gardens and the surrounding groves and vineyards. You will be enchanted by the traditional Burgundy hospitality and the refined decor of the guestrooms and period dining rooms. Savour local specialities enhanced by excellent Burgundies and regional wines.

Lyons (**Intl**) 90 km

Menus
160 FRF (week lunch)
24 €
200-260-310-380 FRF s.i.
30-40-47-58 €
Carte 215-365 FRF s.i.
33-56 €

7 rooms
495-780 FRF s.i.
75-119 €

6 suites
975-1 195 FRF s.i.
149-182 €

75 FRF s.i.
11 €

yes (extra cost)

12 km

1h45 from Paris by the TGV.
Romanesque church tours,
visit of Cluny, walks,
the wine trail, tasting.

www.relaischateaux.fr/ige   FRF : French franc

GEORGES
DUBŒUF

GEORGES DUBŒUF

BEAUJOLAIS-VILLAGES

APPELLATION BEAUJOLAIS-VILLAGES CONTROLÉE

MIS EN BOUTEILLES PAR
LES VINS GEORGES DUBŒUF
71570 ROMANÈCHE-THORINS
FRANCE

75 cl

GEORGES BLANC

France

01540 Vonnas
(Ain)

Tel. : (33) 04 74 50 90 90
Fax : (33) 04 74 50 08 80
E-mail : blanc@relaischateaux.fr

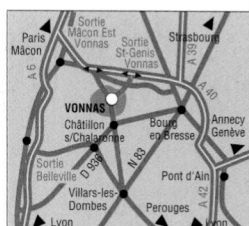

1 h from Geneva between Bourg en Bresse and Macon.
Exits Vonnas on A40 linking A6 and A39.

Owner : Georges Blanc
Weekly closing :
Rest.: Wednesday noon, Monday and Tuesday (except holidays) ; Tuesday noon and Monday only from June 15th to Sept. 15th
Annual closing :
From January 4th to Feb. 12th

✈ Lyons (**Intl**) 80 km

GPS N 46° 13' 120"
E 4° 59' 030"

🍴 Menus **490-890 FRF** s.i.
75-136 €
Carte **500-700 FRF** s.i.
76-107 €
L'Ancienne Auberge
150 FRF s.i.
23 €

I n Vonnas one of the most flower-bedecked villages in France, the Auberge des Blanc has existed since 1872. In the Bresse region, George Blanc's cuisine blends authentic tradition and innovation throughout the seasons. In this unique setting, you will enjoy the warm welcome of the Blanc family and its team. On the nearby market square, another restaurant «L'Ancienne Auberge», upholds traditional family-style cuisine.

☞ 21 rooms
850-1 600 FRF s.i.
130-244 €

🗝 9 suites
1 900-3 500 FRF s.i.
290-534 €

☕ **120 FRF** s.i.
18 €

🐕 yes

⚲ 12 km

FRF : French franc
Visa

169

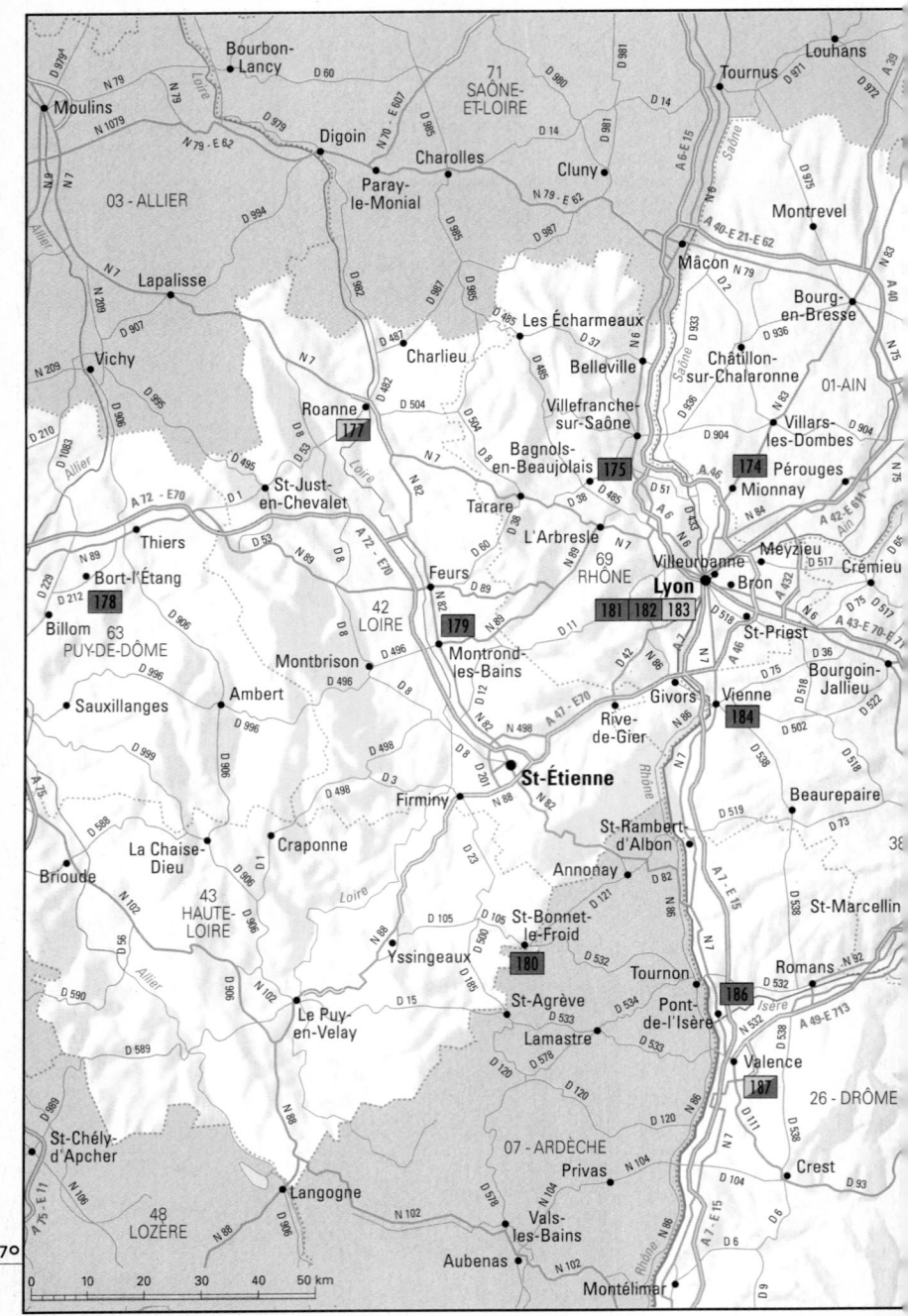

VINTAGES TO DRINK
IN YEAR 2000
BEAUJOLAIS - RHONE VALLEY

Wines recommended by the wine waiters
of the Relais & Châteaux and Relais Gourmands.

* Index of world vintages to drink in year 2000 : page 607

	Name of wine	Wine to enjoy	Noble wine	Outstanding wine
	BEAUJOLAIS			
Red	Beaujolais, Beaujolais Villages	1998		
	St-Amour, Juliénas, Moulin à Vent, Chenas, Fleurie, Morgon, Brouilly, Régnié, Côte de Brouilly, Chiroubles	1998	1996 - 1995	1990
	RHONE VALLEY			
White	Châteauneuf du Pape, Lirac, Vacqueyras	1997	1996	1992 - 1990
	Château Grillet, Condrieu, Hermitage, Crozes-Hermitage, St-Joseph	1997	1995	1989
Rosé wines	Gigondas, Tavel, Lirac, Côtes du Luberon, Côtes du Ventoux	1998 - 1997		
Red	Châteauneuf du Pape, Gigondas, Vacqueyras, Lirac, Coteaux du Tricastin	1995	1990	1985 - 1983
	Hermitage, Côte-Rotie, St-Joseph, Crozes-Hermitage	1996	1989	1991 - 1983

ALAIN CHAPEL

Tel. : (33) 04 78 91 82 02
Fax : (33) 04 78 91 82 37
E-mail : chapel@relaischateaux.fr

01390 Mionnay
(Ain)

France

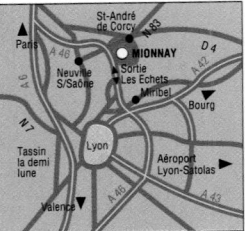

Take the A 46 beltway -
exit Les Echets,
towards Villars-les-Dombes, N 83.

Owners : Chapel Family
Director : Suzanne Chapel
Weekly closing :
Hotel: Monday
Restaurant: Monday and Tuesday
at lunch (except holidays)
Annual closing : January

✈ Lyons (**Intl**) 25 km

🍴 Menus
595-700-800 FRF s.i.
91-107-122 €
Carte **550 FRF** s.i.
84 €
Week lunch **380 FRF** s.i.
58 €

🔑 13 rooms
600-850 FRF s.i.
91-130 €

☕ **57-92 FRF** s.i.
9-14 €

🐎 yes (extra cost)

🎵 3 km

Pérouges (medieval city),
ornithological park.

Enjoy exquisite hospitality at this
elegant country house, set in the
picturesque village of Mionnay. Alain
Chapel's renowned concept of taste, based
on blending regional tradition with refined
gourmet techniques, is today perpetuated
by Suzanne Chapel and chef Philippe
Jousse. Savour «soufflé léger aux noisettes
et thym frais, sorbet au citron de
Menton» and other sublime specialities
accompanied by fine wines.

Visa

FRF : French franc

CHÂTEAU DE BAGNOLS

France

69620 Bagnols en Beaujolais
(Rhône)

Tel. : (33) 04 74 71 40 00
Fax : (33) 04 74 71 40 49
E-mail : bagnols@relaischateaux.fr

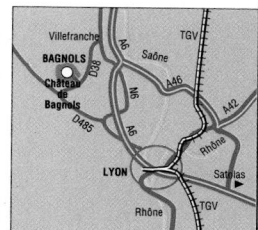

A6 direction Lyons,
exit Villefranche, then direction
Roanne-Tarare via D38 for 12 km.

Owner : Lady Hamlyn
Director : K.H. Zimmermann
Weekly closing :
Rest. : Sunday evening, Monday
and Tuesday at lunch
(November 15th to December 20th)
Annual closing :
From January to March

S et amidst the Beaujolais vineyards and surrounded by a beautiful moat, this 13th century château now a classified historical monument is a luxurious haven of peace. Enjoy the splendour of bygone days in guestrooms ornately decorated with late Renaissance mural paintings where Charles VIII and the Marquise de Sévigné once stayed. Savour refined cuisine in the former Guardroom which possesses of the most impressive Gothic fireplaces in France.

Lyons-Satolas (**Intl**) 60 km

Menus **300-510 FRF** s.i.
46-78 €
Carte **400-590 FRF** s.i.
61-90 €

12 rooms
2 200-3 500 FRF s.i.
335-534 €

8 suites
starting at **2 600 FRF** s.i.
396 €

120 FRF s.i.
18 €

yes (extra cost)
only residence

15 km

Hiking, mountain biking,
horse-riding, hot air ballooning,
classical music concerts...

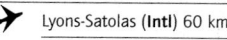

175

www.relaischateaux.fr/bagnols

FRF : French franc

Visa

LE NOUVEAU MILLÉNAIRE SERA CORDON ROUGE

GREY

LA MAISON TROISGROS

France

Place de la Gare
42300 Roanne
(Loire)

Tel. : (33) 04 77 71 66 97
Fax : (33) 04 77 70 39 77
E-mail : troisgros@relaischateaux.fr

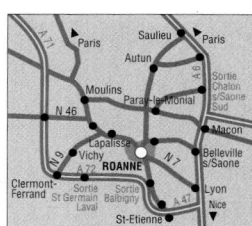

From Paris, A 6 - exit South Chalon, towards Paray-le-Monial and Roanne. From Paris, A 71 - exit Saint-Germain Laval. From Lyons, N7 towards Roanne.

Owners : Troisgros Family
Weekly closing :
Tuesday and Wednesday.
Tuesday evening and Wednesday
from June 1st to Sept. 15th
Annual closing :
February school holidays
and first half of August

The Troisgros Family, today Michel and Marie-Pierre, perpetuate French gastronomic tradition with flair. Savour their «fritot de tomates aux escargots de Bourgogne persillés» and «meringue légère aux fruits des bois» and the fine vintages. Retire to an elegant modern room. There is also «Le Central» next door: a cafe-grocery that proposes dishes combining tradition and fancy and many take-away delicacies.

Lyons (**Intl**) 110 km
Roanne 6 km

Menus **690-830 FRF** s.i.
105-127 €
Carte **800 FRF** s.i.
122 €
Le Central
125 FRF s.i. (lunch)
19 €
170 FRF s.i.
26 €

13 rooms
800-1 600 FRF s.i.
122-244 €

5 suites
1 800-2 000 FRF s.i.
274-305 €

125 FRF s.i.
19 €

yes

6 km

177

FRF : French franc

Visa

CHÂTEAU DE CODIGNAT

SINCE 1975

Tel. : (33) 04 73 68 43 03
Fax : (33) 04 73 68 93 54
E-mail : codignat@relaischateaux.fr

Lezoux
63190 Bort-l'Etang
(Puy-de-Dôme)

France

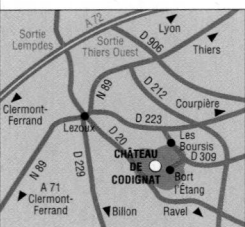

From Clermont-Ferrand, N89
towards Thiers, to Lezoux :
R. de Courpière and Bort-l'Etang.

Owners :
Monique Barberan and Guy Vidal
Directors :
Guy Vidal and Denis Lesage
Annual closing :
From Nov. 3rd to March 20th

 Clermont-Ferrand (**Intl**)
20 mn

 GPS N 45° 46' 52"
E 003° 24' 33"

 Menus 295-360 FRF s.i.
45-55 €
Carte 380-450 FRF s.i.
58-69 €

 15 rooms
790-1 350 FRF s.i.
120-206 €

 4 suites
1 350-2 100 FRF s.i.
206-320 €

 85 FRF s.i.
13 €

 yes (welcome)

35 km

Karting, flight over volcanos in
private plane, riding school.

This 15th-century château with red-tile roofs and medieval turrets offers breathtaking views across the Auvergne volcanos. The grandeur of the past is reflected in the guestrooms' antique furniture, tapestries and four-poster beds, while modern comforts include splendid «trompe l'œil» bathrooms and private jacuzzis. After a helicopter tour of Auvergne's castles and Roman churches, enjoy a romantic dinner by candlelight.

Visa

FRF : French franc

www.relaischateaux.fr/codignat

HOSTELLERIE LA POULARDE

France

42210 Montrond-les-Bains
(Loire)

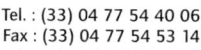

Tel. : (33) 04 77 54 40 06
Fax : (33) 04 77 54 53 14
E-mail : poularde@relaischateaux.fr

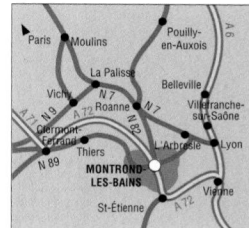

*From Saint-Etienne, A 72
towards Clermont-Ferrand,
exit N°7 Montrond.*

Owners :
Gilles and Monique Etéocle
Weekly closing :
Hotel : Sunday (from Nov. 1st to
April 30th), Monday
Rest. : Sunday evening
(from Nov. 1st to April 30th),
Monday and Tuesday noon
Annual closing :
From January 2nd to 15th

✈ Saint-Etienne (**Intl**) 8 km
Lyons (**Intl**) 70 km

🍴 Menus **250-610 FRF** s.i.
38-93 €
Carte **600-700 FRF** s.i.
91-107 €

T̄rue to its post house origins, La
Poularde's rooms are decorated in a
fusion of traditional and contemporary
style. Virtuoso chef Gilles Etéocle, recipient
of the «Meilleur Ouvrier de France» award,
creates a gastronomic symphony of
flavours. Exquisite dishes such as «sandre de
Loire sur la peau, rates à la forézienne» are
enhanced by superb vintages selected by
the wine waiter, voted Best Young and Best
French Wine Waiter.

⚷ 6 rooms
590 FRF s.i.
90 €

⚷ 8 suites
750-1 200-1 500 FRF s.i.
114-183-229 €

☕ 95 FRF s.i.
14 €

🐎 yes

Forez 3 km

Castle visit, hat-making and
glass Museums, thermal baths,
casino.

179

www.relaischateaux.fr/poularde   FRF : French franc

AUBERGE ET CLOS DES CIMES

SINCE 1997

Tel. : (33) 04 71 59 93 72
Fax : (33) 04 71 59 93 40
E-mail : cimes@relaischateaux.fr

Place de l'Eglise
43290 St Bonnet-le-Froid
(Haute-Loire)

France

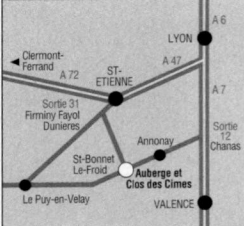

From Lyons: A7 towards Marseille, exit Chanas-Annonay, then towards Le-Puy-en-Velay for 25 kilometres. From Clermont-Ferrand: A47 towards St. Etienne, exit Firminy/ Le-Puy-en-Velay. In Firminy Fayol Nr 31 towards Dunieres. In Dunieres left towards St-Bonnet-le-Froid.

Owner : Régis Marcon
Weekly closing :
Restaurant : Monday evening and Tuesday
Annual closing :
From November 15th to Easter

✈ Lyons **(Intl)** 100 km

🍴 Menus **280-580 FRF** s.i.
43-88 €
Carte **250-600 FRF** s.i.
38-91 €

⊶ 12 rooms
700-1 100 FRF s.i.
107-168 €

☕ **90 FRF** s.i.
14 €

🛏 yes

🎿 12 km

Fishing, skiing, canoeing, mountain biking.

B etween Velay and Vivarais, prolong your stay in one of these lovely comfortable rooms overlooking valleys and mountains. Then meet Régis whose cuisine reflects the magnificent natural surroundings. Savour the «ragoût aux lentilles vertes du Puy et œuf fumé», «brochette "Margaridou"» and «agneau en croûte de foin de cistre». Michelle, his wife, will suggest the fine Rhone valley wines of Condrieu and Croze-Hermitage.

Visa

FRF : French franc

www.relaischateaux.fr/cimes

LÉON DE LYON

France

1, rue Pléney (angle rue du Plâtre)
69001 Lyon
(Rhône)

Tel. : (33) 04 72 10 11 12
Fax : (33) 04 72 10 11 13
E-mail : leon@relaischateaux.fr

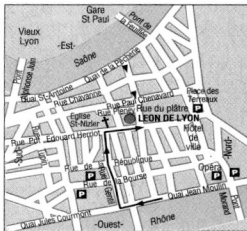

On the peninsula, toward place des Terreaux, before the plaza (at the corner of the rue du Plâtre).

Owners :
Fabienne and Jean-Paul Lacombe
Weekly closing :
Sunday and Monday
Annual closing :
From August 1st to 22nd

Lyons (**Intl**) 20 km

Menus **290 FRF** (lunch)
44 €
590-750 FRF s.i. - 90-114 €
Carte 550 FRF s.i. - 84 €

yes

20 km

New Opera, Traboules visit, Canuts Museum, Basilica of Fourvière.

As the seasons change, Jean-Paul Lacombe reinvents Lyonnaise culinary tradition, using the finest regional produce to create a cuisine with the most delicate aromas. Enjoy «cochon fermier, foie gras, oignons confits en terrine rustique, salades mélangées, vinaigrette au jus de truffes», or the «six petits desserts sur le thème de la praline de Saint-Genix». Regional wines and exceptional vintages.

www.relaischateaux.fr/leon   **FRF : French franc**   Visa

RESTAURANT PIERRE ORSI

SINCE 1981

Tel. : (33) 04 78 89 57 68
Fax : (33) 04 72 44 93 34
E-mail : orsi@relaischateaux.fr

3, place Kléber
69006 Lyon
(Rhône)

France

Near the Tête d'Or park, the Cité Internationale, and the Part-Dieu railway station.

Owner : Pierre Orsi
Director : Geneviève Orsi
Weekly closing : Sunday, Saturday and Sunday in August
Open all year

✈ Lyons-Satolas (**Intl**) 20 km
Lyons-Bron 10 km

🍴 Menus **240-500-600 FRF** s.i.
37-76-91 €
Carte **400-550 FRF** s.i.
61-84 €

🛏 yes

♪ 20 km

Theme nights, dancing, private lounges. Visits to the vaulted cellar, aperitif in the kitchen bar (upon request).

P ierre Orsi, recipient of the «Meilleur Ouvrier de France» award has established his elegant restaurant in an ancient manor near the Tête d'Or park. After being welcomed by his charming wife, Geneviève, savour Orsi's innovative «foie gras chaud de canard poêlé sur nid d'épinards» and «marinière de loup et rouget au basilic». The outstanding wine list features a variety of fine French vintages including an exceptional Mâcon-Clessé.

  Visa

FRF : French franc

www.relaischateaux.fr/orsi

VILLA FLORENTINE

France

25-27, montée Saint-Barthélémy
69005 Lyon
(Rhône)

Tel. : (33) 04 72 56 56 56
Fax : (33) 04 72 40 90 56
E-mail : florentine@relaischateaux.fr

*From the Saône docks
(Vieux Lyon), go to the gare
Saint-Paul, then follow signs to
the basilique Fourvière.*

Owner : Eric Giorgi
Director : Annie Blancardi
Open all year

✈ Lyons-Satolas (**Intl**) 25 km
Lyons-Bron 10 km

🍴 Menus **170-400 FRF** s.i.
26-61 €
Carte **290-420 FRF** s.i.
44-64 €

🔑 16 rooms
1 300-2 100 FRF s.i.
198-320 €

🔑 3 suites
1 600-2 100 FRF s.i.
244-320 €

🍵 100 FRF s.i.
15 €

🦮 yes

♪ 10 km

Visits : Fourvière basilica, St-Jean
cathedral, Gallo-Roman museum...

T his splendid villa, offering sublime panoramic views of Lyon, certainly lives up to its name. Everything from its elegant façade to its sunny rooms, furnished with a mixture of Renaissance refinement and contemporary Italian design, has a sumptuous Florentine feel to it. Savour refined cuisine and superb Rhône vintages at the restaurant «Les Terrasses de Lyon», while contemplating the city lights twinkling below.

183

FRF : French franc

Visa

LA PYRAMIDE

SINCE 1999

Tel. : (33) 04 74 53 01 96
Fax : (33) 04 74 85 69 73
E-mail : pyramide@relaischateaux.fr

14, bd Fernand Point
38200 Vienne
(Isère)

France

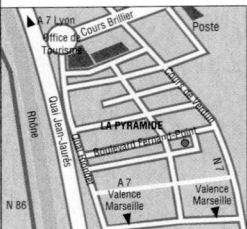

From Vienne, follows signs for «Pyramide». Do not follow signs for «centre ville».

Owners :
Pascale and Patrick Henriroux
Weekly closing :
Rest. : Tuesdays and Wednesdays
Open all year

✈ Lyons (**Intl**) 30 km

🍴 Menus 470-690 FRF s.i.
72-105 €
Carte 650 FRF s.i.
99 €

⚷ 20 rooms
880-1 080 FRF s.i.
134-165 €

⚷ 4 suites
1 380-1 580 FRF s.i.
210-241 €

☕ 90-110 FRF s.i.
14-17 €

🐎 yes (extra cost)

Horseback riding.

« I l n'y a de restaurant que Point. Un point, c'est tout», to paraphrase a famous Sacha Guitry quotation. Yet, for Patrick Henriroux inheriting the restaurant does not signify simply continuing a famous tradition but innovating it as well. A stay at La Pyramide remains an unforgettable experience. The superb cuisine of the South of France and the Dauphiné region is a delight. Savour «rôti d'agneau de lait et cannellonis d'aubergines à la ricotta». Then, retire to one of the extremely charming guestrooms: the best way to know the hotel.

FRF : French franc

www.relaischateaux.fr/pyramide

CHÂTEAU DE FAVERGES-DE-LA-TOUR

France

38110 Faverges-de-la-Tour
(Isère)

Tel. : (33) 04 74 97 42 52
Fax : (33) 04 74 88 86 40
E-mail : faverges@relaischateaux.fr

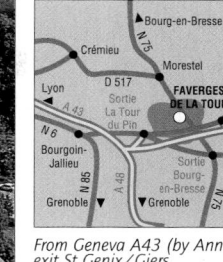

From Geneva A43 (by Annecy),
exit St Genix/Giers.
From Lyons A43 (by Satolas),
exit La Tour-du-Pin.

Owners : Tournier Family
Director : Christophe Bricaud
Annual closing :
From October to May

✈ Lyons (**Intl**) 42 km

GPS N 45° 35' 26''
E 005° 32' 09''

🍴 Menus **210-510 FRF** s.i.
32-78 €
Carte **300-450 FRF** s.i.
46-69 €

🔑 34 rooms
850-2 200 FRF s.i.
130-335 €

🔑 2 suites
1 650-3 000 FRF s.i.
252-457 €

🍵 **70-120 FRF** s.i.
11-18 €

🦮 yes (extra cost)

⛳ private (9 holes)

Hot-air ballooning, flying club,
biking...

G uests will be enchanted by this
elegant residence set amidst a sea
of greenery in the picturesque Dauphiné
countryside. They will also be impressed by
the Tournier family's warm welcome and
generous hospitality. The cosy bedrooms
are bright and comfortable, the lounges
grand and tastefully decorated. Dinner,
served in the candlelit splendour of the
vaulted cellars, is a feast of regional
cuisine and fine Savoy wines.

FRF : French franc

Visa

MICHEL CHABRAN

SINCE 1986

Tel. : (33) 04 75 84 60 09
Fax : (33) 04 75 84 59 65
E-mail : chabran@relaischateaux.fr

Av. du 45ème parallèle, RN 7
26600 Pont-de-l'Isère
(Drôme)

France

On RN7 at Pont-de-l'Isère;
A7, between the Valence nord
and Tain l'Hermitage exits.

Owner : Michel Chabran
Open all year

Lyons (**Intl**) 100 km
Valence 15 km

Menus **350-745 FRF** s.i.
53-114 €
Carte **500-700 FRF** s.i.
76-108 €

yes

(3 x 18 holes) 25 km

Vercors park,
Facteur Cheval palace...

V irtuoso chef Michel Chabran invites guests to savour a symphony of flavours in this elegant restaurant set in the heart of the Hermitage region. This culinary perfectionist blends rustic tradition and haute cuisine to create gourmet specialities such as his «filets de rougets poêlés, purée de pommes de terre à l'huile d'olive, vinaigre balsamique». The cellar is a veritable treasure trove of local vintages.

 Visa

FRF : French franc

www.relaischateaux.fr/chabran

PIC

France

285, avenue Victor-Hugo
26000 Valence
(Drôme)

Tel. : (33) 04 75 44 15 32
Fax : (33) 04 75 40 96 03
Auberge du Pin : (33) 04 75 44 53 86
E-mail : pic@relaischateaux.fr

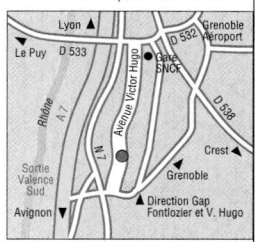

*From Lyons or Marseilles, A7,
exit Valence South; towards City
centre Victor Hugo, follow signs.*

Owner : Anne Pic-Sinapian
Director : David Sinapian
Weekly closing :
Restaurant : Sunday evening,
Monday, Tuesday for lunch from
Nov. to March (except holidays)
Auberge du Pin : o.e.d.
Open all year

G randdaughter of André, daughter of Jacques, Anne Pic upholds tradition with flair, revealing the true nature of products. Enjoy the «pigeon en croûte de noix» and the «filet de loup au caviar» of this innovative hundred-year-old restaurant. The chef's husband David warmly welcomes guests, suggesting vintages from the fine cellar. Minutes away, the Auberge du Pin offers the charms of a simpler Provence-style cuisine.

Lyons (**Intl**) 100 km
Valence 10 km

GPS N 44° 54' 56" E 4° 58' 07"
Valence Chabeuil
(Free shuttle service from
the hotel)

 Menus **290 FRF** s.i. week lunch (drinks included)
44 €
490-690 FRF s.i. -**75-105 €**
Carte **490-700 FRF** s.i.
75-107 €
Auberge du Pin **155 FRF** s.i.
24 €

12 rooms
750-1 350 FRF s.i.
114-206 €

3 suites **1 150-1 800 FRF** s.i.
175-274 €

100-130 FRF s.i. - **15-20 €**

yes (extra cost)

10 km

187

www.relaischateaux.fr/pic

FRF : French franc

Visa

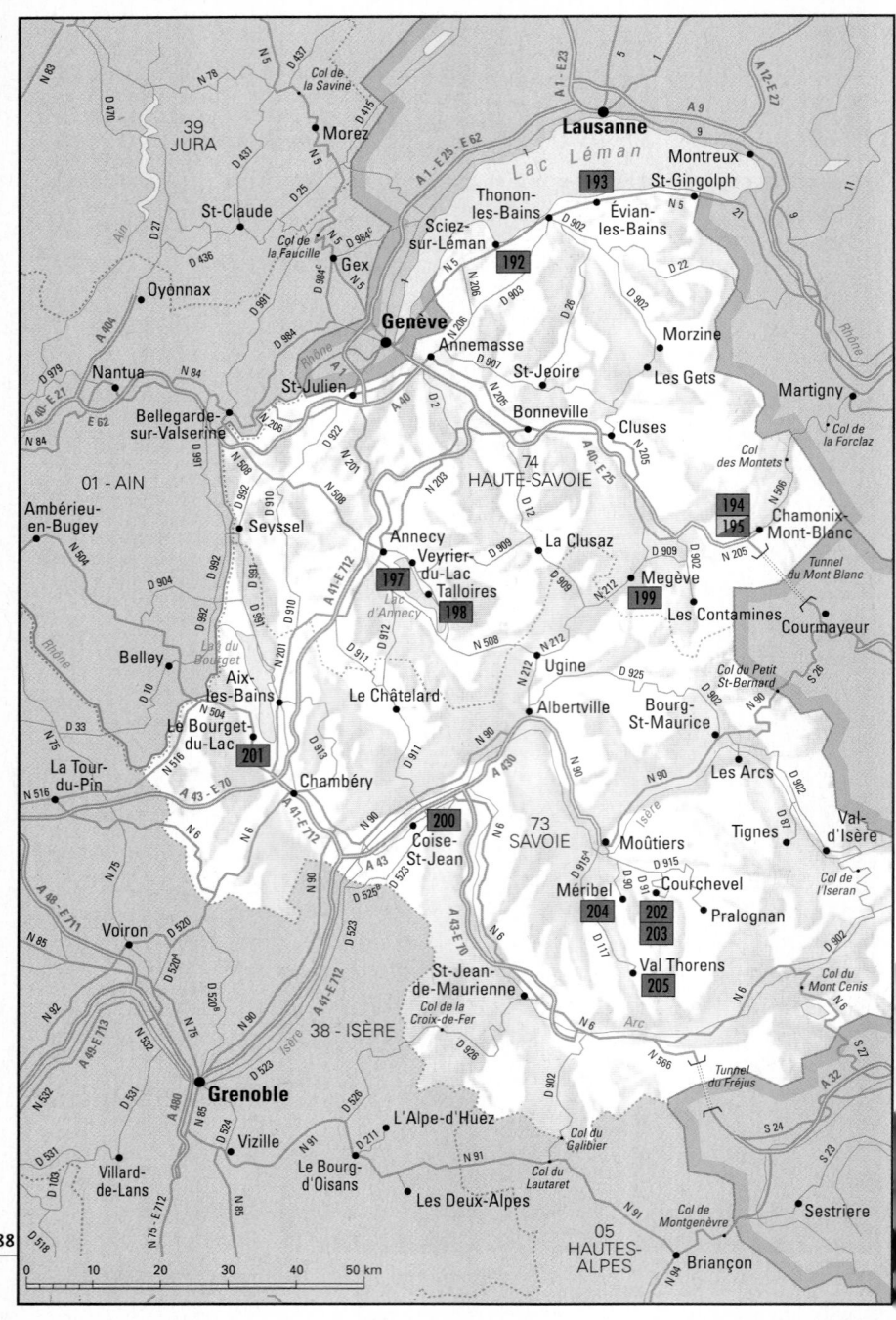

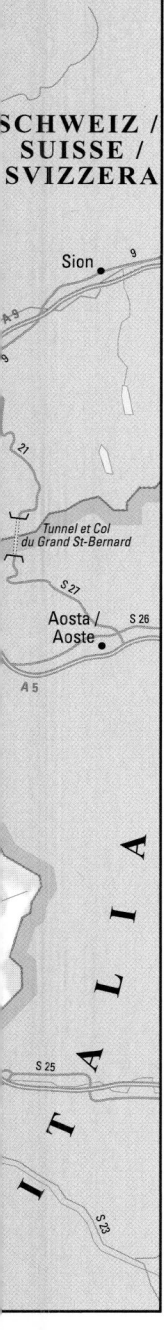

SCHWEIZ /
SUISSE /
SVIZZERA

Sion

Tunnel et Col
du Grand St-Bernard

Aosta /
Aoste

ITALIA

SAVOY MONT-BLANC

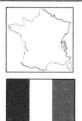

Establishments	Nearest major city	Relais & Châteaux	Relais Gourmands	Page
Alpes Hôtel du Pralong	Courchevel	✿		202
Auberge de l'Eridan	Annecy	✿	⌂	197
Auberge du Bois Prin	Chamonix	✿		194
Auberge du Père Bise	Annecy	✿	⌂	198
Chalet du Mont d'Arbois	Megève	✿		199
Château de Coudrée	Genève	✿		192
Château de la Tour du Puits	Chambéry	✿		200
Fitz Roy Hôtel	Val Thorens	✿		205
Grand Cœur (Le)	Méribel	✿		204
Hameau Albert 1er (Le)	Genève	✿	⌂	195
Hôtel des Neiges	Courchevel	✿		203
Ombremont	Chambéry	✿	⌂	201
Verniaz (La)	Evian	✿		193

TRAVELLER II

Automatique
Fonction réveil
Double fuseau horaire

Automatic
Alarm
Double time zone

GP
GIRARD-PERREGAUX
MANUFACTURE DEPUIS 1791

GIRARD-PERREGAUX
1, place Girardet
CH-2301 La Chaux-de-Fonds
Tel: (+41)32 911 33 33
Fax: (+41)32 913 04 80

http://www.girard-perregaux.ch
com@girard-perregaux.ch

ASSOCIATION
INTERPROFESSIONNELLE
DE LA HAUTE HORLOGERIE

Vintages to drink
in year 2000
Savoie

Wines recommended by the wine waiters
of the Relais & Châteaux and Relais Gourmands.

* Index of world vintages to drink in year 2000 : page 607

	Name of wine	Wine to enjoy	Noble wine	Outstanding wine
	Savoie			
White	Vins de Savoie, Roussette	1998 - 1997	1995	
Red	Vins de Savoie, Mondeuse	1998 - 1997	1996	1990

CHÂTEAU DE COUDRÉE

SINCE 1962

Tel. : (33) 04 50 72 62 33
Fax : (33) 04 50 72 57 28
E-mail : coudree@relaischateaux.fr

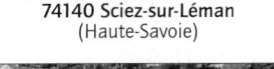

Domaine de Coudrée - Bonnatrait
74140 Sciez-sur-Léman
(Haute-Savoie)

France

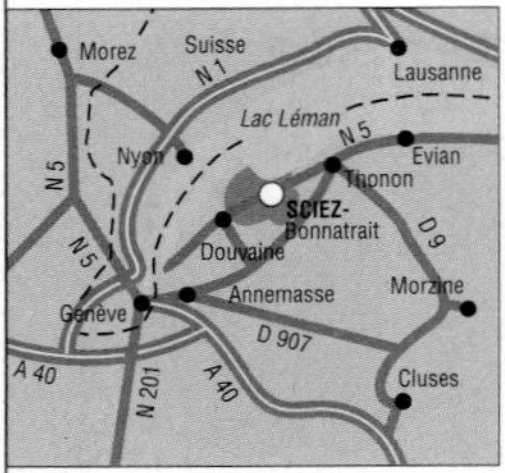

A40 exit Annemasse, Thonon-Evian ; A41 exit Thonon-Evian (via Douvaine), Sciez, Bonnatrait, follow signs.

Owners : S.C.I. J.D.L.
Director : Catherine Réale-Laden
Annual closing :
February and November

Geneva (**Intl**) 28 km

GPS N 46° 20′ 45″
E 006° 23′ 00″

Menus **210-340-510 FRF** s.i.
32-52-78 €
Carte **300-400 FRF** s.i.
46-61 €

14 rooms
780-1 680 FRF s.i.
119-256 €

5 suites
1 580-2 080 FRF s.i.
241-317 €

105 FRF s.i.
16 €

yes (extra cost)

Evian 15 km

This magnificent 12th-century château, once home to the Savoy aristocracy, towers proudly above Lake Geneva. The splendour of bygone days lingers on in the coffered ceilings, monumental fireplaces, stained-glass windows and rich tapestries of its guestrooms, which overlook a floral park with stately plane trees. Savour gourmet cuisine and vintage wines by candlelight and enjoy a private beach, pool and tennis courts.

Visa

FRF : French franc

www.relaischateaux.fr/coudree

LA VERNIAZ ET SES CHALETS

France

Av. d'Abondance, Neuvecelle-Eglise
74500 Evian-les-Bains
(Haute-Savoie)

Tel. : **(33) 04 50 75 04 90**
Fax : **(33) 04 50 70 78 92**
E-mail : verniaz@relaischateaux.fr

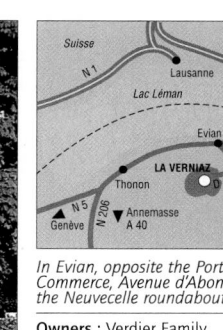

In Evian, opposite the Port de Commerce, Avenue d'Abondance, the Neuvecelle roundabout.

Owners : Verdier Family
Weekly closing : Rest. : Tuesday (except July-August)
Annual closing :
From mid-Nov. to mid-February

Geneva (**Intl**) 45 km
Lyons (**Intl**) 200 km

Menus **200-360 FRF** s.i.
30-55 €
Carte **250-350 FRF** s.i.
38-53 €

30 rooms
550-950 FRF s.i.
(winter) - **84-145 €**
800-1 300 FRF s.i.
(summer) - **122-198 €**

2 suites/5 chalets
1 000-1 600 FRF s.i.
(winter) - **152-244 €**
starting at **1 500 FRF** s.i.
(summer) - **229 €**

85 FRF s.i.
13 €

yes (extra cost)

2 km

N estling between the lake and the mountains above Evian, La Verniaz is an ensemble of old Alpine houses and chalets secluded in beautiful floral parkland. Many of the spacious, individually styled rooms have their own private balcony set amidst the trees. The inventive and generous cuisine, featuring a traditional woodfire «Rôtisserie» and delicious fish freshly caught from Lake Geneva, is enhanced by fine Savoy wines.

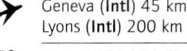

193

www.relaischateaux.fr/verniaz

FRF : French franc

Visa

Auberge du Bois Prin

SINCE 1987

Tel. : (33) 04 50 53 33 51
Fax : (33) 04 50 53 48 75
E-mail : boisprin@relaischateaux.fr

69, Chemin de l'Hermine, Les Moussoux
74400 Chamonix Mont-Blanc
(Haute-Savoie)

France

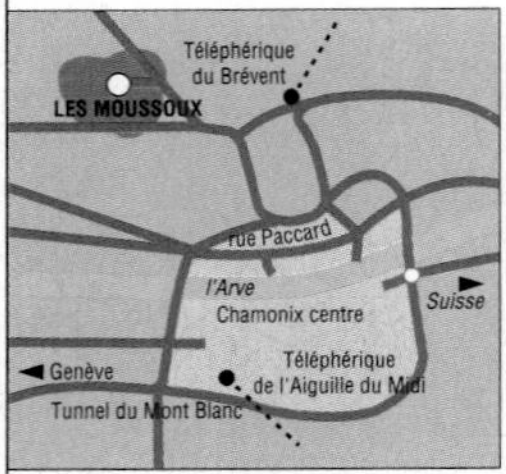

Highway - exit Chamonix south, follow signs to the hotel, towards Les Moussoux.

Owners : Carrier Family
Directors :
Monique and Denis Carrier
Weekly closing :
Rest. : Wednesday at lunch
Annual closing :
From April 25th to May 11th and from October 30th to November 30th

Geneva (**Intl**) 83 km
Annecy 94 km

Menus **180-450 FRF** s.i.
27-69 €
Carte **310-430 FRF** s.i.
47-66 €

11 rooms
920-1 380 FRF s.i.
140-210 €

80 FRF s.i.
12 €

yes (extra cost)

3 km

This picturesque chalet's sunny rooms and balconies offer stunning vistas of Mont-Blanc and the surrounding countryside. In winter the slopes glitter with snow, while in spring the chalet stands amidst a sea of greenery, bathed in the scent of gentian. Monique and Denis Carrier concoct marvellously inventive cuisine and the local cheeses, like the wines -Mondeuse, Ayze and Roussette- are full of rich mountain flavour.

Visa

FRF : French franc

www.relaischateaux.fr/boisprin

SINCE 2000

LE HAMEAU ALBERT Iᴱᴿ

France

119, impasse du Montenvers, BP 55
74402 Chamonix
(Haute-Savoie)

Tel. : **(33) 04 50 53 05 09**
Fax : **(33) 04 50 55 95 48**
E-mail : albert@relaischateaux.fr

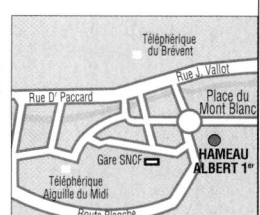

A40 Lyon-Geneva, Chamonix. Enter at Chamonix north, towards Swiss Argentière, 2nd road on the right.

Owner : Pierre Carrier
Director : Martine Carrier
Weekly closing : Rest. Albert Iᵉʳ :
Wednesday and Thursday at lunch
Rest. La Maison Carrier :
Monday and Tuesday at lunch
Annual closing :
Hotel : from Nov. 5th to Dec. 5th
Rest. Albert Iᵉʳ : from May 8th to
18th and from Nov. 5th to Dec. 5th
Restaurant La Maison Carrier :
from Nov. 13th to Dec. 13th

The Carrier family has reigned over the Hameau Albert Iᵉʳ hotel in Chamonix since its 1903 creation. Authenticity, welcome, tradition and gastronomy are master words here from the rooms and chalets in the park to Pierre Carrier's creations. Savour «filet d'omble et miel de bourgeons de sapin», «boudin de la maison, carti à la chirve». Wine list with over 20.000 bottles. In the Hameau's farmhouse, the typical restaurant «La Maison Carrier».

 Geneva (**Intl**) 80 km
Annecy 80 km

 Menus **220-650 FRF** s.i.
34-99 €
Carte **400-700 FRF** s.i.
61-107 €
La Maison Carrier
145 FRF s.i. - **22 €**

 35 rooms
890-1 500 FRF s.i.
136-229 €

5 suites
1 800-4 500 FRF s.i.
274-686 €

 95 FRF s.i. - **14 €**

yes

2 km

Climbing, skiing, kayaking, mountain-biking.

www.relaischateaux.fr/albert

FRF : French franc

Visa

195

AUBERGE DE L'ERIDAN-MARC VEYRAT

SINCE 1991

France

13, vieille route des Pensières
74290 Veyrier-du-Lac
(Haute-Savoie)

Tel. : (33) 04 50 60 24 00
Fax : (33) 04 50 60 23 63
E-mail : veyrat@relaischateaux.fr

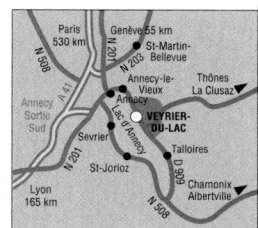

Exit Annecy-Sud, towards the city centre and the lake, RN 59 towards Veyrier-du-lac/Thônes, at Veyrier roundabout, right and right again.

Owner : Marc Veyrat
Weekly closing :
Monday (except July and August)
Tuesday noon and Wednesday noon
Annual closing :
From Dec. 15th to March 1st

T he elegant blue façade of this Savoyard inn looks out across the picturesque shore of Lake Annecy. In these idyllic surroundings, virtuoso chef Marc Veyrat conjures up gastronomic marvels such as «escalope de foie chaud au pain d'épice aux huit arômes» and «coquilles Saint-Jacques et ris de veau au petit lait de coquelicot». Rediscover the flavours and aromas of the Alpine pastures and savour the finest local vintages.

✈ Geneva (**Intl**) 50 km
Annecy 5 km

🍴 Menus **695-995 FRF** s.i.
106-152 €
Carte **500-650 FRF** s.i.
76-99 €

○┱ 9 rooms
1 250-3 250 FRF s.i.
191-495 €

🔒 2 suites
4 250-4 650 FRF s.i.
648-709 €

☕ **245 FRF** s.i.
37 €

🐕 yes (extra cost)

🚶 2 km

197

www.relaischateaux.fr/veyrat

FRF : French franc

Visa

Auberge du Père Bise

SINCE 1973

Tel. : (33) 04 50 60 72 01
Fax : (33) 04 50 60 73 05
E-mail : bise@relaischateaux.fr

Route du Port
74290 Talloires
(Haute-Savoie)

France

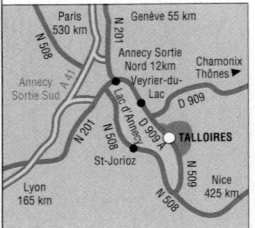

*Highway A 41, exit Annecy Nord,
towards Annecy-le-Vieux,Thônes,
Veyrier-du-Lac, Talloires.*

Owners :
Charlyne and Sophie Bise
Weekly closing : Tues. and Wed.
at lunch from Feb. to May and
from Sept. to Nov.
Annual closing : From the beg.
of Nov. to mid-Feb.

 Geneva (**Intl**) 55 km
Annecy 18 km

 GPS N 45° 50' 23"
E 006° 12' 41"

 Menus **490-820 FRF** s.i.
75-125 €
Carte **600-850 FRF** s.i.
91-130 €

 25 rooms
1 200-1 600 FRF s.i.
183-244 €

 9 suites
2 500-3 000 FRF s.i.
381-457 €

 100-150 FRF s.i.
15-23 €

 yes (extra cost)

 3 km

Mountain biking, water-skiing,
hiking...

P erpetuating a hundred-year-old culinary family tradition, Sophie Bise and her chef reinvent gourmet pleasures with dishes such as the «tatin de pommes de terre, truffes et fois gras». The warm welcome, the superb comfort of the guestrooms which overlook a lake with the purest water in Europe and the prestigious wine cellar with its rare vintages all make the Auberge du Père Bise the ideal place for relaxing and enjoying the dolce vita.

     Visa

FRF : French franc

www.relaischateaux.fr/bise

CHALET DU MONT D'ARBOIS

France

447, chemin de la Rocaille
74120 Megève
(Haute-Savoie)

Tel. : (33) 04 50 21 25 03
Fax : (33) 04 50 21 24 79
E-mail : montarbois@relaischateaux.fr

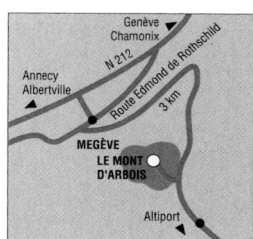

From Paris, highway
exit Sallanches, Megève (11 km).
From the south, exit Albertville.

Owners : B. and N. de Rothschild
Director : Alexandre Faix
Annual closing :
From mid-October to mid-Dec.
and mid-April to mid-June

Geneva (**Intl**) 65 km
Annecy 60 km

Menus **280-700 FRF** s.i.
43-107 €
Carte **400-550 FRF** s.i.
61-84 €

This superb site, set amidst the snow-capped firs of Megève, is a delight all seasons of the year. With the charm of its landscape and swimming pool in summer as in winter, the chalet owned by Benjamin and Nadine de Rothschild, offers refined hospitality, quiet, cosy guestrooms and a cosy lounge. Savour classical yet innovative cuisine and exceptional vintages.

22 rooms
1 100-3 200 FRF s.i.
(summer) - 168-488 €
1 660-4 000 FRF s.i.
(winter) - 253-610 €

2 suites (for 2 to 4 pers.)
2 500-6 500 FRF s.i.
(summer) - 381-991 €
4 000-9 000 FRF s.i.
(winter) - 610-1 372 €

120 FRF s.i.
18 €

yes

300 m

Sauna, jacuzzi, hammam, beauty salon and fitness, carriage rides.

CHÂTEAU DE LA TOUR DU PUITS

Tel. : (33) 04 79 28 88 00
Fax : (33) 04 79 28 88 01
E-mail : tourpuits@relaischateaux.fr

Le Puits
73800 Coise Saint-Jean
(Savoie)

France

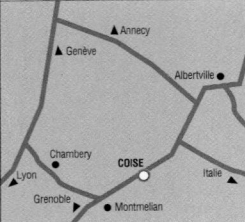

From Chambéry, motorway A43 towards Albertville, exit 23 Châteauneuf. From Albertville and La Maurienne, take N6/N90. At the bridge of Saint-Pierre d'Albigny, turn right towards Châteauneuf. Follow signs.

Owner : Raymond Prévot
Director : Georges Crémilleux
Open all year

✈ Lyons-Satolas (**Intl**) 110 km
Chambéry 30 km

GPS N 45° 32' 03"
E 006° 09' 26"

🍴 Menus **195-550 FRF** s.i.
30-84 €
Carte **280-430 FRF** s.i.
43-66 €

🔑 8 rooms
850-1 250 FRF s.i.
130-191 €

☕ 95 FRF s.i.
14 €

🐕 yes

🏌 30 km
Putting green on the premises

This authentic 18th-century château, set amidst the magnificent Savoie countryside facing the Alps, has been lovingly restored. The elegant guestrooms, each individually decorated, are named after the famous lords who once dwelt here. This tranquil haven, surrounded by wooded parkland, offers endless opportunities for country rambles. Enjoy excellent cuisine, fine Savoie vintages and superb views of the Coisin valley.

Visa

FRF : French franc

www.relaischateaux.fr/tourpuits

France

RN 504
73370 Le Bourget-du-Lac
(Savoie)

Tel. : (33) 04 79 25 00 23
Fax : (33) 04 79 25 25 77
E-mail : ombremont@relaischateaux.fr

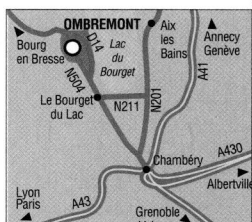

*From Chambéry, follow signs to
Le Bourget-du-Lac, then RN 504
in the direction of Belly,
Bourg-en-Bresse (2 km).*

Owner : Jean-Pierre Jacob
Weekly closing :
Rest. : Tuesday noon
Annual closing :
From the beginning of November
to the beginning of May

Overlooking the Bourget lake, this romantic turn-of-the-century villa is at the heart of park a hundred years old. The sunny rooms with fresh-cut flowers are warmly personalised and have every modern comfort. The regional cuisine gives more than its due to seafood. Savour the «cannellonis de lavaret fumé» and «filet de perche rôti à l'huile de poivrons rouges». Savoy wines have pride of place.

✈ Lyons (**Intl**) 75 km
Geneva (**Intl**) 100 km
Chambéry 4 km

🍴 Menus **250-560 FRF** s.i.
38-85 €
Carte **450-550 FRF** s.i.
69-84 €

⊶ 12 rooms
880-1 400 FRF s.i.
134-213 €

⊶ 5 suites
1 500-1 800 FRF s.i.
229-275 €

🍷 included

🍴 yes (extra cost)

🚶 10 km

Fishing, sailing, water skiing,
kayaking, mountain-biking,
flying club.

🚗 🅿 🛎 👫 ⛱ 🛗 🌊 **201**

FRF : French franc   Visa

ALPES HOTEL DU PRALONG

SINCE 1975

France

Tel. : (33) 04 79 08 24 82
Fax : (33) 04 79 08 36 41
E-mail : pralong@relaischateaux.fr

Route de l'Altiport, B.P. 13
73121 Courchevel 1850 Cedex
(Savoie)

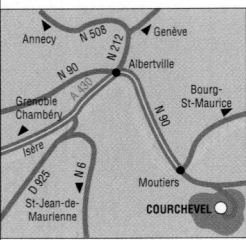

From Albertville, towards
Moutiers and Courchevel 1850,
on the Altiport road.

Owner : SCI Pralong 2000
Director : Albert Parveaux
Annual closing :
From April 15th to Dec. 20th

✈ Lyons (**Intl**) 160 km
Geneva (**Intl**) 160 km

🍴 Menu **420 FRF** s.i.
64 €
Carte **350-480 FRF** s.i.
53-73 €

⚷ 56 rooms
half board/pers.
1 050-1 900 FRF s.i.
160-290 €

⚷ 8 suites
half board/pers.
2 450-3 100 FRF s.i.
373-473 €

🍹 included

🍴 yes

Parasailing, snowmobiling,
hiking.

Perched above the glittering white slopes of Courchevel, at the heart of the Three Valleys ski resort, this comfortable residence offers generous hospitality and calm, spacious rooms decorated with wood panelling. After swooping up to the Olympic slopes on the ski lift, located just outside the hotel, unwind in the covered pool or indulge in a sauna and massage. The cuisine is deliciously fresh and appetizing.

 Visa

FRF : French franc

www.relaischateaux.fr/pralong

SINCE 1980

HÔTEL DES NEIGES

France

B.P. 96
73121 Courchevel 1850 Cedex
(Savoie)

Tel. : (33) 04 79 08 03 77
Fax : (33) 04 79 08 18 70
E-mail : neiges@relaischateaux.fr

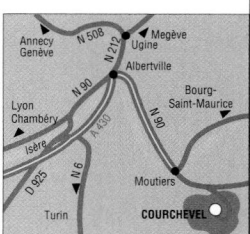

From Lyons, A 43 towards
Chambéry, Albertville, A 430
Moutiers, N 90.

Owner : Henry Benoist
Annual closing :
From April 17th to Dec. 17th

✈ Geneva (**Intl**) 140 km
Lyons (**Intl**) 200 km

 Menus **300-355 FRF** s.i.
46-54 €
Carte **300-400 FRF** s.i.
46-61 €

Aﬁfter an exhilarating morning in the mountains, ski down to this superb chalet and enjoy a delicious lunch on the sun-drenched terrace, accessible from the slopes. The tastefully decorated and cosy rooms, leading into luxurious bathrooms, are wonderfully calm and in the evening guests can recline before a roaring fire and listen to soft piano music. Refined cuisine is enhanced by fine wines and impeccable service.

 37 rooms
half board/pers.
1 320-1 990 FRF s.i.
201-303 €

 5 suites
half board/pers.
2 650 FRF s.i.
404 €

☕ included

🚫 no

Skating, para-sailing, relaxation centre, St-Bon baroque church (17th century)...

     **203**

FRF : French franc

Visa

LE GRAND CŒUR

Tel. : (33) 04 79 08 60 03
Fax : (33) 04 79 08 58 38
E-mail : grandcœur@relaischateaux.fr

73550 Méribel
(Savoie)

France

From Lyons, A 43 towards Chambery, Albertville, N 90 Moutiers, D 90 Méribel.

Owner : Sogeco S.A.
Directors :
Mr. and Mrs. Edouard Ruchti
Annual closing :
From April 7th to December 13th

✈ Lyons (**Intl**) 190 km
Chambéry 80 km

🍴 Menus **210-330 FRF** s.i.
32-50 €
Carte **250-380 FRF** s.i.
38-58 €

🔑 38 rooms
(half board/pers.)
1 000-1 850 FRF s.i.
152-282 €

🔑 3 suites
(half board/pers.)
1 850-2 400 FRF s.i.
282-365 €

☕ 110 FRF s.i.
17 €

🍴 yes
(extra cost) **50 FRF - 8 €**)

Snowmobiling, hangliding, para-sailing, Pracoua observatory...

This authentic Savoyard chalet, nestling at the foot of the slopes in the centre of Méribel, is tastefully decorated with fine wood panelling, sumptuous fabrics and embroidery. After an invigorating day on the slopes, unwind in the sauna, hammam or jacuzzi, sip apéritifs at the piano bar or recline in front of a roaring fire. Savour exquisite candlelit meals at one of the most sought-after restaurants in Méribel.

FRF : French franc

www.relaischateaux.fr/grandcoeur

FITZ ROY HOTEL

France

Tel. : (33) 04 79 00 04 78
Fax : (33) 04 79 00 06 11
E-mail : fitzroy@relaischateaux.fr

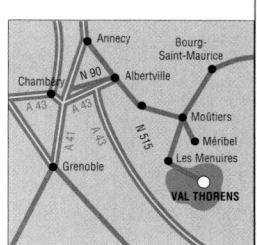

From Lyons, A 43 Chambéry, Albertville, Moutiers; then 36 km of mountain roads.

Owners : S.A. Fitz Roy /
Mrs Claude Loubet
Director : François Prudent
Annual closing :
From May 10th to December 1st

✈ Lyons (**Intl**) 190 km
Chambéry 100 km

GPS N 45° 18′ E 6° 34′

🍴 Menus 250-500 FRF s.i.
38-76 €
Carte 250-600 FRF s.i.
38-91 €

⚷ 30 rooms
half board/pers.
1 050-1 350 FRF s.i.
160-206 €

⚷ 7 suites
half board/pers.
1 250-1 700 FRF s.i.
191-259 €

🍽 included

🛎 yes (extra cost)

Wine cellar.

W ith its snow-covered roof, crafted doors and wood beams, this charming chalet, located in one of the world's most famous ski resorts, makes an idyllic mountain retreat. After an exhilarating day's skiing, its cosy interior is warm and welcoming, a log fire blazing in the hearth, while luxurious whirlpool baths await you in the sunny rooms and suites. Savour regional cuisine or sample the special «light» menu.

FRF : French franc

Visa

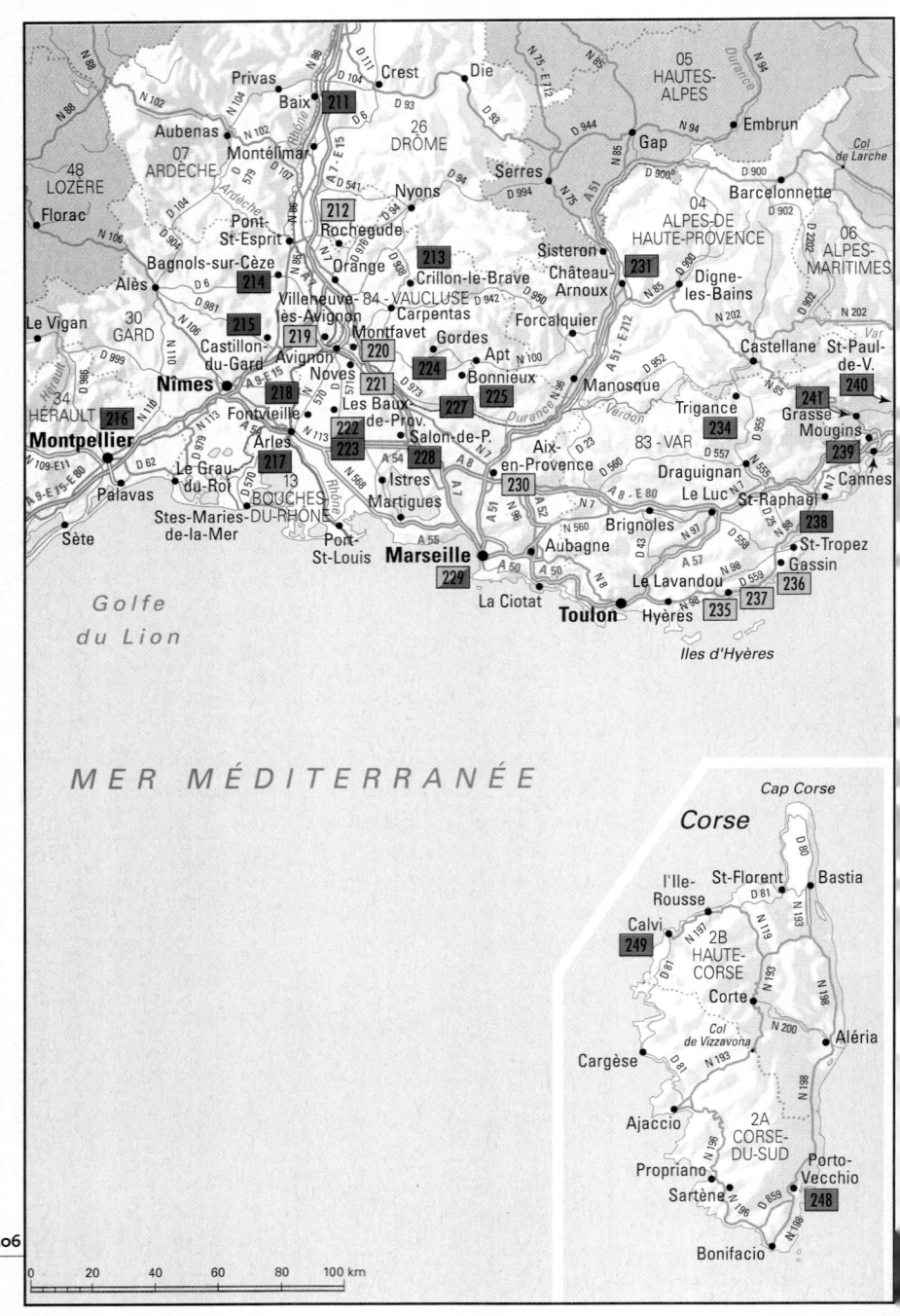

MER MÉDITERRANÉE

Golfe
du Lion

Corse

0 20 40 60 80 100 km

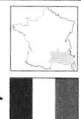

PROVENCE
FRENCH RIVIERA - CORSICA

Establishments	Nearest major city	Relais & Châteaux	Relais Gourmands	Page
Abbaye de Sainte-Croix	Salon de Provence	❀		228
Auberge de Noves	Avignon	❀		221
Auberge la Regalido	Arles	❀		218
Bastide de Capelongue (La)	Avignon	❀		225
Bastide Saint-Antoine (La)	Grasse	❀	♟	241
Bonne Etape (La)	Sisteron	❀	♟	231
Cabro d'Or (La)	Arles	❀		223
Cagnard (Le)	Nice	❀		242
Cardinale (La)	Montélimar	❀		211
Château de Montcaud	Avignon	❀		214
Château de Rochegude	Orange	❀		212
Château de Trigance	Draguignan	❀		234
Château de la Chèvre d'Or	Nice/Monaco	❀		247
Château St-Martin	Nice	❀		243
Club de Cavalière (Le)	Le Lavandou	❀		237
Grand Hôtel de Cala Rossa	Porto-Vecchio	❀		248
Hostellerie de Crillon le Brave	Carpentras	❀		213
Hostellerie Les Frênes	Avignon	❀		220
Hôtel Jules César	Arles	❀		217
Hôtel les Roches	Hyères	❀		235
Jardin des Sens (Le)	Montpellier	❀	♟	216
Mas des Herbes Blanches (Le)	Avignon	❀		224
Métropole (Le)	Nice	❀		246
Moulin de Lourmarin (Le)	Aix-en-Provence	❀	♟	227
Moulin de Mougins (Le)	Cannes	❀	♟	239
Oustau de Baumanière	Arles	❀	♟	222
Petit Nice-Passedat (Le)	Marseille	❀	♟	229
Prieuré (Le)	Avignon	❀		219
Réserve de Beaulieu (La)	Monte Carlo	❀	♟	245
Résidence de la Pinède	St-Tropez	❀		238
Saint-Paul (Le)	Nice	❀		240
Vieux Castillon (Le)	Avignon	❀		215
Villa (La)	Calvi	❀		249
Villa Belrose (La)	Saint-Tropez	❀		236
Villa Gallici	Aix-en-Provence	❀		230

FLAGRANT PLAISIR

LANCEL

Information : 33 1 44 31 41 41

VINTAGES TO DRINK IN YEAR 2000
PROVENCE - CORSICA

Wines recommended by the wine waiters
of the Relais & Châteaux and Relais Gourmands.

* Index of world vintages to drink in year 2000 : page 607

♟	Name of wine	Wine to enjoy	Noble wine	Outstanding wine
	PROVENCE			
White, Rosé wines	Cassis, Palette, Les Baux de Provence, Coteaux d'Aix, Coteaux Varois Côtes de Provence, Bellet	1998 - 1997		
Red	Bandol, Palette...	1996 - 1995	1990 - 1985	1982
	CORSICA			
White	Patrimonio, Vin de Corse Coteaux du Cap Corse	1998 - 1997		
Red	Ajaccio, Patrimonio...	1996	1995	1990
Medium sweet white wines	Muscat du Cap Corse	1998 - 1997	1996	

The House of
Villeroy & Boch
Since 1748

Living with Villeroy & Boch.
Tableware · Furniture · Tiles · Bathrooms

LA CARDINALE ET SA RÉSIDENCE

France

Quai du Rhône
07210 Baix
(Ardèche)

Tel. : **(33) 04 75 85 80 40**
Fax : **(33) 04 75 85 82 07**
E-mail : cardinale@relaischateaux.fr

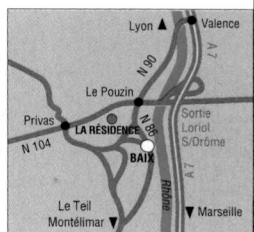

A7, exit Loriol-sur-Drôme, towards Le Pouzin (N 104) and Le Teil (N 86) until Baix.

Owner :
S.A. La Nouvelle Cardinale
Director : Frank Wegener
Weekly closing :
Rest. : Monday from Oct. to April
Annual closing :
End of October to mid-March

This is one of the first Relais & Châteaux founded in this ancient seigniorial estate and its residence with 10 superbly comfortable and charming guestrooms. On the banks of the Rhone at the foot of the Ardèche mountains, this famous establishment perpetuates a hospitality known for its warmth and perfect attentiveness. The delicious sun-drenched cuisine pays tribute to the exquisite flavours of regional products. The wine cellar is a treasure trove of rare vintages.

 Lyons (**Intl**) 150 km
Valence 30 km

🍽 Menus **195-450 FRF** s.i.
30-69 €
Carte **300-550 FRF** s.i.
46-84 €

 5 rooms
800-1 150 FRF s.i.
122-175 €

5 suites
1 500-1 950 FRF s.i.
229-297 €

☕ 100 FRF s.i.
15 €

yes

 25 km

Kayaking, hiking.

P ✳ 👥 ⛵ 🛗 〰 🖋 **211**

www.relaischateaux.fr/cardinale

FRF : French franc

Visa

CHÂTEAU DE ROCHEGUDE

Tel. : (33) 04 75 97 21 10
Fax : (33) 04 75 04 89 87
E-mail : rochegude@relaischateaux.fr

26790 Rochegude
(Drôme)

France

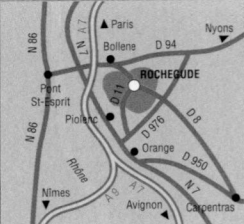

A7, exit Bollène, towards
Carpentras (D8), follow signs for
Relais & Châteaux.

Owner :
S.A.R.L. Abbaye de Bouchet
Director : André Chabert
Weekly closing :
Sunday evening, Monday and
Tuesday at lunch (low season)
Open all year

✈ Marseilles (**Intl**) 110 km
Avignon 45 km

GPS N 44° 14' 49"
E 004° 49' 38"

🍴 Menus **250-550 FRF** s.i.
34-84 €
Carte **380-550 FRF** s.i.
58-84 €

🔑 26 rooms
700-2 000 FRF s.i.
107-305 €

🔑 3 suites
1 900-3 000 FRF s.i.
290-457 €

☕ **100 FRF** s.i.
15 €

🐾 yes (extra cost)

⚜ Practice on the premises
10 km

T his magnificent 12th-century fortress,
once the summer residence of the
Marquis de Rochegude, towers majestically
above the Côtes-du-Rhône and its
sumptuously furnished, air-conditioned
rooms offer superb vistas of the vineyards.
Unwind in the green haven of its 25-acre
park, recline by the pool or enjoy the tennis
courts. Delicious meals, served in the
medieval armoury, are enhanced by the
finest regional wines.

Visa

FRF : French franc

www.relaischateaux.fr/rochegude

HOSTELLERIE DE CRILLON-LE-BRAVE

France

Place de l'Eglise
84410 Crillon-le-Brave
(Vaucluse)

Tel. : (33) 04 90 65 61 61
Fax : (33) 04 90 65 62 86
E-mail : crillonbrave@relaischateaux.fr

*At the top of the village,
facing the Mont-Ventoux,
next to the church.*

Owners :
Peter Chittick and Craig Miller
Weekly closing :
Rest. : for lunch for the week
Annual closing :
From January 3rd to March 10th

T his elegant residence, perched above the village roofs, welcomes you into a green haven secluded behind tall, ochre walls. Its rooms, bathed in the scent of clematis and jasmine wafting up from the Italian-style gardens, offer stunning views across the vineyards to the Mont-Ventoux, once cherished by Mistral and Cézanne. Enjoy sun-drenched cuisine and regional wines beneath the fig trees or in the vaulted dining room.

✈ Marseilles (**Intl**) 100 km
Avignon 40 km

🍽 Menus 230-370 FRF s.i.
35-56 €
Menu (lunch) 160 FRF s.i
24 €
Carte 300-400 FRF s.i.
46-61 €

🔑 18 rooms
850-1 900 FRF s.i.
130-290 €

🔑 5 suites
1 600-2 600 FRF s.i.
244-396 €

☕ 90 FRF s.i.
14 €

🐾 yes (extra cost)

🏃 35 km

www.relaischateaux.fr/crillonbrave

FRF : French franc

Visa

213

CHÂTEAU DE MONTCAUD

France

Tel. : (33) 04 66 89 60 60
Fax : (33) 04 66 89 45 04
E-mail : montcaud@relaischateaux.fr

Route d'Alès (4 km)
30200 Bagnols-sur-Cèze
(Gard)

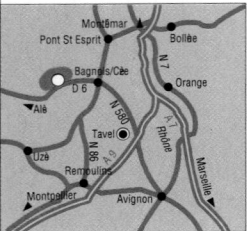

A7 from the south, exit Avignon Sud, A7 from the north, exit Bollène, A9 from the south, exit Remoulins. Continue towards Bagnols-sur-Cèze then D6 towards Alès.

Owner : Rudy Baur
Weekly closing :
Rest. (except residents) : Sunday evening, Monday, Tuesday noon and Saturday noon (off season), Monday noon and Saturday noon (season) and November
Annual closing :
From January 2nd to April 13th

✈ Marseilles (**Intl**) 120 km
Avignon 40 km

🧭 GPS N 44° 10′ 23″
E 004° 34′ 19″

🍴 Menus **175-400 FRF** s.i.
27-61 €
Carte **300-430 FRF** s.i.
46-66 €

🔑 22 rooms
795-1 660 FRF s.i.
121-253 €

🔑 7 suites
1 660-3 330 FRF s.i.
253-508 €

☕ buffet **110 FRF** s.i. - **17 €**

🛏 yes (extra cost)

🎵 20 km

The sound of local festivals is barely discernible in this haven of well-being and light. Tastefully decorated rooms open onto peaceful parkland, and guests spend calm, serene days lounging by the pool, playing tennis or strolling through the rose garden. Dine al fresco on the patio of a charming farmhouse and savour superb cuisine which pays tribute to the sea and the Provençal markets. Excellent Côtes-du-Rhône.

 Visa

FRF : French franc

www.relaischateaux.fr/montcaud

France

Castillon-du-Gard
30210 Remoulins
(Gard)

Tel. : (33) 04 66 37 61 61
Fax : (33) 04 66 37 28 17
E-mail : vieuxcastillon@relaischateaux.fr

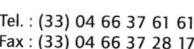

From Paris, Marseilles or Montpellier, A9 exit Remoulins. From Remoulins, N86 towards Montélimar then to the left, at Croisées, D19A towards Alès (5km).

Owners : Walser Family
Director : Patrick Walser
Annual closing :
Beg. of January to mid. February

B etween Nîmes and Avignon, close to the Cévennes national park, the Camargue and the Alpilles, this hilltop hamlet offers breathtaking vistas of the Ventoux valley. With its magnificent patios, medieval architecture and honey-coloured stone terraces set in the heart of a Provençal village, Le Vieux Castillon is a truly unique domain. Enjoy musical evenings, sun-drenched cuisine and an exceptional selection of Côtes-du-Rhône.

Marseilles (**Intl**) 110 km
Nîmes 27 km

Menus 290 FRF s.i. (lunch)
44 €
590 FRF s.i.
90 €
Carte approx. 570 FRF s.i.
87 €

33 rooms
980-1 695 FRF s.i.
149-258 €

2 suites
1 920 FRF s.i.
293 €

90 FRF s.i.
14 €

yes

15 km

FRF : French franc

Visa

LE JARDIN DES SENS

France

Tel. : (33) 04 99 58 38 38
Fax : (33) 04 99 58 38 39
E-mail : jardinsens@relaischateaux.fr

11, avenue Saint-Lazare
34000 Montpellier
(Hérault)

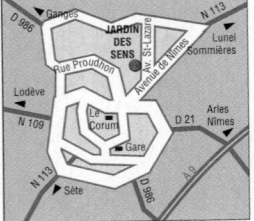

City centre, then «Le Corum»
(Convention centre), Nîmes road,
then avenue St-Lazare.

Owners :
Jacques and Laurent Pourcel,
Olivier Chateau
Weekly closing :
Rest: Sunday and Monday noon
Annual closing :
From January 2nd to 15th

✈	Montpellier (**Intl**) 5 km Nîmes 60 km
🍴	Menu **240 FRF** s.i. **37 €** Carte **410-620 FRF** s.i. **62-95 €**
⚷	12 rooms **900-1 300 FRF** s.i. **137-198 €**
⚷	2 suites **1 600-2 500 FRF** s.i. **244-381 €**
☕	**100 FRF** s.i. **15 €**
🍴	yes
🎿	15 km

J acques and Laurent Pourcel's refined cuisine, which pays tribute to rich Mediterranean flavours and the regional produce of Languedoc, is a veritable festival for the senses. The Pourcel's exquisite creations are accompanied by superb wines carefully selected by Olivier Chateau. Enjoy a true gourmet experience in the glass-fronted dining-room overlooking the beautiful garden, then retire to a charming guestroom.

 Visa

FRF : French franc

www.relaischateaux.fr/jardinsens

HÔTEL JULES CÉSAR

France

9, boulevard des Lices
13631 Arles cedex
(Bouches-du-Rhône)

Tel. : (33) 04 90 93 43 20
Fax : **(33) 04 90 93 33 47**
E-mail : julescesar@relaischateaux.fr

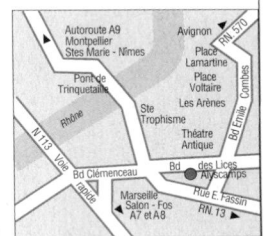

From Nîmes, highway A54 - exit n°5, towards bd. G. Clemenceau then blvd. des Lices.

Owners :
Michel and Jacqueline Albagnac
Director : Christian Filiol
Annual closing :
From Nov. 12th to Dec. 23rd

This sumptuous 17th-century Carmelite convent, converted into a luxury hotel in 1929, is bathed in an aura of charm and serenity. Today the elegant chapel, a protected historical site, still echoes with the strains of heavenly music when it hosts private classical and baroque concerts. Gourmets seek out the Cloître and the Lou Marquès, renowned for their delicious regional specialities and outstanding wine lists.

Marseilles (**Intl**) 80 km
Nîmes-Arles 25 km

Menus **210-420 FRF** s.i.
32-64 €
Carte **300-400 FRF** s.i.
46-61 €

 49 rooms
750-1 250 FRF s.i.
114-191 €

 5 suites
starting at **1 650 FRF** s.i.
252 €

85-130 FRF s.i.
13-20 €

yes (extra cost)

20-25 km

Hunting in Camargue,
deep-sea fishing...

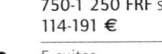

217

FRF : French franc

Visa

AUBERGE LA REGALIDO

Tel. : (33) 04 90 54 60 22
Fax : (33) 04 90 54 64 29
E-mail : regalido@relaischateaux.fr

Rue Frédéric-Mistral
13990 Fontvieille
(Bouches-du-Rhône)

France

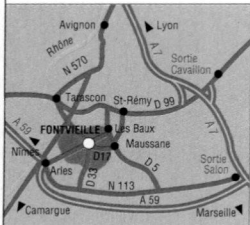

On A59, exit Arles N°7.
From Lyons, A7, exit Cavaillon,
towards St Rémy,
Maussane and Fontvieille.

Owners : Michel Family
Weekly closing :
Restaurant : Monday
(except evening in the summer)
and Tuesday noon
Annual closing :
From beginning of January
to the end of February

✈ Marseilles (**Intl**) 90 km
Nîmes-Arles 30 km

🍴 Menus **270-420 FRF** s.i.
41-64 €
Carte **340-450 FRF** s.i.
52-69 €

🔑 15 rooms
730-1 690 FRF s.i.
111-258 €

🛎 **48-88-108 FRF** s.i.
7-13-16 €

🐾 yes (extra cost)

⛳ Les Baux-Mouriès 10 km

Moulin de Daudet, local products,
hiking, horse-riding, mountain
biking.

I n a tiny village immortalised by
Alphonse Daudet, this picturesque old
mill cloaked in twining ivy and flowers,
appears to have sprung to life from an
artist's palette. Many of its charming
rooms, named after flowers and herbs,
possess private terraces with enchanting
views across the old village roofs. If you're
seeking the authentic flavour of Provence,
look no further than La Regalido's delicious
regional cuisine.

 Visa

FRF : French franc

www.relaischateaux.fr/regalido

Le Prieuré

France

7, place du Chapitre
30400 Villeneuve lez Avignon
(Gard)

Tel. : (33) 04 90 15 90 15
Fax : (33) 04 90 25 45 39
E-mail : leprieure@relaischateaux.fr

From Paris or Spain : A9, exit
Villeneuve, Roquemaure.
From Nice or Marseilles :
A7, exit Avignon North, towards
Nîmes - Villeneuve.

Owner : Marie-France Mille
Director : François Mille
Weekly closing :
Rest.: Wednesday in March, April
and October, and May 1st
Annual closing :
From November 2nd to March 20th

Y ou will be totally enchanted by this elegant 14th-century priory, secluded in a secret garden decorated with rose bowers and a Provençal pergola. The ambience of «elegant idleness» praised by the writer Colette imbues its spacious, comfortable guestrooms and shaded patios as the evening breeze wafts the scent of flowers past the tables. Superb sun-gorged cuisine is complemented by excellent Côtes-du-Rhône.

✈ Marseilles (**Intl**) 78 km
Avignon 12 km

 Menus **210-340-510 FRF** s.i.
32-52-78 €
Carte **250-500 FRF** s.i.
38-76 €

� 26 rooms
570-1 350 FRF s.i.
87-206 €

� 10 suites
1 550-1 900 FRF s.i.
236-290 €

☕ **90 FRF** s.i.
14 €

✡ yes

♪ 12 km

P ▯
❄ ❖ ✦ ⛲ ⛳ 〜 ⚐ **219**

www.relaischateaux.fr/leprieure

FRF : French franc

Visa

HOSTELLERIE LES FRÊNES

SINCE 1981

Tel. : (33) 04 90 31 17 93
Fax : (33) 04 90 23 95 03
E-mail : lesfrenes@relaischateaux.fr

645, av. des Vertes Rives
84140 Avignon-Montfavet
(Vaucluse)

France

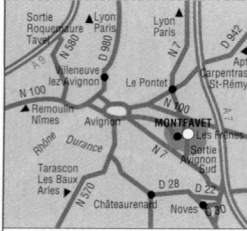

A7, exit Avignon south, towards Avignon, exit n°8. A9, exit Tavel towards Avignon, towards Marseilles, exit n°8. Montfavet, at the church, turn right at the traffic light.

Owners : Biancone Family
Director : Hervé Biancone
Annual closing :
From November to April 1st

✈ Marseilles **(Intl)** 75 km
Avignon 3 km

🍴 Menus **200-420 FRF** s.i.
30-64 €
Carte **250-400 FRF** s.i.
38-61 €

⊶ 15 rooms
880-1 790 FRF s.i.
134-273 €

⊶ 4 suites
starting at **1 880 FRF** s.i.
287 €

☕ 100 FRF s.i.
15 €

🍴 yes

⌂ Châteaublanc 2 km
Grand Avignon 5 km

W elcomed with warm hospitality by the Biancone family and dazzled by the culinary talent of their son, Antoine, it is impossible to resist the charms of Les Frênes. This beautiful 19th-century bourgeois home and its annexes are set in sumptuous parkland and the elegantly decorated, spacious rooms and tree-lined heated pool invite you to la dolce vita. The exquisite Provençal cuisine is enhanced by superb regional wines.

FRF : French franc

www.relaischateaux.fr/lesfrenes

AUBERGE DE NOVES

France

Domaine du Devès - route de Châteaurenard
13550 Noves
(Bouches-du-Rhône)

Tel. : (33) 04 90 24 28 28
Fax : (33) 04 90 90 16 92
E-mail : noves@relaischateaux.fr

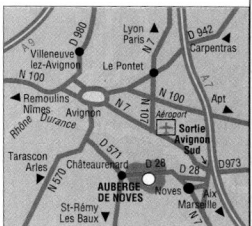

By A7, exit Avignon South,
then towards Aix, Marseilles,
then towards Châteaurenard.

Owners : Lalleman Family
Annual closing :
From mid-November
to mid-December

 Marseilles **(Intl)** 65 km
Avignon 7 km

 GPS N 43° 52' 87"
E 004° 53' 02"

 Menus
230-375-455-535 FRF s.i.
35-57-69-82 €
Carte **425-550 FRF** s.i.
65-84 €

E ncased in a lovingly maintained, wooded 15-hectare park, this resplendent, peaceful manor looked after by the Lalleman family for three generations, has an irresistible magical air of enchantment. The serene setting, elegant rooms, delicious Provençal cuisine, varied choice of wines, fragrant air and swimming pool all majestically express the quality of life.

 19 rooms
1 195-1 650 FRF s.i.
182-252 €
low season
950-1 375 FRF s.i.
145-210 €

 4 suites
1 950 FRF s.i.
297 €
low season **1 700 FRF** s.i.
259 €

 105 FRF s.i.
16 €

 yes

nearby

Fishing, hunting,
horseback riding (3 km).

221

www.relaischateaux.fr/noves

FRF : French franc

Visa

OUSTAU DE BAUMANIÈRE

Tel. : (33) 04 90 54 33 07
Fax : (33) 04 90 54 40 46
E-mail : oustau@relaischateaux.fr

13520 Les-Baux-de-Provence
(Bouches-du-Rhône)

France

From the north, A 7 - exit Avignon South, towards Noves, then St-Rémy-de-Provence, Les Baux.

Owners : Charial Family
Directors :
Jean-André and Geneviève Charial
Weekly closing :
Hotel : Wednesday
Rest. : Wed. and Thursday at lunch from Nov. 1st to March 31st
Annual closing :
From the beginning of January to the beginning of March

✈ Marseilles (**Intl**) 60 km
Nîmes 45 km

🛬 GPS N 43° 45' 5"
E 004° 48' 30"

🍴 Menus **495-750 FRF** s.i.
75-114 €
Carte **500-700 FRF** s.i.
76-107 €

🛏 13 rooms
1 450-1 500 FRF s.i.
221-229 €

🛏 9 suites
1 900-2 200 FRF s.i.
290-335 €

☕ **120 FRF** s.i.
18 €

🐎 yes (extra cost)

⚹ Les Baux 3 km
Mouriès 10 km

This 14th-century farmhouse, imbued with traditional Provençal charm, is set in idyllic natural surroundings straight out of a Cézanne painting. Jean-André Charial perpetuates the culinary traditions of his grandfather, Raymond Thuilier, and gourmet guests will be delighted by his «ravioli de truffes aux poireaux» and «gigot d'agneau en croûte», enhanced by superb wines. Enjoy exquisite hospitality and spacious rooms.

FRF : French franc

www.relaischateaux.fr/oustau

LA CABRO D'OR

France

13520 Les-Baux-de-Provence
(Bouches-du-Rhône)

Tel. : (33) 04 90 54 33 21
Fax : (33) 04 90 54 45 98
E-mail : cabro@relaischateaux.fr

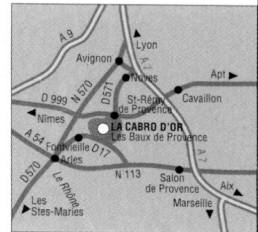

From the South-East: A 7 exit Salon, towards Arles N 113, D5 Maussane-Les Baux.

Owners : Charial Family
Directors :
Jean-André and Geneviève Charial
Weekly closing :
Hotel : Monday evening
from October 15th to March 15th
Restaurant : Monday
from October 15th to March 15th,
Tuesday lunch all year
Annual closing :
From Nov. 11th to Dec. 20th

I f you are seeking an elegant country stopover on the way to L'Oustau de Baumanière, you will be enchanted by the pure simplicity and the ambience of total liberty at the Cabro d'Or. Set amidst luxuriant foliage overlooking a landscape of olive trees, its comfortable rooms open onto an exceptional garden. The Mediterranean cuisine draws its inspiration from regional produce and the hotel garden's herbs and vegetables.

Marseilles **(Intl)** 60 km
Nîmes-Arles 45 km

GPS N 43° 45' 5"
E 4° 48' 30"

Menus **290-450 FRF** s.i.
44-69 €
Carte **300-400 FRF** s.i.
46-61 €

22 rooms
700-1 250 FRF s.i.
107-191 €

8 suites
1 400-1 900 FRF s.i.
213-290 €

85 FRF s.i.
13 €

yes (extra cost **50 FRF - 8 €**)

3 km

223

www.relaischateaux.fr/cabro

FRF : French franc

Visa

LE MAS DES HERBES BLANCHES

SINCE 1976

Tel. : (33) 04 90 05 79 79
Fax : (33) 04 90 05 71 96
E-mail : masherbes@relaischateaux.fr

Joucas
84220 Gordes
(Vaucluse)

France

*A7, exit Cavaillon,
towards Apt (D2). In Coustellet,
towards Gordes, Joucas (D 102).*

Owner :
Paul Juillard
Director : Jean-Luc Laborie
Annual closing :
From January 3rd to March 11th

 Marseilles (**Intl**) 85 km
Avignon 40 km

 GPS N 43° 56' 08"
E 005° 14' 39"

 Menus **205-395 FRF** s.i.
31-60 €
Carte **360-460 FRF** s.i.
55-70 €

 13 rooms
750-1 640 FRF s.i.
114-250 €

 6 suites
1 620-2 350 FRF s.i.
247-358 €

 95 FRF s.i.
14 €

 yes (extra cost)

 Saumane 23 km

This traditional Provençal farmhouse offers superb views of the breathtaking Luberon landscape. The calm of the marvellously comfortable guestrooms, bathed in the scent of juniper and wild thyme, is broken only by the sound of the cicadas and the soft murmuring of the patio fountain. Enjoy local wines and delicately flavoured regional cuisine, before discovering the joys of the Avignon and Gordes festivals.

 Visa

FRF : French franc

www.relaischateaux.fr/masherbes

LE PETIT NICE-PASSÉDAT

France

Anse de Maldormé, Corniche J. F. Kennedy
13007 Marseille
(Bouches-du-Rhône)

Tel. : (33) 04 91 59 25 92
Fax : (33) 04 91 59 28 08
E-mail : passedat@relaischateaux.fr

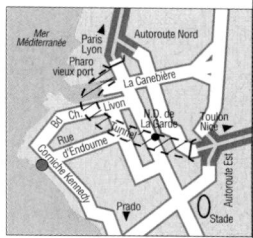

From Marseilles, exit East/North Highway, towards the beach via the Kennedy corniche «hauteur 160».

Owners : Passédat Family
Directors :
Jean-Paul and Gérald Passédat
Weekly closing :
Rest. : Saturday noon, Sunday
(from Nov. to the end of March)
Open all year

The Passédat Family welcomes you to its Greek villa with its luxurious rooms overlooking the Mediterranean. Gérald Passédat has a talent for contemporary cuisine with specialities from Provence and Marseilles: «beignets d'anémones de mer», «brandade de morue truffée», «poissons et crustacés de Méditerranée», «grand dessert Passédat». A fine selection of wines.

✈ Marseilles (**Intl**) 25 km

🍴 Menus **350 FRF** s.i. - **53 €**
(drinks included)
week lunch except holidays
480 FRF s.i. (dinner) - **73 €**
620-750 FRF s.i. - **95-114 €**
Carte **600-800 FRF** s.i.
91-122 €

⊶ 12 rooms
Off seas. **1 000-2 200 FRF** s.i.
152-335 €
Season **1 200-2 600 FRF** s.i.
183-396 €

⊶ 3 suites
Off season **3 100 FRF** s.i.
473 €
Season **4 300 FRF** s.i.
656 €

☕ **41-120 FRF** s.i. - **6-18 €**

🛏 yes (extra cost)

🏌 10 km

Fishing, water sports, thalassatherapy nearby.

www.relaischateaux.fr/passedat

FRF : French franc

Visa

Villa Gallici

SINCE 1996

France

Tel. : (33) 04 42 23 29 23
Fax : (33) 04 42 96 30 45
E-mail : gallici@relaischateaux.fr

Av. de la Violette
13100 Aix-en-Provence
(Bouches-du-Rhône)

From the city centre,
follow the yellow signs.

Owners :
MM. Dez, Jouve, Montemarco
Director : Daniel Jouve
Weekly closing :
Restaurant closed at noon
and Monday evening
(from Nov. 1st to March 31st)
Open all year

✈ Marseilles **(Intl)** 25 km

🍴 Hotel restaurant
(reserved for guests)
Carte **350-500 FRF** s.i.
53-76 €

⚷ 18 rooms
season
1 350-2 650 FRF s.i.
206-404 €
offseason
1 000-2 050 FRF s.i.
152-313 €

⚷ 4 suites
season
2 650-3 050 FRF s.i.
404-465 €
offseason
2 150-2 500 FRF s.i.
328-381 €

☕ 100-130 FRF s.i.
15-20 €

🐾 yes (extra cost)

⚲ 5 km

T his country house overlooking Aix is
bathed in the soft Provençal light so
often depicted by Cézanne. Set amidst an
elegant Florentine garden, where cypress
trees are reflected in a luxurious pool, it
offers sumptuous rooms with terraces and
private gardens. Linger over an aperitif in
the shade of the plane trees, then savour
traditional Provençal cuisine accompanied
by the finest Bordeaux, Burgundies and
Aix wines.

Visa

FRF : French franc

www.relaischateaux.fr/gallici

LA BONNE ETAPE

France

Chemin du Lac
04160 Château-Arnoux
(Alpes-de-Hte-Provence)

Tel. : (33) 04 92 64 00 09
Fax : (33) 04 92 64 37 36
E-mail : bonneetape@relaischateaux.fr

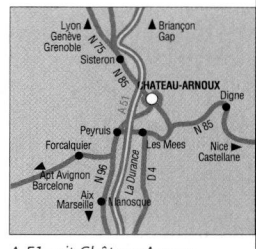

*A 51 exit Château-Arnoux
follow Château-Arnoux then
follow signs to «La Bonne Etape».*

Owners : Pierre and Jany Gleize
Weekly closing :
Monday and Tuesday at lunch
(from Nov. to March only)
Annual closing :
From Jan. 3rd to February 12th
and from Nov. 29th to Dec. 9th

The Gleizes's innovative cuisine is inspired by the subtle aromas of the Haute-Provence region. Their «agneau de Sisteron» with all its preparations and the «crème glacée au miel de lavande» are veritable works of art. Excellent regional wines. Retire to one of the 18 tastefully decorated rooms to prolong this gourmet stay. According to your fancy, simple cuisine «Au Goût du Jour».

Marseilles (**Intl**) 120 km
Nice (**Intl**) 160 km

GPS N 44° 06' 26''
E 006° 00' 00''

La Bonne Etape
Menus **220-550 FRF** s.i.
34-84 €
Carte **350 FRF** s.i.
53 €
Au Goût du Jour
130 FRF s.i.
20 €

10 rooms
850-1 200 FRF s.i.
130-183 €

8 suites
1 100-1 800 FRF s.i.
168-274 €

90 FRF s.i.
14 €

yes

18 km

231

FRF : French franc

Visa

New Audi S3 quattro 210 hp.

Not everyone is lucky

http://www.audi-france.com

enough to have a PlayStation.

CHÂTEAU DE TRIGANCE

SINCE
1966

Tel. : (33) 04 94 76 91 18
Fax : (33) 04 94 85 68 99
E-mail : trigance@relaischateaux.fr

83840 Trigance
(Var)

France

A8 exit Le Muy ; Draguignan then D 955 Comps towards Castellane. After Jabron 4 km to the left.

Owners : Thomas Family
Weekly closing :
Rest. : Wednesday at lunch (low season)
Annual closing :
From Nov. 1st to March 24th

✈	Nice (**Intl**) 100 km Toulon 120 km
🧭	GPS E 06° 26' N 43° 45'
🍴	Menus **220-320 FRF** s.i. **34-49 €** Carte **280 FRF** s.i. **43 €**
⚷	8 rooms **650-950 FRF** s.i. **99-145 €**
⚷	2 suites **950 FRF** s.i. **145 €**
☕	**75 FRF** s.i. **11 €**
🍴	yes
🚶	20 km

Hiking,
rafting on the Verdon river.

S et at the entrance to the Gorges du Verdon, this 11th-century fortress built by the Saint-Victor monks offers breathtaking views of the Provençal landscape. Trigance flourished in the Middle Ages during the reign of the Demandolx, whose coat of arms still adorns the magnificent medieval rooms, furnished with four-poster beds, oak chests and tapestries. A candlelit dinner in the vaulted cellar is a magical experience.

 Visa

FRF : French franc

www.relaischateaux.fr/trigance

France

1, av. des Trois-Dauphins, Aiguebelle
83980 Le Lavandou
(Var)

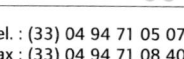
Tel. : (33) 04 94 71 05 07
Fax : (33) 04 94 71 08 40
E-mail : lesroches@relaischateaux.fr

From Toulon, A 57 - towards
Hyères, le Lavandou,
D 559 until Aiguebelle.

Owner : Les Roches S.A.
Directors :
Ivan and Gérard Goujon
Annual closing :
From mid-October to April 7th

✈ Nice **(Intl)** 130 km
Toulon 28 km

🍽 Menus **220-475 FRF** s.i.
34-72 €
Carte **250-450 FRF** s.i.
38-69 €

🛏 35 rooms
1 350-2 700 FRF s.i.
206-412 €

🔑 5 suites
starting at 2 950 FRF s.i.
450 €

☕ included

🍴 yes

🏊 1,5 km

Tuna fishing, diving, sailing,
water-skiing.

iscover this charming hotel nestled in a rocky inlet on the Mediterranean waterfront. Decorated with beautiful antique furniture and original paintings, the rooms overlook the exotic garden and the Iles d'Or. Like an ocean liner, the restaurant invites you to enjoy the superb local seafood while contemplating the stunning sea view. «Being in the right place at the right time»...

www.relaischateaux.fr/lesroches   FRF : French franc   Visa

VILLA BELROSE

SINCE 1999

France

Tel. : (33) 04 94 55 97 97
Fax : (33) 04 94 55 97 98
E-mail : belrose@relaischateaux.fr

Boulevard des Crêtes
83580 Gassin
(Var)

A 8 exit Le Muy, towards
Ste Maxime, St.Tropez, follow the
route along the seacoast and the
signs for «La Villa Belrose».

Owner : Thomas Althoff
Director : Jean-Pierre Hall
Annual closing :
From January 5th to March 5th

✈ Nice (**Intl**) 100 km
Toulon 55 km

🍴 Menus **190-450 FRF** s.i.
29-69 €
Carte **310-540 FRF** s.i.
47-82 €

⚷ 32 rooms
900-3 600 FRF s.i.
137-549 €

⚷ 6 suites
2 800-4 600 FRF s.i.
427-701 €

☕ **120-160 FRF** s.i.
18-24 €

🐎 yes (extra cost)

⛳ 5 km (18 holes)

Deep-sea fishing, go-carting,
water sports.

E njoy the unique panoramic view of this magnificient villa overlooking the Mediterranean, where you can see the port of St Tropez with its village to the right, Ste Maxime and the limitless horizon beyond. This is a perfect haven of calm and enchantment. With its superbly decorated guestrooms and suites, its elegant and intimate restaurant where the chef will delight you with innovative cuisine inspired by Florentine culinary traditions. Linger on the terrace and taste the Mediterranean dishes.

Visa

FRF : French franc

www.relaischateaux.fr / belrose

France

LE CLUB DE CAVALIÈRE

83980 Le Lavandou
(Var)

Tel. : (33) 04 94 05 80 14
Fax : (33) 04 94 05 73 16
E-mail : cavaliere@relaischateaux.fr

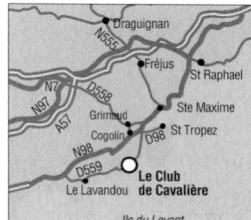

A7 motorway: Aix-en-Provence, A50 Toulon-Hyères. Le Lavandou, Cavalière. From Nice, A57 Hyères, Le Lavandou, Cavalière.

Owner : Sogeco S.A.
Directors :
Marielle and Edouard Ruchti
Annual closing :
From October 4th to May 8th

This ochre provençal villa near Lavandou overlooks the Mediterranean, as you have always imagined it. Surrounded by umbrellas pines, bougainvillea, and exotic gardens, the hotel with its private beach, the rooms and bungalows with private balconies combine to offer you an idyllic stay in the land of the cicadas. Savour the refined Mediterranean cuisine in the restaurant with its superb view of the bay of Cavalière.

✈ Marseilles (**Intl**) 90 km
Nice (**Intl**) 120 km
Toulon 18 km

🍴 Menu 370 FRF s.i.
56 €
Carte 300-450 FRF s.i.
46-69 €

🔑 39 rooms
1 650-2 410 FRF s.i.
252-367 €

🔑 3 suites
2 160-2 860 FRF s.i.
329-436 €

☕ included

🐎 yes (extra cost)

🎿 20 km

Polo, sailing, kayaking,
mountain-biking, jet ski.

FRF : French franc

Visa

RÉSIDENCE DE LA PINÈDE

SINCE 1987

Plage de la Bouillabaisse - B.P. 74
83991 St Tropez
(Var)

France

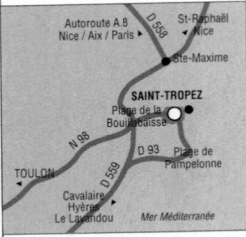

A8, exit Le Muy, towards Ste-Maxime; Saint-Tropez, left after the 1st light 50 m coast side.

Owners : Delion Family
Annual closing :
From October 5th to April

✈ Nice (**Intl**) 100 km
Toulon 55 km

🍴 Menus **300-700 FRF** s.i.
46-107 €
Carte **650 FRF** s.i.
99 €

⚷ 39 rooms
1 450-4 250 FRF s.i.
221-457 €

⚷ 4 suites
starting at **2 750 FRF** s.i.
419 €

🍷 **130 FRF** s.i.
20 €

🍽 yes (extra cost)

♪ 5-10 km

Water sports, private beach.

The his opulent white villa is set next to its own private beach overlooking the Citadelle, the gulf and the magnificent St.Tropez peninsula. Constantly embellished by its owners, this sumptuous Côte d'Azur paradise is ideally located near the world's most famous fishing village. Relax on the shaded terrace and enjoy delightfully flavoursome cuisine while contemplating a truly magical landscape.

Visa

FRF : French franc

www.relaischateaux.fr/pinede

Le Moulin de Mougins

France

Quartier Notre-Dame-de-Vie
06250 Mougins
(Alpes-Maritimes)

Tel. : (33) 04 93 75 78 24
Fax : (33) 04 93 90 18 55
E-mail : mougins@relaischateaux.fr

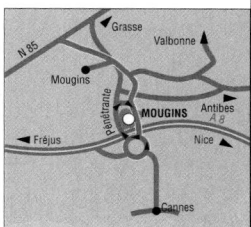

A8, exit Cannes/Mougins.
At the 1st traffic circle,
Grasse/Mougins expressway,
exit «Mougins-Village».

Owners :
Roger and Denise Vergé
Director : Thomas Hartleyb
Weekly closing :
Restaurant : Monday
Annual closing :
From January 28th to March 7th

R oger Vergé has transformed this picturesque mill into a paradise of French gastronomy. Guests will be enchanted by this virtuoso chef's «chartreuse de frais légumes de printemps à l'ail doux confit et huile de basilic», and «poupeton de fleur de courgette à la truffe noire de Valréas et son jus crémeux», accompanied by rare wines. There are 7 guestrooms for those who wish to prolong their stay in this kingdom of pleasure.

 Nice (**Intl**) 30 km

 Menus **300-740 FRF** s.i.
46-113 €
Carte **600-850 FRF** s.i.
91-130 €

 3 rooms
850-950 FRF s.i.
130-145 €

 4 suites
1 800 FRF s.i.
274 €

 90 FRF s.i.
14 €

yes (extra cost)

2 km

www.relaischateaux.fr/mougins

FRF : French franc

Visa

LE SAINT-PAUL

France

SINCE 1992

Tel. : (33) 04 93 32 65 25
Fax : (33) 04 93 32 52 94
E-mail : stpaul@relaischateaux.fr

86, rue Grande
06570 Saint-Paul-de-Vence
(Alpes-Maritimes)

A8, exit Cagnes-sur-Mer,
towards Vence then
La Colle-sur-Loup/Saint-Paul.

Owners : Olivier Borloo
and Charles-Eric Hoffmann
Open all year

 Nice (**Intl**) 15 km

 Menus **250 FRF** s.i.
(week lunch) - **38 €**
310-560 FRF s.i.
(dinner) - **47-58 €**
Carte **320-380 FRF** s.i.
49-58 €

 15 rooms
850-1 600 FRF s.i.
130-244 €

 3 suites
1 300-2 600 FRF s.i.
198-396 €

 95 FRF s.i.
14 €

 yes (extra cost)

 12 km

Maeght Foundation, art galleries,
tourist excursions.

Set in the heart of the famous medieval village of Saint-Paul-de-Vence, this 16th-century bourgeois home offers elegantly decorated rooms bathed in the scent of lavender. Choose between two dining rooms, one with a magnificent vaulted ceiling and frescos, the other set around a fountain. Alternatively, enjoy a romantic candlelit dinner on the flower-covered terrace, savouring Provençal cuisine beneath the stars.

240

Visa

FRF : French franc

www.relaischateaux.fr/stpaul

SINCE 2000

LA BASTIDE SAINT-ANTOINE

France

48, avenue Henri Dunant
06130 Grasse
(Alpes-Maritimes)

Tel. : (33) 04 93 70 94 94
Fax : (33) 04 93 70 94 95
E-mail : saintantoine@relaischateaux.fr

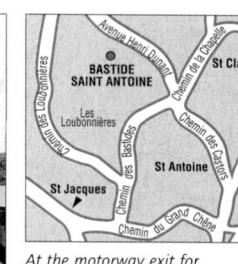

At the motorway exit for Cannes/Grasse/Mougins, follow signs to Grasse. Go to the end of the Grasse axial road, after the tunnel at the roundabout on the right follow signs to St Antoine/St Jacques, then take the first right «Chemin des Castors» for 1.5 km, the Bastide Saint-Antoine is on the left in a large olive grove.

T his elegant 18th country provençal house near Grasse overlooks the Bay of Cannes in the shade of its thousand-year-old olive tree park. From the tranquillity of the tastefully decorated sumptuous rooms with their balconies, you will then savour the delicious cuisine of Jacques Chibois who will delight your palate with a veritable symphony of new flavours such as «fraîcheur de fraises à l'huile d'olive vanillée et olives confites». Excellent wine list.

Owner : Jacques Chibois
Director : Patrice Dubois
Open all year

✈ Nice (**Intl**) 30 km

🍴 Menus **250 FRF** (lunch) s.i.
38 €
550-700 FRF s.i.
84-107 €
Carte 450-600 FRF s.i.
69-91 €

⊙━ 8 rooms
1 020-1 440 FRF s.i.
155-220 €

⊙━ 3 suites
1 620-2 160 FRF s.i.
247-329 €

☕ 135 FRF s.i.
21 €

🍴 yes (extra cost)

🏊 3 km

Horse-riding, fishing, bowling pitch, sailing, flying club, diving.

241

www.relaischateaux.fr/saintantoine

FRF : French franc

Visa

LE CAGNARD

Tel. : (33) 04 93 20 73 21
Fax : (33) 04 93 22 06 39
E-mail : cagnard@relaischateaux.fr

Rue Sous Barri, Haut de Cagnes
06800 Cagnes-sur-Mer
(Alpes-Maritimes)

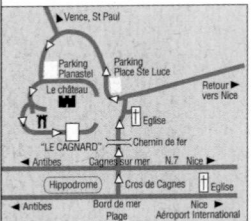

A8 Cagnes or RN 98 (coast)
centre ville, bd Mal Juin,
rue Hôtel des Postes; to the left,
follow signs Château-Musée.

Owners : Mr and Mrs Félix Barel
Director : Françoise Laroche
Weekly closing :
Restaurant: Thursday at lunch
Annual closing :
Restaurant: from the end of Oct.
to mid-December

✈ Nice (**Intl**) 10 km

🍴 Menus **310 FRF** s.i.
(lunch wine included) - **47 €**
330-400-540 FRF s.i.
50-61-82 €
Carte **400-500 FRF** s.i.
61-76 €

⚷ 21 rooms
900-1 500 FRF s.i.
137-229 €

⚷ 4 suites
1 500-2 500 FRF s.i.
229-381 €

🍷 **100 FRF** s.i.
15 €

🦞 yes

♒ 15 km Mougins/Opio

This 13th-century Provençal residence with its elegant ochre facade and cascades of flowers is perched on the ramparts of a medieval village. The Cagnard's rooms are spacious yet intimate and romantic. You will admire the splendid vaulting and mural paintings of the former guard room and appreciate the terrace which opens onto an eternally blue sky. Mediterranean-style cuisine. Excellent wine list.

FRF : French franc

www.relaischateaux.fr/cagnard

Château Saint-Martin

France

Avenue des Templiers - BP 102
06142 Vence cedex
(Alpes-Maritimes)

Tel. : (33) 04 93 58 02 02
Fax : (33) 04 93 24 08 91
E-mail : stmartin@relaischateaux.fr

A8, exit Cagnes-sur-Mer;
Vence, follow Autres directions,
Col de Vence-Coursegoules.

Owner : S.A.H. Eden Roc
Director : Andrée Brunet
Annual closing :
From mid-October
to mid-December

 Nice (**Intl**) 20 km

 Menus 300 FRF s.i.
(lunch) - **46 €**
430-490 FRF s.i.
66-75 €
Carte 430-600 FRF s.i.
66-91 €

 34 rooms
2 000-4 500 FRF s.i.
305-686 €

 6 suites
8 000-12 000 FRF s.i.
1 220-1 829 €

 125 FRF s.i.
19 €

 no

 20 km

20 mn from the sea, museums,
galleries.

T his magnificent château, nestling amidst olive trees just a few steps from the Matisse Chapel, offers a superb panoramic view across 100 kilometres of hills and Mediterranean coastline. No wonder Konrad Adenauer described this former residence of the Templar Knights as «The antechamber to paradise!» The guestrooms are havens of calm and the flavour some cuisine is enhanced by the finest Provençal wines.

LA RÉSERVE DE BEAULIEU

France

5, bd Général Leclerc
06310 Beaulieu-sur-Mer
(Alpes-Maritimes)

Tel. : (33) 04 93 01 00 01
Fax : (33) 04 93 01 28 99
E-mail : reservebeaulieu@relaischateaux.fr

From Nice or from Monoco: follow the seacoast towards Beaulieu.

Owners : Delion Family
Director : Jean-Claude Delion
Annual closing :
From January 16th to March 3rd and from Oct. 29th to Dec. 22nd

✈ Nice (**Intl**) 15 km

🍴 Menus
300-580-850 FRF s.i.
46-88-130 €
Carte **500-800 FRF** s.i.
76-122 €

E legance, refinement, a gentle way of life and comfort are the watchwords which best describe the decor of this splendid Florentine residence where tradition and renewal have been so skilfully blended. In the restaurant, savour the delicious Mediterranean dishes. A sumptuous pool heated to 30° all year round.

⚷ 27 rooms
low saison
990-2 450 FRF s.i.
151-373 €
high saison
2 450-4 700 FRF s.i.
373-717 €

⚷ 10 suites
low saison
3 400-5 750 FRF s.i.
518-877 €
high saison
4 300-9 000 FRF s.i.
656-1 372 €

☕ **125-165 FRF** s.i.
19-25 €

🐎 yes (extra cost)

⛳ Mont-Agel 15 km (18 holes)

Water sports, thalassatherapy and thermal baths nearby, private harbor.

245

FRF : French franc

Visa

LE MÉTROPOLE

SINCE 1979

Tel. : (33) 04 93 01 00 08
Fax : (33) 04 93 01 18 51
E-mail : metropole@relaischateaux.fr

15, bd du Maréchal Leclerc
06310 Beaulieu-sur-Mer
(Alpes-Maritimes)

France

From Nice or Monaco, follow the coast towards Beaulieu.

Owner : S.A. Hôtel Métropole
Director : Jean Rauline
Annual closing :
From October 20th to Dec. 20th

✈ Nice (**Intl**) 15 km

🍴 Menus **410-520 FRF** s.i.
62-79 €
Carte **350-580 FRF** s.i.
53-88 €

⚷ 35 rooms
half board 2 pers.
1 900-4 100 FRF s.i.
290-625 €

⚷ 5 suites
half board 2 pers.
3 400-6 800 FRF s.i.
518-1 037 €

☕ **130 FRF** s.i.
20 €

🍴 yes (extra cost)

⚑ Mont-Agel 15 km

Single room rates upon request
(1-3 days).

This opulent gold and white villa, built in the style of an Italian palace, is set in magnificent gardens opening onto a private beach and pier. Guests will discover elegance, discretion and comfort and enjoy the luxury of the sumptuous pool heated to 30° all year round. Dine on the terrace beneath a beautiful white canopy, savouring superb regional cuisine which brings out the full splendour of seasonal produce.

 Visa

FRF : French franc

`www.relaischateaux.fr/metropole`

Château de La Chèvre d'Or

France

Moyenne corniche, rue du Barri
06360 Eze-Village
(Alpes-Maritimes)

Tel. : **(33) 04 92 10 66 66**
Fax : **(33) 04 93 41 06 72**
E-mail : chevredor@relaischateaux.fr

From Nice (A8), exit La Turbie,
Moyenne corniche towards
Eze-Village.

Owner : S.C.I. La Chèvre d'Or
Director : Thierry Naidu
Annual closing :
From November 26th
to March 1st

 Nice (**Intl**) 12 km

Perched between the mountains and the Mediterranean in the medieval village of Eze, the Château de la Chèvre d'Or has a superb view. The elegant rooms are set in the village. Its three restaurants offer a choice of cuisine suited to every fancy: «La Chèvre d'Or», gastronomic restaurant with its fine vintages and collection of cognacs and armagnacs, minutes away, «Le Grill du Château» and Italian-style «L'Oliveto».

 Menus **280 FRF** s.i.
(week lunch) - **43 €**
390 FRF s.i.
(lunch) - **59 €**
620 FRF s.i. - **95 €**
Carte 490-690 FRF s.i.
75-105 €
Grill du Château
160 FRF s.i. - **24 €**
Oliveto
190 FRF s.i. - **29 €**

 22 rooms
1 600-3 100 FRF s.i.
244-473 €

  9 suites
starting at **3 200 FRF** s.i.
488 €

130-230 FRF s.i.
20-35 €

yes

7 km

247

www.relaischateaux.fr/chevredor

FRF : French franc

Visa

GRAND HÔTEL DE CALA ROSSA

SINCE 1993

Tel. : (33) 04 95 71 61 51
Fax : (33) 04 95 71 60 11
E-mail : calarossa@relaischateaux.fr

20137 Porto-Vecchio
(Corse)

France

Sea (Cie SNCM) and air connections: TAT, Air France.

Owners : Canarelli Family
Director : Patricia Biancarelli
Annual closing :
From mid-November to mid-April

✈ Figari (**Intl**) 35 km
Bastia (**Intl**) 90 km

🚢 GPS N 41° 37' 37"
E 009° 20' 37"

🍴 Menus 200-450 FRF s.i.
30-69 €
Carte 400-550 FRF s.i.
61-84 €

🔑 48 rooms
800-3 000 FRF s.i.
122-457 €

🔑 3 suites
1 600-2 600 FRF s.i.
244-396 €

☕ 120 FRF s.i.
18 €

🐕 no

🚶 Spérone 30 km

Waterskiing, sailing.

Tucked away amidst pink laurels and fragrant pines, La Cala Rossa is set in a luxuriant garden which winds down towards a fine sand beach. The elegant white guestrooms, decorated with juniper-wood panelling and beautifully crafted earthenware, are havens of calm. Enjoy divine cuisine, which blends Mediterranean flavours with the finest seafood, beneath the superb vaulted ceiling of the dining room.

248

FRF : French franc

www.relaischateaux.fr/calarossa

France

Chemin de Notre-Dame-de-la-Serra
20260 Calvi
(Corse)

Tel. : (33) 04 95 65 10 10
Fax : (33) 04 95 65 10 50
E-mail : lavilla@relaischateaux.fr

Avenue Christophe Colomb, take the Notre-Dame-de-la-Serra path.

Owner : Jean-Pierre Pinelli
Director : Patricia Criqui
Annual closing :
From January 2nd to March 31st

✈ Calvi (**Intl**) 7 km
Bastia (**Intl**) 95 km

🍴 Carte **350-500 FRF** s.i.
53-76 €

⌘ 27 rooms
950-3 800 FRF s.i.
145-579 €

⌘ 15 suites
1 500-4 300 FRF s.i.
229-656 €

☕ 120 FRF s.i.
18 €

🐎 no

🏃 6 km

Sailing, fishing, flying club.

T his elegant residence, part Corsican monastery, part Roman villa, is set in the picturesque hills of Calvi between the sea and the mountains. La Villa's exquisite guestrooms, sunny sitting rooms and flower-covered terraces are an open invitation to la dolce vita and the cuisine is a festival of Corsican flavours. Discover the forests of Bonifato, the Scandola nature reserve and the stunning views across Calvi Bay.

BENELUX COUNTRIES

BELGIUM

Establishments	Nearest major city	Relais & Châteaux	Relais Gourmands	Page
Auberge du Moulin Hideux	**Bouillon**	⚜		262
Clos St. Denis	**Tongeren**		👨‍🍳	258
Hof Van Cleve	**Gent**		👨‍🍳	255
Hôtel de Snippe	**Bruges**	⚜		253
Hostellerie Lafarque	**Liège**	⚜	👨‍🍳	261
Hostellerie Saint-Roch	**Liège**	⚜		259
Hostellerie Shamrock	**Ronse**	⚜		254
Moulin des Ramiers	**Dinant**	⚜		260
Restaurant Barbizon	**Brussel**		👨‍🍳	256
Scholteshof	**Hasselt**	⚜	👨‍🍳	257

LUXEMBOURG

Establishments	Nearest major city	Relais & Châteaux	Relais Gourmands	Page
Gaichel (La)	**Arlon**	⚜		264
Table des Guilloux (La)	**Luxembourg**		👨‍🍳	263

Wines recommended by the wine waiters of the Relais & Châteaux and Relais Gourmands.

🍾	Name of wine	Wine to enjoy	Noble wine	Outstanding wine
White	Pinot Gris, Riesling, Pinot Blanc	1996 - 1997		

NETHERLANDS

Establishments	Nearest major city	Relais & Châteaux	Relais Gourmands	Page
Kasteel Wittem	**Maastricht**	⚜		265
Manoir «Inter Scaldes»	**Middelburg**	⚜	👨‍🍳	267
Prinses Juliana	**Maastricht**	⚜	👨‍🍳	266

Cherchez
la femme !

Femme

HOTEL DE SNIPPE

Belgium

53, Nieuwe Gentweg
B-8000 Bruges
(Flandre occidentale)

Tel. : (32) (050) 33 70 70
Fax : (32) (050) 33 76 62
E-mail : desnippe@relaischateaux.fr

Towards the city-centre.
After the belfry, to the right.

Owners :
Luc and Francine Huysentruyt
Weekly closing :
Hotel : Sunday in winter
Restaurant : Sunday and Monday
for lunch
Annual closing :
From Feb. 27th to March 16th
and from November 26th
to December 8th

✈ Ostende (**Intl**) 30 km
Brussels (**Intl**) 100 km

🍴 Menus 1 950-3 650 BEF s.i.
48-90 €
Carte 3 000-4 000 BEF s.i.
74-99 €

⚷ 5 rooms
5 750 BEF s.i.
143 €

⚷ 4 suites
starting at 7 250 BEF s.i.
180 €

☕ included

🛏 yes

🏌 Knokke-Le Zoute 16 km
Damme-Sijsele 10 km

S et in the heart of Bruges, the «Venice of Northern Europe», this magnificent hotel was once the mayor's residence. Its beautiful 18th-century decor has been lovingly restored by Luc and Francine Huysentruyt and the stylish rooms have been designed to ensure utmost comfort. After a romantic stroll by the «Lac d'Amour» or a visit to one of the famous local museums, enjoy refined cuisine in the elegant winter garden.

www.relaischateaux.fr/desnippe

BEF : Belgian franc

Visa

HOSTELLERIE SHAMROCK

SINCE 1976

Tel. : (32) (055) 21 55 29
Fax : (32) (055) 21 56 83
E-mail : shamrock@relaischateaux.fr

Muziekbos
B-9680 Maarkedal
(Flandre orientale)

Belgium

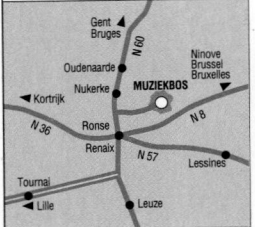

*On the Ronse/Oudenaarde
road (N 60), follow signs
towards Muziekbos, Zottegem.*

Owners :
Livine and Claude Debeyter
Weekly closing :
Monday and Tuesday
(except holidays)
Annual closing :
2nd fortnight in July

✈ Brussels (**Intl**) 60 km

🍴 Menus **2 200-3 750 BEF** s.i.
55-93 €
Carte **2 500-4 000 BEF** s.i.
62-99 €

⊶ 5 rooms
starting at **6 800 BEF** s.i.
169 €

⊶ 1 suite
starting at **8 800 BEF** s.i.
218 €

🍷 included

🍴 no

🏃 Petegem 10 km

Hiking.

B athed in soft, hazy sunlight, this elegant English-style manor, set in a sumptuous park designed by the famous landscape artist J. Wirtz, would not look out of place in an Impressionist painting. This idyllic country retreat is the perfect setting in which to enjoy Claude Debeyter's innovative cuisine, flavoured with herbs from his own garden. The Shamrock is ideally situated near Bruges, Belœil and Gand.

Visa

BEF : Belgian franc

www.relaischateaux.fr/shamrock

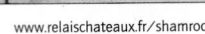

HOF VAN CLEVE

Belgium

Riemegemstraat, 1
B-9770 Kruishoutem

Tel. : (32) (09) 383 58 48
Fax : (32) (09) 383 77 25
E-mail : vancleve@relaischateaux.fr

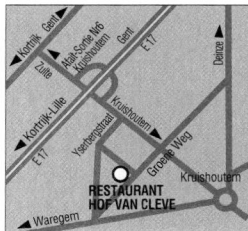

*Motorway E17 Lille-Courtrai
(Kortrÿk)-Anvers (Antwerpen),
exit n°6 for Kruishoutem. Follow
signs to Kruishoutem, after 1 km
on the right, follow the signs.*

Owner : Peter Goossens
Weekly closing :
Sunday and Monday
Annual closing :
From Dec. 20th to January 5th.
1 week to Easter and 3 weeks in
August

✈ Brussels (**Intl**) 60 km
Lille-Lesquin 40 km

🍴 Menus 1 950-5 500 BEF s.i.
48-136 €
Carte 2 750-5 000 BEF s.i.
68-124 €

🐕 no

🏃 5 km

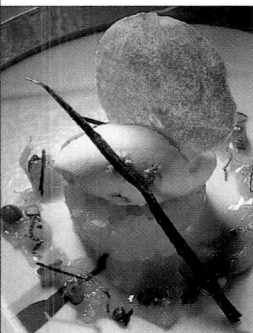

I n the Flemish Ardennes countryside 20 kms from Gand, you will find this rural farmhouse decorated with contemporary paintings. Here, the chef Peter Goossens offers you his wonderful symphony of natural flavours. How can you ever tire of inventive and delicious recipes such as «la salade de caille laquée aux carottes» and «dos d'agneau aux jeunes poireaux et girolles». Heaven for the most demanding palates.

P 🍼 ✈

255

RESTAURANT BARBIZON

SINCE 1964

Tel. : (32) (02) 657 04 62
Fax : (32) (02) 657 40 66
E-mail : barbizon@relaischateaux.fr

95, Welriekendedreef
B-3090 Jezus-Eik (Overijse)
(Brabant)

Belgium

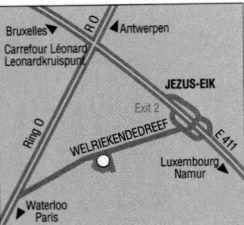

From Brussels, E411, towards Namur, exit n° 2 to Jezus-Eik Hœilaart, then take a right.

Owner : Alain Deluc
Weekly closing :
Tuesday and Wednesday
Annual closing : In February and 3 weeks in July-August

Brussels (**Intl**) 12 km
Namur 40 km

GPS N 50° 47' 318" E 004° 28' 122"

Menus **1 425 BEF** s.i. (week lunch) - **35 €**
starting at **1 800 BEF** s.i. **45 €**
Carte **2 500-4 000 BEF** s.i. **62-99 €**

yes

Tervuren 6 km

Visits : Church of Notre-Dame-au-Bois, arboretum of Tervuren...

For forty years, this elegant mansion near Brussels has welcomed gourmets from around the world. After studying with Troisgros and Chapel, Alain Deluc has created his own culinary masterpieces such as «compression de homard et huîtres, vinaigrette aux herbes», «homard en chemise, beurre Barbizon», and «carré de veau de lait braisé, persillade aux 4 épices et primeurs à l'estragon». Enjoy fine wines, cigars and old Armagnacs.

256

 Visa

BEF : Belgian franc

www.relaischateaux.fr/barbizon

SCHOLTESHOF

Belgium

Kermtstraat 130
B-3512 Stevoort Hasselt
(Limbourg)

Tel. : (32) (011) 25 02 02
Fax : (32) (011) 25 43 28
E-mail : scholteshof@relaischateaux.fr

From Brussels (70km), E314 (A2)
towards Louvain/Leuven,
exit 25, towards Hasselt via N2.

Owner : Roger Souvereyns
Weekly closing : Wednesday
Annual closing :
From January 1st to 21st

✈	Brussels **(Intl)** 75 km Kiwiet 15 km
🛰	GPS N 50° 56' 26'' E 5° 14' 76''
🍴	Menus **3 800-5 100 BEF** s.i. **94-126 €** Carte **3 200-5 500 BEF** s.i. **79-136 €**

Virtuoso chef Roger Souvereyns is also a passionate antique collector and gardener. He has lovingly restored this magnificent 18th-century farmhouse and tends a 28-acre garden, where he grows the herbs and vegetables which flavour his gourmet cuisine. Savour «le croquant de légumes en mille-feuille», «la crème de petits pois glacés, carpaccio de coquilles et caviar» and sublime «gâteau chocolat et compotée d'oranges confites».

⚿	9 rooms **5 500 BEF** s.i. **136 €**
⚿	9 suites starting at **9 000 BEF** s.i. **223 €**
🍷	**600 BEF** s.i. **15 €**
✝	yes (extra cost)
🏃	10 km

www.relaischateaux.fr/scholteshof

BEF : Belgian franc

Visa

CLOS ST. DENIS

Tel. : (32) (012) 23 60 96
Fax : (32) (012) 26 32 07
E-mail : stdenis@relaischateaux.fr

Grimmertingenstraat 24
B-3724 Kortessem
(Limburg)

Belgium

*Motorway E40 dir. Louvain.
At Louvain, take A2 - (E314)
dir. Genk. At Lummen take A13
(E313) dir. Hasselt - Liège. At
Hasselt take exit 29 dir. Tongeren
N20 - (13 km).*

Owners :
Denise and Christian Denis
Weekly closing :
Mondays and Tuesdays
Annual closing :
From January 1st to 16th
and from July 3rd to 18th

 Brussels (**Intl**) 95 km
Liège 25 km

 GPS L 50° 49' 27"
l 005° 25' 52"

 Menus **3 600-5 000 BEF** s.i.
89-124 €
Carte **3 500-5 000 BEF** s.i.
87-124 €

 no

T his magnificent 17th-century farm-house, overlooking a picturesque courtyard, is decorated with oak panelling, Louis XIII furniture and sumptuous tapestries. An idyllic setting in which to savour Christian Denis's gourmet compositions. Enjoy «friandise de crabe et de saumon, sauce à l'avocat, mousse de sole garnie de caviar osciètre», «feuilleté de pigeonneau de Bresse, un confit de ses cuisses, foie d'oie et truffes», accompanied by a superb wine list.

 Visa

BEF : Belgian franc

www.relaischateaux.fr/stdenis

HOSTELLERIE SAINT-ROCH

Belgium

Rue du Parc - Vallée de l'Ourthe
B-4180 Comblain-la-Tour
(Liège)

Tel. : (32) (04) 369 13 33
Fax : (32) (04) 369 31 31
E-mail : saintroch@relaischateaux.fr

From Liege: follow «Ardennes»; motorway E25; take exit n°45 at Sprimont; cross Sprimont; towards Chanxhe; after the bridge over the Ourthe river, follow signs «Hostellerie St. Roch» to the left.

Owners :
Mr and Mrs Dernouchamps-Cawet
Weekly closing :
Hotel: Monday and Tuesday
(except July-August)
Rest. : Monday and Tuesday
(Tuesday in July-August)
Annual closing :
From January 3rd to March 10th

This beautiful residence, formerly a post house, is set in the heart of a magnificent valley, and its flower-bedecked terrace looks out over the River Ourthe. Lovingly restored by owners Francis and Nicole Dernouchamps, the Saint-Roch offers an intimate atmosphere and peaceful rooms decorated with period furniture. Enjoy exceptional hospitality, superb seasonal cuisine and an outstanding selection of wines and brandies.

✈   Brussels (**Intl**) 110 km
Liege 30 km

🍴   Menus
1 300-2 600 BEF s.i.
32-64 €
Carte
2 000-3 000 BEF s.i.
50-74 €

⚷   9 rooms
5 000-6 600 BEF s.i.
124-164 €

⚷   6 suites
starting at **7 700 BEF** s.i.
191 €

☕   included

🐕   yes (extra cost)

🏌   18-28 km (5 golf courses)

259

www.relaischateaux.fr/saintroch   **BEF : Belgian franc**

Visa

LE MOULIN DES RAMIERS

Tel. : (32) (083) 699 070
Fax : (32) (083) 699 868
E-mail : ramiers@relaischateaux.fr

31-32, rue Basse
B-5332 Crupet

Belgium

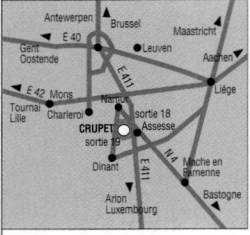

From E 411, exit 19 Spontin,
Crupet 7 km away. From N4,
exit Assesse, Crupet 6 km away.

Owners :
André and Jeanine Fieuw
Weekly closing :
Monday evening and Tuesday
Annual closing :
From March 5th to 20th
and from December 5th to 20th

✈	Gosselies (**Intl**) 50 km Brussels (**Intl**) 78 km
🍴	Menus **1 650-2 150 BEF** s.i. **41-53 €** Carte **1 850-2 400 BEF** s.i. **46-59 €**
🔑	6 rooms starting at **4 450 BEF** s.i. **110 €**
☕	included
🛏	yes (extra cost)
⛳	16 km (18 holes)

Fishing.

S et amidst the luxuriant foliage of Wallonie, the Ramiers is one of the great tables of Belgium thanks to the renowned talent and warm welcome of its hosts, Jeanine and André Fieuw. In this 18th century mill, transformed into a hotel, you will appreciate the beamed ceilings of the superb rooms elegantly decorated with china, pewter, and baroque furniture. As for the restaurant, you will enjoy the classically-inspired yet contemporary cuisine of the chef, the owners' son, Hugues.

BEF : Belgian franc

www.relaischateaux.fr / ramiers

HOSTELLERIE LAFARQUE

Belgium

Chemin des Douys 20
B-4860 Pepinster - Goffontaine
(Liège)

Tel. : (32) (087) 46 06 51
Fax : (32) (087) 46 97 28
E-mail : lafarque@relaischateaux.fr

Highway E42, exit Pepinster RN61 towards Chaudfontaine; hotel indicated at Goffontaine. Highway «des Ardennes» E25, exit n° 45, towards Pepinster.

Owners :
Michel and Agnès Lafarque
Weekly closing :
Monday and Tuesday
(except holidays)
Annual closing :
From March 15th to April 7th
and from September 4th to 24th

 Brussels (**Intl**) 100 km
Liege 30 km

GPS N 50° 34' E 5° 46'

 Menus
2 500-2 775 BEF s.i.
62-69 €
Carte
2 750-3 500 BEF s.i.
68-87 €

3 rooms
4 950 BEF s.i.
123 €

2 suites
5 550 BEF s.i.
138 €

395 BEF s.i.
10 €

no

Gomzé 15 km

Victor Hugo once wrote, «On a clear day, under a blue sky, the Vesdre Valley sometimes resembles a ravine, sometimes a garden, but always a paradise». Hosts Michel and Agnès Lafarque invite you to stay in their elegant 1920's house set in such a garden. This idyllic country haven is the perfect place to enjoy gourmet cuisine - «dos de loup de mer au raisiné», «mousse glacée à l'ananas confit» - fine wines and «joie de vivre».

P

BEF : Belgian franc

Auberge du Moulin Hideux

SINCE 1960

Tel. : (32) (061) 46 70 15
Fax : (32) (061) 46 72 81
E-mail : hideux@relaischateaux.fr

B-6831 Noirefontaine
(Luxembourg)

Belgium

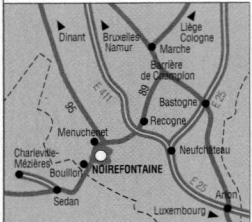

*From Brussels or Luxemburg,
E411, exit 25, towards Bouillon ;
from Paris, A4 Reims
towards Liège.*

Owners :
Charles and Martine Lahire
Weekly closing :
Restaurant : Wednesday
and Thursday for lunch
(March to June only)
Annual closing :
From Dec. 1st to March 15th

✈ Luxemburg (**Intl**) 95 km
   Brussels (**Intl**) 160 km

🍴 Menus
   2 000-2 800 BEF s.i.
   50-69 €
   and **3 800 BEF** s.i. with wine
   94 €
   Carte
   2 000-3 500 BEF s.i.
   50-87 €

🔑 9 rooms
   starting at **7 000 BEF** s.i.
   174 €

🔑 3 suites
   starting at **8 000 BEF** s.i.
   198 €

☕ included

🍴 yes (extra cost)

🚶 40 km

N estling in the picturesque Semois
valley, this 18th-century millhouse
has been an idyllic country inn for the past
50 years. When you discover its cosy
ambience, its comfortable rooms, spacious
tennis courts and indoor heated pool, you
will understand why the Auberge du
Moulin Hideux became the very first Relais
de Campagne outside France. Enjoy
romantic strolls through the forest and
excellent regional cuisine.

BEF : Belgian franc

www.relaischateaux.fr/hideux

LA TABLE DES GUILLOUX

Luxemburg

17-19, rue de la Résistance
L-4996 Schouweiler

Tel. : (352) 37 00 08
Fax : (352) 37 11 61
E-mail : guilloux@relaischateaux.fr

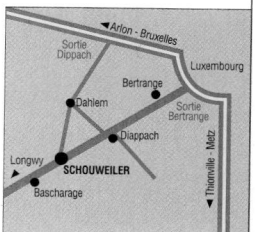

From the airport :
take the Motorway to Brussels,
exit Bertrange.
After Dippach, Schouweiler.
From France : follow directions
to Brussels. Exit Bertranges.

Owners :
Pierrick and Lysiane Guilloux
Weekly closing :
Monday, Tuesday
and Saturday at lunch
Annual closing :
From August 1st to 15th
and from December 23rd
to January 5th

Gourmets flock to Pierrick and Lysiane Guilloux's picturesque country house to savour some of the finest cuisine in Luxemburg. Discover a sublime «tournedos de morue fraîche poêlée, purée grand-mère», a remarkable «queue de bœuf farcie au foie gras» and a superb «turbot rôti aux échalotes confites». Heavenly desserts and a wonderfully eclectic wine list complete this extraordinary gastronomic experience.

Luxemburg (**Intl**) 12 km

Menus
1 600-2 000 LUX s.i.
40-50 €
Carte
1 500-2 000 LUX s.i.
37-50 €

yes

LUX : Luxemburg franc

LA GAICHEL

SINCE 1971

Tel. : (352) 39 01 29
Fax : (352) 39 00 37
E-mail : gaichel@relaischateaux.fr

L-8469 Gaichel/Eischen

Luxemburg

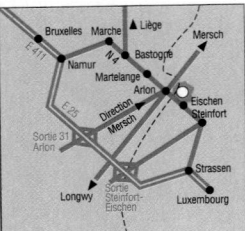

*From Belgium, E411, E25 exit
Arlon, «autres directions» sign,
then towards Mersch, Gaichel..*

Owners : Michel and
Claudine Gaul-Jacquemin
Weekly closing :
Sunday evening and Monday
Annual closing :
From January 9th to February 9th
and from August 20th to 30th

✈ Luxemburg (**Intl**) 25 km
Brussels (**Intl**) 185 km

🍴 Menus
1 600-2 700 LUX s.i.
40-67 €
Carte
2 100-2 700 LUX s.i.
52-67 €

🔑 13 rooms
3 750-5 500 LUX s.i.
93-136 €

☕ included

🐴 no

🏌 on the premises (9 holes)

S ince 1852 this elegant rose-coloured
residence has preserved the tradition
of family hospitality and fine living. La
Gaichel's comfortable guestrooms open
out onto pretty balconies overlooking a
country stream meandering through 35
acres of luxuriant parkland. The hotel is
also renowned as a gourmet retreat where
guests can dine al fresco on the beautiful
garden terrace or enjoy the refined
ambience of the restaurant.

Visa

LUX : Luxemburg franc

www.relaischateaux.fr/gaichel

KASTEEL WITTEM

Netherlands

Wittemer Allée 3
NL-6286 AA Wittem
(Limburg)

Tel. : (31) (043) 4501208
Fax : (31) (043) 4501260
E-mail : wittem@relaischateaux.fr

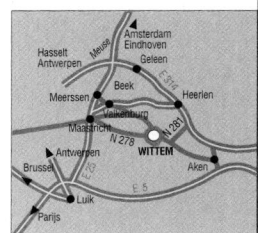

E25, exit Maastricht, N278 towards Vaals; E314, exit N281, towards Vaals, Maastricht.

Owners : Ritzen Family
Directors : Peter and Marc Ritzen
Open all year

✈ Brussels (**Intl**) 130 km
Amsterdam (**Intl**) 200 km

Discover the history of the Netherlands at this magnificent medieval castle, surrounded by an ancient moat and a picturesque park. Kasteel Wittem certainly lives up to its motto «Hospitality and Aptitude». You will find this impeccable service everywhere from the elegant rooms of the castle to the suites in the dungeon. Enjoy a country luncheon on the terrace by the moat and a divine candlelit dinner in the restaurant.

🍴 Menus 110-150 NLG s.i.
50-68 €
Carte 110-145 NLG s.i.
50-66 €

🔑 10 rooms
325-350 NLG s.i.
147-159 €

🔑 2 suites
450 NLG s.i.
204 €

☕ 30 NLG s.i.
14 €

🍴 no

♪ 7 km

Walks, biking, thermal baths.

NLG : Dutch florin

Visa

PRINSES JULIANA

Tel. : (31) (043) 6012244
Fax : (31) (043) 6014405
E-mail : juliana@relaischateaux.fr

Brœkhem 11
NL-6301 HD Bad Valkenburg A/d Geul
(Limburg)

Netherlands

From Liege, A2 Maastricht-Eindhoven then A79 towards Heerlen, exit Valkenburg.

Owners : Paul and Doris Stevens
Weekly closing :
Restaurant : Saturday (lunch)
Annual closing :
From January 1st to 7th

✈ Brussels (**Intl**) 110 km
Amsterdam (**Intl**) 200 km

🍴 Menus **110-185 NLG** s.i.
50-84 €
Carte **100-175 NLG** s.i.
45-79 €

⚷ 16 rooms
325-375 NLG s.i.
147-170 €

⚷ 5 suites
starting at **425 NLG** s.i.
193 €

☕ **32,50 NLG** s.i.
15 €

🐕 yes (extra cost)
except restaurant

⛳ 6-35 km (8 golf courses)

Walks, historic monuments.

G ourmets from around the world have flocked to this sumptuous residence since 1914 to savour the Prinses Juliana's renowned cuisine. Offering exquisite dishes, accompanied by the very finest vintages, the menu is indeed fit for a king. Savour «bisque de homard crémeuse» and «carré d'agneau des prés-salés au romarin». Superb wine list. Parlor for cigars and aged armagnacs.

 Visa

NLG : Dutch florin

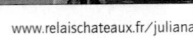 www.relaischateaux.fr/juliana

MANOIR «INTER SCALDES»

Netherlands

Zandweg 2
NL-4416 NA Kruiningen Yerseke
(Zealand)

Tel. : (31) (113) 381753
Fax : (31) (113) 381763
E-mail : scaldes@relaischateaux.fr

From Anvers, A 12, then A 58 towards Vlissingen, exit n°33 Yerseke/Hansweert to the left, thirdway to the left.

Owner : Kees Boudeling
Weekly closing :
Rest. : Monday and Tuesday
Annual closing :
First 3 weeks of January

✈ Brussels (**Intl**) 100 km

🚤 GPS N 51° 27' 24"
E 04° 01' 17"

🍴 Menus **152,50-190 NLG** s.i.
69-86 €
Carte **150-260 NLG** s.i.
68-118 €

🔑 12 suites
345-470 NLG s.i.
157-213 €

☕ **30 NLG** s.i.
14 €

🐕 yes (extra cost)

♪ 11 km

Hunting, fishing, sailing...

This magnificent manor, with its picturesque thatched roof and English-style gardens, is set near one of the most beautiful deltas in Europe. Here, Maartje Boudeling creates seafood dishes such as you have never tasted before. Her «homard entier fumé à la minute au caviar» is extraordinary and the «turbot à la vapeur en robe de truffe» divine. Enjoy heavenly desserts and superb wines, then retire to an elegant guestroom.

www.relaischateaux.fr/scaldes

NLG : Dutch florin

Visa

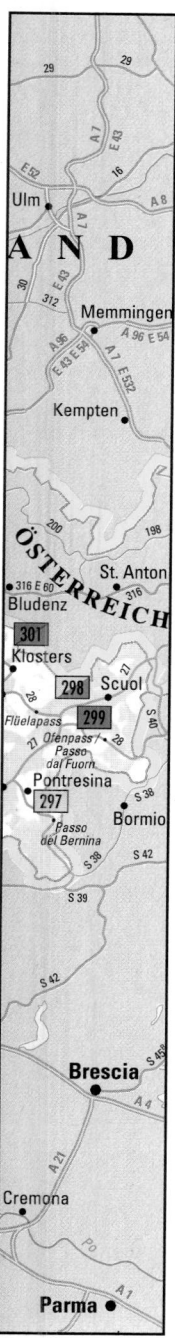

SWITZERLAND
LIECHTENSTEIN

SWITZERLAND

Establishments	Nearest major city	Relais & Châteaux	Relais Gourmands	Page
Albergo Giardino	Locarno	⚜		293
Auberge du Raisin	Lausanne	⚜	🍴	282
Castello del Sole	Locarno	⚜		292
Ermitage Am See	Zürich	⚜		275
G. Wenger-Hôtel de la gare	La Chaux de Fonds	⚜	🍴	277
Grand Hôtel Park	Gstaad	⚜		286
Grandhôtel Schönegg	Zermatt	⚜		291
Hostellerie Alpenrose	Gstaad	⚜		285
Hostellerie du Débarcadère	Lausanne	⚜		280
Hostellerie du Pas de l'Ours	Crans-Montana	⚜		287
Hôtel de la Cigogne	Genève	⚜		279
Hotel Haus Paradies	St Moritz	⚜	🍴	298
Hôtel Rosalp	Martigny	⚜		289
Hotel Splügenschloss	Zürich	⚜	🍴	274
Hôtel Victoria	Montreux	⚜		284
Hotel Walserhof	Davos	⚜		301
Hotel Walther	St Moritz	⚜	🍴	297
Les Sources des Alpes	Sion	⚜		290
Pont de Brent (Le)	Montreux		🍴	283
Restaurant Bruderholz	Basel		🍴	272
Rest. de l'Hôtel de Ville - Ph. Rochat	Lausanne		🍴	281
Restaurant Jöhri's Talvo	St Moritz		🍴	296
Restaurant Kunststuben	Zürich		🍴	276
Rheinhotel Fischerzunft	Schaffhausen	⚜	🍴	273
Shlosshotel Chastè	Scuol	⚜		299
Vieux Manoir au Lac (Le)	Bern	⚜		278
Villa Margherita	Lugano	⚜		294
Villa Principe Leopoldo	Locarno Ascorna	⚜		295

LIECHTENSTEIN

Establishments	Nearest major city	Relais & Châteaux	Relais Gourmands	Page
Parkhotel Sonnenhof	Vaduz	⚜		303
Real (Le)	Vaduz	⚜		302

ℬℬ
1735
BLANCPAIN

SINCE 1735 THERE HAS NEVER BEEN A QUARTZ BLANCPAIN WATCH
AND THERE NEVER WILL BE.

World exclusivity
Half-Hunter Moon Phase.
Power reserve of 100 hours.
Case in red gold or white gold.

VINTAGES TO DRINK IN YEAR 2000
SWITZERLAND

Wines recommended by the wine waiters
of the Relais & Châteaux and Relais Gourmands.

Index of world vintages to drink in year 2000 : page 607

	Name of wine	Wine to enjoy	Noble wine	Outstanding wine
	SWITZERLAND			
White	Chasselas, Arvine, Ermitage, Amigne Pinot Blanc, Chardonnay	1998	1996	1995
Red	Pinot Noir, Syrah, Cornalin, Humagne, Merlot	1997	1996	1995
Overripe	Pinot Gris, Ermitage (Valais)	1997	1996	1995

RESTAURANT BRUDERHOLZ

Tel. : (41) (061) 361 82 22
Fax : (41) (061) 361 82 03
E-mail : bruderholz@relaischateaux.fr

Bruderholzallee 42
CH-4059 Basel

Switzerland

From the Basel train station, follow signs for «Bruderholz».

Owner : Pierre Buess
Weekly closing :
Sunday and Monday
Open all year

✈ Basel (**Intl**) 5 km

🍴 Menus **85-185 CHF** s.i.
Carte **45-75 CHF** s.i.

⚶ yes

🏌 Hagenthal 10 km

Contemporary Art Museum, Tinguely Museum, Puppen Museum, Kunst Museum, Sacher Foundation (music), Beyeler Foundation.

 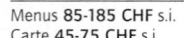

It is thanks to the regretted Hans Stucki that the Bruderholz restaurant attained its international renown. His successor, Pierre Buess and Jean-Claude Wicky, 10 years in the kitchen of this temple of gastronomy, have ensured this transition in a spirit of creation and continuity. Refined French cuisine, respecting the rhythm of the seasons. Excellent vintage wines. Not to be missed.

CHF : Swiss franc

www.relaischateaux.fr/bruderholz

RHEINHOTEL FISCHERZUNFT

Switzerland

Rheinquai 8
CH-8202 Schaffhausen

Tel. : (41) (052) 625 32 81
Fax : (41) (052) 624 32 85
E-mail : fischerzunft@relaischateaux.fr

From Zurich, green signs to St. Gallen, Winterthur. Highway exit Schaffhausen.

Owner : André Jaeger
Weekly closing : Tuesday
Open all year

✈ Zurich (**Intl**) 40 km

🍽 Menus **105-190 CHF** s.i.
    Carte **40-75 CHF** s.i.

⚷ 10 rooms
    270-415 CHF s.i.

☕ **25 CHF** s.i.

🍴 yes

R elax on the waterside terrace of this splendid 17th-century estate, set on the picturesque banks of the Rhine, and enjoy idyllic surroundings and complete tranquillity. The supremely comfortable guestrooms are bathed in natural light. Virtuoso chef André Jaeger has blended European gourmet tradition with Asiatic inspiration and his innovative menus, enhanced by the finest vintages, are a veritable feast for the senses.

www.relaischateaux.fr/fischerzunft

CHF : Swiss franc

Visa

HOTEL SPLÜGENSCHLOSS

SINCE 1986

Tel. : (41) (01) 289 99 99
Fax : (41) (01) 289 99 98
E-mail : splugenschloss@relaischateaux.fr

Splügenstrasse 2/Genferstrasse
CH-8002 Zürich

Switzerland

From central station, follow Limmatquai, quay Brücke, then quay General Guisan. Turn right at Rentenanstalt, then take Jenatschstraße.

Owners :
Christoph and Ingrid Suter
Open all year

✈   Zurich (**Intl**) 6 km

🍴   Menus **65-95 CHF** s.i.
     Carte **75-115 CHF** s.i.

⊶   50 rooms
     395-600 CHF s.i.

⊶   2 suites
     starting at **690 CHF** s.i.

☕   included

🍴   yes (extra cost)

🎿   10 km

Special weekend rates.
Shopping, tourism, festivals of Zurich, opera, theatre.

This beautiful Art Nouveau residence, just a few steps from the Bahnhofstrasse shopping and business district, attracts bons vivants from all over the world. Guests will appreciate Christoph and Ingrid Suter's exquisite hospitality and the intimate comfort of their refined home. After a romantic stroll around the lake, savour the inventive Franco-Swiss cuisine and superb wines at the Restaurant du Château.

    Visa

CHF : Swiss franc

www.relaischateaux.fr/splugenschloss

ERMITAGE AM SEE

Switzerland

Seestrasse 80
CH-8700 Küsnacht
(Zürich)

Tel. : (41) (01) 914 42 42
Fax : (41) (01) 914 42 43
E-mail : ermitage@relaischateaux.fr

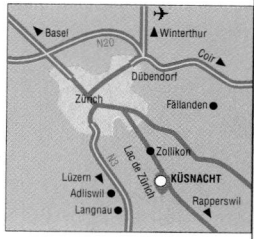

Zurich, place «Bellevue»,
follow signs to Rapperswil
via the Seestrasse (N17),
continue for about 7 km.

Owner :
Hotel Ermitage Am See AG
Directors :
Lisbeth and Kurt Schmid
Open all year

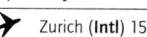 Zurich (**Intl**) 15 km

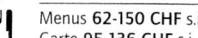 Menus **62-150 CHF** s.i.
Carte **95-136 CHF** s.i.

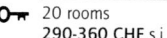 20 rooms
290-360 CHF s.i.

 6 suites
440-740 CHF s.i.

buffet **17 CHF** s.i.

yes (extra cost)

3 km

Water-skiing, sailing, fishing, museums.

N ear Zurich, in the heart of a picturesque landscape of lakes and forests, the Ermitage offers you the charm of its comfortable rooms with a spectacular view on the lake. Between two strolls through the vineyards, enjoy a romantic candlelit dinner savouring a subtle and refined cuisine served with the excellent regional wines. Visit an unusual site: the Fraumünster church with its stained glass windows by Chagall.

   275

CHF : Swiss franc

Visa

RESTAURANT KUNSTSTUBEN

SINCE 1992

Tel. : (41) (01) 910 07 15
Fax : (41) (01) 910 04 95
E-mail : kunststuben@relaischateaux.fr

Seestrasse 160
CH-8700 Küsnacht
(Zürich)

Switzerland

Zurich, place Bellevue, towards Rapperswil via the Seestrasse.

Owner : Horst Petermann
Weekly closing :
Sunday and Monday
Annual closing :
From August 23rd to Sept. 14th
and 2 weeks in February

✈ Zurich (**Intl**) 15 km

🍴 Menus **125-185 CHF** s.i.
Carte **34-85 CHF** s.i.

🐕 yes (no extra cost)

🎿 3 km

C.G. Jung Institute.

G ourmets flock to this elegant restaurant near Zurich to savour Horst Petermann's inspired cuisine. A master of precise timing, Petermann draws the most exquisite flavours from his ingredients and dazzles guests with his repertoire of culinary innovation. Savour «homard de Bretagne sur lit d'épices thaï», «mignon de veau pané à la mie de pain d'amandes et ris de veau aux écrevisses» and the finest Swiss and French wines.

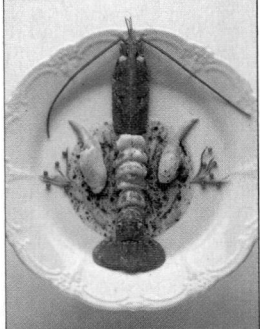

CHF : Swiss franc

www.relaischateaux.fr/kunststuben

GEORGES WENGER - HÔTEL DE LA GARE

Switzerland

2, rue de la Gare
CH-2340 Le Noirmont
(Jura)

Tel. : (41) (032) 953 11 10
Fax : (41) (032) 953 10 59
E-mail : wenger@relaischateaux.fr

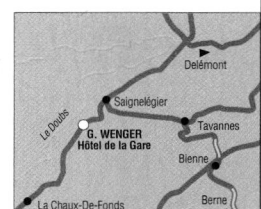

From Geneva, A1 dir. La Chaux de Fonds, then N18 dir. Bâle.

Owner : Georges Wenger
Weekly closing :
Restaurant : Monday and Tuesday
Annual closing :
From January 10th to 31st

Berne (**Intl**) 80 km
Zurich (**Intl**) 100 km

Menus **88-170 CHF** s.i.
Carte **85-120 CHF** s.i.

1 room
240 CHF s.i.

4 suites
290-370 CHF s.i.

included

yes (extra cost)

6 km

Hunting, fishing, climbing,
flying club, skiing, canoeing,
mountain biking, ice-skating,
dog sled races (January),
hot-air balloon festival (October).

Nestling in the heart of a picturesque village in the Swiss Jura, this elegant restaurant serves the most exquisite gourmet cuisine. Virtuoso chef Georges Wenger creates a symphony of flavours and colours, using the finest market-fresh produce. His «tarte tatin de navets au fois gras» and «poulette de Houdan en daubière à l'échalote et laurier» are masterpieces and the wine list is superb. Prolong your stay in one of the cosy, sun-filled guestrooms.

277

Le Vieux Manoir au Lac

Tel. : (41) (026) 678 61 61
Fax : (41) (026) 678 61 62
E-mail : vieuxmanoir@relaischateaux.fr

Route de Lausanne
CH-3280 Murten-Meyriez
(Fribourg)

Switzerland

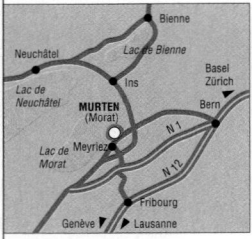

From the north, towards Bern/Neufeld, exit Murten/Morat.
From the south, N12, exit Fribourg Nord.

Owner : Mrs A. Leu
Directors :
Erich and Elisabeth Thomas
Annual closing :
From mid-Dec. to mid-Feb.

✈ Berne (**Intl**) 30 km
Zurich (**Intl**) 120 km
Geneva (**Intl**) 120 km

🍴 Menus **75-130 CHF** s.i.
Carte **80-110 CHF** s.i.

⚷ 26 rooms
300-490 CHF s.i.

⚷ 4 suites
470-540 CHF s.i.

☕ included

🚭 yes (extra cost)

🎣 Wallenried 7 km

Fishing, sailing, rowboats...

This beautiful manor is set in a romantic park overlooking the tranquil waters of Lake Morat. Its spacious guestrooms, tastefully decorated with period furniture, offer vistas of idyllic green countryside stretching away to the horizon. Seasonal cuisine, prepared with the finest local produce, is enhanced by an exceptional Vully. Relax at the private beach, take a bicycle tour or experience the wonders of outdoor opera.

 Visa

CHF : Swiss franc

www.relaischateaux.fr/vieuxmanoir

HÔTEL DE LA CIGOGNE

Switzerland

17, place Longemalle
CH-1204 Genève

Tel. : (41) (022) 818 40 40
Fax : (41) (022) 818 40 50
E-mail : cigogne@relaischateaux.fr

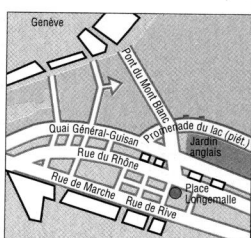

From the Paris highway,
Annemasse, Geneva-Vallard,
city centre before the Mt Blanc
bridge, turn left.

Owner : René Favre
Director : Richard Bischoff
Open all year

✈ Geneva (**Intl**) 8 km

🍴 Menus **58-90 CHF** s.i.
Carte **70-95 CHF** s.i.

🗝 41 rooms
430 CHF s.i.

🗝 9 suites
740-890 CHF s.i.

💼 25 CHF s.i.

🐕 yes (extra cost) except rest.

🏊 2 km

Sauna, jacuzzi, hammam
100 m away...

T his beautiful 19th-century residence lies in the heart of Geneva, just a short stroll from the lake and the old city centre - an ideal setting which is greatly appreciated by La Cigogne's distinguished clientele. The rooms, furnished with impeccable taste, are supremely comfortable. Savour refined cuisine beneath the restaurant's elegant glass roof and choose from an exceptional wine list featuring over 350 vintages.

279

www.relaischateaux.fr/cigogne

CHF : Swiss franc

Visa

HOSTELLERIE DU DÉBARCADÈRE

SINCE 1983

Tel. : (41) (021) 691 57 47
Fax : (41) (021) 691 50 79
E-mail : debarcadere@relaischateaux.fr

Chemin du Crêt 7
CH-1025 St-Sulpice-Lausanne
(Vaud)

Switzerland

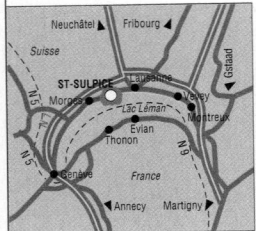

From the highway, towards Lausanne süd, exit Saint-Sulpice.

Owners :
Tony and Caroline Kluvers
Weekly closing :
Sunday from Nov. to February
Annual closing :
From December 20th
to January 20th

✈	Geneva (**Intl**) 40 km
🍴	Menus 78-95 CHF s.i. Carte 25-49 CHF s.i.
⚷	12 rooms **170-300 CHF** s.i.
⚷	3 suites **300-400 CHF** s.i.
☕	21 CHF s.i.
🐕	yes (extra cost)
🏃	15 km

Trips, biking, water sports, jogging, museums.

The Kluvers' elegant hotel, set on the picturesque banks of Lake Geneva, is renowned for its exceptional hospitality. Its comfortable rooms, resplendent with pastel walls and rustic furniture, offer superb panoramic vistas of the lake and the winter garden is a sheer delight. Enjoy generous cuisine featuring salmon trout, char and perch from the lake, accompanied by fine wines from Switzerland and France.

 Visa

CHF : Swiss franc

www.relaischateaux.fr/debarcadere

280

REST. DE L'HÔTEL DE VILLE - PH. ROCHAT

Switzerland

1, rue d'Yverdon
CH-1023 Crissier
(Vaud)

Tel. : (41) (021) 634 05 05
Fax : (41) (021) 634 24 64
E-mail : hoteldeville@relaischateaux.fr

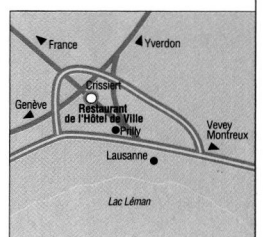

5 km from Lausanne,
motorway exit Crissier,
take direction Crissier centre.

Owner : Philippe Rochat
Weekly closing :
Sunday and Monday
Annual closing :
Last week of July
and first two weeks of August

✈ Geneva (**Intl**) 50 km
Lausanne 5 km

🍴 Menus **200-225 CHF** s.i.
Carte **50-100 CHF** s.i.

yes

10 km

Skiing, water sports,
numerous museums
(the Hermitage 6 km away).

This elegant restaurant near Lausanne is a temple of gastronomy where chef Philippe Rochat delights gourmet palates with his exquisite culinary masterpieces and fine wines. The «chartreuse de pointes d'asperges vertes aux morilles à la fricassée de grenouilles» is excellent, the «canard nantais cuit rosé au vin de Brouilly» superb and the «conversation tiède de fraises des bois, glace à la vanille» simply divine.

　　　　CHF : Swiss franc　　　　Visa

Auberge du Raisin

Tel. : (41) (021) 799 21 31
Fax : (41) (021) 799 25 01
E-mail : raisin@relaischateaux.fr

1, place de l'Hôtel-de-Ville
CH-1096 Cully
(Vaud)

Switzerland

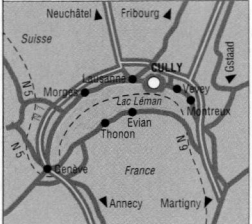

From Lausanne, exit Belmont;
at Lutry towards Villette,
3,2 miles later, towards Cully.

Owner : Jean-Jacques Gauer S.A.
Directors :
Mr and Mrs A. Blokbergen
Open all year

✈	Geneva (**Intl**) 70 km Sion 80 km
⑪	Menus **69-180 CHF** s.i. Carte **79-130 CHF** s.i.
⚷	7 rooms **220-320 CHF** s.i.
⚷	3 suites **380-550 CHF** s.i.
☕	included
🐎	yes (extra cost)
⚐	9 km

Hunting, fishing, climbing,
sailing...

In this elegant old Swiss inn, Adolfo Blokbergen creates innovative gourmet cuisine, drawing the most subtle flavours from his ingredients. You will be enchanted by his superb «gâteau de homard Dubarry à l'estragon» and his «dos de saumon sauvage à la moutarde de raisins rouges». The cellar, filled with Swiss, French and Californian vintages, includes famous white wines from the Lavaux vineyard.

Visa

CHF : Swiss franc

www.relaischateaux.fr/raisin

SINCE 1991

LE PONT DE BRENT

Switzerland

CH-1817 Brent/Montreux
(Vaud)

Tel. : (41) (021) 964 52 30
Fax : (41) (021) 964 55 30
E-mail : brent@relaischateaux.fr

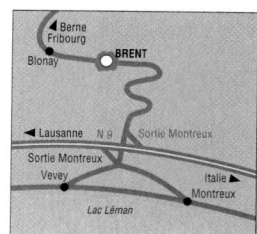

Highway N9, exit Montreux West, towards Blonay-Brent, go through the village.

Owner : Gérard Rabaey
Weekly closing :
Sunday and Monday
Annual closing :
15 days in July and
at the end of the year

✈ Geneva **(Intl)** 100 km

🍽 Menus **80-195 CHF** s.i.
Carte **90-160 CHF** s.i.

🐓 yes

♦ 15 km

Walks and trips (Chillon castle), mountain sports.

alented Norman chef Gérard Rabaey, now accepted as an honorary Vaudois, welcomes gourmets to this picturesque residence above Montreux. Rabaey's inventive French cuisine is prepared with the finest local produce. Savour : «morilles farcies sur truffes, poireaux et asperges vertes», «rougets aux choux nouveaux, sabayon au poivron», «éventail à la rhubarbe, glace noix et miel». The cellar is a treasure trove of Swiss and French vintages.

P   ♿

283

HÔTEL VICTORIA

SINCE 1975

Tel. : (41) (021) 963 31 31
Fax : (41) (021) 963 13 51
E-mail : victoria@relaischateaux.fr

CH-1823 Glion
(Vaud)

Switzerland

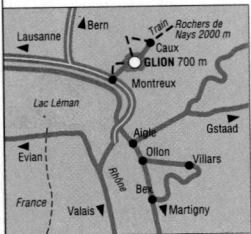

Highway exit Montreux, towards the Lake for 500 m, Caux Glion.

Owner : Toni Mittermair
Open all year

✈	Geneva (**Intl**) 85 km
🍴	Menus **60-85 CHF** s.i. Carte **50-100 CHF** s.i.
🔑	50 rooms **240-350 CHF** s.i.
🔑	9 suites **450-600 CHF** s.i.
🍷	included
🐕	yes (extra cost)
♗	15 km, private practice

Skiing, fishing, climbing, fitness.

This splendid residence, set in a beautiful park on a hillside sloping down to Lake Geneva, benefits from an invigorating climate all year round. The morning sun bathes the spaciously comfortable guestrooms with soft light and guests can contemplate the lake and the snow-capped peaks from a private balcony. Enjoy hunting, fishing or hiking, then savour inventive, light cuisine and excellent Swiss and French wines.

Visa

CHF : Swiss franc

www.relaischateaux.fr/victoria

HOSTELLERIE ALPENROSE

Switzerland

CH-3778 Schönried-Gstaad
(Berne)

Tel. : (41) (033) 744 67 67
Fax : (41) (033) 744 67 12
E-mail : alpenrose@relaischateaux.fr

From Geneva, Lausanne, N 12 exit Bulle, then Saanen, towards Zweisimmen.

Owners :
M. von Siebenthal Family
Weekly closing :
Rest. : Monday and Tuesday noon
Annual closing :
From mid-Oct. to mid-December

 Geneva (**Intl**) 120 km
Zurich (**Intl**) 150 km

 Menus **50-130 CHF** s.i.
Carte **25-120 CHF** s.i.

 14 rooms
130-460 CHF s.i.

 4 suites
320-510 CHF s.i.

 included

 yes (extra cost)

 2 km

With its flower-bedecked terraces, this chalet has a timeless quality. For three generations, the von Sieberthal family have welcomed guests in this small paradise in the heart of the skiing and hiking area surrounding Gstaad-Saanen. The spacious rooms, resplendent with pinewood panelling, feature private balconies with a superb view of the glaciers. Enjoy a candlelight dinner, savouring French cuisine and local specialities enhanced by excellent Swiss and French wines.

285

www.relaischateaux.fr/alpenrose

CHF : Swiss franc

GRAND HOTEL PARK

SINCE 1993

Tel. : (41) (033) 748 98 00
Fax : (41) (033) 748 98 08
E-mail : grandpark@relaischateaux.fr

CH-3780 Gstaad
(Bern)

Switzerland

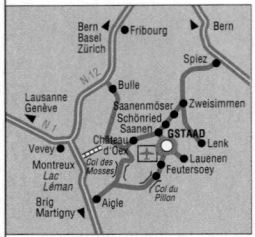

From Geneva, N1 towards Lausanne, N 12 Fribourg, exit Bulle, Château d'Oex, Gstaad.

Owners : Theo Gerlach Family
Directors :
Jan and Regula Brucker
Annual closing :
April to May and
October to mid-December

✈	Geneva (**Intl**) 160 km
🍴	Menus **50-150 CHF** s.i. Carte **25-120 CHF** s.i.
⚬⇁	82 rooms **300-910 CHF** s.i.
8⇁	11 suites **765-1 760 CHF** s.i.
🍷	included
🇭	yes (extra cost)
⏏	10 km

Thalassatherapy, shiatsu, beauty treatments and plastic surgery.

The Luxurious Grand Hotel Park is superbly equipped with every modern convenience yet retains an elegant and traditional ambience. Rooms and luxury suites. Restaurants Le Grill, Le Grand Restaurant, Le Greenhouse with winter garden and south terrace, saltwater pool, sauna, steam-bath, massage, fango, beauty salon and relaxation centre, hairdresser, garden with heated pool and tennis.

 Visa

CHF : Swiss franc

www.relaischateaux.fr/grandpark

GRANDHOTEL SCHÖNEGG

Switzerland

CH-3920 Zermatt
(Valais)

Tel. : (41) (027) 967 44 88
Fax : (41) (027) 967 58 08
E-mail : schonegg@relaischateaux.fr

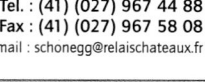

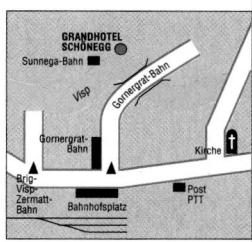

In Täsch, leave your car in the parking lot then train or taxi (10-15 mn) to Zermatt (hotel shuttle).

Owners : Konrad Metry Family
Annual closing :
Hotel: from April 25th
to June 1st and from October 6th
to November 30th
Rest.: from April 25th to
June 20th and from September
15th to December 15th

A fter being picked up at the station by the hotel car, guests are whisked up into the mountains to this picturesque chalet where flower-bedecked balconies offer stunning views of the Matterhorn. Enjoy an invigorating day on the ski slopes, then relax in a sauna before enjoying a romantic candlelit dinner. Impeccable service, refined cuisine and exceptional Valais wines will make your stay unforgettable.

Geneva (**Intl**) 234 km
Sion 73 km

GPS N 46° 01' 49"
E 07° 45' 20"

Menus **52-125 CHF** s.i.
Carte **52-110,50 CHF** s.i.

34 rooms
270-510 CHF s.i.

2 suites
436-750 CHF s.i.

included

yes (extra cost)

www.relaischateaux.fr/schonegg

CHF : Swiss franc

Visa

CASTELLO DEL SOLE

SINCE 1985

Tel. : (41) (091) 791 02 02
Fax : (41) (091) 792 11 18
E-mail : castellosole@relaischateaux.fr

CH-6612 Ascona
(Tessin)

Switzerland

*From Lucern, N2, towards
Bellinzona, exit Bellinzona sud,
towards Locarno.*

Owner : Terreni alla Maggia SA
Director : Bruno Kilchenmann
Annual closing :
From Nov. 1st to March 24th

✈	Lugano (**Intl**) 40 km Milan (**Intl**) 110 km
🍴	Menus **65-90 CHF** s.i. Carte **45-120 CHF** s.i.
⚷	64 rooms **480-620 CHF** s.i.
⚷	15 suites **720-1 400 CHF** s.i.
☕	included
🐕	no
♪	Driving-range, private putting green, Ascona golf course 2 km

This elegant 18th-century residence, a
marvel of ochre and terracotta stone,
nestles amidst 20 acres of luxuriant
parkland. This idyllic holiday paradise
offers a private beach on Lago Maggiore
and unlimited sporting activities. Relax in
the comfortable guestrooms or the
elegant drawing room hung with works of
art, sip an aperitif in the piano bar, then
savour French and Italian cuisine at the
«Locanda Barbarossa».

292

Visa

CHF : Swiss franc

www.relaischateaux.fr/castellosole

ALBERGO GIARDINO

Switzerland

Via Segnale 10
CH-6612 Ascona
(Tessin)

Tel. : (41) (091) 785 88 88
Fax : (41) (091) 785 88 99
E-mail : giardino@relaischateaux.fr

Highway N2 via Gotthard,
towards Bellinzona, exit South
Bellinzona, towards Locarno.

Owner : Albergo Giardino S.A.
Director : Hans C. Leu
Annual closing :
From mid-Nov. to mid-March

The exquisitely romantic guestrooms in this Mediterranean country home are bathed in the scent of flowers wafting up from the exotic gardens. Enjoy an aperitif by the water-lily covered pond, then choose between refined gourmet cuisine at the Ristorante Aphrodite or more traditional Italian fare at the Osteria. Relish excellent Tessin wines and enjoy open-air performances beneath the stars at the «Théâtre Giardino».

Lugano (**Intl**) 40 km
Milan (**Intl**) 110 km

GPS N 46° 09' 39"
E 08° 52' 43"

Menus **59-115 CHF** s.i.
Carte **60-115 CHF** s.i.

54 rooms
590-630 CHF s.i.

18 suites
800-840 CHF s.i.

included

yes (**35 CHF** s.i./day)

1 km

www.relaischateaux.fr/giardino

CHF : Swiss franc

293

VILLA MARGHERITA

SINCE 1986

Tel. : (41) (091) 611 51 11
Fax : (41) (091) 611 51 10
E-mail : margherita@relaischateaux.fr

CH-6935 Bosco Luganese
(Tessin)

Switzerland

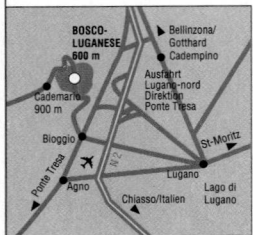

From the N2, exit Lugano north, towards Ponte Tresa, right at the 1st light, after round about towards Cademario.

Owners :
Herzog and Poretti Families
Director :
Margherita Poretti-Herzog
Annual closing :
From October 26th to Easter

✈	Lugano (**Intl**) 6 km Milan (**Intl**) 80 km
🍴	Menus **72-96 CHF** s.i. Carte **40-96 CHF** s.i.
⚷	26 rooms **344-500 CHF** s.i.
⚷	7 suites starting at **520 CHF** s.i.
☕	included
⚗	yes (extra cost) except rest.
♪	Magliaso 10 km

The red-tiled roofs and white walls of this 18th-century belvedere villa and its residences overlook the picturesque countryside surrounding Lugano. The cool, spacious rooms, bathed in early morning sunlight, open out onto the picturesque «Green Path» wending its way through the magnificent park. Dine in the midst of this lush Mediterranean vegetation, in a restaurant serving delicious regional dishes and choice wines.

     Visa

CHF : Swiss franc

www.relaischateaux.fr/margherita

SINCE 2000

VILLA PRINCIPE LEOPOLDO & RESIDENCE

Switzerland

Via Montalbano, 5
CH-6900 Lugano
(Tessin)

Tel. : (41) (091) 985 88 55
Fax : (41) (091) 985 88 25
E-mail : leopoldo@relaischateaux.fr

Leave the motorway at Lugano south, follow signs to Lago. Stay on the left side of the road, at the first traffic lights turn left, towards Ponte Tresa. At the second traffic lights, turn left and follow signs for the hotel.

Owners : GEAL SA
Director : Maurice R.L. Urech
Open all year

This magnificent villa, built for Prince Leopold Von Hohenzollern in 1868, is set on the beautiful Collina d'Oro, overlooking the sparkling waters of Lake Lugano. The splendours of the Belle Epoque are still evident in the luxurious suites and the sumptuous drawing room decorated with marble fireplaces and works of art. Enjoy traditional Swiss hospitality and savour refined cuisine enhanced by superb Piedmontese wines.

✈ Lugano (**Intl**) 5 km

🍴 Menus **59-110 CHF** s.i.
Carte **26-68 CHF** s.i.

⚷ 71 rooms
440-700 CHF s.i.

⚷ 4 suites
1 000-1 800 CHF s.i.

🍷 included

yes (extra cost)

on site

Hiking, climbing, sailing, mountain-biking.

CHF : Swiss franc

Visa

RESTAURANT JÖHRI'S TALVO

Tel. : (41) (081) 833 44 55
Fax : (41) (081) 833 05 69
E-mail : talvo@relaischateaux.fr

Via Gunels 15
CH-7512 St. Moritz/Champfèr
(Grisons)

Switzerland

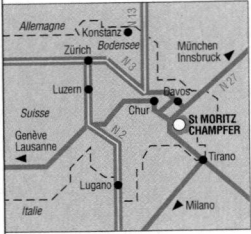

From Italy, Silvaplana, towards St. Moritz, follow signs to Suvretta/Champfèr.

Owners :
Roland and Brigitte Jöhri
Weekly closing :
Monday (except holidays) and
Tuesday (summer low season)
Annual closing :
From mid-April to mid-June and
mid-October to mid-December

 Zurich (**Intl**) 180 km
Samedan 10 km

 Menus **52-195 CHF** s.i.
Carte **80-100 CHF** s.i.

 no

 nearby

Skiing, polo, hunting,
windsurfing...

On the edge of Saint-Moritz, this fine 17th century Graubünden house with its sunny terrace, decorated porch and wooden shutters is the meeting place of all enlightened gourmets. Roland and Brigitte Jöhri's infectious good humour creates an ideal setting in which to enjoy the delicious combination of French gastronomy and regional specialities. Open all day with a wide variety of dishes and a heavenly wine list.

CHF : Swiss franc

www.relaischateaux.fr/talvo

HOTEL WALTHER

Switzerland

CH-7504 Pontresina
(Grisons)

Tel. : (41) (081) 842 64 71
Fax : (41) (081) 842 79 22
E-mail : walther@relaischateaux.fr

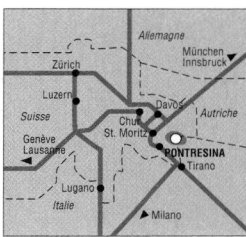

To 8 km from St Moritz.

Owners : Walther Family
Directors :
Thomas and Anne-Rose Walther
Annual closing :
From April 10th to June 10th and
from Oct. 8th to December 16th

 Zurich (**Intl**) 220 km
Samedan 6 km

 Menus **65-100 CHF** s.i.
Carte **60-90 CHF** s.i.

 64 rooms
370-620 CHF s.i.

 9 suites
half board
550-950 CHF s.i.

 included

 yes (extra cost)

 6 km

Hiking, mountain-biking,
all winter sports.

This magnificent baroque manor, perched at 1,800 metres in the Engadine mountains, is set amidst some of the most stunning Swiss countryside. With its modern comfort and the warm hospitality of its owners, Hotel Walther offers you perfectly relaxing holidays in summer as in winter. The light, inventive cuisine which changes with the seasons is accompanied by the finest Swiss, French and Italian vintages.

www.relaischateaux.fr/walther

CHF : Swiss franc

Visa

HOTEL HAUS PARADIES

Tel. : (41) (081) 861 08 08
Fax : (41) (081) 861 08 09
E-mail : paradies@relaischateaux.fr

CH-7551 Ftan
(Grisons)

Switzerland

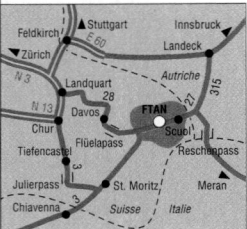

From Landeck (Austria), exit at Scuol; mountain road towards Ftan.

Owners : Paradies Touristik A.G.
(Rahe and Schmittner Families)
Directors :
Waltraud and Eduard Hitzberger
Annual closing :
From mid-April to the end of May
and from the end of October
to mid-December

✈	Zurich (**Intl**) 210 km Samedan 50 km
⑪	Menus **63-170 CHF** s.i. Carte **65-140 CHF** s.i.
☦	20 rooms single **230-265 CHF** s.i. double **330-440 CHF** s.i.
☦	6 suites **520-790 CHF** s.i.
☕	**20 CHF** s.i.
☂	yes (except restaurant)
♫	6 km

Health centre.

S urrounded by picturesque forests and green or snow-covered meadows depending on the season, this elegant hotel lives up to its name. Its rooms are bright and furnished with impeccable taste, some offering South-facing balconies drenched in summer sun. Enjoy the superb traditional cuisine at «La Bellezza» restaurant or the local specialities in the 150-year-old «Stüva Paradis» dining room. This is the perfect retreat for nature lovers who seek a gourmet experience in a haven of peace.

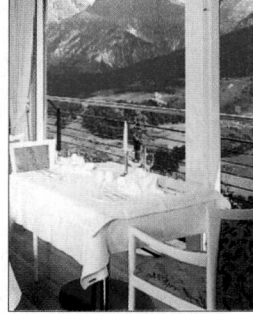

Visa

CHF : Swiss franc

SCHLOSSHOTEL CHASTÈ

Switzerland

CH-7553 Tarasp Sparsels
(Grisons)

Tel. : (41) (081) 864 17 75
Fax : (41) (081) 864 99 70
E-mail : chaste@relaischateaux.fr

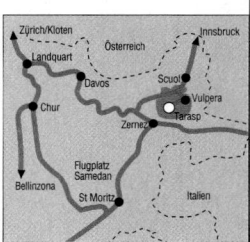

*From Zurich via Landquart-Davos,
Col de Flüela, exit before Scuol.
From Landeck (Austria) last exit
before Scuol, mountain road
towards Tarasp Vulpera.*

Owners :
Daniela and Rudolf Pazeller
Weekly closing :
Rest. : Monday and Tuesday
Annual closing :
From April 1st to May 27th
and from Oct. 22nd to Dec. 22nd

 Zurich (**Intl**) 210 km
Samedan 50 km

 Menus **65-120 CHF** s.i.
Carte **45-80 CHF** s.i.

 13 rooms
240-280 CHF s.i.

 7 suites
280-380 CHF s.i.

 18-22 CHF s.i.

 yes (except rest.) extra cost

 3 km

This picturesque engadin house, covered in snow throughout winter and bedecked with flowers in summer, is a tribute to the finest Swiss woodwork. Cross its charming threshold and discover a cosy ambience in which your attentive hosts, the Pazellers, do their utmost to ensure your well-being. An invigorating stroll through the idyllic countryside will whet your appetite for the Pazellers' delicious traditional cuisine.

www.relaischateaux.fr/chaste

CHF : Swiss franc

Visa

JAQUET-DROZ

MAITRE HORLOGER

depuis 1758

STILL MADE AS IF IT WERE THE ONLY WRISTWATCH IN THE WORLD

DOUBLE TIME. Man's watch in steel with manually-wound movement in a cambered, tonneau-shaped case. Black dial with an auxiliary 24-hour time display (second time zone). Sapphire-crystal case back, tonneau-shaped movement engraved with a Jaquet-Droz motif. Ref. 5195 JS. CHF 6,900.–.

MONTRES JAQUET-DROZ SA
CH-La Conversion (Switzerland)
Telephone: + 41 21 796 00 70 - Fax: + 41 21 791 63 80

SIMKO

HOTEL WALSERHOF

Switzerland

Landstrasse 141
CH-7250 Klosters
(Grisons)

Tel. : (41) (081) 410 29 29
Fax : (41) (081) 410 29 39
E-mail : walserhof@relaischateaux.fr

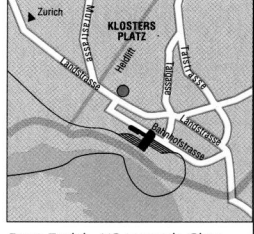

From Zurich, N3 towards Chur,
exit Landquart, towards Davos.

Owners : Beat and Gabi Bolliger
Director : Beat Bolliger
Annual closing :
From April 18th to June 18th
and from October 17th to
December 4th

✈ Zurich (**Intl**) 160 km

🍴 Menus **65-150 CHF** s.i.
Carte **75-180 CHF** s.i.

⚷ 9 rooms
180-360 CHF s.i.

⚷ 6 suites
400-750 CHF s.i.

☕ **24 CHF** s.i.

🐎 yes (extra cost)

🏌 13 km (18 holes)

Horse-riding, sauna, fishing,
climbing, skiing, sailing,
parapenting, sleighing, skating,
moutain-biking.

A stay at the Walserhof means vast fields of snow in winter and long sunny walks in summer. In this beautiful mountain chalet, Beat Bolliger will show you the full extent of his talent. Savour his «millefeuille de volailles fumées au foie de canard» or his «truite aux écailles de pommes de terre sur lentilles», traditional seasonal dishes, spiced with the chef's modernist touch. Fine international wine cellar.

🏃 P 🛗 👫 ↕

301

www.relaischateaux.fr/walserhof

CHF : Swiss franc

Visa

LE REAL

SINCE 1984

Tel. : (423) 232 22 22
Fax : (423) 232 08 91
E-mail : real@relaischateaux.fr

Städtle 21
FL-9490 Vaduz

Liechtenstein

From Zurich, N3, exit Vaduz, towards the centre; under the castle.

Owners : Felix Real Family
Annual closing :
From December 24th to 26th

✈ Altenrhein **(Intl)** 35 km
Zurich **(Intl)** 120 km

🍴 Menus **80-130 CHF** s.i.
Carte **120-160 CHF** s.i.

🔑 10 rooms
195-250 CHF s.i.

🔑 2 suites
330-370 CHF s.i.

☕ included

🐎 yes

⛷ 20 km

Visits : several museums.

The Real family's charming home offers an intimate ambience and generous hospitality. Relax in a comfortable modern guestroom, then descend to the elegant dining room resplendent with white linen and glittering chandeliers. Felix Real's cuisine is considered as one of the finest in the Principality and guests will be enchanted by his delicious local specialities and the remarkable Pinot noir from the family vineyard.

Visa

CHF : Swiss franc

www.relaischateaux.fr / real

PARKHOTEL SONNENHOF

Liechtenstein

Mareestrasse, 29
FL-9490 Vaduz

Tel. : (423) 232 11 92
Fax : (423) 232 00 53
E-mail : sonnenhof@relaischateaux.fr

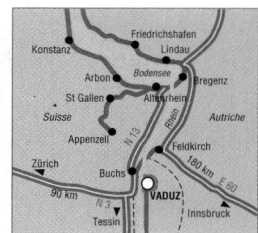

From Zurich, highway towards
Chur, exit Vaduz / Liechtenstein,
towards Schloss Vaduz.

Owners : Emil Real Family
Annual closing :
Hotel : from December 22nd
to January 6th
Rest. : from December 22nd
to February 28th

T his elegant hotel is set in luxuriant parkland overlooking the picturesque town of Vaduz and its medieval castle. The comfortable guestrooms open onto private terraces which offer stunning vistas of the Rhine Valley, the vineyards and the snow-capped peaks of the Swiss Alps. After a luxurious sauna, a dip in the covered pool or a hike through the magnificent countryside, savour seasonal specialities and fine wines.

Altenrhein (**Intl**) 35 km
Zurich (**Intl**) 120 km

Menus **85-160 CHF** s.i.
Carte **72-110 CHF** s.i.

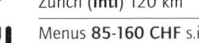 17 rooms
310-400 CHF s.i.

12 suites
starting at **420 CHF** s.i.

included

yes in room only
(extra cost)

25 km

Sauna, hiking...

   303

CHF : Swiss franc

Visa

VINTAGES TO DRINK IN YEAR 2000

GERMANY

Wines recommended by the wine waiters
of the Relais & Châteaux and Relais Gourmands.

* Index of world vintages to drink in year 2000 : page 607

	Name of wine	Wine to enjoy	Noble wine	Outstanding wine
	GERMANY			
White	Weissburgunder, Riesling, Müller-Thurgau	1998	1996	1990
Red	Spätburgunder, Lemberger	1996	1997	1990
Dessert	Riesling, Scheurebe	1995	1990	1989 - 1959

HOTEL STADT HAMBURG

SINCE 1979

Germany

Tel. : (49) (04651) 8580
Fax : (49) (04651) 858220
E-mail : stadthamburg@relaischateaux.fr

Strandstrasse 2
D-25980 Westerland/Sylt
(Schleswig-Holstein)

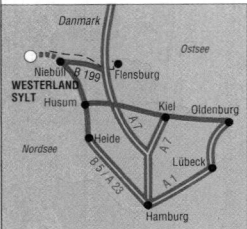

*From Hamburg, A 7 Flensburg,
B 199 Niebüll, a 45 min. crossing.*

Owner : Harald Hentzschel
Director : Bernd Knochenhauer
Open all year

✈ Hamburg **(Intl)** 240 km
Westerland 2 km

🍴 Menus **69-135 DEM** s.i.
35-69 €
Carte **39-62 DEM** s.i.
20-32 €

🔑 50 rooms
325-480 DEM s.i.
166-245 €

🔑 22 suites
520-590 DEM s.i.
266-302 €

☕ 28 DEM s.i.
14 €

🛏 yes (except restaurant)

🧍 5 km

Mountain biking, water sports,
horse-riding.

I magine 40 kilometres of fine sand beaches, a stunning natural landscape of billowing dunes and an invigorating climate. This elegant 19th-century residence, set on a picturesque island in the North Sea, offers idyllic surroundings and supreme comfort. Its charming rooms, decorated with country house furniture and flowers, are havens of calm. Enjoy romantic walks along the shore and savour delightful regional cuisine.

Visa

 DEM : Deutsche Mark

www.relaischateaux.fr/stadthamburg

LANDHAUS SCHERRER

Germany

Elbchaussee 130
D-22763 Hamburg

Tel. : (49) (040) 8801325/8801011
Fax : (49) (040) 8806260
E-mail : scherrer@relaischateaux.fr

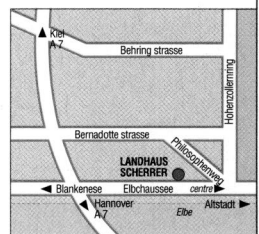

At the corner of Elbchaussee and Hohenzollernring.

Owners : Emmi Scherrer and Heinz Wehmann
Weekly closing : Sunday
Open all year

 Hamburg (**Intl**) 30 km

 Menu lunch (3 courses)
65 DEM s.i.
33 €
Menus **165-198 DEM** s.i.
84-101 €
Carte **45-60 DEM** s.i.
23-31 €

 1 km

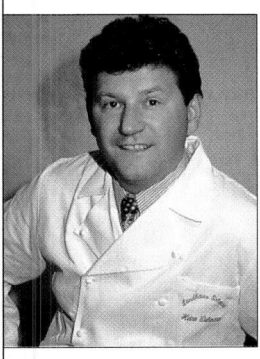

T his magnificent modern restaurant, resplendent with elegant furniture and fine wood panelling, lies on the north bank of the Elbe near Hamburg's Ottensen district. It is in these refined surroundings that master chef Heinz Wehmann creates his gourmet wonders, reinventing the culinary heritage of Northern Germany with inspired talent. Enjoy exquisite courtesy, an excellent cigar service and a superb wine list.

309

HOTEL LOUIS C. JACOB

Tel. : (49) (040) 822550
Fax : (49) (040) 822554 44
E-mail : jacob@relaischateaux.fr

Elbchaussee 401-403
D-22609 Hamburg

Germany

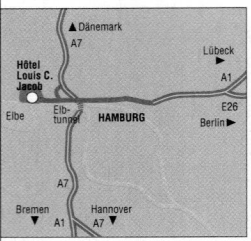

A7 (E3), exit Hamburg/Othmarschen. Walderseestraße towards Blankenese. At the end, turn left in the Reventlowstraße until Elbchaussee, and after right.

Owners : Elbchaussee Immobilienverwaltung Rahe KG
Director : Jost Deitmar
Open all year

✈	Hamburg (**Intl**) 20 km
🍴	Menus **92-145 DEM** s.i. 47-74 € Carte **42-65 DEM** s.i. 21-33 €
⚷	75 rooms **330-580 DEM** s.i. 169-297 €
⚷	11 suites **650-1 500 DEM** s.i. 332-767 €
☕	29 DEM s.i. 15 €
🍴	yes (except restaurant)
🚶	3 km

Located between parks and villas in one of the most elegant quarters of Hamburg, this prestigious hotel has maintained a tradition of hospitality and gastonomy for five generations. Besides the superbly decorated rooms and suites, the famous terrace of linden trees painted by Max Liebermann and the renowned restaurant, guests will enjoy breathtaking views of the river and its boats.

MasterCard · AMERICAN EXPRESS · Diners · Visa

DEM : Deutsche Mark

www.relaischateaux.fr/jacob

Hotel Abtei

Germany

Abteistrasse 1.4
D-20149 Hamburg

Tel. : (49) (040) 442905
Fax : (49) (040) 449820
E-mail : abtei@relaischateaux.fr

*In Hamburg, follow signs
to Zentrum, Hauptbanhof,
Außenalster.*

Owners : Petra and Fritz Lay
Director : Fritz Lay
Weekly closing :
Restaurant : Sunday and Monday
Annual closing :
One week in January
and one week in the summer

This elegant residence, set in a wonderfully calm street near Lake Außenalter, is imbued with 19th century splendour and charm. The sumptuous guestrooms and suites, decorated in luxurious style, overlook a beautiful private garden where guests can breakfast amidst the flowers during the summer months. Hotel Abtei's stylish restaurant features exquisite classical cuisine and excellent Bordeaux.

Hamburg (**Intl**) 5 km

Menus **75-150 DEM** s.i.
38-77 €
Carte **40-55 DEM** s.i.
20-28 €

9 rooms
250-450 DEM s.i.
128-230 €

2 suites
450-500 DEM s.i.
230-256 €

30 DEM s.i.
15 €

yes (extra cost) except rest.

17 km

Polo, sailing.

www.relaischateaux.fr/abtei

DEM : Deutsche Mark

Visa

HOTEL BRANDENBURGER HOF

SINCE 1995

Tel. : (49) (030) 21405-0
Fax : (49) (030) 21405-100
E-mail : brandenburger@relaischateaux.fr

Eislebener Strasse 14
D-10789 Berlin (Wilmersdorf)

Germany

*Berliner Ring (A 110)
exit «Wilmersdorf»,
then «Kurfürstendamm»,
4 km to «Gedächtniskirche».*

Owner : Richard Sauter
Director : Daniela Sauter
Weekly closing :
Restaurant «Die Quadriga» :
Saturday-Sunday
Restaurant «Der Wintergarten» :
open every day
Annual closing :
Restaurant «Die Quadriga» :
from January 1st to 9th
and July 17th to August 20th
Restaurant «Der Wintergarten» :
open all year

Berlin-Tegel **(Intl)** 12 km
Berlin-Schönefeld **(Intl)** 20 km

Menus **125-165 DEM** s.i.
64-84 €
Carte **44-58 DEM** s.i.
22-30 €

78 rooms
single **295-415 DEM** s.i.
151-212 €
double **345-465 DEM** s.i.
176-238 €

4 suites
745 DEM s.i.
381 €

included

yes (extra cost) except rest.

12 km

Polo (15 km), flying club (25 km),
sailing, concerts, massage.

312

Visa

T his magnificient turn-of-the-century manor house is located in a quiet street near the Kurfürstendamm. The interior of the house leaves an impression of timeless elegance and a certain artistic ambition. Many of the rooms, fitted out in the Bauhaus style, overlook the winter garden, an oasis of greenery for unforgettable moments. The «Die Quadriga» restaurant proposes classical Grande Cuisine.

DEM : Deutsche Mark

www.relaischateaux.fr/brandenburger

SCHLOSS HUBERTUSHÖHE

Germany

Robert-Koch-Str. 1
D-15859 Storkow
(Brandenburg)

Tel. : (49) (033678) 430
Fax : (49) (033678) 43100
E-mail : hubertushohe@relaischateaux.fr

By car from Berlin or Potsdam on the A12, exit at Storkow, cross Rieplos, at Storkow follow signs to Beeskow.

Owners :
H.F. and Ph.F. Reemtsma GmbH
Director : Petra Gündel
Weekly closing : Monday
Annual closing : January

✈ Berlin-Schönefeld (**Intl**) 20 km

🍴 Menus **88-135 DEM** s.i.
45-69 €
Carte **92-113 DEM** s.i.
47-58 €

6 0 kms from Berlin on the banks of the magnificent Storkow lake, the hotel awaits you like an oasis of calm and greenery. This splendid turn-of-the-century house, decorated in period style, offers luxurious and refined services. An exceptional moment, enhanced by the superb cuisine of one of today's finest German chefs, Kurt Jäger. The charm and natural surroundings of this setting make it a perfect stopping place.

🔑 18 rooms
210-650 DEM s.i.
107-332 €

🔑 4 suites
490-850 DEM s.i.
251-435 €

🍸 **38 DEM** s.i.
19 €

🍴 yes (extra cost)

♪ 10 km, 2 courses

Hunting, fishing, sailing, kayaking.

313

BÜLOW RESIDENZ

SINCE 1997

Tel. : (49) (0351) 800 30
Fax : (49) (0351) 800 3100
E-mail : bulow@relaischateaux.fr

Rähnitzgasse 19
D-01097 Dresden
(Sachsen)

Germany

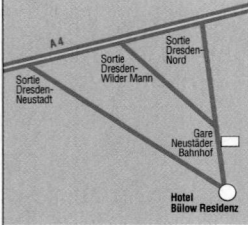

From the airport, take Königsbrücker Landstrasse, follow dir. town centre, at Albertplatz, 1st on the right (Königstrasse), then Dreikönigskirche on the left (Rähnitzgasse).

Owner : Horst Bülow
Director : Ralf J. Kutzner
Annual closing :
From January 2nd to 9th

✈	Klotzsche (**Intl**) 10 km
🍴	Menus 62-148 DEM s.i. **32-76 €** Carte 69-96 DEM s.i. **35-49 €**
🔑	25 rooms single **290 DEM** s.i. **148 €** double 370-390 DEM s.i. **189-199 €**
🔑	5 suites 460-600 DEM s.i. **235-307 €**
☕	25 DEM s.i. **13 €**
🐕	yes (extra cost)
🏌	12 km

The elegant façade of the Bülow Residenz, built in 1730, is a marvel of palatial architecture. This luxury hotel, set in the very heart of Dresden, combines the splendour of bygone days with the utmost in modern comfort. Delicious seasonal cuisine, served in the beautiful courtyard or at the «Caroussel» restaurant, features regional specialities enhanced by the finest French and German vintages.

Visa

DEM : Deutsche Mark

www.relaischateaux.fr/bulow

FÜRSTENHOF CELLE

Germany

Hannoversche Strasse 55/56
D-29221 Celle
(Niedersachsen)

Tel. : (49) (05141) 2010
Fax : (49) (05141) 201120
E-mail : furstenhof@relaischateaux.fr

From the South, A7 exit Celle.
From the North,
A7 exit Soltau-South.

Owners :
Grafen Hardenberg Families
Director : Andreas Schmitt
Open all year

 Hanover (**Intl**) 40 km

 Menus **138-158 DEM** s.i.
71-81 €
Carte **20-69 DEM** s.i.
10-35 €

 71 rooms
245-480 DEM s.i.
125-245 €

 5 suites
345-950 DEM s.i.
176-486 €

 25 DEM s.i.
13 €

 yes (extra cost) except rest.

5 km

Hunting, tennis, biking, fishing,
sauna, theme dinners, theatre,
castles and museums.

This baroque manor containing rooms of historical interest is set in the heart of the medieval town of Celle, shaded by chestnut trees. Its «Endtenfang» restaurant is among the most renowned in Germany and gourmets will appreciate the French cuisine of its talented chef. They will also enjoy «Cucina Casalinga», the Italian cuisine of the «Palio» Taverna & Trattoria, and the culinary compositions «Savoir Vivre» and «Plaisirs de la Table».

Visa

315

HOTEL LANDHAUS AMMANN

SINCE 1987

Tel. : (49) (0511) 830818
Fax : (49) (0511) 8437749
E-mail : ammann@relaischateaux.fr

Hildesheimer Strasse 185
D-30173 Hannover
(Niedersachsen)

Germany

*A 7 exit Hannover-Anderten,
B 65 exit Hannover-Döhren,
turn right towards center.*

Owner : Ammann GmbH
Director : Helmut Ammann
Open all year

✈   Hannover (**Intl**) 25 km

🍴   Menus **98-175 DEM** s.i.
50-89 €
Carte 26-62 DEM s.i.
13-32 €

⚷   12 rooms
275-380 DEM s.i.
141-194 €

⚷   2 suites
370-490 DEM s.i.
189-251 €

☕   27 DEM s.i.
14 €

🐎   yes (except restaurant)

🏇   25 km

Water sports.

H elmut Ammann welcomes guests to
an idyllic haven of calm, set in the
heart of Hannover near the Ellenriede forest
and the Herrenhauser baroque gardens. The
guestrooms in this picturesque cottage,
resplendent with Louis XVI furniture, are
all supremely comfortable and feature
spacious bathrooms. Sip an aperitif on the
romantic atrium terrace, then savour refined
cuisine accompanied by one of the cellar's
800 wines.

Visa

DEM : Deutsche Mark

www.relaischateaux.fr/ammann

BURGHOTEL HARDENBERG

Germany

Im Hinterhaus 11a
D-37176 Nörten-Hardenberg
(Niedersachsen)

Tel. : (49) (05503) 9810
Fax : (49) (05503) 981666
E-mail : hardenberg@relaischateaux.fr

BAB 7 exit Nörten-Hardenberg, go towards Nörten-Hardenberg. Turn left after the service station, turn right after the church, the hotel is 1 km away.

Owner :
Carl Graf von Hardenberg
Director : Ralf O. Leidner
Weekly closing :
Rest. : Sunday
Annual closing : December 24th

N ot far from Göttingen, there is a region of rolling hills and forests: the Bever valley. At the foot of the century-old château of Hardenberg, you will find the elegant 18th century residence the Burghotel. In a festive setting, you will discover the pleasures of nature, rest and modern comfort and for gourmets, those of a flavourful regional cuisine in the Novalis restaurant.

Frankfurt **(Intl)** 250 km
Hannover 100 km

Menus **42,50-125 DEM** s.i.
22-64 €
Carte **67-92 DEM** s.i.
34-47 €

43 rooms
240-300 DEM s.i.
123-153 €

1 suite
350-450 DEM s.i.
179-230 €

included

yes (extra cost)

5 km

317

DEM : Deutsche Mark

HOTEL SCHLOSS WILKINGHEGE

SINCE 1992

Tel. : (49) (0251) 213045
Fax : (49) (0251) 212898
E-mail : wilkinghege@relaischateaux.fr

Steinfurter Strasse 374
D-48159 Münster
(Nordrhein-Westfalen)

Germany

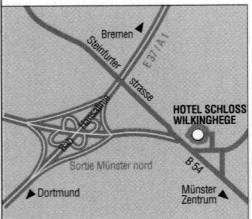

A1, towards Bremen, exit Münster North, towards centre, left at the 2nd light after the exit towards Kinderhaus.

Owner : Lubert Winnecken
Open all year

✈ Münster (**Intl**) 20 km
Düsseldorf (**Intl**) 120 km

🍽 Menus **90-120 DEM** s.i.
46-61 €
Carte **40-48 DEM** s.i.
20-25 €

⚷ 22 rooms
single **195-320 DEM** s.i.
100-164 €
double **270-580 DEM** s.i.
138-297 €

⚷ 13 suites
starting at **350 DEM** s.i.
179 €

☕ included

🐕 yes (extra cost) except rest.

⛳ on the premises (18 holes)

Biking.

This romantic Renaissance château, set in the heart of the magnificent Westphalian countryside, combines modern comfort with a unique historical ambience. Rediscover 16th-century splendour beneath its beautiful white stucco ceilings, as you relax in the elegant rooms hung with silk tapestries and decorated with period furniture. The contemporary cuisine is accompanied by excellent white wines and vintage Bordeaux.

DEM : Deutsche Mark

www.relaischateaux.fr/wilkinghege

HOTEL KRAUTKRÄMER

Germany

Zum Hiltruper See
D-48165 Münster
(Nordrheinwestfalen)

Tel. : (49) (02501) 8050
Fax : (49) (02501) 805104
E-mail : krautkramer@relaischateaux.fr

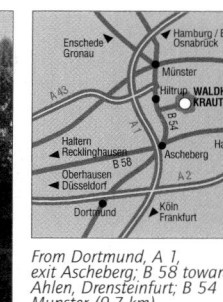

From Dortmund, A 1,
exit Ascheberg; B 58 towards
Ahlen, Drensteinfurt; B 54
Munster (9.7 km).

Owners : Krautkrämer Family
Annual closing : Christmas

✈ Munster (**Intl**) 30 km
Düsseldorf (**Intl**) 120 km

🍽 Menus **55-120 DEM** s.i.
28-61 €
Carte **36-55 DEM** s.i.
18-28 €

⚷ 68 rooms
190-340 DEM s.i.
97-174 €

⚷ 4 suites
450-650 DEM s.i.
230-332 €

☕ included

🐕 yes (extra cost)

♪ 10, between 8 and 20 km

Horseback riding (3 km),
biking, fishing, beauty salon...

The Krautkrämer's luxurious modern guestrooms overlook idyllic natural surroundings. Stroll through the beautiful countryside and visit the region's magnificent «Wasserschlösser» (small castles surrounded by moats) then relax in the sauna or the indoor pool. After an aperitif on the romantic terrace overlooking Lake Hiltrup, enjoy regional specialities enhanced by wines from one of Germany's most outstanding cellars.

www.relaischateaux.fr/krautkramer   DEM : Deutsche Mark   Visa

HOTEL SCHLOSS HUGENPŒT

SINCE 1975

Tel. : (49) (02054) 12040
Fax : (49) (02054) 120450
E-mail : hugenpoet@relaischateaux.fr

August Thyssen Strasse 51
D-45219 Essen (E-Kettwig)
(Nordrheinwestfalen)

Germany

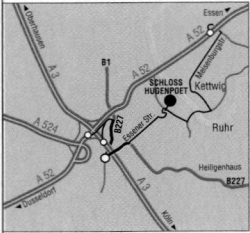

*Take the Rat.-Breitscheid exit
at the Breitscheid interchange
(A3/A52). Take the B227 towards
Velbert, then towards E.-Kettwig.*

Owners : Schloß Hugenpœt
Betiebs GmbH
Directors : Michael Lübbert
and Jürgen Neumann
Open all year

✈ Düsseldorf (**Intl**) 18 km

🍴 Menus **128-168 DEM** s.i.
65-86 €
Carte **45-68 DEM** s.i.
23-35 €

🔑 23 rooms
single **340-380 DEM** s.i.
174-194 €
double **410-495 DEM** s.i.
210-253 €

🔑 2 suites
620-850 DEM s.i.
317-435 €

☕ included

🐕 yes (extra cost) except rest.

🎿 Oefte 5 km

Concerts.

his magnificent Renaissance château, nestling in the picturesque Ruhr Valley, is surrounded by a sea of forest greenery. Guests will be enchanted by the château's historical ambience and its sumptuous interior decor, while gourmets will appreciate the superb cuisine inspired by the finest French traditions. The remarkable cellar, stocked with more than 300 vintages, features some of the finest German white wines.

DEM : Deutsche Mark

www.relaischateaux.fr/hugenpoet

HOTEL RESTAURANT «ZUR TRAUBE»

Germany

Bahnstrasse 47
D-41515 Grevenbroich
(Nordrheinwestfalen)

Tel. : **(49) (02181) 68767**
Fax : **(49) (02181) 61122**
E-mail : zurtraube@relaischateaux.fr

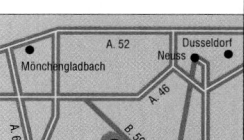

From Dusseldorf, A46 towards Aachen, exit 13, towards the city centre.

Owners :
Dieter and Elvira Kaufmann
Weekly closing :
Sunday and Monday
Annual closing :
From Dec. 20th to January 19th and July 15th to 31st

Behind the magnificent façade of this 19th-century residence lies an elegant dining room renowned as one of Germany's finest restaurants. Gourmets will marvel at Dieter Kaufmann's creative flair and be enchanted by this virtuoso chef's inventions, inspired by traditional French cuisine. The exceptional cellar features over 30,000 vintages and guests can prolong their stay in a stylish room, named after a famous wine.

Düsseldorf (**Intl**) 35 km
Cologne 35 km

Menus **78-188 DEM** s.i.
40-96 €
Carte **49-62 DEM** s.i.
25-32 €

4 rooms
320-410 DEM s.i.
164-210 €

2 suites
starting at **450 DEM** s.i.
230 €

included

no

2 km

www.relaischateaux.fr/zurtraube

DEM : Deutsche Mark

Visa

SCHLOSSHOTEL LERBACH

Tel. : (49) (02202) 2040
Fax : (49) (02202) 204940
E-mail : lerbach@relaischateaux.fr

Lerbacher Weg.
D-51465 Bergisch Gladbach
(Nordrheinwestfalen)

Germany

*A4, towards Olpe,
exit Gladbach-Bensberg
then Bergisch-Gladbach centre.*

Owner : Thomas H. Althoff
Director : Kurt Wagner
Open all year

✈   Cologne-Bonn 25 km

⌖   GPS O 7° 9' 15"
    N 50° 58' 50"

🍴   Menus **99-210 DEM** s.i.
    45-107 €
    Carte **102-145 DEM** s.i.
    52-74 €

⌗   42 rooms
    390-700 DEM s.i.
    199-358 €

⌗   12 suites
    790-1 300 DEM s.i.
    404-665 €

☕   included

🛏   yes (extra cost)

🏃   5 km

L eave the toil of everyday life behind you and follow the winding alley through this magnificent estate to the manor, to enjoy a peaceful, delightful stay, bearing in mind that «Everyone is entitled to a dream come true». The chef, Dieter Müller, renowned for his refined gastronomy, celebrates an aroma-based French Nouvelle Cuisine, while serving the best wines from the most prestigious wine-growing regions.

Visa

DEM : Deutsche Mark

www.relaischateaux.fr/lerbach

HOTEL HOHENHAUS

Germany

D-37293 Herleshausen-Holzhausen
(Hessen)

Tel. : (49) (05654) 9870
Fax : (49) (05654) 1303
E-mail : hohenhaus@relaischateaux.fr

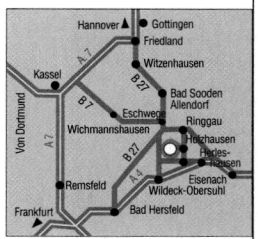

From Bad Hersfeld, A4 towards
Eisenach, exit Herleshausen,
or Wildeck-Obersuhl, B400.

Owner : Hohenhaus GmbH
Director : Hannes Horsch
Weekly closing :
Rest.: Sunday evening, Monday
and Tuesday noon
Open all year

Nestling in a wooded valley, just a few miles from Eisenach, the birthplace of Bach and Luther, this elegant family manor offers comfortable guestrooms, decorated in a contemporary style. Relax in the indoor pool where wide bay windows overlook acres of unspoilt countryside, then enjoy an aperitif in front of a roaring fire. Savour seasonal specialities of the region accompanied by a vast collection of German wines.

✈ Erfurt **(Intl)** 80 km
   Frankfurt **(Intl)** 180 km

🛬 GPS N 50° 58' - E 10° 18'

🍴 Menus **80-150 DEM** s.i.
   41-77 €
   Carte **55-100 DEM** s.i.
   28-51 €

🔑 26 rooms
   300-380 DEM s.i.
   153-194 €

☕ 25 DEM s.i.
   13 €

🐾 yes (extra cost) except rest.

♫ 10 and 45 km

www.relaischateaux.fr/hohenhaus

DEM : Deutsche Mark

323

JOHANN LAFER'S STROMBURG

SINCE 1997

Tel. : (49) (06724) 93100
Fax : (49) (06724) 931090
E-mail : johannlafer@relaischateaux.fr

D-55442 Stromberg
(Rheinland-Pfalz)

Germany

A 61 - Cologne - Ludwigshafen, exit Stromburg, follow the Johann Lafers Stromburg signs for 1 kilometre.

Owner : Johann Lafer
Director : Silvia Buchholz-Lafer
Weekly closing :
Restaurant «Le Val d'Or» : Monday
Open all year

✈ Frankfurt (**Intl**) 75 km

🍴 Menus **169-198 DEM** s.i.
86-101 €
Carte **42-69 DEM** s.i.
21-35 €

🔑 13 rooms
180-380 DEM s.i.
92-194 €

🔑 1 suite
800 DEM s.i.
409 €

☕ 29 DEM s.i.
15 €

🎋 yes (extra cost)

⚓ 1,5 km

T his elegant château, set amidst idyllic natural surroundings in a landscape dotted with mountains and rivers, offers charming, comfortable rooms and exceptional hospitality. The «Val d'Or» restaurant is renowned for the chef's inventive specialities which include the extraordinary «Singapurnudeln mit Hummer Wan Tan, Frühlingsrolle von Edelfischen und Scampi in Kartoffelspaghetti». A veritable gourmet paradise!

324

Visa

DEM : Deutsche Mark

www.relaischateaux.fr/johannlafer

HOTEL BURG WERNBERG

Germany

Schlossberg 10
D-92533 Wernberg-Köblitz
(Bayern)

Tel. : (49) (09604) 939 0
Fax : (49) (09604) 939 139
E-mail : burgwernberg@relaischateaux.fr

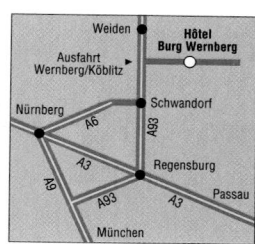

From the A93, take the Wernberg-Köblitz exit in the direction of Wernberg-Köblitz centre. After the yellow church turn right, after 200 m turn left uphill towards the castle.

Owner : Klaus Conrad
Director : Dieter Rehm
Weekly closing :
Rest. «Kastell» :
Monday and Tuesday
Annual closing :
3 weeks in January

This 12th century historical site in the Bayern region, fully restored with all the modern comforts, offers you a romantic and unique setting for your stay. Perched on a hill and flanked by feudal turrets, the château will astound you with its gothic rooms, vaulted dining room and contrapuntal design touches. Guests who appreciate fine cuisine will savour the candlelight dinners prepared with sublime regional products.

 Munich (**Intl**) 180 km
Nurenberg 85 km

 Menus **110-125 DEM** s.i.
56-64 €
Carte **50-90 DEM** s.i.
26-46 €

 25 rooms
230-350 DEM s.i.
118-179 €

 5 suites
450-650 DEM s.i.
230-332 €

 30 DEM s.i.
15 €

 yes (extra cost)

10 km

Hunting, fishing, hiking, canoeing, biking.

DEM : Deutsche Mark

325

PFLAUMS POSTHOTEL PEGNITZ

SINCE 1981

Tel. : (49) (09241) 7250
Fax : (49) (09241) 80404
E-mail : pflaums@relaischateaux.fr

Nürnberger Strasse 8-16
D-91257 Pegnitz
(Bayern)

Germany

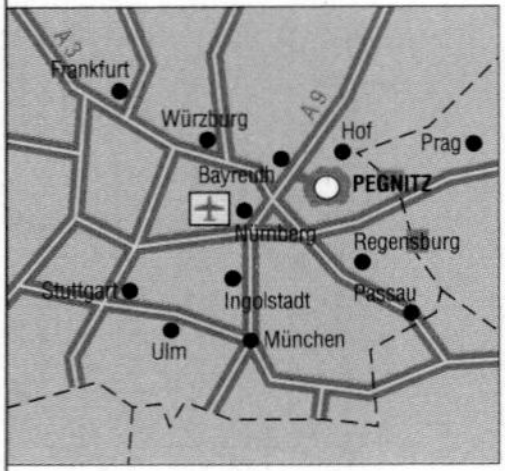

Take the A3 from Frankfurt to the Nuremberg interchange, then follow the A9 towards Berlin. Take the Pegniz exit after 5 km.

Owners :
Andreas and Hermann Pflaum
Director : Andreas Pflaum
Open all year

Nuremberg (**Intl**) 57 km
Bayreuth 27 km

GPS N 49° 45′ 48″
E 11° 54′ 34″

Menus **59-165 DEM** s.i.
30-84 €
Carte **28-55 DEM** s.i.
14-28 €

7 rooms
175-590 DEM s.i.
89-302 €

26 suites
395-1 800 DEM s.i.
202-920 €

28 DEM s.i.
14 €

yes (extra cost)

10 km (27 holes)

Art and Design Gallery, free car service to the Bayreuth Festival Hall, helicopter shuttle, exhibition of Hanover, art gallery, Modern Art museum, billiards, polo, fly fishing, beauty salon 24 hours a day.

Behind the picturesque façade of this 18th-century inn discover the stunning contemporary design which earned the Posthotel Pegnitz the 1991 Gold Award in New York. Wagner aficionados will be delighted to find works by their favourite composer performed at special musical soirées, while gourmets will be enchanted by a symphony of culinary delights. The hotel is also an idyllic retreat for golf and fly-fishing.

Visa

DEM : Deutsche Mark

www.relaischateaux.fr/pflaums

SCHWEIZER STUBEN

Germany

Geiselbrunnenweg, 11
D-97877 Wertheim-Bettingen
(Baden-Württemberg)

Tel. : (49) (09342) 3070
Fax : (49) (09342) 307155
E-mail : stuben@relaischateaux.fr

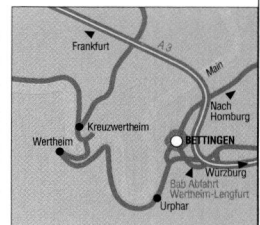

From Frankfurt, A 3, exit Wertheim-Lengfurt, follow signs to «Tennis-Hotel».

Owner : Adalbert Schmitt
Directors : Schmitt Family
Open all year

✈ Frankfurt (**Intl**) 95 km
Nuremberg (**Intl**) 130 km

GPS N 49° 46' 56"
E 9° 33' 62"

🍴 Menus 145-185 DEM s.i.
74-95 €
Carte 85-135 DEM s.i.
43-69 €

⚷ 22 rooms
single 240-400 DEM s.i.
123-205 €
double 290-450 DEM s.i.
148-230 €

⚷ 11 suites
single starting at
470 DEM s.i.
240 €
double starting at
520 DEM s.i.
266 €

☕ included

🛁 yes (extra cost)

⛳ Golf Club
Main-Spessart 9 km
(18 holes)

Sauna, tanning salon, beauty salon, mountain-biking...

This is an idyllic gourmet retreat. Tillmann Hahnn, one of Europe's greatest chefs, is renowned for his innovative cuisine. Drawing on present gastronomy, the «Schweizer Stuben» creates dishes that will enchant you by their diverse inspiration. Guests can also enjoy Italian specialities at the «La Vigna» tavern and Swiss cuisine in the cozy «Schober» restaurant. Relax in the pool, enjoy tennis or golf.

327

DEM : Deutsche Mark

Visa

DER SCHAFHOF AMORBACH

Tel. : (49) (09373) 97330
Fax : (49) (09373) 4120
E-mail : schafhof@relaischateaux.fr

D-63916 Amorbach
(Bayern)

Germany

On the B47, reach Amorch-West, then turn left and follow the signs. Before Amorsbrunner chapel, follow the road to the left along the edge of the forest to Schafhof.

Owner : Dr. Lothar Winkler
Director : Ralf-Peter Spietz
Open all year

 Frankfurt (**Intl**) 80 km

 Menus 50-150 DEM s.i.
26-77 €
Carte 60-100 DEM s.i.
31-51 €

 19 rooms
single 190-250 DEM s.i.
97-128 €
double 240-300 DEM s.i.
123-153 €

 4 suites
450-500 DEM s.i.
230-256 €

 25 DEM s.i.
13 €

 yes (only at the restaurant)

18-27 holes / 15 km

Outdoor chess, ping-pong, pétanque, sauna, solarium, tennis court, organ recitals...

This superb 18th-century residence, once a Benedictine abbey, is set amidst acres of meadows and forests near the baroque village of Amorbach. Enjoy the exceptional hospitality of the Winkler family in this idyllic country retreat where the rooms are elegantly furnished in rustic style. Stroll through the Odenwald or enjoy a romantic carriage ride, then savour typical Franconian cuisine and fine wines at the «Abtstube».

Visa

DEM : Deutsche Mark

www.relaischateaux.fr/schafhof

HOTEL DEIDESHEIMER HOF

Germany

Am Marktplatz
D-67146 Deidesheim
(Rheinland-Pfalz)

Tel. : (49) (06326) 96870
Fax : (49) (06326) 7685
E-mail : deidesheimer@relaischateaux.fr

From Bad Dürkheim or Neustadt, follow the wine route (B 271) to Deidesheim.

Owners : Artur and Anita Hahn
Directors : Manfred Schwarz, Norbert Stadler
Weekly closing :
«Schwarzer Hahn»: Sunday and Monday, from January 1st to 6th and from July 5th to August 25th
Open all year

This beautiful Renaissance manor house, overlooking the most picturesque market square in the region, welcomes a distinguished clientele to its charming country ambience. Exquisite regional cuisine is served in the «St. Urban» tavern, while in the elegant «Schwarzer Hahn» virtuoso chef Manfred Schwarz conjures up gastronomic delights for appreciative gourmets. The cellar is a veritable treasure trove.

✈ Frankfurt (**Intl**) 90 km

🍴 Menus 68-174 DEM s.i. **35-89 €**
Carte 25-62 DEM s.i. **13-32 €**

🛏 18 rooms 240-295 DEM s.i. **123-151 €**

🔑 3 suites 360-470 DEM s.i. **184-240 €**

☕ 20 DEM s.i. **10 €**

🐎 yes (extra cost)

🏃 10 km

329

DEM : Deutsche Mark   Visa

WALD & SCHLOSSHOTEL

SINCE 1965

Tel. : (49) (07941) 60870
Fax : (49) (07941) 61468
E-mail : waldschloss@relaischateaux.fr

D-74639 Friedrichsruhe-Zweiflingen
(Baden-Württemberg)

Germany

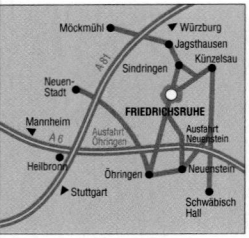

A6 – exit Öhringen; cross the town, then follow signs for Friedrichsruhe (6 km).

Owner : Fürst Kraft zu Hohenlohe-Œhringen
Director : Lothar Eiermann
Open all year

✈	Stuttgart (**Intl**) 80 km
🍴	Menus **80-200 DEM** s.i. **41-102 €** Carte **45-75 DEM** s.i. **23-38 €**
🔑	28 rooms **245-370 DEM** s.i. **125-189 €**
🔑	16 suites **440-650 DEM** s.i. **225-332 €**
☕	25-40 DEM s.i. **13-20 €**
🐕	yes (extra cost)
⛳	18 holes (on the premises)

Sauna, beauty salon, hunting, walks...

Three elegant residences await you, nestling in a magnificent 7-acre park. Combining the charms of an unusual habitat and exquisite menus, Prince Zu Hohenlohe-Œhringen's former summer palace and hunting pavillion have become one of Germany's most renowned gourmet retreats. Savour sublime fish and game specialities and extraordinary desserts and discover the excellent Verrenberg, a wine from the estate's vineyard.

Visa

DEM : Deutsche Mark

www.relaischateaux.fr/waldschloss

MÖNCH'S POSTHOTEL

Germany

Dobler Strasse 2
D-76328 Bad Herrenalb
(Baden-Württemberg)

Tel. : (49) (07083) 7440
Fax : (49) (07083) 744122
E-mail : monchs@relaischateaux.fr

On the A5 from Basel,
take the Rastatt, Gernsbach,
Bad Herrenhalb exit;
from Frankfurt, take the
Karlsruhe, Bad Herrenhalb exit.

Owner : Hubert Mönch
Open all year

✈ Strasbourg (**Intl**) 90 km
Frankfurt (**Intl**) 170 km

🍴 Menus **45-90 DEM** s.i.
23-46 €
Carte **28-45 DEM** s.i.
14-23 €

 18 rooms
150-325 DEM s.i.
77-166 €

6 suites
355-420 DEM s.i.
182-215 €

included

yes

1 km

Fitness room, beauty salon.

This picturesque residence, built as a monastery in 1148, retains all the splendour and traditional charm of the era when it was converted into a luxurious royal post house. Today the fifth generation of owners welcome guests to supremely comfortable rooms overlooking a swimming pool set in a luxuriant park. Enjoy renowned gourmet cuisine at the «Klosterschänke» or savour Mediterannean delights at the «Locanda».

HOTEL VILLA HAMMERSCHMIEDE

SINCE 1996

Tel. : (49) (07240) 601 0
Fax : (49) (07240) 601 60
E-mail : hammerschmiede@relaischateaux.fr

Hauptstrasse 162
D-76327 Pfinztal-Söllingen
(Baden-Württemberg)

Germany

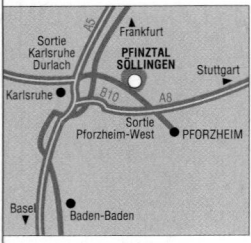

From Frankfurt, A5 towards Bâle,
exit Karlsruhe-Durlach,
B10 towards Pforzheim,
500 m after exit Pfinztal-Söllingen.

Owner : Norbert Schwalbe
Directors :
Annette Schwalbe-Feldmann
and Sebastian Feldmann
Open all year

✈ Baden-Baden (**Intl**) 50 km
Stuttgart (**Intl**) 70 km

🍽 Menus **75-165 DEM** s.i.
38-84 €
Carte **80-110 DEM** s.i.
41-56 €

🔑 25 rooms
258-368 DEM s.i.
132-188 €

🔑 1 suite
698 DEM s.i.
357 €

☕ **27 DEM** s.i.
14 €

🍴 yes (extra cost)

🏊 8 km

E njoy the exceptional hospitality of the Schwalbe family at this splendid Art Nouveau villa, set between Heidelberg and Baden-Baden. The elegant rooms, many furnished in sumptuous Italian Art Deco style, are havens of comfort. Relax in the extraordinary pool dug into rock, then savour refined seasonal cuisine and exceptional wines in the English winter garden or beneath the restaurant's superb vaulted ceiling.

 Visa

DEM : Deutsche Mark

www.relaischateaux.fr/hammerschmiede

HOTEL BAREISS

Germany

Gärtenbühlweg 14
D-72270 Baiersbronn-Mitteltal
(Baden-Württemberg)

Tel. : (49) (07442) 470
Fax : (49) (07442) 47320
E-mail : bareiss@relaischateaux.fr

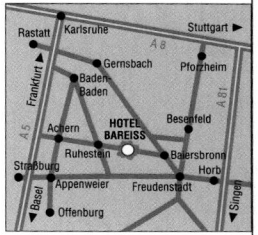

A 5 - exit Rastatt,
Murg valley, Baiersbronn.
A 81, exit Horb, Freudenstadt.

Owner : Hermann Bareiss
Weekly closing :
Restaurant «Bareiss» : Monday and
Tuesday, from June 26th to July 28th
and from November 20th
to December 24th
Open all year

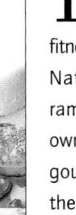

T his paradise in the heart of the Black Forest offers saunas, jacuzzis, pools, a fitness and beauty centre and balneotherapy. Nature lovers will appreciate country rambles, while children will adore their own house, the «Villa Kunterbunt». As for gourmets, they will enjoy the cuisine at the «Dorfstuben» and «Kaminstube» and relish the gastronomic delights of the «Bareiss», one of the ten best restaurants in Germany.

 Strasbourg (**Intl**) 70 km
Stuttgart (**Intl**) 120 km

 Menus 158-189 DEM s.i.
81-97 €
Carte 100-120 DEM s.i.
51-61 €

 45 rooms
440-610 DEM s.i.
225-312 €

 55 suites
starting at 550 DEM s.i.
281 €

 included

 yes (extra cost) rooms only

12 km

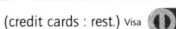

333

RESTAURANT SCHWARZWALDSTUBE

SINCE 1984

Tel. : (49) (07442) 4920
Fax : (49) (07442) 492692
E-mail : schwarzwaldstube@relaischateaux.fr

Hotel Traube Tonbach, Tonbachstrasse 237
D-72270 Baiersbronn-Tonbach
(Baden-Württemberg)

Germany

*From Strasbourg, Karlsruhe
highway, exit Achern,
Rühestein pass, Baiersbronn.*

Owner : Heiner Finkbeiner
Weekly closing :
Rest. : Monday and Tuesday
(except holidays)
Annual closing :
Rest. : from Jan. 10th to Feb. 4th
and from August 3rd to 27th

✈ Strasbourg (**Intl**) 80 km
Stuttgart (**Intl**) 100 km

🍴 Menus **170-215 DEM** s.i.
87-110 €
Carte **100-120 DEM** s.i.
51-61 €

🐎 yes

🏇 Freudenstadt 10 km

Ride in a horse and carriage,
hiking, fitness.

Gourmets flock to this sumptuous restaurant to savour Harald Wohlfahrt's culinary marvels, inspired by the finest French tradition. The «chartreuse de radis noirs aux truffes noires et au foie gras d'oie, beurre de truffes» is sublime and the «saumon d'Ecosse en croustillant de légumes sur un coulis de tomates au coriandre» a veritable masterpiece. With an exceptional wine list and impeccable service, the Schwarzwaldstube is a gastronomic experience you will never forget.

DEM : Deutsche Mark

www.relaischateaux.fr/schwarzwaldstube

KUR-UND SPORTHOTEL DOLLENBERG

Germany

Dollenberg 3
D-77740 Bad Peterstal - Griesbach
(Baden-Württemberg)

Tel. : (49) (07806) 78-0
Fax : (49) (07806) 1272
E-mail : dollenberg@relaischateaux.fr

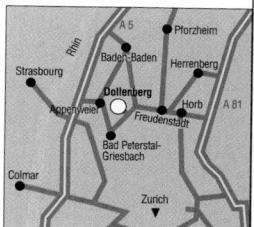

From Frankfurt and Basel:
A5 exit Appenweier, turn left
100 metres after Bad Griesbach.
From Stuttgart: A 81, exit Horb.
Follow the B 28 (Strasbourg).
Turn right before Bad Griesbach.

Owner : Meinrad Schmiederer
Open all year

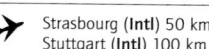

✈ Strasbourg (**Intl**) 50 km
Stuttgart (**Intl**) 100 km

🍴 Menus 38-140 DEM s.i.
19-72 €
Carte 34-58 DEM s.i.
17-30 €

🔑 33 rooms
220-280 DEM s.i.
112-143 €

🔑 38 suites
330-620 DEM s.i.
169-317 €

☕ 24 DEM s.i.
12 €

🐕 yes (extra cost)

♪ 15 km

Meinrad Schmiederer and his sister Ulrike Herrmann perpetuate the tradition of German hospitality in this charming family-style hotel. Welcomed like an old friend, you will be shown to a tastefully decorated comfortable room and looked after with exceptional care and courtesy throughout your stay. Martin Herrmann's light gourmet cuisine, based on seasonal regional produce, is a festival of flavours and aromas.

Beauty treatment, swimming pool, sauna, outdoor chessboard, petanque ground.

DEM : Deutsche Mark

Visa

SCHWARZWALD - HOTEL ADLER

Tel. : (49) (07672) 4170
Fax : (49) (07672) 417150
E-mail : adler@relaischateaux.fr

Fridolinstrasse 15
D-79837 Häusern
(Baden-Württemberg)

Germany

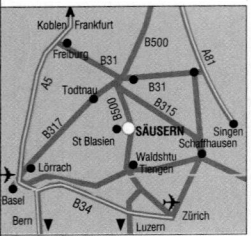

From Frankfurt A5 exit «Freibourg Mitte», B31 Titisee. From Stuttgart A81 exit «Donaueschingen», B31 then B500 via Waldshut.

Owner : Winfried Zumkeller
Weekly closing :
Rest. : Monday and Tuesday
Annual closing :
Rest. : from Nov. 6th to Dec. 15th
Hotel : from Nov. 20th to Dec. 15th

✈ Zurich (**Intl**) 60 km

🍴 Menus **70-140 DEM** s.i.
36-72 €
Carte **58-95 DEM** s.i.
30-49 €

⊶ 28 rooms
194-298 DEM s.i.
99-152 €

⚷ 17 suites
300-450 DEM s.i.
153-230 €

☕ included

🛏 yes (extra cost)

⌇ 30 km

Health and beauty centre.

This charming hotel, set in the south of the Black Forest, has been managed for five generations by the Zumkeller family. A high quality cuisine to delight gourmets and those who love regional specialities, a redesigned landscape of ornamental ponds and swimming pools, a health and beauty centre, tastefully decorated rustic-style rooms and the wide variety of sports available all explain why the Adler is a favourite holiday venue.

MasterCard Visa

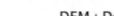
DEM : Deutsche Mark

www.relaischateaux.fr/adler

HOTEL SCHWARZMATT

Germany

Schwarzmattstrasse, 6a
D-79410 Badenweiler
(Baden-Württemberg)

Tel. : (49) (07632) 8201 0
Fax : (49) (07632) 8201 20
E-mail : schwarzmatt@relaischateaux.fr

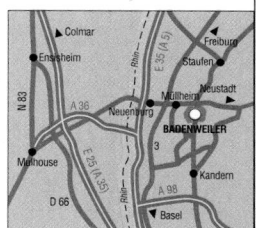

*A5 - exit Müllheim, Badenweiler,
follow signs to centre.*

Owner : Heidemarie Mast-Bareiss
Open all year

 Basel (**Intl**) 35 km
Zurich (**Intl**) 150 km

 Menus 65-120 DEM s.i.
33-61 €
Carte 75-130 DEM s.i.
38-66 €

You will be enchanted with the hospitality of the Mast-Bareiss family and the refined, rustic atmosphere. The comfortable rooms open out onto large sunkissed balconies. The dining rooms, with their delicately coloured decor, are finished off with floral compositions. The cuisine gives pride of place to fresh market produce, combining traditional dishes with the flavour some creations of nouvelle cuisine. Bade, French and Italian wines.

 24 rooms
360-420 DEM s.i.
184-215 €

 14 suites
430-520 DEM s.i.
220-266 €

 30 DEM s.i.
15 €

 yes (extra cost)

 12 golf courses
between 9 and 40 km

Fishing.

   337

| DEM : Deutsche Mark | Crédit cards : rest., shop

SEEHOTEL SIBER

SINCE 1986

Tel. : (49) (07531) 63044
Fax : (49) (07531) 64813
E-mail : siber@relaischateaux.fr

Seestrasse 25
D-78464 Konstanz
(Baden-Württemberg)

Germany

From Stuttgart, A 81
towards Singen, to Constance,
opposite the Constance «Casino».

Owner : Bertold Siber
Annual closing :
10 days in February

✈ Zurich (**Intl**) 65 km
Stuttgart (**Intl**) 120 km

🍴 Menus 115-185 DEM s.i.
59-95 €
Carte 30-75 DEM s.i.
15-38 €

⚷ 11 rooms
330-460 DEM s.i.
169-235 €

⚷ 1 suite
660 DEM s.i.
337 €

🍷 35-50 DEM s.i.
18-26 €

🐕 yes (extra cost)

♪ 10 km

Sauna, water sports, fishing,
dancing...

T|he terraces of this elegant white
villa offer superb views across Lake
Constance. Wander through the sumptuous
Mediterranean-style garden, bathed in
the scent of hortensias and wisteria, or
enjoy a stroll to the Rhine waterfall. Then
relax in a comfortable room before savouring imaginative cuisine accompanied
by exceptional Baden, Burgundy and
Bordeaux wines. The town's renowned Jazz
festival should not be missed.

 Visa

DEM : Deutsche Mark

www.relaischateaux.fr/siber

VILLINO

Germany

Hoyerberg 34
D-88131 Lindau-Bodensee
(Bayern)

Tel. : (49) (08382) 93 450
Fax : (49) (08382) 93 4512
E-mail : villino@relaischateaux.fr

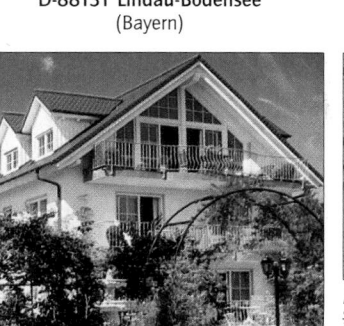

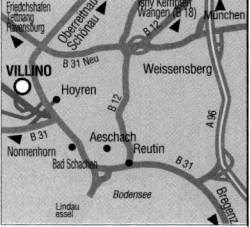

From the A 96 motorway, follow signs to Wasserburg-Nonnenhorn. Turn right after the hospital and follow signs to Oberreitnau-Schönau. After 200 meters, at lights, turn left. Villino is on the right, after about 500 meters.

Owners :
Sonja and Reiner Fischer
Weekly closing :
Rest. : Monday
Annual closing :
From January 10th to 30th

✈ Zurich (**Intl**) 130 km
Friedrichshafen 20 km

🍴 Menus **108-128 DEM** s.i.
55-65 €
Carte **95-120 DEM** s.i.
49-61 €

⚷ 8 rooms
220-300 DEM s.i.
112-153 €

⚷ 8 suites
340-400 DEM s.i.
174-205 €

☕ included

🍴 yes (extra cost)

🏊 3 km

Sailing, biking, tennis.

I f you travel in the beautiful region of Lake Constance, you absolutely must stop at the flower-bedecked and idyllic country residence of Villino. You will appreciate the warm welcome of the hosts, the refined comfort of the rooms and savour the pleasures of the German and Italian cuisine. In the surrounding area, you can visit the lake, the baroque church of Birnau and the falls of the Rhine river.

ALPENHOF MURNAU

SINCE 1972

Tel. : (49) (08841) 4910
Fax : (49) (08841) 5438
E-mail : murnau@relaischateaux.fr

Ramsachstrasse 8
D-82418 Murnau
(Bayern)

Germany

A 95 Munich-Garmisch, take Murnau exit, turn right on to U 21 towards Murnau. In Murnau, straight on to the main crossroads, then left towards Garmisch.

Owner : Erivan Haub
Director : Didier Morand
Weekly closing :
Gourmet restaurant : Monday and Tuesday (nov. to march)
Annual closing :
Gourmet restaurant : from the beginning of January to the beginning of February
«Moosberg-Castell» : open all year

✈ Munich (**Intl**) 110 km

🍽 Menus **62-175 DEM** s.i. **32-89 €**
Carte **15-55 DEM** s.i. **8-28 €**

⊶ 60 rooms
single **170-220 DEM** s.i. **87-112 €**
double **260-475 DEM** s.i. **133-243 €**

⊶ 17 suites
starting at **495 DEM** s.i. **253 €**

🛎 included

🍴 yes (extra cost)

🎿 15 km

Royal Palaces, art and culture, cycling.

The balconies of this elegant manor house, bedecked in colourful flowers, offer a magnificent view of country meadows stretching away to the Alpine foothills in the distance. This idyllic, bucolic retreat is renowned for its remarkable cuisine and its excellent cellar, a veritable treasure trove of local wines. The Alpenhof also boasts the most beautiful sun-drenched terrace in Upper Bavaria.

Visa

DEM : Deutsche Mark

www.relaischateaux.fr/murnau

RESIDENZ HEINZ WINKLER

Germany

Kirchplatz 1
D-83229 Aschau
(Bayern)

Tel. : (49) (08052) 1799 0
Fax : (49) (08052) 1799 66
E-mail : winkler@relaischateaux.fr

*From Munich, A 8 towards
Salzburg, Chiemsee,
exit Frasdorf-Aschau.*

Owner : Heinz Winkler
Open all year

A t the Munich-Salzburg-Kitzbuhl crossroads, near the fairytale castles of Ludwig II of Bavaria and the great backdrop of the Alps, legendary cuisine awaits you at the «Residenz» where you can sample Heinz Winkler's fine game specialities enhanced by rare vintages. The ideal place to stay, complete with a health and beauty centre. Visit the Salzburg Festival and the internationally famous Riedel glassworks.

✈ Salzburg (**Intl**) 60 km
Munich (**Intl**) 120 km

🍴 Menus **145-215 DEM** s.i.
74-110 €
Carte **18-45 DEM** s.i.
9-23 €

⚷ 18 rooms
250-420 DEM s.i.
128-215 €

⚷ 14 suites
490-620 DEM s.i.
251-317 €

🍵 **30 DEM** s.i.
15 €

🛏 yes (extra cost) hotel only

🎿 8 km

Opera Festival of Munich,
festival of Salsbourg,
beauty salon.

341

 Visa

www.relaischateaux.fr/winkler   **DEM : Deutsche Mark**

CZECH REPUBLIC

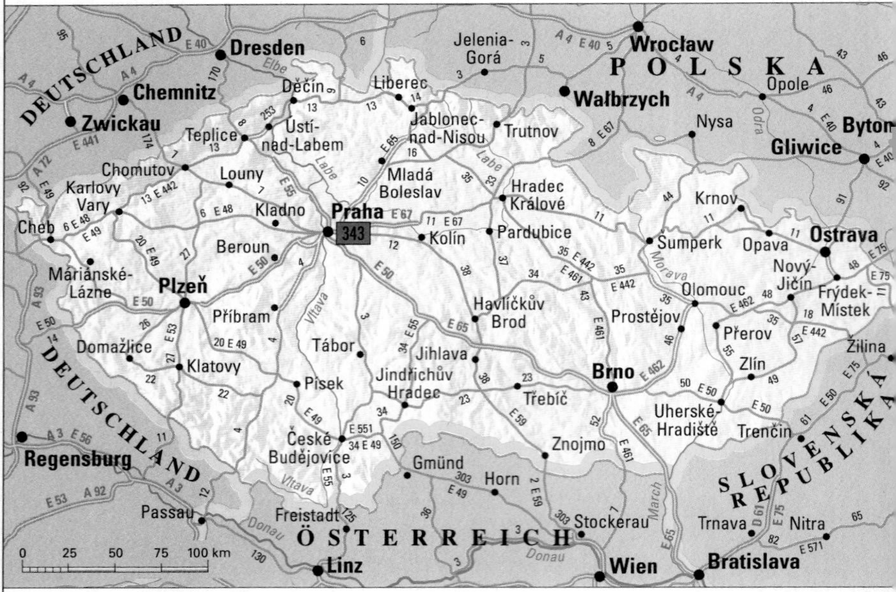

Map of the Czech Republic and surrounding regions showing:

DEUTSCHLAND · Dresden · Chemnitz · Zwickau · Jelenia-Góra · Wrocław · POLSKA · Opole · Byton · Gliwice · Děčín · Liberec · Jablonec-nad-Nisou · Trutnov · Walbrzych · Nysa · Teplice · Ústí-nad-Labem · Chomutov · Louny · Mladá Boleslav · Hradec Králové · Krnov · Ostrava · Karlovy Vary · Kladno · Praha 343 · Kolín · Pardubice · Šumperk · Opava · Nový-Jičín · Frýdek-Místek · Cheb · Beroun · Mariánské-Lázne · Plzeň · Příbram · Havlíčkův Brod · Prostějov · Olomouc · Přerov · Žilina · Domažlice · Klatovy · Tábor · Jihlava · Brno · Zlín · Písek · Jindřichův Hradec · Třebíč · Uherské-Hradiště · Trenčín · SLOVENSKÁ REPUBLIKA · DEUTSCHLAND · České Budějovice · Gmünd · Horn · Znojmo · Regensburg · Passau · Freistadt · ÖSTERREICH · Stockerau · Trnava · Nitra · Linz · Wien · Bratislava

0 25 50 75 100 km

Establishments	Nearest major city	Relais & Châteaux	Relais Gourmands	Page
Hotel Hoffmeister	Prague	⚜		343

HOTEL HOFFMEISTER

Czech Republic

Pod Bruskou 7
CZ-11800 Prague 1

Tel. : (420) (2) 5101 7111
(420) (2) 5731 0942
Fax : (420) (2) 5101 7120
(420) (2) 5732 0906
E-mail : hoffmeister@relaischateaux.fr

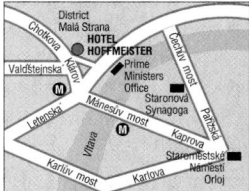

*Located in the Malà Strana
quarter beneath the hills
of the château near the Vltava
river and the bridge of Mánes.*

Owners :
Radomira and Martin Hoffmeister
Director : Martin Hoffmeister
Open all year

 Prague (**Intl**) 16 km

 Menus **500-800 CZK** s.i.
Carte **600-2 500 CZK** s.i.

12 rooms
4 800-7 800 CZK s.i.

5 suites
7 250-14 000 CZK s.i.

330 CZK s.i.

yes (small)

20 km

T his beautifully restored residence, nestling at the foot of the citadel steps, about 300 m from the Prague castle, is renowned for its 1920's decor and its elegant interior, hung with paintings and collages by Adolf Hoffmeister, a close friend of Max Ernst, Cocteau and Picasso. The tastefully furnished rooms, completely soundproofed, are havens of comfort. As for the cuisine, prepared with the finest regional produce, it is one of the best in Prague.

343

www.relaischateaux.fr/hoffmeister

CZK : Czech crown

Visa

344

ARLBERG HOSPIZ

Austria

A-6580 St. Christoph 118
(Tirol)

Tel. : (43) (05446) 2611
Fax : (43) (05446) 3545
E-mail : arlberg@relaischateaux.fr

From Innsbruck, towards Arlberg, exit St.-Anton.
From Switzerland, towards Innsbruck. Exit Arlberg.

Owners :
Adolf and Gerda Werner
Director : Florian Werner
Annual closing :
From May 1st to Dec. 1st

✈ Innsbruck (**Intl**) 100 km
Zurich (**Intl**) 200 km

🍴 Menus **480-1 000 ATS** s.i.
35-73 €
Carte **250-480 ATS** s.i.
18-35 €

🔑 35 rooms
4 200-8 300 ATS s.i.
per person
305-603 €

🔑 60 suites
5 800-12 700 ATS s.i.
per person
421-923 €

☕ included

🍴 yes (extra cost)

🎿 30 km

Childcare, cross-country skiing, alpine skiing, snowboard.

A t the foot of the ski area of Arlberg, this hotel has a tradition of hospitality that is as legendary as its six centuries of history. Intimate and comfortable rooms and suites. Relaxation and entertainment are guaranteed thanks to the wide selection of sports activities, a fitness centre and varied daily programme. Savour delicious food and fine vintages from one of the world's biggest Bordeaux wine cellars.

www.relaischateaux.fr/arlberg

ATS : Austrian schilling

Visa

GASTHOF POST

SINCE 1976

Tel. : (43) (05583) 22060
Fax : (43) (05583) 220623
E-mail : gasthof@relaischateaux.fr

A-6764 Lech am Arlberg
(Vorarlberg)

Austria

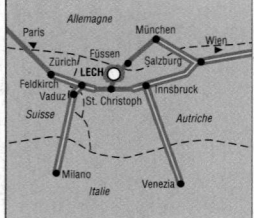

From Zurich towards Innsbruck, exit Arlberg. From Innsbruck, towards Arlberg, exit St. Anton.

Owners : Moosbrugger Family
Annual closing :
From beginning of May to mid-June and from beginning of October to end of November

✈ Zurich (**Intl**) 180 km
Munich (**Intl**) 240 km

🍴 Menus **490-980 ATS** s.i.
36-71 €
Carte **320-560 ATS** s.i.
23-41 €

🔑 21 rooms
summer
2 380-3 180 ATS s.i.
173-231 €
winter
3 380-7 380 ATS s.i.
246-536 €

🔑 18 suites
summer
3 180-4 780 ATS s.i.
231-347 €
winter
4 980-9 580 ATS s.i.
362-696 €

🍽 included

🍴 yes (extra cost)

♪ 20 km

T he memory of the expedition of the imperial post in 1871 is still alive in mountain country culture. This hotel's antique furniture endows each room with a unique character. Its spacious guestrooms overlook spectacular summits or the idyllic garden. In winter, you will take advantage of a famous ski area, and in summer the various cultural and sports activities will provide you with relaxation and entertainment.

Visa (Credit cards : Rest. only)   ATS : Austrian schilling   www.relaischateaux.fr/gasthof

SPORTHOTEL SINGER

Austria

A-6622 Berwang
(1340 m above sea level)
(Tirol)

Tel. : (43) (05674) 8181
Fax : (43) (05674) 818183
E-mail : singer@relaischateaux.fr

From Stuttgart, Ulm,
A7 towards Füssen,
then B314 Reutte, Bichlbach
or via Fernpass, Berwang.

Owners : Günter and Gerti Singer
Annual closing :
From March 26th to May 27th
and from Oct. 3rd to Dec. 17th

 Innsbruck **(Intl)** 75 km
Munich **(Intl)** 160 km

 Menus 350-750 ATS s.i.
25-54 €
Carte 350-580 ATS s.i.
25-42 €

 27 rooms
1 580-2 650 ATS s.i.
115-193 €

 27 suites
1 960-4 340 ATS s.i.
142-315 €

 buffet included

 yes (extra cost)
only rooms

♩ 30 km

S et in a stunning mountain landscape, this elegant hotel seems to have been purpose-built for your pleasure, with a warm cordial atmosphere and tastefully furnished comfortable rooms. Relax in either of the two bars or in the large, original Tyrolian-style lounge with its roaring log fires and enjoy a wonderful candlelit dinner in the restaurants or on the terrace, savouring the best European vintage wines. Visit the castles of King Ludwig II of Bavaria nearby.

Jacuzzi, fitness centre, fishing, sauna, skiing, children's garden.

   351

ATS : Austrian schilling
 Visa

SCHLOSSHOTEL IGLS

SINCE 1985

Tel. : (43) (0512) 377217
Fax : (43) (0512) 378679
E-mail : schlossigls@relaischateaux.fr

Viller Steig 2
A-6080 Igls
(Tirol)

Austria

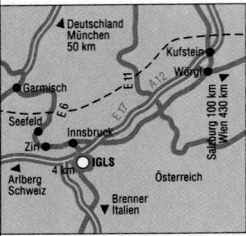

Inntal Highway -
Innsbruck-Ost exit. Continue
to Olympic Stadium. Turn left.
Follow signs to Igls.

Owners : Beck Family
Annual closing :
From October 26th to Dec. 19th

✈ Innsbruck (**Intl**) 8 km
  Munich (**Intl**) 160 km

🍴 Menus **250-600 ATS** s.i.
  18-44 €
  Carte **270-500 ATS** s.i.
  20-36 €

🔑 14 rooms
  3 600-4 800 ATS s.i.
  262-349 €

🔑 6 suites
  4 200-9 200 ATS s.i.
  305-669 €

☕ included

🍴 yes (extra cost)

🎵 2 and 7 km

Sauna, jacuzzi, hammam,
beauty salon, mountain sports,
horse riding...

Perched on a wooded plateau above Innsbruck, this beautiful 19th-century residence, set amidst landscaped gardens, offers breathtaking views of the Tyrol mountains. Enjoy the exquisite comfort of your guestroom, then linger over cocktails in the bar before savouring refined cuisine. Those seeking relaxation will adore the indoor pool, sauna and steam baths while sporting enthusiasts will enjoy golf and skiing.

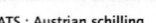

Visa

ATS : Austrian schilling

www.relaischateaux.fr/schlossigls

HOTEL DER BÄR

Austria

Kirchbichl, 9
A-6352 Ellmau
(Tirol)

Tel. : (43) (05358) 2395
Fax : (43) (05358) 239556
E-mail : derbar@relaischateaux.fr

From Innsbruck, A12 exit
Wörgl-Ost, B312 until Ellmau.
From Munich, A8/E45
exit Kufstein-Süd, B173,
B312 until Ellmau.

Owner : Joachim Strickrodt
Directors :
Karl-Heinz and Lorette Windisch
Annual closing :
From April 3rd to the beginning
of June and from mid-October
to mid-December

D iscover traditional Tyrolian charm in a mountain landscape. In winter, the ski slopes are at your door, while in summer meadows and forests stretch as far as the eye can see. Relax in one of the comfortable suites, all with marvellous fireplaces, then enjoy a sauna, swim or massage and a session at the Shiseido Beauty Salon. International and regional cuisine is served with the finest Austrian, French and Italian wines.

✈ Innsbruck (**Intl**) 80 km
Munich (**Intl**) 130 km

🍽 Menus **390-620 ATS** s.i.
28-45 €
Carte **375-540 ATS** s.i.
27-39 €

🔑 31 rooms
2 100-3 440 ATS s.i.
153-250 €

🔑 24 suites
2 800-5 120 ATS s.i.
203-372 €

☕ included

🐕 yes (extra cost) except rest.

⛳ 9 and 18 holes nearby

353

www.relaischateaux.fr/derbar

ATS : Austrian schilling

Visa

HOTEL SCHLOSS MÖNCHSTEIN

Tel. : (43) (0662) 8485550
Fax : (43) (0662) 848559
E-mail : moenchstein@relaischateaux.fr

Mönchsberg Park 26-rch
A-5020 Salzburg-City Center

Austria

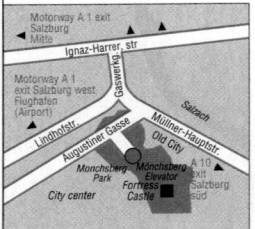

In Salzburg: Müllner Hauptstrasse, Augustiner Gasse, Mönchsberg hill, follow signs.

Owners : Von Mierka Family
Director : Hubert Hirz
Open all year

✈ Salzburg (**Intl**) 5 km

🍴 Menus 440-1 300 ATS s.i.
32-94 €
Carte 320-720 ATS s.i.
23-52 €

🔑 9 rooms
2 900-6 500 ATS s.i.
211-472 €

🛏 7 suites
5 400-30 000 ATS s.i.
392-2 180 €

☕ included

🍴 yes (extra cost) only hotel

🎵 5 km

Baroque district, festival, culture.

I n the centre of Salzburg, you will find the «most charming city hotel in the world». Staying in this castle has become a privilege and dining in its castle-restaurant «Paris Lodron», a must. Enjoy harp concerts on the garden-terrace «Apollo» every Saturday and Sunday or in the castle-café «Maria Theresia». The «Mönchstein Panorama Weg» will take you to Salzburg's historic centre in a matter of minutes.

ATS : Austrian schilling

www.relaischateaux.fr/moenchstein

HOTEL SCHLOSS DÜRNSTEIN

A-3601 Dürnstein
(Niederösterreich)

Tel. : (43) (02711) 212
Fax : (43) (02711) 212-30
E-mail : durnstein@relaischateaux.fr

Austria

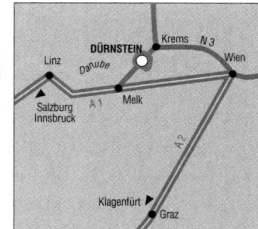

From Salzburg, A1 exit Melk,
cross the Danube,
N3 towards Krems.

Owners :
Johann and Rosemarie Thiery
Director : Rosemarie Thiery
Annual closing :
From November 5th to April 5th

✈ Vienna (**Intl**) 100 km

🍽 Menus **300-380 ATS** s.i.
22-28 €
Carte **390-530 ATS** s.i.
28-39 €

⊶ 35 rooms
950-1 800 ATS s.i.
per person
69-132 €

⊶ 3 suites
1 700-2 100 ATS s.i.
per person
124-153 €

☕ included

🍴 yes (extra cost)

🎿 15 km

Fishing, sauna.

This picturesque castle, built in 1630, is said to have inspired the Grimm Brothers' fairytales. Its sumptuous interior, decorated with parquet floors, antiques, crystal chandeliers and an elegant Biedermeier bar, certainly looks the part. Dinner on the magnificent terrace overlooking the Danube is a truly magical experience. As for the luxurious indoor pool, it is reputed to be one of the most beautiful in Austria.

355

ATS : Austrian schilling

Visa

HOTEL IM PALAIS SCHWARZENBERG

SINCE 1978

Tel. : (43) (01) 798 45 15
Fax : (43) (01) 798 47 14
E-mail : schwarzenberg@relaischateaux.fr

Schwarzenbergplatz 9
A-1030 Wien

Austria

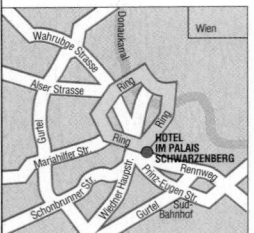

*Access from the «Ring»
surrounding the centre of Vienna:
exit between Kärntner Ring
and Schubertring and go through
the Schwarzenbergerplatz.*

Owner :
SHS the Prince of Schwarzenberg
Director : Gerhard Schwendner
Open all year

✈	Vienna (**Intl**) 20 km
🍴	Menus 390-980 ATS s.i. **28-71 €** Carte 450-1 330 ATS s.i. **33-97 €**
⚷	36 rooms **3 000-5 600 ATS** s.i. **218-407 €**
⚷	8 suites **5 600-12 000 ATS** s.i. **407-872 €**
🍽	190-290 ATS s.i. **14-21 €**
🐕	yes (extra cost)
⛳	7 km

Oe of the most sumptuous baroque buildings of imperial Vienna, this magnificent palace was the summer residence of the Schwarzenberg princes from 1716. Private 7.5 hectare park with fountains and statues. Six stately baroque rooms for all kinds of events. Guestrooms with antique furniture and individually decorated suites. Six new designer park suites and rooms are located in the left side wing. Savour delicious cuisine in the terrace restaurant by the park.

    Visa

ATS : Austrian schilling

www.relaischateaux.fr/schwarzenberg

RESTAURANT STEIRERECK

Austria

Rasumofskygasse 2
Ecke Weissgerberlände
A-1030 Wien

Tel. : (43) (01) 713 31 68
Fax : (43) (01) 713 51 68 2
E-mail : steirereck@relaischateaux.fr

*A23 Vienna centre, Pratercity,
Schüttel Strasse, Donaukanal,
Rotunden Brücke bridge.*

Owners : Reitbauer Family
Weekly closing :
Saturday and Sunday
Open all year

✈ Vienna (**Intl**) 11 km

🍴 Menus **395-880 ATS** s.i.
202-450 €
Carte **480-680 ATS** s.i.
245-348 €

 yes

3 km

Opera, festivals...

I deally located in the heart of imperial Vienna just a short stroll from the Prater, the Steirereck is renowned as the city's finest restaurant. Indeed, master chef Helmut Österreicher has won numerous awards for his subtly flavoured cuisine which reinterprets traditional specialities from the Austrian provinces. Enjoy impeccable service, superb cigars and excellent wines from Wachau, Langenlois, Styria and Europe.

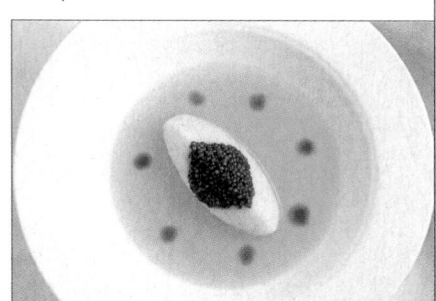

www.relaischateaux.fr/steirereck   **ATS : Austrian schilling**   Visa

HOTEL GRÜNER BAUM

SINCE
1983

Tel. : (43) (06434) 25160
Fax : (43) (06434) 251625
E-mail : grunerbaum@relaischateaux.fr

Kötschachtal 25
A-5640 Badgastein
(Salzburg)

Austria

From Salzburg A10 Bischofshofen,
St Johann, Schwarzach,
Gasteiner valley.

Owners :
Hannes and Monica Blumschein
Annual closing :
From October 26th to Dec. 8th

 Salzburg (**Intl**) 95 km
Munich (**Intl**) 280 km

 GPS 13° 09,80
47° 07,70

 Menus **240-750 ATS** s.i.
17-54 €
Carte **280-750 ATS** s.i.
20-54 €

 37 rooms
1 **640-3 350 ATS** s.i.
119-243 €

 21 suites
2 **040-4 350 ATS** s.i.
148-316 €

 buffet included

⊣ yes (extra cost)

⌡ 2 km

Fitness club, cures,
beauty salon, sauna, miniclub,
children's activities, fishing,
hunting...

Archduke John of Austria built this
magnificent hunting lodge in the
Gastein valley in 1831. Today the valley
has become a national park and the lodge
and its «village» have been transformed
into a luxury hotel. The guestrooms feature
beautiful balconies decorated with fresh
flowers and looking out across the mountain
slopes. Relax in the thermal baths, visit the
beauty centre or enjoy fishing, hiking, skiing
and tennis.

358

ATS : Austrian schilling

www.relaischateaux.fr/grunerbaum

HOTEL SCHLOSS SEEFELS

Austria

Töschling 1
A-9210 Pörtschach
(Kärnten)

Tel. : (43) (04272) 2377
Fax : (43) (04272) 3704
E-mail : seefels@relaischateaux.fr

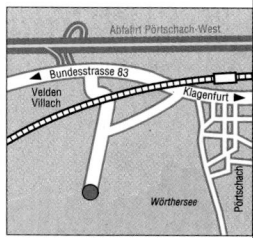

From Klagenfurt airport,
A 2 towards Villach,
exit Pörtschach-West.

Owners :
Hotel Schloss Seefels
Besitz-und Management GmbH
Director : Egon Haupt
Annual closing :
From October to April

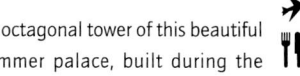

The octagonal tower of this beautiful summer palace, built during the reign of Emperor Franz Joseph, is reflected in the clear blue waters of Pörtschach Lake. What could be more romantic than dining beneath the elegant glass roof of the Belle Epoque veranda or eating on the terrace as the breeze wafts the scent of flowers past your table ? Visit the marina, relax on the private beach, enjoy tennis or a sauna. Paradise !

✈ Klagenfurt (**Intl**) 23 km

🍴 Menus **230-690 ATS** s.i.
16-50 €
Carte **220-500 ATS** s.i.
16-36 €

🔑 60 rooms
1 680-4 680 ATS s.i.
122-340 €

🔑 10 suites
starting at **3 680 ATS** s.i.
267 €

🍵 included

🛏 yes (extra cost)
except restaurants

🏃 5 km

Sauna, solarium, beauty salon,
fishing, water sports...

359

ATS : Austrian schilling

Slovenia

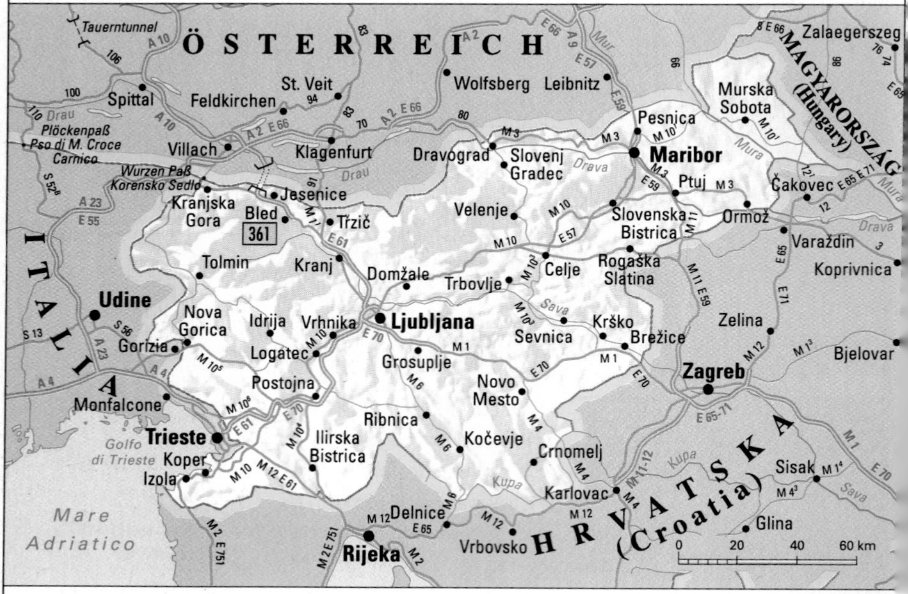

Establishments	Nearest major city	Relais & Châteaux	Relais Gourmands	Page
Hotel Vila Bled	Ljubljana	⚜		361

SINCE
1987

HOTEL VILA BLED

Slovenia

Cesta svobode 26
SI-4260 Bled

Tel. : (386) (064) 7915
Fax : (386) (064) 741 320
E-mail : vilabled@relaischateaux.fr

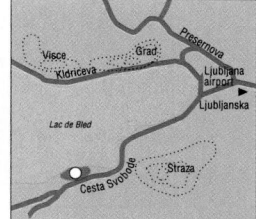

Austrian border
Karawankentunnel E 61∕A1.

Owner : G.H.T. Bled
Director : Janez Fajfar
Open all year

 Ljubljana (**Intl**) 35 km

Menus **45-60 DEM** s.i.
Carte **70-90 DEM** s.i.

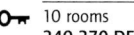 10 rooms
240-270 DEM s.i.

20 suites
270-600 DEM s.i.

included

yes (approval needed)

4 km

Fishing, hunting, canoeing,
private beach, cross-country,
skiing, golf special rates...

S et amidst 12 acres of luxuriant
foliage and dazzling flowers on the
picturesque shore of Lake Bled, this elegant
residence is bathed in soft Alpine sunlight
throughout the year. The comfortable
rooms offer superb vistas of the lake, and
the pure air, spa waters and surrounding
forests will do wonders for your health.
Enjoy light, refined cuisine on the waterside
terrace and savour Slovenia's famous
«black» red wines.

361

www.relaischateaux.fr∕vilabled

DEM : Deutsche Mark

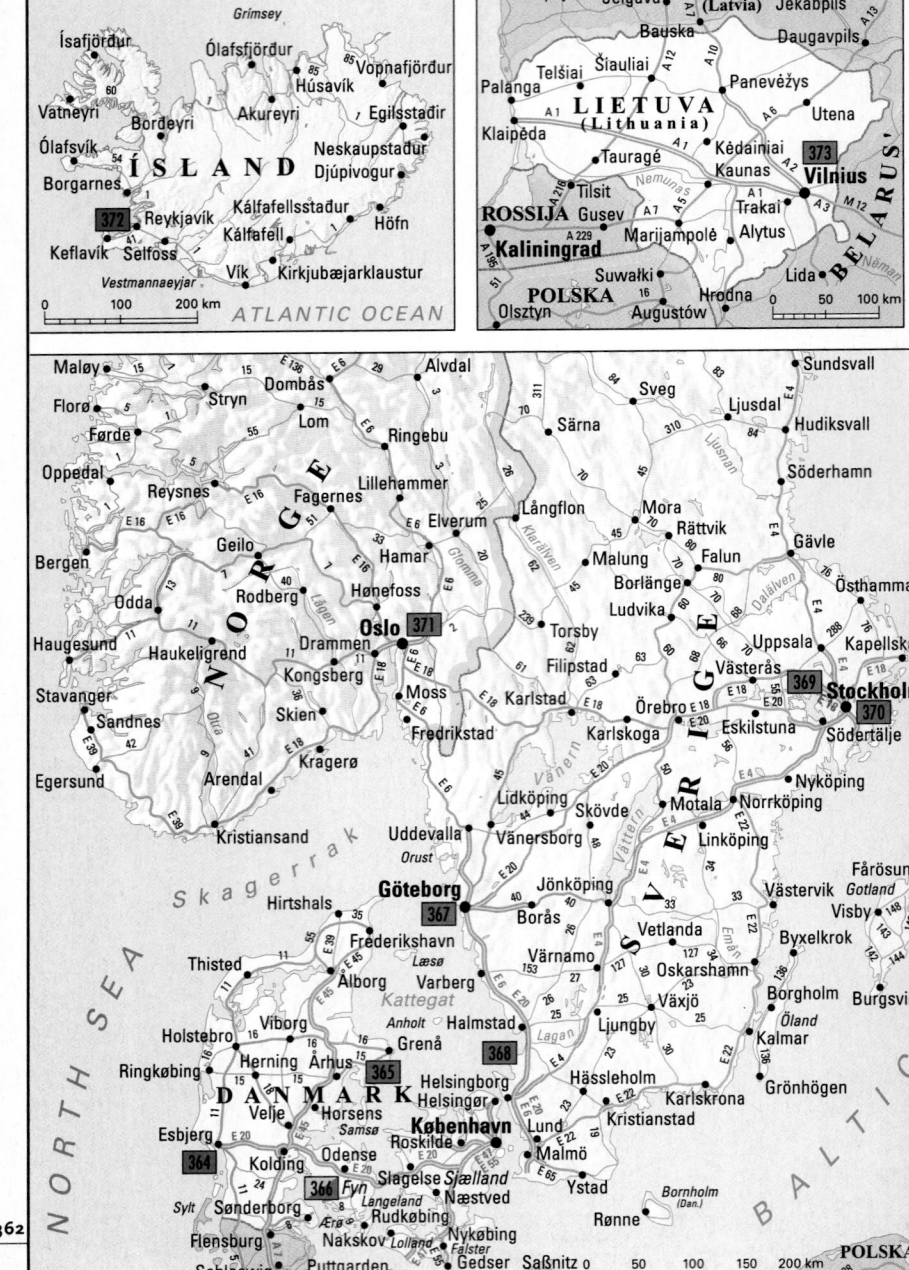

Ísland

Grímsey

Ísafjörður · Ólafsfjörður · Vopnafjörður
· Húsavík
Vatneyri · 60 · 85 · 85
· Borðeyri · Akureyri · Egilsstaðir
Ólafsvík · 54 · Neskaupstaður
Borgarnes · Í S L A N D · Djúpivogur
372 · Reykjavík · Kálfafellsstaður
· Kálfafell · Höfn
Keflavík · Selfoss
Vestmannaeyjar · Vík · Kirkjubæjarklaustur

0 · 100 · 200 km

ATLANTIC OCEAN

Latvija / Lietuva

Liepāja · Jelgava · **LATVIJA** · Jēkabpils
· · **(Latvia)**
· Bauska · Daugavpils
· Telšiai · Šiauliai
Palanga · Panevėžys
· A 12 · A 10 · Utena
Klaipėda · **L I E T U V A** · A 6
· **(Lithuania)**
· Tauragė · Kėdainiai · **373**
· Kaunas · **Vilnius**
ROSSIJA · Gusev · Tilsit · Trakai · A 3 · M 12
· A 7 · Alytus
Kaliningrad · A 229 · Marijampolė · **B E L A R U S**
· Suwałki · Lida · Nëman
POLSKA · 16 · Hrodna
Olsztyn · Augustów · 0 · 50 · 100 km

Norge / Sverige / Danmark

Måløy · 15 · 15 · E 136 · E 6 · 29 · Alvdal · · Sundsvall
Florø · 5 · Stryn · Dombås · 311 · 84 · Sveg · Ljusdal
Førde · 55 · Lom · 15 · · 70 · Särna · 310 · 84 · Hudiksvall
Oppedal · 5 · Ringebu · E 6 · · · Söderhamn
Reysnes · E 16 · Fagernes · Lillehammer · 76 · Långflon · Mora · Rättvik
Geilo · E 16 · E 16 · Elverum · · 70 · Gävle
Bergen · 40 · Hamar · 33 · E 6 · Malung · 70 · Falun
Odda · 13 · Rodberg · E 16 · Hønefoss · Borlänge · 80 · Östhamma
Haugesund · 11 · **Oslo** · **371** · Ludvika · E 4 · 288
· Haukeligrend · Drammen · 239 · Torsby · Uppsala · Kapellsk
Stavanger · 11 · Kongsberg · E 18 · Filipstad · 63 · 80 · Västerås
Sandnes · 42 · Skien · Moss · Karlstad · E 18 · **369** · **Stockhol**
Egersund · E 39 · E 18 · Fredrikstad · Karlskoga · Örebro · E 18 · E 20 · **370**
· Arendal · Karlskoga · Eskilstuna · Södertälje
Kristiansand · · Lidköping · Skövde · Motala · Nyköping
· Uddevalla · Vänersborg · Linköping · Norrköping
· *Orust* · · 34 · Fårösun
Hirtshals · **Göteborg** · Jönköping · Västervik · *Gotland*
· **367** · Borås · 33 · Visby · 148
Thisted · Frederikshavn · Vetlanda · Byxelkrok · 143
· *Læsø* · Värnamo · 127 · 144
Ålborg · Varberg · 153 · Oskarshamn · Borgholm · Burgsvi
Holstebro · Viborg · *Anholt* · Halmstad · Växjö · *Öland*
Ringkøbing · Herning · Århus · **368** · Ljungby · Kalmar
· Velje · **365** · Helsingborg · Hässleholm · Grönhögen
D A N M A R K · Helsingør · · Karlskrona
· Horsens · *Samsø* · Lund · Kristianstad
Esbjerg · **364** · Roskilde · **København** · Malmö
· Kolding · Odense · · Ystad · *Bornholm*
· **366** · *Fyn* · Slagelse · *Sjælland* · *(Dan.)*
Sønderborg · *Langeland* · Næstved · Rønne
· *Ærø* · Rudkøbing · · **POLSKA**
Flensburg · Nakskov · *Lolland* · Nykøbing · *Falster*
Schleswig · Puttgarden · Gedser · Saßnitz · 0 · 50 · 100 · 150 · 200 km
· Kiel · **DEUTSCHLAND** · Gdynia

North Sea
Skagerrak
Kattegat
BALTIC

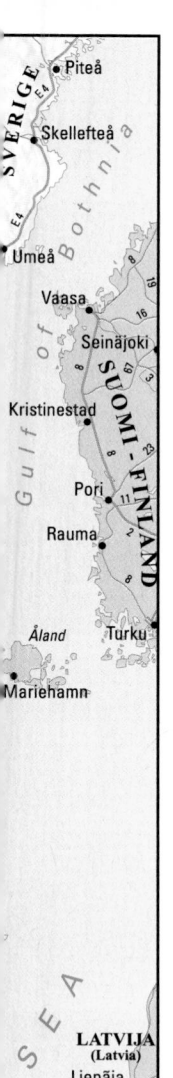

SCANDINAVIA

DENMARK

Establishments	Nearest major city	Relais & Châteaux	Relais Gourmands	Page
Falsled Kro	Odense	✦	♛	366
Molskroen	Ebeltoft	✦		365
Sønderho Kro	Esbjerg	✦		364

SWEDEN

Establishments	Nearest major city	Relais & Châteaux	Relais Gourmands	Page
Kattegat Gastronomi	Ängelholm		♛	368
Krägga Herrgård	Bålsta	✦		369
Leijontornet & Victory Hotel	Stockholm	✦	♛	370
Restaurant Westra Piren	Göteborg		♛	367

NORWAY

Establishments	Nearest major city	Relais & Châteaux	Relais Gourmands	Page
Restaurant Bagatelle	Oslo		♛	371

ICELAND

Establishments	Nearest major city	Relais & Châteaux	Relais Gourmands	Page
Hotel Holt	Reykjavik	✦		372

LITHUANIA

Establishments	Nearest major city	Relais & Châteaux	Relais Gourmands	Page
Stikliai Hotel	Trakai	✦		373

Sønderho Kro

SINCE 1979

Tel. : (45) (075) 164009
Fax : (45) (075) 164385
E-mail : sonderho@relaischateaux.fr

Kropladsen 11
DK-6720 Fanø

Denmark

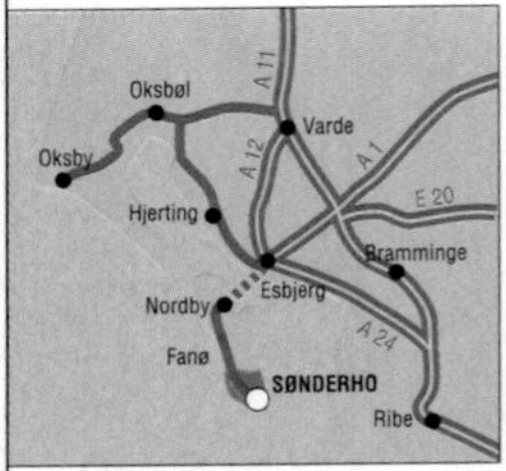

In Esbjerg, ferry (12 mn) to Fanø; take the Sønderho road (13 km).

Owners :
Birgit and Niels Sørensen
Annual closing :
Christmas and February

Hamburg (**Intl**) 270 km
Esbjerg 17 km

Menus **325-415 DKK** s.i.
Carte **396-450 DKK** s.i.

13 rooms
710-1 200 DKK s.i.

95 DKK s.i.

yes (**40 DKK** per night)

12 km

Walks, horse-riding, museums, swimming (in summer).
Discovery of nature: dunes and moors, pebble beaches.

Birgit and Niels Sørensen chose an idyllic setting for the Sønderho Kro, building their hotel on the North Sea Isle of Fanø, in the gardens of one of the oldest inns in Denmark (1722). The inn is a living museum situated 50 m from the marsh-land and 2 km from one of the best beaches in Europe with white dunes. Enjoy Sønderho, a well-preserved 18th century village, before savouring specialities in the cosy restaurant.

Visa

DKK : Danish krone

www.relaischateaux.fr/sonderho

SINCE 2000

MOLSKROEN

Denmark

Hovedgaden 16
DK-84000 Ebeltoft

Tel. : (45) 863 622 00
Fax : (45) 863 623 00
E-mail : molskroen@relaischateaux.fr

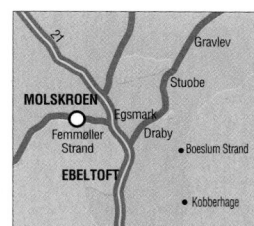

From Arhus, take routes 15 and 21 towards Elbeltoft Femmøller strand. From the Molslinien ferry, route 21. At the Elbeltoft exit, turn left towards Femmøller strand.

Owners : Arne Fremmich
and Dorte Jensen
Director : Ellen Schmith
Open all year

✈	Århus (**Intl**) 12 km
🍴	Menus **310-480 DKK** s.i.
🔑	2 rooms 1 480-1 680 DKK s.i.
🔑	16 suites 1 280-3 200 DKK s.i.
🍽	298-331 DKK s.i.
🛏	yes
♪	6 km

Surfing, sailing, kayaking,
water-skiing, fishing.

Between the sea and the country, discover this large and luminous Danish house built in the 20's and 30's, and totally redecorated in contemporary style: Molskroen, a privileged stopping place near the resort of Ebeltoft. Dinners before a crackling fire, superb seafood, and natural products all contribute to offering you moments of perfect relaxation, enlivened by visits to nearby castles, museums and churches.

P · 🍴 · 🚻 · ♿ · ✈

365

www.relaischateaux.fr/molskroen

DKK : Danish krone

FALSLED KRO

Tel. : (45) (62) 681111
Fax : (45) (62) 681162
E-mail : falsled@relaischateaux.fr

Assensvej 513
Falsled DK-5642 Millinge
(Fyn)

Denmark

From Odense, route 43 towards Faaborg, then routes 8 and 329 towards the village of Falsled.

Owners : Grønlykke Family and Jean-Louis Lieffroy
Weekly closing :
Restaurant : Monday
(except dinner from May to Sept.)
Open all year

✈ Billund (**Intl**) 130 km
Copenhagen (**Intl**) 200 km

GPS N 55° 09' 12"
E 10° 08' 55"

🍴 Menus **420-750 DKK** s.i.
Carte **630 DKK** s.i.

🛏 11 rooms
975-1 850 DKK s.i.

8 suites
starting at **2 250 DKK** s.i.

🍷 **150 DKK** s.i.

yes

🎣 Faaborg 7 km

Lulled by the Fionie mermaids' song, your stay at Falsled Kro will be a magical experience. This idyllic haven set in the midst of beautiful countryside is the ideal place to enjoy Jean-Louis Lieffroy's culinary marvels, prepared with forest game, delicacies from the sea and fruit and vegetables from the garden. Savour «aiglefin fumé au caviar d'aubergine», «pigeon en pot-au-feu à la scandinave» and exquisite «crêpes caramélisées».

 Visa

DKK : Danish krone

 www.relaischateaux.fr/falsled

RESTAURANT WESTRA PIREN

Sweden

Dockepiren
S-417 64 Göteborg
(Västra Götalands län)

Tel. : (46) (031) 519555
Fax : (46) (031) 239940
E-mail : westrapiren@relaischateaux.fr

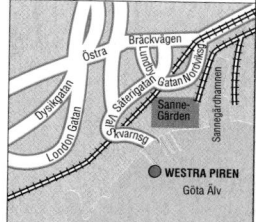

WESTRA PIREN
Göta Älv

In Göteborg, cross the Göta Älvbron bridge, towards Lundbyleden, 3 km then towards Eriksberg.

Owners : Öster Family
Weekly closing : Sunday
Annual closing :
From July 3rd to August 7th and from Dec. 20th to January 15th

✈ Göteborg **(Intl)** 35 km

 GPS N 57° 42' 00"
E 11° 55' 01"

 Menus **269-640 SEK** s.i.
Carte **395-650 SEK** s.i.

 no

Concerts, opera...

T he tall bay windows and marvellous futuristic architecture of «Westra Piren» overlook the old Gothenburg docks. This spectacular restaurant is renowned for Mikael Öster's gourmet cuisine, inspired by French culinary tradition and Swedish seafood delicacies. Savour «marbre de bouillabaisse froide aux merveilles de la mer du Nord, homard, noix de St Jacques et nos poissons» accompanied by an excellent selection of wines.

SEK : Swedish krone

Kattegat Gastronomi

Tel. : (46) (0431) 36 30 02
Fax : (46) (0431) 36 30 03
E-mail : kattegat@relaischateaux.fr

Storgatan 46
S-26093 Torekov

Sweden

*From South E6 towards
Margaretetorp, then Torekov (24 km).
From North E6, towards Ostra karup,
then Torekov (17 km) or route 115.*

Owners :
Rikard and Robert Nilsson
Weekly closing : Monday
(from Sept. 1st to May 31st)
Annual closing :
From Dec. 22nd to Jan. 15th

 Sturup (**Intl**) 130 km
Angelholm 20 km

 Menus **450-795 SEK** s.i.
Carte **450-720 SEK** s.i.

 no

🐎 no

🏌 1 km (18 holes)

Beach, horse-riding, sauna,
jacuzzi, hammam, hunting,
fishing, climbing, skiing, sailing.

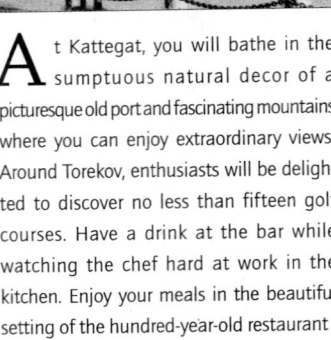

A t Kattegat, you will bathe in the sumptuous natural decor of a picturesque old port and fascinating mountains where you can enjoy extraordinary views. Around Torekov, enthusiasts will be delighted to discover no less than fifteen golf courses. Have a drink at the bar while watching the chef hard at work in the kitchen. Enjoy your meals in the beautiful setting of the hundred-year-old restaurant - voted one of the best in Sweden in 1999.

   Visa

SEK : Swedish krone

www.relaischateaux.fr/kattegat

Sweden

S-74693 Bålsta
(Uppsala län)

Tel. : (46) (0171) 532 80
Fax : (46) (0171) 532 65
E-mail : kragga@relaischateaux.fr

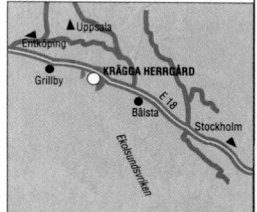

From Stockholm, E18 towards
Enköping, 2nd exit Balsta,
straight to Kragga, follow signs.

Owner : Leif Bonér
Director : Louise Bonér
Weekly closing :
Restaurant : Sunday
Annual closing :
From December 26th to 30th

✈	Stockholm (**Intl**) 51 km
	GPS N 59° 36' 30'' E 17° 22' 00''
🍴	Menus **475-695 SEK** s.i. Carte **280-580 SEK** s.i.
⚷	39 rooms **950-2 000 SEK** s.i.
⚷	4 suites starting at **2 900 SEK** s.i.
☗	**95 SEK** s.i.
☍	yes
🏌	15 km

This charming 19th-century manor is an idyllic setting in which to enjoy country rambles along the shore of Lake Mälaren, a picnic lunch in the rose gardens or a game of tennis on the manicured lawn. The rooms are exquisitely comfortable, and the old library a haven of calm. Here, the seasons not only determine the pace of life they also inspire the cuisine. Visit Skokloster Castle, Linné's House and Ekolsundsviken Bay.

LEIJONTORNET & VICTORY HOTEL

Tel. : (46) (08) 506 400 00
Fax : (46) (08) 506 400 10
E-mail : leijontornet@relaischateaux.fr

Lilla Nygatan 5, Gamla Stan
S-11128 Stockholm

Sweden

*In Stockholm, follow signs
to the centre of the city
and Gamla Stan.*

Owners :
Bengtsson and Lindberg Families
Director : Rickard Bengtsson
Weekly closing :
Rest. : Sunday and holidays
Annual closing :
From Dec. 22nd to January 7th
Restaurant : July

✈	Stockholm-Arlanda (**Intl**) 42 km Stockholm-Bromma 16 km
🍴	Menus **240-395 SEK** s.i. Carte **385-520 SEK** s.i.
⚷	41 rooms **1 650-2 700 SEK** s.i.
⚷	4 suites starting at **2 700 SEK** s.i.
🍵	included
🍴	no
♪	20 km

T his magnificent 17th-century residence in the heart of Stockholm's Old City offers sumptuous guestrooms and warm hospitality. In the restaurant you will find the remains of Stockholm's medieval fortification wall and on the crude limestone tables, Jörgen Andersson's kitchen serve the specialities of shellfish, game and fowl from Scandinavia's best suppliers. The wine cellar is one of the finest in Scandinavia.

SEK : Swedish krone

www.relaischateaux.fr/leijontornet

RESTAURANT BAGATELLE

Norway

Bygdoy Alle 3
N-0257 Oslo

Tel. : (47) 221 21 440
Fax : (47) 224 36 420
E-mail : bagatelle@relaischateaux.fr

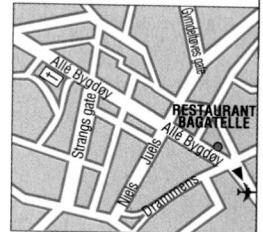

From the south: motorway E6 or E18, exit at Oslo V in the Oslo tunnel. From the north: E18 motorway, exit at Oslo V before the Oslo tunnel. The restaurant is next to the National Library opposite the Hydro Park.

Owners : AS. Holding, Christen Sveaas, Eyvind Hellstrom
Director : Eyvind Hellstrom
Weekly closing : Sunday
Anual closing :
Easter, three weeks late July/early August and Christmas

✈ Oslo (**Intl**) 50 km

🍴 Menus **550-950 NOK** s.i.
Carte **560-850 NOK** s.i.

🛏 no

In Oslo, you must go to Hege and Eyvind Hellstrom's restaurant. The Bagatelle's decor with its large bouquets and contemporary paintings is by Mary. Eyvind is the master of flavours. Savour the «asperges et petits pois au beurre de truffes», «morue aux langues d'oursin et aux crosnes», «foie gras chaud "multifruits"» and «cabillaud truffé rôti en peau». Freshness, elegance and a fine Franco-Italian cellar.

371

www.relaischateaux.fr/bagatelle

NOK : Norvegian krone

Visa

HOTEL HOLT

Tel. : (354) 552 5700
Fax : (354) 562 3025
E-mail : holt@relaischateaux.fr

Bergstadastraeti 37
IS-101 Reykjavik

Iceland

In the heart of Reykjavik, a few minutes from the Parliament and Government House.

Owner : Skuli Thorvaldsson
Director : E. Ingi Fridgeirsson
Annual closing :
From December 24th to 26th

✈	Reykjavik **(Intl)** 5 km Keflavik 50 km
🍴	Menus **1 795-4 000 ISK** s.i. Carte **950-3 800 ISK** s.i.
⚷	30 rooms **12 400-16 100 ISK** s.i.
⚷	12 suites **18 300-23 800 ISK** s.i.
🍷	**1 240 ISK** s.i.
🍖	yes
🚶	5 km

Fishing, walks...

This splendid hotel in the heart of Reykjavik not only offers the ultimate in modern comfort, it also presents 300 works by Icelandic artists. The stylish «Gallery» is Iceland's most renowned restaurant. The Gallery's superb cuisine offers a variety of delicacies from Iceland's pristine fishing grounds as well as an impressive selection of fine wines. After visiting the sights, linger over an aperitif and gaze out across the sea glittering under a summer sun that never sets.

ISK : Icelandic crown

www.relaischateaux.fr/holt

STIKLIAI HOTEL

Lithuania

Gaono Str. 7
2024 Vilnius

Tel. : (370) (2) 62 79 71
Fax : (370) (2) 22 38 70
E-mail : stikliai@relaischateaux.fr

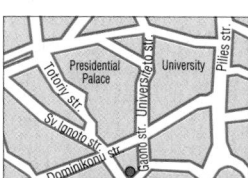

Straight from the airport to the town centre to Basanauicius street. Go to the end of this street to the hotel via Traku street and Domininkonu street.

Owner :
Romualdas Zakarevicius
Director : Alfreda Mikulskiene
Open all year

✈ Vilnius **(Intl)** 10 km

🍴 Carte **120-280 LTL** s.i.

⚷ 18 rooms
660-840 LTL s.i.

⚷ 11 suites
840-1 400 LTL s.i.

🍷 **40 LTL** s.i.

🕎 no

I n the centre of the historic city of Vilnius, listed as belonging to world heritage by Unesco, this beautiful 17th century residence lovingly restored is named after the glass blowers who worked in the narrow streets where it is located. The decoration highlights the warm colours of Lithuania. The elegant comfort of the rooms, the winter garden and the remarkable hospitality of the hosts will leave you captivated.

373

www.relaischateaux.fr/stikliai

LTL : Litas

Visa

CHANNEL ISLANDS

ENGLISH CHANNEL

Alderney (GB)
Cap de la Hague
Cherbourg

St. Peter Port
Guernsey (GB)
Carteret

FRANCE

St-Hélier
Jersey (GB)
387

Coutances

Golfe de St-Malo

St-Malo
Avranches

St-Brieuc
Le Mont-St-Michel

0   20   40   60 km

ATLANTIC OCEAN

Stromness   Kirkwall
Hoy   Mainland
Pentland Firth   Orkney

St. Kilda   Lewis
Thurso
A 836

Outer Hebrides   The Minch   A 894   A 837   A 839   A 9   A 836

Lochmaddy   Ullapool   A 835   Moray Firth
North Uist   A 9
Dunvegan   Elgin
South Uist   Skye   Kyle-of-Lochalsh   Inverness   A 96   A 96
Barra   A 87   Loch Ness   Spey   A 96   A 90
Rhum   Mallaig   A 82   Aberdeen
399   398   Fort William   Dee
Coll   Pitlochry
Tiree   397   396   Perth   A 90
Oban   A 85   Crianlarich   Dundee
Mull   A 82
Colonsay   Kirkcaldy   Firth of Forth
Jura   Scotland   Edinburgh
Islay   Glasgow   A 8   M 8
Kintyre   Arran   Berwick-upon-Tweed
Ayr   A 76   A 1

North Channel   Campbeltown   A 77   Moffat   A 68   A 1

Ballycastle   A 2   Dumfries   A 74
Londonderry   A 6   Ballymena   Stranraer   Carlisle   Newcastle-Upon-Tyne
Donegal   N 15   Omagh   Larne   A 75   Penrith   A 69   Sunderland
Donegal Bay   Enniskillen   Northern   M 2   395   Tyne
Sligo   Ireland   Belfast   394   A 66   Darlington   A 171
Achill   Armagh   A 3   Kendal   Scarborough
Westport   N 5   N 16   Dundalk   Man   A 595   A 66   A 1
N 60   N 2   Douglas   393   A 64
IRELAND   Boyne   IRISH   Blackpool   York   Kingston-upon-Hull
Galway   Athlone   N 4   SEA   Blackburn   M 180
Aran   N 6   Holyhead   Anglesey   A 5   Liverpool   Bradford   Leeds
River Shannon   Lough Derg   Llandudno   Birkenhead   Manchester   M 62
N 18   Dublin   392   Chester   A 6   Sheffield
Limerick   Portlaoise   N 7   M 1   Stoke-on-Trent   Derby   England
N 24   N 9   Cardigan   Schrewsbury   A 41   Nottingham
Caher   N 11   Arklow   Bay   Aberystwyth   A 470   Leicester   A 17
Wolverhampton   391   A 6
Fishguard   Birmingham   Coventry   Cambridge
Wales   A 470   A 46   A 428
Worcester   A 50   390   Oxford   Luton
389   Cheltenham   A 40   381
Swansea   A 465   A 46   380   379   London
Bristol   M 4   Reading   377   378
Cardiff   Channel   Bath   Windsor
388   A 36   Crawley   382
Barnstaple   Taunton   Salisbury   Southampton   A 27   Brighton   Hasting
Exeter   A 303   384   Portsmouth
386   385   383   Bournemouth   Wight
Plymouth   Dorchester   A 27
Penzance   A 30
Scilly

ENGLISH CHANNEL

0   50   100   150   200   250 km

LONDON

Bayswater Road   Oxford Street   SOHO   COVENT GARDEN
MAYFAIR   377
Speaker's Corner   Grosvenor Square   Piccadilly Circus   Charing Cross   Strand
Hyde Park   Park Lane   St James's Park   Embankment   Waterloo Station
Albert Memorial   Hyde Park Corner   Buckingham Palace   Houses of Parliament
Kensington Road   KNIGHTSBRIDGE   378   WESTMINSTER
BROMPTON   Victoria Street   Victoria Station
Natural History Museum   Sloane Square   The Tate Gallery
CHELSEA   King's Road   PIMLICO

0   1 000 metres

374

UNITED KINGDOM

Establishments	Nearest major city	Relais & Châteaux	Relais Gourmands	Page
Airds Hotel (The)	Fort William	⚜		397
Arisaig House	Fort William	⚜		399
Bodysgallen Hall	Cherster	⚜		392
Buckland Manor Hotel	Cheltenham	⚜		389
Chewton Glen Hotel	Bournemouth	⚜		383
Farlam Hall Hotel	Carlisle	⚜		395
Gavroche (Le)	London		🍳	377
Gidleigh Park	Exeter	⚜	🍳	386
Gravetye Manor	East Grinstead	⚜		382
Hambleton Hall	Leicester	⚜		391
Hartwell House	Oxford	⚜		381
Inverlochy Castle	Fort William	⚜		398
Kinnaird	Perth	⚜		396
Longueville Manor	St-Hélier	⚜		387
Mallory Court	Leamington Spa	⚜		390
Manoir aux Quat' Saisons (Le)	Oxford	⚜	🍳	380
Middlethorpe Hall	York	⚜		393
Sharrow Bay Country House	Penrith	⚜		394
Stock Hill Country House	Salisbury	⚜		384
Ston Easton Park	Bath	⚜		388
Summer Lodge	Dorchester	⚜		385
Tante Claire (La)	London		🍳	378
Waterside Inn (The)	Windsor	⚜	🍳	379

NORTH

SEA

The Wash

King's Lynn

Norwich

Great Yarmouth

Ipswich

Harwich

Southend-on-Sea

Dover · Channel Tunnel

Dunkerque

Folkestone

Calais

Boulogne

FRANCE

Strait of Dover

RUINART

La *plus* Ancienne
Maison
De CHAMPAGNE   *Depuis*
1729

LE GAVROCHE

U.K.

43 Upper Brook Street
London W1Y1PF

Tel. : (44) (020) 7 408 0881
Fax : (44) (020) 7 491 4387
E-mail : gavroche@relaischateaux.fr

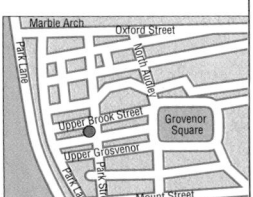

In the centre of London, near Hyde Park and Marble arch.

Owner : Michel Roux Jr.
Director : Silvano Giraldin
Weekly closing :
Saturday and Sunday
Annual closing :
From December 24th to January 3rd

✈ London City Airport (**Intl**)
23 km
London Heathrow (**Intl**)
25 km

🍴 Menus **37-78 GBP**
t.17,5% s.12,5%
Carte **60-100 GBP**
t.17,5% s.12,5%

🐴 no

Jacket and tie required.

S ituated in the heart of London, the Gavroche is the ambassador of classical and modern French cuisine. Following the tradition of his father, Michel Roux Jr. proposes a seasonal menu which has the «Gavroche touch». All wine lovers will be amazed by the selection of prize-winning vintages offered on the wine-list. Thanks to the comfort of the surroundings and to the impeccable service of the dedicated staff, guests can entirely relax and savour their meal.

377

GBP : Pound sterling
Visa

LA TANTE CLAIRE

SINCE 1987

Tel. : (44) (020) 7823 20 03
Fax : (44) (020) 7823 20 01
E-mail : tanteclaire@relaischateaux.fr

Wilton Place
Knightsbridge
London SW1X 7RL

U.K.

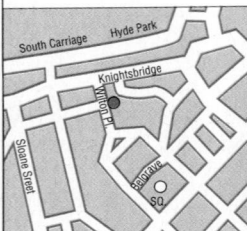

In Knightsbridge, on Wilton Place, to the right of the main entrance of the «Berkeley».

Owner/Chef : Pierre Koffmann
Weekly closing :
Saturday noon and Sunday
Annual closing :
From Dec. 24th to January 1st
and holidays

✈ Heathrow (**Intl**) 23 km

🍴 Menu **28 GBP** s.n.i.
Carte **75 GBP** s.n.i.

🐎 no

Formal dress required for dinner.

London's elite are enraptured by «La Tante Claire». Now established in one of the most discreet, stylish places in the very heart of Knightsbridge, Pierre Koffmann displays all his immense talent in this superb restaurant. Savour the «lotte rôtie bardée de calamars, jus de moules», the French cheeses and the divine desserts such as the «bombe glacée aux fruits de la passion» enhanced by vintage Bordeaux. A veritable delight.

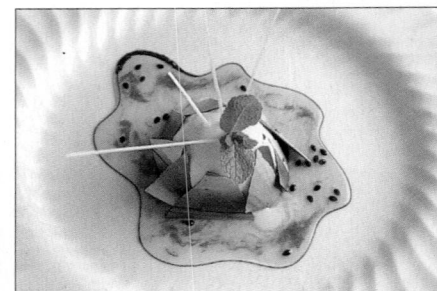

 Visa, Access

GBP : Pound sterling

www.relaischateaux.fr/tanteclaire

THE WATERSIDE INN

U.K.

Ferry Road
Bray
Berkshire SL6 2AT

Tel. : (44) (01628) 620691
Fax : (44) (01628) 784710
E-mail : waterside@relaischateaux.fr

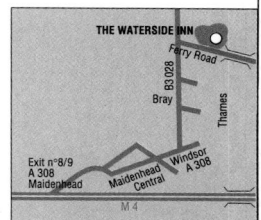

THE WATERSIDE INN
Ferry Road
B3 028
Bray
Thames
Exit n°8/9
A 308
Maidenhead
Maidenhead Central
Windsor A 308
M 4

M4, exit 8/9, Maidenhead Central;
towards Windsor (A 308);
B 3 028 Bray.

Owner : Michel Roux
Director : Diego Masciaga
Weekly closing :
Hotel : Monday
Rest. : Monday, Tuesday noon
Hotel and rest. : Sunday evening
from Oct. 1st to April 30th
Annual closing :
From December 26th
to January 27th

The Waterside Inn certainly lives up to its name. Its wide bay windows frame a picturesque view of the Thames. Michel Roux's menu, complemented by an excellent wine list, boasts delicacies such as «tronçonnettes de homard poêlées minute au porto blanc», «filets de lapereau grillés aux marrons glacés». Guests can also enjoy the luxury of the riverside terrace or an overnight stay in one of the cosy, modern guestrooms.

✈ Heathrow (**Intl**) 25 km

🍴 Menus
29,50-45-69 GBP s.n.i.
Carte **80 GBP** s.n.i.

⚷ 8 rooms
145-175 GBP s.i.

⚷ 1 suite
260 GBP s.i.

☕ included

🍴 no

🏃 5 km

379

Le Manoir aux Quat' Saisons

SINCE 1987

Tel. : (44) (01844) 278881
Fax : (44) (01844) 278847
E-mail : 4saisons@relaischateaux.fr

Church Road
Great Milton
Oxford, OX44 7PD

U.K.

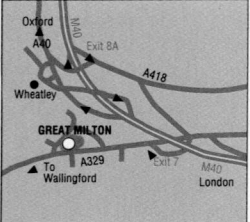

From London, M 40 towards Oxford, exit 7 Wallingford, A 329 towards Great Milton Manor.

Owner : Raymond Blanc
Open all year

 Heathrow (**Intl**) 60 km

 Menus **32-79 GBP** s.i.
Carte **70-85 GBP** s.i.

 25 rooms
230-395 GBP s.i.

 7 suites
475-550 GBP s.i.

 9,50-14,50 GBP s.i.

 no

 10 km

Fishing, clay pigeon shooting, hunting...

Raymond Blanc's contemporary classic is set in elegant gardens in the Oxfordshire countryside and provides an idyllic setting in which to savour his magical cuisine. «Trois bouchées gourmandes aux parfums d'ailleurs». Dishes to delight the palate are created from the freshest of foods, using as many organic products as possible and vegetables from the Manoir's garden when in season. The thirty two rooms are each a unique example of the best in design and comfort. Home to Raymond Blanc's famous Ecole de Cuisine.

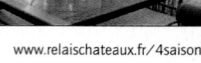

GBP : Pound sterling

www.relaischateaux.fr/4saisons

380

Hartwell House

Oxford Road (near Aylesbury)
Buckinghamshire HP17 8NL

U.K.

Tel. : (44) (01296) 747444
Fax : (44) (01296) 747450
E-mail : hartwell@relaischateaux.fr

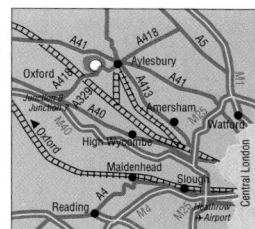

*From London, M40 to junction 7,
then A329/A418
towards Thame/Aylesbury.*

Owner : Richard Broyd
Director : Jonathan Thompson
Open all year

✈ Heathrow (**Intl**) 56 km
Gatwick (**Intl**) 99 km

GPS N 51° 48' 43''
W 000° 50' 88''

🍴 Menus **22-29 GBP** s.i.
Carte **44 GBP** s.i.

☛ 34 rooms
205-305 GBP s.i.

🔑 13 suites
305-600 GBP s.i.

☕ 11,50-15,90 GBP s.i.

🐾 yes (no extra cost)

♪ 2 km

Fishing, croquet, hot-air
ballooning, walking, Oxford,
Waddesdom Manor, spa, sauna,
jacuzzi, hammam.

T his beautifully restored 18th-century stately home is set in a large park in the countryside only one hour from London. The magnificent rooms, once lived in by exiled Louis XVIII and his court, are now superbly furnished with antiques and hung with fine paintings. Enjoy tennis, or relax in the spacious indoor pool or sauna. Dine on delicious food in the elegant setting of the Soane Dining Room overlooking the garden.

381

GBP : Pound sterling

Visa Mastercard

GRAVETYE MANOR

Tel. : (44) (01342) 810567
Fax : (44) (01342) 810080
E-mail : gravetye@relaischateaux.fr

Near East Grinstead
West Sussex, RH19 4LJ

U.K.

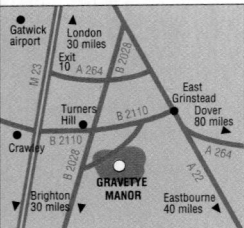

From M23, J10 East Grinstead, A264 The Dukes Head, B2028 towards Turners Hill.

Owners : Peter G. Herbert and Leigh S. Herbert
Director : Andrew Russell
Open all year

✈	Gatwick (**Intl**) 16 km Heathrow (**Intl**) 76 km
¶¶	Menus **28-38 GBP** s.i. Carte **40-55 GBP** s.i.
O⊷	18 rooms **98-290 GBP** s.i.
☕	**10-15 GBP** s.i.
ⴼ	no
♪	Royal Ashdown 8 km

Trout fishing, croquet.

his peaceful 16th-century Elizabethan manor in William Robinson's Natural English garden, is surrounded by a forest, yet only 30 miles from London. Relax in oak panelled sitting rooms warmed by open log fires and furnished with antiques. Every bedroom enjoys vistas of the tranquil gardens. Dine by candlelight, savouring classical British dishes, home-grown vegetables and fruits, with wines from one of Britain's finest cellars.

Visa

GBP : Pound sterling

www.relaischateaux.fr/gravetye

CHEWTON GLEN

U.K.

Christchurch Road
New Milton
Hampshire, BH256QS

Tel. : (44) (01425) 275341
Fax : (44) (01425) 272310
E-mail : chewton@relaischateaux.fr

From London, M3 then M27;
Bournemouth, A337 Lyndhurst,
and A35, then Walkford.

Owners :
Martin and Brigitte Skan
Director : Peter Crome
Open all year

 Southampton (**Intl**) 30 km
Heathrow (**Intl**) 120 km

GPS N 50° 45'
W 01° 40'

 Lunch **28 GBP** s.i.
Dinner **42 GBP** s.i.

35 rooms
220-355 GBP s.i.

18 suites
340-500 GBP s.i.

 english breakfast
17,50 GBP s.i.
continental **14 GBP** s.i.

no

on the premises (9 holes)
10 courses in 30 km

2 indoor and outdoor
tennis courts.

This splendid residence, set in a tranquil landscape of gardens and woodlands, 145 km from London, is imbued with the generous hospitality of its owners. Dine on the finest seasonal fish and game, and savour delicious local produce. Body and soul are rejuvenated in the gym, indoor pool, spa and sauna at the Health Club, where treatments include facials and aromatherapy. Enjoy long country walks, fishing and golf.

www.relaischateaux.fr/chewton

GBP : Pound sterling

Visa

STOCK HILL COUNTRY HOUSE

Tel. : (44) (01747) 823626
Fax : (44) (01747) 825628
E-mail : stockhill@relaischateaux.fr

Gillingham
Dorset SP8 5NR

U.K.

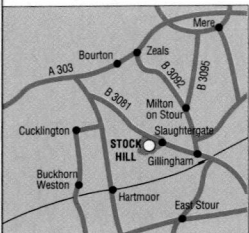

London M3, exit 8 - A 303
towards Exeter turn off B 3081
towards Gillingham.

Owners : Peter and Nita Hauser
Open all year

 Bristol (**Intl**) 50 km
Heathrow (**Intl**) 140 km

 GPS N 51° 2' 2"
W 2° 21' 20"

 Menus :
lunch **19,50-22 GBP** s.i.
dinner **30-32,50 GBP** s.i.

 8 rooms
half board
230-280 GBP s.i.

 included

 no

30 km
putting green on the premises

Hunting, fishing (trout, carp...)
in a private lake, flying club,
horseback riding, sauna.

The blond stone façade of this elegant Victorian house, set in the tranquil Dorset countryside, looks out onto acres of beautiful parkland studded with hundred-year old trees. Owners Peter and Nita Hauser have decorated the intimate guestrooms and lounges with impeccable taste and you will feel truly at home in this idyllic country retreat. Marvellously inventive cuisine is prepared with delicious local produce.

 Visa

GBP : Pound sterling

www.relaischateaux.fr/stockhill

Summer Lodge

U.K.

Evershot-Dorchester
Dorset DT2 OJR

Tel. : (44) (01935) 83424
Fax : (44) (01935) 83005
E-mail : summer@relaischateaux.fr

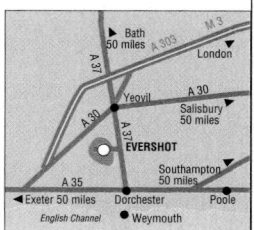

From London, M3, exit 8, A 303 then A 37 towards Dorchester then Evershot, Summer Lane.

Owners :
Nigel and Margaret Corbett
Director : Daniel Hostettler
Open all year

Heathrow (**Intl**) 160 km
Bournemouth 50 km

 GPS N 50° 50′ 1″
W 2° 36′ 3″

 Menu **36 GBP** s.i.
Carte **25-40 GBP** s.i.

 17 rooms
125-275 GBP s.i.

included

yes (extra cost)

5 km

Hunting, clay pigeon shooting, fishing, horseback riding, croquet...

Summer Lodge, a beautiful manor built in the heart of Thomas Hardy's Dorset in 1789, certainly lives up to its name. Everything from the elegant white façade and grey slate roof, to the pretty pastel rooms and the magnolias in the garden is imbued with summer splendour. Hosts Nigel and Margaret Corbett offer generous hospitality. Enjoy a classic English afternoon tea and refined cuisine enhanced by vintage Bordeaux.

385

www.relaischateaux.fr/summer

GBP : Pound sterling

Visa

GIDLEIGH PARK

SINCE 1984

U.K.

Tel. : (44) (01647) 432367
Fax : (44) (01647) 432574
E-mail : gidleigh@relaischateaux.fr

Chagford
Devon TQ13 8HH

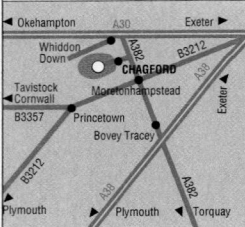

From London, M4 and M5;
after Exeter, take the A30,
then the A382 towards Chagford.

Owners :
Kay and Paul Henderson
Director : Catherine Endacott
Open all year

✈	Heathrow (**Intl**) 300 km Exeter 35 km
🛰	GPS N 50° 40' 58" W 3° 52' 36"
🍴	Menus **35-60 GBP** s.i. (lunch) **60-65 GBP** s.i. (dinner)
⚬⊸	12 rooms half board **375-475 GBP** s.i.
⚬⊸	3 suites half board **400-475 GBP** s.i.
☕	included
🛏	yes
⌇	10 km

Fishing, hunting, croquet...

K ay and Paul Henderson's idyllic
manor house stands in the midst
of Dartmoor National Park, renowned for
its wealth of prehistoric remains. Enjoy
rambling and horse riding in the beautiful
Devon countryside or fishing in the North
Teign River. Savour the delights of Devon
cuisine, prepared with the finest local
produce and fish from the nearby sea, and
relish one of the 400 fine wines from
France, Italy and America.

Visa

GBP : Pound sterling

www.relaischateaux.fr/gidleigh

LONGUEVILLE MANOR

U.K.

Longueville Road
St Saviour
Jersey JE2 7WF

Tel. : (44) (01534) 725501
Fax : (44) (01534) 731613
E-mail : longueville@relaischateaux.fr

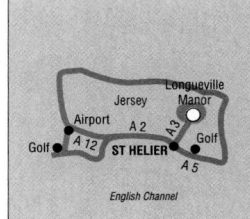

St Helier, A3 for 1,25 miles
towards Gorey, 0,125 miles
from the Derek Warwich Garage.

Owners :
Malcolm Lewis and Susan Dufty
Director : Malcolm Lewis
Open all year

✈ Jersey 10 km

🍴 Menus **20-36 GBP** s.i.
Carte **40-50 GBP** s.i.

⚷ 30 rooms
175-260 GBP s.i.

⚷ 2 suites
320-370 GBP s.i.

🏆 8-12,50 GBP s.i.

🎠 yes

♪ 5 km

Walks, horseback riding,
water sports...

Nestling in lush green countryside near high cliffs and blonde dunes, this 13th-century manor offers all the natural charms of Jersey and adds many of its own. Its elegant interior, fine antique furniture and carved oak panelling is tastefully combined with the height of modern comfort, while outside a heated swimming pool and lawn tennis courts await you. Enjoy impeccable service and delicious local cuisine.

387

www.relaischateaux.fr/longueville   **GBP : Pound sterling**   Visa

Ston Easton Park

SINCE 1990

Tel. : (44) (01761) 241631
Fax : (44) (01761) 241377
E-mail : stoneaston@relaischateaux.fr

Ston Easton-near Bath
Somerset, BA3 4DF

U.K.

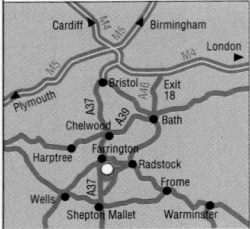

To reach Ston Easton,
take the A37 between Bristol
and Shepton Mallet.

Owners :
Peter and Christine Smedley
Director : Robin Hill
Open all year

✈ Bristol (**Intl**) 16 km
Heathrow (**Intl**) 158 km

🍴 Menus
26-50 GBP s.i. (lunch)
39-50 GBP s.i. (dinner)

🔑 15 rooms
185-305 GBP s.i.

🔑 6 suites
starting at **305 GBP** s.i.

🍽 included

🐾 yes

🚶 within the park

Croquet, fishing, hunting,
hot-air ballooning, billiards.

Y ou will be enchanted by the exquisite
18th-century decor of this Palladian
mansion set amidst romantic gardens and
parkland. The aristocratic guestrooms,
decorated with antique furniture and fine
artwork, look out across manicured lawns
to the River Norr. Savour refined cuisine
and excellent vintages. Enjoy croquet,
golf and horse riding, discover the charms
of Bath or take an exhilarating trip in a
hot-air balloon.

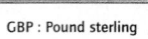

GBP : Pound sterling

www.relaischateaux.fr/stoneaston

BUCKLAND MANOR HOTEL

U.K.

Buckland near
Broadway
Worcestershire WR12 7LY

Tel. : (44) (01386) 852626
Fax : (44) (01386) 853557
E-mail : buckland@relaischateaux.fr

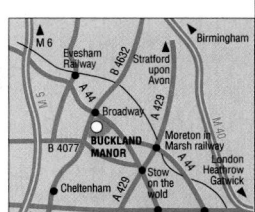

1 1/2 miles from Broadway,
Worcestershire, on the B4632;
Broadway to Winchcombe road.

Owners :
Roy and Daphné Vaughan
Director : Nigel Power
Open all year

 Birmingham (**Intl**) 72 km
Heathrow (**Intl**) 136 km

 GPS N 52° 01' 27"
W 1° 52' 90"

 Menus **29,50 GBP** s.i.
(lunch, except Sunday)
25 GBP s.i. (Sunday noon)
Carte
44-57 GBP s.i. (dinner)

 13 rooms
205-345 GBP s.i.

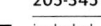 included

 no

 Putting green on the premises
3 km

Polo, hunting, fishing, horseback
riding. Stratford-upon-Avon
and Shakespeare.

T his historic 13th-century manor, mentioned in William the Conqueror's Domesday Book, lies amidst beautiful floral gardens in a peaceful valley in the Cotswolds. Decorated with fine artwork, period furniture and hand-woven tapestries, its elegant interior reflects the history and traditions of Worcestershire. Savour fine wines and local cuisine and enjoy Shakespeare's greatest works in nearby Stratford-upon-Avon.

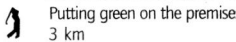

GBP : Pound sterling

Visa

MALLORY COURT

Tel. : (44) (01926) 330214
Fax : (44) (01926) 451714
E-mail : mallory@relaischateaux.fr

Harbury Lane
Bishops Tachbrook, Leamington Spa
Warwickshire CV33 9QB

U.K.

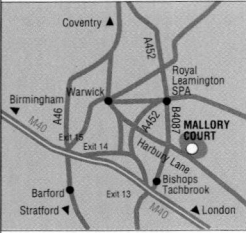

M40, from London J13,
from Birmingham J14, 2 miles
on B4087, to Leamington Spa.

Owners :
Allan Holland and Jeremy Mort
Open all year

 Birmingham (**Intl**) 30 km
Heathrow (**Intl**) 175 km

 Menu **37 GBP** s.i.
Carte **45-60 GBP** s.i.

 18 rooms
165-295 GBP s.i.

 Continental : included
English breakfast : à la carte

 no

 3 km

Trout fishing, horseback riding,
Warwick Castle Cotswolds.

This magnificent manor, surrounded by ten acres of landscaped gardens, lies in the heart of the Warwickshire countryside. You might begin the evening sipping champagne on the terrace before setting off for nearby Stratford-upon-Avon to visit the Royal Shakespeare Theatre. Or you may prefer to enjoy the manor's fine restaurant after a busy day roaming around the Cotswold villages and browsing in the antique shops.

Visa

GBP : Pound sterling

www.relaischateaux.fr/mallory

HAMBLETON HALL

U.K.

Hambleton
Oakham - Rutland LE15 8 TH

Tel. : (44) (01572) 756991
Fax : (44) (01572) 724721
E-mail : hambleton@relaischateaux.fr

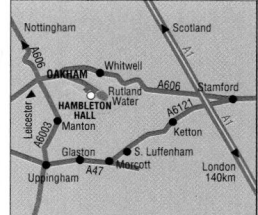

From London, A1 to Stamford,
then A 606; Whitwell
then Hambleton.

Owners : Tim and Stefa Hart
Open all year

 East Midlands (**Intl**) 45 km
Heathrow (**Intl**) 170 km

 GPS N 52° 39' 4''
W 000° 40' 1''

 Menus **14,50-60 GBP** s.i.
Carte **30-60 GBP** s.i.

 15 rooms
145-295 GBP s.i.

 included

 yes

8 km

Hunting, fishing, sailing,
horseback riding.

This 19th-century hunting lodge sits on a wooded hilltop surrounded by rolling grassland and the expanse of Rutland Water. Stefa Hart has decorated the sumptuous interior with impeccable taste. The motto «Fay ce que voudras» inscribed above the entrance, is most appropriate given the Harts' exceptional hospitality. Pleasure is the watchword at Hambleton Hall.

GBP : Pound sterling

BODYSGALLEN HALL

Tel. : (44) (01492) 584 466
Fax : (44) (01492) 582 519
E-mail : bodysgallen@relaischateaux.fr

Llandudno
North Wales LL30 1RS

U.K.

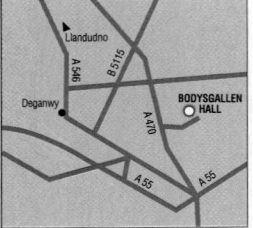

A55 to its intersection with A470.
Then follow A470 towards
Llandudno. The hotel is 2 miles on
the right.

Owner : Richard Broyd
Director : Matthew Johnson
Open all year

✈	Manchester (**Intl**) 128 km Chester 72 km
🍽	Menu **32,50 GBP** s.i.
⚷	19 rooms **140-230 GBP** s.i.
⚷	16 suites **160-230 GBP** s.i.
☕	**8,50-11,50 GBP** s.i.
🐾	yes (cottages only)
🏌	2 km

Historic Houses, castles, gardens,
preserved railways
and mountains scenery.

This magnificent 17th-century residence, set amidst luxuriant parkland in North Wales, has been beautifully restored. Bodysgallen Hall offers 19 spacious rooms decorated with antique furniture, while 16 charming cottages with private gardens await you in the park. Stroll through the elegant gardens, relax in the spa or indoor pool, play tennis and savour superb cuisine. The views of Snowdonia are breathtaking.

GBP : Pound sterling

www.relaischateaux.fr/bodysgallen

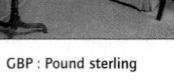

MIDDLETHORPE HALL

U.K.

Bishopthorpe Road
York
Yorkshire YO23 2GB

Tel. : (44) (01904) 641 241
Fax : (44) (01904) 620 176
E-mail : middlethorpe@relaischateaux.fr

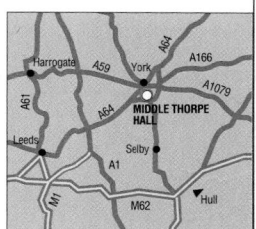

From A1, join the A64, following signs to York West (A1036). Follow signs to Bishopthorpe, then Middlethorpe.

Owner : Richard Broyd
Director : Stuart McPherson
Open all year

✈ Leeds-Bradford (**Intl**) 40 km
Manchester (**Intl**) 113 km

GPS N 53° 55' 80"
W 00° 105' 60"

🍴 Menus
starting at **32 GBP** s.i.
Carte
34,95-36,95 GBP s.i.

🔑 23 rooms
145-170 GBP s.i.

🔑 7 suites
185-255 GBP s.i.

☕ 9,50-12,50 GBP s.i.

no

4 km

This distinguished William III house, set in gardens and parkland, was built in 1699. Now restored with many antiques and pictures, its individually designed bedrooms are both in the house and nearby classical courtyard. Superb cuisine in the oak-panelled dining room. Health and beauty spa. Only 5 minutes from the historic city of York, and ideally situated for the many other attractions of Yorkshire.

Country Houses, abbey-church ruins, city of York, museums.

393

www.relaischateaux.fr/middlethorpe

GBP : Pound sterling

Visa

SHARROW BAY COUNTRY HOUSE

SINCE 1967

Tel. : (44) (017684) 86301
Fax : (44) (017684) 86349
E-mail : sharrow@relaischateaux.fr

Lake Ullswater
Howtown
Penrith Cumbria CA10 2LZ

U.K.

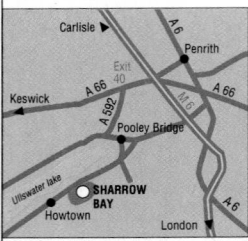

M6, exit 40; A 66 West; A 592; Pooley Bridge; turn right after the church, towards Howtown.

Owner : Brian Sack
Director : Nigel Lightburn
Annual closing :
From December to March

✈ Manchester (**Intl**) 160 km

🍴 Menus
32,25-48,25 GBP s.i.

🔑 19 rooms
half board/2 persons
300-400 GBP s.i.

🔑 7 suites
half board/2 persons
380-400 GBP s.i.

🍹 included

🛏 no

🎿 12 km

Water sports.

The terrace of this elegant family mansion, built in 1840, offers breathtaking views of Lake Ullswater. This idyllic country retreat has been impeccably run on very personal lines by the proprietor, assisted by the director and their caring staff, for the past fifty years. Savour traditional English cuisine. Sharrow is an oasis where one can escape the cares of the world and you will love the intimate relaxed atmosphere.

Visa

GBP : Pound sterling

www.relaischateaux.fr/sharrow

FARLAM HALL HOTEL

U.K.

Brampton
Cumbria CA8 2NG

Tel. : (44) (016977) 46234
Fax : (44) (016977) 46683
E-mail : farlam@relaischateaux.fr

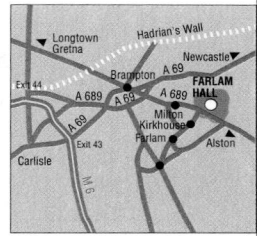

From the A 69 towards Newcastle, take the A 689 towards Alston for 2 miles to Farlam Hall (not Farlam Village).

Owners :
Quinion and Stevenson Families
Director : Alastair Stevenson
Annual closing :
From December 26th to 30th

T he elegant façade of this 17th-century manor, set in beautiful green parkland studded with hundred-year-old trees, is reflected in the waters of the ornamental lake and fountain. The 12 comfortable guestrooms in its interior are charming, and the seasonal cuisine a feast for the senses. Stroll through the magnificent countryside or visit Hadrian's Wall and the region's historic castles, abbeys and stately homes.

✈ Newcastle (**Intl**) 75 km
Manchester (**Intl**) 170 km

GPS N 54° 56' 08''
W 002° 40' 28''

🍴 Menus
30-31 GBP s.n.i.

⚷ 12 rooms
half board
220-250 GBP s.n.i.

☕ included

✦ yes

🎿 Brampton 5 km

Fishing, hiking.

P H

395

KINNAIRD

U.K.

Tel. : (44) (01796) 482440
Fax : (44) (01796) 482289
E-mail : kinnaird@relaischateaux.fr

Kinnaird Estate
By Dunkeld
Perthshire PH8 OLB

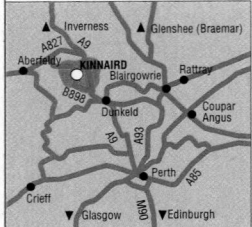

From Perth, A9 towards Inverness, do not enter Dunkeld, continue North, then B898 towards Dalguise.

Owner : Constance Ward
Director : Douglas Jack
Weekly closing :
Monday, Tuesday, Wednesday
from January 1st to March 1st
Open all year

✈	Edinburgh (**Intl**) 95 km Glasgow (**Intl**) 130 km
	GPS N 56° 38' W 3° 38'
🍽	Carte **45 GBP** s.i.
⚷	8 rooms **255-325 GBP** s.i.
⚷	1 suite **350 GBP** s.i.
🍷	included
	heated kennels
	6 km

Hunting, fishing, walking,
clay pigeon shooting, billiards...

T his elegant family home, built in 1770 near the River Tay, offers a majestic view of the Scottish Highlands. Set in the midst of its own 9,000 acre estate, Kinnaird offers salmon and loch fishing, deer stalking and country walking. After an invigorating day in the outdoors, relax beside a fire in your lovely room and enjoy a fine malt whisky in preparation for an excellent dinner.

Visa

GBP : Pound sterling

www.relaischateaux.fr/kinnaird

THE AIRDS HOTEL

U.K.

Port Appin
Appin Argyll PA38 4DF

Tel. : **(44) (01631) 730236**
Fax : **(44) (01631) 730535**
E-mail : airds@relaischateaux.fr

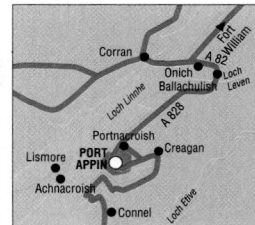

From Edinburgh or Glasgow, A82 towards Ballachulish, A828 towards Appin towards Loch Linnhe.

Owners : Allen Family
Director : Graeme R. Allen
Annual closing :
From January 7th to Feb. 4th
and from Dec. 21st to 27th

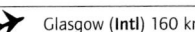

✈	Glasgow (**Intl**) 160 km
	GPS N 56° 33' 26" W 005° 24' 44"
🍴	Menu **40 GBP** s.i.
⚷	11 rooms **141-186 GBP** s.i.
⚷	1 suite **210 GBP** s.i.
☕	included
🛏	no

Skiing, water sports, climbing...

S et amidst beautiful scenery, the Airds Hotel, a former Ferry Inn dating from the early 18th century, offers elegantly furnished accommodation. The dining-room overlooks Loch Linnhe and the Morvern mountains, and guests can appreciate spectacular sunsets whilst enjoying fine cuisine prepared by Graeme Allen. Airds provides an ideal base for exploring the surrounding area which is steeped in history from Celts to Jacobites.

GBP : Pound sterling

INVERLOCHY CASTLE

Tel. : (44) (01397) 702177
Fax : (44) (01397) 702953
E-mail : inverlochy@relaischateaux.fr

Torlundy-Fort William
Scotland PH33 6SN

U.K.

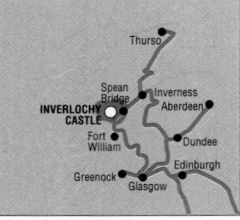

Inverlochy is situated
3 miles north of Fort William on
the main A82 towards Inverness.

Owner :
Inverlochy Castle Hotel Ltd
Director : Michael Leonard
Annual closing :
From mid January to February 12th

✈	Glasgow (**Intl**) 160 km Inverness 110 km
¶¶	Menus **35-50 GBP** s.i. Carte **30-50 GBP** s.i.
⊶	16 rooms **250-450 GBP** s.i.
⊶	1 suite **390-450 GBP** s.i.
☕	included
⚞	no
♪	3 km

Fishing, skiing, pheasant
shooting, stalking for red deer,
guided hill walking...

Inverlochy Castle built in 1863 near the site of the original 13th century fortress, nestles in the foothills of Ben Nevis, sitting amidst some of Scotland's finest scenery once enjoyed by queen Victoria herself. The beauty and tranquillity of the castle's setting is remarkable, and in keeping with the grandeur of its surroundings.

  Visa

GBP : Pound sterling

www.relaischateaux.fr/inverlochy

ARISAIG HOUSE

U.K.

Beasdale
By Arisaig
Inverness-shire, PH 39 4NR

Tel. : (44) (01687) 450622
Fax : (44) (01687) 450626
E-mail : arisaig@relaischateaux.fr

From Glasgow, towards Fort William, A 830 Mallaig; 3 miles East from the village of Arisaig.

Owners :
Ruth, John and Andrew Smither and Alison Wilkinson
Directors :
David and Alison Wilkinson
Annual closing :
From November to April

 Glasgow (**Intl**) 220 km
Inverness 160 km

 GPS N 56° 53' 50''
W 005° 48' 33''

 Menu **40 GBP** s.i.

 10 rooms
160-275 GBP s.i.

 2 suites
260 GBP s.i.

 included

 no

15 km

Fishing, water sports.

This charming stone manor house, set in sumptuous parkland studded with century-old beech trees and brightly-coloured rhododendrons, lies on the spectacular Highland coast. Its elegant wood-panelled rooms, with magnificent fireplaces and vaulted ceilings, are tastefully decorated with floral-print fabrics and china figurines. The local produce, seafood and game served at dinner are a veritable feast for the palate.

ATLANTIC OCEAN

Aran Island

Belmullet
Erris Head

Buncrana
Coleraine
R 238
R 241
Lough Foyle

Letterkenny
N 56
N 13
N 13
N 14
A 2
A 37
Londonderry
A 6
A 5

N 56
Donegal
N 15
Northern
Ireland
A 5
Omagh
A 32
A 505
A 31

Castlebar
Ballina
N 57
N 59
N 59
Sligo
N 16
Enniskillen
GREAT BRITAIN
A 28
M 1

408
Clew Bay
Westport
N 5
N 17
N 5
N 4
Boyle
Lower Lough Erne
Upper Lough Erne
A 4
A 3
Armagh
A 26

Clifden
406
N 59
Lough Mask
Claremorris
N 60
N 5
N 61
N 4
Cavan
N 87
N 3
N 54
N 2
Newry
N 53

407
N 59
Lough Corrib
Roscommon
N 63
N 61
Longford
N 55
N 3
N 52
Dundalk
N 52
Ardee
N 1

Galway
N 17
N 63
Lough Ree
Athlone
Mullingar
N 52
N 51
Navan
N 52
Drogheda
N 2
N 1

Galway Bay
N 6
Loughrea
N 65
Shannon
N 62
N 52
Tullamore
N 4
Boyne
M 4
Dublin
N 1

Aran Islands
N 67
Lough Derg
N 52
N 52
N 62
Roscrea
N 7
N 80
N 7
M 7
N 7
Naas
N 7
Dún Laoghaire

Ennistimon
N 18
Ennis
N 7
Nenagh
N 62
Portlaoise
N 80
N 9
N 81
Wicklow
N 11

Kilrush
River Shannon
N 68
A18
Limerick
N 24
N 8
Carlow
N 77
N 9
N 80
Slaney
N 11
Arklow
N 11

Tralee
Dingle
N 86
N 21
N 69
Kilkenny
N 10
N 9
N 11
409

Dingle Bay
Valentia Island
N 70
N 23
N 21
N 20
Tipperary
N 74
Cashel
N 76
N 10
N 24
Barrow
N 80
N 30
N 11
Enniscorthy

Cahersiveen
N 70
Killarney
N 72
405
Mallow
N 8
Caher
N 24
Clonmel
Suir
N 24
N 25
N 11
Wexford
N 25

Kenmare
403
N 71
Blackwater
N 22
N 20
N 8
N 72
N 25
Waterford
Rosslare

Glengarriff
404
N 71
Lee
Cork
N 25
Dungarvan

Bantry Bay
Bantry
N 71
Cobh
St. George's

Clear Island
Skibbereen

400

0   20   40   60   80   100 km

CELTIC SEA

IRELAND

SHEEN FALLS LODGE

Kenmare
Co. Kerry

Tel. : (353) (064) 41600
Fax : (353) (064) 41386
E-mail : sheenfalls@relaischateaux.fr

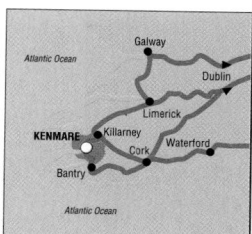

From Kenmare, N 71 direction
Glengarriff, left after the
suspension bridge.

Owner : Bent Hoyer
Director : Adriaan Bartels
Annual closing :
From January 4th to February 6th
and from Nov. 29th to Dec. 23rd

✈ Kerry (**Intl**) 48 km
Cork (**Intl**) 96 km

🛬 GPS N 51° 50' W 09° 35'

🍴 Menu **37,50 IEP** s.i.
48 €

🔑 51 rooms
168-258 IEP s.i.
213-328 €

🔑 9 suites
268-378 IEP s.i.
340-480 €

☕ 15 IEP s.i.
19 €

🐎 no

🎵 Kenmare 2 km
Ring of Kerry 6 km

Fishing, clay-pigeon shooting,
horse-riding, fitness centre,
croquet, hill walking, mountain
biking.

W hen the first stones were laid in 1691, the famous Sir William Petty could not have imagined that this magnificent lodge would become so renowned. A 300-acre haven of woodland and cascading waterfalls, with its luxurious rooms, extensive cellar of fine wines, and rare books, the lodge retains the welcoming atmosphere of a country manor house. Outstanding service and cuisine combine to make your stay as unique as Ireland itself.

IEP : Irish punt

Visa

BALLYLICKEY MANOR HOUSE

SINCE 1967

Tel. : (353) (027) 50071
Fax : (353) (027) 50124
E-mail : ballylickey@relaischateaux.fr

Ballylickey
Bantry bay
Co. Cork

Ireland

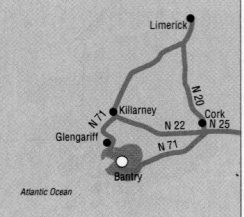

N 71 between Bantry and Glengariff, exit T 64 Ballylickey.

Owners :
Mr and Mrs George Graves
Annual closing :
From November to mid-March

✈ Cork (**Intl**) 80 km

🍴 Menus **20-30 IEP** s.10%
25-38 €
Carte **25-40 IEP** s.10%
32-51 €

🔑 5 rooms
130-150 IEP s.10%
165-190 €

🔑 5 suites
180-220 IEP s.10%
229-279 €

🛏 included

🏊 yes

🎣 2 km and 5 km
(2 golf courses)

Salmon and trout fishing, walks...

S et against a backdrop of wild moors, mountains and sweeping coastlines, Ballylickey offers breathtaking views, and its gleaming white façade opens onto magnificent ornamental gardens winding down to the sea. After a day's fishing or golfing, unwind beside a log fire and enjoy a gourmet meal by candlelight. Choose between a comfortable, sunny room in the manor or a charming cottage hidden in the gardens.

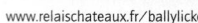

IEP : Irish punt

www.relaischateaux.fr/ballylickey

LONGUEVILLE HOUSE

Ireland

Mallow
Co. Cork

Tel. : (353) (022) 47156
Fax : (353) (022) 47459
E-mail : longuehouse@relaischateaux.fr

*3 miles west of Mallow
via N 72 road to Killarney.
Follow signs. Cork Ferry 35 km.*

Owners : O'Callaghan Family
Annual closing :
From Dec. 20th to February 12th

✈ Cork (**Intl**) 35 km
Shannon (**Intl**) 85 km

🍴 Menus **31-40 IEP** s.n.i.
39-51 €
Carte **28-40 IEP** s.n.i.
36-51 €

 13 rooms
140-170 IEP s.i.
178-216 €

 7 suites
starting at **170 IEP** s.i.
216 €

 included

 no

 Mallow 6 km

Horse-riding, horse racing
(2 km), salmon and trout fishing
on estate, hiking, walking on
estate grounds.

This 1720 Georgian Heritage Mansion is set on a 500-acre wooded estate, in the heart of Blackwater Valley. The O'Callaghan Family have preserved their beautiful home with loving care. William O'Callaghan's cuisine is complemented by 150 fine vintages. The house is surrounded by several top golf courses. The Blackwater river runs through the estate and fishing is private to our house guests. The valley is a walking enthusiasts paradise! Horse racing is available at Mallow race track 2 km away.

405

IEP : Irish punt

Visa

ASHFORD CASTLE

SINCE 1990

Tel. : (353) (092) 46003
Fax : (353) (092) 46260
E-mail : ashford@relaischateaux.fr

Cong
Co. Mayo

Ireland

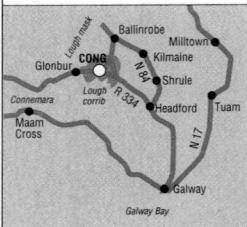

From Galway, towards Castlebar until Headford (N84), then towards Cong (R334).

Owner : Ashford Hotel Ltd
Director : Rory J.C. Murphy
Open all year

✈ Shannon (**Intl**) 205 km
Galway 35 km

🍽 Menu **40 IEP** s.15%
51 €
Carte **55-75 IEP** s.15%
70-95 €

🔑 72 rooms
140-312 IEP s.i.
178-396 €

🔑 11 suites
330-550 IEP s.i.
419-698 €

🍷 9,50-14,50 IEP s.15%
12-18 €

🚫 no

🏌 on the premises (9 holes)

Horseback riding (on the premises), hunting, fishing, clay pigeon shooting, archery, health centre.

A shford Castle, built in 1228 on the banks of Lough Corrib, Ireland's second largest lake, was formerly the home of the Guinness family. Voted best hotel in Ireland for several years now, Ashford offers the highest accommodation standards. Its sumptuous rooms are decorated with wood panelling, old masters and magnificent fireplaces, and the cuisine is simply sublime. Evening entertainment is provided in the Dungeon Bar.

    Visa

IEP : Irish punt

www.relaischateaux.fr/ashford

CASHEL HOUSE HOTEL

Ireland

Cashel
Connemara, Co. Galway

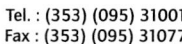
Tel. : (353) (095) 31001
Fax : (353) (095) 31077
E-mail : cashel@relaischateaux.fr

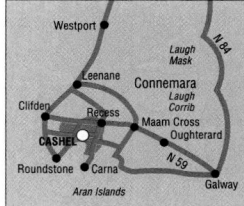

From Galway, take N 59 towards Recess, then take Cashel (1 mile West of Recess).

Owner : Dermot Mc Evilly
Director : Kay Mc Evilly
Annual closing :
From January 3rd to February 3rd

✈ Shannon (**Intl**) 152 km
Galway 72 km

🍴 Menus **32-35 IEP** s.12,5%
41-44 €
Carte **24-35 IEP** s.12,5%
30-44 €

⚷ 19 rooms
110-175 IEP s.i.
140-222 €

⚷ 13 suites
150-215 IEP s.i.
190-273 €

☕ included

🐴 yes (from G.B. only)

🎿 Connemara 24 km

Horseback riding (on the premises), canoeing...

G eneral and Madame de Gaulle were enchanted by this elegant mid-19th century house, nestling amidst the most beautiful garden in Ireland. Its Georgian guestrooms offer superb views of the Atlantic coastline and the rolling green hills of Connemara. After an invigorating walk through the magnificent Connemara wilderness, recline by a traditional peat fire, then savour delicious regional cuisine accompanied by vintage wine.

407

www.relaischateaux.fr/cashel

IEP : Irish punt

NEWPORT HOUSE

Tel. : (353) (098) 41222
Fax : (353) (098) 41613
E-mail : newport@relaischateaux.fr

Newport
Co. Mayo

Ireland

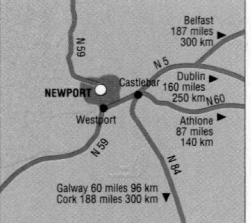

*Main roads to Westport, N 59
from Newport village (9,5 miles).*

Owners :
Kieran and Thelma Thompson
Annual closing :
From October 1st to March 18th

✈ Shannon (**Intl**) 200 km
Knock 70 km

GPS N 53° 53' 5''
W 9° 32' 50''

🍴 Menu (6 courses) dinner
33 IEP s.i.
42 €

⚷ 18 rooms
126-192 IEP s.i.
160-244 €

☕ included

🛏 no

⌣ 12 km

Fishing, clay pigeon shooting,
sailing, horseback riding.

The O'Donnell family, princes of Tir Connell, built their historic home in 1720. Its classical façade looks out across the Newport river which is famous for its salmon fishing. The house with its charming interior is decorated with elegant furniture and fine artwork. The delicious cuisine features freshly caught fish and fine garden produce. It is an idyllic haven in County Mayo.

Visa

IEP : Irish punt

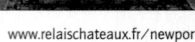
www.relaischateaux.fr/newport

MARLFIELD HOUSE

Ireland

Gorey
Co. Wexford

Tel. : (353) (055) 21124
Fax : (353) (055) 21572
E-mail : marlfield@relaischateaux.fr

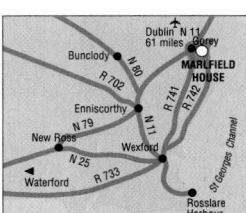

From Dublin, N 11 towards Wexford. Before Gorey, left towards Courtown Harbour.

Owners : Mary and Ray Bowe
Director : Margaret Bowe
Annual closing : January

 Dublin (**Intl**) 80 km
Shannon (**Intl**) 160 km

 GPS N 52° 39' 50"
W 06° 16' 00"

 Menus 37-40 IEP s.i.
47-51 €

 13 rooms
168-176 IEP s.i.
213-223 €

 6 suites
270-490 IEP s.i.
343-622 €

 included

 upon request

 Courtown 2 km

Sauna, fishing, horseback riding, beaches nearby.

This elegant 19th-century house, formerly the residence of the Earls of Courtown, is set amidst stunning flower gardens and woodland walks. Superbly renovated by hosts Mary and Ray Bowe, Marlfield's sumptuous interior is adorned with gleaming antiques, blazing fires and captivating paintings. The blooming conservatory, overlooking the garden, provides a most romantic setting in which to enjoy superb modern Irish cuisine.

www.relaischateaux.fr/marlfield   **IEP : Irish punt**

409

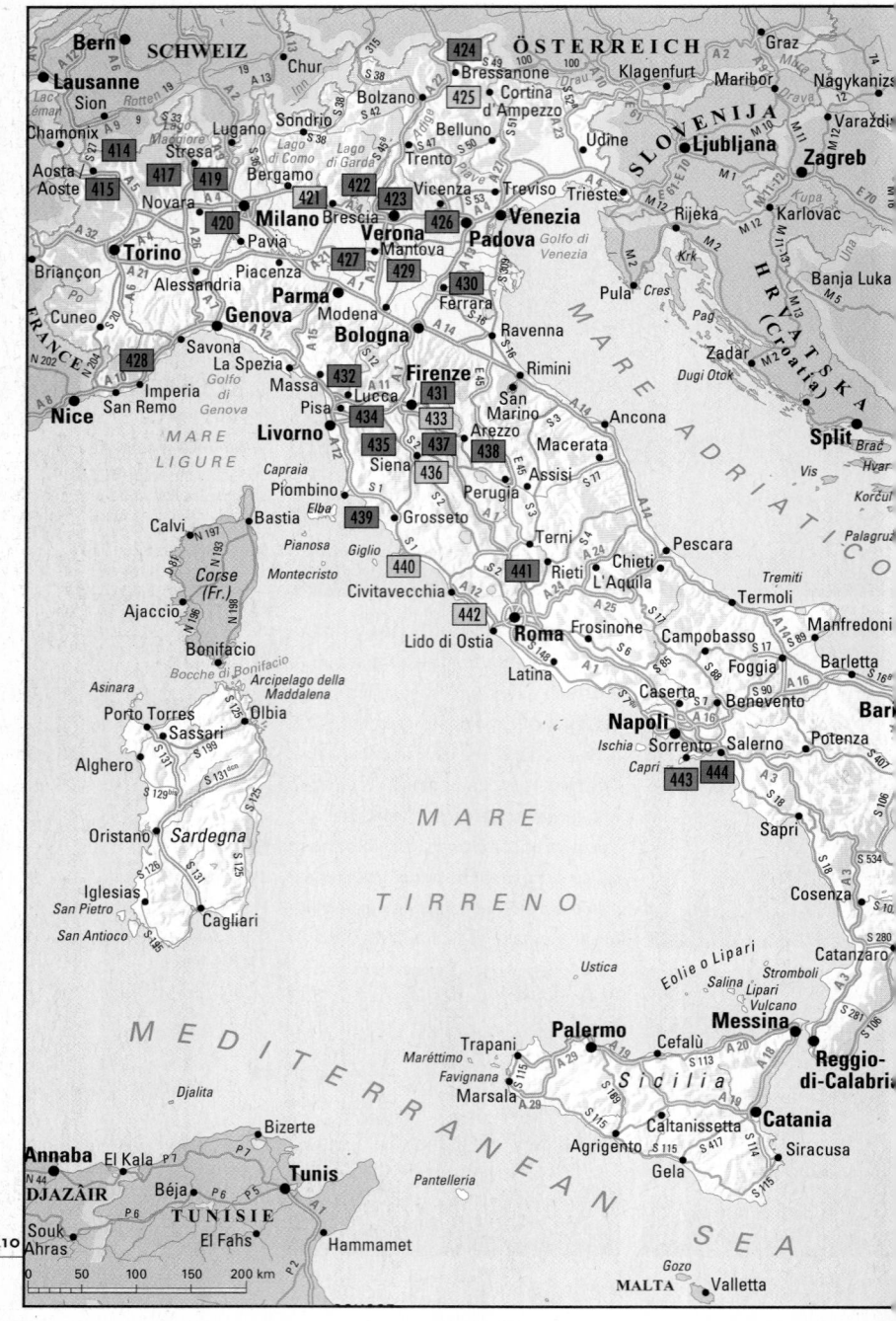

410

ITALY

Establishments	Nearest major city	Relais & Châteaux	Relais Gourmands	Page
Albereta - Rest. G. Marchesi (L')	Bergamo	⚜	👨‍🍳	421
Al Sorriso	Orta	⚜	👨‍🍳	417
Antica Osteria del Ponte	Milano		👨‍🍳	420
Borgo Paraelios	Roma	⚜		441
Bottaccio di Montignoso (Il)	Pisa	⚜		432
Don Alfonso 1890	Napoli		👨‍🍳	443
Gallia Palace Hôtel	Siena	⚜		439
Hotel Bellevue	Aosta	⚜		415
Hotel Certosa di Maggiano	Siena	⚜		436
Hotel Dominik	Bolzano	⚜		424
Hotel Duchessa Isabella	Ferrara	⚜		430
Hotel Hermitage	Aosta	⚜		414
Hotel La Collegiata	San Gimignano	⚜		435
Hotel San Pietro	Napoli	⚜		444
Locanda l'Elisa	Lucca	⚜		434
Melograno (Il)	Bari	⚜		445
Meridiana (La)	Genova	⚜		428
Pellicano (Il)	Roma	⚜		440
Posta Vecchia (La)	Roma	⚜		442
Relais Borgo San Felice	Siena	⚜		437
Relais il Falconiere	Cortona	⚜		438
Restaurant Dal Pescatore	Milano		👨‍🍳	427
Restaurant Enoteca	Firenze		👨‍🍳	431
Ristorante Ambasciata	Mantova		👨‍🍳	429
Ristorante Le Calandre	Venise		👨‍🍳	426
Rosa Alpina	Cortina d'Ampezzo	⚜		425
Sole di Ranco (Il)	Varese	⚜		419
Villa Del Quar	Verona	⚜		423
Villa Fiordaliso	Brescia	⚜		422
Villa la Massa	Firenze	⚜		433

Bon appétit!

www.mastercard.com

Please inquire about exclusive MasterCard® values by calling
Relais & Chateaux reservations, or visit our web site.

Vintages to drink in year 2000

Italy

Wines recommended by the wine waiters
of the Relais & Châteaux and Relais Gourmands.

* Index of world vintages to drink in year 2000 : page 607

	Name of wine	Wine to enjoy	Noble wine	Outstanding wine
	ITALY			
White	Frioul, Vénétie, Julienne	1998 - 1997	1994 - 1993	1990
Red	Toscane : Brunello di Montalcino, Vino Nobile di Montepulciano		1995 - 1993	1990 - 1985 - 1978
	Piémont : Barolo, Barbaresco, Gatinara	1996 - 1995 -1993	1990 - 1989 - 1985	1978 - 1971

HOTEL HERMITAGE

Tel. : (39) 0166 94 89 98
Fax : (39) 0166 94 90 32
E-mail : hermitage@relaischateaux.fr

I-11021 Breuil Cervinia
(Valle d'Aosta)

Italy

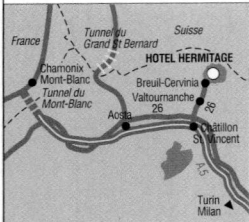

From Turin, A 5 towards Aosta, Châtillon exit,
RR 46 towards Breuil-Cervinia.

Owners : Neyroz Family
Director : Corrado Neyroz
Annual closing :
From beg. May to beg. July
and from beg. Sept. to end Nov.

✈ Milan (**Intl**) 170 km
　 Turin 110 km

🍴 Menus
　 80 000-100 000 ITL s.i.
　 41-52 €
　 Carte
　 90 000-120 000 ITL s.i.
　 46-62 €

⊶ 18 rooms
　 400 000-600 000 ITL s.i.
　 207-310 €

⊶ 18 suites
　 starting at **600 000 ITL** s.i.
　 310 €

☕ **40 000 ITL** s.i.
　 21 €

🚫 no

⛳ 9 holes / 1 km

Heli-skiing, climbing, flying club.
Airport service taxi.

Nestling at the foot of mount Cervin, this marvellous alpine-style chalet offers refined and elegant rooms with antique Aoste Valley furniture. After an invigorating day in the mountains, relax in front of a crackling log fire, then sit down to a romantic candlelit dinner. Enjoy exquisite dishes and vintage wines. Beauty salon and fitness centre. Skiing all year round.

Visa

ITL : Italian lira

www.relaischateaux.fr/hermitage

Italy

Piazza Venezia 5
I-21020 Ranco-Varese
(Lombardia)

Tel. : (39) 0331 97 65 07
Fax : (39) 0331 97 66 20
E-mail : soleranco@relaischateaux.fr

Alessandria-Gravellona highway,
Milan-Laghi, Sesto Calende exit,
towards Angera.

Owners : Brovelli Family
Directors : Carlo and Itala Brovelli
Weekly closing :
Monday and Tuesday
from November to March
Annual closing :
From Dec. 1st to February 14th

I l Sole celebrates its 150th anniversary in the year 2000. Managed, as always, by the Brovelli family, cleverly perpetuating tradition. Andrea will offer you one of the 14 rooms, some of them overlook the lake so that you can fully appreciate your stay in this fragrant, pastoral setting. Then enjoy the delicate flavours of Carluccio's cuisine with many seafood specialities, followed by Davide's delicious desserts.

✈ Milan-Malpensa (**Intl**) 20 km
Milan-Linate (**Intl**) 50 km

GPS N 45° 48.00
E 008° 34.134

🍴 Menu **135 000 ITL** s.i.
70 €
Carte
110 000-140 000 ITL s.i
57-72 €

⚷ 4 rooms
350 000-400 000 ITL s.i.
181-207 €

⚷ 10 suites
450 000-700 000 ITL s.i.
232-362 €

☕ **20 000-30 000 ITL** s.i.
10-15 €

🍴 no

♫ 10 km

Flying club, fishing, sailing,
horse-riding, excursions on
the lake, visits to the botanical
gardens, tennis close nearby...

419

ITL : Italian lira

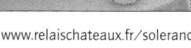

ANTICA OSTERIA DEL PONTE

SINCE 1998

Tel. : (39) 02 942 00 34
Fax : (39) 02 942 06 10
E-mail : osteriaponte@relaischateaux.fr

Piazza G. Negri 9
20080 Cassinetta di Lugagnano
(Lombardia)

Italy

From Milan take the main road to Abbiategrasso, then follow signs for the next 2 km.
From Turin exit Aut. Casello di Arluno, then Corbetta, then Cassinetta di Lugagnano.

Owners : Santin Family
Director : Renata Santin
Weekly closing :
Rest. : Sunday and Monday
Annual closing :
From Dec. 25th to January 12th
and in August

✈ Malpensa (**Intl**) 20 km
Linate (**Intl**) 25 km

🍴 Menu **170 000 ITL** s.i.
88 €
Carte
110 000-180 000 ITL s.i.
57-93 €

 no

Certosa di Pavia 22 km, piazza
di Vigevano 16 km.

Food lovers flock to this select restaurant near Milan to savour Ezio Santin's innovative gourmet cuisine. Sitting on the picturesque veranda or in the elegant white-walled dining room, resplendent with polished wood, sumptuous carpets and antique furniture, savour the exquisite «tarte de pâtes fraîches à la gourge et truffes blanches» and «oie de ferme à la royale», accompanied by the finest Italian vintages.

ITL : Italian Lira

www.relaischateaux.fr/osteriaponte

Italy

Via Vittorio Emanuele n°11
I-25030 Erbusco-Franciacorta
(Lombardia)

Tel. : (39) 03077 605 50
Rest. : (39) 03077 605 62
Fax : (39) 03077 605 73
E-mail : albereta@relaischateaux.fr

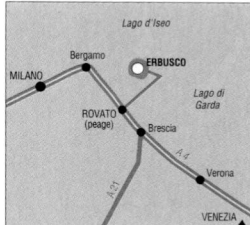

Turn left at the toll.
At crossroads towards Sarnico.
After 3 km turn right. Albereta
is on top of Bellavista Hill.

Owner : Carmen Moretti de Rosa
Director : Eugenio Rigo
Annual closing :
Rest. : from January 10th
to February 20th

This ancient manor is the home of the Moretti Family. It is located in the Alpine forelands, in the heart of the Franciacorta vineyards, famous for their sparkling wines. The estate, transformed into a hotel, boasts modern, bright, luxuriously decorated rooms. The restaurant too has been skilfully transformed by Gualtiero Marchesi, a master in combining Italian savour and inventiveness.

Milan (**Intl**) 65 km
Verona 60 km

GPS N 045°36.440'
E 009°58.781'

Menus
180 000-240 000 ITL
t.10% s.i.
93-124 €

38 rooms
starting at **330 000 ITL**
t.10% s.i.
170 €

6 suites
starting at **600 000 ITL**
t.10% s.i.
310 €

25 000-45 000 ITL
t.10% s.i.
13-23 €

yes (small dogs)

3 km (9 and 18 holes)

421

ITL : Italian lira

Visa

VILLA FIORDALISO

SINCE 1997

Italy

Tel. : (39) 0365 201 58
Fax : (39) 0365 290 011
E-mail : fiordaliso@relaischateaux.fr

Via Zanardelli 150
I-25083 Gardone Riviera
(Lombardia)

From Milan, A4, Brescia East,
exit 45 bis towards Lago di
Garda West. From Venice A4,
Desenzano, towards Salo.

Owner : Rosa Tosetti
Director : Max Tosetti
Weekly closing :
Rest. : Monday (all day)
and Tuesday noon
Annual closing :
From January 1st to March 7th

✈ Verona (**Intl**) 38 km
Milan (**Intl**) 100 km

🍴 Menus
85 000-130 000 ITL s.i.
44-67 €
Carte
75 000-110 000 ITL s.i.
39-57 €

⊙╥ 6 rooms
350 000-650 000 ITL s.i.
181-336 €

&╥ 1 suite
900 000 ITL s.i.
465 €

☕ included

🍴 no

⚇ 4 km

N estling amidst cypresses, pine trees and olive trees, near a private beach, Villa Fiordaliso offers idyllic surroundings and absolute calm. Its elegant neo-classical façade looks out across the tranquil waters of Lake Garda, and it was here that the poet Gabriele D'Annunzio used to gaze out through the villa's beautiful stained glass windows. The seasonal Italian cuisine is excellent and the hospitality exquisite.

Visa

ITL : Italian lira

www.relaischateaux.fr/fiordaliso

HOTEL VILLA DEL QUAR

Italy

Via Quar n° 12
I-37020 Pedemonte, Verona
(Veneto)

Tel. : (39) 045 680 06 81
Fax : (39) 045 680 06 04
E-mail : delquar@relaischateaux.fr

*A22 exit Verona north, take
the Valpolicella motorway all the
way to the end, then take a right
towards S. Floriano; Pedemonte.*

Owners : Montresor Family
Director : M. Evelina Acampora
Weekly closing :
Rest.: Monday (from March to April)
Annual closing :
From January 1st to March 14th

T his elegant Renaissance villa on the outskirts of Verona has been converted into a luxurious hotel. Encircled by an old stone wall, the villa is set on a vast estate, looking out across vineyards, meadows and emerald lawns where a private pool glitters in the sun. Enjoy exquisite calm in the guestrooms, decorated with oak beams and antique furniture, and savour exceptional Italian vintages in the ancient cellar.

Boscomantico 6 km
Catullo 18 km

GPS N 45° 29' 48''
E 010° 55' 49''

Menu-carte
75 000-100 000 ITL s.i.
39-52 €

18 rooms
400 000-470 000 ITL s.i.
207-243 €

4 suites
565 000-660 000 ITL s.i.
292-341 €

included

yes (ground floor only)

18 km

Sauna, gym, jogging course.

423

ITL : Italian Lira

Visa

HOTEL DOMINIK

Tel. : (39) 0472 83 01 44
Fax : (39) 0472 83 65 54
E-mail : dominik@relaischateaux.fr

I-39042 Bressanone/Brixen
(Südtirol)

Italy

Zürich 380 km — München 250 km — Wien 510 km
BRIXEN BRESSANONE — Innsbruck 80 km — Cortina 100 km — *Dolomites*
Meran 70 km — Bozen 40 km — Venezia 250 km
Milano 340 km — Verona 180 km

*Exit : from North Brixen/Bressanone.
From South Klausen/Chiusa.*

Owners : Dominik Demetz Family
Director : A. Dominik Demetz
Weekly closing :
Rest. : Tuesdays (except August)
Annual closing :
From January 10th to Easter and
end of November

✈ Innsbruck (**Intl**) 80 km
Bolzano 40 km

🍴 Menus
70 000-100 000 ITL s.i.
36-52 €
Carte
65 000-110 000 ITL s.i.
34-57 €

⊶ 25 rooms
260 000-360 000 ITL s.i.
134-186 €

⊶ 3 suites
400 000-600 000 ITL s.i.
207-310 €

☕ included

🛏 yes (extra cost)

Sauna, skiing,
hiking in the Dolomite Alps,
Archeology museum.

S et in the magnificent countryside of
the South Tyrol, in the ancient town
of Brixen-Bressanone, this comfortable
hotel is the ideal base for exploring
the Dolomite Alps. The quiet, spacious
guestrooms, decorated with traditional
Tyrolian furniture and featuring loggias or
private terraces, offer superb panoramic
views of the nearby mountains. The
traditional cuisine is delicious and the
regional wines superb.

 Visa

ITL : Italian lira

www.relaischateaux.fr/dominik

ROSA ALPINA

Italy

Str. Micura de Rü
I-39030 S. Cassiano
(Alto Adige)

Tel. : (39) 0471 84 95 00
Fax : (39) 0471 84 93 77
E-mail : alpina@relaischateaux.fr

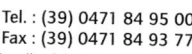

From Venice: motorway A27
to Belluno, follow SS51 to Cortina,
SS48 Passo Falzarego, S. Cassiano.
From Verona: A22 motorway
Bressanone exit, SS49 Val Puteria,
SS244 Val Badia, S. Cassiano.

Owner : Paolo Pizzinini
Director : Marlène Pizzinini
Weekly closing :
Rest. : Tuesday
Annual closing :
From Easter to mid-June
and from October 1st to Dec. 4th

T he Rosa Alpina is an ideal stopping place for those who seek fitness and relaxation. In a typical 1500m-high Dolomite village, this hotel has planned everything for invigorating holidays. After a wonderful day of skiing, enjoy beauty treatments, cures and relaxation in this temple of well-being, decorated with 17th and 19th century style Tyrolean furniture. Excellent regional cuisine and superb wine list.

✈ Venice (Intl) 180 km
　 Bolzano 80 km

🍴 Menus
　 60 000-95 000 ITL s.i.
　 31-49 €
　 Carte
　 62 000-120 000 ITL s.i.
　 32-62 €

🔑 31 rooms
　 350 000-620 000 ITL s.i.
　 181-320 €

🔑 20 suites
　 520 000-840 000 ITL s.i.
　 269-434 €

☕ included

🛏 yes (extra cost)

⛳ 8 km (9 holes)

Hunting, fishing, climbing, skiing...

ITL : Italian lira

Visa

RISTORANTE LE CALANDRE

SINCE 1999

Tel. : (39) 049 63 03 03
Fax : (39) 049 63 30 00
E-mail : calandre@relaischateaux.fr

Via Liguria 1
I-35030 Sarmeola di Rubano, Padova
(Veneto)

Italy

From Milano, A4 exit Grisignano,
take SS 11 towards Padua. From
Venice, A4 exit Padua West.

Owners : Alajmo Family
Director : Raffaele Alajmo
Weekly closing :
Sunday and Monday
Annual closing :
From January 1st to 10th
and from August 6th to 28th

✈ Venice (**Intl**) 20 km

🍽 Menus
150 000-160 000 ITL s.i.
77-83 €
Carte
130 000-160 000 ITL s.i.
67-83 €

🐴 yes

⛳ 6 km (27 holes)

Conference room.

P 🚰 ❄ 🔣

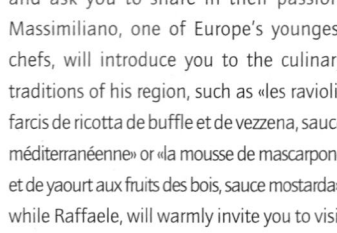

5 minutes from Padua, Raffaele and Massimiliano Alajmo will greet you and ask you to share in their passion. Massimiliano, one of Europe's youngest chefs, will introduce you to the culinary traditions of his region, such as «les raviolis farcis de ricotta de buffle et de vezzena, sauce méditerranéenne» or «la mousse de mascarpone et de yaourt aux fruits des bois, sauce mostarda», while Raffaele, will warmly invite you to visit the wine cevar with its 600 vintages.

   Visa

ITL : Italian lira

www.relaischateaux.fr/calandre

RESTAURANT DAL PESCATORE

Italy

Loc. Runate 17
Canneto S/O - I-46013 Mantova
(Lombardia)

Tel. : (39) 0376 72 30 01
Fax : (39) 0376 703 04
E-mail : pescatore@relaischateaux.fr

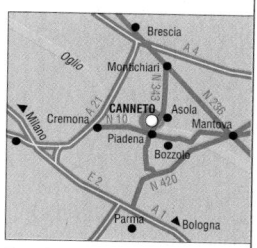

From Parma, Brescia or Mantova towards Piadena.

Owner : Antonio Santini
Weekly closing :
Monday and Tuesday
Annual closing :
From January 2nd to 22nd
and from August 6th
to September 3rd

The picturesque village of Canneto, set on the banks of the Oglio, provides an idyllic setting for this elegant restaurant opened in 1920 by Antonio Santini's grandparents. Today chef Nadia rejuvenates regional Italian cuisine with innovative flair and talent. Her «tortelli de chèvre et truffe blanche» is extraordinary and the «risotto au safran» a true gourmet delight. The cellar is a treasure trove of rare vintages.

Verona (**Intl**) 65 km
Milan (**Intl**) 100 km

Menu **165 000 ITL** s.i.
85 €
Carte
160 000-190 000 ITL s.i.
83-98 €

no

40 km

Historical 15th-century cities
of Cremona and Mantova.

ITL : Italian lira

LA MERIDIANA

Italy

Tel. : (39) 0182 58 02 71
Fax : (39) 0182 58 01 50
E-mail : meridiana@relaischateaux.fr

Via Ai Castelli
I-17033 Garlenda
(Liguria)

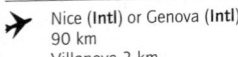

Take the A 10 towards Ventimiglia or Genova, exit Albenga, towards Garlenda (8 km).

Owners : Segre Family
Directors :
Edmondo and Alessandra Segre
Annual closing :
From Nov. to the beg. of March

✈ Nice (**Intl**) or Genova (**Intl**)
90 km
Villanova 2 km

⌖ GPS N 44° 02' 41"
E 08° 07' 35"

🍴 Menus **80 000-100 000 ITL**
t.10% s.i.
41-52 €
Carte **90 000-120 000 ITL**
t.10% s.i.
46-62 €

🔑 14 rooms
starting at **330 000 ITL**
t.10% s.i.
170 €

🔑 16 suites
starting at **500 000 ITL**
t.10% s.i.
258 €

☕ **30 000-32 000 ITL**
t.10% s.i.
15-17 €

🍴 yes (upon request)

🎏 on the premises (18 holes)

Nestling between Monaco and Portofino, La Meridiana is renowned for its traditional Italian hospitality and its magnificent 18-hole golf course. Gourmets will be enchanted by the «Il Rosmarino» restaurant where the finest seafood, infused with the delicate aroma of garden herbs, is enhanced by exceptional vintages. Enjoy a romantic stroll through the ancient Roman villages or relax on the magnificent beach at Alassio.

Visa

ITL : Italian lira

www.relaischateaux.fr/meridiana

RISTORANTE AMBASCIATA

Italy

Via Martiri di Belfiore, 33
I-46026 Quistello-Mantova
(Lombardia)

Tel. : (39) 0376 61 91 69
(39) 0376 61 90 03
Fax : (39) 0376 61 82 55
E-mail : ambasciata@relaischateaux.fr

*Modena-Brennero motorway, exit
at Mantova south or Pegognaga.*

Owners :
Francesco and Romano Tamani
Director : Francesco Tamani
Weekly closing :
Sunday evening and Monday
Annual closing :
From January 1st to 20th
and from August 8th to 30th

I n the Lombardy county village of
Quistello only 20 minutes from
Mantua, Francesco and Romano Tamani
have transformed their home into a stopping
place for superb gastronomy. They will
delight gourmets with their regional cuisine.
Savour the «tagliatelles aux saucisses
fraîches» and the sublime «millefeuille de
tripes de bœuf à la polenta grillées aux
feuilles de laurier». Excellent international
vintages.

Verona (**Intl**) 50 km

Menus
110 000-170 000 ITL s.i.
57-88 €
Carte
90 000-150 000 ITL s.i.
46-77 €

no

ITL : Italian lira

HOTEL DUCHESSA ISABELLA

Tel. : (39) 0532 20 21 21/20 21 22
Fax : (39) 0532 20 26 38
E-mail : isabella@relaischateaux.fr

Via Palestro 68/70
I-44100 Ferrare
(Emilia-Romagnia)

Italy

From Bologna or Padua,
A13 exit Ferrara-North,
straight ahead; Via Palestro and
right after Massari Park.

Owner : Evelina Bonzagni
Weekly closing :
Restaurant : Sunday
and Monday evenings
Annual closing :
From August 1st to 31st

✈ Bologna (**Intl**) 50 km
Venice (**Intl**) 90 km

🍴 Menus
120 000-150 000 ITL s.i.
62-77 €
Carte
140 000-170 000 ITL s.i.
72-88 €

🔑 21 rooms
430 000-540 000 ITL s.i.
222-279 €

🔑 6 suites
740 000-1 400 000 ITL s.i.
382-723 €

🍷 included

🍴 yes (extra cost)

🎿 2 km

Nestling in the heart of Ferrare, the picturesque town built by the dukes of Este, this elegant 16th-century residence is resplendent with coffered ceilings, ancient frescos and a collection of antique clocks. The sumptuous rooms, overlooking the park, are havens of comfort and the cuisine, inspired by the gastronomical traditions of Este, is a sheer delight. The magnificent Ferrare Palio is the oldest in the world.

Visa

 ITL : Italian lira

www.relaischateaux.fr/isabella

SINCE 1984

RESTAURANT ENOTECA PINCHIORRI

Italy

Via Ghibellina, 87
I-50122 Firenze
(Toscana)

Tel. : (39) 055 24 27 77
Fax : (39) 055 24 49 83
E-mail : enoteca@relaischateaux.fr

Piazza Santa Croce, Via Verdi,
and turn right into Via Ghibellina.

Owners : Giorgio Pinchiorri
and Annie Féolde
Weekly closing : Sunday, Monday
and Wednesday for lunch
Annual closing :
August and Christmas

✈ Firenze (**Intl**) 2 km
Pisa (**Intl**) 85 km

🍽 Menu lunch
90 000 ITL s.i. - **46 €**
Gourmet sampling menu
for the dinner
190 000-230 000 ITL s.i.
98-119 €
Carte
125 000-180 000 ITL s.i.
65-93 €

🐎 yes

🎿 Grassina 10 km

Uffizi museum, Duomo...

European gourmets flock to this restaurant set in a magnificent Renaissance palace. Giorgio Pinchiorri himself will help you choose from the 150,000 wines in his prestigious cellar, stocked with French, Italian and Californian vintages. In the kitchens, French chef Annie Féolde adds innovative flair to Tuscan cuisine with her «gnocchis parfumés à la Trévise» and her superb «filet d'agneau, aubergines, tomates séchées au soleil».

431

www.relaischateaux.fr/enoteca   **ITL : Italian Lira**   Visa

IL BOTTACCIO DI MONTIGNOSO

SINCE 1988

Tel. : (39) 0585 34 00 31
Fax : (39) 0585 34 01 03
E-mail : bottaccio@relaischateaux.fr

Via Bottaccio 1
I-54038 Montignoso
(Toscana)

Italy

From the north, A-12, Massa,
seafront towards Viareggio,
Cinquale, towards Montignoso.

Owner : Stefano d'Anna
Director : Sossio Mosca
Open all year

✈ Pisa (**Intl**) 30 km

⚓ GPS N 43° 59' 07''
E 10° 08' 35''

🍴 Menus
95 000-130 000 ITL s.i.
49-67 €
Carte
95 000-130 000 ITL s.i.
49-67 €

☍ 4 rooms
starting at **450 000 ITL** s.i.
232 €

☍ 4 suites
550 000-850 000 ITL s.i.
284-439 €

☕ 25 000-35 000 ITL s.i.
13-18 €

🛏 yes

🏃 3 km

Sauna, fishing, water sports,
flying club...

This beautiful 17th-century oil mill, nestling in the hills sloping down to the Tyrrhenian Sea, offers a perfect balance between authentic tradition and modern comfort. The guestrooms, resplendent with old oak beams, varnished floors and period furniture, are veritable havens of calm. As for the sunny Mediterranean cuisine, enhanced by fine Italian vintages and grappas, it is a sheer delight. Welcome to la dolce vita !

 Visa

ITL : Italian lira

VILLA LA MASSA

Italy

Via della Massa, 24
I-50012 Bagno a Ripoli
(Toscana)

Tel. : (39) 055 62 611
Fax : (39) 055 63 31 02
E-mail : lamassa@relaischateaux.fr

*Milan-Florence-Rome motorway,
exit Florence south, after 3 km,
take direction Bagno a Ripoli.
Follow arrow markings.*

Owner : Villa d'Este SPA
Director : Silvano Mamprin
Annual closing :
From Nov. 15th to March

 Firenze (**Intl**) 18 km
Piza (**Intl**) 50 km

 GPS N 43° 45' 53" E 11° 20' 18"

 Menus
50 000-160 000 ITL s.i.
26-83 €
Carte **110 000 ITL** s.i.
57 €

 24 rooms
off-season
360 000-650 000 ITL s.i.
186-336 €
season
470 000-750 000 ITL s.i.
243-387 €

With its riverside parkland, this 16th century villa is located in the heart of the unique light of the Tuscany countryside. From its 17th century period furniture, refined decoration, and inspired Tuscan cuisine to its superb cellar with its excellent regional vintages: it offers all the ingredients for an idyllic stay. Here you will savour the gentle art of living. For lovers of Italy and its flamboyant Renaissance.

 10 suites
off-season
900 000-1 100 000 ITL s.i.
465-568 €
season
1 000 000-1 300 000 ITL s.i.
516-671 €

 included

 yes

10 km

Fishing, horse-riding, biking...

www.relaischateaux.fr/lamassa

ITL : Italian lira

Visa

LOCANDA L'ELISA

SINCE 1994

Tel. : **(39) 0583 37 97 37**
Fax : **(39) 0583 37 90 19**
E-mail : elisa@relaischateaux.fr

Via Nuova per Pisa 1952
I-55050 Lucca
(Toscana)

Italy

From Rome or Bologna, A 1 exit Firenze, A 11 exit Lucca, follow signs to «Locanda l'Elisa».

Owner : Ruggero Giorgi
Weekly closing :
Restaurant : Sunday
Annual closing :
From January 3rd to Feb. 29th and from Nov. 20th to Dec. 31st

✈	Pisa (**Intl**) 18 km Firenze (**Intl**) 65 km
🍴	Menus 85 000-110 000 ITL s.i. 44-57€ Carte 95 000-120 000 ITL s.i. 49-62 €
🔑	2 rooms 330 000-490 000 ITL s.i. 170-253 €
🔑	8 suites 480 000-690 000 ITL s.i. 248-356 €
☕	32 000 ITL s.i. 17 €
🐕	yes (small dogs)
♘	25 km

This sumptuous mauve and white villa was restored during the Napoleonic era for one of Princess Elisa's civil servants. The soft Tuscan light floods through the windows of its elegant suites, decorated with marble fireplaces, luxurious damask fabrics, canopy beds and beautiful antique furniture. Enjoy a romantic dinner on the «Belle Epoque» veranda overlooking the park and savour one of the exceptional local vintages.

Visa

ITL : Italian Lira

www.relaischateaux.fr/elisa

HOTEL LA COLLEGIATA

Italy

Loc. Strada 27
I-53037 San Gimignano
(Toscana)

Tel. : (39) 0577 943 201
Fax : (39) 0577 940 566
E-mail : collegiata@relaischateaux.fr

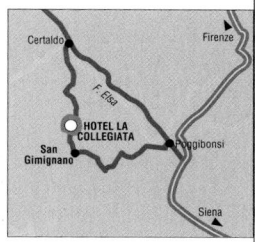

From Firenze, follow Firenze-Siena motorway, exit Poggibonsi north. Follow signs to San Gimignano. The hotel is 1.5 km from the city's historic centre.

Owner : M. Parco dei Cipressi
Director : Silvia Perko
Annual closing :
From January 6th to February 6th

Originally a Franciscan convent built in 1587, this magnificent hotel overlooks the heart of the Chianti wine region and is only a few kilometres away from the medieval city of San Giminiano. The guestrooms are located in the former cloister. You will dine under the Roman vaulting of the ancient chapel richly decorated in the sumptuous red so reminiscent of the Siennese Renaissance. From the uppermost floors, you can discover the 13 towers of San Giminiano.

✈ Pisa (**Intl**) 65 km

🍴 Menus
75 000-95 000 ITL s.i.
39-49 €
Carte
85 000-110 000 ITL s.i.
44-57 €

⚷ 16 rooms
550 000-850 000 ITL s.i.
284-439 €

⚷ 5 suites
850 000-1 300 000 ITL s.i.
439-671 €

☕ **20 000-35 000 ITL** s.i.
10-18 €

🚫 no

⛳ 20 km (18 holes)

Horse-riding, jacuzzi...

P ❄ 🚻 ♦ 🛗 〰️

435

Hotel Certosa di Maggiano

SINCE 1978

Tel. : (39) 0577 28 81 80
Fax : (39) 0577 28 81 89
E-mail : certosa@relaischateaux.fr

Strada di Certosa 82
I-53100 Siena
(Toscana)

Italy

From Florence, Siena South,
towards «Porta Romana»; right
in front of the Porta, 200 m.

Owner : I.T.A.R. S.P.A.
Directors : Anna Recordati,
Margherita Grossi
Open all year

✈ Firenze (**Intl**) 50 km
Pisa (**Intl**) 120 km

◉ GPS N 43° 18' 56"
E 011° 21' 01"

🍴 Menus
80 000-120 000 ITL s.i.
41-62 €
Carte
80 000-150 000 ITL s.i.
41-77 €

⚷ 6 rooms
starting at **700 000 ITL** s.i.
362 €

⚷ 11 suites
starting at **900 000 ITL** s.i.
465 €

☕ **50 000 ITL** s.i.
26 €

🛏 no

🧍 40 km

Horse-riding, biking,
thermal baths, visit of cellars
and gardens.

I n the 14th century, St. Bruno's disciples
used to meditate in the cloisters of
this beautiful Carthusian monastery.
Today gourmets gather here to savour
superb local cuisine and fine wines. The
panoramic view from the guestrooms
encompasses medieval Siena and its
magnificent cathedral, museums and
fountains. Visit the site of the Palio, the
Chianti vineyards and castles and explore
Volterra, Pienza and San Quirico.

ITL : Italian lira

www.relaischateaux.fr/certosa

HOTEL RELAIS BORGO SAN FELICE

Italy

San Felice
I-53019 Castelnuovo Berardenga (Siena)
(Toscana)

Tel. : (39) 0577 39 64
Fax : (39) 0577 35 90 89
E-mail : borgofelice@relaischateaux.fr

From Firenze, expressway towards Siena North, and towards Arezzo-Monteaperti San Felice.

Owner : RAS S.p.A
Director : Lorenzo Righi
Annual closing :
From Nov. 1st to March 31st
except for seminar facilities

✈ Firenze (**Intl**) 90 km

🍽 Menus
100 000-120 000 ITL s.i.
52-62 €
Carte
120 000-180 000 ITL s.i.
62-93 €

🗝 33 rooms
350 000-490 000 ITL s.i.
181-253 €

🗝 12 suites
730 000-840 000 ITL s.i.
377-434 €

☕ **50 000 ITL** s.i.
26 €

🛏 no

♪ 55 km

Beauty salon, painting workshop,
visit of S. Felice wine cellars.

T his charming inn is set in the medieval village of Siena, nestled in the hills of the Chianti Classico, in the heart of the magnificent Tuscan countryside. The inn's elegant stone façade looks out across a labyrinth of winding alleyways and shaded piazzas, and its beautifully decorated rooms are havens of comfort and charm. The superb regional cuisine will complete your experience of authentic Italian dolce vita.

P ❄ 🛗 💄 〽 🏓

437

ITL : **Italian lira**

Visa

RELAIS IL FALCONIERE

SINCE 1998

Tel. : (39) 0575 612 616
Fax : (39) 0575 612 927
E-mail : falconiere@relaischateaux.fr

Localita S. Martino 370
52044 Cortona (Arezzo)
(Toscana)

Italy

A1, exit «Valdichiana» direction Perugia, exit 2,Cortona. Arrival Camucia, direction Arezzo (SS71). Go 2 km and turn right at first crossroad.

Owners : Baracchi Family
Weekly closing :
Rest. : Monday from Nov. to March
Open all year

✈ Perugia (**Intl**) 45 km
Firenze (**Intl**) 100 km

🍴 Menus
80 000-90 000 ITL s.i.
41-46 €
Carte
80 000-100 000 ITL s.i.
41-52 €

🔑 10 rooms
360 000-440 000 ITL s.i.
186-227 €

🔑 2 suites
590 000 ITL s.i.
305 €

☕ buffet **30 000 ITL** s.i.
15 €

🐕 yes (small only)
extra cost

♫ 25 km

S et between Tuscany and Umbria, this elegant residence, built in 1600, was home to poet Antonio Guadagnoli in the 19th century. Today, Il Falconiere, which retains all the splendour of its historical past, has been magnificently restored. 10 guestrooms and 2 suites, resplendent with beautiful antique furniture, offer exquisite comfort. Savour regional cuisine while enjoying superb views of the idyllic Tuscan countryside.

Visa

ITL : Italian lira

www.relaischateaux.fr/falconiere

GALLIA PALACE HOTEL

Italy

Via delle Sughere
I-58040 Punta Ala, Grosseto
(Toscana)

Tel. : (39) 0564 92 20 22
Fax : (39) 0564 92 02 29
E-mail : gallia@relaischateaux.fr

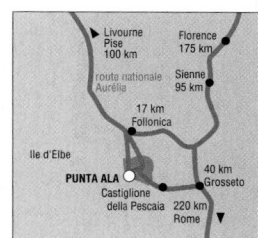

Rome, A 16 Civitavecchia,
Aurelia SS1 Grosseto, towards
Castiglione della Pescaia.

Owners : Gallia Family
Director : Luciano Bonfanti
Annual closing :
From October 1st to May 16th

✈ Pisa (**Intl**) 110 km

🍴 Menus
80 000-95 000 ITL s.i.
41-49 €
Carte
75 000-130 000 ITL s.i.
39-67 €

🔑 75 rooms
385 000-650 000 ITL s.i.
199-336 €

🔑 8 suites
580 000-980 000 ITL s.i.
300-506 €

☕ buffet included

🐾 yes (extra cost)
only in rooms

🏌 Club Punta Ala 2 km

Beauty centre, Turkish bath,
water sports, candlelit dinners in
the garden (Saturdays)...

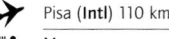

C lear blue skies, fine sand beaches and the turquoise waters of Punta Ala Bay... Experience the dolce vita at the Gallia Palace pool or in the shade of the century-old pine trees on the private beach. After a massage or steam bath at the beauty centre, savour seafood specialities and Tuscan wines. Explore medieval villages and Etruscan ruins and enjoy Grosseto's summer festivities such as the famous Rodeo of the Rose.

439

www.relaischateaux.fr/gallia

ITL : Italian lira

Visa

IL PELLICANO

SINCE 1982

Tel. : (39) 0564 85 81 11
Fax : (39) 0564 83 34 18
E-mail : pellicano@relaischateaux.fr

Cala dei Santi
I-58018 Porto Ercole, Grosseto
(Toscana)

Italy

From Rome, A 12 towards Civitavecchia, exit Orbetello towards Porto Ercole.

Owner : Roberto Sció
Director : Cinzia Fanciulli
Annual closing :
From January 1st to the end of April and from October to Dec. 31st

✈	Rome (**Intl**) 150 km
🍴	Menu **125 000 ITL** s.i. **65 €** Carte **95 000-145 000 ITL** s.i. **49-75 €**
🔑	27 rooms **480 000-1 100 000 ITL** s.i. **248-568 €**
🔑	14 suites **900 000-2 300 000 ITL** s.i. **465-1 188 €**
🍷	included
🐾	no
🏌	50 km

Beauty salon, hunting, fishing, water sports, horseback riding.

This elegant villa, set on the picturesque Argentario peninsula overlooking the Tyrrhenian Sea, is built on several levels. Wander down through flower-bedecked patios to the private beach and the pool by the sea or relax in a spacious room, secluded beneath the cypresses and pine trees. Dine al fresco at the barbecue buffet while contemplating the sunset or enjoy a romantic candlelit dinner at the panoramic restaurant.

Visa

ITL : Italian lira

www.relaischateaux.fr/pellicano

BORGO PARAELIOS

Italy

Valle Collicchia
I-02040 Poggio Catino, Rieti
(Lazio)

Tel. : (39) 0765 26 267
Fax : (39) 0765 26 268
E-mail : borgo@relaischateaux.fr

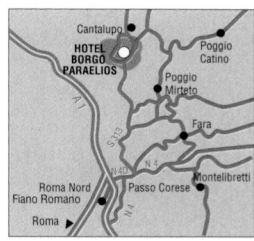

From Rome, A 1 exit Fiano Romano, towards Passo Corese. Left SS 313 towards Terni km 17.600.

Owner : Adolfo Salabé
Director : Andrea Salabé
Weekly closing :
Restaurant : Tuesday
Open all year

✈ Rome (**Intl**) 70 km
Urbe 30 km

🍴 Menus
110 000-140 000 ITL s.i.
57-72 €

 13 rooms
350 000-450 000 ITL s.i.
181-232 €

2 suites
550 000 ITL s.i.
284 €

☕ included

🐕 yes (small dogs only)
extra cost

⛳ on the premises (9 holes)

This magnificent 19th-century villa, surrounded by a beautiful park, is an idyllic haven of calm in which the architect has lovingly preserved the period furniture and marvellous vaulted ceilings of bygone days. The villa's elegant rooms are hung with masterpieces by Canaletto and Attardi and its restaurant pays tribute to the finest Italian gastronomy. The Borgo offers a special mini-bus service to Rome (just 40km away).

441

ITL : Italian lira

Visa

LA POSTA VECCHIA

SINCE 1992

Tel. : (39) 06 994 95 01
Fax : (39) 06 994 95 07
E-mail : posta@relaischateaux.fr

Palo Laziale
I-00055 Ladispoli, Roma
(Lazio)

Italy

From Rome SS 1 Aurelia towards Ladispoli, then follow signs to Palo Laziale.

Owner :
La Posta Vecchia Hotel S.R.L.
Director :
Harry Charles Mills Sció
Weekly closing :
Restaurant : Tuesday
Annual closing :
From November to March

✈ Rome (**Intl**) 20 km

🍴 Menu **120 000 ITL** s.i.
62 €
Carte
120 000-140 000 ITL s.i.
62-72 €

☰ 10 rooms
775 000 ITL t.n.i., s.i.
400 €

☰ 8 suites
starting at **1 550 000 ITL** t.n.i., s.i.
801 €

🍷 included

🔥 no

🏃 30 km

Sauna.

T his elegant residence, overlooking the Tyrrhenian Sea, was once the home of Paul Getty who transformed La Posta Vecchia into a temple of art. Many of the guestrooms, lavishly decorated with Carrara marble bathtubs, Venetian lamps and Gobelins tapestries, are luxuriously comfortable. Laze on the terrace, savour traditional Italian cuisine or visit the sights of Rome (just 35 minutes away). La dolce vita is guaranteed.

ITL : Italian lira

www.relaischateaux.fr/posta

DON ALFONSO 1890

Italy

Corso S. Agata 11
I-80064 S. Agata Sui Due Golfi
(Campania)

Tel. : (39) 081 878 00 26
Fax : (39) 081 533 02 26
E-mail : donalfonso@relaischateaux.fr

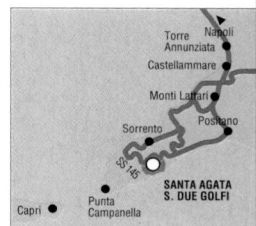

*From Naples A 3, exit
Castellammare di Stabia
towards Sorrento, Positano.*

Owners :
Livia and Alfonso Iaccarino
Weekly closing :
Monday and Tuesday
Monday only from June 1st
to September 30th
Annual closing :
From Jan. 10th to February 25th

A panoramic road on the Gulf of Naples and Salerno leads to the restaurant Don Alfonso where family tradition is at the service of a brilliant cuisine, centred around vegetables and oil which are produced on the premises: «espadon aux pois chiches et au thym», «rougets au romarin et au concombre», «pâtes aux clovisses et courgettes». Everything deserves mention. Built into rock, the cellar has a remarkable selection of the world's wines.

✈ Naples (**Intl**) 60 km

🍽 Menus
120 000-160 000 ITL s.i.
62-83 €
Carte
130 000-170 000 ITL s.i.
67-88 €

🛏 no

Pompei theatre festival
(July-September).
Chamber music in Sorrento.

P 🍷 ❄ ♿ ✈

443

HOTEL SAN PIETRO

SINCE 1988

Tel. : (39) 089 87 54 55
Fax : (39) 089 81 14 49
E-mail : sanpietro@relaischateaux.fr

Via Laurito 2, campania
I-84017 Positano
(Campania)

Italy

*From Naples A3 exit
Castellammare di Stabia towards
Sorrento, Positano.*

Owner : Virginia Attanasio
Annual closing :
From November 1st to April 1st

✈	Naples (**Intl**) 60 km
🧭	GPS N 40° 37' 25" E 14° 30' 00"
🍴	Carte **90 000-120 000 ITL** s.i. **46-62 €**
🔑	55 rooms **660 000-760 000 ITL** s.i. **341-393 €**
🔑	5 suites **850 000-1 200 000 ITL** s.i. **439-620 €**
☕	included
🐕	yes (only in the hotel)

Private beach, water skiing,
jacuzzi, fishing...

Overlooking the stunning Amalfi coastline, the San Pietro's decor is designed to blend in with its idyllic natural surroundings. The terraced gardens cascading down the rocks to the private beach are resplendent with Neapolitan ceramics and luxuriant foliage which spills through the windows of the elegant rooms. The cuisine, a tribute to the flavours of the South, is enhanced by excellent French and Italian vintages.

ITL : Italian lira

www.relaischateaux.fr/sanpietro

IL MELOGRANO

Italy

Contrada Torricella 345
I-70043 Monopoli-Bari
(Puglia)

Tel. : (39) 080 690 90 30
Fax : (39) 080 74 79 08
E-mail : melograno@relaischateaux.fr

From Bari, SS16; towards Monopoli then Alberobello, towards Rizzitello-Tormento, Melograno.

Owners : Guerra Family
Director : Camillo Guerra
Annual closing :
From January 7th to March 31st

✈ Bari **(Intl)** 60 km
Naples **(Intl)** 300 km

👁 GPS N 40° 55'
E 17° 16'

🍴 Menus
60 000-80 000 ITL s.i.
31-41 €
Carte
70 000-100 000 ITL s.i.
36-52 €

⊙╍ 33 rooms
420 000-660 000 ITL s.i.
217-341 €

⊙╍ 4 suites
680 000-1 140 000 ITL s.i.
351-589 €

☕ included

🐎 yes, upon request

♪ 30 km

Private beach (15-06/15-09) nearby.

T his beautiful 16th-century estate, set in the heart of the breathtaking Puglia countryside near the Adriatic beaches, has been restored by antique collector Camillo Guerra. The elegant rooms, decorated with Persian rugs and period furniture, offer vistas of olive groves, orchards and pomegranate trees. Relax on the private beach, located in an ancient Roman fishpond, then savour regional cuisine and fine wines.

ATLANTIC
OCEAN

Golfe de Gascogne
Golfe de Vizcaya

F R A

Périgueux
Cahors
Toulouse
Arcachon
Bordeaux
Bayonne
Pau
Tarbes
Andorra
La Seu d'Urgell
Huesca
Lérida

La Coruña
Santiago de Compostela
Lugo
Gijón
Oviedo
Santander
Donostia / San Sebastián
Irún
Iruñea Pamplona
452
454
455
456
457

Pontevedra
Vigo
Orense
León
Gasteiz / Vitoria
Burgos
Logroño
Aranda de Duero
Soria
Zaragoza

Viana do Castelo
Braga
Benavente
Zamora
453
Valladolid
Palencia
Zaragoza
Alcañiz
463
Tarragona
Tortosa
Cabo de Tortosa

Porto
Salamanca
E S P A Ñ A
Segovia
Viseu
Guarda
Ávila
Madrid
Guadalajara
Teruel
Castellón de la Plana
Golfo de València

Figueira da Foz
Coimbra
450
Plasencia
El Escorial
Cuenca
València
Gandía
S. Anton

Fátima
Cáceres
Toledo
Santarém
Trujillo
Lisboa
451
Cascais
Estremoz
Mérida
Badajoz
Zafra
Ciudad Real
Albacete
465
466
Alicante

Setúbal
Évora
Valdepeñas
Murcia

Sines
Córdoba
Úbeda
Lorca
Cartagena

Sevilla
Jaén
Baza

Sagres
Huelva
Jerez de la Frontera
Golfo de Cádiz
Antequera
Granada
Almería
Faro
Marbella
Málaga
Motril

Cádiz
Gibraltar (G.B.)
Algeciras
Estrecho de Gibraltar
Ceuta (Esp.)
MEDITERRANEAN
Mostaganem

ATLANTIC
OCEAN
Tanger
Tetouan
Al Hoceima
Melilla (Esp.)
Sidi-Bel-Abbès
Wahran (Oran)
Mascara

Larache
Chefchaouen
D J A Z
(Alge)
Saïda

Souk-el-Arba-du-Rharb
Oujda
Tlemcen

M A G H R E B (Morocco)
Guercif
El Bayadh

Rabat
Meknès
Fès
Taza

Casablanca

0   50   100   150   200 km

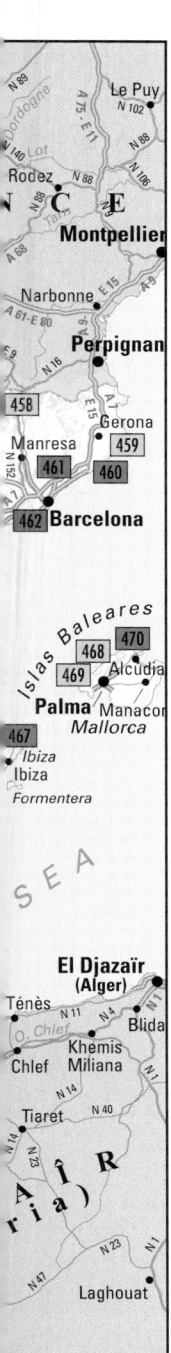

IBERIAN PENINSULA

PORTUGAL

Establishments	Nearest major city	Relais & Châteaux	Relais Gourmands	Page
Fortaleza do Guincho	Cascais	⚜		451
Hotel Quinta Das Lagrimas	Coimbra	⚜		450

SPAIN

Establishments	Nearest major city	Relais & Châteaux	Relais Gourmands	Page
Girasol	Alicante		👨‍🍳	465
Gran Hotel Son Net	Palma	⚜		469
Hotel Cala Sant Vincenç	Pollença	⚜		470
Hotel El Castell	Andorra	⚜		457
Hotel El Montiboli	Villajoyosa	⚜		466
Hotel Hacienda Na Xamena	Ibiza	⚜		467
Hotel Santa Marta	Gerona	⚜		460
Hotel San Romàn de Escalante	Santander	⚜		452
Mas de Torrent	Gerona	⚜		459
Posada de la Casa del Abad	Dueñas	⚜		453
Raco de Can Fabes (El)	Barcelona		👨‍🍳	461
Residencia (La)	Palma	⚜		468
Restaurant Alkelare	San Sebastián		👨‍🍳	454
Restaurant Neichel	Barcelona		👨‍🍳	462
Restaurante Arzak	San Sebastián		👨‍🍳	456
Restaurante Martin Berasategui	San Sebastián		👨‍🍳	455
Torre del Remei	Andorra	⚜		458
Torre del Visco (La)	Valderrobres	⚜		463

447

ONLY ONE ONLY YOU

THREE TIME ZONES Chronograph
The first chronograph
in the world with three time zones
Yellow gold
4 sapphire cabochons
Glass : sapphire crystal
Dial : light blue mother of pearl
Automatic chronograph movement (center)
Water resistant to 30 meters
2 years worldwide guarantee
Registered model

DELANEAU
GENÈVE
SINCE 1880

DELANEAU 29-31, route de l'Aéroport CP 204 CH 1215 Genève 15 Tél. ++ 41 22 799 53 53 Fax ++ 41 22 799 53 54

GENÈVE • PARIS • LONDON • MILANO • BERLIN • BEVERLY HILLS • NEW YORK • CHICAGO • PHOENIX • TOKYO • HONG KONG • SINGAPORE • RIYADH • DUBAI • ABU DHABI

VINTAGES TO DRINK IN YEAR 2000
SPAIN - PORTUGAL

Wines recommended by the wine waiters
of the Relais & Châteaux and Relais Gourmands.

* Index of world vintages to drink in year 2000 : page 607

	Name of wine	Wine to enjoy	Noble wine	Outstanding wine
	SPAIN			
Red	Rioja, Ribera del Duero	1993 - 1991	1989	1987 - 1985
	Navarra, Carinena	1996	1992	1991
	Penedes, Priorato	1996 - 1995	1990	1983 - 1978
White	Ribeiro, Rueda	1998	1995	
	PORTUGAL			
Port	Vintage	1995 - 1994	1977	1963

HOTEL QUINTA DAS LAGRIMAS

SINCE 1999

Tel. : (351) (239) 441 615
Fax : (351) (239) 441 695
E-mail : lagrimas@relaischateaux.fr

Santa Clara - Apartado 5053
P-3041-901 Coimbra
(Beira Litoral)

Portugal

Take exit Lousa-Condeixa or A1,
towards Coimbra.
Continue 12 km, turn left.

Owner :
Jose-Miguel Alarcão Júdice
Director : Mário Stromp de Morais
Open all year

✈	Porto (**Intl**) 100 km Lisbon (**Intl**) 180 km
🍴	Carte **5 000-6 500 PTE** s.i. **25-32 €**
⊶	35 rooms **23 000-29 000 PTE** s.i. **115-145 €**
⚷	4 suites **62 500 PTE** s.i. **312 €**
☕	included
🐕	yes (except in restaurant and rooms)
🏌	Driving-range Pitch and putt

Fishing, water skiing, kayaking,
mountain-biking, walking,
drive in 4x4, horse-riding.

This 18th century palace, surrounded by magnificent gardens, still vibrates with the memory of the famous romance between Prince Pedro and Inès de Castro. Today, this property has been transformed into a superb hotel, beautifully decorated in the traditional colours of Portugal. Enjoy the charm of its elegant guestrooms with inlaid furniture. Savour the delicious local cuisine prepared with fish or game.

PTE : Portuguese escudo

www.relaischateaux.fr/lagrimas

FORTALEZA DO GUINCHO

Portugal

Estrada do Guincho
P-2750-642 Cascais

Tel. : (351) (21) 487 0491
Fax : (351) (21) 487 0431
E-mail : guincho@relaischateaux.fr

A5 to Cascais. Take EN91, at the first roundabout follow signs to Birre. At the second roundabout, follow signs to Torre until you reach the sea. Turn right, continue for 6 km till you reach the fortress on the left.

Owner : Guinchotel Ltd
Director : Bertrand Petton
Open all year

Perched on a hilltop overlooking the ocean, this entirely renovated 17th century fortress will astound and enchant you with its myriad charms. You will appreciate the winter garden in an ancient cloister and the rooms with their balconies that open onto a breathtaking view. The cuisine draws its inspiration from regional French and Portuguese culinary tradition. A privileged site in a main tourist region.

✈ Lisbon (Intl) 30 km

GPS N 38° 43' 54"
W 009° 21' 55"

🍴 Menus **6 500-9 500 PTE** s.i.
32-47 €
Carte **8 100-14 900 PTE** s.i.
40-74 €

⚷ 26 rooms
23 000-43 000 PTE s.i.
115-214 €

⚷ 3 suites
42 000-54 000 PTE s.i.
209-269 €

☕ included

🍴 yes

♪ 3 km

Sailing, horse-riding, fishing, flying club, tennis.

PTE : Portuguese escudo

HOTEL SAN ROMAN DE ESCALANTE

SINCE 1996

Tel. : (34) 942 67 77 45
Fax : (34) 942 67 76 43
E-mail : escalante@relaischateaux.fr

Carretera Escalante, Castillo km. 2
E-39795 Escalante
(Cantabria)

Spain

From Bilbao, A8 towards Santander, exit 182, towards Gama-Santona C629. In Escalante, towards Castillo C402, km 2.

Owners :
Mr J. Melis, J. Iribarnegaray
and Mrs V. Reynes
Director : Juan Melis
Annual closing :
From Dec. 21st to January 22nd

✈ Bilbao (**Intl**) 65 km
    Santander 35 km

🍴 Menus **3 750-5 100 ESP**
    t.7% s.i.
    23-31 €
    Carte **4 500-6 000 ESP**
    t.7% s.i.
    27-36 €

  11 rooms
    13 000-20 000 ESP
    t.7% s.i.
    78-120 €

  2 suites
    23 000-25 000 ESP
    t.7% s.i.
    138-150 €

☕ 1 250 ESP t.7% s.i.
    8 €

  yès (extra cost)

🏃 18 km

Horseback riding (2 km),
hunting, fishing, skiing,
flying club, water sports.

This 17th-century residence and its magnificent gardens, which lie on the route to Saint-Jacques-de-Compostelle, have been beautifully restored by Juan Melis. The elegant rooms bear witness to your host's passion for ancient art, as do the gallery and the antique shop. History buffs will be enchanted by the private archives, preserved in an annex. Enjoy traditional cuisine and the finest Spanish and French vintages.

452

 Visa

ESP : Spanish pesetas

www.relaischateaux.fr/escalante

SINCE 2000

POSADA DE LA CASA DEL ABAD

Spain

Plaza Francisco Martín Grohaz, 12
E-34160 Ampudia-Palencia
(Castilla y Leon)

Tel. : (34) 979 768 008
Fax : (34) 979 768 300
E-mail : abad@relaischateaux.fr

*Madrid : motorway N-VI
(towards Coruña) until Tordesillas,
then towards Valladolia, N-620
fast lane. After Valladolia,
towards Palencia-Burgos until
Duenas. Go through Duenas and
take P.903 until Ampudia.*

Owners : Garcia Puertas Family
Director : Javier Merino
Annual closing :
From January 10th to 21st

Madrid (**Intl**) 220 km

Menu **4 066 ESP** s.i. - **24 €**
Carte **4 815-6 955 ESP** s.i.
29-42 €

13 rooms
off-season
12 840-14 980 ESP s.i.
77-90 €
season
17 120-19 260 ESP s.i.
103-116 €

4 suites
off-season
16 050-18 190 ESP s.i.
96-109 €
season
20 330-22 470 ESP s.i.
112-135 €

963-1 712 ESP s.i.
6-10 €

yes

40 km

Horse-riding, hunting.

A t the heart of the historic town of
Ampudia in the vast Castilla y Leon
region, the Posada brings a touch of colour
and beauty. Built in the 17th century, this
former seigniorial residence was lovingly
transformed into a prestigious and comfortable hotel with a resolutely contemporary
atmosphere. The elegant regional cuisine
gives pride of place to freshly grown
vegetables, country ham, game and the
wines of Duerno.

ESP : Spanish pesetas

RESTAURANT AKELARE

SINCE 1999

Tel. : **(34) 943 21 20 52**
      (34) 943 21 40 86
Fax : **(34) 943 21 92 68**
E-mail : akelare@relaischateaux.fr

P° Padre Orcolaga 56
E-20008 San-Sebastián
(Guipúzcoa)

Spain

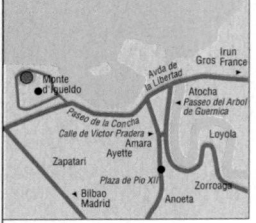

A8 Bilbao/Behobia, exit Ondarreta. Follow the route all along the University area. On arrival in the city, take direction «La montagne d'Igueldo»

Owner : Pedro Subijana
Weekly closing :
Sunday evening and Monday
Annual closing :
February and first half of October

✈ Biarritz **(Intl)** 40 km
    San Sebastian 20 km

🍴 Menu
    10 500 ESP t.7% s.i.
    63 €
    Carte
    11 000-13 000 ESP t.7% s.i.
    66-78 €

🐎 no

⛳ 6 km (18 holes)

Sailing, diving, surfing, kayaking, thalassotherapy.

P 🍽 ❄ 🎿

From the summit of Igueldo, the bay windows of Akelare overlook the Cantabrian sea, offering an idyllic panorama. «Thon blanc à l'aigre-doux de poivrons», «feuillantine aux agrumes caramélisés», the menu constantly changes with every season. The wide variety of vegetables and herbs grown on the premises ensure the freshness and delicate flavour of every dish. The wine cellar, which is continually replenished, has a vast and wide selection of fine vintages.

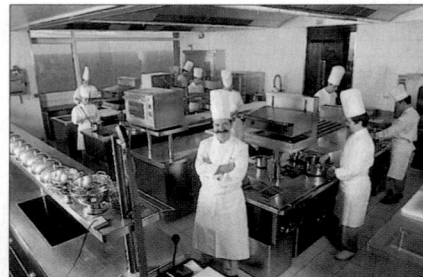

  Visa

ESP : Spanish pesetas

www.relaischateaux.fr/akelare

RESTAURANTE MARTIN BERASATEGUI

Spain

Calle Loidi, 4
E-20160 Lasarte-Oria
(Oria Guipúzcoa)

Tel. : (34) 943 36 64 71
Fax : (34) 943 36 61 07
E-mail : berasategui@relaischateaux.fr

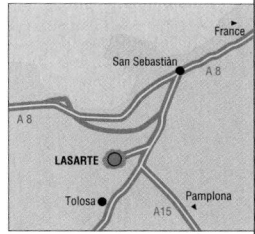

From San-Sebastian, take N1 towards Toulouse, then exit Lasarte and continue 5km.

Owner : Martin Berasategui
Weekly closing :
Sunday evening and Monday
Annual closing :
From Dec. 13th to January 13th

 Bilbao **(Intl)** 100 km
Hondarribia 20 km

 Menu **9 000 ESP** t.7% s.i.
54 €
Carte **9 000-10 000 ESP**
t.7% s.i.
54-60 €

 no

I n this elegant restored residence, located in the heart of the countryside, guests will be amazed by Martin Berasategui's imagination and brilliance. By combining typical Basque cuisine with regional and traditional products, he offers a wide range of novel recipes such as the superb «mille-feuille au caramel d'anguille fumée au fois gras, à l'oignon et à la pomme verte». The wines and the service are exceptional.

 P ★

www.relaischateaux.fr/berasategui   ESP : Spanish pesetas   Visa

RESTAURANTE ARZAK

SINCE 1979

Tel. : (34) 943 28 55 93
(34) 943 27 84 65
Fax : (34) 943 27 27 53
E-mail : arzak@relaischateaux.fr

Alto de Miracruz 21
E-20015 San Sebastián
(Gúipuzcoa)

Spain

*From France, highway
until exit 5, from Bilbao,
highway until exit 6.*

Owners : Juan-Mari Arzak
and Maite Espina
Weekly closing :
Sunday evening and Monday
Annual closing :
From June 18th to July 5th
and from November 5th to 29th

✈ Bilbao (**Intl**) 90 km
Pamplona 90 km

🍴 Menus
10 000-12 000 ESP s.i.
60-72 €
Carte
12 000-16 000 ESP s.i.
72-96 €

🛏 no

🏌 Basozabal 2 km
Jaizquibel 20 km

T he elegant seaside resort of San Sebastian is home to one of Spain's finest chefs. Indeed, international gourmets flock to this picturesque town to savour the gastronomic delights created by Juan-Mari Arzak «Donostiarra» and his daughter Elena. Discover quintessential Basque cuisine and choose from a superb list of vintage wines in this charming restaurant hung with old paintings.

   Visa

ESP : Spanish pesetas

www.relaischateaux.fr/arzak

456

HOTEL EL CASTELL

Spain

Route N-260 km 229, Apto. 53
E-25700 Seu d'Urgell
(Lerida)

Tel. : (34) 973 35 07 04
Fax : (34) 973 35 15 74
E-mail : elcastell@relaischateaux.fr

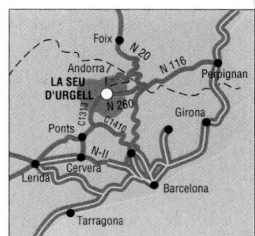

Barcelona, A. Lerida, exit 25 Igualada (N-II), Cervera (L 311), Ponts (C-1313), Adrall (N-260), to Seu d'Urgell.

Owner : Jaume Tápies Travé
Open all year

✈ Barcelona (**Intl**) 200 km
Seu d'Urgell 5 km

GPS N 42° 21' 30"
E 001° 26' 40"

🍴 Menu **8 000 ESP** t.7% s.i.
48 €
Carte
6 500-8 500 ESP t.7% s.i.
39-51 €

⚿ 32 rooms
23 000-25 500 ESP t.7% s.i.
138-153 €

⚿ 5 suites
34 000 ESP t.7% s.i.
204 €

☕ included

🐾 yes except restaurant
(extra cost **1 000 ESP - 6 €**)

⌇ 8 and 40 km

Private concerts, fishing, hunting, rafting, canoeing, cross-country, skiing...

Perched at 650 metres in the Pyrenees, this elegant modern hotel offers breathtaking views of the mountain landscape. The rooms, spacious and comfortable, open out onto private terraces where guests will enjoy magical breakfasts basking in the morning sunlight. The renowned cuisine, inspired by the finest produce from the local rivers and huertas, is enhanced by a wine list featuring over 650 vintages.

ESP : Spanish pesetas

Visa

TORRE DEL REMEI

Tel. : (34) 972 14 01 82
Fax : (34) 972 14 04 49
E-mail : torreremei@relaischateaux.fr

Cami Reial s/n
E-17539 Bolvir
(Girona)

Spain

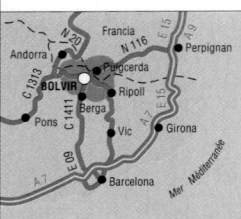

Perpignan, N116 Prades-Andorra;
Barcelona, C 1411
Tunel del Cadi Berga-Puigcerda.

Owners : José Maria Boix
and Loles Vidal de Boix
Open all year

✈ Perpignan (**Intl**) 80 km
   Barcelona (**Intl**) 150 km

⟋ GPS N 42° 25' 16"
   E 01° 53' 27"

🍴 Menus **6 800 ESP**
   t.7% s.i.
   41 €
   Carte **6 000-8 000 ESP**
   t.7% s.i.
   36-48 €

🔑 4 rooms
   starting at **27 000 ESP**
   t.7% s.i.
   162 €

🔑 7 suites
   starting at **41 000 ESP**
   t.7% s.i.
   246 €

☕ **2 500 ESP** t.7% s.i.
   15 €

🐾 yes (extra cost)

⅃ 1 km

S haded by sequoias and nestling in the
Pyrenees amidst an 8-acre forest near
the Cadi National park, this magnificent
summer palace has been transformed into
an elegant hotel. Enjoy peace and calm in
one of the 10 marvellously comfortable
guestrooms, offering superb vistas of the
mountain landscape. Savour refined
regional cuisine, enjoy golf and horse riding
or venture into the Pyrenees with an
experienced mountain guide.

 Visa

ESP : Spanish pesetas

 www.relaischateaux.fr/torreremei

MAS DE TORRENT

Spain

E-17123 Torrent
(Girona)

Tel. : **(34) 972 30 32 92**
(34) 972 30 11 50
Fax : **(34) 972 30 32 93**
E-mail : mastorrent@relaischateaux.fr

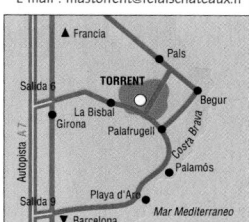

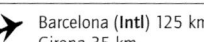

From France, A 7 towards Girona, exit 6 (G 255 - Palamós), follow the Gi 652 Pals-Begur road.

Owners : Figueras Family
Director : Gregori Berengüi
Open all year

Barcelona **(Intl)** 125 km
Girona 35 km

GPS N 41° 56' 92"
E 3° 12'

Menu starting at
6 000 ESP t.7% s.i.
36 €
Carte starting at
5 500 ESP t.7% s.i.
33 €

25 rooms
starting at **31 000 ESP**
t.7% s.i.
186 €

5 suites
starting at **38 000 ESP**
t.7% s.i.
228 €

2 400-3 000 ESP t.7% s.i.
14-18 €

yes (extra cost) except rest.
and main house

6 km

I deally located near the Costa Brava's beaches and golf courses, this beautifully restored 18th-century farmhouse is imbued with traditional Catalan charm. Relax in a superb guestroom, decorated in rustic style, or in the garden of an independent bungalow, set by the pool. In the restaurant, decorated with contemporary Spanish paintings in homage to Picasso, enjoy traditional cuisine accompanied by fine Catalan wines.

459

ESP : Spanish pesetas

Visa

HOTEL SANTA MARTA

Tel. : (34) 972 36 49 04
Fax : (34) 972 36 92 80
E-mail : santamarta@relaischateaux.fr

Playa Santa Cristina
E-17310 Lloret De Mar
(Girona)

Spain

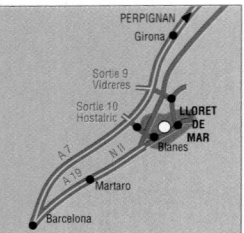

*From Barcelona, A 7, exit 9
Vidreres, Lloret de Mar.*

Owners : Noguera Family
Director : Jorge Noguera
Annual closing :
From Dec. 15th to February 1st.

✈ Barcelona (**Intl**) 80 km

 GPS N 41° 41' 378"
E 02° 49' 003"

🍴 Menu **6 250 ESP** t.n.i., s.i.
38 €
Carte
5 000-7 000 ESP t.n.i., s.i.
30-42 €

⚬⊷ 52 rooms
19 000-37 000 ESP
t.n.i., s.i.
114-222 €

⚬⊷ 8 suites
29 000-50 000 ESP
t.n.i., s.i.
174-300 €

☕ **1 800 ESP** t.n.i., s.i.
11 €

🐾 yes (extra cost)
except restaurant

♪ 5 clubs less than 40 km
away

T he magnificent coastline and fine sand beach of Santa Cristina seem to have been specially designed for this elegant modern hotel, nestling amidst a 15-acre park. Its spacious, sunny rooms open onto terraces overlooking the ocean and the pine forests. After an afternoon playing tennis or relaxing by the marvellous pool, enjoy the «sweet and savoury» flavours of traditional Catalan cuisine at the waterside restaurant.

    Visa

ESP : Spanish pesetas

www.relaischateaux.fr/santamarta

EL RACO DE CAN FABES

Sant Joan 6
E-08470 Sant Celoni
(Barcelona)

Tel. : (34) 93 867 28 51
Fax : (34) 93 867 38 61
E-mail : raco@relaischateaux.fr

*From Barcelona, A 7, exit 11
Sant Celoni; located 200 m
behind the town hall.*

Owners :
Santi and Angels Santamaria
Weekly closing :
Sunday evening and Monday
Annual closing :
From February 1st to 14th
and from June 26th to July 10th

All the aspects of present-day Catalonia - diverse, dynamic, artistic and progressive - are reflected in the modern, inventive cuisine proposed with brio by Santi and Angels Santamaria, in the admirable setting of the Montseny Natural Park. Close to perfection, the culinary creations display the talent of a genius.

Barcelona (**Intl**) 50 km
Gerona 50 km

Menus
12 500-15 500 ESP s.i.
75-93 €
Carte
9 850-12 250 ESP s.i.
59-74 €

yes

Food workshops : herbs (spring)
and mushrooms (autumn).

461

Restaurant Neichel

Spain

Tel. : (34) 93 203 84 08
Fax : (34) 93 205 63 69
E-mail : neichel@relaischateaux.fr

Beltrán i Rózpide
16 bis (antes Av. de Pedralbes)
E-08034 Barcelona

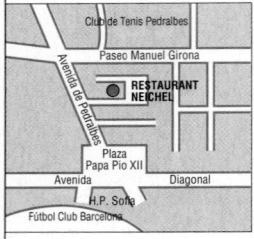

From the Southern entrance to Barcelona (A 2), take the avenue Diagonal to Pie XII plaza.

Owners :
Evelyn and Jean-Louis Neichel
Weekly closing :
Saturday for lunch and Sunday
Annual closing :
From August 1st to Sept. 5th

✈ Barcelona **(Intl)** 10 km

🍴 Menus **7 800-8 800 ESP** s.i.
47-53 €
Carte **8 000-10 000 ESP** s.i.
48-60 €

🛏 yes (small)

Private salon (for 12 and 16).

  ✳

J ean-Louis and Evelyn Neichel keep one of the best tables in Barcelona, in the heart of the Pedralbes area. Catalan products and imagination combine to inspire original fish and seafood dishes, as well as a Flavours and Savours menu. A beautiful view of a Mediterranean garden.

  Visa

ESP : Spanish pesetas

www.relaischateaux.fr/neichel

LA TORRE DEL VISCO

Spain

Fuentespalda
E-44587 Tervel
(Bajo Aragón)

Tel. : (34) 978 76 90 15
Fax : (34) 978 76 90 16
E-mail : visco@relaischateaux.fr

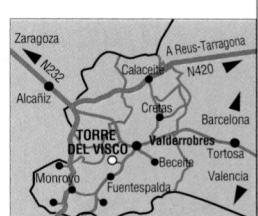

*From Barcelona: A7 motorway south to junction 38.
C233 to Mora La Nova.
N420 to Calaceite. A1413, then A231 to Valderrobres.
A1414 to Fuentespalda. After 6 km, turn right onto un-asphalted tack to hotel at 5 km.*

Owners : Piers Dutton, Jemma Markham
Annual closing :
From January 7th to 21st

✈ Barcelona (**Intl**) 250 km
Zaragoza 150 km

🍴 Menu **6 000 ESP** t.7% s.i.
36 €

⚷ 11 rooms
half board
26 000-30 000 ESP
t.7% s.i.
156-180 €

⚷ 3 suites
half board
40 000 ESP t.7% s.i.
240 €

🏆 included

🍴 no

Restaurant reservations are required for non-hotel guests. Horse-riding, hiking, mountain-biking.

Tucked away in the splendid natural setting of the Teruel region, La Torre is a lovely labyrinth of houses, patios and terraces whose original turret dates back to the 15th century. Expanded over the years, the hotel produces olives, almonds and cereal on its farm. Guests can admire the culinary preparation of «civet de sanglier sauvage» and visit the superb 15th century cellar with its 1500 bottles Spanish wines.

Costa Blanca
PATRONATO PROVINCIAL DE TURISMO
ALICANTE - SPAIN

GIRASOL

Spain

Ctr. Moraira-Calpe, KM 1,5
E-03724 Moraira
(Alicante)

Tel. : (34) 96574 4373
Fax : (34) 96649 0545
E-mail : girasol@relaischateaux.fr

From Alicante, A7 towards Valencia, exit 63, RN 332 towards Teulada, route N° AV 1342 towards Moraira, at the traffic circle take a right, route N° AP1391, Moraira-Calpe.

Owners :
Joachim and Victoria Koerper
Weekly closing :
Monday (except in summer)
Annual closing :
From November 10th to 30th

 Alicante (**Intl**) 90 km
Valencia (**Intl**) 120 km

 Menus
8 900-11 600 ESP t.7% s.i.
53-70 €
Carte
9 500-12 500 ESP t.7% s.i.
57-75 €

 yes

 5 between 1.5 and 30 km

A delightful villa with an elegant decor, suffused in Mediterranean light. This same light illuminates the culinary creations of Joachim Koerper. His reputation is characterised by sophisticated dishes using very high quality seafood such as gambas and surmullet, enhanced by the treasures of a royal cellar. An essential place to stay for the most demanding Epicureans.

465

ESP : Spanish pesetas

Visa

HOTEL «EL MONTIBOLI»

Tel. : (34) 96 589 02 50
Fax : (34) 96 589 38 57
E-mail : montiboli@relaischateaux.fr

Partida Montiboli S/N
E-03570 Villajoyosa
(Alicante)

Spain

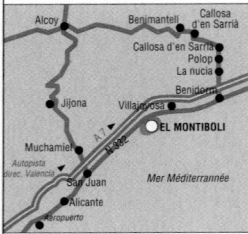

From the airport: A7 towards Valence, exit Villajoyosa, towards Alicante, after 4 km, turn left at the roundabout, follow signs for hotel.

Owner : José Maria Caballé
Director : José Manuel Castillo
Open all year

✈ Alicante (**Intl**) 40 km

🍴 Menu **4 500 ESP** t.7% s.i.
27 €
Carte
5 300-7 500 ESP t.7% s.i.
32-45 €

⊶ 38 rooms
19 600-29 600 ESP
t.7% s.i.
118-178 €

⊶ 12 suites
27 600-42 800 ESP
t.7% s.i.
166-257 €

🍸 included

🍴 yes (extra cost)

⁄ 15 km (18 holes)

Fishing, climbing, skiing, sailing, sauna, fitness room.

T he Arabs believed that the choosen souls flew up to heaven from these very cliff, a natural frontier between El Montiboli and the Mediterranean Sea. Indeed, the hotel, nestled in the midst of moorish gardens, has a paradisiaque charme. In this pleasant setting, the chef combines the flavours of an innovative Mediterranean cuisine with talent and finesse.

ESP : Spanish pesetas

www.relaischateaux.fr/montiboli

HOTEL HACIENDA NA XAMENA

E-07815 San Miguel - Ibiza
(Baléares)

Tel. : (34) 971 33 45 00
Fax : (34) 971 33 45 14
E-mail : xamena@relaischateaux.fr

22 km northwest of Ibiza town, towards San Miguel.

Owner :
Na Xamena - Hotel Hacienda S.A.
Director : Sabine Lipszyc
Annual closing :
From November 2nd to April 27th

✈ Ibiza (**Intl**) 25 km

🍴 Menu 7 500 ESP t.7% s.i.
45 €
Carte
4 500-9 200 ESP t.7% s.i.
27-55 €

⚷ 52 rooms
24 000-55 000 ESP
t.7% s.i.
144-331 €

⚷ 9 suites
54 000-130 000 ESP
t.7% s.i.
325-781 €

☕ 2 450 ESP t.7% s.i.
15 €

🛏 yes (rooms only)

♪ 23 km

52 private jacuzzis with view of the sea, concerts...

T his lavish estate, set in the heart of one of Europe's last unspoilt natural areas, offers breathtaking vistas of shimmering turquoise bays and fine sand beaches. The elegant guestrooms, look out across the ocean and the magnificent cliffs. Enjoy a romantic candlelit dinner, accompanied by the finest Spanish wines, while watching the spectacular Ibiza sunset.

La Residencia

Tel. : (34) 971 63 90 11
Fax : (34) 971 63 93 70
E-mail : residencia@relaischateaux.fr

Finca son Canals
E-07179 Deya-Mallorca
(Baleares)

Spain

From airport, direction Palma and before city, take «Via de cintura». Come off Valldemossa junction. After Valdemossa, follow road to Deià.

Owner : Son Moragues S.A.
Director : Marie Aastrup
Open all year

✈ Palma (**Intl**) 35 km

🍴 Menus
8 500-12 000 ESP t.7% s.i.
51-72 €
Carte
8 000-13 000 ESP t.7% s.i.
48-78 €

⊶ 45 rooms
24 400-59 500 ESP t.7% s.i.
147-358 €

⊶ 18 suites
41 850-126 000 ESP t.7% s.i.
252-757 €

☕ included

🍴 no

🎣 20 km

This stately 17th-century residence with its magnificent flower-bedecked terraces lies in idyllic surroundings between the sea and the mountains. Relish the comfort of the sumptuous rooms appointed with period furniture and exquisite artwork, relax in the shade of eucalyptus and lime trees and enjoy superb panoramic views. The restaurant, set in the old olive press, features local specialities and a superb wine list.

 Visa

ESP : Spanish pesetas

www.relaischateaux.fr/residencia

GRAN HOTEL SON NET

Spain

E-07194 Puigpunyent-Mallorca
(Baleares)

Tel. : (34) 971 1470 00
Fax : (34) 971 1470 01
E-mail : sonnet@relaischateaux.fr

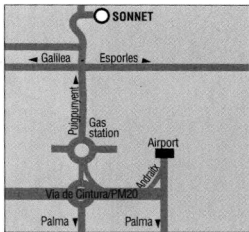

From the airport, take PM19 towards Palma, after 5 km take PM20 towards Andraitz. Exit at Puigpunyent. After the traffic circle, continue straight on for 11 km. The Son Net is on top of the hill.

Owners : David Stein, Norman and Lyn Lear
Director : Antonio Rey
Open all year

Tucked away in the island's hinterland, nestled in its verdant park, this entirely renovated 18th century coral-coloured villa is located 15 minutes from Palma de Majorca. Son Net will enchant you with its superb view, Majorcan decoration, marble bathrooms, swimming pool, splendid gardens, and private music concerts. Its restaurant gives pride of place to refined Mediterranean gastronomy.

✈ Palma (**Intl**) 25 km

🍴 Tasting menu
10 500 ESP t.7% s.i.
63 €
Carte **10 000-12 000 ESP** t.7% s.i.
60-72 €

🔑 17 rooms
35 000-55 000 ESP t.7% s.i.
210-331 €

🔑 7 suites
105 000-125 000 ESP t.7% s.i.
631-751 €

🍲 **2 900 ESP** s.i.
17 €

🛏 no

♪ 15 km

Spa.

www.relaischateaux.fr/sonnet

ESP : Spanish pesetas

Visa

HOTEL CALA SANT VICENÇ

SINCE 1998

Tel. : (34) 971 530 250
Fax : (34) 971 532 084
E-mail : calasantvicenc@relaischateaux.fr

2, rue Maressers
07469 Cala Sant Vicenç-Mallorca
(Baleares)

Spain

From the airport, go to Palma,
then Inca, then Pollença.

Owners : Suau Family
Annual closing :
From Dec. 1st to February 1st

✈ Palma (**Intl**) 60 km

🍴 Menus
7 500-10 000 ESP s.i.
45-60 €
Carte
6 000-11 000 ESP s.i.
36-66 €

⊙⇁ 23 rooms
17 500-35 700 ESP s.i.
105-215 €

⊙⇁ 15 suites
27 500-42 000 ESP s.i.
165-252 €

☕ included

🐕 no

♪ 8 km

Indoor exercice room, sauna,
beauty salon, private room.

S et on the northern coast of
Majorca, this family-run hotel offers
impeccable service and exceptional
hospitality. Its 38 elegant rooms are fully
refurbished and beautifully decorated.
Relax in the calm, cool interior of Italian
sandstone, swim at the pool, surrounded
by palm trees, 200 metres from a limpid,
turquoise sea. Savour Mediterranean
cuisine at the «Cavall Bernat» restaurant.

Visa

ESP : Spanish pesetas

www.relaischateaux.fr/calasantvicenc

Relais & Châteaux invitation cheque:

re-inventing the art of saying thank you

The simple, discrete and sophisticated way of offering dreams à la carte in over 400 establishments throughout the world. For your incentive, promotion and loyalty operations... or simply to make someone happy. For further information, ring (33) 01 45 72 90 01.

RELAIS & CHATEAUX.
Relais Gourmands

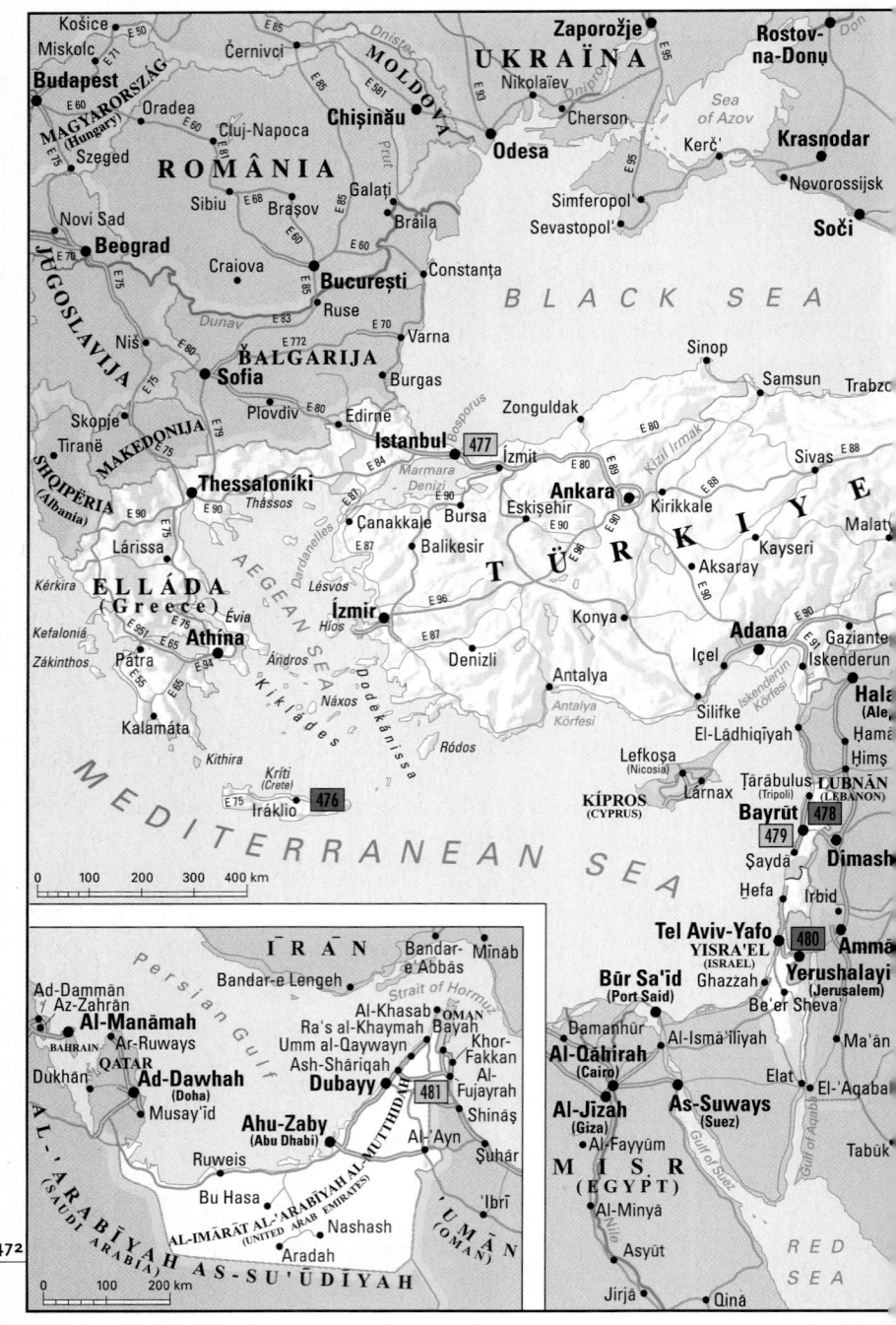

Košice •   E 50   *E 85*   *Dnister*   **Zaporožje** •   **Rostov-**
Miskolc •   E 71   Černivci   **M O L D O V A**   **U K R A Ï N A**   E 95   **na-Donu**   *Don*
Budapest   E 60   Oradea   E 60   Nìkolaïev   Cherson   *Sea*
MAGYARORSZÁG   E 75   Cluj-Napoca   **Chişinău**   E 581   **Odesa**   *of Azov*   Kerč'   **Krasnodar**
(Hungary)   Szeged   **R O M Â N I A**   E 85   Galaţi   Simferopol'   • Novorossijsk
Novi Sad   Sibiu   E 68   Braşov   E 85   Brăila   Sevastopol'   **Soči**
Beograd   E 70   E 60   Craiova   E 60   **Bucureşti**   Constanţa   *B L A C K   S E A*
JUGOSLAVIJA   E 75   *Dunav*   E 83   Ruse   E 70   Varna
Niš   E 80   E 772   **BALGARIJA**   Burgas   Sinop   Samsun   Trabzc
Skopje   E 75   **Sofia**   Plovdiv   E 80   Edirne   Zonguldak
Tiranë   **MAKEDONIJA**   E 79   **Istanbul** [477]   İzmit   E 80   E 80   Sivas   E 88
SHQIPËRIA   E 90   E 84   *Marmara*   **Ankara**   Kirikkale   E 88   Malat
(Albania)   **Thessaloniki**   *Thássos*   E 87   Çanakkale   *Deniz*   E 90   Bursa   Eskişehir   E 90   **T Ü R K İ Y E**   Kayseri
Lárissa   *Lésvos*   Balikesir   Aksaray   E 90
E L L Á D A   *Évia*   *Híos*   **İzmir**   E 96   Konya   **Adana**   Gaziante
(Greece)   E 951   E 75   E 65   *Ándros*   E 96   İçel   İskenderun
Kefaloniá   **Athína**   E 94   *Náxos*   E 87   Denizli   Silifke   *İskenderun*   **Hala**
Zákinthos   Pátra   E 55   Antalya   *Körfezi*   **(Ale,**
Kalamáta   *Kikládes*   *Dodekánissa*   *Antalya*   Ḥamā
Kíthira   *Ródos*   *Körfezi*   El-Ládhiqīyah   Ḥimş
Kríti   E 75 [476]   Lefkoşa   Ṭārābulus   **LUBNĀN**
(Crete)   Iráklio   **KÍPROS**   *(Nicosia)*   Lárnax   *(Tripoli)*   **(LEBANON)**
M E D I T E R R A N E A N   S E A   **(CYPRUS)**   **Bayrūt** [478]   [479]   **Dimash**
0   100   200   300   400 km   Şaydā   Irbid
Ḥefa   **Tel Aviv-Yafo** [480]   **Amm**
YISRA'EL   **(ISRAEL)**   **Yerushalayi**
Būr Sa'īd   Ghazzah   **(Jerusalem)**
(Port Said)   Be'er Sheva'
Damanhūr   Al-Ismā'īliyah   Ma'ān
Al-Qāhirah   **(Cairo)**   Elat   El-'Aqaba
Al-Jīzah   **As-Suways**   *Gulf of Aqaba*   Tabūk
(Giza)   **(Suez)**
• Al-Fayyūm   **M I S R**
(E G Y P T)
Al-Minyā   *Gulf of Suez*
An-Nīle
Asyūt   *R E D*
Jirjā   Qinā   *S E A*

Inset map (bottom left)

Persian Gulf   **Ī R Ā N**   Bandar-   Mīnāb
Bandar-e Lengeh   e'Abbās
Strait of Hormuz
Ad-Dammān   Al-Khasab   **OMAN**
Az-Zahrān   Ra's al-Khaymah   Bayah
Al-Manāmah   Umm al-Qaywayn   Khor-Fakkan
BAHRAIN   Ar-Ruways   Ash-Shāriqah   Al-Fujayrah
Dukhān   **QATAR**   **Dubayy**   [481]   Shināş
Ad-Dawhah   Musay'id   **(Doha)**
Ahu-Zaby   Al-'Ayn   Şuḥār
(Abu Dhabi)
Ruweis   **AL-'ARABĪYAH AL-MUTTAḤID**
AL-'ARABĪYAH   Bu Hasa   'Ibrī
(SAUDI   **AL-IMĀRĀT AL-'ARABĪYAH AL-MUTTAḤIDAH**   **'U M Ā N**
ARABIA)   Nashash   **(UNITED ARAB EMIRATES)**   **(OMAN)**
AS-SU'ŪDĪYAH   Aradah
0   100   200 km

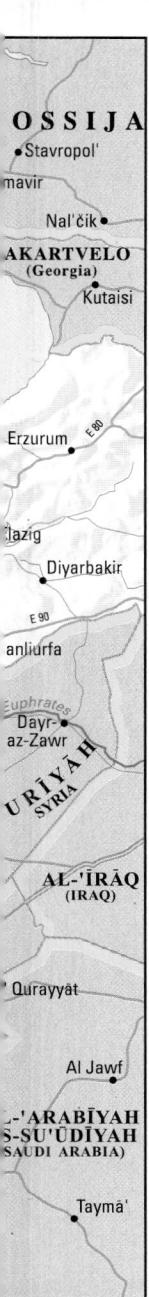

OSSIJA
•Stavropol'
mavir
Nal'čik •
AKARTVELO
(Georgia)
Kutaisi

Erzurum •

lazig
Diyarbakir

E 90
anliurfa

Euphrates
Dayr- •
az-Zawr
URĪYĀH
SYRIA

AL-'IRĀQ
(IRAQ)

Qurayyāt

Al Jawf

-'ARABĪYAH
S-SU'ŪDĪYAH
(SAUDI ARABIA)

Taymā'

GREECE - TURKEY
LEBANON - ISRAEL - DUBAI

GREECE (CRETE)

Establishments	Nearest major city	Relais & Châteaux	Relais Gourmands	Page
Elounda Mare Hotel	Agios Nikolaos	⚜		476

TURKEY

Establishments	Nearest major city	Relais & Châteaux	Relais Gourmands	Page
Bosphorus Pasha	Istanbul	⚜		477

LEBANON

Establishments	Nearest major city	Relais & Châteaux	Relais Gourmands	Page
Auberge de Fakra (L')	Beyrouth	⚜		478
Hotel Albergo	Beyrouth	⚜		479

ISRAEL

Establishments	Nearest major city	Relais & Châteaux	Relais Gourmands	Page
American Colony (The)	Jerusalem	⚜		480

DUBAI

Establishments	Nearest major city	Relais & Châteaux	Relais Gourmands	Page
Hatta Fort Hotel	Dubaï	⚜		481

Le Hub* Roissy - Charles - de - Gaulle.
Il semblerait que tous les coins du monde se soient soudainement rapprochés.

Accueillant en permanence les arrivées et les départs de vols du monde entier, l'aéroport Roissy - Charles - de - Gaulle vous offre chaque jour 1600 possibilités de correspondance en moins de deux heures. Renseignez-vous dans votre agence de voyages, votre agence Air France ou au 0 802 802 802 (0,79 F/mn), 3615 AF (1,29 F/mn) ou www.airfrance.fr

* La plate-forme d'interconnexion.

AIR FRANCE

Faire du ciel le plus bel endroit de la te

VINTAGES TO DRINK IN YEAR 2000
ISRAEL - LEBANON - GREECE

**Wines recommended by the wine waiters
of the Relais & Châteaux and Relais Gourmands.**

* Index of world vintages to drink in year 2000 : page 607

	Name of wine	Wine to enjoy	Noble wine	Outstanding wine
	ISRAEL			
Red	Cabernet Sauvignon	1996 - 1995	1990	
	LEBANON			
Red	Vallée de la Bekaa	1995	1990	1978 - 1972
	GREECE (CRETE)			
Red	Sitia, Dafnes...	1996	1995	1991

ELOUNDA MARE HOTEL

Tel. : (30) (0841) 411 02/03
Fax : (30) (0841) 413 07
E-mail : elounda@relaischateaux.fr

GR-720 53 Elounda
Crète

Greece

North of Aghios Nikolaos (9 km), on the north-eastern coast of the island.

Owners :
Spyros and Eliane Kokotos
Director : Chris Tzianos
Annual closing : From November to the end of March

✈	Iraklion (**Intl**) 70 km
🚁	GPS N 35° 14' 84" E 25° 43' 94"
🍴	Menu **10 000 GRD** s.i. Carte starting at **12 000 GRD** s.i.
🔑	44 rooms **42 000-110 000 GRD** s.i.
🔑	45 bungalows starting at **53 000 GRD** s.i.
🍽	Buffet included
🏇	no
🏃	500 m (9 holes par-3)

Constructed in traditional Cretan style, Elounda Mare offers simple and discreet luxury blending its lucious gardens with the turquoise waters of a romantic cove. Here is a beautiful establishment with a private sandy beach, an orthodox chapel, an art gallery and, above all, serenity. All bungalows have climate control and a private garden with swimming pool. Three diverse restaurants offer fresh fish and Greek gastronomy with fine wines.

Visa

GRD : Greek drachma

www.relaischateaux.fr/elounda

BOSPHORUS PASHA

Turkey

Yaliboyu Cad. N° 64
80210 Beylerbeyi Istanbul

Tel. : (90) (216) 422 00 03
Fax : (90) (216) 422 00 12
E-mail : bosphorus@relaischateaux.fr

There are two main roads from the airport to the hotel. All the taxi drivers know these two routes. Taking these two motorways helps avoid traffic when going to the hotel.

Owner : Ferit Fehmi Meriçten
Director : Elif Camural
Open all year

✈ Atatürk (**Intl**) 20 km

🍴 Menus **29-97 USD** s.i.
Carte **40-70 USD** s.i.

🔑 13 rooms
330-370 USD s.i.

🔑 1 suite
750 USD s.i.

☕ included

🚩 yes

Fishing, jacuzzi.

Located on the eastern banks of the Bosphorus, the Bosphorus Pasha Hotel was once the holiday home of the grand vizir of sultan Selim III. Entirely restored in the Ottoman style, today it is the most perfect example of this rich tradition. Each room carries the mark of the Ottoman architectural style and each detail reflects the wealth of the Eastern civilisation. In the restaurant, formerly the ancient boathouse, enjoy Mediterranean cuisine and Turkish specialities to the sound of waves lapping.

L'AUBERGE DE FAQRA

SINCE 1984

Tel. : (961) (1) 25 73 30/1/2
Fax : (961) (9) 71 02 94
E-mail : faqra@relaischateaux.fr

Centre de Faqra
Kfardébiane
B.P. 11, 2560 Beyrouth

Lebanon

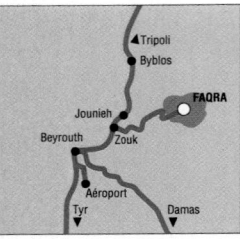

From Beirut, towards Tripoli.
At Zouk take the mountain road
on the right.

Owners : Hôtelière Faqra S.A.L.
Raymond J. Daoud
Director : Nicolas M. Cattan
Annual closing :
May and November

✈ Beirut (**Intl**) 45 km

🍴 Menus
50 000-60 000 LBP s.i.
Carte
60 000-80 000 LBP s.i.

🔑 20 rooms
350 000-400 000 LBP s.i.

🔑 8 suites
starting at **500 000 LBP** s.i.

🍸 15 000-20 000 LBP s.i.

🛏 no

🏃 Beirut 45 km

Winter skiing, tennis in summer.

Perched at 1720 metres, offering superb panoramic views of the sea and 300 days of sunshine a year, L'Auberge de Faqra is a veritable Lebanese paradise. Enjoy hiking and mountain climbing or take advantage of the private ski area, the tennis courts, fitness centre and heated pool. After visiting the ruins of the Roman temple at Faqra and the ancient city of Byblos, savour exquisite traditional cuisine by candlelight.

Visa

LBP : Lebanese Pound

www.relaischateaux.fr/faqra

HOTEL ALBERGO

Lebanon

137, rue Abdel Wahab El Inglizi
Beyrouth

Tel. : (961) (01) 339 797
Fax : (961) (01) 339 999
E-mail : albergo@relaischateaux.fr

*From the airport, take av. de
l'aéroport ; at the roundabout,
take av. Jamel Abdel Nasser ;
at 2nd roundabout, take av. de
Novembre, continue straight on
towards av. Béchara El Khoury ;
after 2 km, take bd de
l'Indépendance to the right and
turn left after Sodeco Square.*

Owner : Sté hôtelière de Vinci
Director : Michel Chardigny
Open all year

Situated in the heart of the oldest
quarter of Beirut, the secret of the
splendid facade of the Hotel Albergo
combines the enchantment of supreme
comfort with the magic of a refined
setting. This residence is a unique
experience where the subtle hospitality
and the friendly atmosphere make this a
privileged hotel. The Albergo will soon
become one of your favourite places to
enjoy a unique and memorable stay.

✈	Beirut (**Intl**) 5 km
🍽	Carte **25-60 USD** t.5% s.16%
🛏	33 suites **215-650 USD** t.5% s.16%
🍷	**15-20 USD** t.5% s.16%
🛎	yes
⛳	5 km (18 holes)

Climbing, skiing, sailing,
mountain-biking, jacuzzi,
thalassotherapy.

Visa

THE AMERICAN COLONY HOTEL

SINCE 1997

Tel. : (972) (2) 627 9777
Fax : (972) (2) 627 9779
E-mail : americancolony@relaischateaux.fr

Nablus Road - PO BOX 19215
97200 Jerusalem

Israël

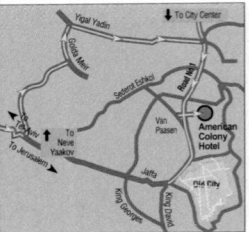

From Tel Aviv, left at 1st lights on reaching Jerusalem till «T». Left then right at lights. Next lights right, one mile till sixth light. Left at hotel sign.

Owner : Valentine Vester
Director : Urs Umbricht
Open all year

✈ Ben-Gurion **(Intl)** 45 km
Jerusalem 15 km

🍴 Menus **15-29 USD**
t.17% s.15%
Carte **15-40 USD**
t.17% s.15%

🔑 75 rooms
140-250 USD
t.17% s.15%

🔑 9 suites
280-380 USD
t.17% s.15%

🍷 **15 USD** t.17% s.15%

🍴 yes

♨ 80 km

Antiques, art galleries, historical tours of the city, business Centre, Reuters on line, car hire, souvenir shop, book shop, travel agency.

S pend a thousand and one magical nights in historic Jerusalem. This authentic Middle-Eastern mansion built in 1860 and with a fascinating history is an oasis of tranquility in this vibrant city. It offers various categories of rooms, each full of atmosphere and charm and three high-class restaurants. The hotel is a ten-minute walk from the Old City and other major tourist sites.

480

USD : US Dollar

www.relaischateaux.fr/americancolony

CHÂTEAU DE FEUILLES

Seychelles

Pointe Cabris - Baie Sainte-Anne
Ile de Praslin

Tel. : (248) 233 316
Fax : (248) 233 916
E-mail : feuilles@relaischateaux.fr

From "the" Praslin airport, follow the route along the beaches.

Owner : Château LTD
Director : Cédric Morel
Open all year

✈ Mahé **(Intl)** 45 km
  Praslin 10 km

🍴 Menus **225-250 SCR** s.i.
  Carte **100-250 SCR** s.i.

🔑 5 rooms
  1 450-1 850 SCR s.i.

🔑 4 suites
  1 850-2 250 SCR s.i.

☕ included

🍴 no

⛳ Mahé (9 holes)

Sailing, fishing, diving, trips to nearby islands, snorkelling, mountain bike, casino.

This privileged place with its breathtaking view of the ocean and the islands has ten rooms, divided between the château and the outbuildings with their splendid local architecture in the shade of the mango and coconut trees. The light inventive cuisine is a homage to sea and sun. Enjoy this charming place with its bougainvillea and relax to the sound of exotic birds singing. A unique experience.

Visa

Imba Matombo Lodge

SINCE 1997

Tel. : (263) (4) 499013/4
Fax : (263) (4) 499071
E-mail : imbamatombo@relaischateaux.fr

3, Albert Glen Close
Glen Lorne
Harare

Zimbabwe

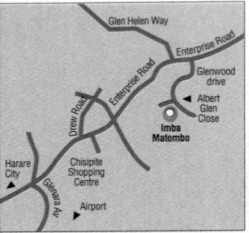

*Leave central Harare,
take Enterprise Road.
10 km drive to Chisipite,
5 km further on turn right into
Glenwood Drive, follow signs.*

Owners :
John and Charlotte Ford
Open all year

✈	Harare (**Intl**) 20 km
🍴	Menus **25-50 USD** t.5% s.i. Carte **30-50 USD** t.5% s.i.
⌂	8 rooms **250-350 USD** t.5% s.i.
⌂	3 suites **400-480 USD** t.5% s.i.
☕	**10 USD** t.5% s.i.
🐴	no
⛳	4 at 10 km

Gymnasium, sauna, jacuzzi.

Perched on a hill on the edge of Harare, this elegant lodge offers supreme comfort, impeccable service and one of the capital's finest restaurants. Imba Matombo is just a short flight from Zimbabwe's famous game reserves and the magnificent Victoria Falls. It is also a golfers' paradise, offering eight first-class courses within a 40 minute drive. Savour warm African hospitality, superb cuisine and undisturbed calm.

Visa

USD : US dollar

www.relaischateaux.fr/imbamatombo

SINGITA PRIVATE GAME RESERVE

South Africa

PO Box 650881
Benmore, 2010
(Mpumalanga)

Tel. : (27) (11) 234 0990
Fax : (27) (11) 234 0535
E-mail : singita@relaischateaux.fr

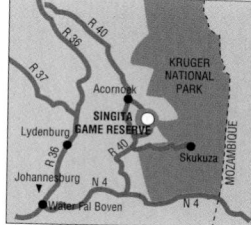

From Skuzuka airport, R536 towards Hazyview, sign board to the right 1 km before Lisbon Store, follow arrows to Singita (28 km).

Owner : Luke Bailes
Director : Bruce Simpson
Open all year

 Johannesburg **(Intl)** 500 km
Singita airstrip 3 km
(private airstrip)

GPS S 24° 48' 18"
E 31° 25' 34"

 Full board

 18 suites
3 900 ZAR s.i. per person

included

no

This magnificent 18,000 hectare reserve overlooking the Sand River offers 18 superb suites, nestling beneath giant ebony trees, each with its own swimming pool. Safaris in an open Land Rover enable you to discover, by day and by night, lion, leopard, rhino, elephant, buffalo and cheetah. Enjoy traditional evenings in the «Boma» and savour refined cuisine accompanied by the finest vintage South African wines from the 12,000 bottle underground wine cellar.

Curio shop, bush walks,
game drives by day and night
with rangers and trackers,
bird watching. Health Spa.

Visa

LONDOLOZI PRIVATE GAME RESERVE

SINCE 1993

Tel. : (27) (011) 775 0001
Fax : (27) (011) 784 7667
E-mail : londolozi@relaischateaux.fr

PO Box 4752
Rivonia, 2128

South Africa

Skukuza airport, towards Hazyview (R536 for 30 km), right towards Kingston Gate, Londolozi.

Owners : David and Shan Varty
Director : Gary Lotter
Open all year

✈ Johannesburg (**Intl**) 500 km
Londolozi Airstrip 1 km

GPS S 24° 48' 37"
E 31° 30' 27"

🍴 full board

O— 24 rooms
600-650 USD s.i.
per person

☕ included

🍴 no

🎿 Hazyview 65 km

Big Game safaris, guided game drives, bush walks, photography...

L ondolozi, the Zulu word meaning «protector of living things», has been acclaimed by President Nelson Mandela as «the model of the dream I cherish for the future of nature preservation in our country». For over 70 years, the Varty family have welcomed guests to experience Africa's most magical safari and wildlife reservation while offering luxury, personalised service and superb Pan-African cuisine.

🏃 P ✳ ✈ 〰

Visa

USD : US dollar

www.relaischateaux.fr/londolozi

CYBELE FOREST LODGE

South Africa

P.O. Box 346
White River 1240
(Mpumalanga)

Tel. : (27) (013) 764 1823
Fax : (27) (013) 764 1810
E-mail : cybele@relaischateaux.fr

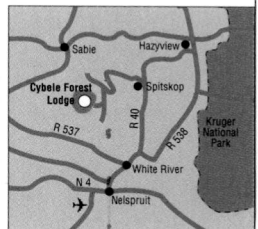

From White River, along the R40 towards Hazyview; left towards Spitskop.

Owners :
Rupert and Barbara Jeffries
Directors :
Alan Swallow and Noami Kuhn
Open all year

 Johannesburg (**Intl**) 400 km
Hazyview 20 km

 GPS S 25° 09' 15"
E 30° 58' 77"

 half-board

This haven of hospitality is set in the mountain forests near the Mpumalanga game reserves. The surrounding 120 hectares feature a river stocked with trout, a waterfall, stables and forest walks. The cottages are surrounded by lush gardens. All suites have private swimming pools. Cocktails are served on the colonial-style verandah. Delicious meals and Cape wines can be enjoyed in the candlelit dining room or in the garden.

 6 cottages
1 250-1 520 ZAR
t.14% s.n.i.

 6 suites
3 000-3 890 ZAR
t.14% s.n.i.

 included

 no

20 km

TSWALU PRIVATE DESERT RESERVE

Tel. : (27) (0) 53 781 9311
Fax : (27) (0) 53 781 9316
E-mail : tswalu@relaischateaux.fr

PO Box 420
Kathu 8446
(The Kalahari, Northern Cape Province)

South Africa

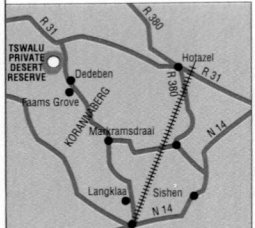

From Upington, N14 until Olifantshoek, then towards Barton then towards Sonstraal. After Healthcare Centre continue 10 km further. Tswalu is on the left.

Owners : Oppenheimer Family
Open all year

	Tswalu
	Full board
	9 suites **2 500 ZAR** s.n.i. per person
	included
	no

Day and night game drives, horse riding, bush walks, bird watching, African open air boma dining, sundowners on the sand dunes, curio shop.

An oasis of luxury in a breathtaking environment. This is the best way to describe Tswalu, the largest privately owned game reserve in South Africa with over 300 species of birds and animals among which you will find the rare desert black rhinoceros. Centred around a main lodge, there are nine individual air-conditioned lodges with private verandas where you can contemplate the spectacular sunsets. After your safari, you will be served dinner under the magnificient Kalahari night skies.

 Visa

ZAR : South African rand

BUSHMANS KLOOF

South Africa

PO Box 53405
Kenilworth 7945
(Cederberg Mountains-Western Cape)

Tel. : (27) (021) 797 09 90
Fax : (27) (021) 761 55 51
E-mail : bushmans@relaischateaux.fr

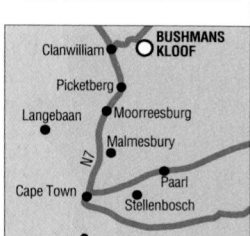

*Three hours drive from Cape Town:
follow N1, then N7 to Clanwilliam.
Continue for 35 km on the R364
gravel road through the Cederberg
Wilderness area and over
the Parkhuis Pass to the lodge.
Road transfers on request,
and Fly in Safaris available from
Cape Town International Airport.*

Owner : Mark McAdam
Director : Bill McAdam
Open all year

L ocated at the foothills of the Cederberg Mountains amidst rivers and rock formations, Bushmans Kloof offers you a note of sophistication and comfort and a unique wilderness experience. The reserve is rich in wildlife, indigenous flora and ancient San rock art, a mere 270 km from Cape Town. Guests will enjoy stylish, contemporary country cuisine, enhanced by South African wines from our award-winning wine list.

Cape Town (**Intl**) 278 km

GPS S 39° 02' 00"
E 19° 02' 32"

Full board

7 rooms
1 590 ZAR s.i.

7 suites
1 900-3 000 ZAR s.i.

included

no

30 km

Roping down, fly-fishing, hiking.

www.relaischateaux.fr/bushmans | ZAR : South African rand | Visa

HUNTER'S COUNTRY HOUSE

SINCE 1998

Tel. : (27) (044) 532 7818
Fax : (27) (044) 532 7878
E-mail : hunters@relaischateaux.fr

P.O. Box 454
Plettenberg Bay 6600
(Cape Province)

South Africa

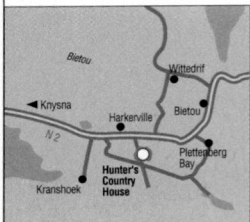

From Plettenberg Bay, take N2 West. 10 km until you see the sign.

Owner : Craig Hunter
Director : Ian Hunter
Open all year

 Cape Town (**Intl**) 530 km
Port Elizabeth 240 km

 Menus **189-295 ZAR** s.n.i.
Carte **97-230 ZAR** s.n.i.

 15 rooms
1 490-1 840 ZAR s.n.i.

 8 suites
2 185-3 500 ZAR s.n.i.

 included

 no

10 km

Fishing, water sports, dolphin and whale watching, Tsitsikamma National Park, hiking trail, bird watching, beaching.

A warm welcome awaits you at Hunter's. Set in a 90-hectare estate, accomodation is in luxurious, antique furnished, thatched cottages, each with fireplace and private patio, nestling in beautiful gardens overlooking indigenous forest. Enjoy intimate baronial dining rooms, the sunny conservatory and the cellar of fine wines. Visit nearby unspoilt beaches. South Africa's Hotel of the year 1996.

 Visa

ZAR : South African rand

www.relaischateaux.fr/hunters

THE PLETTENBERG

South Africa

Look out Rocks- P.O. Box 719
Plettenberg Bay 6600
(Cape Province)

Tel. : (27) (04453) 32 030
Fax : (27) (04453) 32 074
E-mail : plettenberg@relaischateaux.fr

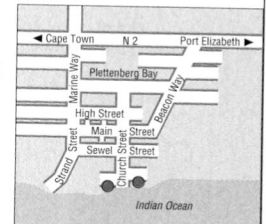

*From Port Elizabeth, N2,
exit Plettenberg Bay Beacon.
Beacon way, to the right.*

Owner : Liz McGrath
Director : Nigel Pace
Open all year

✈ Cape Town (**Intl**) 550 km
Port Elizabeth 220 km

🍴 Menus **100-140 ZAR** s.n.i.
Carte **90-150 ZAR** s.n.i.

⚷ 28 rooms
1 400-1 800 ZAR s.n.i.

⚷ 12 suites
1 800-3 200 ZAR s.n.i.

🍷 50-65 ZAR s.n.i.

🚫 no

♨ 2 km

Water sports, fishing, golf,
squash, walks...

uilt on a rocky headland overlooking
the Indian Ocean, this exclusive hotel
provides elegant accommodation, furnished
with impeccable taste. Enjoy diving, tennis
or golf, or simply laze on the terraces,
enjoying the Tsitsikamma mountains and
watching the whales and dolphins in the
Bay. Dine on seafood delicacies and Karoo
lamb, accompanied by the finest selection
of wines.

www.relaischateaux.fr/plettenberg

ZAR : South african rand

GRANDE ROCHE

Tel. : (27) (021) 863 27 27
Fax : (27) (021) 863 22 20
E-mail : granderoche@relaischateaux.fr

P.O. Box 6038
7622 Paarl
(Western Cape)

South Africa

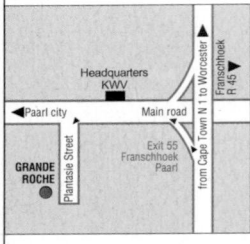

Airport, N 2, towards Somerset West, R 300, towards N 1 to Paarl, exit Paarl main road - 5 km to the left.

Owner : Hans Georg Allgaier
Director : Horst W. Frehse
Annual closing :
From the beginning of June to the end of August

✈	Cape Town (**Intl**) 40 km
	GPS S 33° 44' E 18° 58'
⑪	Menus **149-280 ZAR** s.i. Carte **32-55 ZAR** s.i.
⚷	35 suites **1 200-2 780 ZAR** s.i.
	included
	no
	4 km

Hiking, cycling, horse-riding.

S outh Africa's most hedonistic property, with a white-washed 18th century Cape Dutch manor house, historic and new vine-clad Suites, is in the heart of the Cape Winelands, surrounded by vineyards and exquisite gardens. Renowned «Bosman's» offers Cape delicacies such as Loin of Springbok, Ravioli and Medaillons of Crayfish, and an award-winning Cape Wine Cellar. A Fitness Centre with own masseur, hiking trails, bicycles, nearby Golf Courses satisfy the physical needs.

 Visa

ZAR : South African rand

www.relaischateaux.fr/granderoche

LE QUARTIER FRANÇAIS

South Africa

CNR Berg-Wilhelmina Str.
Franschhoek 7690
(Cape Winelands)

Tel. : (27) (021) 876 2151
Fax : (27) (021) 876 3105
E-mail : quartier@relaischateaux.fr

R54 to Franschhoek, down main road - Huguenot Road -, Police Station on left, Restaurant Le Quartier on right. Right into Berg Street and right into Wilhelmina Street for Auberge

Owners :
Susan Huxter, Richard Friedman and Pauline Friedman
Director : Linda Coltart
Open all year

83 kms from Cape Town, Le Quartier Français is in the heart of the vineyards of the famous Franschhoek valley of the French Huguenots. Located in the village centre, this Victorian residence is a exquisite stopping place on the wine trail and the trace of the history of the Huguenot settlers between Mount Rochelle, Haute Provence, Chamonix. Impeccable decoration and service. Eclectic cuisine by Margot Janse and regional wine, of course!

✈ Cape Town (**Intl**) 83 km
Stellenbosch 26 km

🍴 Menus **85-250 ZAR** s.n.i.
Carte **110-150 ZAR** s.n.i.

🗝 15 rooms
1 100 ZAR t.1% s.n.i.

🗝 2 suites
2 500 ZAR t.1% s.n.i.

☕ 45-65 ZAR s.n.i.

🛏 no

🎿 26 km

Fishing, hiking, horse-riding, hot-air balloon, biking.

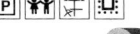

P 🍴 🔼 :L:

495

WILLOWBROOK LODGE

SINCE
1997

Tel. : (27) (021) 851 3759
Fax : (27) (021) 851 4152
E-mail : willowbrook@relaischateaux.fr

PO Box 1892
7129 Somerset West
(Western Cape)

South Africa

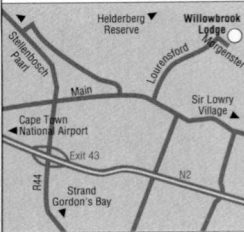

*From the airport, N2
exit 43, to the left R44,
then right onto Main road.
Left onto Lourensford road.*

Owner : Janik Olchanetzky
Director : Serge Olchanetzky
Annual closing :
From June 1st to August 31st

✈	Cape Town (**Intl**) 30 km
🍴	Carte **105-150 ZAR** s.n.i.
⚿	11 rooms **920-1 250 ZAR** s.n.i.
☕	45-85 ZAR s.n.i.
🛏	no
♪	1,5 km

Hunting, fishing, mountain-
climbing, sailing, canoeing,
mountain biking, flying club,
parachuting, concerts, cooking
and wine tasting courses.

When Janik and Serge Olchanetzky saw this magnificent South African landscape they immediately fell in love with Somerset West, as you will too when you discover this oasis of calm and luscious greenery. Relax in one of the comfortable guestrooms, each individually decorated with impeccable taste, then savour French-style cuisine prepared with the finest local ingredients and accompanied by superb local vintages.

496 P 🚻 ⛱ 🛗 🏊

 Visa

ZAR : South African rand

www.relaischateaux.fr/willowbrook

THE MARINE HERMANUS

South Africa

Marine Drive
Hermanus 7200

Tel. : (27) (028) 313 10 00
Fax : (27) (028) 313 01 60
E-mail : hermanus@relaischateaux.fr

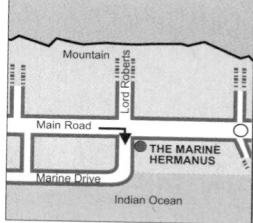

Shortly after the main shopping centre on the Marine road.

Owner : Liz McGrath
Director : Oliver Cooke
Open all year

✈ Cape Town (**Intl**) 100 km

GPS S 34° 25' 00"
E 19° 15' 00"

🍴 Menus
90-150 ZAR t.14% s.i.

⚷ 24 rooms
1 095-1 650 ZAR
t.14% s.i.

⚷ 22 suites
1 925-3 190 ZAR
t.14% s.i.

🍷 **65 ZAR** t.14% s.i.

🛏 no

♪ 1 km

In the famous coastal village of Hermanus, the hotel with its Edwardian architecture overlooks Walker Bay with its hues of blue: The Marine, a totally renovated turn-of-the-century colonial marvel is well-named. Everything about it is marine, clear and luminous from the tables of the orangery to the immense rooms decorated in a contemporary style. Fresh seafood served, of course, in both restaurants and regional wines.

Whale watching, diving, sailing, hiking, horse-riding, squash, tennis.

ELLERMAN HOUSE

Tel. : (27) (021) 439 91 82
Fax : (27) (021) 434 72 57
E-mail : ellerman@relaischateaux.fr

180 Kloof Road
Bantry Bay 8001 Le Cap
(Western Cape)

South Africa

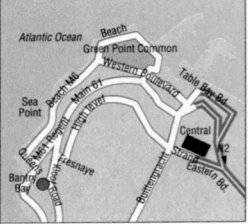

From the airport, N2 towards Cape Town, via Eastern Blvd; Strand Street, High Level Rd, Av. Fresnaye.

Owners :
Peter Bayly and Paul Harris
Director : Peter Bayly
Open all year

✈	Cape Town (**Intl**) 19 km
🍴	Carte **75-150 ZAR** s.i.
⚷	9 rooms **2 200-3 500 ZAR** s.i.
⚷	2 suites **4 900 ZAR** s.i.
☕	included
⚑	no
🏊	5 km

Sauna, private fitness centre, small business meetings (upon request).

In 1962 Sir John Ellerman fell in love with Bantry Bay and undertook the renovation of this beautiful aristocratic villa. Ellerman House has nine elegant rooms and two sumptuous suites, decorated in Edwardian style, which offer superb views of the ocean. Linger over an evening aperitif on the terrace under the deep blue starry night of the southern hemisphere, then savour excellent seafood cuisine and local vintages.

    Visa

ZAR : South African rand

www.relaischateaux.fr/ellerman

THE CELLARS-HOHENORT

South Africa

93, Brommersvlei Rd
Constantia - 7800 Cape Town
(Western Cape)

Tel. : (27) (021) 794 21 37
Fax : (27) (021) 794 21 49
E-mail : cellars@relaischateaux.fr

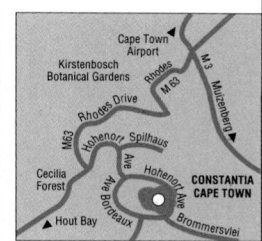

Airport, Cape Town (N2), Muizenberg (M3), Kirstenbosch (M63) and towards Hout Bay.

Owner : Liz McGrath
Director : Fredrik Aspegrén
Open all year

✈	Cape Town (**Intl**) 20 km
🍴	Menus 100-185 ZAR s.i. Carte 90-150 ZAR s.i.
⊶	38 rooms 1 400-2 300 ZAR s.i.
🔑	16 suites 2 500-9 000 ZAR s.i.
☕	55-65 ZAR s.i.
🚭	no
♪	5 km

Excursions.

This elegant hotel situated in the heart of the Constantia Valley is next to the World Famous Kirstenbosch gardens. Beautiful gardens with sweeping views across False Bay and Table Mountain. A beauty salon offers the usual beauty routines. Enjoy swimming, tennis or golf on the one hole golf green designed by Gary Player. Fine cuisine at «Novelli At The Cellars Restaurant» or traditional Cape Malay fare at the «Cape Malay Kitchen». A superior wine list is available.

www.relaischateaux.fr/cellars

ZAR : South African rand

499

NEW ZEALAND

Sydney
Wollongong
AUSTRALIA

TASMAN

SEA

Kaitaia
Whangarei
*Great
Barrier Is.*
Auckland
Hamilton · Tauranga
North Island Rotorua 501
New Plymouth · Gisborne
*Lake
Taupo*
Collingwood · Palmerston
Napier
Westport Nelson North
Greymouth
South Island · Kaikoura
Haast **Wellington**
Milford
Sound Timaru
Alexandra
Invercargill Dunedin
Foveaux Strait
Stewart Is.
Christchurch

PACIFIC OCEAN

0   100   200   300 400 km

Establishments	Nearest major city	Relais & Châteaux	Relais Gourmands	Page
Moose Lodge	Rotorua	⚜		501

Wines recommended by the wine waiters of the Relais & Châteaux and Relais Gourmands.

	Name of wine	Wine to enjoy	Noble wine	Outstanding wine
White	Sauvignon	1998 - 1997	1995	1996
Red	Merlot	1998 - 1997	1995	1996

MOOSE LODGE - GOLF RESORT

New Zealand

State Highway 30, RD4
PO Box 7181 Lake Rotoiti
Rotorua

Tel. : (64) (7) 362 78 23
Fax : (64) (7) 362 76 77
E-mail : moose@relaischateaux.fr

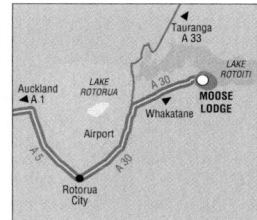

From Auckland: A1 south until Tirau.
Take A5 east towards Roturua.
Take A30 north, 3km after airport
take A30 east until Whakatane.
Continue for 8.2 km to the left.

Owners :
Omni Realty + Services LTD
Director : Shirley Chan
Open all year

E njoy the tranquility of the New Zealand bush, on this 50-hectare estate. Each suite, with its 1930's decor, has its own personalised furniture. You will be seduced by the charm of the candle-lit dinners, in the dining room overlooking the beautiful lake. After golf on our own private golf course, you may enjoy the natural, hot mineral baths or gymnasium and just relax, while literary enthusiasts will enjoy the peaceful atmosphere of the library.

✈   Rotorua 12 km

🍽   Menu **90 NZD**
t.12,5% s.n.i.

🔑   16 rooms
600-760 NZD
t.12,5% s.n.i.

🔑   4 suites
700-960 NZD
t.12,5% s.n.i.

☕   **32 NZD** t.12,5% s.n.i.

🛏   no

⛳   on the premises (18 holes)

Mineral baths, horse-riding,
fitness centre, spa.

501

NZD : New Zealand dollar

Visa

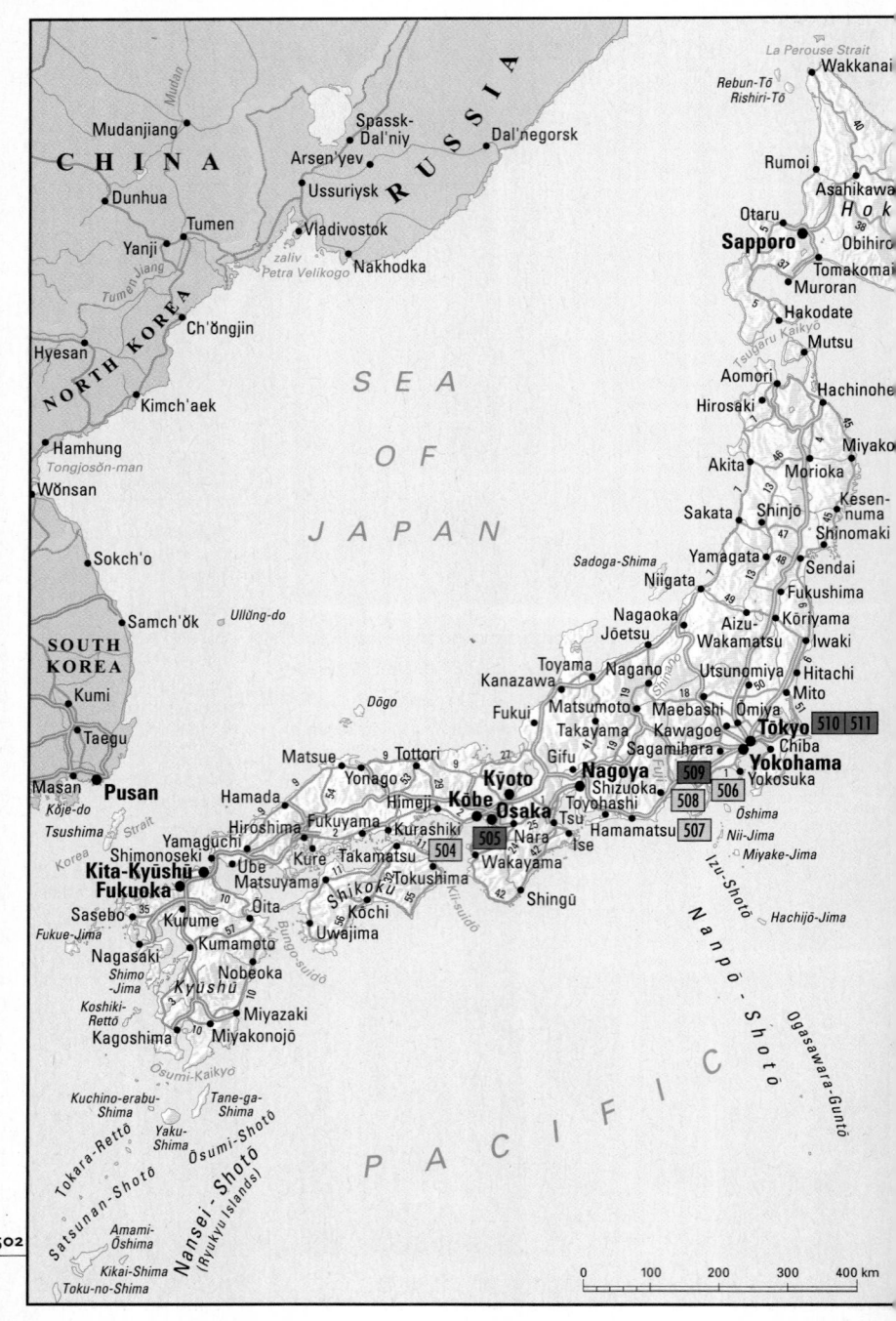

La Perouse Strait

RUSSIA

Wakkanai

Rebun-Tō
Rishiri-Tō

CHINA

Mudanjiang

Spassk-
Dal'niy

Dal'negorsk

Rumoi

Arsen'yev

Asahikawa

Dunhua

Ussuriysk

Hok

Otaru

Sapporo

Obihiro

Tumen

Vladivostok

zaliv
Petra Velikogo

Nakhodka

Tomakomai

Yanji

Muroran

Tumen Jiang

Hakodate

NORTH KOREA

Ch'ŏngjin

Mutsu

Tsugaru Kaikyō

Hyesan

Aomori

Hachinohe

Kimch'aek

SEA

Hirosaki

Miyako

Hamhung

Akita

Morioka

Tongjosŏn-man

OF

Kesen-
numa

Wŏnsan

Sakata

Shinjō

Shinomaki

JAPAN

Yamagata

Sendai

Sadoga-Shima

Niigata

Fukushima

Sokch'o

Nagaoka
Jōetsu

Aizu-
Wakamatsu

Kōriyama

Iwaki

Ullŭng-do

**SOUTH
KOREA**

Samch'ŏk

Dōgo

Toyama

Nagano

Utsunomiya

Hitachi

Kanazawa

Maebashi

Mito

Kumi

Fukui

Matsumoto

Kawagoe

Omiya

Tōkyō 510 511

Taegu

Matsue

Tottori

Gifu

Sagamihara

Yokohama

Masan

Yonago

Himeji

Kyōto

Nagoya

509

Chiba

Pusan

Hamada

Kōbe

Osaka

Shizuoka

Yokosuka

508

506

Kōje-do

Tsushima

Hiroshima

Fukuyama

504

Nara

505

Toyohashi

Tsu

507

Ōshima

Nii-Jima

Tsushima Strait

Korea Strait

Yamaguchi

Kurashiki

Hamamatsu

Miyake-Jima

Shimonoseki

Ube

Kure

Matsuyama

Kita-Kyūshū

Shikoku

Takamatsu

Ise

Wakayama

Izu-Shotō

Hachijō-Jima

Fukuoka

Ōita

Tokushima

Shingū

Kii-suidō

Sasebo

Kurume

Kōchi

Fukue-Jima

Uwajima

Bungo-suidō

Nagasaki

Kumamoto

*Shimo-
Jima*

Nobeoka

Kyūshū

*Koshiki-
Rettō*

Kagoshima

Miyazaki

Miyakonojō

Ōsumi-Kaikyō

N a n p ō - S h o t ō

O g a s a w a r a - G u n t ō

*Kuchino-erabu-
Shima*

*Tane-ga-
Shima*

*Yaku-
Shima*

P A C I F I C

Tokara-Rettō

Ōsumi-Shotō

Satsunan-Shotō

N a n s e i - S h o t ō
(Ryukyu Islands)

*Amami-
Ōshima*

Kikai-Shima

Toku-no-Shima

0   100   200   300   400 km

JAPAN

HOTEL ANAGA

SINCE
1993

Tel. : (81) (0799) 39 11 11
Fax : (81) (0799) 39 11 91
E-mail : anaga@relaischateaux.fr

Anaga, Seidan-cho
Mihara-gun, Hyogo-ken 656-0661

Japan

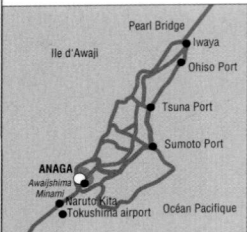

*From Tokushima airport, towards
Naruto then Anaga (30 mn).*

Owner : Sadao Iue
Director : Hidekatsu Matsuoka
Open all year

✈ Kansai (**Intl**) 60 km
Tokushima 20 km

GPS N 34° 16' 12"
E 134° 40' 15"

🍴 Menus **6 000-12 000 JPY**
t.8% s.10%
Carte **2 500-8 000 JPY**
t.8% s.10%

⚬ 56 rooms
18 000-45 000 JPY
t.8% s.10%

⚬ 6 suites
starting at **60 000 JPY**
t.8% s.10%

☕ **2 000-3 000 JPY**
t.8% s.10%

🚫 no

private 25 km

Fishing, cruise, jacuzzi.

H otel Anaga, a veritable jewel of modern luxury and comfort, is set on the tip of Awaji island. After breakfast on a flower-bedecked balcony overlooking the sea, stroll to the beach or the Sumoto golf course or enjoy a cruise through the Strait of Naruto. Linger over cocktails in the elegant Lounge Bar, then savour French seafood specialities at the «Cadeau de la mer» or Japanese cuisine at the «Anaga Restaurant».

504

Visa

JPY : Yen

www.relaischateaux.fr/anaga

LA BÉCASSE

Japan

ARK Bldg. 1F, 1-1-10 Kitahorie
Nishi-ku Osaka 550-0014

Tel. : (81) (06) 6543 4165
Fax : (81) (06) 6543 1268
E-mail : becasse@relaischateaux.fr

From Osaka train station, towards Midoü-Suji, Namba, Suhomachi-Suji, towards Yotsubashi and Umeda.

Owner : Yoshinori Shibuya
Weekly closing : Sunday
Open all year

✈ Kansaï (**Intl**) 30 km

🍴 Menus **4 000-10 000 JPY**
t.8% s.10%
Carte **10 000-15 000 JPY**
t.8% s.10%

🛏 no

Tenjinmatsuri Festival (July), Osaka Palace visit.

Y oshinori Shibuya, one of the highest stars in the firmament of Japanese gastronomy, is renowned for his original Franco-Japanese cuisine, inspired by Robuchon and Chapel who taught him «never to be satisfied». This lesson has certainly borne fruit. Savour Shibuya's exquisite «salade de homard à la coriandre», «paupiettes de sole au foie gras» and «piccata d'agneau» in a tastefully decorated restaurant in the heart of Osaka.

JPY : Yen

HORAI

SINCE 1986

Japan

Tel. : (81) (0557) 80 51 51
Fax : (81) (0557) 80 02 05
E-mail : horai@relaischateaux.fr

750-6 Izusan
Atami-shi, Shizuoka-ken 413-0002

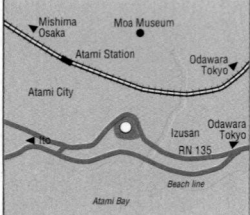

From Tokyo, Super Bullet Train (50 mn) until Atami Station ; 5 mn from Horai.

Owners : Seiyu Furutani
Director : Ryozo Tayama
Open all year

✈	Tokyo-Narita (**Intl**) 170 km Tokyo-Haneda 100 km
🍴	lunch on request
⊶	13 Japanese-style rooms-suites half board **80 000-120 000 JPY** t.8%
⊶	3 Japanese-style apartments half board **160 000-200 000 JPY** t.8%
☕	included
🛏	no
♪	4 km

Fishing, sailing...

T he only sound that you will hear in this idyllic haven, bathed in the aromas of ancient Japan, is the wind murmuring in the cherry trees or the waves rolling onto the sands. The minimalist «sukiya» style apartments, decorated with fresh flowers, open out directly onto the ocean. Relax in the open-air hot springs, then enjoy Japanese seafood in your room or savour French cuisine at the «Nanki Bunko» restaurant.

   Visa

JPY : Yen

www.relaischateaux.fr/horai

SEIRYUSO

Japan

2-2 Kochi
Shimoda-Shi
(Shizuoka-ken 415)

Tel. : (81) (0558) 22 13 61
Fax : (81) (0558) 23 20 66
E-mail : seiryuso@relaischateaux.fr

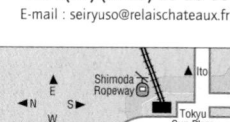

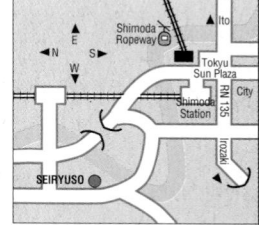

3.5 km from the Shimoda train station; from Tokyo via the Tomei highway and Rte 135.

Owner : Kenichi Tanaka
Director : Hideo Tanaka
Open all year

✈ Narita (**Intl**) 250 km

🍴 Menus **12 000-25 000 JPY**
t.8% s.i.
Dinner on request

⚷ 24 Japanese style
rooms-suites
half board
56 000-90 000 JPY
t.8% s.i.

⚷ 6 Japanese style
apartments
half board
110 000 JPY t.8% s.i.

☕ included

🍴 no

🏃 10 km

Fishing.

S erenity and calm reign in this vast park bathed in Izu's light. A flagstone walk flanked by 100-year-old willows and a lovely stone lantern leads to six pavilions admirably arranged in the purest Japanese style. Pure water from on-site hotsprings replenish the external pool, which is open all year long. Casa Vino, renowned for its refined cuisine, offers primarily fish and wines from around the world.

P ❄ ⬦ 🍴 📶

507

www.relaischateaux.fr/seiryuso

JPY : Yen

Visa

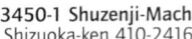

ASABA

SINCE 1989

Tel. : (81) (0558) 72 70 00
Fax : (81) (0558) 72 70 77
E-mail : asaba@relaischateaux.fr

3450-1 Shuzenji-Machi
Shizuoka-ken 410-2416

Japan

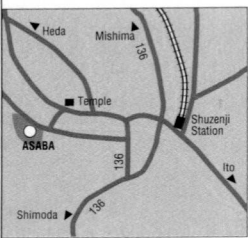

From Mishima, R 136 towards Shuzenji; right after Kokey bridge in front of the Shuzenji Temple, 200m farther on the left.

Owner : Aiko Asaba
Director : Kazuhide Asaba
Open all year

✈	Tokyo-Narita (**Intl**) 200 km Tokyo-Haneda 130 km
🍴	included
⚷	15 rooms half board **60 000-80 000 JPY** t.8% s.n.i.
⚷	4 suites half board **86 000-96 000 JPY** t.8% s.n.i.
☕	included
⚄	no
🏃	3 km

Asaba was built in 1675, amidst the oldest hotsprings on the Izu Peninsula. Its crowning feature is a bamboo forest bordering a magnificent pond. A series of sumptuous buildings seems to float along this stretch of water. Opposite them is the stage of the «No» Theatre, a little bridge, a room of mirrors... Outdoor or family bathing facilities are made of cypress wood. Festive Japanese cuisine.

Visa

JPY : Yen

www.relaischateaux.fr/asaba

GÔRA KADAN

Japan

1300 Gôra
Hakone-Machi
Ashigara-Shimogun, Kanagawa-ken, 250-0408

Tel. : (81) (0460) 2 3331
Fax : (81) (0460) 2 3334
E-mail : gora@relaischateaux.fr

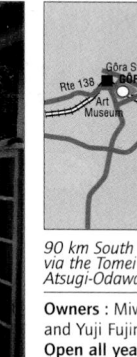

90 km South West of Tokyo, via the Tomei highway then Atsugi-Odawara way and route 1.

Owners : Miwako Fujimoto and Yuji Fujimoto
Open all year

✈	Tokyo-Narita (**Intl**) 170 km Tokyo-Haneda 100 km
🍴	starting at **20 000 JPY** t.8% s.i.
🔑	39 Japanese style rooms-suites half board **100 000-120 000 JPY** t.8% s.i.
🔑	5 Japanese - style apartments half board **140 000-144 000 JPY** t.8% s.i.
☕	included
🍴	no
🏊	2 km

D iscover the wonders of ancient Japan at Gôra Kadan, the former summer residence of the Kan-In-No-Miya imperial family. This noble residence, set in idyllic surroundings at the foot of Mount Fuji, offers beautiful Tatami-style rooms with cypress baths, sumptuous open-air baths, pool and jacuzzi. After a visit to the nearby botanical gardens or the art and tradition museum, savour traditional Kaiseki cuisine.

Sauna, jacuzzi, beauty spa, thermal baths. Limousine service available on request.

JPY : Yen

Visa

MIKUNI

SINCE 1991

Tel. : (81) (03) 33 51 38 10
Fax : (81) (03) 32 25 13 24
E-mail : mikuni@relaischateaux.fr

1-18 Wakaba
Shinjuku-ku Tokyo 160-0011

Japan

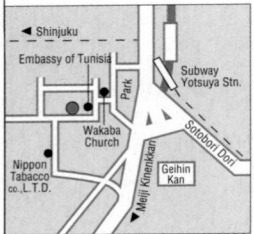

From the Yotsuya railway station,
cross Sotobori-Dori, then the park.
Go straight on to the left
of the church. Turn left
at the first crossroads, then right
to the very end.

Owner/Chef : Kiyomi Mikuni
Weekly closing :
Sunday evening and Monday
Open all year

✈ Tokyo-Narita (**Intl**) 80 km
Tokyo-Haneda 12 km

🍴 Lunch **6 500-10 000 JPY**
t.5% s.15%
Dinner **15 000 JPY**
t.5% s.15%
Carte **5 800-10 000 JPY** s.i.
(Possibility of portions
for tasting)

🐎 no

Kiyomi Mikuni is one of Tokyo's highest rated chefs. Drawing on Girardet, Troisgros and Chapel, he has created his own «cuisine spontanée», blending French and Japanese tradition with innovative flair. Savour his exquisite «Japanized». «salade de homard d'Alain Chapel», and «platinium et menthe fraîche Kiyomi Mikuni», and choose from an excellent selection of French wines.

510

  Visa

JPY : Yen

www.relaischateaux.fr/mikuni

KAKIDEN

Japan

Yasuyo Bldg., 3-37-11 Shinjuku,
Shinjuku-ku, Tokyo to 160-0022

Tel. : (81) (03) 3352-5121
Fax : (81) (03) 3350-5113
E-mail : kakiden@relaischateaux.fr

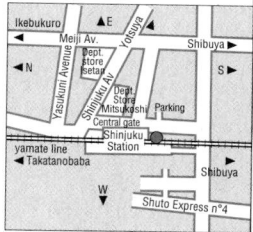

Shinjuku Railway station, near the East-Central exit. In the Yasuyo building (Nippon Saiken Shinyo Ginko is on the first floor).

Owner : Zenichi Yasuda
Director : Mitsuko Yasuda
Annual closing :
From Dec. 30th to January 4th

Tokyo-Narita (**Intl**) 80 km
Tokyo-Haneda 15 km

Lunch **4 000 JPY**
t.5% s.10%
Menus
«Continental Room»
8 000-35 000 JPY
t.8% s.10%
«Tatami Room»
20 000-35 000 JPY
t.8% s.20%

no

Japanese culture in all its variety, from the ancestral mastery of tea ceremonies to that of the refinement of Kaiseki cuisine. The Kakiden sign was calligraphed by Kawabata himself. As you savour the calm and serene architecture of rooms devoted to tea ceremonies, your palate and your eyes will delight in the delicacy of each season's meal, and you will be enthralled by the Koto concerts performed there.

Visa

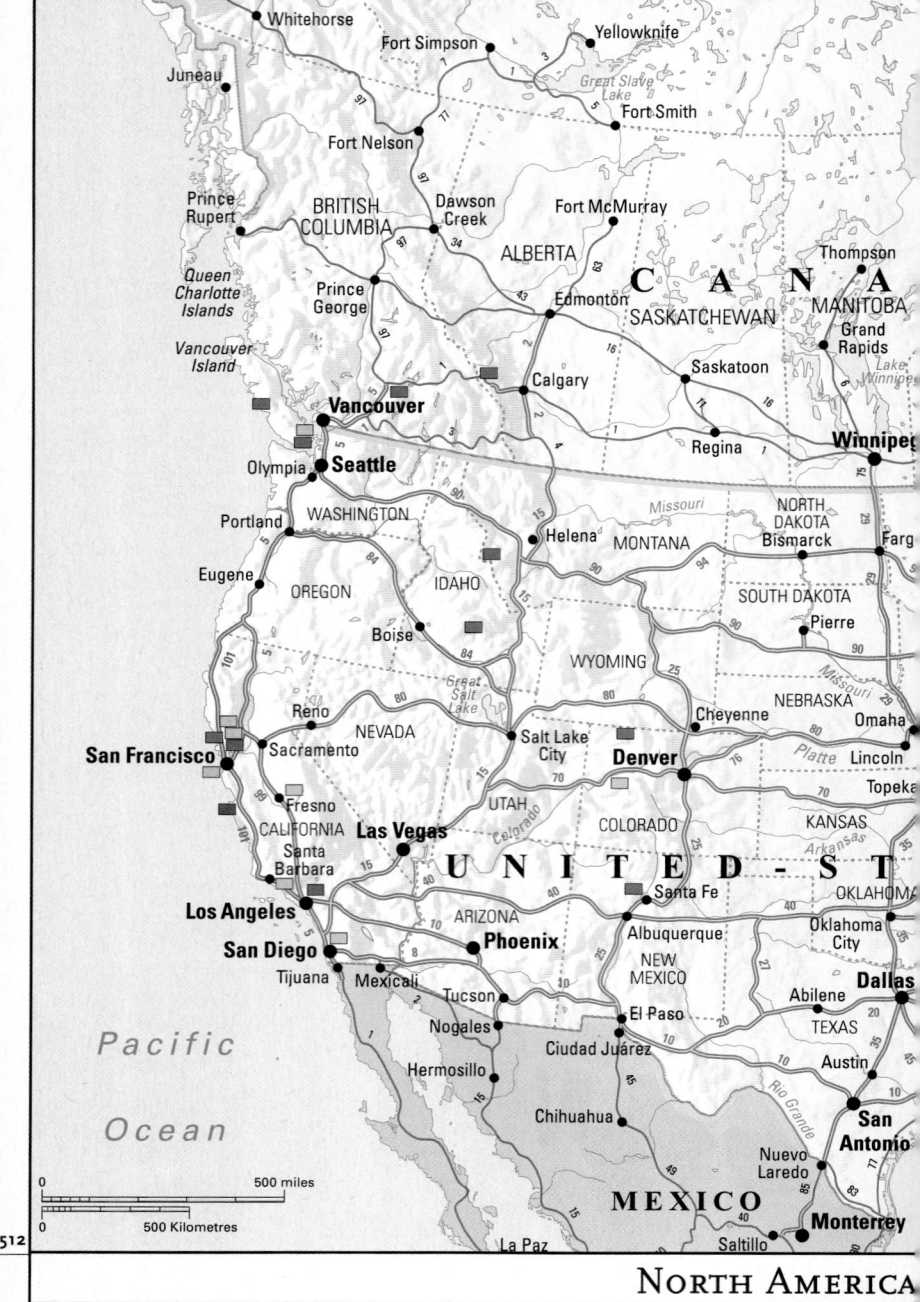

NORTH AMERICA

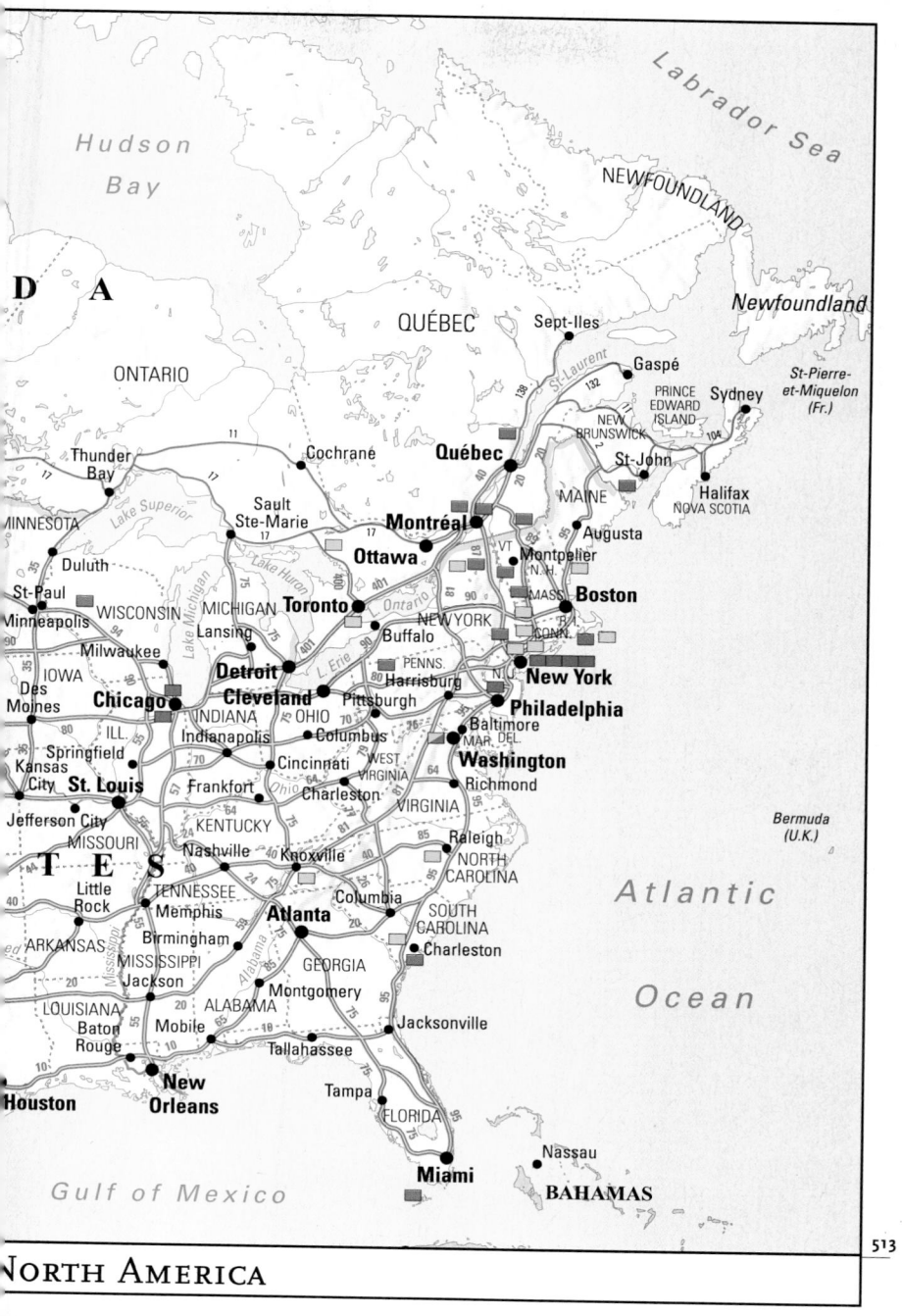

Hudson
Bay

Labrador Sea

NEWFOUNDLAND

Newfoundland

D   A

ONTARIO

QUÉBEC

Sept-Îles

St-Pierre-
et-Miquelon
(Fr.)

Gaspé

PRINCE
EDWARD
ISLAND

Sydney

Cochrane

Québec

St-Laurent

132

NEW
BRUNSWICK

104

St-John

Thunder
Bay

11

17

Sault
Ste-Marie

17

MAINE

Augusta

Halifax
NOVA SCOTIA

MINNESOTA

Lake Superior

75

Montréal

Ottawa

17

401

20

18

VT
N.H.

Montpelier

Duluth

St-Paul

WISCONSIN

MICHIGAN

Lansing

Toronto

Lake Huron

400

90

Ontario

Buffalo

85

80

MASS.

R.I.
CONN.

Boston

Minneapolis

35

94

Milwaukee

75

L. Erie

NEW YORK

New York

Des
Moines

IOWA

Chicago

INDIANA

Detroit

Cleveland

OHIO

75

Pittsburgh

PENNS.

Harrisburg

80

70

Philadelphia

N.J.

90

Springfield

ILL.

Indianapolis

Columbus

70

WEST
VIRGINIA

Washington

MAR. DEL.

Baltimore

Kansas
City

St. Louis

70

Cincinnati

Frankfort

Charleston

Ohio

64

Richmond

Jefferson City

MISSOURI

KENTUCKY

64

VIRGINIA

81

85

Raleigh

Bermuda
(U.K.)

T   E   S

Nashville

Knoxville

40

24

NORTH
CAROLINA

Little
Rock

40

TENNESSEE

24

75

Columbia

85

ARKANSAS

Memphis

Birmingham

59

Atlanta

20

SOUTH
CAROLINA

Charleston

MISSISSIPPI

Jackson

Montgomery

GEORGIA

Atlantic

LOUISIANA

20

ALABAMA

Alabama

75

Jacksonville

Ocean

Baton
Rouge

Mobile

10

Tallahassee

Houston

10

**New
Orleans**

Tampa

75

FLORIDA

95

Gulf of Mexico

Miami

Nassau

BAHAMAS

513

NORTH AMERICA

CHAMPAGNE
Laurent-Perrier
ESTABLISHED 1812

Photo Michel Gibert

VINTAGES TO DRINK IN YEAR 2000
USA - CANADA

Wines recommended by the wine waiters
of the Relais & Châteaux and Relais Gourmands.

* Index of world vintages to drink in year 2000 : page 607

	Name of wine	Wine to enjoy	Noble wine	Outstanding wine
	USA			
Red	Pinot Noir (Oregon)	1996 - 1995	1993	1994
	Pinot Noir, Cabernet Sauvigon, Merlot, Zinfandel (Napa Valley)	1997 - 1996	1994 - 1993	1990 - 1987 - 1975
Dry white wines	Chardonnay (Napa Valley)	1997 - 1996	1995 - 1993	1994 - 1992
	Sauvignon Blanc (Napa Valley)	1997 - 1996	1995	
	CANADA			
Dry white wines	Chardonnay, Riesling, Pinot Blanc	1997 - 1996	1995	
Ice Wein	Vidal Icewine, Riesling Icewine	1997	1995	1989 - 1991
Red	Cabernet Franc, Merlot	1995		

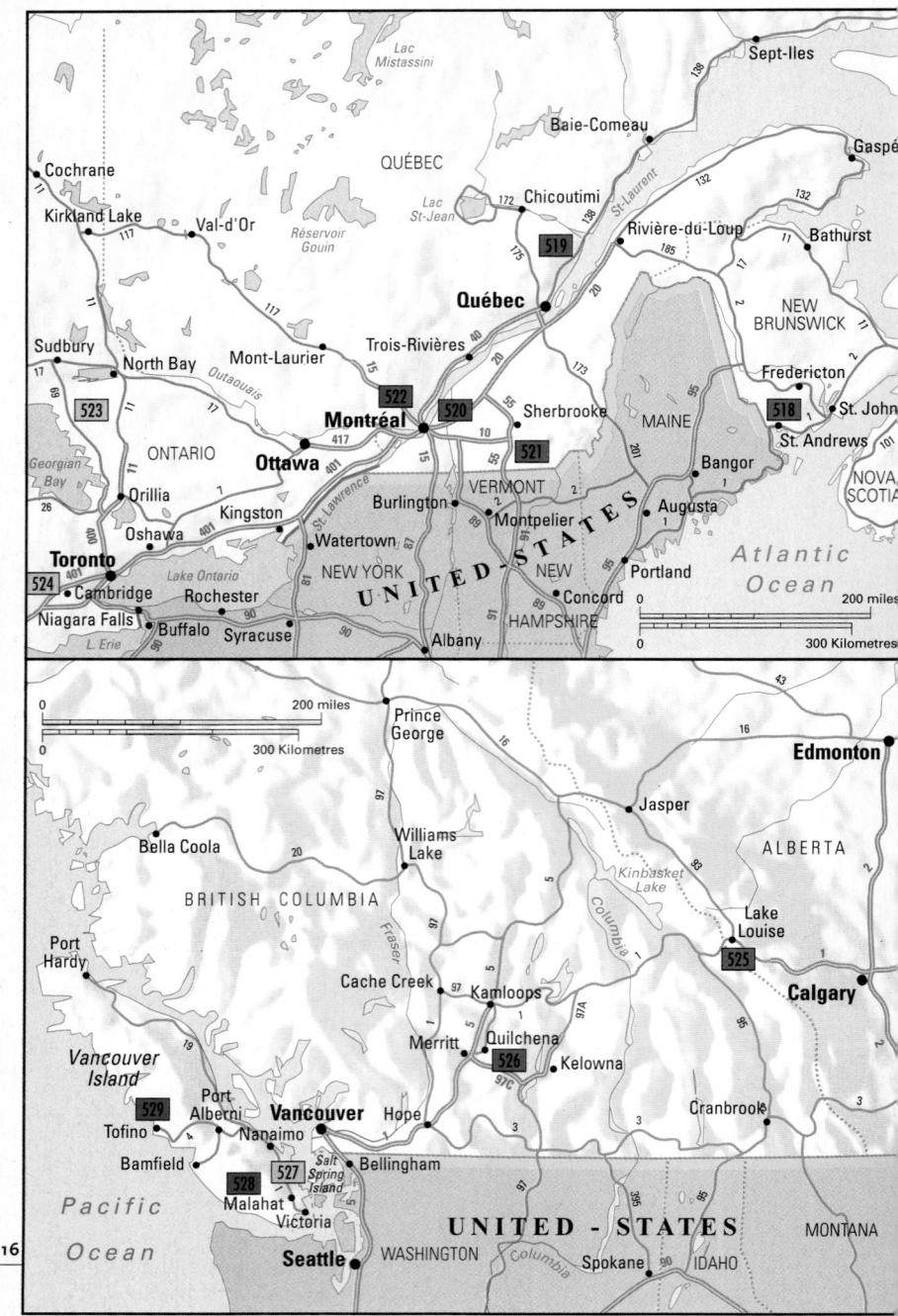

North America

Canada

Establishments	Nearest major city	Relais & Châteaux	Relais Gourmands	Page
Auberge Hatley	Montréal	⚜		521
Hastings House	Victoria	⚜		527
Hostellerie Les Trois Tilleuls	Montréal	⚜		520
Hôtel L'Eau à la Bouche	Montréal	⚜		522
Inn at Manitou (The)	Parry Sound	⚜		523
Kingsbrae Arms	Saint John	⚜		518
Langdon Hall	Cambridge	⚜		524
Little Beaver Creek ranch	Vancouver	⚜		526
Pinsonnière (La)	Québec	⚜		519
Post Hotel	Calgary	⚜		525
The Aerie	Victoria	⚜		528
Wickaninnish Inn	Tofino	⚜		529

KINGSBRAE ARMS

SINCE 1998

Tel. : (1) (506) 529 1897
Fax : (1) (506) 529 1197
E-mail : kingsbrae@relaischateaux.fr

219 King Street
St Andrews
New Brunswick EOG 2X0

Canada

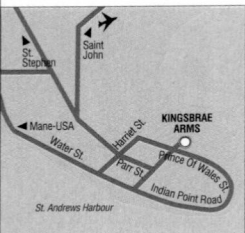

From the Fundy Coastal Drive, Hwy 1, exit St Andrews. Turn up King St. and go to the top of the hill.

Owners : Harry Chancey Jr. and David Oxford
Director : Harry Chancey
Open all year

✈ Saint John (**Intl**) 100 km
Bangor (**Intl**) 145 km

🍴 Menus **75-90 CAD**
t.15% s.15%

🔑 5 rooms
300-375 CAD
t.15% s.5%

🔑 3 suites
450-525 CAD
t.15% s.5%

☕ included

🛏 on request

🏃 1 km

Jacuzzi, deep sea fishing, whale watching, biking.

This sumptuous residence, built in 1897, is adjacent to the magnificent Kingsbrae Horticultural Garden and offers stunning views across Passamaquoddy Bay. Spacious suites and rooms feature fireplaces and whirlpools. The reception rooms are resplendent with period furnishings, Oriental carpets and objets d'art. The superb cuisine is based on the region's seasonal bounty from land and sea.

CAD : Canadian dollar

www.relaischateaux.fr/kingsbrae

LA PINSONNIÈRE

Canada

124, rue St-Raphaël
Cap-à-l'Aigle
Québec GOT 1BO

Tel. : (1) (418) 665 4431
USA/Can Toll free : **(1) (800) 387 4431**
Fax : (1) (418) 665 7156
E-mail : pinsonniere@relaischateaux.fr

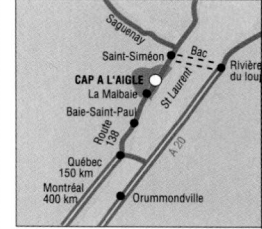

From Québec, route 138 East to Cap-à-l'Aigle, or by 362 East, the scenic route.

Owners : Authier Family
Director : Valérie Andrée Authier
Annual closing :
From Oct. 29th to Dec. 15th

Quebec (**Intl**) 150 km
Montreal (**Intl**) 400 km

Menus **50-95 CAD**
t.15% s.15%

25 rooms
150-500 CAD t.15% s.i.

1 suite
500 CAD t.15% s.i.

15 CAD t.15% s.15%

no

5 km (2)

Massotherapy, trapping, snowbiking, fishing, concerts, casino.

Perched high above the majestic St. Lawrence River, La Pinsonnière embraces the changing seasons and natural splendours of the Charlevoix region, a UNESCO World Biosphere Reserve. The rooms, with four-poster beds, fireplaces and whirlpool baths, offer idyllic views. Outdoor activities include skiing, dogsledding and whale watching cruises. Award-winning cuisine is complemented by an impressive wine cellar.

519

CAD : Canadian dollar

Visa

HOSTELLERIE LES TROIS TILLEULS

SINCE 1983

Tel. : (1) (514) 856 7787
USA/Can Toll free : (1) (800) 263 2230
Fax : (1) (450) 584 3146
E-mail : tilleuls@relaischateaux.fr

290 Richelieu
St-Marc-sur-Richelieu
Québec J0L 2E0

Canada

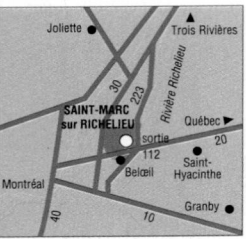

From the airport, A20 towards Quebec City, exit 112; route 223 north, 7 km.

Owner : Michel Aubriot
Open all year

✈ Dorval (**Intl**) 60 km
Mirabel (**Intl**) 100 km

GPS N 39° 12' W 45° 73'

🍴 Menus **20-76 CAD**
t.15% s.15%
Carte **29-40 CAD**
t.15% s.15%

⚷ 23 rooms
95-125 CAD t.15%

⚷ 1 suite
450 CAD t.15%

☕ **3,5-13 CAD** t.15% s.15%

🍽 no

🎣 10 km

Hunting, climbing,
horseback riding.

Deep in the heart of Quebec, maple groves, manors, churches and mills bear witness to the birth of a nation. On the tranquil banks of the Richelieu River, discover a magnificent setting where the comfortable rooms, (decorated with fresh bouquets), open onto terraces and the beautiful riverfront garden. After hunting and sleigh riding in unspoiled natural surroundings, savour superb cuisine and exceptional wines.

CAD : Canadian dollar

www.relaischateaux.fr/tilleuls

AUBERGE HATLEY

Canada

325 Chemin Virgin, C.P. 330
North Hatley
Québec JOB 2CO

Tel. : (1) (819) 842 2451
Fax : (1) (819) 842 2907
E-mail : hatley@relaischateaux.fr

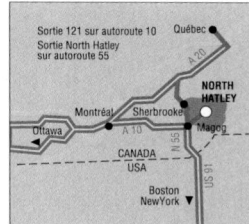

Sortie 121 sur autoroute 10
Sortie North Hatley
sur autoroute 55

*From Montreal, highway n° 10,
exit 121; follow signs to «Auberge
Hatley».*

Owners :
Robert and Liliane Gagnon
Annual closing :
From November 10th to 30th

✈ Dorval (**Intl**) 140 km
Mirabel (**Intl**) 180 km

🍴 Menus **50-95 CAD**
t.16% s.n.i.
Carte **50-95 CAD**
t.16% s.n.i.

⊶ 24 rooms
175-350 CAD t.16% s.i.

🛎 **15 CAD** t. 16% s.n.i.

🛏 no

♪ 3 km

Kayaking, cross-country skiing,
snowbiking, dog sleighing,
swimming, cycle paths.

A charming country house with magnificient views overlooking Lake Massawippi and surrounding forests tinged with purple and gold during the Indian summer. Bright and intimate rooms, many with fireplace, balconies. One of the most celebrated restaurant in Québec. The Hatley grows its salads and herbs in its own greenhouse. Superb wine cellar. Enjoy private access to the lake, bicycle path, golf and winter sports.

Visa

HÔTEL L'EAU À LA BOUCHE

SINCE 1989

Tel. : (1) (450) 229 2991
USA/Can Toll free : (1) (888) 828 2991
Fax : (1) (450) 229 7573
E-mail : eaubouche@relaischateaux.fr

3003 Bd Ste-Adèle
Sainte-Adèle
Québec J8B 2N6

Canada

*Laurentides highway (15 North),
exit 67, route 117 North
(blvd. Sainte-Adèle).*

Owners : Pierre Audette
and Anne Desjardins
Open all year

✈ Mirabel (**Intl**) 35 km
Dorval (**Intl**) 75 km

🍴 Menus **55-120 CAD**
t.15% s.15%
Carte **35-45 CAD**
t.15% s.15%

 25 rooms
165-280 CAD t.15%

 12,5 CAD t.15% s.15%

 no

 3 km

Dog and horse sleighs,
water sports, golf, skiing,
cycle track...

This tiny hotel, nestled in the Laurentian Mountains, looks out across a magnificent landscape resplendent with maples, firs and silver birches. Enjoy the comfort of the charming rooms, the terraces, relax in the outdoor heated pool and indulge in a full range of leisure activities, 40 minutes away from Mont-Tremblant. You will be enchanted by Anne Desjardins' delicious regional cuisine and the outstanding wine list.

 Visa

CAD : Canadian dollar

www.relaischateaux.fr/eaubouche

THE INN AT MANITOU

Canada

Center Road
McKellar
Ontario POG 1CO

Tel. : (1) (705) 389 2171
USA/Can. Toll free : (1) 800 571 8818
Fax : (1) (705) 389 3818
E-mail : manitou@relaischateaux.fr

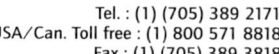

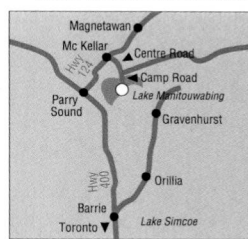

*Toronto, Highway 401, 400
North towards Parry Sound,
Highway 124 Sundridge.*

Owners/Directors :
Ben and Sheila Wise
Annual closing :
From October 21st to May 8th

T his charming estate of 220 hectares near Lake Manitouwabing offers golf, tennis, and spa facilities. The superb guestrooms and suites (antique marble, spacious lounges and fireplaces) have private sun terraces with spectacular views. With its world-renowned restaurant and exceptional wine list, this is a wonderful resort created with utmost care by Ben and Sheila Wise.

Toronto (**Intl**) 250 km
Lake Manitouwabing 1 km

Carte **31-65 CAD**
t.8% and 7% s.16%

22 rooms
pp/pd includes all meals
229-323 CAD
t.8% and 7% s.16%

11 suites
pp/pd includes all meals
320-388 CAD
t.8% and 7% s.16%

21 CAD t.8% and 7% s.16%

yes

Golf Academy
on the premises

Spa, water sports, sailing, fishing, horseback riding, biking, fitness center, sauna, jacuzzi.

CAD : Canadian dollar

LANGDON HALL

SINCE 1990

Tel. : (1) (519) 740 2100
Fax : (1) (519) 740 8161
E-mail : langdon@relaischateaux.fr

Country House Hotel
RR n°33 Cambridge
Ontario N3H 4R8

Canada

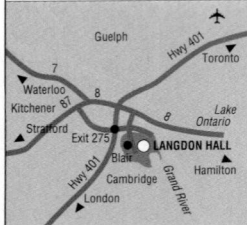

Hwy 401, exit 275, Fountain St. to Blair Rd. to Langdon Drive, 2nd on the right and 1st left.

Owners :
Beaton and Bennett Families
Director : Mark Torrance
Annual closing :
First week of January

✈	Toronto (**Intl**) 105 km
🍴	Menus **20-75 CAD** t.15% Carte **35-55 CAD** t.15%
🔑	40 rooms **269-319 CAD** s.i.
🔑	8 suites **399-699 CAD** s.i.
🍷	**8-15 CAD** t.15%
🐕	yes (extra cost)
🏌	public 2 km

Spa, canoeing, croquet, mountain-biking, hunting, ski, fitness, sauna, jacuzzi, walking trails.

S et amidst 200 acres, our house was built for a descendant of legendary financier John Jacob Astor. Most guestrooms have a fireplace, and all are decorated with period furniture, crisp white linens and the most comfortable feather beds. The dining room offers outstanding cuisine featuring local products and our garden's bounty. Indulge at the Spa, visit Mennonite countryside and enjoy theatre at the Stratford Festival.

Visa

CAD : Canadian dollar

www.relaischateaux.fr/langdon

Canada

POST HOTEL

PO Box 69
Lake Louise
Alberta TOL 1EO

Tel. : (1) (403) 522 3989
Fax : (1) (403) 522 3966
E-mail : posthotel@relaischateaux.fr

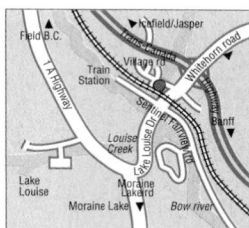

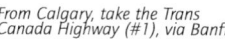

From Calgary, take the Trans
Canada Highway (#1), via Banff.

Owners :
André and Georges Schwarz
Director : Geoffrey Booth
Annual closing :
From October 21st to Dec. 13th

 Calgary (**Intl**) 190 km

 Carte **50-65 CAD**
t.7% s.15%

 71 rooms
300-375 CAD t.12%

27 suites
400-600 CAD t.12%

15 CAD t.7% s.15%

 no

 55 km

Skiing, fishing, climbing, hiking...

The Canadian Rockies at their finest. Perched at 1500 metres amidst the natural wonders of Banff National Park, you will find this cherished Alpine chalet. Canada's largest ski area is just minutes away and the abundance of snow is just one reason a growing number of European skiers visit the area each winter. The dining room features fresh market cuisine complemented by an 850 label, 20,000 bottle Award-winning wine cellar.

525

LITTLE BEAVER CREEK RANCH

SINCE
1998

Canada

Tel. : (1) (250) 371 76 64
Fax : (1) (250) 372 48 93
E-mail : littlebeaver@relaischateaux.fr

Quilchena
Glimpse Lake
British Columbia VOE 2RO

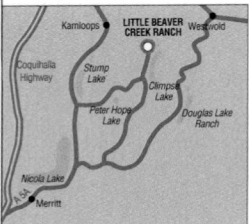

From Vancouver on Coquihalla - Hwy 1/5 via Merritt on Hwy 5A to Quilchena. Follow road signs.

Owner : Alex Schütz
Annual closing :
From October 15th to May 15th

✈ Vancouver (**Intl**) 300 km
Kamloops 80 km

GPS N 50° 15' 14"
W 120° 15' 44"

O⊷ 1 room
350 CAD t.15% s.i.
full board
per person and per day

8⊷ 6 suites
445-650 CAD t.15% s.i.
full board
per person and per day

卉 yes

♪ 30 km

Riding, fishing-boating,
fitness-club.

The spirit of the Wild West lives on at Little Beaver Creek Ranch, built at the beginning of this century. Nested between the Pacific Coast and the mountains, this magnificent ranch is set amidst stunning countryside where deer, bears, coyotes and pumas still roam. Explore the region on horseback, stroll beneath the century-old trees or relax by the lake, then enjoy the superb comfort of the charming guest suites.

526

Visa

CAD : Canadian dollar

www.relaischateaux.fr/littlebeaver

HASTINGS HOUSE

Canada

160 Upper Ganges Rd
Salt Spring Island
British Columbia V8K 2S2

Tel. : (1) (250) 537 2362
USA/Can. Toll free : **(1) (800) 661 92 55**
Fax : (1) (250) 537 5333
E-mail : hastings@relaischateaux.fr

By car-ferry from Vancouver or Victoria, or by seaplane from Vancouver, Victoria or Seattle.

Owners :
Jerry Parks and Bonny O'Connor
Director : Mark Gottaas
Annual closing :
From January 3rd to March 2nd

Vancouver (**Intl**) 67 km
Seattle 117 km

Menu **70 CAD** t.7% s.n.i.

3 rooms
310-410 CAD t.15% s.n.i.

14 suites
365-620 CAD t.15% s.n.i.

Full English breakfast included

no

4 km (2 courses)

Fishing, mountain biking, kayaking, hiking, galleries, crafts market, bird watching, massage therapy.

Return to an era of grace and simplicity. This magnificent half-timbered English manor nestles amidst the forests of Salt Spring Island beside a peaceful harbor. Enjoy acres of vibrant lawns and gardens, breathtaking vistas, abundant wildlife, and a lively arts community. Savor exquisite cuisine prepared with the finest local products, and relax in the comfort of your individually appointed fireplace suite.

527

CAD : Canadian dollar

THE AERIE

Tel. : (1) (250) 743 7115
Fax : (1) (250) 743 4766
E-mail : aerie@relaischateaux.fr

600 Ebadora Lane
Box 108 - Malahat - Vancouver Island
British Columbia, VOR 2LO

Canada

From Victoria Airport,
Trans Canada Highway, exit at
Spectacle Lake; follow road signs.

Owner : Maria Schuster
Director : Markus Griesser
Open all year

✈	Victoria (**Intl**) 40 km
	GPS N 48° 34' 13" O 123° 32' 06"
🍴	Menus **50-75 CAD** t.15% s.i. Carte **27-32 CAD** t.15% s.i.
⊶	10 rooms **150-275 CAD** t.15% s.i.
⊶	13 suites **250-450 CAD** t.15% s.i.
☕	included
⊬	no
♪	3 golf courses (20 mn)

Whale watching, fishing, sailing,
hiking, kayaking, wine tours,
garden-tour's.

The breathtaking views over the fjords and Olympic Mountains inspired owner, Maria Schuster, and her family to design a Mediterranean-style mansion complete with a highly acclaimed dining room and the newly opened Aveda Wellness and Beauty Center. Surrounded by ten acres of meticulously kept grounds and gardens, this setting combined with impeccable service and style has proven to be an ideal match for those seeking a tranquil hideaway.

Visa

CAD : Canadian dollar

www.relaischateaux.fr/aerie

THE WICKANINNISH INN

Canada

Osprey Lane at Chesterman Beach
Tofino
British Columbia VOR 2ZO

Tel. : (1) (250) 725 31 00
Fax : (1) (250) 725 31 10
E-mail : wickaninnish@relaischateaux.fr

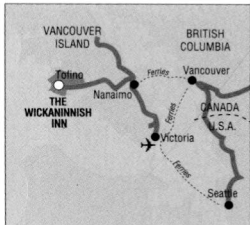

From Nanaimo Highway 19,
then Hwy 4 West until Port
Alberni then Tofino.
Turn left on Lynn Road
and right on Osprey Lane.

Owner : Charles R. Mc Diarmid
Open all year

 Vancouver (**Intl**) 250 km
Long Beach Airport 15 km

 GPS N 49° 4' 7"
W 125° 50' 6"

 Menu **70 CAD**
t.15% s.n.i.
Carte **60-80 CAD**
t.15% s.n.i.

 46 rooms
180-400 CAD
t.15% s.n.i.

 7-18 CAD t.15% s.n.i.

yes (extra cost **20 CAD**)

15 km

Whale watching, diving,
sea kayaking, birding, fishing,
hiking, mountain biking, spa,
stormwatching.

N ature lovers will adore this idyllic retreat nestled on the West Coast of Vancouver Island. Imagine a fine sand beach, surrounded by a forest of giants conifers, and a charming residence, built of cedar wood, whose wide bay windows offer breathtaking views of the open ocean and the islands. Imagine savoring delicious seafood then relaxing in a tranquil room, lulled by the sound of the waves. Wickaninnish Inn : the answer to your dreams.

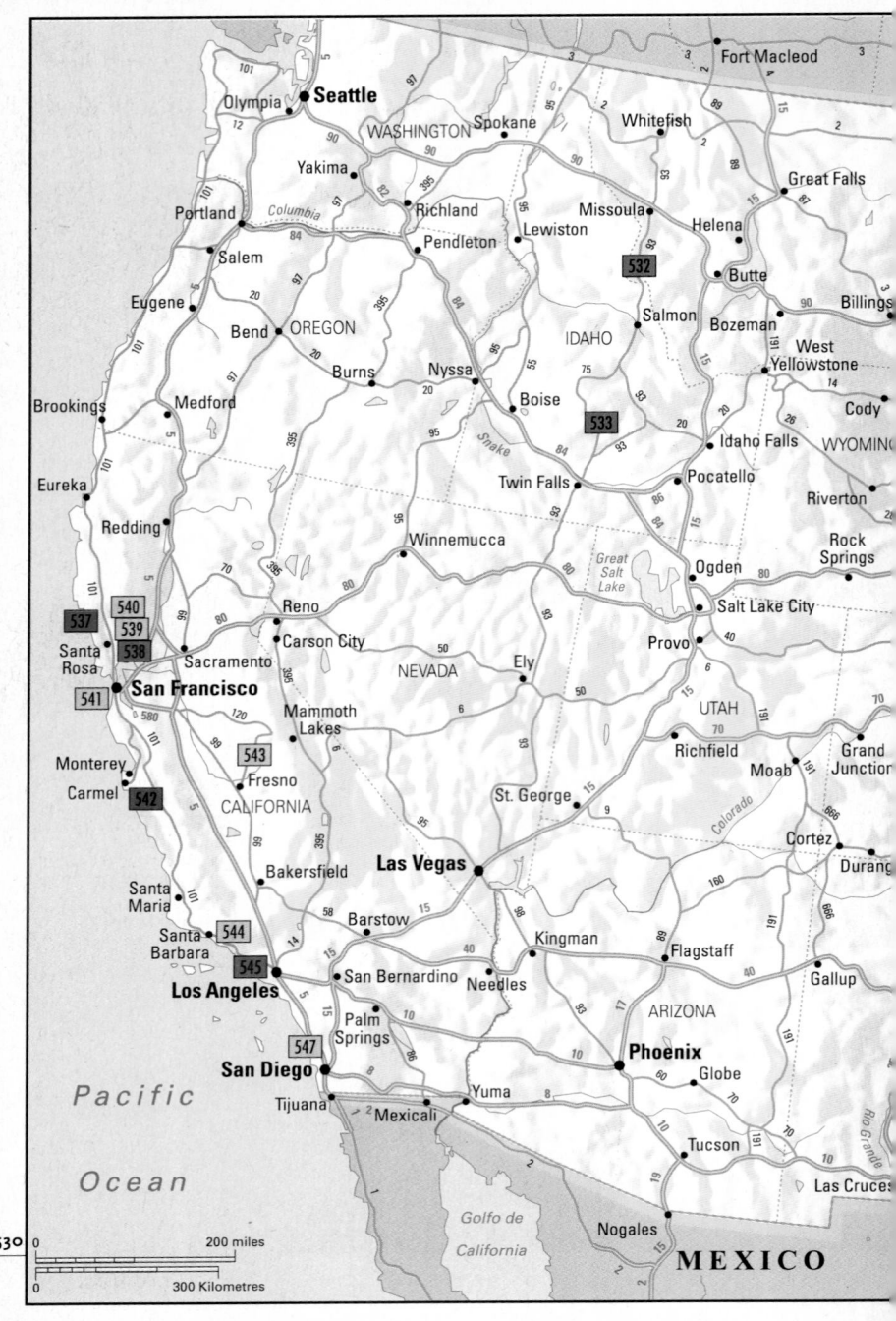

Seattle
Olympia
101
12
5
WASHINGTON
Spokane
Yakima
90
90
97
82
395
95
Whitefish
89
Fort Macleod
3
2
15
Great Falls
87
Billings
90
191
Portland
Columbia
84
Richland
97
Lewiston
Missoula
Helena
15
Butte
90
West
Yellowstone
14
Cody
WYOMING
Salem
Eugene
101
20
Bend
OREGON
Pendleton
Salmon
Bozeman
93
Brookings
5
Medford
97
20
Burns
20
Nyssa
Boise
533
20
Idaho Falls
Pocatello
86
15
84
Riverton
20
Snake
95
84
93
Rock
Springs
20
26
Eureka
101
Redding
70
395
Winnemucca
80
Great
Salt
Lake
80
Ogden
Salt Lake City
80
540
537
539
538
5
80
Reno
Carson City
50
Ely
50
NEVADA
Provo
40
6
15
UTAH
70
191
70
Grand
Junction
Santa
Rosa
541
San Francisco
580
120
Sacramento
395
Mammoth
Lakes
6
93
Richfield
70
Moab
191
866
Monterey
Carmel
542
101
99
543
Fresno
CALIFORNIA
66
395
St. George
95
15
9
Colorado
Cortez
Durango
160
191
666
Santa
Maria
101
58
Bakersfield
Barstow
Las Vegas
15
5
14
15
544
San Bernardino
Needles
40
Kingman
95
93
17
Flagstaff
191
40
Gallup
191
Santa
Barbara
545
Los Angeles
5
Palm
Springs
10
ARIZONA
San Diego
547
Tijuana
15
86
8
2
Mexicali
Yuma
8
10
Phoenix
60
Globe
70
10
191
Pacific
Ocean
Golfo de
California
Nogales
15
2
Tucson
Las Cruces
191
10
MEXICO

530
0   200 miles
0   300 Kilometres

North America

Western United States

Establishments	Nearest major city	Relais & Châteaux	Relais Gourmands	Page
Auberge du Soleil	San Francisco	✿		539
Château du Sureau	Fresno	✿		543
French Laundry (The)	San Francisco		♕	538
Home Ranch (The)	Steamboat Spring	✿		534
Knob Hill Inn	Ketchum	✿		533
Little Nell (The)	Aspen	✿		535
Meadowood Napa Valley	San Francisco	✿		540
Orangerie (L')	Los Angeles		♕	545
Rancho de San Juan	Espanola	✿		536
Rancho Valencia Resort	San Diego	✿		547
San Ysidro Ranch	Los Angeles	✿		544
Sherman House (The)	San Francisco	✿		541
Stonepine	Carmel	✿		542
Timberhill Ranch	San Francisco	✿		537
Triple Creek Ranch	Missoula	✿		532

TRIPLE CREEK RANCH

USA

Tel. : (1) (406) 821 4600
Fax : (1) (406) 821 4666
E-mail : triplecreek@relaischateaux.fr

5551 West Fork Stage Route
Darby
Montana 59829

75 miles south of Missoula via Highway 93; after Darby, right onto West Fork Rd (Highway 473) for 7 miles. Follow signs.

Owners :
Craig and Barbara Barrett
Directors :
Wayne and Judy Kilpatrick
Open all year

✈	Hamilton 45 km Missoula 115 km
GPS	GPS N 45° 52' 87" W 114° 12' 46"
⍩	Meals included
🛏	19 suites **510-995 USD** t.4,5%, s.15%
☕	included
🛏	no
⚑	Putting green on the premises 18 holes 45 km

The American dream lives on in this spectacular landscape in the heart of Montana. Enjoy fishing in the lakes and rivers, or skiing on the mountain slopes. Explore the magnificent valley, resplendent with pine trees and wild flowers, on foot or on horseback. Relax in the ranch's comfortable private lodges, which feature a full range of amenities, before savouring a delicious candlelit dinner accompanied by superb vintages.

MasterCard Visa

USD : US dollar

www.relaischateaux.fr/triplecreek

KNOB HILL INN

USA

960 North Main Street, P.O. Box 800
Ketchum
Idaho, 83340

Tel. : (1) (208) 726 8010
Fax : (1) (208) 726 2712
E-mail : knobhill@relaischateaux.fr

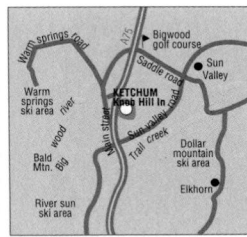

From *Hailey* Airport, the hotel is 12 miles North on *Highway 75*, 2 blocks after the *Warm Springs* traffic light on the right.

Owners : Mr and Mrs Koenig
Annual closing :
From April 15th to May 15th
(May 30th for restaurant)

✈ Hailey 19 km

🍴 Menus **18-25 USD**
t.6% s.15%
Carte **30-40 USD**
t.6% s.15%

 16 rooms
175-240 USD
t.9% s.15%

8 suites
275-375 USD
t.9% s.15%

☕ **7,50-10 USD**
t.9% s.15%

🍴 no

🚶 1 km

Sauna, jacuzzi, horseback riding (1,5 km), skiing, hiking, fishing.

S un Valley, America's finest ski resort and an idyllic haven for fishing, tennis, hiking and golf, provides the setting for Joe and Sandy Koenig's Knob Hill Inn. This magnificent chalet, perched at 1750 metres, offers warm Austrian hospitality and beautiful guestrooms which open onto balconies with stunning mountain views. After an invigorating day on the slopes, savour delicious European cuisine and fine wines.

533

www.relaischateaux.fr/knobhill

USD : US dollar

Visa

THE HOME RANCH

Tel. : (1) (970) 879 1780
Fax : (1) (970) 879 1795
E-mail : homeranch@relaischateaux.fr

P.O. Box 822
Clark
Colorado 80428

USA

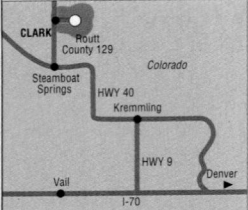

*Denver, I70 West, Hwy 9 North,
Hwy 40 West, Steamboat
Springs; Rte 129 towards Clark.*

Owners :
Kendrick and Cile Jones
Annual closing :
April and from October 15th
to Dec. 20th

 Denver (**Intl**) 350 km
Yampa Valley 70 km

 Full board

 6 rooms
500-600 USD
t.4% s.15%

 8 suites
570-660 USD
t.4% s.15%

 included

 no

 25 km

Downhill skiing at Steamboat,
cross country, snow-shoeing,
horseback riding, hiking, fishing,
sauna, jacuzzi.

Come visit Ken Jones' magnificent
ranch, where 150 horses graze in
the pastures in authentic western
ambiance. In the winter, relax in your
private jacuzzi after an exhilarating day's
skiing in the Rocky Mountains, or after a
summer horseback riding trip in one
million acres of national forest. Later,
watch the sunset from your log cabin
porch before dining on savory western-
style cuisine.

  Visa

USD : US dollar

www.relaischateaux.fr/homeranch

THE LITTLE NELL

USA

675 East Durant Avenue
Aspen
Colorado 81611

Tel. : (1) (970) 920 4600
USA toll free : (888) 843 6355
Fax : (1) (970) 920 4670
E-mail : littlenell@relaischateaux.fr

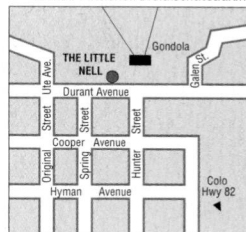

*From Denver, take the I-70
towards Glenwood Springs,
then Highway 82 towards Aspen.*

Owner :
Aspen Skiing Company
Director : Eric Calderon
Open all year

✈ Aspen **(Intl)** 6 km
Denver **(Intl)** 360 km

🍴 Carte **25-45 USD**
t.8,2%

🔑 **77 rooms**
325-450 USD (summer)
t.8,2%
500-700 USD (winter)
t.8,2%

🔑 **15 suites**
700-2 500 USD (summer)
t. 8,2%
900-4 000 USD (winter)
t.8,2%

🍷 **6-11 USD** t.8,2%

🛎 yes

🏌 10 km

Jacuzzi, spa, thalassotherapy...

Nestled in the heart of the Colorado Rockies, Aspen is one of America's finest ski resorts and in summer the town is a centre of music and cultural activities. The «Little Nell», ideally situated at the foot of Aspen mountain, is a haven of comfort and elegance. Its superb rooms, featuring contemporary architecture, open onto gardens, waterfalls and a private pool. Hospitality is generous and the food impeccable.

535

USD : US dollar

RANCHO DE SAN JUAN

USA

SINCE 1996

Tel. : (1) (505) 753 6818
USA toll free : (1) (800) 726 7121
Fax : (1) (505) 753 6818
E-mail : sanjuan@relaischateaux.fr

PO Box 4140
Espanola
New Mexico 87533

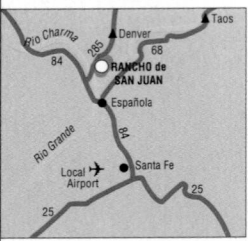

From Sante Fe, Hwy. 84/285 north; 7 miles after Espanola, right on Hwy. 285, Rancho 3.5 miles after the intersection.

Owners : David G. Heath and John H. Johnson III
Weekly closing :
Rest. : Sundays and Mondays
Open all year

✈	Albuquerque (**Intl**) 160 km Denver (**Intl**) 520 km
🍴	Menus **45-95 USD** t.6%
⚷	9 rooms **175-200 USD** t.6%
⚷	8 suites **225-325 USD** t.6%
🛥	included
🚭	no
♪	35 km

Discover sophisticated elegance in the majestic desert overlooking the Ojo Caliente River Valley. The Rancho's luxurious suites and guestrooms are decorated with antiques, art and fireplaces and offer private terraces for outdoor enjoyment. Its elegant restaurant serves award-winning cuisine, enhanced by fine custom porcelain and family silver for candlelight dining: a feast for the senses.

536

 Visa

USD : US dollar

www.relaischateaux.fr/sanjuan

TIMBERHILL RANCH

USA

35755 Hauser Bridge Road
Cazadero
California 95421

Tel. : (1) (707) 847 3258
Fax : (1) (707) 847 3342
E-mail : timberhill@relaischateaux.fr

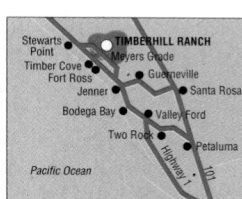

From the San Francisco Airport, towards Santa Rosa, River Rd., Meyers Grade Rd.

Owners :
Tarran Mc Daid, Franklin Watson, Michael Riordan
Open all year

✈ San Francisco (**Intl**) 144 km
Santa Rosa 75 km

GPS N 38° 36' 0"
W 123° 178'

🍴 Dinner included

🔑 15 suites
395-415 USD t.9%
food t.0,75% s.12%

☕ included

🚫 no

🏊 20 km

Biking, hiking, canoeing, kayaking...

Sheltered from the Pacific Coast by Salt Point State Park, this ranch is a haven of calm, infused with the fragrance of cedar. There are no phones or televisions in the 15 cottages, indeed nothing to disturb the utter tranquillity as you sit on a veranda contemplating the sunset. After swimming, tennis or a romantic stroll along the Sonoma coast, savour delicious seafood and local cuisine enhanced by regional wines.

USD : US dollar

THE FRENCH LAUNDRY

USA

Tel. : (1) (707) 944 2380
Fax : (1) (707) 944 1974
E-mail : laundry@relaischateaux.fr

6640 Washington Street
Yountville
California 94599

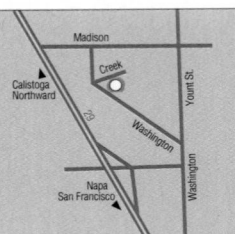

*From Napa take Highway 29
North. Exit at Yountville / Veterans
Home. Turn right at the Stop sign.
Go left on Washington st.
Stay left on Washington st.
and proceed a half mile north to
6640 Washington at Creek st.*

Owner : Thomas A. Keller
Director : Laura Cunningham
Annual closing :
From 1st to 18th January

✈ Oakland (**Intl**) 100 km
San Francisco (**Intl**) 120 km

🍴 Menus **65-85 USD**
t.7,25% s.n.i.

🛏 no

Visit of the Napa Valley.

 ❄

This elegant turn-of-the-century stone residence in the heart of California's famous Napa Valley, is set admist a charming country garden. This idyllic haven is the setting for Chef Thomas Keller's innovative, award-winning cuisine. His contemporary dishes feature a subtle blend of classic French traditions and regional fare. The prix-fixe menus are accompanied by over 350 selections of California and French varietals.

USD : US dollar

www.relaischateaux.fr/laundry

AUBERGE DU SOLEIL

USA

180 Rutherford Hill Road, P.O. Drawer B
Rutherford
California 94573

Tel. : (1) (707) 963 1211
Fax : (1) (707) 963 8764
E-mail : soleil@relaischateaux.fr

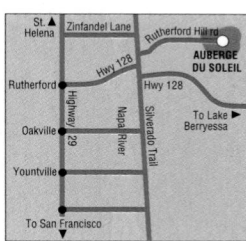

Napa, towards St. Helena
(Hwy 29) to Rutherford, take
Hwy 128 towards Silverado Trail.

Owners : Claude Rouas
and Robert Harmon
Directors : George A. Gœggel
and Philippa J. Perry
Open all year

Nestled amidst olive trees, on a hillside, above a mosaic of vineyards - this superb setting inspired Claude Rouas to open his magnificent restaurant here in 1981. The superb cuisine, which features the full splendor of the region's flavours and colours, is enhanced by 500 of California's finest wines. The romantic guestrooms, each with fireplace and private terrace, are housed in country cottages.

 San Francisco (**Intl**) 120 km
Santa Rosa 60 km

 Carte **45-65 USD**
t.7,25% s.15%

 31 rooms
375-575 USD s.i.

 19 suites
750-2 500 USD s.i.

 10-15 USD t.7,25% s.15%

 no

15 km

Fitness centre, jacuzzi, hammam, beauty salon, yoga, spa.

USD : US dollar

Visa

MEADOWOOD NAPA VALLEY

Tel. : (1) (707) 963 3646
Fax : (1) (707) 963 3532
E-mail : meadowood@relaischateaux.fr

900 Meadowood Lane
St. Helena
California 94574

USA

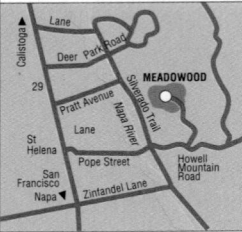

*From the Golden Gate Bridge,
take Hwy 101 towards Marin
County; Hwy 37,
Hwy 121, Hwy 29 North.*

Owners : William Harlan
and John Montgomery
Director : Seamus McManus
Open all year

✈	San Francisco (**Intl**) 110 km Napa 35 km
🍴	Carte **35-55 USD** t.7,75% s.15%
🔑	38 rooms **345-695 USD** t.10,5% s.i.
🔑	47 suites **560-3 000 USD** t.10,5% s.i.
🍷	**9-17,50 USD** t.7,75% s.15%
🚫	no
⛳	9 holes

Sauna, jacuzzi, spa, croquet,
hiking, bicycling.

S urrounded by pristine vineyards and hills roamed by Robert Louis Stevenson, this superb Meadowood Napa Valley estate nestles in a private 250-acre valley. Expect understated elegance with a tradition of intimacy, discreet service and refined comfort. Idyllic setting for golf, tennis, hiking, swimming or pampering at the full-service spa. Savour California wine country cuisine and discover Napa Valley wine with Meadowood's wine tutor.

     Visa

USD : US dollar

www.relaischateaux.fr/meadowood

THE SHERMAN HOUSE

USA

2160 Green Street
San Francisco
California 94123

Tel. : (1) (415) 563 3600
Fax : (1) (415) 563 1882
E-mail : sherman@relaischateaux.fr

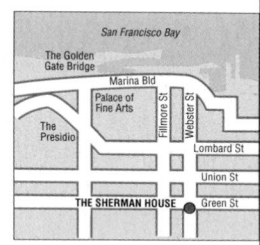

South of Golden Gate Bridge, from Lombard Street, turn right on Fillmore St., turn left on Green St.

Owners :
Manou and Vesta Mobedshahi
Director : Christine Berlin
Open all year

✈ San Francisco (**Intl**) 26 km

🍴 Menus **55-65 USD**
t.8,5% s.20%
Carte **41,50-47,50 USD**
t.8,5% s.20%

⚷ 8 rooms
350-500 USD t.14% s.i.

⚷ 6 suites
700-850 USD t.14% s.i.

☕ included

🍴 no

🏊 10 km

Water sports.

J ust minutes from Fisherman's Wharf, stands a magnificent Victorian residence, built in 1876, where Leander Sherman once played host to the greatest names in music, art and literature. Sherman House is still imbued with the splendour of bygone days, and guests will be enchanted by the exquisite gardens and magnificent rooms, many with superb views of San Francisco Bay. The eclectic menus are wonderfully imaginative.

www.relaischateaux.fr/sherman

USD : US dollar

STONEPINE

Tel. : (1) (831) 659 2245
Fax : (1) (831) 659 5160
E-mail : stonepine@relaischateaux.fr

150 E. Carmel Valley Road
Carmel Valley
California 93924

USA

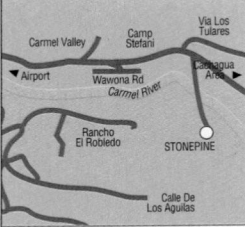

From San Francisco :
Highway 101 south to Carmel.
Turn left on Carmel Valley road.
From Los Angeles :
Highway 101 north, exit Salinas,
route 68 west until Laureles
Grade, left on to Carmel Valley
road.

Owners :
Gordon and Noel Hentschel
Director : Gordon Hentschel
Open all year

✈	San Francisco (**Intl**) 160 km
	Monterey 20 km
🍴	Menu **65 USD**
	t.7,25% s.18%
⊶	8 rooms
	275-500 USD
	t.10,5% s.10%
⊶	6 suites
	375-1 200 USD
	t.10,5% s.10%
☕	included
🛏	no
🚶	7 km

T his fabulous estate is nestled amidst 330 pristine acres in the heart of picturesque Carmel Valley. Only 30 minutes from Carmel pebble beach and Monterey's fisherman's wharf, it offers the very best in country living. Take advantage of the equestrian and numerous other activities and guest services or just relax in the beautiful chateau gardens. The restaurant is excellent and the cellar international.

 Visa

USD : US dollar

www.relaischateaux.fr/stonepine

CHÂTEAU DU SUREAU

USA

48688 Victoria Lane, PO Box 577
Oakhurst, Yosemite National Park
California 93644

Tel. : (1) (559) 683 6860
Fax : (1) (559) 683 0800
E-mail : sureau@relaischateaux.fr

Near Yosemite National Park.

Owners : Erna Kubin-Clanin,
Dr. René Clanin
Annual closing :
January 3rd to 23rd

 San Francisco (**Intl**) 320 km
Fresno 68 km

 Carte **53-85 USD**
t.7,75% s.18%

 10 rooms
325-525 USD t.9% s.12%

 1 villa
2 500 USD t.9% s.12%

 included

no

5 km

Gymnasium, water sports,
rock climbing, fishing,
sporting clay shooting
and cross-country skiing.

T his beautiful Provençal château lies in the heart of the Sierra Nevada forest. Its ten elegant guestrooms and the 2 bedroom Parisian Villa, decorated with sumptuous antique furniture, open onto balconies which offer stunning views of the Californian countryside. After a glass of champagne in the gardens, proprietress and renowned cordon bleu Erna Kubin-Clanin will delight you with superb regional cuisine and an award-winning wine list.

     543

Visa

SAN YSIDRO RANCH

SINCE 1988

Tel. : (1) (805) 969 5046
Fax : (1) (805) 565 1995
E-mail : sanysidro@relaischateaux.fr

900 San Ysidro Lane
Montecito, Santa Barbara
California 93108

USA

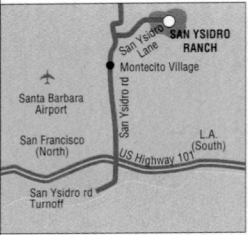

On Highway 101, along the coast, San Ysidro Ranch exit.

Owners :
Claude Rouas and
Robert Harmon
Director : Janis Clapoff
Open all year

✈ Los Angeles (**Intl**) 150 km
Santa Barbara 20 km

🍴 Menus **30-50 USD**
t.8% s.i.

⚷ 13 rooms
399-425 USD
t.10% s.i.

⚷ 25 suites
499-3 000 USD
t.10% s.i.

☕ **10 USD**
t.8% s.i.

🐕 yes (extra cost)

🏃 30 km

Polo, sailing, surfing,
fitness centre.

Vivien Leigh and Laurence Olivier were married at San Ysidro and the Kennedys spent their honeymoon here. You too will be enchanted by this beautiful ranch built in 1893. Nestled beneath orange trees, its bungalows look out over the Santa Ynez hills and the scent of eucalyptus and jasmin will make you forget that Los Angeles is less than an hour away. Enjoy traditional cuisine, an ocean view pool and exercise room.

544

USD : US dollar

www.relaischateaux.fr/sanysidro

NORTH AMERICA

NORTH-EASTERN UNITED STATES

Establishments	Nearest major city	Relais & Châteaux	Relais Gourmands	Page
Auréole	New York		🍳	565
Bernardin (Le)	New York		🍳	569
Blantyre	Boston	⚜		555
Canoe Bay	Minneapolis	⚜		575
Castle at Tarrytown (The)	New York	⚜		563
Charlotte Inn (The)	Boston	⚜		557
Charlie Trotter's Restaurant	Chicago		🍳	573
Daniel	New York		🍳	566
Fearrington House (The)	Chapel Hill	⚜		571
Glendorn	New York	⚜		570
Jean Georges	New York		🍳	567
Inn at Little Washington (The)	Washington	⚜	🍳	572
Inn at National Hall (The)	New York	⚜		562
Inn at Sawmill Farm (The)	Wilmington, VT	⚜		553
Lake Placid Lodge	Albany	⚜		551
Mayflower Inn (The)	New York	⚜		560
Nomades (Les)	Chicago		🍳	574
Old Drovers Inn	New York	⚜		561
Pitcher Inn (The)	Burlington	⚜		554
Point (The)	Burlington	⚜		552
Ryland Inn (The)	New York		🍳	556
Wauwinet (The)	Nantucket Town	⚜		559
White Barn Inn	Boston	⚜		550

WHITE BARN INN

Tel. : (1) (207) 967 2321
Fax : (1) (207) 967 1100
E-mail : whitebarn@relaischateaux.fr

P.O. Box 560 C
Kennebunkport
Maine 04046

US

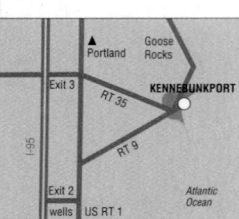

From Boston, 1 95 North to the Maine Turnpike; exit 3, Rte 35, 7 miles to Kennebunkport.

Owner : Laurence Bongiorno
Director : William Mozingo
Annual closing :
Rest. : from January 9th to 24th

✈ Portland (**Intl**) 30 km
   Boston (**Intl**) 100 km

🍴 Menu 67 USD t.7% s.i.
   Carte 67 USD t.7% s.i.

🔑 16 rooms
   160-330 USD t.7% s.i.

🔑 9 suites
   365-450 USD t.7% s.i.

☕ included

🚫 no

🎿 1 km

Mountain and touring bicycles, canoes, boating, beach, water sports, fishing, tennis, cross country skiing.

Since the 1800's, travellers have made their way to the White Barn Inn. Today, not only is the welcome just as warm, but the famous old inn has been transformed into a luxury hotel. Each of the elegant suites and guestrooms are individually decorated, many with fireplaces and jacuzzi. As for the restaurant, its New England cuisine, accompanied by the finest American and European vintages, enjoys a national reputation.

 Visa

USD : US dollar

www.relaischateaux.fr/whitebarn

LAKE PLACID LODGE

USA

PO Box 550
Lake Placid, New York
New York 12946

Tel. : (1) (518) 523 2700
Fax : (1) (518) 523 1124
E-mail : lakeplacid@relaischateaux.fr

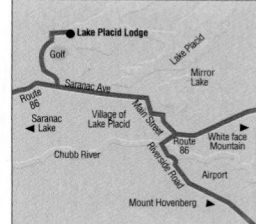

From N.Y. City - I 87 N, exit 30 route 73 NW. At Lake Placid take route 86 west, then Whiteface Inn Road and follow signs to Lake Placid Lodge.

Owners :
David and Christie Garrett
Director : Kathryn Kincannon
Open all year

This magnificent Lodge, nestled on the secluded wood-lined shore of Lake Placid, affords breathtaking views of the age-old Adirondack Mountains. A romantic and rustically elegant retreat, the Lodge offers warm and comfortable decor, stone fireplaces, deep soaking tubs and endless outdoor recreation. The highly acclaimed restaurant serves innovative New American cuisine composed with classical French techniques.

Albany **(Intl)** 200 km
Saranac Lake 30 km

Menus
7,5-32 USD t.7%

12 rooms
300-450 USD t.7% s.15%

22 suites
450-700 USD t.7% s.15%

included

yes (extra cost)

Direct access

551

USD : US dollar

Visa

Tel. : (1) (518) 891 5674
Fax : (1) (518) 891 1152
E-mail : point@relaischateaux.fr

HCR1, Box 65
Saranac Lake
New York 12983

USA

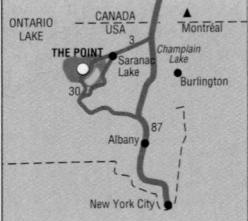

From the airport, take roads 186 and 30, Lake Clear, Saranac Inn Golf Club, 16 km to the left.

Owners :
David and Christie Garrett
Director : Tim Thuell
Annual closing :
From March 15th to April 15th

✈ Montreal (**Intl**) 240 km
Saranac Lake 17 km

🍴 Full board

🔑 11 rooms
950-1 700 USD
t.7% s.15%

☕ included

🛏 yes

🏃 4 km

Fishing, water-skiing, downhill skiing, walks, mountain hiking, canoeing, biking, horseback riding, cross-country skiing, picnics, antiqueing.

Nestled in the Adirondack mountains on a pristine lake, this former Rockefeller estate offers the ultimate civilized wilderness experience. Log architecture, stone fireplaces, sumptuous beds and antique furniture recreate the historic Great Camp Era. A refined and relaxed houseparty atmosphere, superb cuisine and the feeling of total escape have earned this idyllic retreat the rating of «Number One Resort Hotel».

MasterCard Visa

USD : US dollar

www.relaischateaux.fr/point

THE INN AT SAWMILL FARM

USA

Route 100 - Crosstown Road - P.O. Box 367
West Dover
Vermont 05356

Tel. : (1) (802) 464 8131
USA Toll free : (800) 493 1133
Fax : (1) (802) 464 1130
E-mail : sawmill@relaischateaux.fr

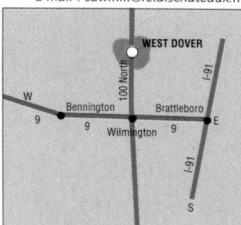

From Boston, Mass. Pike to I91; exit 2, right to VT 9 West to Wilmington. Right at light to 100 North to West Dover.

Owners :
Rodney and Ione Williams
Director : Rodney Williams Jr.
Annual closing :
From March 28th to May 27th

This charming Inn in Southern Vermont is imbued with «Old New England» style. The elegant guestrooms and their canopy beds are swathed in beautiful floral fabrics, as are the armchairs by the magnificent red brick hearth in the living room. After golf, hiking, skiing, biking, fishing, swimming, tennis, or antique-hunting, enjoy inspired cuisine and savour one of the cellar's 34,000 vintages.

✈	Albany (**Intl**) 121 km Bradley (**Intl**) 180 km
🍴	Full board (2 persons)
⚷	10 rooms **330-395 USD** t.s.15%
⚷	10 suites **420-470 USD** t.s.15%
☕	included
🚫	no
🏃	1 km

Downhill skiing, cross-country, fishing, mountain biking...

USD : US dollar

THE PITCHER INN

SINCE 1999

Tel. : (1) (802) 496 6350
USA Toll free : (1) (888) 867 4824
Fax : (1) (802) 496 6354
E-mail : pitcher@relaischateaux.fr

Main Street - PO Box 347
Warren
Vermont 05674

USA

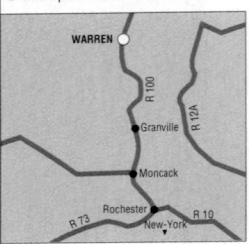

*From New York: take I 95N,
then I 91N , then I 89N, exit 9.
Take R 2E, then R 100B, continue
on R 100S. Exit Warren Village.
The Pitcher Inn is on the left.*

Owners :
Winthrop and Margaret Smith
Directors :
Heather and John Carino
Weekly closing :
Rest. : Tuesday
Open all year

✈	Burlington **(Intl)** 75 km
🍴	Menus **8-24 USD** t.9% s.n.i. Carte **45-55 USD** t.9% s.n.i.
🔑	9 rooms **300-500 USD** t.9% s.n.i.
🔑	2 suites **600 USD** t.9% s.n.i.
☕	included
🚫	no
⛳	5 km (18 holes)

Polo, hunting, fishing, climbing,
crosscountry skiing, hiking,
kayaking canoeing.

Located in a picturesque New England village, the Pitcher Inn provides its guests with the very best of Vermont tradition. In each room, there is a certain harmony between the antiques and the hidden «treasures» of today. The restaurant proposes contemporary American cooking, spiced with regional influences and one of the region's best-stocked wine cellars.

554

USD : US dollar

www.relaischateaux.fr/pitcher

BLANTYRE

USA

Blantyre Road, P.O. Box 995
Lenox
Massachusetts 01240

Tel. : (1) (413) 637 3556
Fax : (1) (413) 637 4282
E-mail : blantyre@relaischateaux.fr

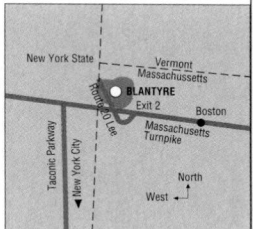

From Boston, Massachusetts Turnpike West, exit 2; Rte 20 Lee West.

Owner : Ann Fitzpatrick
Director : Roderick Anderson
Weekly closing :
Restaurant : Monday
Annual closing :
From November 7th to May 5th

✈	Hartford (**Intl**) 100 km Boston (**Intl**) 200 km
	GPS N 44° 46' W 69° 22'
🍴	Menu **75 USD** t.5% s.18%
🔑	19 rooms **275-500 USD** t.9,7% s.10%
🔑	4 suites **345-700 USD** t.9,7% s.10%
☕	included
🍴	no
🧍	1 km

B uilt in 1902 in the Berkshire hills, just 200 kilometres from Boston, this elegant Tudor-style residence is set amidst 85 acres of lawns and woodland. Its aristocratic interior, resplendent with four-poster beds, magnificent fireplaces and luxurious bathrooms, is decorated with impeccable taste. The country house cuisine, served in the oak-panelled dining room, is delicious, and the cellar's 450 vintages outstanding.

P ❄ ♿ ✈ 🏨 🏊 🎾 **555**

USD : US dollar

THE RYLAND INN

Tel. : (1) (908) 534 4011
Fax : (1) (908) 534 6592
E-mail : ryland@relaischateaux.fr

Route 22 West - Box 284
Whitehouse
New Jersey 08888

USA

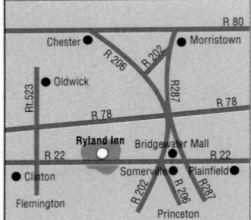

From Princeton, R 206 north until/ R 22, follow this road for 10 km. At sign «Whitehouse», turn right exiting off R 22 and continuing for 180 m.

Owners : Craig Shelton, Steven Pozycki, Paul L. Ferber
Director : Craig Shelton
Weekly closing :
Restaurant : Monday
Annual closing :
Rest. : one week in January

Newark (**Intl**) 35 km

GPS N 40° 36'33" O 74° 44'30"

Menus **75-85 USD**
t.6% s.15%
Carte **65-75 USD**
t.6% s.15%

no

2 km

Polo, hunting, fishing, climbing, skiing, sailing, kayaking, horse-riding.

1 5 minutes from the World Trade Center by helicopter, enter a totally different universe at The Ryland Inn. Located in the very heart of the New Jersey hunting region, this famous restaurant is surrounded by 50 acres of hills and magnificent landscape. Its organic garden produces vegetables and herbs which provide the inspiration behind the French-American cuisine of the owner-chef, Craig Shelton. A refined cuisine, full of elegance, giving pride of place to local American products.

USD : US dollar

www.relaischateaux.fr/ryland

CHARLOTTE INN

USA

South Summer St.
Edgartown
Massachusetts 02539

Tel. : (1) (508) 627 4151
Fax : (1) (508) 627 4652
E-mail : charlotte@relaischateaux.fr

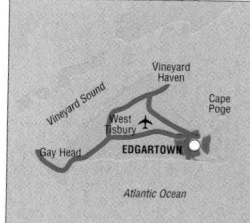

From Boston,
Rte 3 to Woods Hole (Mass.),
ferry to Vineyard Haven.

Owners :
Gerret and Paula Conover
Director : Carol Read
Weekly closing :
Rest. : Monday and Tuesday
(low season)
Annual closing :
Rest. : from January 2nd to
February 13th

I n the heart of a village on Martha's Vineyard island, this beautiful 19th-century inn, surrounded by manicured gardens, is decorated in the best English style. The elegant rooms, each individually decorated, could be in a museum but the ambience is decidedly comfortable. In the restaurant, the crystal, porcelain and silver glisten in soft candlelight. Savour light, refined French cuisine accompanied by the finest wines.

✈	Boston (**Intl**) 120 km Martha's Vineyard 5 km
🍴	Menu starting at **62 USD** t.5% s.i.
🔑	23 rooms **295-495 USD** t.5% s.i.
🔑	2 suites **495-850 USD** t.5% s.i.
☕	15,95 USD t.5% s.i.
🐾	no
🏃	3 km

557

USD : US dollar

SINCE 1993

OLD DROVERS INN

USA

Old Route 22
Dover Plains
New York 12522

Tel. : (1) (914) 832 9311
Fax : (1) (914) 832 6356
E-mail : droversinn@relaischateaux.fr

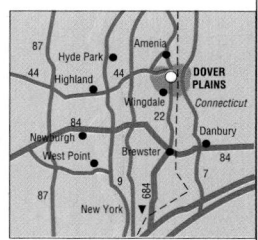

From New York, take the Saw Mill River Parkway towards I 684 Brewster, Route 22 North.

Owner : Kemper Peacock
Weekly closing :
Tuesday and Wednesday
Annual closing :
From January 3rd to 20th

| ✈ | N.Y. J.F.K. (**Intl**) 140 km |
| | N.Y. La Guardia 130 km |

🍴	Menus **14-38 USD**
	t.7,25%
	Carte **25-60 USD**
	t.7,25%

🔑	4 rooms
	150-395 USD
	t.10,25% s.15%

| ☕ | included |

| 🐕 | yes (extra cost) |

| ⛳ | 10 km |

Fishing, skiing, biking, hiking,
antique dealers, HydePark
Museums...

This authentic Colonial house is steeped in American history. Indeed, it is one of the oldest inns in the United States, serving as a stopover from 1750 for cowboys herding their cattle to the city markets. You don't have to reserve the entire Inn, as Elizabeth Taylor and Richard Burton once did, to indulge in its charm and hospitality, and savour superb regional cuisine accompanied by the finest French and American vintages.

561

USD : US dollar

THE INN AT NATIONAL HALL

SINCE 1996

Tel. : (1) (203) 221 1351
Fax : (1) (203) 221 0276
E-mail : nationalhall@relaischateaux.fr

2, Post Road West
Westport
Connecticut 06880

USA

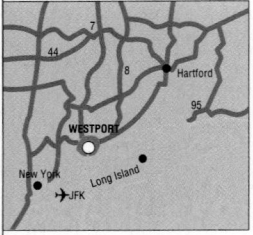

From airports : I-95 north to exit 17, Westport, turn left on to Rte. 33, go 1.5 miles. Directions: cross traffic light at U.S. 1 and turn immediately right.

Owners : Eugene Gorab and James E. Cooper, Jr.
Director : Jane C. Ferruccio
Open all year

✈ N.Y. J.F.K. (Intl) 90 km
N.Y. La Guardia 75 km

🍴 Menu **60 USD**
t.6% s.15%
Carte **16-28 USD**
t.6% s.15%

🔑 8 rooms
225-450 USD t.12% s.i.

🔑 7 suites
400-700 USD t.12% s.i.

☕ Continental breakfast included

🚫 no

🏊 12 km

Sauna, fitness centre, squash, theatre and outdoor concert, museums, antiques.

This historic Inn, an 1873 Italianate restored landmark, is fashioned after Europe's elite manor houses. It offers the luxury and service of a grand hotel. The 15 individually-decorated rooms and suites are a visually stunning collaboration of architecture and interior design. The Inn's award-winning restaurant serves innovative Mediterranean cuisine with fine wines. It is a must for East Coast visitors.

USD : US dollar

www.relaischateaux.fr/nationalhall

JEAN GEORGES

USA

One Central Park West
New York
New York 10023

Tel. : (1) (212) 299 3900
Fax : (1) (212) 299 3914
E-mail : jeangeorges@relaischateaux.fr

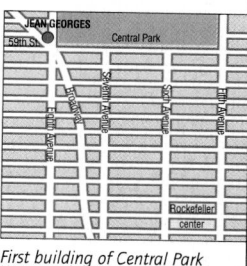

First building of Central Park West, at the corner of Columbus Circle (ground floor of the Trump International Hotel).

Owner :
Jean-Georges Vongerichten
Director : Alain Michel
Weekly closing :
Saturday for lunch and Sunday
Nougatine : open everyday
Open all year

N.Y. JFK (**Intl**) 25 km
N.Y. La Guardia 20 km

Menus
lunch **35-45-60 USD**
t.8,25% s.18-20%
dinner **85 USD**
t.8,25% s.18-20%
Tasting **115 USD**
t.8,25% s.18-20%

no

Discover the «enfant terrible of the French nouvelle cuisine» in Trump International Hotel on Central Park West. In a spare and contemporary setting, chef Jean-Georges Vongerichten offers the superb creations of his inventive gastronomy, reflecting subtle combinations of wild plants and oriental flavours. Savour the «thon blanc et rouge mariné à l'huile d'olive et citron». Superb wine list.

ECRITURE

GIVENCHY

JACQUES BENEDICT S.A.
39, BOULEVARD DE LA RÉPUBLIQUE
92210 SAINT CLOUD - FRANCE
TEL : + 33 (O) 1 46 02 02 03 - FAX : + 33 (O) 1 46 02 34 14
E-MAIL : infos@watches-givenchy.com

LE BERNARDIN

USA

155 West 51st Street
New York
New York 10019

Tel. : (1) (212) 489 15 15
Fax : (1) (212) 265 16 15
E-mail : bernardin@relaischateaux.fr

Between Rockefeller Center and Broadway. Two streets away from the Museum of Modern Art (MOMA).

Owners :
Maguy Le Coze and Eric Ripert
Weekly closing :
Saturday for lunch and Sunday
Annual closing : Holidays

N.Y. JFK **(Intl)** 40 km
N.Y. La Guardia 24 km

Menus :
Lunch **32-42 USD**
t.8,25% s.n.i.
Dinner **70 USD**
t.8,25% s.n.i.
Tasting **90-120 USD**
t.8,25% s.n.i.

no

C hef Eric Ripert and Maguy Le Coze preside over Le Bernardin, innovation and luxury in dining located in Midtown Manhattan. Ripert's interpretations of seafood such as Striped Bass Baked with Shaved Celery Root Perigord Truffles and Salsify have been lauded by critics and diners alike, while the exceptional wine list and beautiful dining room provide the perfect setting for an unforgettable experience.

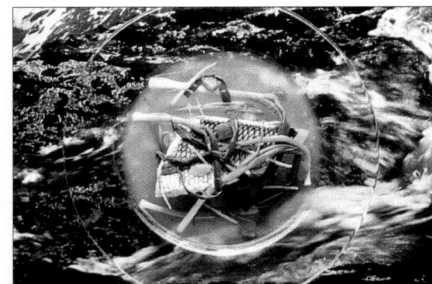

www.relaischateaux.fr/bernardin

USD : US dollar

Visa

❧ GLENDORN - "A LODGE IN THE COUNTRY" ⟨SINCE 1999⟩

Tel. : (1) 814 362 6511
USA toll free : (1) (800) 843 8568
Fax : (1) 814 368 9923
E-mail : glendorn@relaischateaux.fr

1032 West Corydon Street
Bradford
Pennsylvania 16701

USA

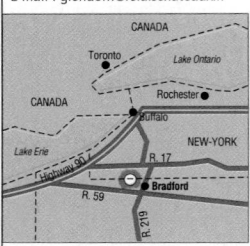

From Buffalo, take I-90 towards Erie. After Seneca West exit, take 219 South to Salamanca, then follow 219 to Bradford.

Owners : Dorn Family
Directors :
Eugene and Linda Spinner
Annual closing :
From January 3rd to February 8th

✈	Buffalo (**Intl**) 135 km Bradford 35 km
🍴	Full board
⚷	2 rooms **375-475 USD** t.6% s.15%
⚷	8 suites **495-675 USD** t.6% s.15%
🍷	included
🐎	yes
⛳	18 km (18 holes)

Walking, mountain-biking, fitness centre, skeet shooting.

Tucked away in the Pennsylvania mountains, this 518 hectare private estate provides a «country» setting for thirty guests. Fishing, clay pigeon shooting, trekking, tennis and swimming will take up your days, while the fireplace and candle-lit atmosphere will add that romantic touch to the cocktail parties and evening meals. The antique furniture, the wood panelling and the quality linen enhance the beauty of the rooms, suites and rustic cabins, veritable havens of tranquillity, cut off from the outside world.

 Visa

USD : US dollar

www.relaischateaux.fr/glendorn

THE FEARRINGTON HOUSE

USA

2000 Fearrington Village
Pittsboro
North Carolina 27312

Tel. : (1) (919) 542 2121
Fax : (1) (919) 542 4202
E-mail : fearrington@relaischateaux.fr

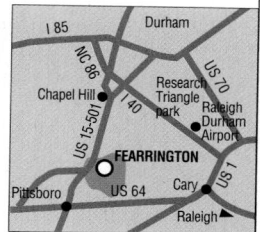

Take I 40 until Chapel Hill, then 15-501 south towards Pittsboro. The hotel is 13 km to the south of Chapel Hill.

Owner : RB Fitch
Director : Richard Delany
Weekly closing : Monday
Open all year

 Raleigh-Durham (**Intl**) 30 km

 Menu **65 USD** t.6% s.n.i.

 16 rooms
175-250 USD t.9% s.i.

 15 suites
250-350 USD t.9% s.i.

 included

 no

10 km

Biking, hiking, sailing, fishing.

Traditional Southern hospitality awaits you at this elegant country inn set amidst floral gardens in the heart of a picturesque village. Relax in the beautiful suites and guestrooms, each individually decorated with antique furniture, original artwork and bouquets of fresh flowers. Experience the charm of regional cuisine by soft candlelight and enjoy poetry readings, wine tastings and garden visits throughout the year.

www.relaischateaux.fr/fearrington

USD : US dollar

THE INN AT LITTLE WASHINGTON

SINCE 1987

Tel. : (1) (540) 675 3800
Fax : (1) (540) 675 3100
E-mail : washington@relaischateaux.fr

Middle and Main Street, PO Box 300
Washington
Virginia 22747

USA

Washington D.C., 66 West, exit 43 A, (Gainesville), Warrenton, Rte. 211 West.

Owners : Patrick O'Connell and Reinhardt Lynch
Open all year

	Washington DC (**Intl**) 70 km
	Menus **98-128 USD** t.7% s.18%
	9 rooms **340-795 USD** t.7%
	5 suites **550-940 USD** t.7%
	18 USD
	no
	30 km

Biking trips, fishing, horseback riding...

T his magnificent inn, one of America's most renowned country retreats, lies in a romantic village in the foothills of the Blue Ridge Mountains. For two decades, Patrick O'Connell and Reinhardt Lynch have welcomed guests with exquisite hospitality. Savour fine wines and gourmet delicacies such as «Medaillons of veal sauté with local morels, Sauternes and Virginia country ham» in idyllic natural surroundings.

Visa

USD : US dollar

www.relaischateaux.fr/washington

CHARLIE TROTTER'S

USA

816 W. Armitage Avenue
Chicago
Illinois 60614

Tel. : (1) (773) 248 6228
Fax : (1) (773) 248 6088
E-mail : charlie@relaischateaux.fr

In Lincoln Park,
1/2 block west of Halsted St.,
on the northern side of the street.

Owner : Charles Trotter
Weekly closing :
Sundays and Mondays
Annual closing :
2 weeks in March

 O'Hare (**Intl**) 20 km
Midway Airport 17 km

 Carte **100 USD**
t.9,75% s.20%

 no

harlie Trotter, one of the brightest stars of American gastronomy, is renowned for his innovative cuisine, which embraces organically raised seasonal products. Experience Trotter's brilliant flavor combinations, such as Marinated Hamachi with Osetra Caviar, Clementine & Pulped Avocado and Roasted Grouse Breast with Root Vegetables and Legume Sauces. The award-winning cellar, stocked with over 1,100 vintages, is superb.

Visits to the kitchen, private salon, great museums: Art Institute, Field Museum of Natural History.

573

LES NOMADES

Tel. : (1) (312) 649 9010
Fax : (1) (312) 649 0608
E-mail : nomades@relaischateaux.fr

222 East Ontario Street
Chicago
Illinois 60611

USA

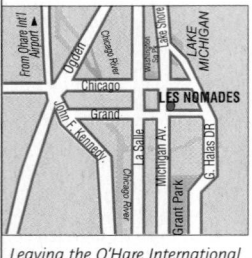

Leaving the O'Hare International airport, take the Kennedy I 90 expressway towards Chicago. Leave the expressway at Ohio Street East in the direction of Fairbanks, turn left, go straight on for one block, turn left, follow signs to Ontario. Go straight on for half a block.

Owner : Roland Liccioni
Director : Mary-Beth Liccioni
Weekly closing :
Sunday and Monday
Open all year

✈ O'Hare (**Intl**) 50 km

🍴 Menu **60 USD**
t.9,75% s.20%
Tasting menu **75 USD**
t.9,75% s.20%

🐾 no

I n a typical turn-of-the-century «brown-stone» of central Chicago, Les Nomades offers you gastronomic cuisine signed Roland Liccioni. Savour : «ris de veau braisé sauce portabella», «loup de mer à l'estragon», foie gras, Chef's own smoked salmon or «consommé de champignons aux asperges», «capuccino». Not to mention the «salade du Français, tendres verdures et haricots verts avec une vinaigrette au Pernod».

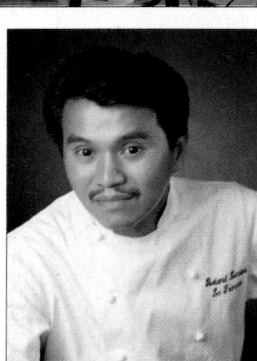

574

CANOE BAY

USA

P.O. Box 28
Chetek
Wisconsin 54728

Tel. : (1) (715) 924 4594
Fax : (1) (715) 924 2078
E-mail : canoebay@relaischateaux.fr

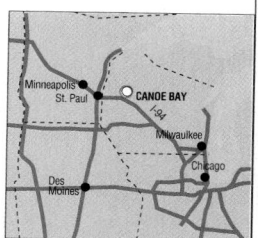

From Minneapolis, follow I-94 E to 53 N, exit Chetek.

Owners :
Dan and Lisa Dobrowolski
Open all year

✈ Minneapolis (**Intl**) 192 km
Eau Claire 72 km

🍽 Menus **55-67,5 USD**
t.5,5% s.n.i.

🔑 9 rooms
285-300 USD
t.5,5% s.n.i.

🔑 10 suites
325-650 USD
t.5,5% s.n.i.

🏆 included

no

🏹 19 km

Jacuzzi, canoeing, hiking, skiing, snow-shoeing, spa services, fishing, mountain biking...

This romantic Wisconsin retreat is set amidst beautiful natural surroundings. Guests will find not one but several magnificent residences, resplendent with incredible views, stone fireplaces and sumptuous fabrics. Enjoy the luxury of the guestrooms, sip aperitifs on your private balcony then savour delicious cuisine. Strolling through the forest, canoeing on two private lakes, discover the taste of paradise.

575

USD : US dollar

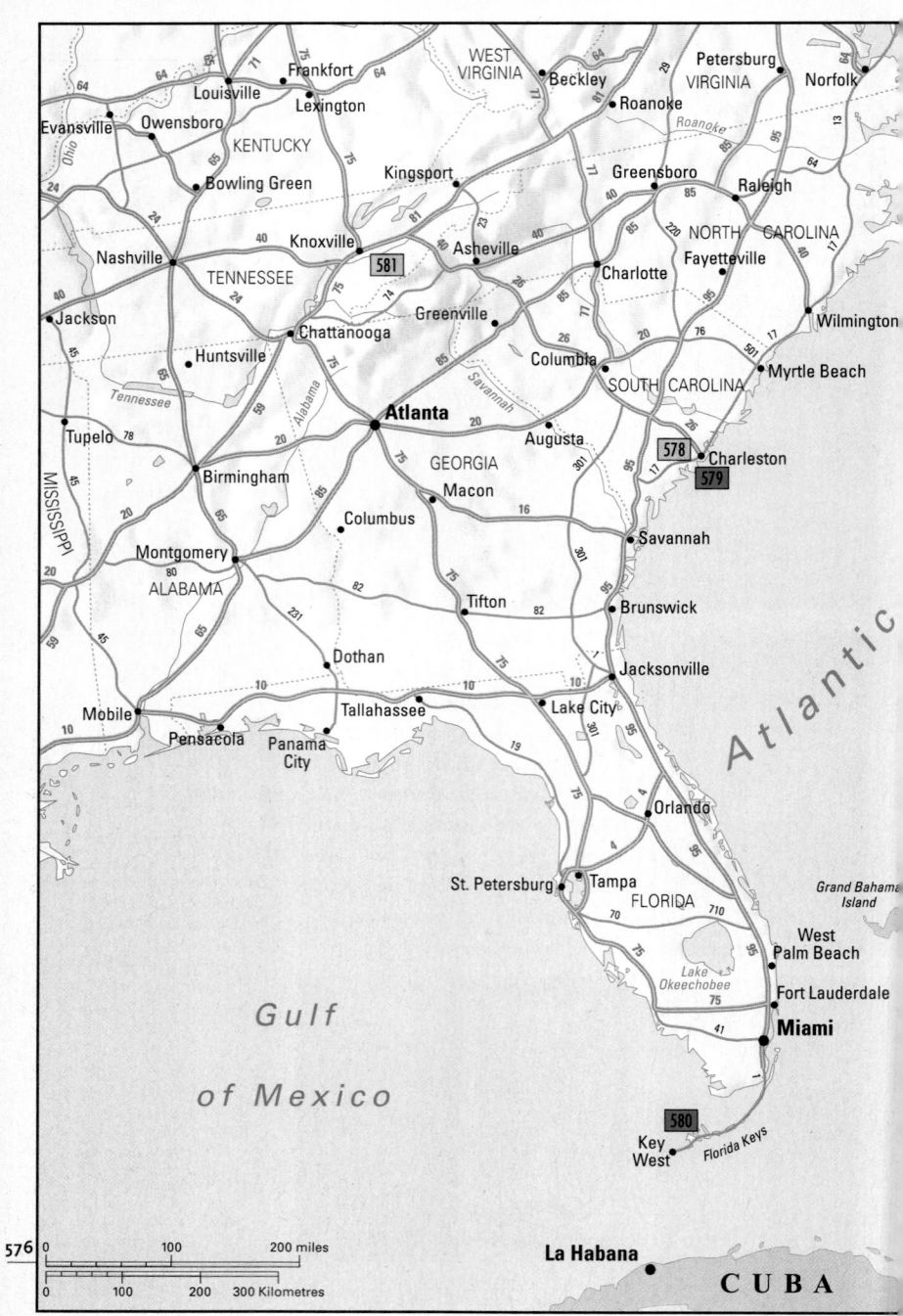

WEST VIRGINIA
VIRGINIA
KENTUCKY
TENNESSEE
NORTH CAROLINA
SOUTH CAROLINA
GEORGIA
ALABAMA
MISSISSIPPI
FLORIDA

Frankfort
Louisville
Lexington
Evansville
Owensboro
Bowling Green
Nashville
Jackson
Huntsville
Tupelo
Birmingham
Montgomery
Columbus
Dothan
Mobile
Pensacola
Panama City
Tallahassee

Beckley
Roanoke
Kingsport
Knoxville
Asheville
Chattanooga
Greenville
Atlanta
Augusta
Macon
Tifton
Lake City
Jacksonville

Petersburg
Norfolk
Greensboro
Raleigh
Fayetteville
Charlotte
Columbia
Wilmington
Myrtle Beach
Charleston
Savannah
Brunswick

St. Petersburg
Tampa
Orlando
West Palm Beach
Fort Lauderdale
Miami
Key West

Chattanooga

Ohio
Tennessee
Alabama
Savannah
Roanoke

581
578
579
580

Atlantic

Gulf

of Mexico

Lake Okeechobee

Grand Bahama Island

Florida Keys

La Habana

CUBA

576 0   100   200 miles
    0   100   200   300 Kilometres

NORTH AMERICA

Map labels:
Hatteras Island

Ocean

Great Abaco Island

BAHAMAS
Nassau

Andros Island

SOUTH-EASTERN UNITED STATES

Establishments	Nearest major city	Relais & Châteaux	Relais Gourmands	Page
Blackberry Farm	Maryville	⚜		581
Little Palm Island	Little Torch Key	⚜		580
Planters Inn	Charleston	⚜		579
Woodlands Resort Inn	Charleston	⚜		578

WOODLANDS RESORT & INN

SINCE 1997

Tel. : (1) (843) 875 2600
Fax : (1) (843) 875 2603
E-mail : woodlands@relaischateaux.fr

125 Parsons Road
Summerville
South Carolina 29483

USA

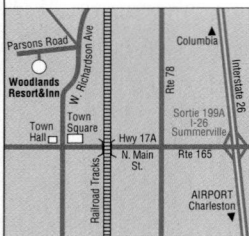

From Interstate I-26, exit 199A, 1.8 miles to West Richardson. On West Richardson, turn right, after 1.25 mile, left into Parsons Road.

Owner : Joe Whitmore
Director : Marty Wall
Open all year

✈ Charleston 35 km

🍴 Menus **89-120 USD**
t.5% s.17%
Carte **44-59 USD**
t.5% s.17%

🔑 19 rooms
295-350 USD t.7% s.i.

☕ **10-15 USD** t.5% s.17%

🛏 no

🎣 10 km

Whirlpools, day spa service, hunting, fishing, museums, plantation visits, antique shops, art galleries.

I n the heart of South Carolina, a region famous for its magnificent blue skies and cotton plantations, is the superb restoration of this 1906 Classic Revival Mansion. Nestled amidst 42 acres of woods and pristine pine forest, not far from the Atlantic Coast and Historic Charleston, Woodlands offers gracious hospitality and luxurious guestrooms. The new American cuisine will delight the most refined palates.

MasterCard · American Express · Visa

USD : US dollar

www.relaischateaux.fr/woodlands

PLANTERS INN

USA

112 North Market Street
Charleston
South Carolina 29401

Tel. : (1) (843) 722 2345
Fax : (1) (843) 577 2125
E-mail : planters@relaischateaux.fr

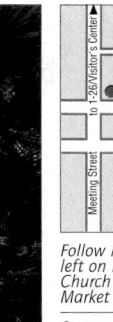

Follow Meeting Street south; turn left on Hayne street then right on Church street and right on North Market Street.

Owner : Hank Holliday
Director : Larry Spelts
Open all year

Charleston 19 km

Menus **45-90 USD** t.8% s.i.
Carte **20-29 USD** t.8% s.i.

56 rooms
160-295 USD t.12% s.i.

6 suites
325-500 USD t.12% s.i.

8-15 USD t.8% s.i.

no

7 km (18 holes)

Spa and fitness center, water sports, historic tours nearby.

Located in the heart of the America's largest historic district, Planters Inn, built in 1844, is the ideal starting point for your visit to Charleston. Its rooms echo the noble accents of the local landscape, by recreating a calm, peaceful, yet luxurious decor. The courtyard and verandas, with their ornate fountains, create an urban oasis. The renowned Peninsula Grill proposes regional American cooking and an award-winning wine list.

USD : US dollar

579

LITTLE PALM ISLAND

Tel. : (1) (305) 872 2524
USA Toll free : (800) 343 8567
Fax : (1) (305) 872 4843
E-mail : littlepalm@relaischateaux.fr

28500 Overseas Highway
Little Torch Key
Florida 33042

USA

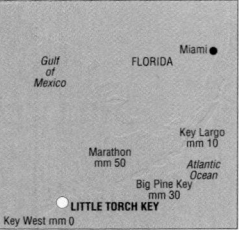

From Miami, US 1 Highway South to Little Torch Key at mm 28.5. Hourly ferry service to the Island.

Owner : Patrick Colee
Director : Heinrich Morio
Open all year

✈ Key West (**Intl**) 45 km
Miami (**Intl**) 192 km

 GPS N 24° 37' 11"
W 81° 24' 42"

🍴 Fullboard
140 USD t.7,5% s.18%
per person
Halfboard
125 USD t.7,5% s.18%
per person

 30 suites
500-1 200 USD
t.11,5% s.10%

 20-30 USD t.7,5% s.18%

 no

🏊 42 km

Fishing, sailing, snorkeling, scuba, watersports fitness center, seaplane excursions, pool, beach and full spa.

This exclusive Island is a paradise for those seeking the ultimate romantic escape with unspoiled natural surroundings. Choose between total relaxation or endless watersport adventure. Nestled among towering palms, each thatched-roof suite offers endless ocean views, private verandahs and exquisite British Colonial furnishings. Enjoy «Floribbean» cuisine accented with French and Asian undertones.

    Visa

USD : US dollar

www.relaischateaux.fr/littlepalm

BLACKBERRY FARM

USA

1471, West Millers Cove
Walland
Tennessee 37886

Tel. : (1) (865) 984 8166
Fax : (1) (865) 681 7753
E-mail : blackberry@relaischateaux.fr

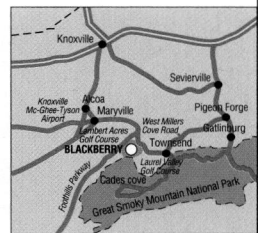

From Mc-Ghee-Tyson airport,
Maryville, A 321,
West Millers Cove Road.

Owners : Kreis and Sandy Beall
Director : John C. Fleer
Open all year

✈ Atlanta **(Intl)** 340 km
  Knoxville 25 km

GPS N 35° 41' 15"
  W 83° 51' 92"

🍴 included

🔑 23 rooms (full board)
  395-645 USD
  t.12% s.15%

🔑 16 suites (full board)
  645-795 USD
  t.12% s.15%

☕ included

🛏 no

🎵 nearby

Mountain biking, trout fishing,
hiking, cardio room,
white water rafting,
spa services, cooking school.

S itting on the veranda of this idyllic country retreat at the foot of the Great Smoky Mountains, gaze out across a magnificent expanse of forests and meadows, crisscrossed with streams and paths. The estate and its cottages are furnished with English-style antiques and the elegant guestrooms are tastefully decorated with chintz and floral arrangements. Savour superb cuisine with delightful Southern accents.

www.relaischateaux.fr/blackberry
USD : US dollar

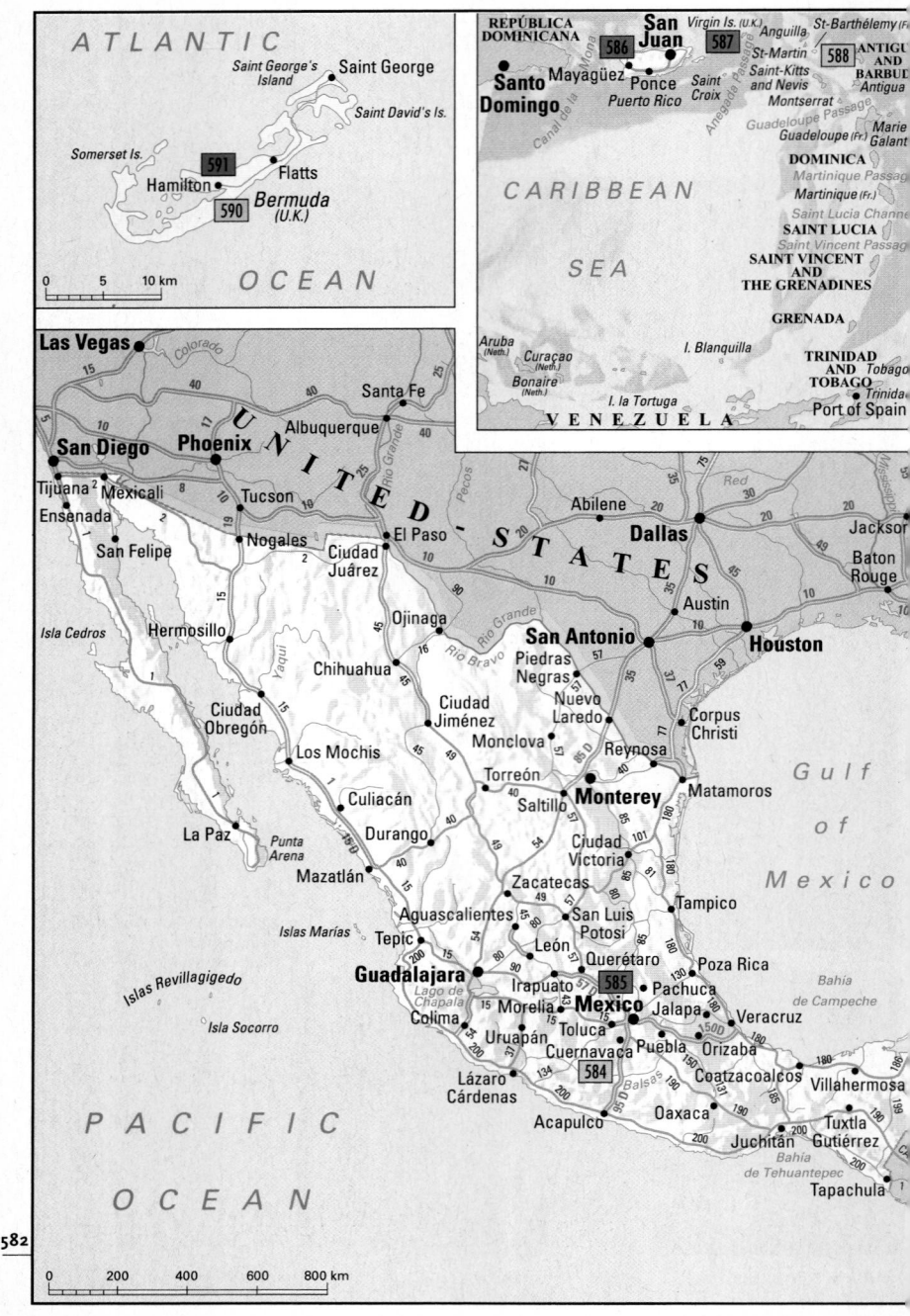

Bermuda (inset, top left)

ATLANTIC

OCEAN

Saint George's Island
Saint George
Somerset Is.
Saint David's Is.
591
Hamilton
Flatts
590
Bermuda (U.K.)

0   5   10 km

Caribbean (inset, top right)

REPÚBLICA DOMINICANA
San Juan
Virgin Is. (U.K.)
Anguilla
St-Barthélemy (Fr
586
587
St-Martin
Saint-Kitts and Nevis
588
ANTIGU AND BARBUD
Antigua
Santo Domingo
Mayagüez
Ponce
Puerto Rico
Saint Croix
Montserrat
Guadeloupe Passage
Guadeloupe (Fr.)
Marie Galant

Canal de la Mona
Anegada Passage

DOMINICA
Martinique Passage
Martinique (Fr.)

CARIBBEAN

Saint Lucia Channe
SAINT LUCIA
Saint Vincent Passag
SAINT VINCENT AND THE GRENADINES

SEA

GRENADA

Aruba (Neth.)
Curaçao (Neth.)
Bonaire (Neth.)
I. Blanquilla
TRINIDAD AND TOBAGO
Tobago
Trinida
Port of Spain

I. la Tortuga

VENEZUELA

Main map (Mexico / United States)

Las Vegas
Colorado
15
40
Santa Fe
25
Albuquerque
40
U N I T E D
San Diego
10
Phoenix
17
Tijuana
Mexicali
8
Tucson
10
19
El Paso
90
S T A T E S
Abilene
20
35
Red
30
20
Dallas
20
49
Jackso
Ensenada
2
5
10
Rio Grande
Ciudad Juárez
10
10
Austin
10
Baton Rouge
San Felipe
2
Nogales
2
Ojinaga
45
Rio Grande
San Antonio
57
10
Houston
Isla Cedros
Hermosillo
15
16
Rio Bravo
Piedras Negras
35
37
77
59
Corpus Christi
Chihuahua
45
Ciudad Jiménez
Nuevo Laredo
Gulf
Ciudad Obregón
Yaqui
15
45
49
Monclova
57
Reynosa
77
Los Mochis
1
Torreón
40
Saltillo
Monterrey
Matamoros
of
La Paz
Culiacán
Ciudad Victoria
101
Mexico
Punta Arena
Durango
40
54
49
180
Islas Marías
Mazatlán
Zacatecas
49
San Luis Potosí
85
81
Tampico
Aguascalientes
80
90
León
Querétaro
130
Poza Rica
Bahía de Campeche
Islas Revillagigedo
Tepic
200
15
15
Irapuato
585
Pachuca
Guadalajara
Lago de Chapala
15
Morelia
Mexico
Jalapa
Veracruz
Isla Socorro
Colima
15
Toluca
Puebla
180
Uruapán
31
Cuernavaca
584
Orizaba
150
Coatzacoalcos
185
Villahermosa
Lázaro Cárdenas
134
Balsas
500
190
PACIFIC
200
Acapulco
200
Oaxaca
190
Tuxtla Gutiérrez
200
Juchitán
200
OCEAN
Bahía de Tehuantepec
Tapachula
1

582

0   200   400   600   800 km

589
BARBADOS

0   100 200 km

Montgomery

Mobile

New Orleans

Cancún
Mérida 180 D 180
Isla Cozumel
Campeche
Chetumal
186
rancisco
scárcega BELIZE
Belmopan
Puerto San
Barrios Pedro
Sula
9 HONDURAS
Tegucigalpa
Guatemala

San Salvador
L SALVADOR

MEXICO - CARRIBEAN BERMUDA

MEXICO

Establishments	Nearest major city	Relais & Châteaux	Relais Gourmands	Page
Las Mañanitas	Mexico City	⚜		584
Restaurant Champs-Elysées	Mexico City		👨‍🍳	585

Wines recommended by the wine waiters of the Relais & Châteaux and Relais Gourmands.

🍷	Name of wine	Wine to enjoy	Noble wine	Outstanding wine
Red	Pinot noir, Cabernet sauvignon, Merlot	1994	1988 - 1986	1989 - 1982

PUERTO RICO

Establishments	Nearest major city	Relais & Châteaux	Relais Gourmands	Page
Horned Dorset Primavera (The)	Mayagüez	⚜		586

VIRGIN ISLANDS

Establishments	Nearest major city	Relais & Châteaux	Relais Gourmands	Page
Biras Creek Resort	Spainish Town	⚜		587

FRENCH WEST INDIES

Establishments	Nearest major city	Relais & Châteaux	Relais Gourmands	Page
Le Toiny	Saint-Barthélémy	⚜		588

BARBADAS

Establishments	Nearest major city	Relais & Châteaux	Relais Gourmands	Page
Coblers Cove	Speightstown	⚜		589

BERMUDA

Establishments	Nearest major city	Relais & Châteaux	Relais Gourmands	Page
Horizons and Cottages	Hamilton	⚜		590
Waterloo House	Hamilton	⚜		591

Las Mañanitas

SINCE
1990

Tel. : (52) (73) 14 14 66
Fax : (52) (73) 18 36 72
E-mail : mananitas@relaischateaux.fr

Ricardo Linares 107, Apdo. 1202
62000 Cuernavaca
(Morelos)

Mexico

Highway 95D Cuernavaca,
E. Zapata blvd.,
A. Obregon street, 2 miles then
turn left R. Linares.

Owners :
Margot Krause and Ruben Cerda
Director : Ruben Cerda
Open all year

✈	Mexico (**Intl**) 80 km Mariano Matamoros 12 km
🍴	Carte **28-43 USD** s.15%
⚬━	1 room **130 USD** s.5%
8━	21 suites **177-286 USD** s.5%
☕	8-15 USD s.15%
卅	no
♪	5 km

Mountain hiking...

R ediscover the unique charm and privileged setting of Cuernavaca, a magnificent mountain town which the Aztecs named «the City of eternal spring». Las Mañanitas's elegant rooms, decorated with beautiful Spanish colonial furniture and paintings by Mexico's finest artists, look out across luxuriant tropical gardens. Explore Mexico's ancient ruins and traditional folklore, and enjoy regional and international cuisine.

USD : US dollar

www.relaischateaux.fr/mananitas

RESTAURANT CHAMPS-ELYSÉES

Mexico

Paseo de la Reforma
316-Col. Juarez
Ciudad de México

Tel. : **(52) (5) 514 0450**
Fax : **(52) (5) 208 2302**
E-mail : champselysees@relaischateaux.fr

In the centre of the Rose zone across from the independence monument (Angel).

Owners :
Paquita and François Avernin
Weekly closing : Sunday
Annual closing : Easter week

Mexico (**Intl**) 15 km
Toluca (**Intl**) 25 km

Carte **200-400 MXP**
s.15%

yes

S et on the Paseo de la Reforma, Mexico City's equivalent of the Champs-Elysées, this elegant restaurant is renowned for its remarkable gourmet cuisine. François and Paquita Avernin welcome guests with exquisite courtesy and serve them gastronomical wonders such as «terrine d'aubergines», «pomme de terre farcie aux escargots de Bourgogne» and «crème brûlée». These French-inspired delicacies are accompanied by admirable wines.

585

www.relaischateaux.fr/champselysees   MXP : Mexican peso

THE HORNED DORSET PRIMAVERA

Tel. : (1) (787) 823 40 30
USA toll free : (800) 633 18 57
Fax : (1) (787) 823 55 80
E-mail : horneddorset@relaischateaux.fr

Apartado 1132, route 429
00677 Rincon

Puerto Rico

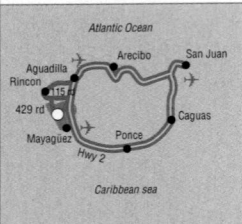

Mayaguez, rte. 2 north, rte. 115 towards Rincon at the Anasco intersection, then route 429.

Owners : Harold Davies, Kingsley Wratten, Wilhelm Sack
Open all year

 San Juan **(Intl)** 200 km
Mayagüez 10 km

 Menu **56** USD s.15%
Carte **56-80** USD s.15%

 30 rooms
280-800 USD t.7% + 3%

 10-15 USD s.15%

 no

 20 km

Water sports, fishing, massage, fitness centre, concerts.

The veranda of this neo-colonial style hacienda opens out onto the azure waters of the Caribbean. The guestrooms, furnished with impeccable taste, are exquisite havens of calm and all feature air-conditioning and luxurious marble bathrooms. Linger over an apéritif at the poolside and contemplate the spectacular Puerto Rican sunset, then enjoy delicious seafood and freshly-caught lobster by romantic candlelight.

USD : US dollar

www.relaischateaux.fr/horneddorset

BIRAS CREEK

British Virgin
Islands

P.O. Box 54
Virgin Gorda

Tel. : (1) (284) 494 3555
Fax : (1) (284) 494 3557
E-mail : biras@relaischateaux.fr

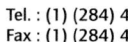

John O Point — Biras Hill
North Sound
Camelia Point — Biras Creek — **BIRAS CREEK RESORT**
Grassy Ground — *South Sound*

*Transportation prearranged
from Beef Island
+ Virgin Gorda Airport.
Both Airports accessible
through San Juan Puerto Rico
+ Antigua WI.*

Owner : Bert Houwer
Directors : Jacques Brouchier
and Pam Berry-Brouchier
Open all year

✈ Virgin Gorda 10 km
Beef Island 30 km

⚓ GPS N 18"29 W 64"21

🍴 Full board

⚷ 30 rooms
425-750 USD
t.7% s.10%

⚷ 4 suites
625-1150 USD
t.7% s.10%

☕ included

🐎 no

A secluded retreat for nature-lovers, far removed from organised activities. Only accessible by boat, the hotel magnificently overlooks the ocean. Contemplating this spectacular view, guests can enjoy cocktails and meals «al fresco». Each of the spacious suites, decorated in the West Indian style, is near the water and has a private lounge, bedroom, patio and garden shower.

Fishing, hiking, snorkeling,
sailing, motor-rigged dinghies,
parasailing, massage.

587

www.relaischateaux.fr/biras

USD : US dollar

LE TOINY

Tel. : 0590 27 88 88
Fax : 0590 27 89 30
E-mail : toiny@relaischateaux.fr

Anse de Toiny
97133 Saint-Barthélémy

French
West Indies

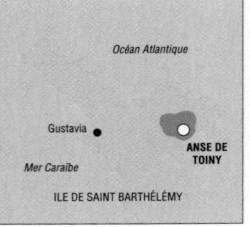

Océan Atlantique

Gustavia ●

ANSE DE TOINY

Mer Caraïbe

ILE DE SAINT BARTHÉLÉMY

*Complementary transport
to and from the airport.*

Owner : Michael Shen
Director : David P. Henderson
Annual closing :
From Sept. 1st to October 18th

✈ Saint-Martin **(Intl)** 20 km
Saint-Barthélémy 6 km

🍴 Carte
300 FRF (lunch) s.i.
46 €
500 FRF (dinner) s.i.
76 €

🔑 12 villas
low season :
2 920 FRF s.i. - **445 €**
high season :
5 520 FRF s.i. - **842 €**

☕ included

🛏 yes

Boat and plane trips, sea fishing.

Discover Caribbean paradise in your own colonial-style villa surrounded by lush tropical gardens. Relax in your private pool overlooking the ocean and enjoy the utmost in modern amenities (personal fax, TV and air conditioning). After a day on the sun-drenched beaches, dine by romantic candlelight at «Le Gaïac» which offers refined French cuisine with a local Caribbean flair and a superb panoramic ocean view.

Visa

FRF : French franc

www.relaischateaux.fr/toiny

COBBLERS COVE

Barbados

St. Peter, Barbados
West Indies

Tel. : (1) (246) 422 2291
Fax : (1) (246) 422 1460
E-mail : cobblers@relaischateaux.fr

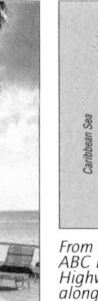

Speightstown
Atlantic Ocean
ST PETER
Caribbean Sea
Bridgestown
Airport

From the airport, take the ABC Highway, then on to Highway 1, travelling North along the West Coast.

Owner : Hayton Ltd.
Director : Hamish Watson
Annual closing :
From September 1st
to October 15th

I magine the elegance of an English country house combined with the charms of a tropical island paradise. Cobblers Cove, nestled beneath palm trees and overlooking fine sand beaches and turquoise waters, offers exceptional hospitality and luxurious accommodation. Relax on the terrace of a sumptuous suite, secluded in the hotel's landscaped gardens, then savour fine wines and cuisine at the «Terrace Restaurant».

✈	Barbados (**Intl**) 29 km
🍴	Menus 45-70 USD t.15% s.10% Carte 45-70 USD t.15% s.10%
⚷	40 suites 250-1 700 USD t.7,5% s.10%
☕	15 USD t.7,5% s.10%
🚭	no
⛳	Royal Westmoreland 3 km

Water sports, polo, golf trips, flying club...

589

USD : US dollar

HORIZONS AND COTTAGES

Tel. : (1) (441) 236 0048
USA Tool free : 800 468 0022
Fax : (1) (441) 236 1981
E-mail : horizons@relaischateaux.fr

P.O. Box PG 198
Paget PGBX

Bermuda

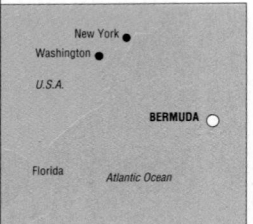

From Bermuda airport, follow the south coast towards Paget.

Owners :
Elfrida Wardman Chappell
and George Wardman
Director : George Wardman
Open all year

✈	Bermuda (**Intl**) 15 km
🍽	Menus included Carte **55 USD** s.15%
⚬⊸	45 rooms **306-470 USD** t.7,25% s.10%
⚬⊸	3 suites **545-735 USD** t.7,25% s.10%
☕	included
🛏	no
🎵	yes

Water sports,
Coral Beach Club 500 metres.

T his 18th-century Plantation Estate offers idyllic natural surroundings and traditional island hospitality. Sporting enthusiasts will enjoy the wide range of leisure pursuits such as golf, putting and tennis, while guests seeking sun and relaxation will adore the coral sand beaches of the South Shore. Enjoy an apéritif in the shade of the hibiscus, then savour fine wines and seafood delicacies on the «Ocean Terrace».

USD : US Dollar

www.relaischateaux.fr/horizons

Bermuda

WATERLOO HOUSE

P.O. Box HM 333
Hamilton HMBX

Tel. : (1) (441) 295 4480
USA toll free : 800 468 4100
Fax : (1) (441) 295 2585
E-mail : waterloo@relaischateaux.fr

From Bermuda Airport, towards Hamilton, then Outskirts via Front Street, the hotel is indicated.

Owners :
Elfrida Wardman Chappell
and George Wardman
Director : Trudy Mulder
Open all year

✈	Bermuda **(Intl)** 15 km
🍴	Menus **40-45 USD** s.15% Carte **45-55 USD** s.15%
⚷	20 rooms **280-390 USD** t.7,25% s.10%
⚷	10 suites **390-600 USD** t.7,25% s.10%
	included
	yes (extra cost)
	Mid Ocean Club 10 km

Sailing, fishing, diving, snorkelling.

Views of shimmering blue water and pink coral beaches stretch to the horizon and the scent of frangipani wafts on the breeze. Paradise awaits you at this manor house which offers luxurious accommodation and an outstanding restaurant. Cruise aboard the private launch, picnic on a deserted island, or snorkel with the tropical fish. After cocktails by the pool, enjoy a romantic dance in the moonlight with a local band.

591

www.relaischateaux.fr/waterloo

USD : US dollar

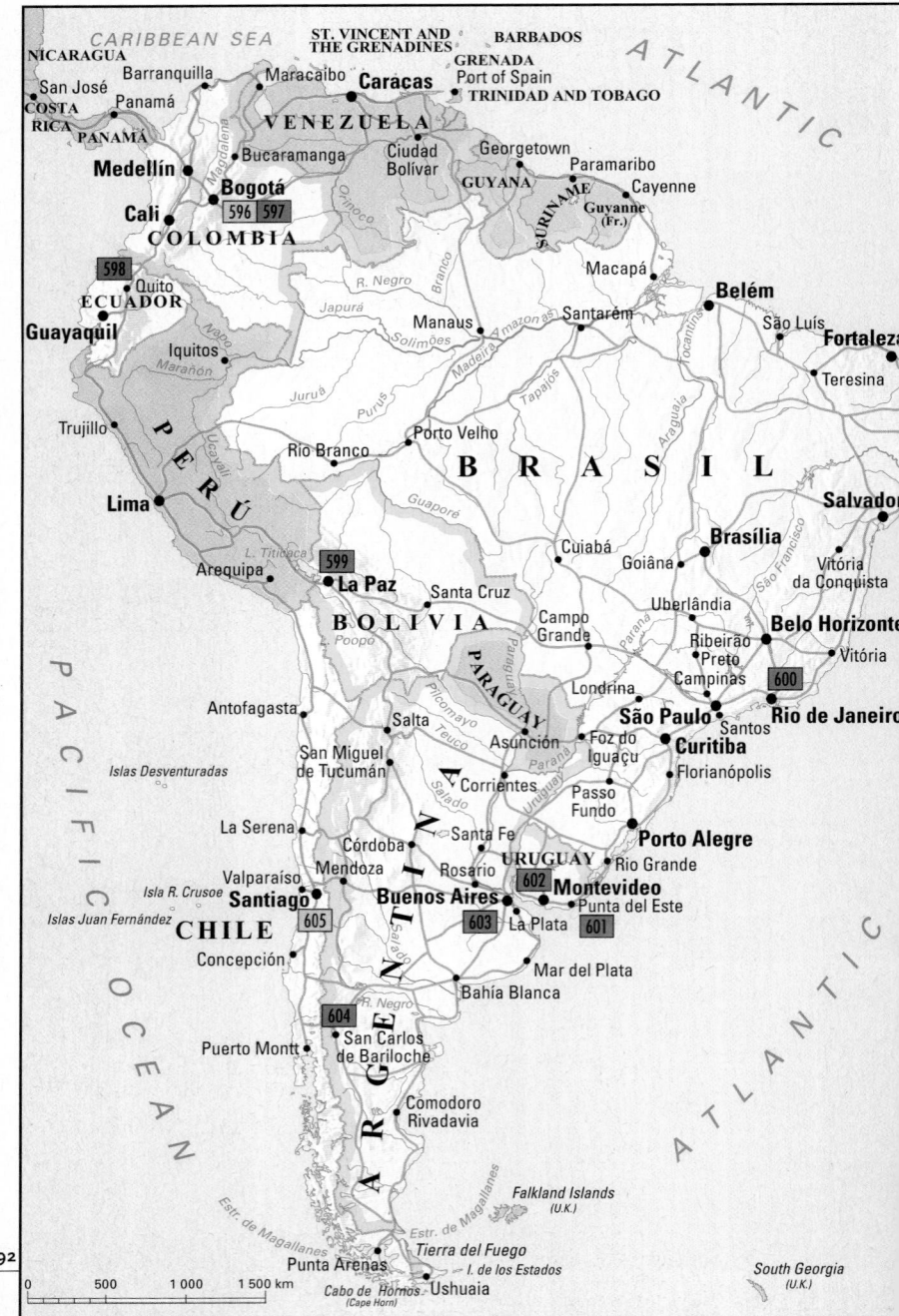

CARIBBEAN SEA

ATLANTIC

NICARAGUA
Barranquilla
San José
COSTA
RICA
Panamá
PANAMÁ

Maracaibo
Caracas
ST. VINCENT AND
THE GRENADINES
GRENADA
Port of Spain
BARBADOS

VENEZUELA

Bucaramanga
Ciudad
Bolívar
Georgetown
Paramaribo
Cayenne
TRINIDAD AND TOBAGO

Medellín
Cali
Bogotá
596 597
COLOMBIA

598
Quito
ECUADOR

GUYANA
SURINAME
Guyane
(Fr.)

Macapá

Belém
São Luís
Fortaleza

Guayaquil
Iquitos
Marañón
Napo

R. Negro
Branco

Manaus
Solimões
Amazonas
Santarém
Teresina

Trujillo
P E R Ú
Juruá
Purús
Madeira
Tapajós

Tocantins
Araguaia
São Francisco

Río Branco
Porto Velho

Lima
Ucayali
Guaporé

B R A S I L

Salvador

Arequipa
L. Titicaca
599
La Paz
Santa Cruz
Cuiabá
Brasília
Goiânia
Vitória
da Conquista

B O L I V I A
L. Poopó
Campo
Grande
Uberlândia
Belo Horizonte
Vitória

Antofagasta
PARAGUAY
Paraguay
Pilcomayo
Teuco
Salta
Asunción
Foz do
Iguaçu
Londrina
Ribeirão
Preto
Campinas
600
São Paulo
Santos
Rio de Janeiro
Curitiba
Florianópolis

Islas Desventuradas
San Miguel
de Tucumán
Corrientes
Salado
Paraná
Uruguay
Passo
Fundo

La Serena
Isla R. Crusoe
Córdoba
Santa Fe
URUGUAY
602
Porto Alegre
Río Grande

Islas Juan Fernández
Valparaíso
Santiago
605
Mendoza
Rosario
Buenos Aires
603
La Plata
Montevideo
601
Punta del Este

CHILE
A R G E N T I N A
Salado

Concepción
Mar del Plata
Bahía Blanca

604
R. Negro
Puerto Montt
San Carlos
de Bariloche

PACIFIC OCEAN

Comodoro
Rivadavia

ATLANTIC

Estr. de Magallanes
Falkland Islands
(U.K.)

592
0   500   1 000   1 500 km
Estr. de Magallanes
Tierra del Fuego
I. de los Estados
Punta Arenas
Cabo de Hornos
(Cape Horn)
Ushuaia
South Georgia
(U.K.)

HOTEL CHARLESTON

Carrera 13 N° 85-46
46 Bogota

Colombia

Tel. : (57) (1) 2571 100
Fax : (57) (1) 6160 687
E-mail : charleston@relaischateaux.fr

From the airport, take carretera 26 then avenida 68, then left on Ave. Chile, right on calle 15, and left on calle 85, the hotel is in the middle of the block.

Owner : Charleston S.A.
Director : Juan Pablo Saiz
Annual closing :
From Dec. 20th to January 8th

✈ Eldorado (**Intl**) 15 km

🍽 Menus **7-15 USD** t.16%
Carte **12-25 USD** t.16%

🔑 32 rooms
165 USD

🔑 26 suites
190-230 USD

🍷 7-15 USD t.16%

🛗 no

🎿 15 km

This charming hotel combines Colombian hospitality with elegant British decor and sophisticated French cuisine. Set in the heart of Bogota's residential district, it also makes an ideal base for discovering the capital's attractions. Dine by candlelight in the «Biblioteca», a beautiful library-dining room which has become the city's most sought-after restaurant, and enjoy fine vintages from South America and France.

HOSTERIA LA MIRAGE

Tel. : (593) (6) 91 52 37
Fax : (593) (6) 91 50 65
E-mail : lamirage@relaischateaux.fr

Cotacachi - Imbabura

Ecuador

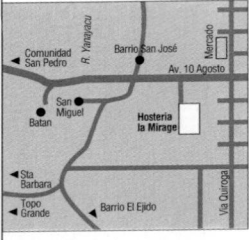

Take the Pan American highway north, pass the village of Tabacundo and the city of Otavalo. After 8 km, take a left at the Cotacachi sign, take the main road, pass 2 traffic lights - approx 300 m then, turn left.

Owner : Jorge Espinosa
Director : Patricio Hidrovo
Open all year

✈ Quito (**Intl**) 120 km

🍴 Menus **20-30 USD**
t.10% s.10%
Carte **25-35 USD**
t.10% s.10%

🔑 12 rooms (half-board)
180-195 USD
t.10% s.10%

🔑 11 suites (half-board)
200-280 USD
t.10% s.10%

🍷 **10-15 USD** t.10% s.10%

🍴 no

Horseback riding, spa, aromatherapy, massages, steambath, jaccuzzi, mountain climbing, fishing, hiking, mountain-biking, festivals.

The Mirage's comfortable and modern rooms offer breathtaking views of the Andes cordillera. Set in luxuriant gardens full of tropical flowers and wildlife, this magical place is a haven of peace. Visit the vibrant colorful Indian market at Otavalo, enjoy riding, swimming and tennis then savour regional specialities at one of the best restaurants in Ecuador.

Visa

USD : US dollar

www.relaischateaux.fr/lamirage

HACIENDA VILLA DEL SOL

Puente Aranjuez-PO BOX 312313
La Paz

Tel. : (591) (2) 74 00 08
Fax : (591) (2) 74 00 32
E-mail : villadelsol@relaischateaux.fr

Bolivia

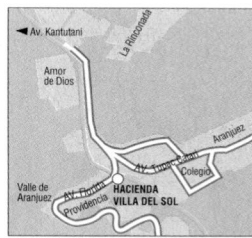

Follow av. Kantutani towards av. Costanera. Stay right along the river and take av. Florida. The Puente Aranjuez is 800m farther.

Owners :
Jorge and Ana-Maria Plaza
Director : Jorge Plaza
Open all year

✈	JFK El Alto **(Intl)** 15 km
🍴	Carte **60-120 BOB** s.i.
🛏	16 suites **690-1 800 BOB** s.i.
🍷	17-32 BOB s.i.
	yes (extra cost)
	1 km

Climbing, biking, horse-riding, fitness room, sauna, jacuzzi, spa.

T he Hacienda del Sol is a haven of peace. In this idyllic place, the only sounds you will hear are birds chirping and water gurgling. The hotel was built respecting Bolivian tradition: with earthenware tiles and adobe walls. Every guestroom has its own fireplace, private patio and balcony. In the restaurant, enjoy the chef's cuisine prepared with the finest ingredients and the lightly spicy Bolivian specialities.

    599

BOB : Bolivian peso

HOTEL E FAZENDA ROSA DOS VENTOS

SINCE 1991

Tel. : (55) (021) 642 88 33
(55) (021) 532 11 97
Fax : (55) (021) 240 81 25
(55) (021) 642 81 74
E-mail : fazenda@relaischateaux.fr

Km 22, Estrada Teresópolis-Nova Friburgo
25977-400 Teresópolis-R.J.

Brazil

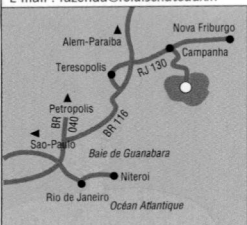

*Exit Rio, Linha Vermelha, BR 040
towards Petrópolis, BR 116
towards Teresópolis, RJ 130.*

Owner : Hotel e Fazenda
Rosa dos Ventos Ltda
Director :
Elizabeth Waddington Agra
Open all year

✈	Rio-Galeao (**Intl**) 110 km Rio-Santos Dumont (**Intl**) 130 km
🍴	Menu **20 USD** s.10% Carte **25-35 USD** s.10%
O⊸	35 rooms **155-182 USD** s.10%
8⊸	5 suites **195-214 USD** s.10%
☕	included
🚭	no
♪	27 km

Sauna, horseback riding,
lake fishing, steam bath,
beauty centre.

P erched at 1250 metres, this
elegant hotel is set amidst 250
acres of luxuriant foliage in the heart of
the Serra dos Orgaos National Park. Its
marvellously comfortable guestrooms are
housed in three alpine-style chalets
overlooking flower gardens, stables and
a mountain lake. Savour regional
specialities or classic international cuisine
and enjoy exquisite hospitality in this
haven of peace and eternal sunshine.

USD : US dollar

www.relaischateaux.fr/fazenda

LA BOURGOGNE

Uruguay

Pedragosa Sierra,
20100 Punta Del Este
(Maldonado)

Tel. : (598) (042) 4820 07
Fax : (598) (042) 4878 73
E-mail : bourgogne@relaischateaux.fr

From Parada 5 straight ahead,
intersection: av. Del Mar and
Pedragosa Sierra.

Owners :
Evelyne and Jean-Paul Bondoux
Annual closing :
From March 31st to October 15th

 Montevideo (**Intl**) 120 km
Laguna del Sauce 22 km

 Menus
lunch **300 UYU** t.23% s.i.
dinner **750 UYU** t.23% s.i.

 yes

 4 km

500 m away from the beach,
museums and galleries.

This elegant restaurant set in a cool jasmine-scented garden near magnificent beaches and the local yacht club, is renowned for its superb French cuisine. Jean-Paul Bondoux is a true perfectionist, cultivating fresh vegetables, herbs and spices on his own farm. Savour «terrine de jeunes poireaux aux langoustines» and «gigot d'agneau rôti aux herbes du jardin», accompanied by the finest French and South American vintages.

601

BELMONT HOUSE HOTEL

Uruguay

Tel. : (5982) 600 0430
Fax : (5982) 600 8609
E-mail : belmont@relaischateaux.fr

Av. Gral Rivera 6512
11500 Montevideo

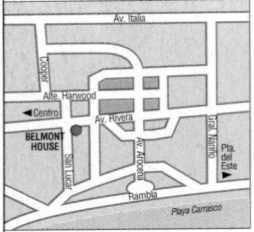

From the airport, take avenue de Las Americas, av. Italia, Paul Harris, av. Rivera.

Owner : Alfredo Folle
Open all year

✈	Carrasco (**Intl**) 7 km
🍽	Menu **25 USD** t.23% Carte **38 USD** t.23%
⊙⊤	24 rooms **275-310 USD** t.14%
8⊤	4 suites **400-582 USD** t.14%
☕	included
🐴	no
♪	15 km

Fitness, sauna, jacuzzi ;
carnaval (February).

This elegant English-style residence, set in the heart of Carrasco's residential quarter, lies just 300 metres from the capital's most beautiful beach. The sumptuous suites and guestrooms (many measuring up to 110 m²) are resplendent with 19th-century English furniture, antiques and French and Italian paintings. Relax in the tranquil gardens or take a dip in the luxurious pool. One of Montevideo's most idyllic spots.

Visa

USD : US dollar

www.relaischateaux.fr/belmont

JEAN-PAUL BONDOUX

Argentina

c/o Alvear Palace
2027 Ayacucho, Buenos Aires
(Rio de la Plata)

Tel. : **(54) 11 4805 3857**
Fax : **(54) 11 4805 5332**
E-mail : bondoux@relaischateaux.fr

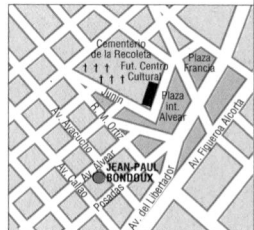

*In the centre of Buenos Aires,
at the corner of avenue Alvear
and Ayacucho.*

Owners :
Evelyne and Jean-Paul Bondoux
Weekly closing :
Saturday noon and Sunday
Open all year

✈ Buenos Aires (**Intl**) 40 km

🍴 Menus **45-65 USD** s.i.
Carte **50-80 USD** s.i.

🐾 no

J ean-Paul Bondoux has chosen this elegant restaurant, tastefully decorated in contemporary style, to showcase his gourmet delicacies inspired by Burgundy tradition. The menu features a superb «faisan en deux cuissons au muscat de Beaumes de Venise», a «merluza au coulis de petits pois» and an extraordinary «carré de veau service voiture aux sauces de votre choix», accompanied by Argentine wines or an exceptional Pommard.

603

www.relaischateaux.fr/bondoux

USD : US dollar

Visa

HOSTERIA LAS BALSAS

Tel. : (54) (2944) 49 4308
Fax : (54) (2944) 49 4308
E-mail : lasbalsas@relaischateaux.fr

Villa La Angostura
8407 Neuquen

Argentina

*From Bariloche, Route 231
towards Villa La Angostura.
After Cerro Bayo signs, 300 m
to the left.*

Owners :
Hosteria Las Balsas S.A.
Director : Romina Cambiasso
Open all year

✈ San Carlos de Bariloche
    80 km

🍴 Menu **40 USD** s.i.
    Carte **40 USD** s.i.

⊶ 13 rooms
    250 USD s.i.

⊶ 2 suites
    450 USD s.i.

☕ included

🛏 no

Jacuzzi, spa, water sports, trout
fishing, skiing, horseback riding,
walks, hiking, mountain biking.

Magnificent forests and snow-capped peaks surround the sparkling waters of Lake Nahuel Huapi. In the midst of these idyllic natural surroundings, the blue wooden walls and octagonal tower of Las Balsas overlook a peaceful cove. Relax in one of the thirteen beautiful rooms and enjoy the exquisite hospitality of Las Balsas. Enjoy riding, hiking, or a boat tour and savour delicious cuisine and fine wines.

Visa

USD : US dollar

www.relaischateaux.fr/lasbalsas

HACIENDA LOS LINGUES

Chile

Av. Providencia 1100
Torre, C OF. 205 Santiago
Del libertador Bernardo O' Higgins

Tel. : (56) (2) 235 5446
Fax : (56) (2) 235 7604
E-mail : loslingues@relaischateaux.fr

From Santiago,
Pan American Highway
(route 5), exit «Los Lingues».

Owner : German Claro-Lira
Director : German Claro-Lyon
Open all year

Santiago (**Intl**) 130 km
San Fernando 11 km

GPS S 70° 53' 40"
W 34° 31' 10"

Menus
46-62 USD s.15%

10 rooms
186 USD s.15%

2 suites
406 USD s.15%

19 USD s.15%

yes

This colonial-style residence, tucked away in the Andes, is set amidst tropical gardens. Covered galleries lead to its beautiful guestrooms, hung with old paintings and decorated with period furniture. Amidst this ancestral family home's exquisite crystal, porcelain and silver, savour Chilean cuisine and superb wines. The Hacienda has been renowned for its thoroughbred stud farm, the oldest in the Americas, since 1760.

Billiards, horseback riding, hunting, fly fishing, mountain biking, water-skiing, flying club, wine tours, rafting...

USD : US dollar

Visa

Wine, passion and internet

WORLD VINTAGES
TO BE SAVOURED IN THE YEAR 2000
INDEX OF THE COUNTRIES AND REGIONS

BY THE SOMMELIERS OF THE RELAIS & CHÂTEAUX AND THE RELAIS GOURMANDS

F or each wine region, you can discover in the pages indicated opposite, the mature vintages that we recommend tasting in the Year 2000. Some vintages of great renown are not mentioned as we think they require additional ageing.

Celebratory wines, wines to keep, wines to enjoy, each vintage has its character. To guide you, we have grouped them into three families:

Wine to enjoy	*Noble wine*	*Outstanding wine*
Pleasant	*depth*	*nobility*
charm	*complexity*	*rarity*
convivial	*contrast*	*the reference!*

This information is given to you for information only and may sometimes conceal large quality differences from one property to another. That is why the advice of the sommelier or the maître d'hôtel remains essential: only he can guide you through the subtleties of his wine list.

Enjoy your tasting

International co-ordination:
Philippe Faure-Brac – Best Sommelier in the World 1992

Alcohol abuse is bad for your health.

No card is more accepted for business.

www.mastercard.com

Please inquire about exclusive MasterCard® values by calling
Relais & Chateaux reservations, or visit our web site.

MEETING FACILITIES

Establishments	Meeting Capacity	Conference Capacity	Reception Capacity	Cocktail party Capacity	Number of conference rooms	Audio-visual Equipment	Secretarial services	Number of rooms	Page
FRANCE									51
PARIS REGION									51
Auberge des Templiers	40	50	80	120	3	●	●	30	74
Boyer «Les Crayères»	20	20	80	80	1			19	79
Cazaudehore et «La Forestière»	30	50	120	140	4	●		30	72
Château de Courcelles	50	70	90	120	1	●	●	18	81
Divellec (Le)			12				●		62
Hostellerie Le Clos	15	25			1	●		10	75
Hotellerie du Bas-Bréau	25	40	40	40	4	●	●	20	73
Restaurant Guy Savoy			80		3		●		59
Royal Champagne	30	50	50	50	5	●	●	29	77
BRITTANY - NORMANDY - PAS DE CALAIS									82
Auberge Bretonne (L')	20	20	60	60	1		●	8	96
Bretagne et sa Résidence (Le)	20	35	50	60	2	●	●	9	95
Castel Clara	20		20	30	1	●		43	94
Castel Marie-Louise	25	50	50	80	3	●	●	31	97
Château d'Audrieu	30	60	60	90	3	●	●	30	87
Château de Locguénolé	60	150	240	350	6	●	●	28	93
Château de Montreuil	14	18	18		1	●		14	84

Establishments	Meeting Capacity	Conference Capacity	Reception Capacity	Cocktail party Capacity	Number of conference rooms	Audio-visual Equipment	Secretarial services	Number of rooms	Page
Ferme St-Siméon (La)	50	70	80	80	3	●	●	29	85
Goyen (Le)	26	40	115	150	2	●	●	24	91
Hôtel de la Plage	20	50	100	150	2	●	●	30	90
Manoir de Lan-Kerellec	18	30	80	100	1	●	●	19	89
LOIRE VALLEY									98
Bardet Jean (Château Belmont)	20	50	45	60	3	●		21	104
Château de Marçay	50	80	80	200	3	●	●	34	103
Château de Noirieux	50	60	100	120	3	●	●	19	102
Château de Noizay	21	32	30	50	2	●	●	14	106
Domaine des Hauts de Loire	40	60	50	80	3	●		35	107
Hautes Roches (Les)	30	35	100	180	2	●	●	15	105
THE GREATER SOUTH WEST									110
Auberge de la Galupe	25		60		2	●			138
Bras (Michel)	20	25	50	40	2	●	●	15	129
Chapelle St-Martin (La)	30	120	200	300	5	●	●	13	117
Château Cordeillan-Bages	15	20	24	24	1		●	25	132
Château de Castel Novel	110	250	300	400	3	●	●	37	120
Château de Curzay	40	60	45	60	2	●		22	115
Château de Mercuès	70	120	110	150	2	●	●	30	127
Château de Nieuil	40	80	100	120	3	●		14	118
Château de Puy Robert	35	45		55	1			38	122
Château de Riell	30	120	120	120	5	●	●	22	143
Château de Roumégouse	30		80	100	1	●		15	126
Château de la Treyne	35	60	60	120	2	●		16	125
Domaine d'Auriac	50	100	100	100	7	●	●	26	142
Domaine de Bassibé	20	20	120	120	2	●	●	18	135
Guérard (M) «Les Prés d'Eugénie»	80	120	120	150	7	●	●	40	137
Loges de l'Aubergade (Les)	50	60	60	100	3	●	●	10	131
Longcol	40	60	40	100	1	●		19	130
Moulin de la Gorce (Au)	20	30	40	40	1			10	119

Establishments	Meeting Capacity	Conference Capacity	Reception Capacity	Cocktail party Capacity	Number of conference rooms	Audio-visual Equipment	Secretarial services	Number of rooms	Page
Prinses Juliana	20	50	150	400	2	●		21	266
SWITZERLAND - LIECHTENSTEIN									268
SWITZERLAND									272
Albergo Giardino	20	50	70	100	2		●	72	293
Auberge du Raisin	20	30	50	50	1			10	282
Castello del Sole	20	40	150	150	2	●	●	79	292
Ermitage Am See	14		20	20	1	●	●	26	275
Grand Hôtel Park	130	200	240	240	8	●	●	93	286
Grandhôtel Schönegg			80	100			●	36	291
Hostellerie Alpenrose	20	60	100	150	2			18	285
Hostellerie du Débarcadère	15	15	80	180	2			15	280
Hostellerie du Pas de l'Ours			100	50	1		●	9	287
Hôtel de la Cigogne	25	30	25	40	1	●	●	50	279
Hotel Haus Paradies	20	50	50	50	2	●	●	26	298
Hôtel Rosalp	15	30			1	●		20	289
Hotel Splügenschloss	18	30	60	50	1	●	●	52	274
Hôtel Victoria	100	130	130	140	3		●	59	284
Hotel Walther	25	30	200	200	1			73	297
Les Sources des Alpes	10	40	70	100	1			30	290
Rheinhotel Fischerzunft	40	60	70	70	1		●	10	273
Shlosshotel Chastè	12		40	40	1			20	299
Vieux Manoir au Lac (Le)	34	60	120	180	4	●	●	30	278
Villa Margherita	26	36	60	90	2		●	33	294
Villa Principe Leopoldo	40	120	100	200	7	●	●	75	295
LIECHTENSTEIN									302
Parkhotel Sonnenhof	14		40	40	1	●		29	303
Real (Le)	60	40	60	80	1			12	302
GERMANY									304
Alpenhof Murnau	120	200	160	250	6	●		77	340
Bülow Residenz	24	30	50	60	2	●	●	30	314

Establishments	Meeting Capacity	Conference Capacity	Reception Capacity	Cocktail party Capacity	Number of conference rooms	Audio-visual Equipment	Secretarial services	Number of rooms	Page
Burghotel Hardenberg	60	120	220	220	7	●	●	44	317
Fürstenhof Celle	60	80	80	100	6	●	●	76	315
Hotel Abtei	10		20	30	2			11	311
Hotel Brandenburger Hof	30	40	120	350	5	●	●	82	312
Hotel Burg Wernberg	50	180	80	200	10	●	●	50	325
Hotel Deidesheimer Hof	80	120	150	180	4	●	●	21	329
Hotel Hohenhaus	40	40	40	60	2	●	●	26	323
Hotel Krautkrämer	120	200	150	200	6	●		72	319
Hotel Louis C. Jacob	140	240	140	250	6	●		86	310
Hotel Restaurant Zur Traube			70	120				6	321
Hotel Schloss Hugenpœt	60	110	120	130	5	●	●	25	320
Hotel Schloss Wilkinghege	40	90	80	200	4	●		35	318
Hotel Schwarzmatt	30	60	50	50	1	●		38	337
Hotel Stadt Hamburg	70	100	100	100	3	●	●	72	308
Johann Lafer's Stromburg	80	160	120	200	4	●		14	324
Kur-und Sporthotel Dollenberg	25	40	30	60	2	●		71	335
Landhaus Ammann	140	180	180	250	7	●	●	14	316
Landhaus Scherrer	150	150	150	180	3				309
Mönchs Posthotel	45	100	120	150	4	●	●	24	331
Pflaums Posthotel Pegnitz	100	100	100	100	5	●	●	33	326
Residenz Heinz Winkler	45	45	45	45	2	●	●	32	341
Rest. Schwarzwaldstube	40	60	50	50	4	●	●		334
Schafhof Amorbach (Der)	55	120	80	150	3	●		23	328
Schloss Hubertushöhe	12	20	40	70	4	●	●	22	313
Schlosshotel Lerbach	65	100	120	150	3	●		54	322
Schwarzwald Hotel Adler			60	90	2			45	336
Schweizer Stuben	35	50	80	100	2	●		33	327
Seehotel Siber	25		80	80	1	●	●	12	338
Villa Hammerschmiede	40	80	72	72	5	●	●	26	332
Villino	20	20	20	20	1			16	339
Wald & Schlosshotel	60	120	120	250	3	●	●	44	330

Establishments	Meeting Capacity	Conference Capacity	Reception Capacity	Cocktail party Capacity	Number of conference rooms	Audio-visual Equipment	Secretarial services	Number of rooms	Page
CZECH REPUBLIC									342
Hotel Hoffmeister	30	60	100	150	3	●		17	343
AUSTRIA									344
Arlberg Hospiz	20	100	300	100	6		●	95	349
Deuring Schlössle	40	120	150	150	4	●	●	13	348
Gasthof Post	180	250	150	250	6	●		38	350
Hotel der Bär	70	120	120	120	3	●	●	55	353
Hotel Grüner Baum	30	70	120	120	3	●	●	58	358
Hotel Im Palais Schwarzenberg	250	450	500	1 000	6	●	●	44	356
Hotel Schloss Dürnstein	30	50	100	150	3	●		38	355
Hotel Schloss Mönchstein	30	55	50	70	3	●	●	16	354
Hotel Schloss Seefels	45	100	160	390	4	●		70	359
Schlosshotel Igls	11	20	14	25	1	●	●	20	352
SLOVENIA									360
Hotel Vila Bled	50	90	80	120	2	●	●	30	361
SCANDINAVIA									362
DENMARK									364
Falsled Kro	25	40	80	100	1	●	●	19	366
Molskroen	40	80	80	100		●		18	365
Sønderho Kro	12		45	50	2	●		13	364
SWEDEN									367
Kattegat Gastronomi	14	30	50	150	11	●	●		368
Krägga Herrgård	45	80	200	400	8	●	●	43	369
Leijontornet & Victory Hotel	85	85	85	85	10	●	●	45	370
ICELAND									372
Hotel Holt	40	65	62	130	1			42	372
LITHUANIA									373
Stikliai Hotel	20		100	200	4	●		29	373
UNITED KINGDOM									374
Arisaig House	10		32	40	1			12	397
Bodysgallen Hall	24	50	55	60	3	●	●	35	392

THE SMARTEST LUGGAGE YOU CAN CARRY.

Card

Establishments	Meeting Capacity	Conference Capacity	Reception Capacity	Cocktail party Capacity	Number of conference rooms	Audio-visual Equipment	Secretarial services	Number of rooms	Page
Chewton Glen Hotel	40	150	120	200	6	●	●	53	383
Farlam Hall Hotel	12	25	45	60	1			12	395
Gavroche (Le)	20		20	30	1	●			377
Gidleigh Park	22		28		1	●		15	386
Gravetye Manor	12				1	●		18	382
Hambleton Hall	20	40	60		3	●		15	391
Hartwell House	40	34	60	100	6	●	●	47	381
Inverlochy Castle	22	22	40	50	2			17	398
Kinnaird	20	20			1	●	●	9	396
Longueville Manor	20	30	20	30	2	●	●	32	387
Mallory Court	20		25		3	●		18	390
Manoir aux Quat' Saisons (Le)	44	44	55	55	1	●		32	380
Middlethorpe Hall	25	60	54	60	2	●	●	30	393
Sharrow Bay Country House	12		30	50	1	●		26	394
Stock Hill Country House	12		20	20	1			8	384
Ston Easton Park	22	40	55	80	10	●	●	21	388
Summer Lodge	24	40	71	200	5	●	●	17	385
Tante Claire (La)	40	40	40	40					378
Waterside Inn (The)	8		8	8	1	●		9	379
IRELAND									400
Ashford Castle	54	110	75	75	1	●	●	83	406
Longueville House	14	20	50	50	4	●	●	20	405
Marlfield House	20	40	40	50	2	●		19	409
Sheen Falls Lodge	65	150	120	150	4	●	●	60	403
ITALY									410
Albereta (L') - Rest. G. Marchesi	70	180	180	200	4	●	●	44	421
Al Sorriso	16	16	35	35	1			8	417
Borgo Paraelios	18	35	100	80	3			15	441
Bottaccio di Montignoso (Il)	12	30	40	60	2	●	●	8	432
Gallia Palace Hotel	45	80	120	170	2	●		83	439

Establishments	Meeting Capacity	Conference Capacity	Reception Capacity	Cocktail party Capacity	Number of conference rooms	Audio-visual Equipment	Secretarial services	Number of rooms	Page
Hotel Certosa di Maggiano	18	25	40	60	3	●	●	17	436
Hotel Dominik	35	100	70	200	3	●		28	424
Hotel Hermitage	20	35	50	35	1	●		36	414
Hotel La Collegiata	30		70	80	2	●		21	435
Melograno (Il)	100	600	450	600	6	●	●	37	445
Meridiana (La)	25	30	80	120	1	●	●	30	428
Pellicano (Il)	20		50	50	1	●		41	440
Posta Vecchia (La)	40	100	70	100	4		●	18	442
Relais Borgo San Felice	70	70	80	80	2	●		45	437
Restaurant Dal Pescatore	8		10		1		●		427
Ristorante Le Calandre	20	25	40	40	2		●		426
Rosa Alpina	200	150	150	200	2	●	●	51	425
Sole di Ranco (Il)	14		45	25	1		●	14	419
Villa Del Quar	40	100	120	120	2	●	●	22	423
Villa Fiordaliso	16		300	1 000	1	●		7	422
Villa la Massa	35	60	80	120	5	●	●	34	433
IBERIAN PENINSULA									446
PORTUGAL									450
Fortaleza do Guincho	160	220	180	300	2	●	●	29	451
Hotel Quinta Das Lagrimas	45	100	90	100	4	●	●	39	450
SPAIN									452
Gran Hotel Son Net	17	40	150	250	2			24	469
Hotel Cala Sant Vicenç	22	35	50	50	1	●	●	38	470
Hotel El Castell	70	80	250	400	3	●		37	457
Hotel El Montibolli	25	60	200	250	3	●		50	466
Hotel Hacienda Na Xamena	120	150	250	300	6	●	●	61	467
Hotel San Romàn de Escalante	20	30	140	200	1	●		13	452
Hotel Santa Marta	30	130	250	300	4	●		60	460
Mas de Torrent	30	60	120	160	3	●	●	30	459
Posada de la Casa del Abad	25	25	25	25	1	●		17	453

Establishments	Meeting Capacity	Conference Capacity	Reception Capacity	Cocktail party Capacity	Number of conference rooms	Audio-visual Equipment	Secretarial services	Number of rooms	Page
Residencia (La)	32	50	80	110	2	●		64	468
Restaurant Akelare	120	120	140	70	1	●	●		454
Restaurante Arzak	40				4	●	●		456
Torre del Remei	25		300	800	3	●	●	11	458
Torre del Visco (La)	26		39	50	2	●		14	463
GREECE - TURKEY - LEBANON - ISRAEL - DUBAI									472
GREECE (CRETE)									476
Elounda Mare Hotel	60	90	100	130	3		●	89	476
TURKEY									477
Bosphorus Pasha	35	70	70	120	1			14	477
LEBANON									478
Auberge de Faqra (L')	30	60	1 500	2 000	6	●	●	28	478
ISRAEL									480
American Colony (The)	60	100	120	150	3	●	●	84	480
DUBAI									481
Hatta Fort Hotel	60	200	150	200	5	●		54	481
SOUTHERN AFRICA									482
ZIMBABWE									486
Imba Matombo	14	30	60	80	2	●		11	486
SOUTH AFRICA									487
Bushmans Kloof	28	28	28	28	2	●	●	14	491
Cellars - Hohenort (The)	20	30	35	50	3	●	●	53	499
Grande Roche	160	200	150	200	1	●	●	35	494
Hunter's Country House	32	50	50	50	4	●	●	23	492
Londolozi Game Reserve			24	50				24	488
Marine (The)	24	30	45	60	1	●	●	47	497
Plettenberg (The)	20	12	80	80	2	●	●	40	493
Quartier Français (Le)	10	20	40	80				17	495
Singita Game Reserve			36	36				18	487
Tswalu Private Desert Reserve	12	40	30	40	1	●	●	9	490

Establishments	Meeting Capacity	Conference Capacity	Reception Capacity	Cocktail party Capacity	Number of conference rooms	Audio-visual Equipment	Secretarial services	Number of rooms	Page
Willowbrook Lodge	15	25	30	50	1			11	496
NEW-ZEALAND									500
Moose Lodge	25	40	45	70	1	●	●	20	501
JAPAN									502
Asaba	50	80	65		2			19	508
Gôra Kadan	80		100	150	3	●		44	509
Hotel Anaga	80	100	100	120	1			62	504
Kakiden	100		100	100	1		●		511
Seiryuso	60	100	100		4	●		30	507
NORTH AMERICA									512
CANADA									516
Auberge Hatley	25	40	50	50	2	●	●	24	521
Hastings House	16	20	50	75	2	●		17	527
Hostellerie Les Trois Tilleuls	60	100	120	200	7	●	●	24	520
Hôtel L'Eau à la Bouche	28	50	60	60	4	●	●	25	522
Inn at Manitou (The)	80	120	60	150	5	●	●	33	523
Kingsbrae Arms	12	25	25	50	1	●	●	8	518
Langdon Hall	40	70	60	100	4	●		48	524
Little Beaver Creek Ranch	14	14	24	24	1		●	7	526
Pinsonnière (La)	50	75	75	100	3	●	●	26	519
Post Hotel	55	55	64	64	1	●		98	525
The Aerie	36	50	80	120	3	●		23	528
Wickaninnish Inn	30	60	60	75	1	●	●	46	529
WESTERN UNITED STATES									530
Auberge du Soleil	30	100	150	225	3	●		50	539
Château du Sureau	24	65	110	150	3	●	●	12	543
Home Ranch (The)	20	40	40	40	5	●		14	534
Knob Hill Inn	25	35	60	60	1	●		24	533
Little Nell (The)	20	200	200	250	9	●	●	92	535

LEISURE ACTIVITIES

Establishments	Swimming-pool on site	Tennis on site	9/18-hole golf course	Mountain-biking	Horse-riding	Polo	Hunting	Fishing	Sailing	Water-Skiing	Canoeing Kayaking-Rafting	Skiing	Flying club	Page
FRANCE														51
PARIS REGION														51
Auberge des Templiers	●	●	25 km	●										74
Boyer «Les Crayères»		●	5 km											79
Cazaudehore et «La Forestière»			2 km											72
Château de Courcelles	●	●	18 km	●	●									81
Hostellerie Le Clos		●	7 km	●	●		●	●						75
Hôtel de Vigny			15 km											56
Hotellerie du Bas-Bréau	●	●	3 km		●									73
Royal Champagne			30 km		●									77
BRITTANY- NORMANDY - PAS DE CALAIS														82
Auberge Bretonne (L')			10 km		●	●		●	●				●	96
Bretagne et sa Résidence (Le)			12 km											95
Castel Clara	●	●	8 km	●					●					94
Castel Marie-Louise			6 km	●			●		●	●				97
Château d'Audrieu	●		15 km	●					●					87
Château de Locguénolé	●	●	16 km	●				●	●	●				93
Château de Montreuil	●		15 km	●					●					84
Chaumière (La)			6 km		●	●		●	●					86
Ferme St-Siméon (La)	●		7 km			●								85
Goyen (Le)			38 km	●	●				●					91
Hôtel de la Plage	●	●	35 km	●	●				●	●				90
Maisons de Bricourt			12 km		●									88
Manoir de Lan-Kerellec			5 km	●				●	●	●				89
LOIRE VALLEY														98
Bardet Jean (Château Belmont)	●		7 km		●					●				104
Bernard Robin / Le Relais			9 km				●	●						108
Château de Marçay	●	●	15 km	●	●							●		103

Establishments	Swimming-pool on site	Tennis on site	9/18-hole golf course	Mountain-biking	Horse-riding	Polo	Hunting	Fishing	Sailing	Water-Skiing	Canoeing Kayaking-Rafting	Skiing	Flying club	Page
Château de Noirieux	●	●	15 km	●			●	●					●	102
Château de Noizay	●	●	18 km	●										106
Domaine des Hauts de Loire	●	●	15 km	●										107
Grand Hôtel du Lion d'Or			25 km	●			●							109
Hautes Roches (Les)	●		10 km	●										105
THE GREATER SOUTH WEST														110
Auberge de la Galupe			15 km		●			●		●	●			138
Bras (Michel)			15 km	●										129
Chapelle St-Martin (La)	●	●	10 km		●									117
Château Cordeillan-Bages			20 km	●										132
Château de Castel Novel	●	●	10 km	●	●						●			120
Château de Curzay	●		6 km		●									115
Château de Mercuès	●	●	30 km		●									127
Château de Nieuil	●	●	25 km	●				●						118
Château de Puy Robert	●		45 km	●	●						●			122
Château de Riell	●	●	12 km		●		●	●						143
Château de Roumégouse	●		30 km		●									126
Château de la Treyne	●	●	10 km	●	●						●			125
Domaine d'Auriac	●	●	on site		●						●			142
Domaine de Bassibé	●		8 km											135
Guérard (M) «Les Prés d'Eugénie»	●	●	1,5 km	●										137
Hôtel du Centenaire	●		25 km	●	●						●			123
Loges de l'Aubergade (Les)			14 km							●				131
Longcol	●	●	60 km	●										130
Moulin de l'Abbaye (Le)			25 km	●	●						●			121
Moulin de la Gorce (Au)			30 km					●						119
Parc Victoria (Le)	●		2 km		●				●					139
Pyrénées (Les)	●		50 km											140
Relais de la Poste	●	●	15 km	●	●		●	●	●		●			134
Réserve (La)	●	●	6 km	●	●						●			141
Rest. Richard Coutanceau			10 km				●	●	●					116
Saint-James	●		20 km											133
Vieux Logis (Le)	●		25 km		●					●	●			124
ALSACE-LORRAINE														144
Abbaye La Pommeraie			30 km	●							●			153
Arnsbourg (L')			20 km		●		●	●					●	149
Château d'Adoménil	●				●									148
Hostellerie La Cheneaudière	●	●	45 km		●									152
BURGUNDY - FRANCHE COMTÉ														154
Blanc (Georges)	●	●	12 km	●										169

Establishments	Swimming-pool on site	Tennis on site	9/18-hole golf course	Mountain-biking	Horse-riding	Polo	Hunting	Fishing	Sailing	Water-Skiing	Canoeing Kayaking-Rafting	Skiing	Flying club	Page
Château d'Igé			12 km		●						●			167
Château de Germigney			30 km	●			●	●			●			165
Côte Saint-Jacques (La)	●	●	18 km	●	●					●				158
Espérance (L')	●			●	●			●			●			159
Hostellerie de Levernois		●	100 km		●									163
Lameloise			15 km	●										164
Loiseau (Bernard) - La Côte d'Or			27 km	●				●						161
Restaurant Greuze			15 km											166
LYON - RHONE VALLEY														170
Auberge et Clos des Cimes			12 km	●	●			●	●		●	●		180
Chabran (Michel)	●		25 km		●									186
Chapel (Alain)			3 km											174
Château de Bagnols	●		15 km	●										175
Château de Codignat	●	●	35 km	●	●									178
Château de Faverges	●	●	on site	●										185
Hostellerie La Poularde	●		3 km		●									179
Léon de Lyon			20 km											181
Maison Troisgros (La)			6 km	●					●	●	●			177
Pic	●		10 km											187
Pyramide (La)					●					●	●			184
Restaurant Pierre Orsi			20 km											182
Villa Florentine	●		10 km		●									183
SAVOY - MONT BLANC														188
Alpes Hôtel du Pralong	●											●		202
Auberge de l'Eridan			2 km		●				●	●	●			197
Auberge du Bois Prin			3 km	●	●							●		194
Auberge du Père Bise			3 km	●						●				198
Chalet du Mont d'Arbois	●		300 m		●							●		199
Château de Coudrée	●	●	15 km	●	●				●	●	●			192
Château de la Tour du Puits	●		30 km									●		200
Fitz Roy Hotel	●											●		205
Grand Cœur (Le)												●		204
Hameau Albert 1er (Le)	●		2 km	●	●			●			●	●	●	195
Hôtel des Neiges												●		203
Ombremont	●		6 km	●	●				●	●	●	●	●	201
Verniaz (La)	●	●	2 km	●	●					●	●	●		193
PROVENCE - FRENCH RIVIERA - CORSICA														206
Abbaye de Sainte-Croix	●		10 km	●	●									228
Auberge de Noves	●	●	20 km	●	●		●	●						221
Auberge la Regalido			10 km	●	●									218

Establishments	Swimming-pool on site	Tennis on site	9/18-hole golf course	Mountain-biking	Horse-riding	Polo	Hunting	Fishing	Sailing	Water-Skiing	Canoeing Kayaking-Rafting	Skiing	Flying club	Page
Bastide de Capelongue (La)	●		25 km	●	●	●								225
Bastide Saint-Antoine (La)	●		3 km	●	●	●	●	●	●	●	●		●	241
Bonne Etape (La)	●		18 km	●	●				●					231
Cabro d'Or (La)	●	●	3 km		●									223
Cagnard (Le)			15 km	●	●			●	●	●				242
Cardinale (La)	●		25 km		●						●			211
Château de Montcaud	●	●	20 km	●	●						●		●	214
Château de Rochegude	●	●	10 km	●										212
Château de Trigance			20 km		●		●	●			●			234
Château de la Chèvre d'Or	●		7 km					●	●	●				247
Château St-Martin	●	●	20 km	●				●	●	●				243
Club de Cavalière (Le)	●	●	15 km	●				●	●	●	●		●	237
Grand Hôtel de Cala Rossa			30 km	●	●			●	●	●				248
Hostellerie de Crillon le Brave	●		35 km	●	●									213
Hostellerie Les Frênes	●		2 km											220
Hôtel Jules César	●		20 km				●	●			●			217
Hôtel les Roches	●		1,5 km	●	●			●	●	●				235
Jardin des Sens (Le)	●		15 km					●	●					216
Mas des Herbes Blanches (Le)	●	●	23 km	●	●									224
Métropole (Le)	●		15 km	●				●	●	●				246
Moulin de Lourmarin (Le)			20 km	●	●	●		●	●		●		●	227
Moulin de Mougins (Le)			2 km		●			●	●	●				239
Oustau de Baumanière	●	●	3 km		●									222
Petit Nice-Passedat (Le)	●		10 km					●	●					229
Prieuré (Le)	●	●	12 km	●										219
Réserve de Beaulieu (La)	●		15 km	●	●			●	●	●				245
Résidence de la Pinède	●		5 km	●	●	●								238
Saint-Paul (Le)			12 km		●			●	●	●				240
Vieux Castillon (Le)	●		15 km	●	●			●			●			215
Villa (La)	●	●	6 km		●			●	●	●			●	249
Villa Belrose (La)	●		5 km	●	●			●	●	●				236
Villa Gallici	●		5 km		●			●						230
BENELUX COUNTRIES														250
BELGIUM														253
Auberge du Moulin Hideux	●	●	40 km	●							●			262
Hof Van Cleve			5 km											255
Hôtel de Snippe			10 km											253
Hostellerie Lafarque			15 km											261
Hostellerie Saint-Roch		●	18 km	●							●			259

Establishments	Swimming-pool on site	Tennis on site	9/18-hole golf course	Mountain-biking	Horse-riding	Polo	Hunting	Fishing	Sailing	Water-Skiing	Canoeing Kayaking-Rafting	Skiing	Flying club	Page
Hostellerie Shamrock			10 km											254
Moulin des Ramiers			16 km	●				●						260
Restaurant Barbizon			6 km											256
Scholteshof		●	10 km											257
LUXEMBOURG														263
Gaichel (La)		●	on site											264
NETHERLANDS														265
Kasteel Wittem			7 km	●	●			●						265
Manoir «Inter Scaldes»			11 km					●	●	●				267
Prinses Juliana			6 km											266
SWITZERLAND - LIECHTENSTEIN														268
SWITZERLAND														272
Albergo Giardino	●	●	1 km											293
Auberge du Raisin			9 km				●	●	●	●				282
Castello del Sole	●	●	2 km											292
Ermitage Am See			3 km	●	●	●		●	●	●				275
Georges Wenger Hôtel de la Gare			6 km	●			●	●			●	●	●	277
Grand Hôtel Park	●	●	10 km	●	●						●	●		286
Grandhôtel Schönegg												●		291
Hostellerie Alpenrose			2 km	●	●			●			●	●		285
Hostellerie du Débarcadère			15 km	●					●	●				280
Hostellerie du Pas de l'Ours	●		500 m									●		287
Hôtel de la Cigogne			2 km		●			●						279
Hotel Haus Paradies			6 km									●		298
Hôtel Rosalp			1 km	●								●		289
Hotel Splügenschloss			10 km	●										274
Hôtel Victoria	●	●	15 km					●				●		284
Hotel Walserhof			13 km	●	●			●	●			●		301
Hotel Walther	●	●	6 km	●		●		●				●		297
Les Sources des Alpes	●		40 km	●							●	●		290
Pont de Brent (Le)			15 km											283
Restaurant Bruderholz			10 km											272
Rest. de l'Hôtel de Ville - Ph. Rochat			10 km						●					281
Restaurant Jöhri's Talvo			10 km	●		●	●					●		296
Restaurant Kunststuben			3 km											276
Shlosshotel Chastè			3 km									●		299
Vieux Manoir au Lac (Le)			7 km					●	●					278
Villa Margherita	●		10 km					●		●				294

632

Establishments	Swimming-pool on site	Tennis on site	9/18-hole golf course	Mountain-biking	Horse-riding	Polo	Hunting	Fishing	Sailing	Water-Skiing	Canoeing Kayaking-Rafting	Skiing	Flying club	Page
Villa Principe Leopoldo & Residence	●	●	6 km	●	●		●	●	●	●	●		●	295
LIECHTENSTEIN														302
Parkhotel Sonnenhof	●		25 km											303
Real (Le)			20 km											302
GERMANY														304
Alpenhof Murnau	●		15 km	●	●									340
Bülow Residenz			12 km											314
Burghotel Hardenberg			5 km	●	●		●	●					●	317
Fürstenhof Celle	●		5 km	●			●	●						315
Hotel Abtei			17 km			●			●				●	311
Hotel Bareiss	●	●	12 km											333
Hotel Brandenburger Hof			12 km			●			●				●	312
Hotel Burg Wernberg			9 km	●	●			●			●			325
Hotel Deidesheimer Hof			10 km											329
Hotel Hohenhaus	●	●	10 km		●									323
Hotel Krautkrämer	●	●	8 km	●	●	●		●	●	●				319
Hotel Louis C. Jacob			3 km	●	●	●		●						310
Hotel Restaurant Zur Traube			2 km											321
Hotel Schloss Hugenpœt		●	5 km	●										320
Hotel Schloss Wilkinghege		●	on site	●										318
Hotel Schwarzmatt	●		9 km		●			●						337
Hotel Stadt Hamburg	●		5 km	●				●						308
Johann Lafer's Stromburg			1,5 km											324
Kur-und Sporthotel Dollenberg	●	●	15 km	●										335
Landhaus Ammann			25 km						●					316
Landhaus Scherrer			1 km											309
Mönchs Posthotel	●		1 km											331
Pflaums Posthotel Pegnitz	●		10 km		●	●		●						326
Residenz Heinz Winkler	●		8 km		●		●	●						341
Restaurant Schwarzwaldstube			10 km											334
Schafhof Amorbach (Der)		●	15 km											328
Schloss Hubertushöhe	●		7 km	●	●		●	●	●	●			●	313
Schlosshotel Lerbach	●	●	5 km	●	●									322
Schwarzwald Hotel Adler	●	●	30 km	●										336
Schweizer Stuben	●	●	9 km	●										327
Seehotel Siber			10 km					●	●					338
Villa Hammerschmiede	●		8 km											332
Villino			3 km	●	●		●	●	●	●	●		●	339

BAL
du
Moulin Rouge

Féerie

BAL DU
Moulin
Rouge
PARIS

DINNER & SHOW AT 7.PM FROM 790 F- SHOW AT 9.PM : 560F & AT 11.PM : 500 F
MONTMARTRE - 82, BOULEVARD DE CLICHY - 75018 PARIS
RESERVATIONS : 01 53 09 82 82 - WWW.MOULIN-ROUGE.COM

Establishments	Swimming-pool on site	Tennis on site	9/18-hole golf course	Mountain-biking	Horse-riding	Polo	Hunting	Fishing	Sailing	Water-Skiing	Canoeing Kayaking-Rafting	Skiing	Flying club	Page
Wald & Schlosshotel	●	●	on site	●			●							330
CZECH REPUBLIC														342
Hotel Hoffmeister			20 km											343
AUSTRIA														344
Arlberg Hospiz	●		30 km									●		349
Deuring Schlössle			10 km					●		●		●		348
Gasthof Post	●		20 km									●		350
Hotel der Bär	●	●	5 km									●		353
Hotel Grüner Baum	●	●	2 km				●	●				●		358
Hotel Im Palais Schwarzenberg	●	●	7 km											356
Hotel Schloss Dürnstein	●		15 km					●						355
Hotel Schloss Mönchstein		●	5 km											354
Hotel Schloss Seefels	●	●	5 km	●	●			●	●	●	●			359
Restaurant Steirereck			3 km											357
Schlosshotel Igls	●		2 km		●									352
Sporthotel Singer			30 km	●				●				●		351
SLOVENIA														360
Hotel Vila Bled		●	4 km				●	●			●	●		361
SCANDINAVIA														362
DENMARK														364
Falsled Kro			7 km											366
Molskroen			7 km	●	●		●	●	●	●	●		●	365
Sønderho Kro			12 km					●						364
SWEDEN														367
Kattegat Gastronomi			1 km		●		●	●	●					368
Krägga Herrgård		●	15 km		●									369
Leijontornet & Victory Hotel			20 km											370
ICELAND														372
Hotel Holt			5 km					●						372
LITHUANIA														373
Stikliai Hotel	●				●								●	373
UNITED KINGDOM														374
Airds Hotel (The)									●	●				397
Arisaig House			16 km					●	●					399
Bodysgallen Hall	●	●	2 km											392
Buckland Manor Hotel	●	●	3 km		●	●	●	●						389
Chewton Glen Hotel	●	●	on site	●										383
Farlam Hall Hotel			5 km	●	●			●						395

635

Establishments	Swimming-pool on site	Tennis on site	9/18-hole golf course	Mountain-biking	Horse-riding	Polo	Hunting	Fishing	Sailing	Water-Skiing	Canoeing Kayaking-Rafting	Skiing	Flying club	Page
Gidleigh Park		●	10 km		●		●	●						386
Gravetye Manor			8 km		●			●						382
Hambleton Hall	●	●	8 km		●		●	●	●					391
Hartwell House	●	●	2 km		●			●						381
Inverlochy Castle		●	3 km		●		●	●	●			●		398
Kinnaird		●	6 km		●		●	●						396
Longueville Manor	●	●	5 km		●				●					387
Mallory Court	●	●	3 km		●			●						390
Manoir aux Quat' Saisons (Le)			10 km	●			●	●						380
Middlethorpe Hall	●		4 km		●									393
Sharrow Bay Country House			12 km						●					394
Stock Hill Country House		●	30 km		●		●	●					●	384
Ston Easton Park		●	on site		●		●	●						388
Summer Lodge	●	●	5 km		●		●	●						385
Waterside Inn (The)			5 km											379
IRELAND														**400**
Ashford Castle		●	on site	●	●		●	●						406
Ballylickey Manor House	●		2 km					●						404
Cashel House Hotel		●	24 km		●									407
Longueville House			6 km		●			●						405
Marlfield House		●	2 km					●						409
Newport House			12 km		●			●	●					408
Sheen Falls Lodge	●	●	2 km	●	●			●		●	●			403
ITALY														**410**
Albereta (L') - Rest. G. Marchesi	●	●	3 km	●	●				●					421
Al Sorriso			15 km		●		●	●		●				417
Borgo Paraelios	●	●	on site		●									441
Bottaccio di Montignoso (Il)	●		3 km		●		●	●					●	432
Gallia Palace Hotel	●	●	2 km	●	●				●	●				439
Hotel Bellevue	●		37 km	●	●			●				●		415
Hotel Certosa di Maggiano	●	●	40 km	●	●									436
Hotel Dominik	●											●		424
Hotel Duchessa Isabella			2 km											430
Hotel Hermitage	●		500 m		●							●	●	414
Hotel La Collegiata	●		20 km		●									435
Hotel San Pietro	●	●						●		●				444
Locanda l'Elisa	●		25 km		●									434
Melograno (Il)	●	●	30 km		●				●					445

636

Establishments	Swimming-pool on site	Tennis on site	9/18-hole golf course	Mountain-biking	Horse-riding	Polo	Hunting	Fishing	Sailing	Water-Skiing	Canoeing Kayaking-Rafting	Skiing	Flying club	Page
Meridiana (La)	●		on site											428
Pellicano (Il)	●	●	50 km		●	●	●	●	●	●	●			440
Posta Vecchia (La)	●		30 km		●									442
Relais Borgo San Felice	●	●	55 km	●										437
Relais il Falconiere	●		25 km		●									438
Restaurant Dal Pescatore			40 km											427
Restaurant Enoteca Pinchiorri			10 km											431
Ristorante Le Calandre			6 km											426
Rosa Alpina	●		10 km	●	●		●	●				●	●	425
Sole di Ranco (Il)			10 km		●			●	●				●	419
Villa Del Quar	●		18 km											423
Villa Fiordaliso			4 km											422
Villa la Massa	●		8 km	●	●			●						433
IBERIAN PENINSULA														446
PORTUGAL														450
Fortaleza do Guincho			3 km	●	●			●	●	●	●		●	451
Hotel Quinta Das Lagrimas	●	●	on site	●	●			●		●	●			450
SPAIN														452
Girasol			1,5 km				●	●	●					465
Gran Hotel Son Net	●	●	15 km	●	●			●	●	●	●		●	469
Hotel Cala Sant Vicenç	●		8 km	●	●				●	●				470
Hotel El Castell			8 km	●	●		●	●			●	●		457
Hotel El Montibolli	●	●	15 km	●	●			●	●	●				466
Hotel Hacienda Na Xamena	●	●	23 km	●	●				●					467
Hotel San Romàn de Escalante			18 km		●		●	●	●	●			●	452
Hotel Santa Marta	●	●	3 km	●				●	●					460
Mas de Torrent	●	●	6 km	●	●									459
Posada de la Casa del Abad	●	●	40 km	●	●		●	●						453
Residencia (La)	●	●	20 km							●				468
Restaurant Akelare			6 km						●		●			454
Restaurante Arzak			2 km											456
Torre del Remei	●		1 km	●	●			●						458
Torre del Visco (La)				●	●		●	●						463
GREECE - TURKEY - LEBANON - ISRAEL - DUBAI														472
GREECE (CRETE)														476
Elounda Mare Hotel	●	●	500 m							●	●			476
TURKEY														477
Bosphorus Pasha				●	●			●						477

637

Establishments	Swimming-pool on site	Tennis on site	9/18-hole golf course	Mountain-biking	Horse-riding	Polo	Hunting	Fishing	Sailing	Water-Skiing	Canoeing Kayaking-Rafting	Skiing	Flying club	Page
LEBANON														478
Auberge de Faqra (L')	●	●	45 km	●	●								●	478
Hotel Albergo	●		5 km	●					●	●				479
ISRAEL														480
American Colony (The)	●		80 km		●									480
DUBAI														481
Hatta Fort Hotel	●	●	on site											481
SOUTHERN AFRICA														482
SEYCHELLES														485
Château de Feuilles	●			●				●	●	●				485
ZIMBABWE														486
Imba Matombo	●	●	10 km											486
SOUTH AFRICA														487
Bushmans Kloof			37 km	●				●						491
Cellars - Hohenort (The)	●	●	5 km	●										499
Cybele Forest Lodge	●		20 km		●			●						489
Ellerman House	●		5 km		●				●					498
Grande Roche	●	●	4 km	●	●			●						494
Hunter's Country House	●		10 km					●	●					492
Londolozi Game Reserve	●		65 km											488
Marine (The)	●		1 km					●	●	●				497
Plettenberg (The)	●		2 km					●	●					493
Quartier Français (Le)	●		26 km	●	●									495
Singita Game Reserve	●													487
Tswalu Private Desert Reserve	●		45 km											490
Willowbrook Lodge	●		1,5 km	●	●		●	●	●		●		●	496
NEW ZEALAND														500
Moose Lodge		●	on site		●			●		●	●			501
JAPAN														502
Asaba			3 km							●				508
Gôra Kadan	●		2 km											509
Horai			4 km					●	●					506
Hotel Anaga	●	●	25 km					●						504
Seiryuso	●		10 km					●						507
NORTH AMERICA														512
CANADA														516
Auberge Hatley	●		3 km	●	●			●			●	●		521
Hastings House			4 km	●				●	●		●			527

Establishments	Jacuzzi	Sauna	Hammam	Solarium	Fitness	Spa	Beauty Salon	Page
Saint-James		●		●				133
ALSACE-LORRAINE								144
Hostellerie La Cheneaudière	●	●	●					152
BURGUNDY - FRANCHE COMTÉ								154
Côte Saint-Jacques (La)		●						158
SAVOY - MONT BLANC								188
Alpes Hôtel du Pralong		●		●	●			202
Auberge du Bois Prin	●	●						194
Chalet du Mont d'Arbois	●	●	●		●		●	199
Château de la Tour du Puits					●			200
Fitz Roy Hotel	●	●	●	●	●	●	●	205
Grand Cœur (Le)	●	●	●		●			204
Hameau Albert 1er (Le)	●	●	●	●	●		●	195
Hôtel des Neiges	●	●			●			203
Ombremont		●						201
PROVENCE - FRENCH RIVIERA - CORSICA								206
Cabro d'Or (La)				●				223
Château de Montcaud		●	●		●			214
Château de la Chèvre d'Or				●				247
Hostellerie Les Frênes		●		●				220
Métropole (Le)				●				246
Vieux Castillon (Le)		●	●					215
Villa (La)			●					249
Villa Belrose (La)					●			236
BENELUX COUNTRIES								250
LUXEMBOURG								263
Gaichel (La)		●						264
SWITZERLAND - LIECHTENSTEIN								268
SWITZERLAND								272
Albergo Giardino	●	●	●	●	●	●	●	293
Castello del Sole		●		●	●		●	292
Grand Hôtel Park	●	●	●	●	●	●	●	286

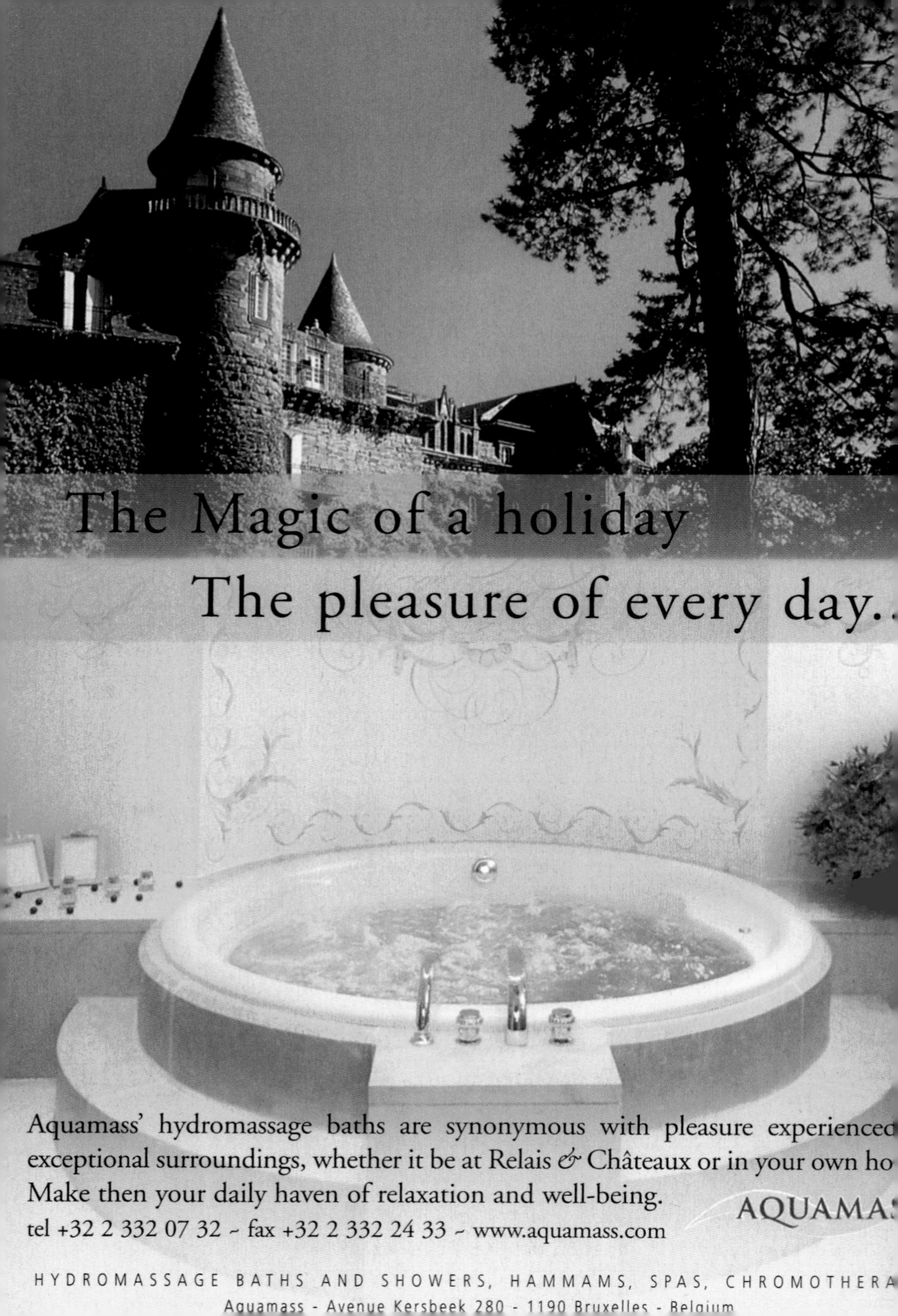

The Magic of a holiday
The pleasure of every day..

Aquamass' hydromassage baths are synonymous with pleasure experienced
exceptional surroundings, whether it be at Relais *&* Châteaux or in your own ho
Make then your daily haven of relaxation and well-being.
tel +32 2 332 07 32 ~ fax +32 2 332 24 33 ~ www.aquamass.com

AQUAMAS

Establishments	Jacuzzi	Sauna	Hammam	Solarium	Fitness	Spa	Beauty Salon	Page
Grandhôtel Schönegg	●	●	●	●	●			291
Hostellerie Alpenrose	●	●		●				285
Hotel Haus Paradies	●	●	●	●	●	●	●	298
Hôtel Rosalp	●	●	●					289
Hôtel Victoria	●	●		●				284
Hotel Walserhof		●						301
Hotel Walther	●	●	●	●	●	●	●	297
Les Sources des Alpes	●	●	●	●	●	●	●	290
Shlosshotel Chastè	●	●	●	●				299
Villa Margherita		●		●	●			294
Villa Principe Leopoldo	●	●		●	●			295
LIECHTENSTEIN								302
Parkhotel Sonnenhof		●		●				303
GERMANY								304
Alpenhof Murnau	●	●	●	●			●	340
Burghotel Hardenberg	●	●		●				317
Fürstenhof Celle		●		●				315
Hotel Bareiss	●	●	●	●	●	●	●	333
Hotel Brandenburger Hof			●	●		●	●	312
Hotel Burg Wernberg		●		●				325
Hotel Hohenhaus		●		●				323
Hotel Krautkrämer		●		●		●	●	319
Hotel Louis C. Jacob		●		●				310
Hotel Schwarzmatt				●				337
Kur-und Sporthotel Dollenberg	●	●	●	●	●	●	●	335
Mönchs Posthotel					●		●	331
Pflaums Posthotel Pegnitz	●	●	●	●	●	●	●	326
Residenz Heinz Winkler		●	●	●	●	●	●	341
Schafhof Amorbach (Der)		●		●				328
Schlosshotel Lerbach		●		●			●	322
Schwarzwald Hotel Adler	●	●	●	●	●	●	●	336
Schweizer Stuben		●	●	●				327

Establishments	Jacuzzi	Sauna	Hammam	Solarium	Fitness	Spa	Beauty Salon	Page
Villa Hammerschmiede	●	●	●	●				332
Villino		●		●				339
Wald & Schlosshotel		●	●			●	●	330
AUSTRIA								344
Arlberg Hospiz	●	●	●	●				349
Gasthof Post	●	●	●	●	●	●		350
Hotel der Bär		●	●	●	●	●	●	353
Hotel Grüner Baum		●	●	●	●	●	●	358
Hotel Schloss Dürnstein		●	●	●	●			355
Hotel Schloss Seefels		●						359
Schlosshotel Igls	●	●	●	●				352
Sporthotel Singer	●	●		●				351
SCANDINAVIA								362
SWEDEN								367
Krägga Herrgård	●	●		●				369
Leijontornet & Victory Hotel	●	●						370
LITHUANIA								373
Stikliai Hotel		●			●			373
UNITED KINGDOM								374
Bodysgallen Hall	●	●		●	●	●	●	392
Chewton Glen Hotel	●	●	●		●		●	383
Hartwell House	●	●	●	●	●	●	●	381
Middlethorpe Hall	●	●		●	●		●	393
Stock Hill Country House		●						384
IRELAND								400
Ashford Castle	●	●			●		●	406
Sheen Falls Lodge	●	●		●	●		●	403
ITALY								410
Albereta (L') - Rest. G. Marchesi	●	●		●	●			421
Al Sorriso	●							417
Gallia Palace Hotel	-		●				●	439
Hotel Bellevue	●	●	●	●				415

646

Establishments	Jacuzzi	Sauna	Hammam	Solarium	Fitness	Spa	Beauty Salon	Page
Hotel Certosa di Maggiano					●			436
Hotel Dominik		●		●	●			424
Hotel Hermitage	●	●	●	●	●		●	414
Hotel La Collegiata	●							435
Hotel San Pietro				●				444
Melograno (Il)	●							445
Meridiana (La)		●						428
Pellicano (Il)	●	●		●	●			440
Posta Vecchia (La)		●			●			442
Relais Borgo San Felice				●	●		●	437
Rosa Alpina	●	●	●	●	●	●	●	425
Villa Del Quar	●	●			●			423
IBERIAN PENINSULA								446
SPAIN								452
Gran Hotel Son Net		●			●			469
Hotel Cala Sant Vicenç		●			●		●	470
Hotel El Montibolli		●			●			466
Posada de la Casa del Abad		●			●			453
Residencia (La)	●		●		●		●	468
Torre del Remei	●			●				458
GREECE - TURKEY - LEBANON - ISRAEL - DUBAI								472
GREECE (CRETE)								476
Elounda Mare Hotel	●	●	●					476
LEBANON								478
Auberge de Faqra (L')		●		●	●		●	478
Hotel Albergo	●							479
SOUTHERN AFRICA								482
ZIMBABWE								486
Imba Matombo	●	●			●		●	486
SOUTH AFRICA								487
Bushmans Kloof		●						491
Cellars - Hohenort (The)	●	●			●	●	●	499

Establishments	Jacuzzi	Sauna	Hammam	Solarium	Fitness	Spa	Beauty Salon	Page
Ellerman House		●			●			498
Grande Roche		●	●		●			494
Singita Game Reserve		●	●		●			487
JAPAN								502
Gôra Kadan	●	●				●	●	509
Hotel Anaga	●							504
NORTH AMERICA								512
CANADA								516
Inn at Manitou (The)	●	●		●	●	●	●	523
Kingsbrae Arms	●							518
Langdon Hall	●	●			●	●	●	524
Little Beaver Creek Ranch	●		●		●			526
Pinsonnière (La)		●				●	●	519
Post Hotel	●	●						525
The Aerie	●	●			●	●	●	528
Wickaninnish Inn		●				●	●	529
WESTERN UNITED STATES								530
Auberge du Soleil	●		●		●			539
Château du Sureau					●		●	543
Home Ranch (The)	●	●	●					534
Knob Hill Inn	●	●			●			533
Little Nell (The)	●				●			535
Meadowood Napa Valley	●	●			●		●	540
Rancho Valencia Resort	●	●			●			547
San Ysidro Ranch					●		●	544
Stonepine	●				●			542
Timberhill Ranch	●			●				537
Triple Creek Ranch	●	●			●			532
NORTH-EASTERN UNITED STATES								548
Blantyre	●	●			●			555
Canoe Bay	●							575
Castle at Tarrytown (The)	●				●			563

OUR PARTNERS

Relais & Châteaux has selected three internationally renowned partners
to guarantee you high-quality service.

/// M I L E A G E P L U S ®
United Airlines

With each of our partners, we have established exclusive offers :

earn flying miles, obtain a reduction on your stay,
benefit from preferential rates on car rentals...

To learn more about these offers,
please contact our Information Central (see page 15)

Establishments	Jacuzzi	Sauna	Hammam	Solarium	Fitness	Spa	Beauty Salon	Page
Fearrington House (The)					●			571
Inn at Sawmill Farm (The)	●							553
Mayflower Inn (The)	●	●			●	●		560
Pitcher Inn (The)	●					●	●	554
SOUTH-EASTERN UNITED STATES								576
Blackberry Farm					●			581
Little Palm Island	●				●		●	580
Planters Inn	●							579
Woodlands Resort Inn	●						●	578
MEXICO - CARRIBEAN - BERMUDA								582
PUERTO RICO								586
Horned Dorset Primavera	●				●		●	586
BARBADOS								589
Cobblers Cove					●			589
BERMUDA								590
Horizons and Cottages	●				●	●	●	590
Waterloo House	●				●	●	●	591
SOUTH AMERICA								592
COLOMBIA								596
Casa Medina					●			596
Hotel Charleston			●		●			597
ECUADOR								598
Hosteria La Mirage	●	●		●		●	●	598
BOLIVIA								599
Hacienda Villa del Sol	●	●	●	●	●	●	●	599
BRAZIL								600
Hotel Fazenda Rosa-dos-Ventos		●			●			600
URUGUAY								601
Belmont House	●	●			●			602
ARGENTINA								603
Hosteria Las Balsas	●			●				604

CHANEL

HAUTE JOAILLERIE

BAGUES "NUIT" ET "JOUR" EN OR BLANC OU JAUNE 18 CARATS, SAPHIRS ET DIAMANTS.

EXCLUSIVEMENT DANS LES BOUTIQUES CHANEL JOAILLERIE

18, PLACE VENDÔME · 01 55 35 50 05 · 40, AVENUE MONTAIGNE · 01 40 70 12 33 · PARIS.

ES · NEW YORK · BAL HARBOUR · BEVERLY HILLS · CHICAGO · COSTA MESA · HAWAI · PALM BEACH · LAS VEGAS · TOKYO · OSAKA · NAGOYA · HONG KONG · TAIPEI

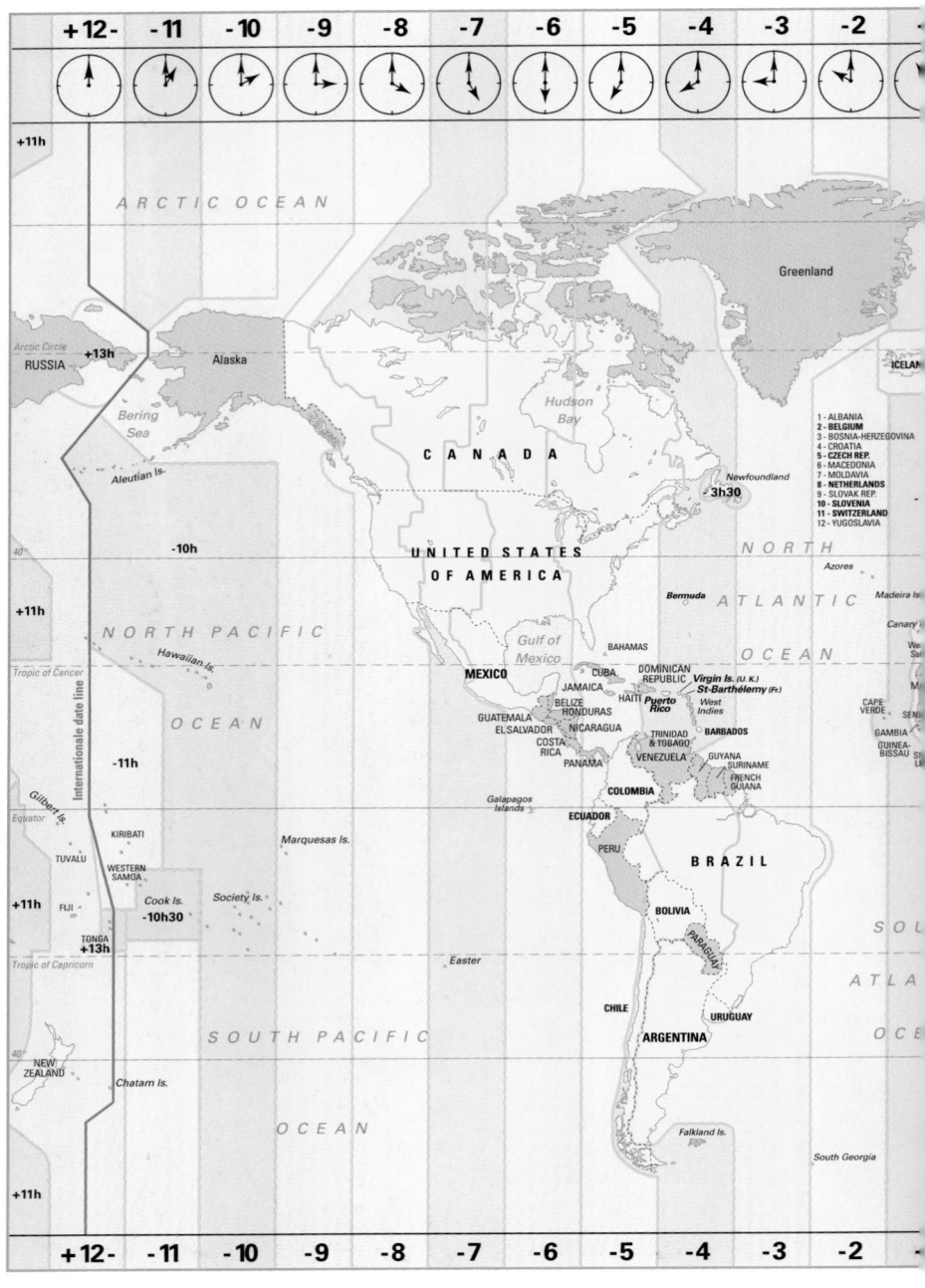

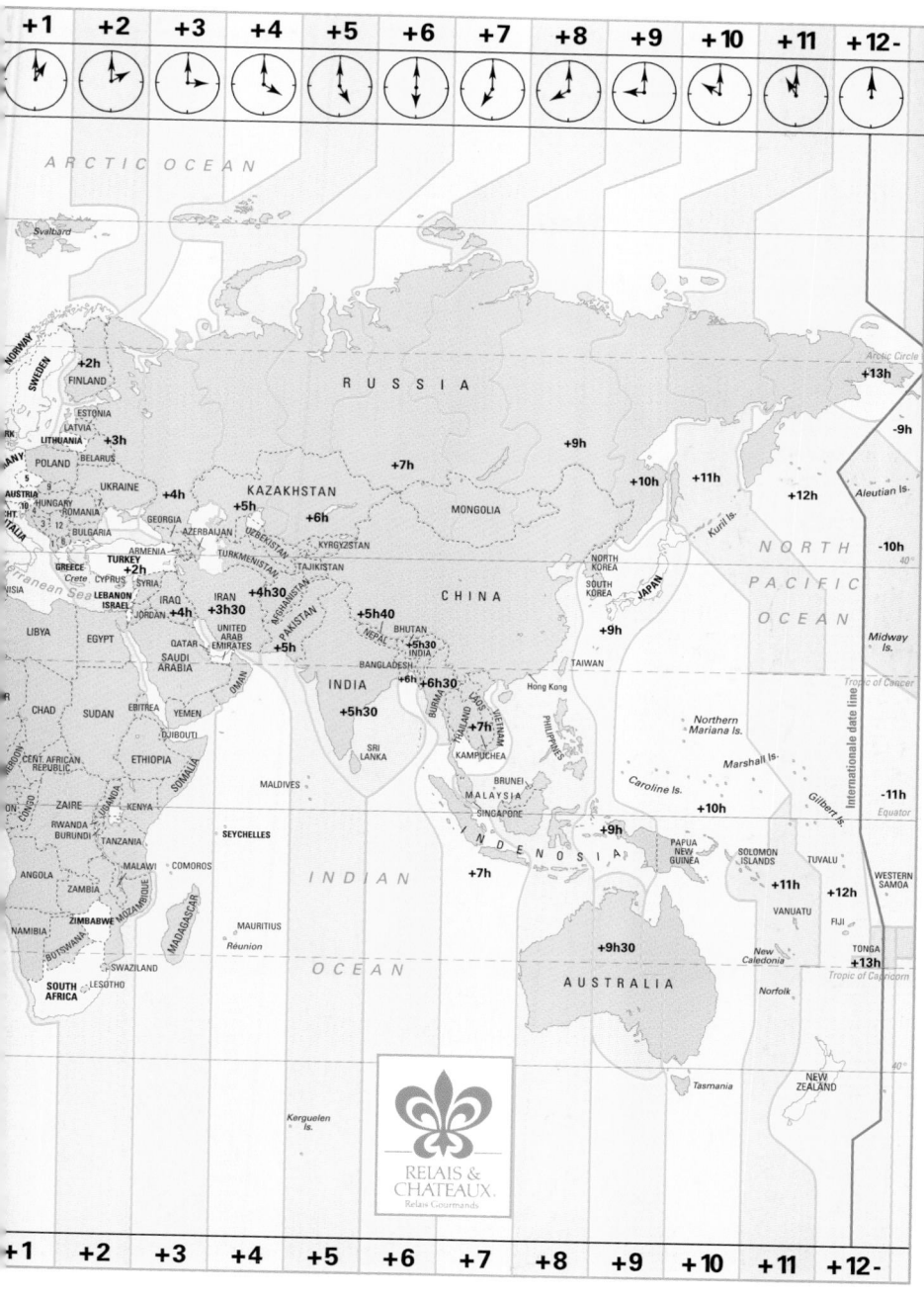

Apprenez à lire dans nos bul...

CHAMPAGNE

MAREUIL-SUR-AŸ

BILLECART-SALMON

1818
B S

40, rue Carnot
B.P. 8 - 51160 Mareuil-sur-Aÿ
Tél. : 03 26 52 60 22